41: *Afro-American Poets Since 1955*, edited by Trudier Harris and Thadious M. Davis (1985)

42: *American Writers for Children Before 1900*, edited by Glenn E. Estes (1985)

43: *American Newspaper Journalists, 1690-1872*, edited by Perry J. Ashley (1986)

44: *American Screenwriters*, Second Series, edited by Randall Clark, Robert E. Morsberger, and Stephen O. Lesser (1986)

45: *American Poets, 1880-1945*, First Series, edited by Peter Quartermain (1986)

46: *American Literary Publishing Houses, 1900-1980: Trade and Paperback*, edited by Peter Dzwonkoski (1986)

47: *American Historians, 1866-1912*, edited by Clyde N. Wilson (1986)

48: *American Poets, 1880-1945*, Second Series, edited by Peter Quartermain (1986)

49: *American Literary Publishing Houses, 1638-1899*, 2 parts, edited by Peter Dzwonkoski (1986)

50: *Afro-American Writers Before the Harlem Renaissance*, edited by Trudier Harris (1986)

51: *Afro-American Writers from the Harlem Renaissance to 1940*, edited by Trudier Harris (1987)

52: *American Writers for Children Since 1960: Fiction*, edited by Glenn E. Estes (1986)

53: *Canadian Writers Since 1960*, First Series, edited by W. H. New (1986)

54: *American Poets, 1880-1945*, Third Series, 2 parts, edited by Peter Quartermain (1987)

55: *Victorian Prose Writers Before 1867*, edited by William B. Thesing (1987)

56: *German Fiction Writers, 1914-1945*, edited by James Hardin (1987)

57: *Victorian Prose Writers After 1867*, edited by William B. Thesing (1987)

58: *Jacobean and Caroline Dramatists*, edited by Fredson Bowers (1987)

59: *American Literary Critics and Scholars, 1800-1850*, edited by John W. Rathbun and Monica M. Grecu (1987)

60: *Canadian Writers Since 1960*, Second Series, edited by W. H. New (1987)

61: *American Writers for Children Since 1960: Poets, Illustrators, and Nonfiction Authors*, edited by Glenn E. Estes (1987)

62: *Elizabethan Dramatists*, edited by Fredson Bowers (1987)

63: *Modern American Critics, 1920-1955*, edited by Gregory S. Jay (1988)

64: *American Literary Critics and Scholars, 1850-1880*, edited by John W. Rathbun and Monica M. Grecu (1988)

65: *French Novelists, 1900-1930*, edited by Catharine Savage Brosman (1988)

66: *German Fiction Writers, 1885-1913*, 2 parts, edited by James Hardin (1988)

67: *Modern American Critics Since 1955*, edited by Gregory S. Jay (1988)

68: *Canadian Writers, 1920-1959*, First Series, edited by W. H. New (1988)

69: *Contemporary German Fiction Writers*, First Series, edited by Wolfgang D. Elfe and James Hardin (1988)

70: *British Mystery Writers, 1860-1919*, edited by Bernard Benstock and Thomas F. Staley (1988)

71: *American Literary Critics and Scholars, 1880-1900*, edited by John W. Rathbun and Monica M. Grecu (1988)

72: *French Novelists, 1930-1960*, edited by Catharine Savage Brosman (1988)

73: *American Magazine Journalists, 1741-1850*, edited by Sam G. Riley (1988)

74: *American Short-Story Writers Before 1880*, edited by Bobby Ellen Kimbel, with the assistance of William E. Grant (1988)

75: *Contemporary German Fiction Writers*, Second Series, edited by Wolfgang D. Elfe and James Hardin (1988)

76: *Afro-American Writers, 1940-1955*, edited by Trudier Harris (1988)

77: *British Mystery Writers, 1920-1939*, edited by Bernard Benstock and Thomas F. Staley (1988)

78: *American Short-Story Writers, 1880-1910*, edited by Bobby Ellen Kimbel, with the assistance of William E. Grant (1988)

79: *American Magazine Journalists, 1850-1900*, edited by Sam G. Riley (1988)

(Continued on back endsheets)

Dictionary of Literary Biography • Volume One Hundred Twelve

British Literary Publishing Houses, 1881-1965

British Literary Publishing Houses, 1881-1965

8614

Edited by
Jonathan Rose
Drew University
and
Patricia J. Anderson
Simon Fraser University

A Bruccoli Clark Layman Book
Gale Research Inc.
Detroit, London

Printed in the United States of America

Published simultaneously in the United Kingdom
by Gale Research International Limited
(An affiliated company of Gale Research Inc.)

The paper used in this publication meets the minimum requirements
of American National Standard for Information Sciences—Permanence
Paper for Printed Library Materials, ANSI Z39.48-1984. ∞™

ISBN 0-8103-4592-7
91-31918 CIP

Contents

Contents

Plan of the Series

... Almost the most prodigious asset of a country, and perhaps its most precious possession, is its native literary product—when that product is fine and noble and enduring.

Mark Twain*

The advisory board, the editors, and the publisher of the *Dictionary of Literary Biography* are joined in endorsing Mark Twain's declaration. The literature of a nation provides an inexhaustible resource of permanent worth. We intend to make literature and its creators better understood and more accessible to students and the reading public, while satisfying the standards of teachers and scholars.

To meet these requirements, *literary biography* has been construed in terms of the author's achievement. The most important thing about a writer is his writing. Accordingly, the entries in *DLB* are career biographies, tracing the development of the author's canon and the evolution of his reputation.

The purpose of *DLB* is not only to provide reliable information in a convenient format but also to place the figures in the larger perspective of literary history and to offer appraisals of their accomplishments by qualified scholars.

The publication plan for *DLB* resulted from two years of preparation. The project was proposed to Bruccoli Clark by Frederick G. Ruffner, president of the Gale Research Company, in November 1975. After specimen entries were prepared and typeset, an advisory board was formed to refine the entry format and develop the series rationale. In meetings held during 1976, the publisher, series editors, and advisory board approved the scheme for a comprehensive biographical dictionary of persons who contributed to North American literature. Editorial work on the first volume began in January 1977, and it was published in 1978. In order to make *DLB* more than a reference tool and to compile volumes that individually have claim to status as lit-

erary history, it was decided to organize volumes by topic, period, or genre. Each of these freestanding volumes provides a biographical-bibliographical guide and overview for a particular area of literature. We are convinced that this organization—as opposed to a single alphabet method—constitutes a valuable innovation in the presentation of reference material. The volume plan necessarily requires many decisions for the placement and treatment of authors who might properly be included in two or three volumes. In some instances a major figure will be included in separate volumes, but with different entries emphasizing the aspect of his career appropriate to each volume. Ernest Hemingway, for example, is represented in *American Writers in Paris, 1920-1939* by an entry focusing on his expatriate apprenticeship; he is also in *American Novelists, 1910-1945* with an entry surveying his entire career. Each volume includes a cumulative index of subject authors and articles. Comprehensive indexes to the entire series are planned.

With volume ten in 1982 it was decided to enlarge the scope of *DLB*. By the end of 1986 twenty-one volumes treating British literature had been published, and volumes for Commonwealth and Modern European literature were in progress. The series has been further augmented by the *DLB Yearbooks* (since 1981) which update published entries and add new entries to keep the *DLB* current with contemporary activity. There have also been *DLB Documentary Series* volumes which provide biographical and critical source materials for figures whose work is judged to have particular interest for students. One of these companion volumes is entirely devoted to Tennessee Williams.

We define literature as the *intellectual commerce of a nation*: not merely as belles lettres but as that ample and complex process by which ideas are generated, shaped, and transmitted. *DLB* entries are not limited to "creative writers" but extend to other figures who in their time and in their way influenced the mind of a people. Thus the series encompasses historians, journalists, publishers, and screenwriters. By this means readers of *DLB* may be aided to perceive litera-

---

*From an unpublished section of Mark Twain's autobiography, copyright © by the Mark Twain Company.

ture not as cult scripture in the keeping of intellectual high priests but firmly positioned at the center of a nation's life.

DLB includes the major writers appropriate to each volume and those standing in the ranks immediately behind them. Scholarly and critical counsel has been sought in deciding which minor figures to include and how full their entries should be. Wherever possible, useful references are made to figures who do not warrant separate entries.

Each *DLB* volume has a volume editor responsible for planning the volume, selecting the figures for inclusion, and assigning the entries. Volume editors are also responsible for preparing, where appropriate, appendices surveying the major periodicals and literary and intellectual movements for their volumes, as well as lists of further readings. Work on the series as a whole is coordinated at the Bruccoli Clark Layman editorial center in Columbia, South Carolina, where the editorial staff is responsible for accuracy of the published volumes.

One feature that distinguishes *DLB* is the illustration policy–its concern with the iconography of literature. Just as an author is influenced by his surroundings, so is the reader's understanding of the author enhanced by a knowledge of his environment. Therefore *DLB* volumes include not only drawings, paintings, and photographs of authors, often depicting them at various stages in their careers, but also illustrations of their families and places where they lived. Title pages are regularly reproduced in facsimile along with dust jackets for modern authors. The dust jackets are a special feature of *DLB* because they often document better than anything else the way in which an author's work was perceived in its own time. Specimens of the writers' manuscripts are included when feasible.

Samuel Johnson rightly decreed that "The chief glory of every people arises from its authors." The purpose of the *Dictionary of Literary Biography* is to compile literary history in the surest way available to us–by accurate and comprehensive treatment of the lives and work of those who contributed to it.

The *DLB* Advisory Board

Foreword

This volume covers a period of growth, reorganization, and crisis in the British publishing industry. It was an era that began with a movement away from the unbridled competition of the mid-Victorian years, which had cut into the earnings of publishers, booksellers, and authors. After 1881 these three interest groups would introduce an element of organization and regulation into the book business. They began by organizing themselves: the Society of Authors was founded in 1884, the Associated Booksellers of Great Britain and Ireland in 1895, the Publishers' Association in 1896. International copyright protection was secured by the Berne Convention of 1886 and, in the United States, by the Chace Act of 1891. The 1900 Net Book Agreement, following a proposal Frederick Macmillan had made a decade earlier, fixed retail prices and thus controlled the destructive competition that had bankrupted so many Victorian booksellers. Recently, the Net Book Agreement has been challenged by powerful retailers.

In 1881 British publishing still consisted of many small family firms. Over the next 110 years most of those companies would disappear or be absorbed into large corporations. The literary agent, practically unheard of before A. P. Watt went into the business around 1875, became a powerful mediator between author and publisher. Britain's first successful book club, the Book Society, commenced in 1929.

This period of publishing history, however, was not exclusively a story of commercialization and corporate growth. The Kelmscott Press, launched in 1891, inspired a succession of private presses devoted to the art of the book. Other publishers found ways to sell quality literature to a mass market without sacrificing profit: J. M. Dent founded Everyman's Library, his series of shilling classics, in 1906; and Allen Lane began the paperback revolution with Penguin Books in 1935.

The industry struggled through two world wars, coping with staff shortages, paper rationing, and steep inflation. The blackest night in the history of British publishing came on 29-30 December 1940, when German bombers devastated the offices of many venerable houses around Paternoster Row in London. (The destruction of business records is still mourned by publishing historians, and it seriously hampered the compilation of several company histories for this volume and its companion, *DLB 106: British Literary Publishing Houses, 1820-1880*.)

After World War II émigrés from central Europe—such as André Deutsch and George Weidenfeld—injected new energy into what had become a fairly stodgy profession. Production of new titles increased dramatically, from about ten thousand in 1950 to more than forty thousand in the mid 1980s. Dickensian methods of invoicing and record keeping gave way to computerization; marketing became increasingly scientific and aggressive.

Indeed, postwar British publishers had to become more businesslike to survive. As former colonies developed indigenous publishing industries, London firms found their export markets shrinking. In the 1980s budget cuts by the government of Prime Minister Margaret Thatcher reduced book purchases by public libraries and educational institutions. One by one, independent houses found themselves swallowed up by conglomerates. At the same time, new small presses continued to sprout up and prosper. It is too early to tell which of these will make literary history, and which will prove ephemeral. Accordingly, the editors have excluded from this volume any firm founded after 1965.

We hope that this volume and *DLB 106* will encourage scholarship in the largely unmapped field of publishing history. Only the more prominent British publishing houses have been adequately chronicled; for a great many firms no complete account exists. Each entry in our two volumes, with its accompanying bibliography, is designed to be a starting point for further research.

The varieties of book history, and the enormous potential of the field, are laid out by Robert Darnton in *The Kiss of Lamourette* (New York: Norton, 1990) and his article "Histoire du livre—Geschichte des Buchwesens: An Agenda for Comparative History" in *Publishing History*, 22 (1987): 33-41. The contributors to this volume and to *DLB 106* have written concise individual company histories, but scholars in the field have employed many other approaches: they have reconstructed the publishing histories of particular books, authors, editors, and literary agents; they have analyzed the business of printing and bookselling, the organization of the book trade, the sociology and economics of authorship, and the politics of literary criticism; they have traced the legal history of copyright, censorship, and underground publishing; they have shown how publishers select, solicit, and edit manuscripts; they have traced the diffusion of books to public and home libraries; they have built up a large body of historical literature measuring the spread and the extent of literacy; and, most recently, they have begun to study how people in past times read, and how they responded to what they read.

The contributors to this volume and to *DLB 106* teach in departments of history, literature, communications, art, and sociology; they also include librarians, bibliophiles, and members of the publishing industry. They have been drawn from all over the English-speaking world: most are from Britain and the United States, and some work in Canada, Australia, and Ireland. Because they are dispersed so widely both by discipline and by geography, publishing historians have brought a rich variety of methodologies to their subject; for the same reason, however, they are often unaware of each other's work. As we write, efforts are already under way to organize an international scholarly society for the history of authorship, reading, and publishing. Our two volumes will, we trust, help forge these scattered researchers into an organized and cooperative group.

—*Jonathan Rose and Patricia J. Anderson*

Acknowledgments

This book was produced by Bruccoli Clark Layman, Inc. Karen L. Rood is senior editor for the *Dictionary of Literary Biography* series. Philip B. Dematteis was the in-house editor.

Production coordinator is James W. Hipp. Projects manager is Charles D. Brower. Photography editors are Edward Scott and Timothy C. Lundy. Permissions editor is Jean W. Ross. Layout and graphics supervisor is Penney L. Haughton. Copyediting supervisor is Bill Adams. Typesetting supervisor is Kathleen M. Flanagan. Systems manager is George F. Dodge. The production staff includes Rowena Betts, Teresa Chaney, Patricia Coate, Gail Crouch, Margaret McGinty Cureton, Mary Scott Dye, Sarah A. Estes, Robert Fowler, Cynthia Hallman, Ellen McCracken, Kathy Lawler Merlette, Catherine A. Murray, John Myrick, Pamela D. Norton, Cathy J. Reese, Laurrè Sinckler-Reeder, Maxine K. Smalls, Teri C. Sperry, and Betsy L. Weinberg.

Walter W. Ross and Henry Cunningham did library research. They were assisted by the following librarians at the Thomas Cooper Library of the University of South Carolina: Jens Holley and the interlibrary-loan staff; reference librarians Gwen Baxter, Daniel Boice, Faye Chadwell, Jo Cottingham, Cathy Eckman, Rhonda Felder, Gary Geer, Jackie Kinder, Laurie Preston, Jean Rhyne, Carol Tobin, Virginia Weathers, and Connie Widney; circulation-department head Thomas Marcil; and acquisitions-searching supervisor David Haggard.

J. O. Baylen, the contributor of the Faber and Faber Limited entry, would like to thank Mr. John Bodley, the Faber and Faber archivist, for information about the firm. The editors would like to thank Mr. William McMullan for information that was used in the Pan Books Limited entry.

British Literary
Publishing Houses,
1881-1965

Dictionary of Literary Biography

George Allen and Unwin Limited
(London: 1914-1986)
Unwin Hyman Limited
(London: 1986-   )

See also the George Allen, George Bell and Sons, William Bemrose, Swan Sonnenschein Limited, and T. Fisher Unwin entries in *DLB 106: British Literary Publishing Houses, 1820-1880*.

The origins of George Allen and Unwin Limited lay in the 1870s, when the writer John Ruskin decided to sell his own books direct to the public with the help of an assistant, George Allen, who had been an engraver and joiner and later an art teacher. The first work published and sold in this way was *Fors Clavigera*, a series of letters to the "workmen and labourers of Great Britain." The series appeared monthly from January 1871 to March 1878, then at irregular intervals until 1884. Allen's press at Orpington, Kent, eventually handled all of Ruskin's books. With Ruskin's permission, Allen began to act for other authors and opened an office in London at Bell Yard, behind the Old Bailey, in 1882. In 1893 he moved to 156 Charing Cross Road, where he published the first of Gilbert Murray's translations of Greek plays. Allen died in 1907 and was succeeded by

his children. In 1909 the firm purchased the London publishing business of the Derby printers Bemrose and Sons and moved to Rathbone Place, off Oxford Street. In 1911 it amalgamated with Swan Sonnenschein and Company (founded in 1878), which specialized in sociology and politics. Swan Sonnenschein had published *Capital* (1887), by Karl Marx; *Towards Democracy* (1883-1911), by Edward Carpenter; the Library of Philosophy (1890-1911), edited by John Henry Muirhead; and a Social Science series including work by Beatrice Webb. Authors of more general interest on Sonnenschein's list were George Bernard Shaw, George Moore, and J. M. Barrie.

The enlarged firm, renamed George Allen and Company, was acquired in 1914 by Stanley Unwin, who was descended from printers and papermakers. Stanley Unwin was born in 1884 to Edward and Elizabeth Spicer Unwin in a suburban villa at Handen Road, southeast London; Edward Unwin and his brother George were partners in the printing firm of Unwin Brothers. After Stanley Unwin's birth the family, which in-

Sir Stanley Unwin

cluded six boys and two girls, moved to The Mount, a vast Victorian residence near Bromley, Kent. Edward Unwin, a deacon of the Congregational church, allowed no drink in the house, nor any Sunday newspapers. The day of rest was given up almost entirely to religious observance, and family prayers were held every day.

Stanley Unwin was educated first at a school for sons of missionaries at Blackheath and afterwards at Abbotsholme School under Dr. Cecil Reddie, author of a book on the school published by George Allen in 1900. Reddie's school was not notably academic: pupils took lessons in the morning, did manual work in the afternoon, and devoted their evenings to social life. Unwin's chief literary recollection of his early days was reading J. A. Hobson's radical work *The War in South Africa* (1900), which made Unwin permanently skeptical of jingoism, and fourteen of the novels of Sir Walter Scott, one after the other. At the age of fifteen he left school and worked for about a year in a shipping and brokering office in London. On a weekend visit to Thomas Fisher Unwin, his father's stepbrother, he was asked if he would like to join his uncle's publishing business. Stanley agreed on the condition that he

first be allowed to spend some time in Germany, as his three older brothers had. Thomas Fisher Unwin readily assented.

On arriving in Germany in 1903 Stanley Unwin enrolled at a school in Sachsen Meiningen to improve his German. But in his typically energetic way, he also set out to explore the German book trade, the organization of which he came to admire. For a time he worked in Leipzig and attended the Leipzig Book Fair, the hub of the European trade. In Berlin he managed to sell £120 worth of T. Fisher Unwin's books. After traveling in Switzerland and Czechoslovakia he returned to England, joining T. Fisher Unwin in September 1904. He familiarized himself with type and typesetting in his father's printing works and "traveled" British bookshops as a publisher's representative for his uncle. By his early twenties he had risen to become office manager at 1 Adelphi Terrace, two doors away from Fisher Unwin's flat, where the firm moved in 1905. He visited the Leipzig Book Fair every year and in 1907 traveled to the United States, where he found American publishers to be much less efficient than the Germans. His main personal acquisitions for the firm's list were *Songs of a Sourdough* (1908), by Robert W. Service, and *Ann Veronica* (1909), a feminist story by H. G. Wells that Unwin bought for fifteen hundred pounds. He also obtained the valuable agencies for the Baedeker Guides and the Ordnance Survey maps. But Unwin found his uncle an exacting and jealous taskmaster, and in 1912 he resigned and set out with his future brother-in-law, Severn Storr, on a world tour.

It was not in Unwin's nature to regard this or any other tour as a holiday pure and simple. Wherever he went, he made careful notes on possible markets for books; on his return to London in December 1913 he probably knew more about those markets, as well as the Continental and American ones explored while working for his uncle, than any other member of the British book trade. To insatiable curiosity and energy, he joined a remarkable talent for business; his Nonconformist upbringing had given him a "Protestant" attitude to work, some moderately radical political views, and, ironically, the same somewhat dictatorial ideas as T. Fisher Unwin about how to run a firm. It was his fixed opinion that the best publishing businesses were the creation of one man; staff conferences, if held at all, should be merely advisory.

Not long after returning to England, Unwin discovered an ailing firm which appeared to suit

Unwin (second row, seventh from left) at the 1934 Ripon Hall publishers and booksellers conference that he helped organize

his management principles. George Allen and Company was to be wound up on 1 January 1914. The firm's collapse derived chiefly from a decline in the sales of Ruskin's books. Unwin made his own valuation of its bound and unbound stock, stereo plates, molds, copyrights, illustrations, furniture, and liens against the company held by printers and binders. He made his offer for the firm "subject to liens," which meant that the whole of the amount offered would be available to the receiver, whereas from all other offers the value of the liens would have to be deducted. It was a characteristically shrewd variant on normal practice. The debenture holders retained their debentures in full and actually had a majority holding in the new firm, George Allen and Unwin Limited, registered on 4 August 1914 with a nominal capital of five thousand pounds. Unwin was made managing director for life, and, conscious that only reinvestment would save the firm, agreed with the other directors that none of them would take more than three hundred pounds a year in salary unless they unanimously voted otherwise. Since Unwin had been getting twelve hundred pounds a year from T. Fisher Unwin in 1911, the new venture meant for him a considerable drop in pay. He did, however, increase the pay of his staff. He also moved the business from Rathbone Place to 40 Museum Street, near the British Museum.

Unwin felt from the first that the ship had too many captains. World War I helped him here: his three fellow directors were called up for military service, but he was declared medically unfit; thus he was able to run the business more or less single-handedly. Dead stock was successfully remaindered, including paperbound copies of Thomas Gray's *Elegy Written in a Country Churchyard* that were sold to the vicar of Stoke Poges, where the poem was written, for a penny apiece. Ruskin's life story, published as *Praeterita* from 1885 to 1900, was retitled *The Autobiography of John Ruskin* in 1915 and sold out completely. Never one to miss an opportunity, Unwin commissioned an autobiography on his wedding day from the minister who married him, Dr. R. F. Horton. It was published in 1917. He was not, however, able to persuade his fellow directors, who had returned from the war, to publish *Married Love*, by Marie Stopes; the book, which openly discussed topics previously shrouded in Victorian prudery, was published in 1918 by

A. C. Fifield and sold more than a million copies. This defeat exemplified Unwin's willingness to propagate new ideas, so long as they did not carry an excessive business risk. The modest sales of *Rain before Seven* (1915), a novel by Eric Leadbitter, confirmed his determination not to depend on fiction. The basis of prosperity was, for him, a sound backlist of books steadily in demand; few novels met this criterion. The first book to appear with the George Allen and Unwin imprint, *The Diplomatic History of the War* (1915), by Morgan Philips Price, did meet it. It was highly topical, widely reviewed, offered only a minimal risk, and would be read by students of the war long after the Armistice.

It was the war that brought the philosopher Bertrand Russell to George Allen and Unwin as an author; thereafter, the firm published almost all of Russell's books. Cambridge University Press had published Russell's highly technical *The Principles of Mathematics* (1903) and *Principia Mathematica* (1910, coauthored with Alfred North Whitehead), but the war diverted Russell from mathematics and logic to ethics and social philosophy. His pacifism led to his imprisonment and the loss of his fellowship at Trinity College, Cambridge. At this point Unwin, to whom Russell's combination of liberal resistance to war and rational criticism of society were wholly congenial, invited him to submit manuscripts. The first of Russell's books to be published by George Allen and Unwin was *Principles of Social Reconstruction* (1916), a collection of articles written for American magazines. Russell continued to write copiously on philosophical topics: *Introduction to Mathematical Philosophy* (1919) and *The Analysis of Mind* (1921) appeared in George Allen and Unwin's Library of Philosophy series, edited by John Henry Muirhead. But it was his forays into the mine fields of economics, education, morals, and politics in rigorous, well-written, provocative studies such as *Marriage and Morals* (1929), *The Conquest of Happiness* (1930), *Education and the Social Order* (1932), *Power* (1938), and *Authority and the Individual* (1949), as well as searching critiques of religion, communism, and nuclear warfare, that made him familiar to the wider reading public. Russell's *History of Western Philosophy and Its Connection with Political and Social Circumstances from the Earliest Times to the Present Day* (1946), often reprinted, brought together—as its title shows—several of his preoccupations. So did his typically candid autobiography, published in three volumes from 1967 to 1969, just before his death.

Frank Mumby's claim that George Allen and Unwin Limited contributed more than any other publisher to the common stock of knowledge gains ample proof from the books of Russell alone.

Unwin encouraged other authors of a late-Victorian and Edwardian liberal cast of mind such as Murray, whose translations from the Greek he continued to publish and whose efforts on behalf of the League of Nations after 1918 he applauded; J. A. Hobson, whose criticisms of imperialism touched a sympathetic chord in Unwin; L. T. Hobhouse, the analyst of social tensions; H. M. Hyndman, the Marxist product of Eton and Trinity who led the Socialist Democratic Federation; J. M. Robertson, the freethinking scholar and writer; and Ramsay MacDonald, leader of the Independent Labour party. Books of a politico-sociological type were often recommended to Allen and Unwin by A. R. Orage, the Fabian editor of the *New Age*, and G. P. Gooch, the historian of historiography.

Some unfounded criticism of Unwin's actions in acquiring George Allen and Company blocked his first application to join the Publishers Association. This rejection was no great loss: the association concerned itself with little more than the defense of the Net Book Agreement of 1900, designed to prevent booksellers from undercutting the prices set by publishers. Though fully opposed to this practice, Unwin had his own views about discounts from publishers to booksellers, which never wavered up to the 1950s. He would not allow more than a 21-percent discount on single orders (which were obviously expensive to fulfill), whereas the normal discount was 25 percent. Such a policy exemplified his attention to detail, for which his fellow directors had no taste. They worked in private offices, while he occupied a small office on the ground floor from which he could see every visitor. They started at the civilized hour of 10:00 A.M., while he was on duty at 9:00. He saw all the incoming mail and copies of every letter sent. They were involved less with the growth of the firm than with the safety of their investments. One by one, Unwin eased them out.

Eager to introduce foreign literature to English readers, Unwin engaged two wandering scholars, Eden and Cedar Paul, as translators. They rendered A. F. A. Hamon's *Bernard Shaw: Le Molière du XXᵉ siecle* (1913) as *The Twentieth Century Molière: Bernard Shaw* (1915) and produced *Treitschke: His Life and Works* (1914) and the seven-

Philip Unwin, nephew of Sir Stanley Unwin, at age sixty

volume *History of Germany in the 19th Century* (1915-1918), by Heinrich von Treitschke. Among Czechoslovakian books which the Pauls translated into English were *The Spirit of Russia* (1916), by Tomâŝ Masaryk, the first president of the Czech Republic; and *The Cheat* (1941), by Karel Capek. One unexpected best-seller from the German was *Napoleon* (1927), by Emil Ludwig. Although Unwin published *In Days to Come* (1921), by the German industrialist and philosopher Walter Rathenau, he turned down *Mein Kampf* (1925-1927), by Adolf Hitler, on the ground that Hitler's rise to power was then uncertain. Other notable Continental authors whose works were published by Unwin were Benedetto Croce, Oswald Spengler, August Strindberg, Albert Sorel, Albert Schweitzer, and Sigmund Freud. As early as 1919 Unwin published Arthur Waley's translations of Chinese poetry and even accepted his six-volume English version (1925-1933) of the Japanese novel *The Tale of Genji*, by Shikibu Murasaki.

In his twenties Unwin had belonged to the National Liberal Club; he resigned after founding his business and joined the more radical 1917 Club, a forum for left-wing intellectuals and Lib-

eral and Labour politicians. Determined that his firm should lead rather than follow in the world of ideas, he published extensively for the London School of Economics and the Fabian Society. In December 1920 he took over the Swarthmore Press, a Quaker pacifist firm which published books on the social relevance of Christianity. Despite his strong Congregationalist roots, he was—like his mother—attracted by the Quaker idea of the "Inner Light," which left him unconcerned with the opinions of others if he was satisfied with his own actions. It is not difficult to see how this attitude expressed itself in the management of George Allen and Unwin Limited.

In 1919 the firm published Unwin's pamphlet *British Literature and the United States*, which dealt with the vexing problem of American copyright. Seven years later he published *The Truth about Publishing* at his own expense. The eighth edition, revised and partly rewritten by Unwin's nephew Philip, appeared in 1976; it has been translated into thirteen languages, including Hindi, Japanese, and Turkish. Its purpose was threefold: to strip the mystery from publishing, to help inexperienced authors, and to secure status for Unwin himself. It has also served to educate the book trade: no beginner in publishing now ignores it.

The main practical effect of the book was to immerse Unwin in the politics of the book trade. He had been a leader in the Society of Bookmen since its foundation in 1921; membership was confined to fifty people connected with authorship and the production and distribution of books. Its function, congenial to Unwin, was the discussion of new ideas in trade practice. The society evolved in 1925 into the National Book Council (which became the National Book League after World War II), which published bibliographies, maintained a library, and urged the importance of books on the British government, local authorities, and the general public. Unwin had attended meetings of the Publishers' Association since his days with T. Fisher Unwin; but after the failure of his first application for membership as head of his own firm, he waited ten years before trying again. *The Truth about Publishing* quickly drew him onto the council of the Publishers' Association; he became treasurer in 1931 and served as president from 1933 to 1935 and vice-president from 1935 to 1937. He promoted the first joint conference between publishers and booksellers, held at Ripon Hall near Oxford in 1934. He was likewise active in the International Publishers' As-

Trade advertisement comparing the sales of Allen and Unwin's edition of Thor Heyerdahl's The Kon-Tiki Expedition *to those of Eric Williams's* The Wooden Horse, *published by Collins*

sociation and helped to revive the International Congress of Publishers, which had lain dormant since before World War I.

Unwin was determined to preserve his business as a family firm rather than as a public company. On 1 March 1927 he took his nephew Philip Unwin into the production department at a salary of fourteen pounds a month. Philip was the son of George Soundy Unwin, joint managing director of the Unwin Brothers printing firm, and had, like Stanley himself, worked for T. Fisher Unwin. In 1926 Fisher Unwin had sold out to Ernest Benn, with whom Philip Unwin spent five months before joining his uncle.

The Depression decimated export markets for British books, led to cuts in library expenditures, and put many publishing firms out of business. Unwin's practice of reinvesting not less than half of each year's profits carried him through some bad times; in 1934, when a loss seemed inevitable, he refunded part of his own salary to keep the company afloat. In 1928 he had acquired the firm of Williams and Norgate; in 1934, when George Allen and Unwin needed capital, he sold Williams and Norgate to his last remaining co-director, E. L. Skinner. George Allen and Unwin

Limited was now completely his. It had taken Unwin twenty years to achieve the kind of complete authority over his business which he had somewhat resented at T. Fisher Unwin.

Unwin picked out from the Williams and Norgate theological and philosophical list one author, Lancelot Hogben, in whom he saw promise; Hogben's *Mathematics for the Million* (1936) and *Science for the Citizen* (1938) proved highly successful for George Allen and Unwin as the Depression lifted. Also in the 1920s, Unwin bought Maunsell of Dublin, publisher of the playwrights J. M. Synge and St. John Ervine. In 1937 George Allen and Unwin Limited obtained a controlling interest in The Bodley Head, previously run by John Lane and his distant cousin Allen Lane. Unwin thought it would be "amusing" to own the firm cooperatively with his competitors Jonathan Cape and J. M. Dent, as long as they held no more than one-sixth of the equity each. As it turned out, the Bodley Head would pay no dividend until 1947 and would be sold to Max Reinhardt in 1957 for seventy-two thousand pounds. Since the Bodley Head general list did not sit easily with Unwin's more academic publishing, he had no desire to absorb any of its authors into his own firm. This reluctance also applied, for different reasons, to the Phaidon Press, a Jewish artbook publisher founded in Vienna in 1923 and acquired by Unwin in 1938 to protect it from the Nazis.

Unwin's progressive outlook led him to publish books on India and by Indians at a time when British imperial sentiment was strong. *The Hindu View of Life* (1927), by the philosopher and statesman Sarvepalli Radhakrishnan; *The True India* (1939), by C. F. Andrews; Radhakrishnan's translation of *The Bhagavadgita* (1948); and *The Story of My Experiments with Truth* (1949), by Mahatma Gandhi, helped to create a new understanding of the subcontinent.

The hunger for books that occurred in Britain during World War II was frustrated by a shortage of paper. George Allen and Unwin Limited bought up as much paper as possible before rationing was introduced in April 1940, forcing publishers to make do with 60 percent of their average consumption in the years 1936 to 1938. In 1937 the British book trade had published some 11,300 titles; the number had fallen to 7,500 by 1943. Unwin wrote to the *Times* and badgered Whitehall in the hope of increasing the paper supply. He complained that many small publishers escaped rationing because they did not exist in the years on which the quotas were based. Yet established firms simply could not meet the rising demand from the armed services, the Red Cross, the British Council, and the Ministry of Information. Unwin's own situation worsened when the Allen and Unwin storehouse at Edmonton in north London was bombed on 8 November 1940: sheet stock of 1.4 million books, representing some 2,100 titles, was lost. Unwin published some of his lectures on paper rationing and related topics as *Publishing in Peace and War* (1944) but with no effect on the government; rationing remained in force until 1949. One victory he could claim: with the support of the publisher Geoffrey Faber he persuaded the government to exempt books from the purchase tax. In return, he got the Publishers' Association to sign the Book Production War Economy Agreement, which governed the appearance of British books throughout the war. Gray, speckled paper; narrow margins; blank endpapers; new chapters beginning on the same page on which the previous chapter ended; and plain covers unmistakably mark wartime typography after 1941.

Unwin's reforming streak touched a chord in public opinion during the war, when service-

men and civilians alike began to expect radical change after the Armistice. Books in the backlist by left-wing writers, such as *A Grammar of Politics* (1925) and *Liberty in the Modern State* (1930), by Harold J. Laski, and, above all, *Full Employment in a Free Society* (1944), by Sir William Beveridge, helped to propagate some of Unwin's own ideas on a fairer distribution of wealth, a better-regulated economy, and wider educational opportunity. Books designed to improve morale and technical efficiency also sold well, such as *Their Finest Hour* (1940), by Alan Michie and Walter Graebner; *Home Guard Goings On* (1941), by Basil Boothroyd; and books on astronavigation by the yachtsman Francis Chichester. It was Chichester who suggested a series of spotters' handbooks for the Observer Corps and others; more than twenty thousand were sold.

Toward the end of the war Unwin bought the assets of Elkin Mathews and Marrot, previously noted for belles lettres and then beginning to publish educational books; shortly afterward he acquired Thos. Murby and Company, the leading geological publisher. But these additions were probably less important to the firm than translations. Unwin claimed that George Allen and Unwin published more translations than any other two English publishers put together. Translations from Czech, Danish, Flemish, Icelandic, and Turkish and a series of ethical and religious classics from East and West had a modest but steady sale. Then came *The Kon-Tiki Expedition* (1950), by the Norwegian writer and explorer Thor Heyerdahl. Philip Unwin had been offered the book in the summer of 1948, while on holiday in Norway, by the head of Gyldendal Norsk Forlag; at that time some 140,000 copies had already been sold in Scandinavia.

Heyerdahl's four-thousand-mile voyage across the Pacific on a balsa-wood raft, undertaken to prove a theory about ancient migration, had attracted little attention in the British press. But when the book appeared, it served as the perfect diversion from postwar austerity for thousands of readers. Heyerdahl's was the first great peacetime adventure. Unwin doubled the normal number of review copies: when the reviews came out on 31 March 1950 the first printing of 40,000 copies and a second impression of 27,000 were sold before publication. Each reprint thereafter was of at least 20,000 copies. The demand for translations from the English led to world sales in one year of 875,000 copies. Some half a million hardback copies were sold by Allen and

Unwin; book club sales amounted to almost as many. It became a Reader's Digest Condensed Book; it was set as a text for the General Certificate of Education; the Penguin edition was reprinted several times. *The Kon-Tiki Expedition* was the most successful book published by Allen and Unwin in the firm's first thirty-five years. Two other books by Heyerdahl, *American Indians in the Pacific* (1952) and *Aku-Aku* (1958), about Easter Island, were also in considerable demand.

Profits on *The Kon-Tiki Expedition* enabled the normally thrifty Unwin to pay staff bonuses; some senior men even got company cars. But his management style remained as cautious as ever. Although Philip Unwin and Charles Furth, a respected editor, had become directors in 1948, Stanley Unwin continued to preside as governing director with a veto at board meetings. He was by this time also a director of other businesses, not all associated with his own: Methuen, Chapman and Hall, The Bodley Head, and Unwin Brothers, the family printers. He retained his lively interest in the international book trade, which took him on frequent journeys across the globe. Allen and Unwin sales by the early 1950s had increased to five times the prewar amount, even though the demand for books dropped sharply. Unwin argued that the books were underpriced in that inflation had made them relatively cheap. His rule was never to fix the published price at less than three times the unit cost of manufacture, but delays in printing and paper supply meant that costs rose after the estimates had been made. Unwin's solution was to raise the formula to three and a half times the unit cost and always to measure the estimate against inflationary trends.

If publishing was to Unwin an art of rational calculation, he could hardly deny that luck also played its part. Soon after the success of *The Kon-Tiki Expedition*, he was equally fortunate with another book having Nordic overtones. In October 1936 a student of the Oxford professor J. R. R. Tolkien had sent the typescript of Tolkien's fantasy novel *The Hobbit* to Allen and Unwin. Unwin, assuming the book to be a fairy story, had asked his ten-year-old son Rayner to read it. On Rayner's approval, it had been published on 21 September 1937. After good reviews by C. S. Lewis, himself a writer of fantasies and a friend of Tolkien, the book had sold out by Christmas. Thus encouraged, Tolkien had offered another story, *The Silmarillion*, but it was not quite what Unwin wanted. In February 1938 Tolkien

Dust jacket for the first of J. R. R. Tolkien's fantasy novels, published by Allen and Unwin in 1937

had sent a third manuscript, about a ring; Rayner Unwin had enjoyed it, but his father, averse to publishing fiction and uncertain that *The Hobbit* was not a seasonal fluke, turned it down. As a student at Oxford in 1947, Rayner Unwin had read an expanded version of the third story, which Tolkien then called *The Lord of the Rings*, and thought it brilliant and gripping. Tolkien, still smarting from Stanley Unwin's rejection of *The Silmarillion*, hoped that Collins rather than Allen and Unwin would publish *The Lord of the Rings*. Collins took until 1952 to decide against doing so. In September 1952 Rayner Unwin brought the huge typescript back to his father. With typical caution, Stanley Unwin felt that, if published at all, the work should appear in three or four self-contained volumes; a waning of interest might then easily bring the book to a halt before too much money was lost on it. He also suggested that the work should be subject not to conventional royalty payments but to an arrangement under which profits would be shared with the author after the costs of production had been recovered. This scheme—Unwin's preferred method for potentially unprofitable books—would have the effect of reducing the price and of reaping greater benefits for the author if the book sold well. Tolkien finally accepted the arrangement, and *The Lord of the Rings* appeared in three volumes: *The Fellowship of the Ring* (1954), *The Two Towers* (1954), and *The Return of the Ring* (1955). Unwin had thirty-five hundred copies of the first volume printed and slightly fewer of the others. To his great surprise, he had to reprint the first volume after six weeks. Wide sales in America led to the formation of a Tolkien Society, foreign translations proliferated, and the creatures of Tolkien's fantasy became a cult; by the end of 1968 some three million copies of *The Lord of the Rings* had been sold. Rayner Unwin, who became chairman of the firm after his father's death, finally published *The Silmarillion* in 1977. (Tolkien had died in 1973.)

It is ironic that near the end of Stanley Unwin's publishing career he should enjoy the benefits of gambling, against which his careful temperament had thus far revolted. It was for his sound, steady predictability that friends and colleagues valued him. Public recognition of his contribution to the British and international book trade had begun at the end of World War II. In 1945 he had received an honorary LL.D. from Aberdeen University; he had been knighted in 1946; twenty years later he was made Knight Commander of the Order of St. Michael and St. George (KCMG). To mark his close links with the European trade, he also received Belgian, French, and Czech decorations. Oskar Kokoschka painted a portrait of him sitting characteristically at his desk in 40 Museum Street; this painting still hangs in the chairman's office.

By 1968, when Stanley Unwin died, only the directors and the editorial office remained in London. The warehouse had been moved to larger premises at Hemel Hempstead, Hertfordshire, in 1960, and by 1974 the trade and accounts departments were also there. These changes, in part the result of advice from management consultants, corresponded with similar migrations from London by firms such as Longmans and the Cape-Bodley Head-Chatto group.

On 29 July 1986 George Allen and Unwin Limited and Bell and Hyman Limited merged to form Unwin Hyman Limited, most shares being held by the Unwin and Hyman families. Robin Hyman had formed Bell and Hyman Limited in 1977 from the former George Bell and Sons Limited, a firm dating from 1839 and noted for schoolbooks, books on chess, and above all for *The Diary of Samuel Pepys* (1893-1899). The merger meant that the combined firm covered the whole range of educational literature up to the university level. As of 1989 Unwin Hyman, with Rayner Unwin as nonexecutive chairman and Robin Hyman as managing director, had more than three thousand books in print and sales exceeding twelve million pounds. Since 1 October 1986 warehousing and distribution have been carried out from Maidstone, Kent. In 1987 the two component firms left their separate premises in Museum Street, Hemel Hempstead, and Queen Elizabeth Street to settle in Broadwick House, Broadwick Street, Soho, London.

References:

H. H. Bemrose, *The House of Bemrose 1826-1926* (Derby: Bemrose, 1926);

Humphrey Carpenter, *J. R. R. Tolkien: A Biography* (London: Allen & Unwin, 1977);

J. W. Lambert and Michael Ratcliffe, *The Bodley Head 1887-1987* (London: Bodley Head, 1987);

F. A. Mumby and Frances H. S. Stallybrass, *From Swan Sonnenschein to George Allen and Unwin Ltd* (London: Allen & Unwin, 1955);

David Unwin, *Fifty Years with Father: A Relationship* (London: Allen & Unwin, 1982);

Philip Unwin, *The Printing Unwins: A Short History of Unwin Brothers, the Gresham Press 1826-1926* (London: Allen & Unwin, 1976);

Unwin, *The Publishing Unwins* (London: Heinemann, 1971);

Stanley Unwin, *The Truth about a Publisher* (London: Allen & Unwin, 1960; New York: Macmillan, 1960);

Unwin, *The Truth about Publishing*, eighth edition, revised by Philip Unwin (London: Allen & Unwin, 1976).

Papers:
The archives of George Allen and Unwin Limited are held by the Library of the University of Reading.

—*J. A. Edwards*

Angus and Robertson (UK) Limited
(London: 1968-)
Angus and Robertson (London)
(London: 1954-1968)

The London house of Angus and Robertson began publishing books in 1954. It is a subsidiary of the large Australian publishing firm Angus and Robertson, which has been an important part of Australia's literary history.

The firm began as a bookshop set up by David Mackenzie Angus, who arrived in Sydney in 1882. Having worked as a bookseller's assistant in Edinburgh, Angus found work in a Sydney bookstore before leaving in 1884 to set up his own shop with fifty pounds of savings. Then aged twenty-nine, Angus rented half a shop at 110 1/2 Market Street, received his first shipment of (mainly secondhand) books from a former colleague in Edinburgh, and sent out his first circular, dated 10 June 1884, advertising the shop and encouraging mail orders from country towns.

George Robertson had been apprenticed to a bookseller and publisher in Glasgow before immigrating to New Zealand and then to Sydney in 1882. He and Angus worked at the same bookstore after their arrival in Sydney, and after Angus set up his own shop, Robertson would go there after work to assist with the sorting and marking of books.

In January 1886 the twenty-six-year-old Robertson left his job and paid fifteen pounds for a half share in Angus's business. During its first year as Angus and Robertson the shop had healthy sales of four thousand pounds. In 1887 the other half of 110 Market Street became available, and the bookshop doubled in size.

Angus was a specialist in the craft of bookselling, particularly secondhand books, whereas Robertson was an energetic entrepreneur who anticipated a world market and foresaw the possibilities of publishing. The first titles bearing the Angus and Robertson imprint were published in 1888: two books of verse, *A Crown of Wattle*, by H. Peden Steel, and *Sun and Cloud on River and Sea*, by Ishmael Dare (the pen name of Arthur W. Jose); and *Facsimile of a Proposal for a Settlement on the Coast of New South Wales*, written by Sir George Young in 1785 and printed from a copy in Robertson's antiquarian collection of Australiana.

At the end of 1890 the partners acquired a much larger property at 89 Castlereagh Street, around the corner from the original premises. The new shop, formerly a coach factory, had to be extensively renovated, a process which lasted until 1895. The new layout, featuring cupboard-tables, movable shelving, and plenty of light and space for browsing, was the prototype of modern Sydney bookshops until the 1950s. A regular clientele of doctors, lawyers, academics, and politicians frequented the shop, as well as writers such as Henry Lawson and A. B. (Banjo) Paterson. Overseas visitors of the 1890s included John Galsworthy, Joseph Conrad, and Robert Louis Stevenson.

In 1895 the firm published *The Man from Snowy River*, by Paterson, followed by Lawson's *In the Days When the World Was Wide and Other Verses* in 1896. Both poets, then in their twenties, had had work published regularly in the *Bulletin*, the most influential Australian literary and political journal of its day, and Lawson's mother had published his first volume of poems and stories in 1894; but these were their first books to be published by a commercial publishing house. The two books made an enormous impact on the Australian reading public, capturing as they did the

David Mackenzie Angus, the Scottish immigrant to Australia whose bookshop, opened in 1884, became the Angus and Robertson publishing firm

spirit of colonial Australia as it existed in the minds of most city dwellers. Together with Lawson's next volume, a collection of bush stories titled *While the Billy Boils* (1896), the books established Angus and Robertson as a major Australian publishing house. The first Angus and Robertson catalogue, circulated in 1895, was the earliest catalogue ever to contain only Australian publications.

In 1899 Angus was forced by ill health to retire from the business. The next year he sold his share to Fred Wymark and Richard Thomson, two employees. Angus died from tuberculosis on

21 February 1901 in Edinburgh.

Robertson ran the publishing side of the business, assisted first by Hugh MacCallum and then, beginning in 1899, by Fred Shenstone, who worked for Robertson for the next thirty years. During the early 1900s the work of Lawson and Paterson was kept in print and was joined by new work such as Paterson's *Old Bush Songs* (1905) and his long-awaited first novel, *An Outback Marriage* (1906). Bertram Stevens's *Anthology of Australian Verse* also appeared in 1906, and nonfiction and schoolbooks helped to keep the business profitable.

Robertson received a regular supply of unsolicited manuscripts, employing literary men and women such as his daughter Bessie, Jose, Stevens, and Christopher Brennan on a free-lance basis to read and edit them. In 1899 Miles Franklin submitted the manuscript of *My Brilliant Career* to Angus and Robertson on the advice of Lawson, only to have it rejected. It was published by Blackwood of Edinburgh in 1901. Robertson later claimed that he was away in England at the time and that it was Thomson who was responsible for rejecting the manuscript. But Franklin had no better luck in 1905 when her *Some Everyday Folk and Dawn* was also rejected by Angus and Robertson; it was published by Blackwood in 1909.

In 1907 the Angus and Robertson bookshop and publishing business was converted into a public company, Angus and Robertson Limited. The chairman was Robertson, with Wymark, Thomson, and Arthur Wigram Allen as directors. Shenstone was company secretary and manager of the publishing department. The first meeting of the board of directors took place on 12 February 1907. The following year Angus and Robertson bought the premises at 89 Castlereagh Street and also the adjoining property, allowing the shop to be renovated and extended.

Robertson had been trying since 1899 to establish an Angus and Robertson agency in London. He succeeded in 1913, when Henry George set up the Australian Book Company in the basement and ground floor of a building on Farringdon Road. The purpose of the firm was to import and distribute Angus and Robertson titles in England and to export British and American books to Australia. It functioned more as a shipping agent than a bookselling company.

During World War I Angus and Robertson continued to flourish despite paper shortages and other restrictions. Popular titles were repub-

George Robertson, who went into partnership with Angus in 1886

lished in Special Pocket Editions for the troops in the trenches, as well as new titles such as Will Ogilvie's *The Australian and Other Verses* (1916) and Paterson's *Saltbush Bill JP and Other Verses* (1917). The bookshop set up its own Military Department, selling not only service pamphlets but also boots, hats, belts, camp beds, whistles, and other equipment for soldiers.

The great success of the war years was C. J. Dennis's long narrative poem *The Songs of a Sentimental Bloke* (1915). With spelling and colloquialisms capturing the speech and sentiments of "ordinary Australians," the book became enormously popular with readers at home, with soldiers in the trenches nostalgic for Australia, and with British readers fascinated by this glimpse of a culture intriguingly different from class-bound, war-preoccupied Britain. Within three months *The Songs of a Sentimental Bloke* had outsold every previous Australian book of verse, and it was into its third impression by the beginning of 1916. Two thousand copies of the fourth impression were

sent to the Australian Book Company in London, with instructions from Robertson that George was to negotiate with Oxford University Press to publish and distribute the book in Britain and North America. After six impressions, the book went into a second edition late in 1916, with a Pocket Edition for the trenches. Altogether, more than fifty-five thousand copies were sold in the first year of publication.

This success was quickly followed by another Dennis book, *The Moods of Ginger Mick*, published in October 1916. It also sold well, though not as spectacularly as *The Songs of a Sentimental Bloke*, which is still regarded as an Australian classic. In 1918 Robertson published *The Magic Pudding*, written and illustrated by Norman Lindsay. Already an established artist, Lindsay was persuaded by Stevens to create a book for children, and Robertson, recognizing a best-seller, published it immediately.

A new company, with the same name, was registered on 21 September 1920, taking over the old Angus and Robertson Limited. The move generated capital which Robertson used in 1923 to buy a printery, Eagle Press; in 1929 he renamed it the Halstead Printing Company after his birthplace in Essex, England. It became the largest book printer in Australia and was incorporated in 1937 as Halstead Press Proprietary Limited, a subsidiary of the parent company.

The 1920s saw two major publications for Angus and Robertson. The first was the *Official History of Australia in the War of 1914-18*, edited by C. E. W. Bean, financed by the Commonwealth Government and published in twelve volumes from 1921 to 1942. The second was the *Australian Encyclopædia*, edited by Jose, Herbert Carter, and T. G. Tucker, published in two volumes in 1925-1926. The encyclopedia expanded to ten volumes in 1958 and was sold by Angus and Robertson in 1962 to the Grolier Society of Australia.

Robertson died on 27 August 1933. Shortly before his death he gave to the Mitchell Library in Sydney (now part of the State Library of New South Wales) his collection of publishing records, which he had edited, annotated, and bound into volumes. These volumes remain the single most valuable source for the early history of Angus and Robertson.

Thomson succeeded Robertson as chairman of the board, with Arthur Wigram Allen, Walter G. Cousins, W. T. Jones, Albert A. Ritchie, and William Kirwan as directors. In 1936 Robertson's

Angus and Robertson's second premises at 89 Castlereagh Street, Sydney, as they appeared in 1916

grandson George A. Ferguson was appointed to the board.

Cousins and Jones went to London in 1937 and decided to buy the London agency, the Australian Book Company, then operating from larger premises at 37 Great Russell Street. Its director was still George, assisted by Hector MacQuarrie together with an accounting assistant, two clerks, and two packers. The following year, Angus and Robertson's first London catalogue was issued from Great Russell Street. It advertised books published by Angus and Robertson in Sydney, such as *The Australian Aborigines: How to Understand Them* (1937), by A. P. Elkin; *Over the Range* (1937) and *Forty Fathoms Deep* (1937) by Ion Idriess, whose outback stories helped to popularize Australian writing at home as well as in Britain; and *Australian Parrots* (1938), by Neville Cayley.

Also during 1938, Ferguson was sent to London to supervise the establishment of the new Angus and Robertson (London) office at 48 Bloomsbury Street. On the death of George, MacQuarrie took over as the director of the company, presiding over a small staff of mainly female clerks and one packer during World War II.

During the war paper rationing in Britain affected book publishing, and Australian authors who could have expected their work to be published in Britain found it more likely to be produced by Australian publishers. In 1942 Cousins was appointed chairman of the Angus and Robert-

son board in Sydney, succeeding Thomson. After Cousins's death in 1948 Ritchie became chairman.

In November 1951 the London office opened a small bookshop in Australia House in the Strand to sell books about Australia to prospective migrants and visitors. In 1953 the parent company acquired new premises at 105 Great Russell Street with the intention of establishing a London publishing house. Under the British Empire Agreement, which took effect just after the war, United Kingdom publishers had sole rights to the Australian market, which meant that European and American books could only find their way to Australia via British publishers. Ferguson, MacQuarrie, and MacQuarrie's assistant of six years, Barry Rowland, therefore built up the London office of Angus and Robertson specifically to circumvent the British Empire Agreement. Rowland was made publishing manager in 1953, and he and MacQuarrie and their staff of fourteen moved to the converted house at 105 Great Russell Street in 1954. Their aim, as MacQuarrie reported to the Angus and Robertson in-house magazine *Fragment* (May 1954), was "to make Angus & Robertson London a first-rate London publishing house."

The first books published by Angus and Robertson (London) were *Esquire Etiquette* (1954), one of a series of popular books from the American *Esquire* magazine, and *White Coolies* (1954), by

Cartoon by David Low showing Robertson besieged by writers

Betty Jeffrey, a story of Australian nurses held by the Japanese in World War II.

The London branch became increasingly active during the 1950s, publishing British as well as American and Continental titles. It also supplied books to British stores, exported books to Australia, and imported Angus and Robertson books to sell in Britain. *The Shiralee*, by D'Arcy Niland, published by Angus and Robertson in Sydney, was the Book Society Choice for 1955 in London.

By 1954 Angus and Robertson comprised three almost separate businesses of retailing, publishing, and printing; the firm employed about 550 people, including the London staff. About seventy-five new titles a year were published in Sydney and London, and a similar number of reprints. The London office was run as a self-contained business, though MacQuarrie and Rowland were in close contact with Ferguson, director of publishing in Sydney, and were answerable to Ritchie, the chairman of the board. Walter Vincent Burns was appointed to the Angus and Robertson board of directors in 1959. The following year, when Ritchie resigned, Burns was appointed chairman. Under his leadership the

company underwent major reorganization and expansion. Retail outlets and other properties were bought in Sydney; Melbourne; Wellington, New Zealand; and London; and new subsidiary companies were formed reflecting Burns's business interests, especially in real estate. Staff turnover was high, with several appointments to and resignations from the board of directors occurring within the same year. At the end of 1960 Burns sold his shares to Consolidated Press and resigned from the Angus and Robertson board. He was succeeded as chairman by Norman Cowper. Consolidated Press made an unsuccessful takeover bid before selling its 30 percent holding of Angus and Robertson in 1962. These shares were bought by three groups of investors: William Collins, the British publisher; a group of smaller British publishers; and a company formed by some of the Angus and Robertson directors.

In London, Rowland was replaced in 1959 by a Burns appointee, Stanley Amor. Amor was replaced by Walter Butcher in 1961. In 1962 the London office moved to 54-58 Bartholomew Close and in the same year represented Australia at the Frankfurt Book Fair—the first time Australian publishers had ever been represented at the fair. Angus and Robertson has exhibited at Frankfurt every year since then, selling titles originating in Australia to British and European publishers.

Between 1962 and 1969 the parent company of Angus and Robertson acquired two more retail operations; expanded publishing activities in Australia, London, and Singapore; and extended printing activities in Sydney and Melbourne. The Singapore office was set up in 1968 by John Ferguson, George Ferguson's son; its function was primarily to sell books, though some publishing—mainly Asian editions of textbooks for the Asian market—was also undertaken. In the same year the London business was transferred to an incorporated company, Angus and Robertson (UK) Limited.

By 1969 the parent company in Sydney was suffering a serious cash crisis. When William Collins and the other British shareholders decided to sell their 24.6 percent holding, Angus and Robertson was ripe for takeover. The Collins shares were sold in 1970 to Tjuringa Securities, an associate of Ipec Insurance Limited, and in 1971 Ipec Insurance, under the chairmanship of Gordon Barton, became the parent company and 100 percent owner of Angus and Robertson and its subsidiaries. Most of the subsidiary companies acquired during the previous decade were sold off, but Angus and Robertson (UK) Limited survived as part of a move to strengthen publishing operations in London, Singapore, and Manila. There was a brief association with Paul Hamlyn's Octopus Books, which were marketed in Australia through Angus and Robertson. The Angus and Robertson bookshop in Australia House was closed in 1972.

The London office moved to 2 Fisher Street in 1971, and John Ferguson succeeded Butcher as director, with responsibility for the Singapore branch as well as for the London office. He closed down the book-buying facility in London as the larger British publishers by this time had their own branches in Australia. By 1972 all the pre-takeover directors had retired or resigned, and many senior staff members in retail and publishing had resigned. The Angus and Robertson group consisted of the parent company, Angus and Robertson Holdings Limited, which discontinued trading; Angus and Robertson (Bookshops) Proprietary Limited; Angus and Robertson (Publishers) Proprietary Limited; Angus and Robertson (S.E. Asia) Proprietary Limited; Angus and Robertson (Wholesalers) Proprietary Limited; and Angus and Robertson (UK) Limited.

John Ferguson was responsible for establishing the children's list, which remained strong for the London office throughout the 1970s, and he continued to publish American and British titles for the Commonwealth market. Important publications of this period include *Tracy and Hepburn*, by Garson Kanin (1972), and *The Undersea World of Jacques Cousteau* (1972), both American titles. In 1973 Ferguson returned to Sydney and was replaced in London by David Harris. The British office moved to Lewes, Sussex, in 1974 and to 16 Ship Street, Brighton, in 1975.

In the 1960s and 1970s Angus and Robertson lost its preeminence in Australian publishing, partly as a result of competition from the Australian branches of British publishers such as Collins and Penguin. Under the ownership of Ipec, Angus and Robertson's Australian publishing division showed losses from 1972 to 1975, but after dropping everything extraneous, including its own distributing, the publishing division was again making a profit in 1976-1977 with sales of four million Australian dollars.

In 1978 the chain of Angus and Robertson bookshops in Sydney was sold to Gordon and Gotch, then Australia's only surviving large book and magazine distributor and now part of Rupert Murdoch's News International empire. In 1979 Angus and Robertson (UK) moved from Brighton to 10 Earlham Street, London.

Early in 1981 the former Ipec Insurance, which had become Australian National Hotels, put Angus and Robertson up for sale. An approach was made to the New South Wales premier Neville Wran, by a committee of authors led by Frank Moorhouse, to propose that Angus and Robertson be bought by the New South Wales government to become a low-profit publisher supporting Australian writing. But in May 1981 Bay Books, a subsidiary of Murdoch's News International Limited, bought the Angus and Robertson publishing house for something close to the asking price of four million dollars. The London office remained a subsidiary of Angus and Robertson Australia. In 1981 Harris was replaced as director by Peter Ackroyd, who was succeeded by Barry Winkleman in 1982. Winkleman was managing director of another Murdoch-owned publishing company, Times Books Limited, so the Angus and Robertson (UK) office was moved to the Times Books office at 16 Golden Square.

From 1981 to 1987 publishing activities by Angus and Robertson (UK) were greatly reduced, and the company was restricted mainly to importing books and acting as the marketing arm for Australian books and books purchased jointly with Angus and Robertson in Australia. Since 1987 the company has again built up its own publishing list, concentrating mainly on humor, entertainment, and popular health. The London office has its own separate publishing program as well as copublishing titles originating from Angus and Robertson in Australia.

News International Limited also gained control of William Collins and Harper and Row, creating the new international company of HarperCollins. In 1989 Angus and Robertson's publishing division in Australia was merged with Collins (Australia) to form Collins/Angus and Robertson, whose parent company is HarperCollins and which is ultimately owned by News International Limited. Angus and Robertson (UK) is a subsidiary company of HarperCollins, and its books are sold and distributed by Collins.

Angus and Robertson (UK) published sixty-four new titles in 1987 and seventy-five in 1988. Its imprints were Angus and Robertson, Arkon Paperbacks, Eden Books, Sirius Quality Paperbacks, and Bay Books. Publications in the late 1980s include *Charles and Diana: Inside a Royal Mar-*

riage (1987), by Ralph G. Martin; *Neighbours: Behind the Scenes* (1988), by James Oram; and *Topping: The Autobiography of the Police Chief in the Moors Murders Case* (1989), by Peter Topping with Jean Ritchie. The company's address was 16 Golden Square, London W1R 4BW, and its managing director was Barry Winkleman.

In 1990 all imprints owned by HarperCollins in the United Kingdom, including Angus and Robertson, were moved to 77-85 Fulham Palace Road, Hammersmith. Angus and Robertson (UK) Limited mainly publishes books as joint productions with Collins/Angus and Robertson in Sydney. Jonathan Lloyd became managing director in 1991.

References:

A. W. Barker, *Dear Robertson* (Sydney: Angus & Robertson, 1982);

Gordon McCarthy, *The Great Big Australian Takeover Book* (Sydney: Angus & Robertson, 1973);

James R. Tyrrell, *Old Books, Old Friends, Old Sydney* (Sydney: Angus & Robertson, 1987);

Barry Watts, "Literary Masterpiece: The Building of the Angus & Robertson Empire," *Weekend Australian* (Melbourne), 8-9 November 1986, p. 7;

William H. Wilde and others, *The Oxford Companion to Australian Literature* (Melbourne: Oxford University Press, 1985).

Papers:

The Angus and Robertson archive is in the Mitchell Library, Sydney, Australia.

—*Helen Fulton*

Edward Arnold
(London: 1890-1921)
Edward Arnold and Company
(London: 1921-1953)
Edward Arnold (Publishers) Limited
(London: 1953-1987)
Edward Arnold, a Division of Hodder and Stoughton Limited
(London: 1987-   )

See also the Hodder and Stoughton, Limited entry in *DLB 106: British Literary Publishing Houses, 1820-1880.*

Edward Augustus Arnold was born at Plymouth on 5 July 1857. His father, Edward Penrose Arnold, was an inspector of schools; his grandfather was the great public-school reformer Dr. Thomas Arnold; one of his uncles was the poet and critic Matthew Arnold, and one of his cousins the novelist Mrs. Humphry Ward. Arnold attended Eton and Oxford, and then, in 1883, joined the publishing firm of Richard Bentley, where he wo.ked in the trade department and looked after the company's advertising. At Bentley, Arnold edited a volume of Lord Randolph Churchill's speeches titled *Plain Politics for the Working Classes* (1885) and took on the editorship of *Imperial Federation*, the magazine of the Imperial Federation League.

In 1886 Arnold persuaded John Murray that there was room for a new magazine which should cost one shilling and be complementary to Murray's *Quarterly Review*. Arnold was appointed editor, and the first issue of *Murray's Magazine* was published early in 1887. In 1889 Arnold rejected Thomas Hardy's *Tess of the D'Urbervilles* because of its "frequent and detailed reference to immoral situations"; the novel was published by Osgood, McIlvaine in 1891.

In 1889, while continuing to act as editor of *Murray's Magazine*, Arnold took on the United Kingdom agency of Ginn and Company of Boston and New York. In the same year he approached Murray to see if there were any likelihood of his being taken into partnership. On being told that there was no vacancy, Arnold determined to start his own publishing business and did so on 1 January 1890 as Mr. Edward Arnold, Publisher, at 18 Warwick Square, Paternoster Row.

In April of that year Arnold published his first book, Jeremiah Lynch's *Egyptian Sketches*, described by the *Times* (7 June 1890) as "a book on Egypt at once so fresh and so comprehensive." Fifteen hundred copies were printed, and a reprint of five hundred copies was ordered for November. During the year Arnold published one political, one medical, one scientific, and one humorous book; the latter was *My Wife's Politics*, by Horace Hutchinson. He was to develop all these fields later. At the same time he began what was to be a distinguished school and college list with nine English and arithmetic textbooks. He continued to represent Ginn and Company until 1902, by which time his own list occupied him fully.

In 1891 Arnold published ten general books and seven schoolbooks. Although he had a small staff, it was Arnold himself who commissioned the books and played a large part in their production and promotion. In the middle of the year he moved to more commodious premises at 37 Bedford Street. Among the books Arnold published that year were Hutchinson's *That Fiddler Fel-*

low, a humorous golfing story set in St. Andrews; Mrs. W. K. Clifford's *Love Letters of a Worldly Woman*, an epistolary novel about three women's romantic crises; and Sir Gerald Porter's *My Mission to Abyssinia*, the first in a long line of reminiscences and memoirs by distinguished politicians, soldiers, and administrators.

During 1892 and 1893 Arnold published twenty-six general books, including his first historical and religious titles. His most influential book of that period was Alfred (later Viscount) Milner's *England in Egypt* (1892). A new edition was published in 1894 and a thirteenth in 1920. The *Dictionary of National Biography* described the book as "probably the greatest service that Milner rendered to his country's task in Egypt." An extremely popular book of reminiscences, W. R. Le Fanu's *Seventy Years of Irish Life* (1893), remained in print until 1949. In 1892-1893 Arnold added forty books to his educational list.

In 1894 Arnold took into partnership A. L. Mumm, who invested seven thousand pounds. Mumm was essentially a silent partner, but, as honorary secretary of the Alpine Club, he could introduce Arnold to many famous authors of travel, exploration, and mountaineering books. The first of these books to be published by Arnold was *The Exploration of the Caucasus* (1896), by D. W. Freshfield—a classic which was to remain in print for thirty years.

In 1895 Arnold established a New York office at 70 Fifth Avenue to protect his copyrights in the United States. As well as publishing simultaneous editions of his own books, such as Stephen Crane's *George's Mother* (1896), Arnold also published in New York books not published by him in London, including H. G. Wells's *Thirty Strange Stories* (1897) and *The Invisible Man* (1897). He closed the New York office in 1898.

By the end of his first ten years as a publisher Arnold, working largely on his own, had published some 250 general books and 250 books for schools. Probably the most successful of the latter was a delightful three-book course, *French-Without-Tears* (1895-1897), by Lady Florence E. E. Bell. Not only did these books give a phrase to the English language but they remained in print for more than sixty years.

Of the general books, the largest sections were travel books and biographies. The most remarkable and successful work in these categories was Rudolf Carl Slatin's *Fire and Sword in the Sudan* (1896), in which the author describes his twelve years held in captivity by the Mahdi. The

book went through three editions; the last, in 1907, remained in print for forty years. Of the twenty or so works of fiction, the two most notable were Mary Cholmondeley's *Red Pottage* (1899), which had thirteen impressions in its first two years; and *Moonfleet* (1898), by J. Meade Falkner, a classic adventure story of smuggling that is still in print. Falkner's other masterpiece, *The Nebuly Coat*, was published in 1903. Arnold's small list of critical works included Walter (later Sir Walter) Raleigh's first book, *Robert Louis Stevenson* (1895). This perceptive and readable critic went on to write three further books for Arnold: *Style* (1897), *Milton* (1900), and *Wordsworth* (1903). Arnold also scored hits with several illustrated humorous books. Hilaire Belloc's *More Beasts (for Worse Children)* (1897) was followed by his *The Modern Traveller* (1898) and *A Moral Alphabet* (1899). *Tails with a Twist*, by "A Belgian Hare," was published in 1898; the author was Oscar Wilde's lover Lord Alfred Douglas, who had just returned from his voluntary exile. The first of Harry Graham's books of comic verse, *Ruthless Rhymes for Heartless Homes*, came out in 1899 under the pseudonym "Col. D. Streamer." He wrote ten other humorous books, including *Misrepresentative Women, and Other Verses* (1906) and *More Ruthless Rhymes for Heartless Homes* (1930). The two *Ruthless Rhymes* books, classics of their kind, remain in print today in one volume.

By the end of 1902 the growth of his business forced Arnold to seek new premises. During 1903-1904 he was personally involved in acquiring a site and in the design of a new building, which was probably the first in London to be built as a publisher's office and warehouse. Arnold moved into 41-43 Maddox Street, off Bond Street, in May 1904. The handsome building still stands, although its interior is much changed. Arnold continued to publish about ninety new books each year. In 1904 he brought out M. R. James's first book, *Ghost Stories of an Antiquary*, which quickly established James as one of the finest writers of ghost stories in the English language. *More Ghost Stories of an Antiquary* (1911) was followed by *A Thin Ghost* (1919) and finally by *A Warning to the Curious, and Other Ghost Stories* (1925). All these volumes were consolidated in 1931 as *Collected Ghost Stories*, which is still in print.

The fiction list continued to grow steadily. In 1908 Upton Sinclair's *The Metropolis* was published; in the same year E. M. Forster's third novel, *A Room with a View*, appeared. Forster's first two books had been published by Blackwood, but Forster was attracted to Arnold not only because of his more generous royalties but also because Arnold showed a keen critical interest in Forster's work. Arnold urged Forster to write another novel, and *Howards End* was published in 1910. Arnold rejected Forster's two volumes of short stories, however, as he held that there was no public demand for them (they were published by Sidgwick and Jackson in 1911 and 1928, respectively). Forster's great novel *A Passage to India* appeared in 1924; that year Arnold took over the first two books, *Where Angels Fear to Tread* (1905) and *The Longest Journey* (1907), and published them together with *A Room with a View* and *Howards End* in a uniform edition to which *A Passage to India* was added in 1926. Forster's *Aspects of the Novel*, based on the Clark lectures given in Cambridge, was published in 1927. The happy partnership between the company and Forster continued until Forster's death.

Among many other novels published by Arnold before World War I notable ones were Walter de la Mare's *The Return* (1910) and both of Leonard Woolf's novels, *The Village in the Jungle* (1913) and *The Wise Virgins* (1914).

In the prewar years Arnold developed the other main strands of his list: travel, memoirs, and politics. Many of these books were not only successful but often of great influence. Edmund Candler's *The Unveiling of Lhasa* (1905) described the dramatic opening up of Tibet; Jenny Spencer Churchill's *The Reminiscences of Lady Randolph Churchill* (1908), written under her new married name, Mrs. George Corwallis-West, was a great success, but, oddly, her son Winston makes only a few one-line appearances. Arnold was concerned about developments in Europe and published several books advocating military reform, including two by Erskine Childers, *War and the Arme Blanche* (1910) and *German Influence on British Cavalry* (1911). The most remarkable book in this field was the translation *Germany and the Next War* (1912), by Gen. Friedrich von Bernhardi, which plainly asserted that war was inevitable between Britain and Germany. It was difficult to keep the book in stock, and, after many reprints, two new editions were published in 1914.

In 1912 Arnold published 130 titles, the largest yearly output he was to achieve. Fifty were schoolbooks covering the arts, science, and commerce. The list of literary criticism was greatly strengthened that year by the first two volumes, *1780-1830*, of Oliver Elton's *A Survey of English Literature*. The next two volumes, *1830-1880*, were published in 1920, and the last two, *1730-1780*, in 1928. These six volumes remained in print for fifty years.

During World War I Arnold's output decreased. The firm published several works concerning the war, ranging from eyewitness accounts to books on technical and medical aspects of modern warfare. Arnold continued to build his medical list; many of the books remain standard works. Two examples, both by Ten Teachers, are *Midwifery* (1917), now published as *Obstetrics*, and *Diseases of Women* (1919), retitled *Gynaecology*.

In 1918 Arnold started his school music list under the editorship of the composer Thomas F. Dunhill. Over the years the list grew to more than five hundred songs, piano pieces, and operettas.

In 1919 some former staff members returned from the war; among them was F. P. Dunn, the science editor. During the 1920s and 1930s Dunn built up a fine list of science research monographs and texts, including a key work in nuclear energy, F. W. Aston's *Isotopes* (1922), and Morris W. Travers's *The Discovery of the Rare Gases* (1928). A newcomer in 1919 was Brian W. Fagan, who took over the schoolbook and university arts lists. He became a partner in the firm in 1921, at the same time as Dunn, and was responsible for such distinguished books as J. Huizinga's *The Waning of the Middle Ages* (1924), W. L. Renwick's *Edmund Spenser* (1925), and W. W. Tarn's *Hellenistic Civilisation* (1927).

During the 1920s Arnold remained personally in charge of publishing memoirs and books on travel, religion, and field sports. He also maintained his fiction list until 1929, adding between five and ten titles each year. Two of his most popular novelists of the time were Anne Sedgwick and Mary Skrine.

In 1926 Mumm retired from the partnership, withdrawing his £7,000 investment and a profit of £3,742. His links with the Alpine Club had allowed Arnold to publish four books on the Everest expeditions. C. K. Howard-Bury's *Mount Everest: The Reconnaissance* (1922) was followed by C. G. Bruce's *The Assault on Mount Everest* (1923) and E. F. Norton's *The Fight for Everest: 1924* (1925). The whole dramatic story was retold by Sir Francis Younghusband in his classic *The Epic of Mount Everest* (1926).

In the 1920s Arnold published several outstanding medical books which immediately established themselves internationally and which still hold their place. The most successful are Robert Muir's *Text-book of Pathology* (1924), which reached its twelfth edition in 1987, and W. W. C. Topley and G. S. Wilson's *The Principles of Bacteriology and Immunity* (1929), in its eighth edition in 1990 as *Topley and Wilson's Principles of Bacteriology, Virology and Immunology.*

When Arnold retired at the end of 1930, his company had fifteen hundred titles in print, of which about six hundred were schoolbooks. He had taken an active part in trade affairs, serving on the Publishers' Association Council and several of its committees; in 1928-1929 he had been president of the association. Arnold always believed that a publisher should not publish more books than he could treat as living entities. In following this belief for forty years, he created a wide list in which many books had long lives. He died in 1942.

It was difficult for Fagan and Dunn to raise the forty-four thousand pounds to buy Arnold's share of the partnership, but with considerable personal austerity and the help of Coutts Bank they did so. Arnold was paid off at the end of 1932, and the substantial overdraft Coutts had provided was fully redeemed in 1937. This double repayment had to be made during the Depression, a difficult enough time in any event; there were staff cuts and salary reductions, and publishing had to be done with great care. Fagan, the senior partner, took over the general list. Two books emerge as being of great importance: Forster's *Abinger Harvest* (1936), which had to be temporarily withdrawn on account of a libelous chapter; and H. A. L. Fisher's *A History of Europe* (1936). The original publisher of Fisher's book was Eyre and Spottiswoode, but the author insisted that a separate edition should be published at the same time by a schoolbook publisher. It did more than any other single title to help the firm emerge from the slump in the late 1930s. In 1949 Eyre and Spottiswoode sued, claiming that Arnold's price had become too close to its own and that this constituted a breach of the agreement. The suit was settled in Arnold's favor.

The schoolbook list was not very active during the 1930s, as Fagan had withdrawn from this field; his eventual successor, John Morgan, joined the firm only in 1934, and his career was interrupted by World War II. Tom Clare was active in technical and commercial publishing and made a splendid start in publishing for nurses with W. Gordon Sears's *Medicine for Nurses*

(1935). It was Dunn who was the most productive during this decade, with a stream of scientific textbooks and reference works. Many of these are still in print in revised editions.

In 1939 the war brought a new set of problems: disappearance of staff into the armed forces, acute shortage of paper, and destruction of stock by enemy bombing. To avoid the latter, the warehouse and accounts were sent for the duration to Frome in Somerset, home of the firm's main printer. Dunn went to supervise this operation; Fagan remained in Maddox Street, spending many of his nights fire-watching. The destruction of stock was not entirely avoided, as the main trade binder was severely bombed twice; many Arnold schoolbooks went up in flames. Fewer titles were published; apart from schoolbooks, the most productive areas were publishing for technical schools and colleges and developing the nursing list.

In 1945 the firm was able to reassemble under one roof in Maddox Street. Fagan became president of the Publishers' Association in 1945; he was also chairman of the association's Paper Committee, which administered the rationing. Clare and Morgan were made partners, and it was these two who developed the distinguished educational and professional list which gave the firm its identity for the next forty years. Morgan was quick to enter the new market provided by the Secondary Modern schools, created by R. A. Butler's 1944 Education Act. The need for more extensively illustrated textbooks, in which pictures were an integral part of the instruction, was filled by several works, most notably *Our World* (1949), by E. W. Young and J. Mosby. Morgan also published prolifically for the more academic market in the grammar schools with such works as V. H. H. Green's *The Hanoverians* (1948) and C. P. Hill's *British Economic and Social History, 1700-1914* (1957). Clare was equally active in publishing texts for technical colleges (E. C. Rollason's *Metallurgy for Engineers* [1939]); science books (L. T. Draycott's *Elementary Practical Physics* [1954]); and, most of all, books in medicine (Cedric Keith Simpson's *Forensic Medicine* [1947; ninth edition, 1985]; J. G. Greenfield's *Neuropathology* [1958]). He was also responsible for keeping up to date the many grand old medical books on the Arnold list, such as Topley and Wilson's *The Principles of Bacteriology and Immunity.*

Dunn continued to publish scientific works at an advanced level and produced several long-lived reference books, such as J. K. Charlesworth's *The Quaternary Era* (1957) and U. R. Evans's *The Corrosion and Oxidation of Metals* (1960). The general list was far less active, partly because Fagan's activities in the Publishers' Association were highly demanding and partly because of a decision to make the firm entirely educational and academic. Three books by Forster appeared during the 1950s, however: *Two Cheers for Democracy* (1951), a collection of previously published pieces; *The Hill of Devi* (1953), describing Forster's early visits to India and interesting as background to *A Passage to India*; and *Marianne Thornton* (1956), a charming family memoir. All of these rather low-key works later flourished in Penguin editions. The list of sheet music for schools, started in 1918, was sold to Novello in 1959.

The increased level of publishing activity necessitated some changes in the organization. It was no longer possible for the general manager to be responsible for all aspects of the company's business except for building the list and company finance; a sales manager was appointed for the first time in 1953, and the general manager's function became a combination of production and office manager. That year the business was changed from a partnership into a private limited company. Also in the 1950s the importance of export sales began to be appreciated. Several overseas trips were made, most notably a long visit by Morgan to Africa in 1954. Overseas agencies were set up, with John Cochrane appointed to sell Arnold books in Australia and New Zealand.

Toward the end of the 1950s Fagan and Dunn announced their intention to retire at the end of 1960 and the end of 1962, respectively. It thus became necessary to arrange for the first time for a permanent source of external capital, and funding was provided by the Industrial and Commercial Finance Corporation (ICFC). Anthony Hamilton was appointed a director in 1958, followed by Bryan Bennett in 1962 and Paul Price in 1964.

During the 1960s the schoolbook department continued to be the largest division of the firm, first under Morgan and then under Bennett. In addition to strengthening the secondary list Bennett developed the firm's program in the increasingly important field of further (that is, adult) education, with particular success in catering: by 1990 the two books by Victor Ceserani and Ronald Kinton, *Practical Cookery* (1962) and *The Theory of Catering* (1964), had, between them,

sold nearly one and a quarter million copies. Price was active in biology, with two substantial series: Studies in Biology, begun in 1966, and Contemporary Biology, started in 1967. Hamilton developed the humanities list, which he had started in the late 1950s, in English literature with the Stratford-upon-Avon Studies, begun in 1960; in history with Sigfrid Henry Steinberg's *Dictionary of British History* (1963); and in geography with Peter Haggett's *Locational Analysis in Human Geography* (1965). Only the medical list was relatively quiet at this time: Clare had become chairman after Dunn's retirement, and a suitable successor as medical publisher had not yet been found.

Clare's sudden death in October 1965 was a severe blow to the company. Morgan became chairman and Hamilton managing director, the functions being formally separated for the first time. The Maddox Street buildings were no longer large enough to contain the whole business, including distribution; and the crypt of St. George's, Hanover Square, was a nearby but hardly efficient location for the firm's reserve stocks. Distribution and warehousing were moved in 1968 to Woodlands Park, near Maidenhead, and Mike Husk was appointed to the board as resident director there. By 1972 it had become impossible to house all the publishing departments at Maddox Street, so a handsome Mayfair house, built in 1830, at 25 Hill Street was leased.

Takeovers became a common part of the London publishing scene during the 1960s. Edward Arnold received many approaches; they were not welcomed but had to be taken seriously as the expansion of the business was causing a need for further funds. ICFC was helpful, but it was part of its philosophy not to acquire a majority holding. After much discussion it was decided in 1969 to invite James Martyn, who had experience both of publishing and of private companies, to join the board. He bought shares and introduced other shareholders, many of whom were helpful to the management in a variety of ways. The company was thus enabled to maintain its independence for a further eighteen years.

Forster died in 1970, leaving his literary estate in the hands of King's College, Cambridge, where he had spent much of his later life. It was agreed with the executors that the bulk of Forster's work, published and unpublished, should appear in a scholarly edition, to be called the Abinger Edition, under the editorship of Oliver Stallybrass. This edition would replace Arnold's pocket edition of Forster's works, the sales of which had long since been eclipsed by the Penguin paperbacks. Penguin agreed to convert its own texts to those of the Abinger Edition as these volumes appeared and stocks of its current paperback reprint became exhausted. The most important of the unpublished works was *Maurice*, a novel about homosexuality, completed in 1914 and revised in 1919, 1932, and 1959-1960. It was agreed that the book should be published as soon as possible and separately from the Abinger Edition, which it might join later. *Maurice* appeared in 1971, followed in 1972 by a collection of short stories, *The Life to Come*.

Various board changes took place around 1970. Bennett took over responsibility for sales and marketing. He consequently withdrew from direct management of schoolbooks, and Nicolas McDowall joined the board to take this place. In 1969 Jim Peck had been appointed chief accountant, and he joined the board as financial director in 1973. Morgan retired as chairman in 1971, handing over the position to Hamilton, but remained on the board for a further five years as president.

Sales and profits continued to perform well throughout the 1970s, with only a slight dip in the middle of the decade. A computer was installed at Woodlands Park to perform the invoicing and accounting functions; it also produced a detailed analysis of sales and costs by title and by territory. The Australian agency became Edward Arnold Australia on Cochrane's retirement in 1974. This company soon began to publish in Melbourne, though for some time on a limited scale. Worldwide distribution was further expanded by selling individual titles or series to appropriate publishers in the United States, by selling to agencies owned by larger publishers in Canada and Japan, and by forming a consortium of likeminded publishers to found agencies in East Africa, New Zealand, and particularly South Africa. In India, Arnold joined Heinemann Educational Books to form Arnold-Heinemann, India, managed by Gulab Vazirani. The 1970s also saw the rise of Nigeria as an important market; though sales had been disrupted by the civil war, they began to increase substantially in 1977.

In the 1970s Price took charge of the medical list, which had been somewhat dormant since the death of Clare. He quickly produced some "advances" series; the first was Current Topics in Immunology, begun in 1974 and edited by John Turk. Another successful series was Current Surgi-

cal Practice, begun in 1976 and edited on behalf of the Royal College of Surgeons by John Hadfield and Michael Hobsley. Early in the decade Dr. John Roberts joined the company, at first to take charge of the physical sciences program but later to be head of all publishing in science, including engineering. The humanities department was headed by John Davey, who had joined the firm in the middle 1960s; he published actively in geography and in history, notably The New History of England series, begun in 1977 under the editorship of A. G. Dickens and Norman Gash. Davey was also responsible in 1977 for publishing the first journals the firm had brought out in many years. These geography journals, including *Progress in Human Geography*, became the start of a new activity in academic journal publishing. At about the same time a change in teaching techniques, which seemed to be moving away from course textbooks, and a higher level of schoolbook funding, which permitted the purchase of supplementary material, led McDowall to publish a large quantity of small books, mainly in English, religious education, and social studies; for some years these books were extremely successful.

After six years of more or less uninterrupted expansion, the Hill Street house was no longer large enough. Two adjoining houses at 41 and 42 Bedford Square, easily found toward the end of a property slump, provided about 50 percent more accommodation in an ideal location for an educational publisher, being close to the British Museum, London University, and some major hospitals. Life there started well, with a large sales increase in 1978 and record profits in spite of the expenses of the move. The company's problems, however, began to increase shortly afterward.

The arrival of the Conservative government in 1979 brought severe cutbacks in schoolbook funding. The sale of Arnold schoolbooks held up well, but in the middle 1980s, after a continuing squeeze on expenditures and the introduction of the new General Certificate of Secondary Education examinations, the list began to suffer from a lack of solid textbooks; those that did exist, such as Peter Bishop's *Comprehensive Computer Studies* (1981), sold well.

Partly as a response to the reduced schoolbook market, it was decided to increase the company's publishing in further education. The quite substantial list in this field, which had been subsumed by other departments, was gathered together as one list. It prospered, drawing much of its revenue from the established catering books but also adding some excellent new titles such as Richard D. Gross's *Psychology* (1987).

Scientific publishing became more difficult, with the biology market a shadow of its former self. This decline was compensated for to some extent by the boom in computer books. Medicine was not exempt from the problems of the 1980s. The various Current Topics series, formerly successful, began to suffer diminished sales. It was still possible, however, to do well with outstanding and substantial books, such as Norman L. Browse's *An Introduction to the Symptoms and Signs of Surgical Disease* (1978); and there was a rich crop of new editions, including the great *Topley and Wilson's Principles of Bacteriology, Virology and Immunity*, the seventh edition of which appeared in four volumes in 1983-1984.

The humanities department, having suffered from a too rapid turnover of managers, settled down to produce some textbooks and reference books of high quality. New journals were also added to the list; and the firm further developed its publishing in English-language teaching and its list designed for overseas markets. This last brought the firm closer to the problems of the African market, especially Nigeria.

In the late 1970s and early 1980s Nigeria became a market of great importance to educational publishers. Funding of the Nigerian school program was, for a time, extremely lavish, and huge orders were being received for Arnold textbooks. Obviously, books written specially for the market could be expected to do even better. A small, well-thought-out list was produced; but its appearance coincided with the collapse of the Ethiopian economy, which resulted in a substantial sum being written off in the 1985 accounts.

Progress in the Australian market was also slow, and the company's financial performance was much hampered by the fluctuations of the Australian dollar. Management changes were made in the Australian firm in 1979 and 1984; after that the company settled down under Managing Director Terry Coyle and was shortly able to recruit an experienced and talented educational publisher, Marie Kelly.

The American market also became more difficult, as a result of Reaganomics. The library market was so reduced that purchases by importing publishers of all but the most outstanding titles became unviably small, and some publishers ceased importing altogether. It was therefore decided to set up a modest operation housed in the office of a friendly Baltimore publisher, University Park Press, and managed by Geoffrey Mann. This operation made an excellent start, but in its third year the host publisher was abruptly closed by its parent company. It therefore became necessary to find staff, premises, and a computer system in a great hurry. All of this was accomplished, but the increased costs of running the operation were not helpful to the business.

In 1985 Arnold acquired Lloyd-Luke, a small but distinguished medical house whose list contained one or two "plums" of the sort that all medical publishers covet—notably *Clinical Chemistry in Diagnosis and Treatment* (1971), by Joan F. Zilva. In 1986 the board decided, with great reluctance, that it was becoming impossible to continue as an independent company. Sales and profits had declined sharply in 1983, and although there was a recovery in 1984, mainly due to a splendid year of medical publishing, 1985 proved to be far worse than 1983 had been. Interest in acquiring Edward Arnold had never ceased, though the approaches usually came from unattractive quarters. The board therefore paid careful attention when Hodder and Stoughton made a discreet advance, and during the many subsequent meetings an encouraging similarity of outlook became apparent. Arnold's need to join a larger group was clear; on its side, Hodder and Stoughton was anxious to increase the size of its small educational business. On 6 May 1987 Edward Arnold (Publishers) Limited became Edward Arnold, the educational, academic, and professional division of Hodder and Stoughton.

Reference:

Bryan Bennett and Anthony Hamilton, *Edward Arnold: 100 Years of Publishing* (London: Hodder & Stoughton, 1990).

Papers:

The Edward Arnold archives are held by Hodder and Stoughton at Dunton Green, near Sevenoaks, Kent.

—Bryan Bennett and Anthony Hamilton

Ashendene Press

(Bayford, Hertfordshire: 1894-1899; London: 1899-1935)

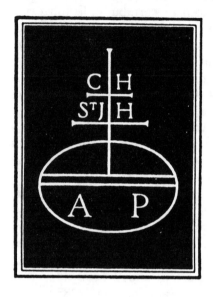  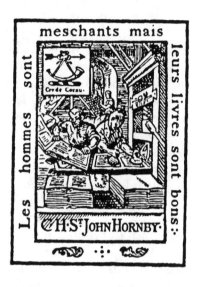

The Ashendene Press is considered one of the three great English private presses, along with the Kelmscott Press and the Doves Press. Unlike that of the other two, the work of the Ashendene Press was for pleasure and not for reform. As its founder, St. John Hornby, wrote in 1935, "In the choice of books to print I have been influenced partly by my own personal taste in literature and partly by the suitability of a book from a purely typographical standpoint—or perhaps it would be more true to say by a combination of these two factors. My choice has therefore fallen in the majority of cases upon books which gave scope for a certain gaiety of treatment in the use of coloured initials and chapter-headings; or, as in the case of *Utopia* [1906] and *Thucydides* [1930], marginal notes in colour. Such books present a more interesting problem to the printer, and as I have worked for my own pleasure and amusement without having to keep too strict an eye upon the cost, personal indulgence in this respect has been easy."

Charles Harry St. John Hornby was born on 25 June 1867 in Hertfordshire. In 1890 he graduated from Oxford, where he knew of the work of the Daniel Press, a private press active in Oxford from 1874 until 1903. Hornby was called

to the bar in 1892 but gave up law the same year to enter the firm of W. H. Smith and Son, printers, booksellers, and stationers; he became a partner in 1894. At W. H. Smith, Hornby learned to set type and to work a handpress. In December 1894 he began work on the first Ashendene Press book, *The Journal of Joseph Hornby, February-March 1815*, which was finished in February of the following year in an edition of thirty-three copies. The work was a diary kept by his grandfather on a visit to Paris a few months before the Battle of Waterloo. Hornby's printing press was an Albion Crown, set up in the summerhouse in the garden of his father's estate, Ashendene, in the Hertfordshire parish of Bayford.

In March 1895 Hornby visited William Morris's Kelmscott Press, where work on *The Works of Geoffrey Chaucer* (1896) was under way. Sydney Cockerell recalled that Morris and Hornby "got on capitally together." This was the only time that the two were to meet. Of Morris, Hornby wrote, "The spirit which infused his work has done more than anything else during the past forty years to influence the printing craft not only in England but throughout the world."

Like those of the Daniel Press, the first books of the Ashendene Press were family produc-

St. John and Cicely Hornby in 1900, and a few were sold for two guineas each. The next book printed by the press was its first to be sold by prospectus: William Tyndale's translation of *The Boke off the Revelacion off Sanct Jhon the Devine*, offered in an edition of fifty-four copies at two guineas each. It was finished in July 1901. The prospectus also announced Hornby's plan to print an Italian edition of Dante's *Inferno* (1321), "for which I am having cut a new fount of type, modelled closely upon an old 15th century fount, a very noble type."

From 1896 until 1901 Hornby had used various fonts of the seventeenth-century Fell type of the Oxford University Press, fonts that had been revived by Henry Daniel at the Daniel Press in 1877. Following the lead of the Kelmscott Press and Doves Press, however, Hornby desired a private type for the Ashendene Press. With the aid of Robert Proctor of the British Museum, Hornby and the engravers and photographers Cockerell and Emery Walker spent many hours during the spring of 1901 looking at examples of fifteenth-century roman types. They chose the work of Conrad Sweynheym and Arnold Pannartz and photographed pages from their press's three earliest books, in particular the first book printed in Italy, Cicero's *De Oratore* (circa 1465). A nearly complete font of type was created by selecting the best example of each letter; these were then enlarged and perfected by Walker and Cockerell with the constant advice of Hornby. A few letters, such as *k*, *w*, and *y*, had to be newly designed. There followed meticulous criticism by all three men of the work of Walker's draftsman, who redrew every letter; E. P. Prince, who cut the punches; and Miller and Richard, the Edinburgh typefounder that cast a full font of the type. The type was named Subiaco, after the town where Sweynheym and Pannartz began printing before they moved to Rome.

Finished in 1902, the *Inferno* was the first volume of the three-volume *La Commedia di Dante*, completed in 1905. St. John and Cicely Hornby and Turton printed 149 copies of the *Inferno*: 135 on paper, sold for three guineas, and 14 on vellum, sold for ten guineas. In addition to new type they used a new press, a large Albion Royal made in 1853. The *Inferno* had woodcuts adapted by R. Catterson Smith from a 1497 Venetian edition and cut by Charles Keates. It was the first Ashendene Press book to have initial letters by Graily Hewitt; these were drawn by hand in gold, red, blue, and green at the beginning of each

St. John Hornby and his Albion printing press (woodcut by Robert Ashwin Maynard)

tions; Hornby was assisted by three of his sisters, a brother, and a cousin, Meysey Turton. Nine more books were printed in the garden house between 1895 and 1899, most in editions of fifty copies; none was for sale. Hornby printed his edition of *The Prologue to the Tales of Caunterbury* in 1897, one year after the appearance of the Kelmscott Chaucer. Containing "zincotype" reproductions of the woodcuts in William Caxton's 1478 edition of Chaucer, it was the first illustrated Ashendene book. In January 1898 Hornby married Cicely Barclay, and in September 1899 they moved to Shelley House, Chelsea, London, taking the Ashendene Press with them. It was eventually set up in its own small house adjoining the stables, the composing room on the ground floor and the pressroom above.

The first Ashendene Press book to be offered for sale was its eleventh book and its first book printed in London: Andrew Lang's translation of the thirteenth-century *The Song-Story of Aucassin and Nicolete*. Forty copies were printed by

Page from the Ashendene Press edition of the works of Dante, printed between 1906 and 1909

canto. Hewitt's work appears in all but one of the twenty-six books produced by the Ashendene Press after the *Inferno*. The strain of printing 149 copies of the *Inferno* in his spare time led Hornby in January 1904 to hire a part-time pressman, George Faulkner, who had been trained at the Oxford University Press. In January 1905 Faulkner began work on a full-time basis. He also helped with the typesetting. Between work on the Dante volumes the press printed 44 copies of *The Song of Solomon* (1902) on vellum, all illuminated by Florence Kingsford, and selections from St. Francis of Assisi's *Fioretti* (1904).

In 1906 Hornby began to print a complete edition of the works of Dante, *Tutte le Opere di Dante Alighieri*, which was finished in 1909. This book, the Kelmscott Chaucer, and the Doves Bible (1903-1905) have been called the three greatest works of the three greatest English private presses. To have reset the entire *Divine Comedy* a second time as part of the larger work shows Hornby's devotion to Dante. The 150 paper copies were sold for ten guineas each, 6 vellum copies for fifty guineas.

For the complete Dante, Charles M. Gere drew a series of illustrations that were cut on wood by W. H. Hooper, who had also cut the blocks for the Kelmscott Chaucer. Gere, whose work was rooted in the turn-of-the-century Arts and Crafts school, also drew the illustrations for Sir Thomas Malory's *Morte Darthur* [sic] (1913) and for the selections from and the complete edition (1922) of the *Fioretti*. Hewitt's designs for an almost complete alphabet were made into metal blocks by Wilfred Merton and printed in red in the complete Dante. This alphabet was used again in the *Morte Darthur*.

In November 1914 there began a correspondence that produced the only original work of literary importance to be published by the Ashendene Press: *Poems Written in the Year MCMXIII by Robert Bridges Poet-Laureate*. At Bridges's request the book was dated 1914, but it was not completed until June 1915. Hornby typeset the book himself and had eighty-five paper and six vellum copies printed, none for sale. Most of Bridges's work between 1883 and 1903 had first appeared in small editions printed by the Daniel Press; after Henry Daniel closed his press in 1903, Bridges had stopped writing poetry for a time. In a letter to Hornby dated 18 November 1914 Bridges wrote, "About the poems. A mood for writing came on me last Autumn, & I wrote all these poems then except No 5 & two

of the classical epigrams, which are earlier." There were eleven poems in all, and Bridges had much to say about line lengths, punctuation, and spelling. For the paper copies Hewitt's initial letters were printed in some copies in blue, in others in red and blue.

Giovanni Boccaccio's *Il Decameron*, intended as a companion to the complete Dante, was discontinued until after World War I. Finished by the end of 1920, *Il Decameron* was printed in an edition of 105 paper copies at twelve guineas and 10 vellum copies at seventy-five guineas. It occupies a place in the history of censorship, as the United States Post Office in Kansas City seized and destroyed one copy in August 1926 for violating Section 305 of the Tariff Act of 1922, which prohibited the importation of immoral books. This action raised a storm of protest on both sides of the Atlantic. John Henry Nash wrote in a letter to the *San Francisco Chronicle*, "St. John Hornby's 'Decameron' is, to my mind, not only one of the most beautiful examples of fine printing ever achieved, but is also a real contribution to art. . . . Anyone who would lay profane hands on it should be outcast."

In 1920 Hornby printed one of Henry James's last works, *Refugees in Chelsea*, which had first been published in the *Times Literary Supplement* just before James's death in 1916. Crosby Hall, where James wrote the work, was a few doors away from Hornby's Shelley House. Another work of historical importance was the Ashendene printing of a fifteenth-century manuscript life of St. Clare of Assisi, by Ugolino Verino, that Hornby had purchased at auction in 1918: from this *Vita di S. Chiara Vergine* (1921) was printed in 236 paper copies at 2.5 guineas and 10 vellum copies at 10 guineas. Walter W. Seton of University College, London, provided an introduction and notes to the text, which was written for the nuns of Sancta Clara Novella in Florence in 1496. From 1922 to 1925 the Ashendene Press produced an edition of Edmund Spenser's works that appeared in two volumes: *The Faerie Queene* in 1923 (180 copies on paper for 16 guineas, 12 on vellum for 105 guineas) and *The Minor Poems* in 1925 (200 on paper for 12 guineas, 15 on vellum for 60 guineas).

For Miguel de Cervantes' *The History of Don-Quixote* (1927-1928) Hornby had Walker design a second type, "Ptolemy," based on the type used by Leonard Holle for printing Ptolemy's *Geographia* in Ulm in 1482. Published in two volumes, *The History of Don-Quixote* was the longest

Hornby (seated, second from left) with the other partners in W. H. Smith and Son, 1935

of the Ashendene Press books and the most expensive to produce. The 225 copies on paper sold for 20 guineas if bound in patterned boards or 28 guineas if bound in leather, and the 20 vellum copies sold for 150 guineas each. Ptolemy type was used for three of the four subsequent books of the press, *Thucydides* (1930), *Daphnis et Chloé* (1933), and *A Descriptive Bibliography of the Books Printed at The Ashendene Press* (1935).

The illustrations in *Daphnis et Chloé* are wood engravings by Gwen Raverat. All but ten copies of the first printing of this book, on Japanese vellum, were destroyed after it was discovered that the sheets had been folded before the ink was completely dry. (A leaf from the canceled edition is included in all copies of the 1935 bibliography.) For the second edition Batchelor handmade paper was used, and the engravings do not have the same clarity as in the original edition. In addition to the illustrations, the second printing has open blue initials drawn by Hewitt and his assistants.

Even with the disaster of the destroyed edition, expenses for *Daphnis et Chloé* were probably covered. The first edition cost £666, which included £210 to the artist and 5 guineas to Hewitt for designing the initial letters. The second printing cost £1,221, including £305 paid to W. H. Smith for binding and £312 to Hewitt for draw-

ing the initials in all copies. Hornby offered the second printing for 6 guineas for each of the 250 paper copies and 40 guineas for each of the 17 vellum copies. In the foreword to the bibliography Hornby wrote: "To the curious in such matters it may be of interest to know that over a period of years the Press has about paid its way without gain or loss. If the interest which it has added to life be put upon the credit side, it has brought a more than rich return."

After the first edition of *Daphnis et Chloé* was finished in February 1931 Faulkner, Hornby's pressman since 1902, died. In a March 1933 prospectus Hornby wrote, "his careful work and faithful service deserve more than a passing tribute." For *The Book of Ecclesiasticus* (1932) and the reprinted *Daphnis et Chloé* (finished in April 1933) H. Gage-Cole was hired to take Faulkner's place. Gage-Cole had served his apprenticeship with Morris and had also worked at the Doves and Cranach Presses.

The bibliography was probably inspired by Falconer Madan's bibliography of the Daniel Press, *Memorials of C. H. O. Daniel with a Bibliography of the Press, 1845-1919* (1921), printed on the Daniel Press and containing reset pages of Daniel Press books with a few original leaves tipped in. The Ashendene bibliography is in many ways the best of all the Ashendene Press books; it contains many reprinted pages, some with hand-drawn initial letters; type specimens; prospectuses; title pages; illustrations of bindings; and reprintings of woodcuts. Of the 390 copies printed, all on paper, 340 were for sale at seven guineas each.

Unlike the work of many other private presses, Ashendene Press books always had excellent bindings. The first Ashendene books were bound by Zaehnsdorf, whose manager, A. L. Marlow, had taken Hornby to meet Morris in 1895. Later, all regular binding was done by the W. H. Smith bindery under Douglas Cockerell's direction. Special bindings were made for a few copies of each book, in particular the vellum copies, the majority by Katharine Adams and Cockerell.

Hornby died on 26 April 1946. His influence on printing and typography through the work of the Ashendene Press was augmented by his lifelong association with the firm of W. H. Smith and Son. Although the major work of W. H. Smith was book and newspaper distribution in provincial towns, the printing and binding departments, under Hornby's direction, maintained the highest standards of design and workmanship; Smith became the first large commercial establishment to incorporate the principles of the private-press movement into mechanical book production. On 30 August 1935, after receiving his gift copy of the bibliography, Hewitt wrote Hornby, "You must be happy to know (not think) that you, of all the moderns, have done more & better for printing than all of them. I do congratulate you."

References:

A Descriptive Bibliography of the Books Printed at The Ashendene Press MDCCCXCV-MCMXXXV (London: Ashendene Press, 1935);

Colin Franklin, *The Ashendene Press* (Dallas: Bridwell Library, Southern Methodist University, 1986);

Franklin, *The Private Presses* (Chester Springs, Pa.: Dufour Editions, 1969);

Kelmscott, Doves and Ashendene, The Private Press Credos with an Introduction by Will Ransom (New York: Typophiles, 1952).

Papers:

The Ashendene Press archives are in the Bridwell Library, Southern Methodist University.

—Jennifer B. Lee

Athlone Press

(London: 1949-   )

See also the Hodder and Stoughton, Limited entry in *DLB 106: British Literary Publishing Houses, 1820-1880*.

The Athlone Press, established in 1949 as the publishing house of the University of London, derives its name from the earl of Athlone, Alexander Cambridge. At that time he was chancellor of the university, but perhaps the world knew him better as the brother of Queen Mary (the wife of George V) and as a former governor-general of Canada and South Africa. The launching of the Athlone Press revealed to the public that the University of London Press, a well-known imprint, had nothing whatsoever to do with the university. This situation, surely unique among the world's great universities, came about through a chain of events which can only be termed bizarre.

Until the first decade of the twentieth century the University of London, founded in 1836, was primarily an examining body. But an expansion of the teaching function, and the probability that other academic activities would follow, encouraged what Negley Harte has called "an over-enthusiastic drive for the reconstituted university to take on all the trappings of the traditional universities." Among these trappings was a university press. Since the 1840s the printing of examination papers and syllabi had been carried out under the supervision of Her/His Majesty's Stationery Office, which had put the work out for bids. The university senate decided that alternatives should be considered, and deliberations over the founding of a press lasted from 1904 to 1908. The senate eventually disappointed enthusiasts for a press by concluding that the arrangements with the stationery office were adequate for current needs.

Unknown to the university authorities, the secretary to the Royal Society of Medicine, J. Y. W. (later Sir James) MacAlister, sometime earlier had quietly registered a private company under the name London University Press Limited. This was an astute move, as the value of such an imprint most certainly would increase with the university's growth. In 1908 MacAlister advised the university of the existence of his firm and offered to sell the name; but the senate refused to approve the purchase, believing that MacAlister could not use the imprint for commercial purposes. He came back with a fresh proposal, offering to raise the capital for a new printing and publishing company. Eventually a compromise was reached, and the University of London Press Limited came into being. The agreement between the university and the new company was signed on 15 August 1910 over the objections of the university's solicitors, Freshfields, who thought MacAlister's position was weak. It contained forty-five clauses and bound the university to the press for all printing and publishing work for fifty years. The press was to be paid the cost of work executed plus 10 percent; not less than one-sixth of the profits was to be paid into a fund to finance the publication of academic works by University of London scholars. To the senate such an arrangement, which required no outlay of funds and seemed to promise early and easy profits, was too good to pass up. So the university plunged ahead, encouraged by the principal, Sir Henry Miers, who understood little about financial operations of this kind. As a result, the University of London found itself tied to MacAlister, who had secured a long-term contract on conditions exceptionally favorable to himself: in effect, he had obtained legal title to the university's name for the full period of the contract.

Before long the disadvantages of the arrangement to the University of London became painfully apparent. There were constant disputes about the prices charged for printing; since the press had the right to add 10 percent to its printing bills, the university's printing costs were always that much above market prices. The hoped-for profits to subsidize academic publications never materialized. Scarcely any works written by faculty members of the University of London were published by the press, though the agreement had called for such publications. What one account has called "the embarrassing absurdity of this situation" prompted the formation of a senate committee of inquiry in 1916, but it became bogged down in futile arguments. To conceal the humiliating position in which the university had been placed, the report of the committee of inquiry was not bound in the senate minutes but remained confidential for many years. In 1917 relations between the press and the university deteriorated still further when the press attempted to establish a new scale of charges. Arbitration failed, and matters reached the High Court. Though Mr. Justice Astbury gave his opinion that the university had legal grounds for terminating the agreement, the situation continued much as before.

In the mid 1920s the University of London attempted once again to extricate itself. A new and much stronger committee of inquiry under Sir Josiah (later Lord) Stamp delved into the financial history of the arrangement and, after a study lasting more than three years, condemned it out of hand. The committee proposed that a more realistic scale of charges be adopted. On 8 November 1927, scarcely six weeks after the new rates were put into effect, the press asked to be released from the agreement signed in 1910. The following year the contract was ended, but as part of the settlement the company was allowed to retain the name University of London Press. Another clause in the new agreement gave the university the right to buy back the imprint at some unspecified future date, but the University of London Press Limited steadily expanded its business, and the cost of repurchase became almost prohibitive.

What had complicated matters further over the years was that ownership of the press and the University of London imprint had slipped away from MacAlister into the hands of others who were even more remote from the university. In 1910 he had contracted with the firm of Richard

Clay and Sons, then printers to the Universities of Cambridge and Liverpool, to be "printers to the University of London Press" for fifty years. In the same year he had arranged with the firm of Hodder and Stoughton to be publishers for the University of London Press for the same period. As a result, the University of London Press became little more than a post office for the bills of the printers and publishers. Richard Clay and Sons dropped out of the arrangement in 1921, leaving Hodder and Stoughton in control through its majority shareholding in the press. For many years thereafter Hodder and Stoughton made great profits from use of the University of London imprint for textbooks sold throughout the British Empire, none of the buyers guessing the true state of affairs. Possibly the creation of the Athlone Press proved sufficiently embarrassing to the firm that it concluded that it would be best to terminate a most lucrative operation. But any embarrassment felt in that quarter was as nothing compared with what the University of London had suffered for so many years. It was not until 1973, more than two decades after the founding of the Athlone Press, that a final settlement was reached. At long last the imprint was returned to the University of London, and the owners were to be paid ten thousand pounds in five annual installments.

The Athlone Press in its early days earned a reputation as an academic publishing house which produced a limited number of works of high quality. It published only three titles in its first year, but the figure increased steadily until it reached thirty-five titles in 1969-1970. As befitted the press of a large university, Athlone endeavored to cover the spectrum of academic disciplines, and it did so with some success. Works on literature and history were most prominent in the annual catalogues, but such diverse fields as anthropology, Slavonic studies, religion, and law were also well represented. Distinguished scholars and others whose works were published by Athlone in the 1950s and 1960s included the historians R. H. Tawney, Sir Lewis Namier, Sir John Neale, Sir Keith Hancock, and Hugh Trevor-Roper; the astronomer Sir Martin Ryle; the statesman Sir John Anderson (Viscount Waverley); the archbishop of Canterbury, Michael Ramsey; and such other notable figures as Sir Stephen Runciman, K. D. Wheare, Sir Maurice Bowra, and G. D. H. Cole. In addition to its list of books, Athlone was also responsible for publishing university journals such as the *Bulletin of the In-*

stitute of Historical Research and the *Slavonic and East European Review*, along with the Creighton, Stamp, and L. T. Hobhouse lecture series. It cannot be doubted, however, that the Athlone Press from the 1950s to the 1970s was not the success it might have been had its name been University of London Press.

The Athlone Press had not come into existence for the primary purpose of turning a profit but to publish academic works by scholars associated with the university. Not unnaturally, it operated at a loss from the beginning and required an annual subsidy, which increased at a steady rate from the 1950s through the 1970s. In the year from 1 August 1954 to 31 July 1955 the subsidy, around five thousand pounds, amounted to more than nine-tenths of the press's general account. In the early 1960s a change in accounting procedures reduced the size of the subsidy for a short time, but it rose rapidly in the 1970s, exceeding fifty thousand pounds for the year 1976-1977. By this time University of London administrators had become alarmed at rising costs in almost every sector of their operation and had decided that they must retrench heavily or risk institutional disaster. In what now seems like a panic-stricken move, the senate decided to discontinue altogether the subsidy to the Athlone Press. This decision was a strange one, as the university might well have looked into ways of making Athlone profitable—for example, by cutting back on its generous staffing and vacating its more than adequate premises on Gower Street. Many leading academics of the University of London labeled the senate decision scandalous, for it ensured that a great university would be deprived of its press. Gloomy prognoses were quickly borne out by events. In January 1979 the Athlone Press was sold by the University of London to the Bemrose Corporation, a large printing firm which was seeking to establish a publishing division. Two years later the Bemrose Corporation withdrew from publishing, and Athlone became, and seems likely to remain, a wholly independent publisher. In the course of these changes the press abandoned Gower Street for more modest quarters on Bedford Row, also in Bloomsbury; later it moved to premises near Golders Green in North London.

Since 1981 the Athlone Press has retained a formal connection with the University of London through an advisory board consisting of several leading figures from the university. Otherwise, ownership and control are in private hands, with Brian Southam as managing director. Under his guidance the Athlone Press has maintained its traditional role as an academic publisher, building up a considerable list of titles ranging from sixth-form and undergraduate texts to specialized monographs. While there is still heavy emphasis on scholarly works in history, language, and literature, Athlone has also moved in new directions. It has developed a publishing program in the area of Japanese studies, listing thirty titles, many of them translations, in its 1989-1990 catalogue. Perhaps better known are such series as Monographs on Social Anthropology, sponsored by the London School of Economics and Political Science, in which sixty volumes have been published and thirty-five remain in print. No less significant is the European Thought series, with thirty-eight titles in print, including the complete *Tolstoy's Letters* (1978) and *Lev Tolstoy's Diaries* (1985); Jacques Derrida's *Disseminations* (1981) and *Positions* (1981); *Norse Poems* (1981), by W. H. Auden and Paul B. Taylor; and *Turgenev's Letters* (1983). Further evidence of Athlone's interest in great figures from philosophy and literature is to be found in works on Plato, Jane Austen, and Aleksandr Pushkin. In a class by itself is the Survey of London series, with forty-two volumes published as of 1990, a monumental work described by Mark Girouard in *Architectural Review* as "the undisputed leader among the various juggernauts that are working their way through British topography and architecture." As of 1989 Athlone had approximately 350 titles in print, reflecting the company's policy of keeping most titles in print for many years after publication.

If the antecedents of the Athlone Press were highly unusual because of the "University of London Press" legacy, the firm has now established an identity of its own. After an existence of just over forty years, comparatively brief in the annals of British publishing, it seems to have entered smooth waters. The University of London, however, remains without a press of its own.

Reference:
Negley Harte, *The University of London, 1836-1986* (London: Athlone Press, 1986).

—*John M. McEwen*

Arthur Barker Limited

(London: 1932-1939; London: 1946-1959; London: 1959-1991)

Arthur Barker Limited was founded in July 1932 at 21 Garrick Street, London, by Arthur Barker, who had trained with William Heinemann and with the Book Society. His earliest titles were James Agate's *English Dramatic Critics: An Anthology 1660-1932* (1932) and H. C. Armstrong's *Grey Wolf* (1932), a biography of Turkish president Kemal Atatürk. In its first five years the firm built up a list of which, in retrospect, the star author was Robert Graves. In 1934 appeared Graves's *Claudius, the God and His Wife, Messalina* and *I, Claudius*, along with works by Naomi Royde-Smith, E. F. Benson, and Anthony Weymouth; a life of Franz Anton Mesmer, by Margaret Goldsmith; and a reprint of Charles Dickens's *The Life of Our Lord*. The firm's first full-time sales representative, E. J. Sloane, joined in December of that year. The senior reader was L. A. G. Strong. In 1935 Barker began to draw attention to his list by issuing monthly bulletins.

Dashiell Hammett's *The Thin Man* was published in May 1935. By 1936 the list amounted to 140 titles, among them books of poetry by Graves and by Laura Riding; verse, however, never became a main feature of the firm's output. Also on the 1936 list were works by Charlotte Haldane, Alexander Woollcott, and Hugh Kingsmill.

In his memoirs the literary agent David Higham records that "in the late 30s Barker lost his independence because Margery Sharp's new novel couldn't be delivered on time," but he gives no further details. The firm was liquidated at the beginning of World War II, much of which Barker spent in a Japanese prisoner-of-war camp. When he restarted the business he was a sick man; he soon handed over the running of the firm to Herbert Van Thal, while he spent half of each year in Spain. Arthur Barker Limited was reregistered on 8 October 1946 at Castle Street, Edinburgh, the office of the printing firm Morrison and Gibb, which had acquired the firm.

All publishing operations were based at 30 Museum Street, London.

Van Thal was a bookman, author, and editor whose own short-lived firm, Home and Van Thal, had been taken over. The firm kept its general character, but the Van Thal influence was apparent in series such as English Novelists and Museum Street Thrillers. The firm also published westerns and the Blyton Bedside Books. Noel Langley contributed light fiction. In a list not notable for biographies, *Gide* (1951), a study by George Painter, future biographer of Marcel Proust, stands out. The firm was producing more than forty titles a year, by authors including Mickey Spillane, Lillian Roth, and Marjorie Kinnan Rawlings. Barker began publishing *The Bedside Esquire* in 1951.

In December 1954 the firm was acquitted of the charge of publishing an obscene libel in a case arising from H. McGraw's *The Man in Control* (1953). In July 1958 Norma Sykes, an actress known as "Sabrina," brought an action for libel, claiming she was portrayed adversely in Robert Muller's *Cinderella Nightingale* (1958). The book was withdrawn.

In 1959 Van Thal arranged the sale of Arthur Barker Limited to George Weidenfeld. He stayed on to manage the list but soon left because of a personality clash with Weidenfeld. Arthur Barker Limited became a separate imprint of Weidenfeld and Nicolson. The 1990 list was confined to two books on sport, and in 1991 the imprint was terminated.

References:

David Higham, *Literary Gent* (London: Cape, 1978);

Herbert Van Thal, *The Tops of the Mulberry Trees* (London: Allen & Unwin, 1971).

—*John Hewish*

Barrie and Jenkins
(London: 1965-)
James Barrie
(London: 1947-1957)
Barrie and Rockliff
(London: 1957-1965)

In 1947 James Barrie, the great-nephew and namesake of the playwright, established his own imprint to publish such popular books as Lady Cynthia Asquith's diaries, *Haply I May Remember* (1950), *Remember and Be Glad* (1952), and *Portrait of Barrie* (1954). Asquith, a novelist, had been Sir James Barrie's secretary from 1918 until 1937, and she inherited a good deal of his estate.

In 1957 Barrie Books purchased Rockcliff Books, which had been founded by R. H. Rockliff, the publisher of the annual *Theatre World*. Rockliff's art and antique books complemented the belletristic publications of Barrie, then directed by Leopold Ullstein and John Bunting.

In 1965 Barrie and Rockliff purchased Herbert Jenkins, Limited and Hammond, Hammond, which brought the firm P. G. Wodehouse and Radclyffe Hall, respectively. In 1967 Barrie and Jenkins purchased the Cresset Press, founded in 1927 by Dennis Cohen; with this purchase came many distinguished authors, including Arthur Miller, Carson McCullers, Sir John Summerson, and Jacquetta Hawkes, and the Cresset Classics series. The company was then directed by Richard Wadleigh and Christopher MacLehose, with Ullstein remaining as manager.

In the 1960s Barrie and Jenkins began producing distinguished lines of art books and popular nonfiction such as Alexander Werth's *Russia at War* (1964), Dee Brown's *Bury My Heart at Wounded Knee* (1971), and David Thomson's *Woodbrook* (1974). In 1972 Barrie and Jenkins was taken over first by Communica Europe, then by Hutchinson and Company. In 1985 Hutchinson was taken over by Century Publishing Limited, and Century Hutchinson was formed.

In 1987 Barrie and Jenkins reemerged as a partially independent publishing company by merging with Shuckburgh Reynolds. Barrie and Jenkins still publishes high-quality art and illustrated books, as exemplified by *Irish Gardens and Demesnes from 1830* (1980), by Edward Malins and Patrick Bowe. The firm also publishes general nonfiction and fiction. In 1989 Random House bought Century Hutchinson, forming Random Century.

Reference:

"Who Owns Whom—A Guide to Ownership Change in the UK Booktrade, 1982/1987," *Bookseller* (4 September 1987): 988-989, 991-994.

—Beverly Schneller

Geoffrey Bles
(London: 1923-1939)
Geoffrey Bles Limited
(London: 1939-)

Born in 1886, Geoffrey Bles served in the Indian army and the Indian civil service before returning to England and beginning a career in publishing. After obtaining practical experience under Herbert Jenkins, the publisher of P. G. Wodehouse, he founded his own firm in 1923. Bles was a learned man, well read in the classics, who throughout his long career was to have an uncanny eye for discovering writers of major importance: previously unpublished British writers and foreign writers whose work had yet to be translated into English.

Bles's first premises were at 22 Suffolk Street, Pall Mall, London. His first publication was *A. S. F.: The Story of a Great Conspiracy* (1924), a detective novel by John Rhode. Detective fiction was to continue to be a staple of Bles's publishing, although he just missed out on the most prolific and profitable writer of the genre, Agatha Christie. Her second book, the collection of poems *The Road of Dreams* (1925), was to be her only work published by Bles. From the start there was considerable variety in the firm's output: Bles also published expensively produced books on the fine arts, such as the limited edition of *Rare English Glasses of the XVII & XVIII Centuries* (1924), by Joseph Bles.

Many significant translations were published for the first time in Britain by Bles, such as Karel Capek's *Letters from England* (1925). Translations of writings on the arts included *The Art of the Theatre* (1924), by Sarah Bernhardt, and, in the same year, Konstantin Stanislavsky's seminal text on acting, *My Life in Art*. The firm was to continue publishing Stanislavsky's works up to *Creating a Role* (1963).

In 1927 additional premises were taken up at 66-68 Haymarket. This same year, Bles described his ideas about publishing in *The Commercial Side of Literature* by Michael Joseph: "I am specially interested in books on fine arts . . . books of travel . . . tales of mystery and adventure . . . the 'really fine love story'—praying that I shall recognise it when I get it!"

Jocelyn Gibb, who became Geoffrey Bles's partner in 1952 and took over the firm on Bles's retirement in 1954

Bles could certainly recognize a popular work where others could not. *Grand Hotel* (1930), translated by Basil Creighton, was Vicki Baum's first novel to be published in English; it had been rejected by several other British publishers. It was an immediate best-seller for Bles, and the following year in the United States for Doubleday, Doran. Bles continued publishing her work until *Grand Opera* (1942). It was also in 1930 that Bles began to publish theological and religious works, such as *The Message of Francis of Assisi*, by H. F. B. Mackay. The writings of the physician Halliday

Gibson Sutherland were typical Bles publications: the autobiographical *The Arches of the Years (the Adventures of a Doctor)* (1933) was another instance of a book that had been ignored by other publishers but proved to be a best-seller when published by Bles; the sequel, *A Time to Keep* (1934), which recounts Sutherland's conversion to Roman Catholicism, was one of Bles's many religious publications; and Sutherland's *Hebridean Journey* (1939) exemplifies the firm's interest in travel books.

In 1934 the firm moved to 2 Manchester Square. The 1930s saw a growing emphasis on theological works. Nikolay Aleksandrovich Berdyaev had been professor of philosophy at Moscow University after the Bolshevik Revolution, but his disillusionment with Lenin led him to immigrate to Paris and abandon Marxism for Eastern Orthodox Christianity. Bles introduced this philosophical theologian to the English-speaking world with *Freedom and the Spirit* (1935); he went on to publish subsequent works by Berdyaev, as well as *Introduction to Berdyaev* (1950), edited by O. Fielding Clarke. Another discovery was Jacques Maritain, a Thomist whose works included *The Rights of Man and Natural Law* (1944). Bles declared his policy on religious writing to be "quite non-denominational, the writers ranging from Roman Catholic priests to free Churchmen, although Anglicans predominate." In 1935 Bles started using the device of a thick, irregular arrow pointing downward. It is said that the device originated in a doodle Bles drew on some blotting paper.

In 1939 Bles converted his firm from a private to a limited company. The same year he acquired the Centenary Press, along with its editor, Ashley Sampson, and Sampson's series of popular theological publications, the Christian Challenge. Sampson invited a relatively unknown Oxford don, C. S. Lewis, to contribute a book on suffering and pain to the series. *The Problem of Pain* was published in October 1940; Lewis wished to remain anonymous but was dissuaded by Sampson from doing so. The book was immediately acclaimed; it was reprinted twice in 1940 and four times the following year.

Lewis's *The Screwtape Letters* was first published in the *Guardian*, a Christian weekly, in 1941. Sampson persuaded Bles to publish the work in book form, for which Lewis added a preface and epigraphs. The first edition of two thousand copies was sold out before its publication in February 1942; the book was reprinted twice in March and six more times before the end of the year. By 1991 paperback sales in England and America had easily surpassed the million mark, with two million copies sold worldwide. Lewis gave two-thirds of his royalties from the work to the poor.

In 1942 Bles moved to 37 Essex Street. That year the firm published a book by Lewis's friend Charles Williams, *The Forgiveness of Sins*, which included a passage arguing for the forgiveness of the Germans after they were defeated but predicting that such forgiveness would not occur. The work appeared in the Christian Challenge series, as did *The Resurrection of Christ* (1945), by Professor Arthur Michael Ramsey, who was to serve as archbishop of Canterbury from 1961 to 1974.

Another friend of Lewis's, Sister Penelope of the Community of St. Mary the Virgin in Wantage, had had a translation of St. Athanasius's *The Incarnation of the Word of God* turned down as too literal by the Society for Promoting Christian Knowledge. Lewis persuaded Bles to publish it in 1944; Lewis provided an introduction. Similarly, in 1943 the Reverend J. B. Phillips had sent Lewis a translation of Paul's Letter to the Colossians into modern colloquial English. Lewis encouraged him to translate the remaining epistles and arranged for Bles to publish them under the title *Letters to Young Churches* (1947). At first they sold slowly, but when Lewis added an introduction sales picked up quickly.

Meanwhile, Bles had continued to publish Lewis's religious works throughout the 1940s, among them *Broadcast Talks* (1942), *The Great Divorce: A Dream* (1945), and *Miracles: A Preliminary Study* (1947). The year 1950, however, marked a departure for both Lewis and Bles. The firm had published little in the line of children's stories, but Bles encouraged Lewis to write a whole series of such tales even before the publication of the first of his "Narnia" stories, *The Lion, the Witch and the Wardrobe*. The book came out in the autumn of 1950 in time for the Christmas gift market, and sales proved phenomenal. Also successful were the next four tales in the series: *Prince Caspian: The Return to Narnia* (1951); *The Voyage of the Dawn Treader* (1952); *The Silver Chair* (1953); and *The Horse and His Boy* (1954), for which Bles provided the title. Lewis had sent him a letter worrying about "Narnia and the North" as a title for the tale and suggesting several others. Bles replied, "I like best 'The Horse and the Boy,' but what about 'The Horse and his Boy,' which is a little startling and conveys the idea of your other title 'The Horse Stole the Boy.' "

In 1952 the firm moved to 52 Doughty Street, and Bles acquired a partner, Jocelyn ("Jock") Gibb. Despite the sales of Lewis's works, however, Geoffrey Bles Limited could not maintain its independence. In 1953 William Collins, Sons and Company Limited acquired the firm. The following year Bles retired and handed over the management of the firm to Gibb.

The character of the firm's publishing was maintained under Gibb with Lewis's autobiography, *Surprised by Joy: The Shape of My Early Life* (1955), and further religious works such as *Reflections on the Psalms* (1958). Phillips provided a translation of the Acts of the Apostles, *The Young Church in Action* (1955). Geoffrey Bles Limited continued to publish much travel writing, notably *Letters from Africa* (1957), by Stephen King-Hall. Among the firm's many writers of detective fiction, some had quite specific niches in regard to subject matter; the pseudonymous Glyn Carr (Frank Showell Styles), for example, throughout the 1950s and 1960s wrote endlessly about murders on mountains in tales such as *The Corpse in the Crevasse* (1952) and *Death Finds a Foothold* (1961). Bles detective novels were often conspicuous by their dust jackets, consisting of a photograph of a dramatic scene from the novel which was also a clue to the solution of the crime.

Bles died on 3 April 1957. In the autumn of that year the firm began a house journal called *Fifty-Two* after its address, 52 Doughty Street, and including short extracts from books to be published or articles of introduction by the authors. The journal was discontinued in the autumn of 1959.

Publications of this period included *The Story of the Trapp Family Singers* (1953), by Maria von Trapp, which had previously been published in the United States, and *Vale of Laughter: An Autobiography* (1957), by the playwright Ben Travers. Phillips continued his translations of the Bible with *The Book of Revelation* (1957) and *The New Testament in Modern English* (1958), which was republished in a pocket edition in 1960.

Lewis formed a close friendship with Gibb,

who, like Sampson and Bles before him, was able to nurture Lewis's creativity into publication. In 1952 Lewis had started and abandoned a book on prayer; it was only with Gibb's encouragement that he recommenced it many years later, and it was finally published as *Letters to Malcolm: Chiefly on Prayer* (1964). In a letter to Lewis (13 June 1963), Gibb enthused: "By Jove, this is something of a present to a publisher!"

After Lewis's death in 1963 Geoffrey Bles Limited published several anthologies of his writings edited by Walter Hooper, including *Poems* (1964), as well as a tribute edited by Gibb, *Light on C. S. Lewis* (1965), and *Letters of C. S. Lewis* (1966), edited by W. H. Lewis. The firm published Lewis's posthumous works up to *Undeceptions: Essays on Theology and Ethics* (1971), edited by Hooper.

There seem to have been fewer significant publications by Geoffrey Bles Limited since around the time of Lewis's death. The religious vein was continued with *The Compassion of God and the Passion of Christ* (1963), by the dean of Westminster Abbey, Eric Symes Abbott. The only important secular writers to be added to the Bles list were Catherine Dupré, whose novels include *The Chicken Coop* (1967), and Josephine Bell, whose historical novel *Tudor Pilgrimage* (1967) achieved success.

Dupré's work now appears under the Collins imprint, as do Phillips's translations. Although Geoffrey Bles Limited is included in the 1990 *ISBN Directory of Publishers*, with the address given as Barlavington Farm House, Barlavington, Petworth, West Sussex, no publications have appeared under the imprint since 1974.

References:

Fifty-Two: A Review of Books and Authors from Geoffrey Bles (London: Bles, 1957-1959);

Roger Lancelyn Green and Walter Hooper, *C. S. Lewis: A Biography* (London: Collins, 1974);

Michael Joseph, *The Commercial Side of Literature* (London: Hutchinson, 1925), p. 230.

—Tim Randall

Bodley Head
(London: 1887-1921)
Bodley Head Limited
(London: 1921-1987)

The Bodley Head is one of the best-known publishing houses of the modern era, responsible for works by some of the most significant writers and artists of the late nineteenth and twentieth centuries. Its fame was established in the early 1890s, when the Bodley Head imprint appeared on such significant books as the two Rhymers' Club volumes (1892, 1894); Arthur Symons's *Silhouettes* (1892); Richard Le Gallienne's *English Poems* (1892); Michael Field's *Sight and Song* (1892); Lord De Tabley's (John Byrne Leicester Warren) *Poems Dramatic and Lyrical* (1893); Kenneth Grahame's *Pagan Papers* (1893); John Davidson's *Fleet Street Eclogues* (1893); and Oscar Wilde's *Salome* (1894), with its many superb illustrations by Aubrey Beardsley. At that time, the Bodley Head also published several important journals, among them the finely designed and printed *Hobby Horse* (1893), edited by Herbert P. Horne; and the most sensational journal of the period, the *Yellow Book* (1894-1897), edited by Henry Harland and Beardsley. It continued to earn the public's attention in the early twentieth century by publishing works by H. G. Wells, Stephen Leacock, J. B. Priestley, James Joyce, and Graham Greene.

In 1887 Charles Elkin Mathews owned an antiquarian bookshop in Cathedral Yard, Exeter. A young bibliophile, John Lane, was working under Mathews's brother as a clerk in the Railway Clearing House at Euston Station in London. Anxious for a chance to get into the book business, Lane persuaded Mathews to move his shop to London, where his chances of success both as antiquarian bookseller and as publisher might be better. Lane became Mathews's silent partner and found quarters at 6B Vigo Street, where the business was set up in September 1887.

The shop, which had previously been known as the Cabinet of Fine Arts, still displayed over its door a sign depicting Rembrandt's head. Since Mathews had associated his Exeter shop with the name of that city's most famous son, Sir Thomas Bodley, the founder of the Bodleian Library at Oxford, he and Lane decided to replace the Rembrandt's head with that of Bodley, which became the logo for the new firm. The shop in Vigo Street was indeed a "cabinet," what one observer described as "a little box of a place." At the rear was a trapdoor leading to a storeroom and privy, where Mathews often took refuge to avoid meeting importunate authors and dissatisfied customers. The entire front of the shop, except for the door, was formed by a large window filled with displays of books which figures prominently (along with Mathews as Pierrot) in Beardsley's cover design for the prospectus for the *Yellow Book*.

Charles Elkin Mathews, cofounder of the Bodley Head, in 1893 (pencil drawing by John Butler Yeats; collection of Michael B. Yeats)

Mathews had dabbled in publishing at Exeter, but he and Lane soon developed plans to publish on a larger scale. With the appearance on the London literary scene of the young, Byronic-looking Le Gallienne, these plans became a reality. Sharing the partners' love of old tomes, Le Gallienne had a firsthand knowledge of publishing, and Mathews and Lane found his enthusiasm for beautiful books of verse infectious. Le Gallienne's first book of poems, *My Ladies' Sonnets and Other "Vain and Amatorious" Verses, with Some of Graver Mood*, privately printed in his native Liverpool in 1887, was in almost every way a model for the first Bodley Head book, Le Gallienne's *Volumes in Folio* (1889). Published in 250 small-paper and 50 large-paper copies, it set the pattern for Bodley Head books to come. Printed at the Chiswick Press on Van Gelder handmade paper, the book had a tastefully designed title page lettered in red and black—so different from the poorly designed, "spidery" title pages that had become a hallmark of the Victorian book. With *Volumes in Folio* and other equally beautiful books that followed it, Mathews and Lane created a vogue for daintily packaged poetry and

thus gave impetus to what the periodical press dubbed "the remarkable poetical renascence of the early nineties." The Bodley Head became a mecca for the young poets, artists, and "New Woman" writers of the period, many of whom might not have found an audience without the assistance of Mathews and Lane.

Mathews and Lane developed ingenious production practices that cut their costs to a minimum. They employed larger-than-usual type sizes (above ten-point) and more leading than normal between lines, creating what Wilde's friend Ada Leverson described as "the tiniest rivulet of text meandering through the very largest meadow of margin." This habitual use of relatively little text per book substantially reduced the cost of typesetting. Moreover, the partners printed their editions on remainders of fine paper that they bought at far below the usual price. In addition, they negotiated agreements that paid their authors at best a modest royalty only after production costs had been paid, and they limited the editions to the number of copies the poetry market would bear—usually between three hundred and six hundred. By these means Mathews and Lane were able to sell Bodley Head books for less than the five shillings normally charged at the time for a book of poetry and still make a good profit.

In January 1892 Lane ceased to be a silent partner and came into the business full time. Soon, however, he and Mathews found that their quite different temperaments and business styles caused friction between them. They increasingly took divergent courses, with Lane prone to involve the firm with authors and artists about whom Mathews had grave moral reservations. Mathews was especially uneasy about Wilde's association with the Bodley Head. Not only did Wilde seduce Edward Shelley, a clerk Lane had planted in the firm in 1890 to spy on Mathews, but he arranged with Lane during the summer of 1893 for the Bodley Head to publish his ill-fated *The Portrait of Mr. W. H.*, a story about homosexual love. (The book was to be published in the autumn of 1894, but the breakup of the partnership and Wilde's legal problems stopped the publication process. *The Portrait of Mr. W. H.* was privately printed in 1904.) Mathews viewed his deliberate exclusion from the April 1894 dinner celebrating the first number of the *Yellow Book* as the last in a series of provocations and affronts engineered by Lane.

*John Lane, who took over the Bodley Head when he and
Mathews dissolved their partnership in 1894*

After a struggle between Mathews and Lane over the firm's authors, the partnership was dissolved on 30 September 1894. Mathews remained in the premises at 6B Vigo Street, while Lane, taking the Bodley Head sign with him, moved to new quarters across the street in the Albany.

In contrast to Mathews, who carried on the antiquarian book business and favored poetry, Lane devoted his firm exclusively to publishing and focused mainly on fiction. The Keynotes series was named for the first book in the series, an 1893 volume of short stories by George Egerton (Mary Chavelita Dunne). The books in the series were decorated with a key design unique to each volume, the first few of which were the work of Beardsley. Already popular before the dissolution of the partnership, the Keynotes series was taken over by Lane and became one of his first great successes in publishing. Its titles included Florence Farr's *The Dancing Faun* (1894), M. P. Shiel's *Prince Zaleski* (1895), Ella D'Arcy's trendy *Monochromes* (1895), and Victoria

Cross's controversial reply to Grant Allen's *The Woman Who Did* (1895), *The Woman Who Didn't* (1895). Other series, such as the Arcady Library, the Bodley Head Anthologies, and Pierrot's Library, helped Lane provide his talented authors with further means of publication. A staunch supporter of the "New Woman" movement of the 1890s, Lane also founded the Eve's Library series, which included works such as Roy Devereux's (Margaret Pember-Devereux) *The Ascent of Woman* (1896) and Elizabeth Rachel Chapman's *Marriage Questions in Modern Fiction, and Other Essays on Kindred Subjects* (1897).

Arthur Machen's *The Great God Pan and the Inmost Light* (1894), Max Beerbohm's *The Happy Hypocrite: A Fairy Tale for Tired Men* (1897), and Baron Corvo's (Frederick William Rolfe) *Stories Toto Told Me* (1898) were great Lane successes. Proceeding into the twentieth century with his skillful eye for new talent, Lane built the Bodley Head into one of the most successful publishing houses in the world. The firm became the house of choice for avant-garde talent and for fashionable authors who prided themselves on being "a cut above," such as Alice Meynell, G. K. Chesterton, Edmund Gosse, and Harold Frederic.

As partners, Mathews and Lane had entered into joint publishing ventures with several American firms, in particular such avant-garde houses as Copeland and Day, Stone and Kimball, and Way and Williams. In 1896 Lane established his own office in New York with the young Mitchell Kennerley, whom Lane had trained, as manager. Under the later guidance of Temple Scott, the New York Bodley Head prospered into the new century; it was sold to Dodd, Mead in 1921.

His trips to America led to Lane's acquaintance with a wealthy American widow, Mrs. Annie Eichenberg King, whom he married in 1898. With her money, he expanded his business into a general publishing enterprise, producing books on gardening, art, biography, and travel. Among Lane's most celebrated ventures was the beautiful deluxe edition (1908-1928) of the complete works of the French novelist Anatole France.

Lane's principal organ of advertisement was the *Bodleian: A Journal of the Books at the Bodley Head*, published monthly from 1909 to 1931. It announced the latest works of the Bodley Head's authors, among them Wilde, Wells, Priestley, Kenneth Grahame, Arnold Bennett, Saki (H. H. Munro), Ford Madox Ford, and W. J. Locke. Agatha Christie's first six books and C. S. Fores-

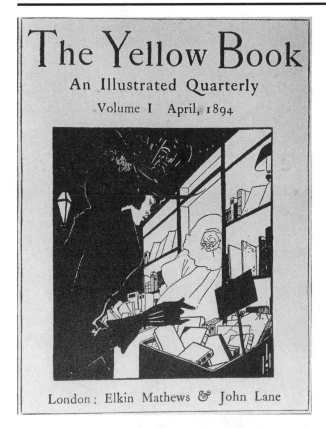

Prospectus for Aubrey Beardsley's journal. The drawing by Beardsley depicts the front of the original Bodley Head premises in Vigo Street; Mathews, as Pierrot, stands in the doorway.

ter's first thirteen novels all appeared with the Bodley Head imprint. The Bodley Head became a private limited-liability company in 1921.

By the time of Lane's death on 2 February 1925, the Bodley Head was in decline. At this point, Allen Lane, who had joined his "uncle" at the Bodley Head at the age of sixteen in 1919, emerged as the dominant figure at the firm. In actuality a distant cousin of the publisher, Allen, who had changed his surname from Williams, got the firm into one of its gravest crises. In 1926, emboldened by the current appetite for slightly risqué memoirs, he threw caution to the wind and accepted for publication *The Whispering Gallery: Being Leaves from a Diplomat's Diary* (1926), ostensibly edited by Hesketh Pearson and touted as recollections of conversations with such significant persons as Kaiser Wilhelm, Czar Nicholas II, King Alphonso XIII, and the novelists Wells, Henry James, and Thomas Hardy. Review copies of the book appeared on 19 November 1926. Shortly thereafter, the *Daily Mail* of London ran the headlines: "A SCANDALOUS FAKE EXPOSED. MONSTROUS ATTACK ON PUB-

LIC MEN. REPUDIATIONS BY FIVE CABINET MINISTERS." It appears that the book was actually written by Pearson himself. The Bodley Head board of directors had Pearson arrested on a charge of obtaining money under false pretenses. Found not guilty, he then brought an action against the Bodley Head. The firm finally had to pay Pearson the total profits received from sales of the book before it had been withdrawn.

Despite this setback, Lane did much to keep the firm afloat during the lean years of the late 1920s and early 1930s. He published some major books, such as Gertrude Stein's *The Autobiography of Alice B. Toklas* (1933) and James Joyce's *Ulysses* (1936). Nevertheless, such successes were few. Lane became chairman of the board in 1930 and moved the firm to Galen Place, off Bury Street, in 1935. He staved off bankruptcy until 1936, when the firm went into receivership. In 1937 the Bodley Head was bought by a consortium of publishers: George Allen and Unwin Limited, Jonathan Cape, and J. M. Dent. In 1935 Lane had founded Penguin Books, his greatest achievement in publishing. Although Penguin Books was never part of the Bodley Head, the Bodley Head imprint appeared on its first eighty titles.

In 1956 the Bodley Head was bought by Max Reinhardt, under whose direction the firm once again prospered; it moved from Little Russell Street to Earlham Court in 1957. Among its authors was Graham Greene, who also served as a director. The Bodley Head Limited moved to 9 Bow Street in 1966, to 30 Bedford Square in 1985, and to 32 Bedford Square in 1986. Because of illness, Reinhardt sold the firm in May 1987 to Random House, at which time it ceased to exist.

References:

R. D. Brown, "The Bodley Head Press: Some Bibliographical Extrapolations," *Papers of the Bibliographical Society of America*, 61 (1967): 39-50;

J. W. Lambert and Michael Racliffe, *The Bodley Head 1887-1987* (London: Bodley Head, 1987);

J. Lewis May, *John Lane and the Nineties* (London: Bodley Head, 1936);

James G. Nelson, *The Early Nineties: A View from the Bodley Head* (Cambridge, Mass.: Harvard University Press, 1971);

John Ryder and others, *The Bodley Head, 1887-1957* (London: Bodley Head, 1970);

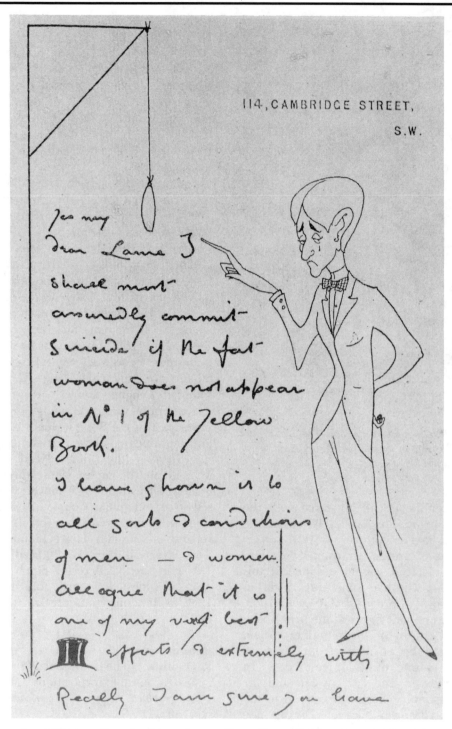

First page of an 1894 letter from Beardsley to Lane, with a self-portrait (from J. Lewis May, John Lane and the Nineties, *1936)*

Margaret D. Stetz and Mark Samuels Lasner, *England in the 1890s: Literary Publishing at the Bodley Head* (Washington, D.C.: Georgetown University Press, 1990);

Oscar Wilde, *Letters to the Sphinx from Oscar Wilde, with Reminiscences of the Author by Ada Le-*verson (London: Duckworth, 1930), pp. 19-20.

Papers:

Bodley Head records are in the library of the University of Reading.

—*James G. Nelson*

British Academy

(London: 1901-)

The British Academy, founded in 1901 and granted a royal charter the following year, is a private learned society devoted to the humanities and the social sciences; its full title is the British Academy for the Promotion of Historical, Philosophical, and Philological Studies. It is a self-governing fellowship of scholars elected for their distinction in one or more of the academic disciplines that the academy exists to promote. One of its chief functions is to act as a scholarly publisher, and its Publications Committee, composed of fellows of the academy under the chairmanship of the publications secretary, supervises this area of activity. Since its creation, the academy has maintained a close relationship with the Oxford University Press, which distributes almost all of its volumes.

The academy's principal publication is the *Proceedings of the British Academy*, which first appeared in 1903 and has been published annually since 1927. By 1990 it had reached its seventy-fifth volume. The *Proceedings* consists of the papers read to the academy in a given calendar year, most of them in long-established endowed series such as the Shakespeare Lectures, the Warton Lectures on English Poetry, the Chatterton Lectures on English Poets, the Keynes Lectures in Economics, the Raleigh Lectures on History, the Dawes Hicks Lectures in Philosophy, the Mortimer Wheeler Archaeological Lectures, and the Radcliffe-Brown Lectures in Social Anthropology. The list of lecturers includes T. S. Eliot, G. M. Trevelyan, M. R. James, Bertrand Russell, Kenneth Clark, Benedetto Croce, R. H. Tawney, L. B. Namier, F. A. Hayek, C. S. Lewis, J. R. R. Tolkien, Karl R. Popper, Isaiah Berlin, A. J. Ayer, and A. J. P. Taylor. Individual papers have been much reprinted; generations of British history students have been brought up on W. Notestein's "The winning of the initiative by the House of Commons," first published in 1926, and Sir Lewis Namier's "1848: the Revolution of the Intellectuals," first published in 1946. Four selections of Shakespeare, history, and philosophy lectures were published by the Oxford University Press between 1964 and 1968; further collections of Shakespeare, philosophy, and English lectures

appeared under the imprint of the Oxford University Press between 1985 and 1988 and two on Anglo-Saxon England and Middle English literature under the academy's own imprint in 1989 and 1990. Also included in the *Proceedings* are memoirs of deceased fellows of the academy, which cumulatively form a unique record of British scholarship in the humanities and social sciences.

The papers that appear in the *Proceedings* are of single lectures. Other series are published separately, such as the Schweich Lectures on Biblical Archaeology, which contain the texts of three related lectures on some aspect of the archaeology, art, history, languages, and literature of ancient civilizations with reference to biblical study. The first volume in this series was S. R. Driver's *Modern Research as Illustrating the Bible* (1909); later volumes have included G. R. Driver's *Semitic Writing: From Pictograph to Alphabet* (1948; third edition, 1976), H. H. Rowley's *From Joseph to Joshua: Biblical Traditions in the Light of Archaeology* (1950), R. de Vaux's *Archaeology and the Dead Sea Scrolls* (1961; revised, 1977), and Yigael Yadin's *Hazor* (1972). The thirty-eight volumes of annual Schweich Lectures that were published annually between 1909 and 1948 have been reprinted by Kraus Reprint of New York and are still available. The fiftieth volume of Schweich Lectures appeared in 1989.

For many years the British Academy has joined with other scholarly academies in organizing occasional symposia on topics of mutual interest and publishing the proceedings. Meetings with the Royal Society have concentrated on subjects of concern both to scholars in the humanities and those in the natural sciences; resulting volumes have included *The Place of Astronomy in the Ancient World* (1974), *The Early History of Agriculture* (1977), *The Emergence of Man* (1981), *The Psychological Mechanisms of Language* (1981), and *Predictability in Science and Society* (1986). Meetings with the Royal Irish Academy on important topics in the shared history of Britain and Ireland have produced *The English in Medieval Ireland* (1984) and *Ireland after the Union* (1989). Other volumes have dealt with the Anglo-Dutch contribu-

Members and guests of the British Academy at the opening of its first official quarters at 6 Burlington Gardens, 24 July 1928; left to right: Dr. J. W. Mackail; Sir Frederic Kenyon; Sir Charles Wakefield; Arnold Mitchell, architect of the building; Cosmo Lang, the Archbishop of Canterbury; Col. Sir John Edward Kynaston Studd, the Lord Mayor of London; A. J. Balfour, president of the academy; H. A. L. Fisher; and Sir Israel Gollancz, secretary of the academy

tion to the civilization of early modern society and Anglo-American intellectual relations.

The British Academy is also a publisher of scholarly monographs. In earlier years volumes were occasional and of a somewhat miscellaneous character, ranging from the esoteric *A Dictionary of Assyrian Botany* (1949), by R. Campbell Thomson, to the pioneering field survey *Offa's Dyke* (1955), by Sir Cyril Fox; *Roman and Early Byzantine Portrait Sculpture in Asia Minor* (1966), by Jale Inan and Elisabeth Rosenbaum; and the three-volume *Gascon Register A (Series of 1318-1319)* (1975-1976), by G. P. Cuttino. Such volumes, of acknowledged scholarly excellence (the Cuttino work was awarded the Haskins Medal of the Medieval Academy of America), were expensive to produce, with necessarily limited print runs, and were at best "slow sellers" by the standards of commercial and even most university presses.

Since the 1970s there has been a marked expansion of the academy's activities, which has led to an increased commitment to publication. In the main the policy now is to publish only works which come forward as the outcome of the academy's own Research Projects program. This program comprises some thirty projects; about two-thirds of the resulting books are published by the academy, while others appear under the imprints of other academic publishers and university presses. Many of the projects form the British contribution to international enterprises, and their publications conform to an agreed international format. Academy projects are chiefly concerned to produce fundamental works of scholarship on which subsequent research may be based; volumes are planned first and foremost on the criterion of scholarly importance and designed to have a long scholarly life. Virtually all academy Research Projects fall within one of three categories: illustrated catalogues of artifacts; editions and texts, either of a single author or (often loosely) related works; and dictionaries and other reference works.

The first category includes four series of comprehensively illustrated catalogues concerned, respectively, with the pre-Conquest Anglo-Saxon stone sculpture (two volumes published by 1990, twelve volumes projected), sculpture from

The second home of the British Academy, Burlington House, occupied from 1968 to 1982

The second category of British Academy Research Projects publications, editions and texts, ranges from editions of Anglo-Saxon charters (pre-Conquest title deeds relating to grants of land and liberties) to editions of British authors of the Middle Ages writing in Latin (in which texts by Robert Grosseteste are prominent), English Episcopal Acta (the output of medieval bishops' chanceries), and more modern material in series concerned with African history and oriental historical and archival documents. The Records of Social and Economic History Series, of which nine influential volumes were published between 1914 and 1935, has been reprinted by Kraus Reprint of New York. A new series was established in 1972 and by 1990 contained some fifteen volumes. Another productive series is Early English Church Music, with nearly forty volumes appearing between 1963 and 1990. The aim of the series is to make available church music by English composers from the Norman Conquest to the Commonwealth, and it is designed to serve the needs of both scholars and performers. It includes work by anonymous and undeservedly neglected figures as well as much of the output of acknowledged masters such as Thomas Tallis, John Taverner, John Sheppard, Christopher Tye, and Orlando Gibbons. The series is published on commission for the academy by Stainer and Bell.

The third category of Research Projects publications, dictionaries and reference works, is best represented by the *Dictionary of Medieval Latin from British Sources*, of which four fascicles, covering the letters *A* to *H*, appeared between 1975 and 1990. When complete, the dictionary will be an indispensable guide to the study of the Latin of the Middle Ages in Britain from the sixth to the sixteenth centuries, drawing on literary sources from Gildas's *De Excidio Britanniae* (circa 540) to William Camden's *Britannia* (1586). In the meantime, *The Revised Medieval Latin Word-List, from British and Irish Sources* (1965), in its fifth impression in 1989, serves as an introductory tool to meet the needs of students and scholars of medieval Latin.

Roman Britain (six fascicles published by 1990, with five more projected), ancient Greek vases and pottery in public and private collections (four volumes devoted to British collections published by 1990, with two volumes planned on collections in New Zealand and Canada), and medieval stained glass (five volumes published, including the definitive 1981 study of the medieval glass of Canterbury Cathedral by M. H. Caviness). Two other series are concerned with coins, the first (forty volumes published by 1990) detailing coins of the British Isles in British and important overseas collections (principally containing material from the Viking and Slav hoards of the Baltic region) and the second examining collections of Greek coins in the British Isles, in which each volume is devoted to a major collection (for example, that of the Ashmolean Museum at Oxford) and publication is in fascicles. A pendant to the British coins series is *Coinage in Tenth-Century England* (1990), the first detailed study of the coinage of a formative period of English history. It stands as a memorial to its principal author, the great numismatist C. E. Blunt, who died in 1987.

Under its secretary from 1949 to 1968, the archaeologist Sir Mortimer Wheeler, the British Academy became associated with various archaeological enterprises. In 1962 the academy published *Charsada: A Metropolis of the North-West Frontier*, the report of an excavation carried out jointly with the Pakistani government on the site of the former capital of Gandhara on the Peshawar plain. The academy is also responsible for the continuing publication of the excavations of the British mission which worked in Carthage between 1973 and 1978 under the UNESCO-Tunisian "Save Carthage" project. A first double volume appeared in 1984, and two further volumes are in preparation. Finally, in 1990 British Academy Monographs in Archaeology was launched to include the work of the British Schools and Institutes (funded by the British Academy), concentrating initially on work in the Near East and Africa. The first volumes, both of which appeared in 1990, were Judith S. McKenzie's *The Architecture of Petra* and the latest installment of Kathleen Kenyon's *Excavations in Jerusalem.* Fur-

ther volumes are in preparation.

The British Academy's first headquarters, occupied in 1928, were at 6 Burlington Gardens, London. In 1968 it moved into Burlington House. Since 1982 it has been at 20-21 Cornwall Terrace.

Reference:

Mortimer Wheeler, *The British Academy 1949-1968* (London: Published for the British Academy by the Oxford University Press, 1970).

—*Peter W. H. Brown*

John Calder (Publishers) Limited
(London: 1949-1964; 1975-   )
Calder and Boyars
(London: 1964-1975)

John Calder (Publishers) Limited was started in 1949 to publish general quality literature and to fill the many gaps in current and classical literature created by wartime shortages. While at Zurich University studying political economy, John Calder had read European literature in the original languages. Returning to England, he found that many important works were out of print in English or had never been translated. Eighteenth- and nineteenth-century classics translated from the German, French, Italian, and Russian appeared in the firm's list together with new English and American novels and books on the arts, in particular music, opera, and drama. In 1958 Calder took in a partner, Marion Boyars. The company's name was changed to Calder and

Boyars in 1964; it was changed back in 1975 after the partnership broke up. Calder analyzed his forty years of publishing in his contribution to the 1989-1990 edition of *The Waterstone's Guide to Books*: "Creative literary publishing is totally different from general publishing and is more like running an art gallery. It needs the capital to endure a small and slow return, enough knowledge and energy to function effectively with little outside help, a small staff able to do anything and a missionary belief that the effort is worthwhile. It also needs a flair to publicise a personal taste so that the author one is trying to build up gets some benefit and recognition in his lifetime. Because a literary publisher starts with little competition, making his own discoveries, it is usually

Card from Samuel Beckett, written shortly before the playwright's death, paying tribute to John Calder (Sotheby's auction catalogue, 13 December 1990)

some time before he has to worry about larger, predatory publishers seducing his authors, and he must use that honeymoon period to get the confidence and affection of his writers. Then, provided he does his job well, he has a good chance of keeping his authors once they are established and profitable. He should also have the good luck to find at least one really unusual and important new talent whose name will become synonymous with the imprint: this will give him the energy and pride to ride the waves of adversity that will inevitably attack him periodically."

In the mid 1950s Calder had found such a talent in Samuel Beckett, whom he would later describe as his "lucky genius, friend and guru." Calder also published the *nouveau roman* of Alain Robbe-Grillet, Nathalie Sarraute, Robert Pinget, Marguerite Duras, and Claude Simon; works by important German and Eastern European writers; and innovative novels by such British writers as Alan Burns, Aidan Higgins, Ann Quin, and Alexander Trocchi. Not all of these writers have remained with Calder, for when the fourteen-year partnership with Boyars dissolved, she acquired half the list. During the partnership Calder and Boyars gained both profit and notoriety with works such as Henry Miller's *Tropic of Cancer* (1963) and *Tropic of Capricorn* (1964), as well as Hubert Selby's *Last Exit to Brooklyn* (1966). The latter was the subject of a much-publicized obscenity case at the Old Bailey. The company eventu-

ally won on appeal and reprinted twenty thousand copies of the book in response to widespread interest aroused by the case. As so often happens, the attempted suppression of the book only served to enhance its appeal for a larger public than it might otherwise have attracted. The firm is also noteworthy for having introduced absurdist theater in the 1950s to Britain through the work of Eugène Ionesco, Fernando Arrabal, Pinget, René de Obaldia, and some British writers. There has been a continuing policy to publish British, American, and European plays, most notably the works of Howard Barker. The firm has also brought out expressionist and surrealist series of literature. As Calder expressed it in *The Waterstone's Guide to Books,* "Literature is an art, or should be: it is influenced by, and influences in its turn, the other arts." This view has led him into a deeper investigation of music, drama, philosophy, and politics, the result of which is an expanded list of books on these subjects and on related new ideas and critical approaches. Little by little he has abandoned general publishing in favor of what he calls "a more specialised list of books of and on literature and the related arts, with a large section devoted to opera."

Calder believes that the independent publisher and bookseller have an important role to play "in a time when libraries decline, universities are forced to abandon culture, and newspapers increasingly avoid the intellectual in their review coverage"; it is the happy combination of "writers, publisher and booksellers, working together to spread the joy of reading and learning, on which so much of our culture and civilisation is based, which provides an alternative to lives and values based on greed and ignorance, and enhances,

rather than diminishes, what is best and most promising in the human character." His firm is located at 9-15 Neal Street.

—*John Calder*

Jonathan Cape Limited
(London: 1924-   )
Jonathan Cape
(London: 1921-1924)

See also the Robert O. Ballou, Jonathan Cape and Harrison Smith, and Random House entries in *DLB 46: American Literary Publishing Houses, 1900-1980: Trade and Paperback.*

As Michael S. Howard put it, the firm of Jonathan Cape is an institution that never became institutional. It combined risk-taking with respectability; it also united flexibility and enterprise with rigorous production standards. From the beginning it earned impressive profits with a list that included modern classics and experimental literature as well as best-sellers.

The son of a builder, Herbert Jonathan Cape was born on 15 November 1879 in Hammersmith. Almost uniquely among contemporary publishers, he served an apprenticeship in bookselling and thus acquired a close familiarity with the literary marketplace. He entered the trade at age sixteen as an errand boy for Hatchards bookshop; four years later he became a traveling salesman for the London office of Harper and Brothers, and in 1904 he moved to Gerald Duckworth and Company. In 1907 he married Edith Louisa Creak. He became manager at the Duckworth firm in 1911 and supervised the

business when Duckworth was away during World War I.

Cape enlisted in the army in December 1915. His wife died just when he returned to civilian life in 1919. Realizing that he could never become a director with Duckworth, who thought he lacked the necessary breeding for the job (in fact, Cape was quite well-read, though he had little formal education), Cape placed an advertisement in the *Times* offering to found a publishing imprint with any interested party. There was a response from Geoffrey Faber, but as both men were looking for capital and neither had much, nothing came of their meeting. Instead, Philip Lee Warner hired Cape as trade distributor for the Medici Society, which produced fine art volumes. At about the same time, Cape—using his mother's maiden name—started his own firm, Jonathan Page and Company. He had a tiny office in Buckingham Street and one employee, Olyve Vida James, who would become his second wife in 1927.

Cape got off to a profitable start in early 1920 by securing reprint rights from Duckworth for the spicy novels of Elinor Glyn. He produced them in huge quantities as shilling paperbacks

Jonathan Cape

and sold them outright to the wholesale firm of Simkin Marshall Hamilton Kent and Company. That summer Cape took on as junior partner George Wren Howard, who brought five thousand pounds in capital to the firm. Howard was a collector of private-press books—including the work of the Kelmscott, Doves, Ashendene, and Cuala Presses—and had worked for the Medici Society.

Learning that Warner was planning to publish a five-hundred-copy Medici Society edition of Charles Montagu Doughty's *Travels in Arabia Deserta* (first published by Cambridge University Press in 1888 and in a condensed version by Gerald Duckworth and Company in 1908) with a new introduction by T. E. Lawrence, Cape saw the opportunity to inaugurate a new publishing company with an impressive first production. He persuaded Warner to publish *Travels in Arabia Deserta* jointly with the firm of Jonathan Cape, which was launched on the first day of 1921 from offices at 11 Gower Street. Cape and How-

ard shrewdly offered free copies to selected newspapers on condition that they review the book—a reasonable request, they explained, for a nine-guinea limited-edition volume. The strategy worked: *Travels in Arabia Deserta* was widely reviewed and quickly sold out. Further profits accrued from a three-guinea edition published in 1923 and a thirty-shilling version in 1926.

A few weeks after he set up shop, Cape hired Edward Garnett as his chief literary adviser. Garnett was perhaps the most perceptive and influential publisher's reader of his generation, having worked for T. Fisher Unwin, William Heinemann, Gerald Duckworth, and the Bodley Head. For two hundred pounds a year he would at least look at all manuscripts that Cape received and would carefully read eight to ten a week.

Cape then visited America, where, acting on Garnett's advice, he secured British publication rights to an impressive list of books: Sherwood Anderson's *Poor White* (American edition, 1920; Cape edition, 1921) and *Windy MacPherson's Son* (revised American edition, 1922; Cape edition, 1923) from Ben Huebsch, and H. L. Mencken's *Prejudices: First Series* (American edition, 1919; Cape edition, 1921) from Alfred A. Knopf. He also acquired works by Carl Sandburg and Dorothy Canfield from Harcourt, Brace; by Van Wyck Brooks from E. P. Dutton; and by Eugene O'Neill from Boni and Liveright. From Harcourt, Brace, Cape also secured Sinclair Lewis's *Babbitt* (American and Cape editions, 1922), which he printed with a glossary of 125 Americanisms. Apparently one American idiom escaped the London publisher: when Lewis told him "I'll want to see my name in lights," Cape took him literally and displayed an illuminated advertisement for *Babbitt* in Picadilly Circus. The publicity may have been effective: the first printing of twelve thousand was sold out by the end of the year.

For the rest of his career Cape would visit the United States on a fairly regular basis and would lead the British publishing industry in importing works by American authors. In his first efforts at publishing books by British writers, however, he stumbled. Clare Sheridan's *Russian Portraits*, E. L. Grant Watson's *Shadow and Sunlight: A Romance of the Tropics*, and Marjorie Strachey's *David the Son of Jesse* led off the 1921 list; in each case Cape overspent on publicity, printed too many copies, and ended up with a substantial loss. One 1921 book that did enjoy large and sustained sales was Percy Lubbock's *The Craft*

Cape (seated, center) in 1922 with his partner George Wren Howard (seated, left); Olyve Vida James, his first employee and later his second wife; and the staff of the company

of Fiction, which remained in print as late as 1970.

In May 1921 Cape paid two thousand pounds to acquire the A. C. Fifield list, including works by H. G. Wells, W. H. Davies, Lancelot Hogben, and Laurence Housman. Fifield had also published works by Samuel Butler, and Cape would bring out the Shrewsbury edition of Butler's collected works between 1923 and 1926. In September Cape started *Now & Then*, an occasional journal to publicize his books. Except for an interval from 1944 to 1948, when it was interrupted by World War II, it would continue until 1961.

By the end of its first year the firm had built up a list of 120 books. Combined sales for Cape and Page, which published light novels and technical books, were £10,954, though profits were a scant £103. The partners could not afford to draw salaries until 1922, when the sister companies earned £1,954 on sales of £25,000.

In 1922 Cape scored a critical and commer-cial success with Lubbock's childhood memoir *Earlham*, which won the James Tait Black Memo-rial Prize. Ten Cape books would garner that award by 1969, a record equaled by no other pub-lisher. Liam O'Flaherty's *The Informer* (1925), E. H. Young's *Miss Mole* (1930), and Elizabeth Bowen's *Eva Trout* (1969) were among the win-ners. In 1922 Cape also began the six-shilling Nov-els of Today series with C. E. M. Joad's *The High-brows* and Camille Mallarmé's *The House of the Enemy*.

For a one-thousand-pound advance Cape published Wells's novel *The Dream* (1924) and sold more than fifteen thousand copies in a month. Wells demanded lavish royalties, but the firm was able to profit from his next book, *Chris-tina Alberta's Father* (1925), by selling the Ameri-can rights to Harcourt, Brace for twelve thou-sand dollars. Cape refused Wells's demands for his cumbersome novel *The World of William Clissold* (1926), which went instead to Ernest Benn. In 1938 Wells would return to Cape for one more novel, *Apropos of Dolores*.

In 1916 Cape had tried unsuccessfully to persuade Duckworth to publish James Joyce's *A Portrait of the Artist as a Young Man*; the book was published in the United States by Huebsch in 1916 and in England by Harriet Shaw Weaver's Egoist Press in 1917. Cape took over the work as well as Joyce's *Chamber Music* (published by Elkin Mathews in 1907) and *Exiles* (published by Grant Richards in 1918) in 1924. He refused *Ulysses* (published in Paris and also by the Egoist Press in 1922) because he feared it would be suppressed, and in any case he found it a "penance" to read. Cape did publish Joyce's early draft manuscript *Stephen Hero* in 1944, followed by a revised and expanded edition in 1956.

To attract badly needed capital, the firm was incorporated as Jonathan Cape Limited in February 1924. Piers Gilchrist Thompson, who had come to work for Cape the previous year, became secretary of the company and invested four thousand pounds in it. Page and Company was absorbed into the new enterprise. The following January the expanding company moved to more spacious offices at 30 Bedford Square.

When Lawrence saw Roy Campbell's manuscript for *The Flaming Terrapin* in the studio of Augustus John, he sent a note to Cape: "Get after this man." The firm published the poem in 1924. Garnett became a mentor and helper to Campbell, as he did to many other authors. In the late 1920s he nursed along O'Flaherty, who later paid tribute to his influence: "Like a father he took me under his protection, handling me with a delicacy with which one handles a highly-strung young colt, which the least mistake might make unfit for racing.... I was only too willing that he should fashion the development of my literary talent in whatever way he pleased." Garnett secured O'Flaherty a grant of two hundred pounds from the Royal Literary Fund and tried to place his articles in magazines. In turn, O'Flaherty introduced Garnett to Seán O'Faoláin, who received similar encouragement and support, along with some frank criticism. O'Faoláin's *Midsummer Night's Madness and Other Stories* (1932) had an introduction by Garnett scolding the Irish nation for ignoring or censoring its best writers. The book was critically acclaimed in Britain and suppressed in Ireland.

"[Garnett's] just discovered another bloody genius," Cape supposedly snorted on receiving a recommendation to publish H. E. Bates's novel *The Two Sisters* (1926). Once again Garnett assumed the role of literary godfather: he meticu-

lously criticized Bates's work, placed his stories in magazines, invited him out to his country home, and found him work as a clerk in the J. and E. Bumpus bookstore (even paying part of his salary). Bates would have twenty-two books published by Cape, and in 1950 he expressed his appreciation in *Edward Garnett: A Memoir*.

In 1926 Cape's sales exceeded fifty thousand pounds, boosted by Bates's *The Two Sisters*, Lewis's *Mantrap*, Naomi Mitchison's *The Laburnam Branch Poems*, O'Flaherty's *The Tent, and Other Stories*, and Sandburg's *Abraham Lincoln: The Prairie Years*. Cape also began the Travellers' Library, a uniform line of well-produced reprints selling for three shillings, sixpence, and the Story Series. The latter, consisting of collections of short stories, did not last long, but it is notable for including *In Our Time: Stories* (1926), by Ernest Hemingway. According to legend Cape, on having Hemingway pointed out to him in a Paris café in 1926, said: "Ask him to come over. Tell him I should like to publish him." Cape published *The Sun Also Rises* (1926) under the title *Fiesta* (1927), followed by *A Farewell to Arms* in 1929. Hemingway was gratified by the "very generous" royalties he received for *Fiesta*, but he confessed in 1947 that "I have never been able to like Cape." The author lashed out at the publisher for removing four-letter words from the English edition of *Death in the Afternoon* (1932); and one can hardly blame Hemingway for being upset by Cape's dust jacket for *The Old Man and the Sea* (1952), which portrayed a tuna rather than the marlin of the story. Nevertheless, Hemingway acknowledged that "We always got along well.... He keeps his word . . . and all his faults are obvious."

T. E. Lawrence believed that no work could be truly creative unless it involved handwork. Not content merely to write a book, he had to oversee every aspect of its production, and for a time he considered setting up a private press with Vyvyan Richards. Lawrence had studied with delight the Kelmscott Press edition of *The Works of Geoffrey Chaucer* (1896), and he aimed for the same standard of excellence when he embarked on printing his own limited edition of his *Seven Pillars of Wisdom*. For purely visual reasons—to avoid glaring patches of white space, for instance—Lawrence would repeatedly rewrite the text after it was set in type, sometimes running through fourteen sets of proofs. In December 1926 he finally published an edition of 190 copies, 128 of which were sold to subscribers for thirty guineas each; about 100 were in distinctive fine bindings,

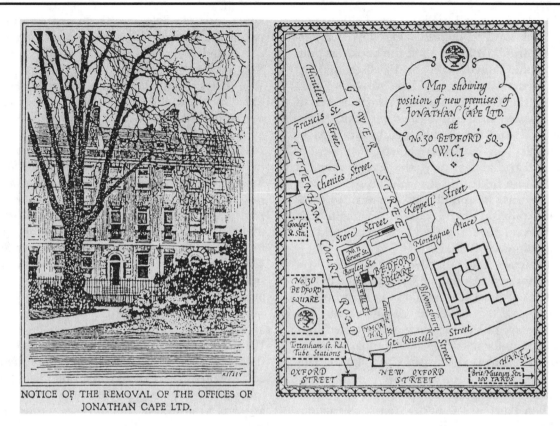

NOTICE OF THE REMOVAL OF THE OFFICES OF
JONATHAN CAPE LTD.

Announcement of the firm's move to new premises, January 1925

no two of them alike. Since the costs of the project, thirteen thousand pounds, were far greater than expected, Lawrence offered to let Cape publish an abridgment provided that Lawrence could withdraw the volume once it had covered his deficit. The book appeared in March 1927 under the title *Revolt in the Desert* in a five-guinea edition of 300 copies and a popular thirty-shilling edition. The latter sold more than 30,000 copies in a few months and clearly could have sold many more; but having earned his thirteen thousand pounds in royalties, Lawrence exercised his option to halt sales.

Thanks largely to *Revolt in the Desert*, the firm's sales increased in 1927 by 150 percent, and profits soared from two thousand pounds to almost twenty-eight thousand. Other popular successes of that year included Robert Graves's biography *Lawrence and the Arabs*, Katherine Mayo's *Mother India*, and Hugh Lofting's *Doctor Dolittle's Caravan*. By this time Cape was making a major investment in poetry with Campbell's *The Wayzgoose*, Davies's *A Poet's Calendar*, and Edna St. Vincent Millay's opera libretto *The King's Henchman*. Buoyed by the annus mirabilis of 1927, Cape was able to attract important new authors in 1928,

among them Christopher Isherwood with *All the Conspirators* and Henry Williamson with *The Pathway*.

Also in 1928, posthumous success came to Mary Webb. Cape had published her last completed novel, *Precious Bane*, in 1924. At first, like her earlier works, it had enjoyed critical acclaim but modest sales, though after winning the Femina-Vie Heureuse prize in 1926 it had gone into a fourth printing. Hamish Hamilton, a former Cape employee, had managed to interest Prime Minister Stanley Baldwin in the novel, which was set in a part of Shropshire where Baldwin's family had lived for generations. Baldwin had written Webb a letter of appreciation not long before she died in October 1927. The following April, at a dinner for the Royal Literary Society, Baldwin hailed *Precious Bane* as an unknown classic; the book was transformed into a bestseller and has enjoyed sustained popularity ever since. Baldwin's speech mobilized Cape to publish a collected edition of Webb's works—something he had earlier refused to do—in 1928 as *Seven for a Secret*. He also published her *Poems: and, The Spring of Joy* (1928), her novel *Armour wherein He Trusted* (1929), *A Mary Webb Anthology*

(1939), *Fifty-One Poems* (1946), and *The Essential Mary Webb* (1949). (In 1943 Katherine Webb, the widow of Mary Webb's widower, would become Cape's third wife; Vida died in 1931.)

In 1928 Cape plunged into the most notorious controversy of his career by publishing Radclyffe Hall's lesbian novel *The Well of Loneliness*. The manuscript had been rejected by J. W. Arrowsmith, Cassell, Heinemann, and Martin Secker. Cape paid a five-hundred-pound advance and secured a brief introduction by the psychologist Havelock Ellis. The price was set high at fifteen shillings, fifteen hundred copies were printed in plain wrappers, and review copies were sent only to magazines and newspapers that were likely to give it a fair reading. The critics were mostly sympathetic, but on Saturday, 18 August, posters announced that James Douglas, editor of the *Sunday Express*, would condemn the book in the next day's edition. That morning booksellers snapped up every available copy of *The Well of Loneliness*; Cape had already ordered a second printing of three thousand copies. Douglas was in the habit of denouncing "sexual inversion and perversion," and that Sunday he was in rare form. "I would rather give a healthy boy or a healthy girl a phial of prussic acid than this novel," he wrote, and he appealed to the home secretary to suppress the book if the publisher did not withdraw it. Infuriated, Cape sent the home secretary some favorable reviews and a copy of the novel, offering to halt sales if the minister thought it obscene. That was an unwise strategy: the home secretary, the comically puritanical guardian of public morals Sir William Joynson-Hicks, threatened to ban the book if it was not withdrawn.

Without consulting Hall, Cape announced in the *Times* that he would cease publication of *The Well of Loneliness*. Immediately, however, he subleased the rights to the Pegasus Press in Paris and sent papier-mâché molds for the casting of new stereo plates; Pegasus put out a new edition and tried to smuggle copies into Britain. The police seized volumes sent to Leonard Hill, a bookseller who distributed Pegasus books in London, and summonses were issued to Hill and Cape "to show cause why the articles so seized should not be destroyed." Leonard and Virginia Woolf, E. M. Forster, Rose Macaulay, A. P. Herbert, Vita Sackville-West, Desmond MacCarthy, Laurence Housman, Storm Jameson, and Julian Huxley were all prepared to defend *The Well of Loneliness*; but the presiding magistrate, Sir Chartres Biron,

did not allow them to testify, declaring that it was up to him to decide the question of obscenity. The defense was bungled by Cape's barrister, Norman Birkett. He never called on Cape to testify or to explain why he had first withdrawn the book and then had it republished in a rather underhanded manner. After arriving in court two hours late, Birkett claimed that the book merely depicted normal friendship between women. That contention was manifestly untrue: Hall had frankly portrayed lesbianism in her novel, just as she openly professed it in her own life. During the luncheon break she furiously scolded Birkett for trying to conceal the whole point of the book, and that afternoon he was compelled to make a retraction in court, effectively destroying his case. J. B. Melville, defense counsel for the Pegasus Press, more honestly argued that *The Well of Loneliness* was a plea for "toleration and understanding for those who are God's creatures," a book "which has been said on all sides to be a fine literary work." Unmoved, Sir Chartres declared that the novel portrayed the seduction of a married woman (it did not) and ruled that any book that defended such "horrible practices" was by definition obscene. (Despite the ruling, the Travellers' Library would in 1932 publish a collection of Samuel Johnson's witticisms assembled by Sir Chartres Biron.)

The Well of Loneliness fared better in the United States. The firm of Alfred A. Knopf agreed to take it on but backed out when the censorship storm broke in England. Cape then placed the book with Covici-Friede, which published it in December 1928. John S. Sumner of the New York Society for the Suppression of Vice persuaded the authorities to prosecute the publishers, but attorney Morris L. Ernst secured an acquittal.

After *The Well of Loneliness*, the Cape firm tried to avoid entanglements with the censors. In 1932 Garnett missed a chance to acquire Samuel Beckett's novel "Dream of Fair to Middling Women" ("I wouldn't touch this with a bargepole"). Because it graphically described sexual encounters and contraceptives, both Garnett and Cape balked at Mitchison's novel *We Have Been Warned*, which was published by Constable in 1935. In 1928 Lawrence had sent Garnett the manuscript for *The Mint*, his brutally frank portrait of life in the Royal Air Force, but had stipulated that it not be published before 1950. It appeared in 1955 in a limited unexpurgated edition and in a standard edition in which the obscenities were re-

MEMORANDUM OF AGREEMENT made and entered into this   day of
One thousand nine hundred and twenty five BETWEEN
THOMAS EDWARD LAWRENCE (Esq), of Cloud's Hill, Moreton, Dorsetshire,
(hereinafter called the author) of the one part A N D the Firm of
JONATHAN CAPE LTD 30, Bedford Square, W.C.1., (hereinafter called
the Publishers) of the other part. WHEREBY it is mutually agreed
as follows:-

1.   The Author hereby agrees to grant to the Publishers, their
successors and assigns the exclusive licence to publish in volume
form in the English language throughout the British Empire during
the legal term of copyright an original work (provisionally entitled
being an abridgement of THE SEVEN PILLARS OF WISDOM of which he
is the author.

2.   The author undertakes to deliver to the Publishers the MS of
this abridgement on or before the thirty first day of March 1926.
The length shall not be less than one hundred and twenty thousand
words.   Should the author not have himself prepared the abridgement by that date the Publishers shall be at liberty to have an
abridgement made themselves from the original book THE SEVEN PILLARS
OF WISDOM and the author undertakes to supply the Publishers with
a copy of the work for the purpose of making the abridged version

3.   The Author hereby warrants to the Publishers that the said work
is in no way whatever a violation of any existing copyright and
that it contains nothing obscene, indecent (or with the intention
of the author) libellous; and will indemnify the Publishers against
any loss, injury or damage, including any legal costs or expenses
properly incurred, occasioned to, or incurred by the Publishers in
consequence of any breach (unknown to the Publishers) of this war-
ranty. PROVIDED ONLY
And it is hereby further agreed that in the following cases any
loss, injury or damage (including any legal costs, or expenses as afore-
said) occasioned to, or incurred by either the Author or the Publishers or both shall be contributed to and borne and paid by the
Author and the Publishers in equal shares, namely:-

1.   Where any matter contained in the said work shall be
held to constitute a libel upon a person to whom it shall
appear the author did not intend to refer;

2.   Where an unsuccessful action is brought in respect of
an alleged libel contained in the said work; and

3.   Where any proceedings are threatened, instituted or prosecuted for any alleged libel contained in the said work and
the claim is settled before judgement with the consent of
the Author and the Publishers.

4.   The Publishers on being supplied by the Author with the manuscript (or copy) and the proof sheets duly and timely revised shall
publish the said work during the year 1927 unless prevented from
doing so by strikes, lockouts or other circumstances or happenings
beyond their control.   They shall publish the work at their own expense, in such style as they deem best and at a published price of
not less than fifteen shillings in the first instance and shall pay
to the Author on the published price of each copy sold by them the
following royalties:-

Fifteen per cent (15%) on the first two thousand (2,000)
copies and Twenty per cent (20%) thereafter.

Draft agreement for the Cape publication of T. E. Lawrence's Revolt in the Desert, *with annotations by George Bernard Shaw*

10.   In the event of the Author so desiring it the Publishers agree not to place on sale any further copies of the English and Colonial Editions of the said work ~~after they have recovered the sum of Three thousand pounds (£3,000) advanced to the author plus a net profit of fifty per cent (50%) on the amount advanced such profits to be calculated on all copies sold from the beginning.~~

11.   It is hereby agreed that the Publishers shall have the first opportunity to consider for publication the next book by the same author; such book or books shall be the subject of a fresh agreement between the author and the Publishers the terms of which shall be mutually agreed between the parties.

The Publishers undertake to decide within one month from the receipt of the manuscript or manuscripts whether they are willing to make an offer for the publication of such book or books. If within a period of one month no agreement as to the terms of publication shall have been reached, then the Author shall be at liberty to open negotiations for the publication of such book or books elsewhere.

12.   All serial and other rights not specifically mentioned in this contract are reserved to the Author.

13.   The Author hereby authorises the Publishers to pay to his Agent Raymond Savage of 43, Aldwych, London, W.C.2., any monies payable to him under the terms of this Agreement and declares that his receipt shall be a good and valid discharge in respect thereof and further he authorises and empowers the Publishers to ~~treat with~~ his said Agent ~~who will act on his behalf in any matters~~ arising out of this Agreement ~~in any way whatsoever.~~

Rupert Hart-Davis (right), then a director of Jonathan Cape Limited, and the poet Edmund Blunden taking the field during a 1938 cricket match between Cape and the Alden Press in Oxford (Yale University Library)

placed with blank spaces. Cape also cut expletives from Hemingway's fiction and Irwin Shaw's war novel *The Young Lions* (1949). Occasionally he used his blue pencil to make what he thought were improvements. When Simone de Beauvoir, in *The Second Sex* (1953), alluded to a man's habit of lighting up a cigarette after sex, Cape replaced "cigarette" with "pipe." He published Norman Mailer's *Barbary Shore* (1952)—a critical and commercial failure in Britain, as it was in the United States, where it had been published in 1951—but rejected Mailer's next novel, *The Deer Park* (published in America in 1955), fearing that it might be prosecuted for obscenity; *The Deer Park* was published in London by Allan Wingate in 1957. For the same reason, Wren Howard sternly refused Vladimir Nabokov's *Lolita*, which had been published in Paris in 1955 and would be published in England in 1959 by Weidenfeld and Nicolson.

While the controversy over *The Well of Loneliness* was swirling around him, Cape was busy establishing a beachhead in the United States. In January 1929 he joined with Harrison Smith, chief editor at Harcourt, Brace, to set up an independent American company with offices in New York at 139 East 46th Street. Robert O. Ballou, a columnist for *Publishers' Weekly* and literary editor of the *Chicago Daily News*, also invested in the new firm of Jonathan Cape and Harrison Smith Incorporated and became its treasurer.

Harrison Smith was an audacious and enterprising publisher. He offered *Gallows' Orchard* (1930) by Claire Spencer (his wife) to the Book-of-the-Month Club and Maksim Gorky's *Bystander* (1930) to the Literary Guild; when both were rejected, he reversed the submissions and had them both accepted—the first publisher to score such a coup. Compared with his partner, however, he was sloppy and unbusinesslike. As Christopher Morley quipped in the *Saturday Review of Literature*:

> Said Jonathan Cape to Harrison Smith,
> "Here's a sentence that ought to be done something with."
> Said Harrison Smith to Jonathan Cape,
> "We'll leave it to the printer to whip into shape."

On one visit to the New York office, Cape protested that the manuscript for William Faulkner's *As I Lay Dying* (1930) had not been properly edited. He demanded to know the meaning of one sentence in particular; Ballou could not explain it. Finally Cape confronted Faulkner himself, who studied the sentence and then confessed, "Why, damned if I know. I was lookin' at thet the othah day, and wondrin'; and then I remembered that I was pretty co'ned up [intoxicated on corn whiskey] when I wrote that, and didn't know what I was sayin'."

Even as the Great Depression tightened its stranglehold on the American publishing industry, Smith habitually ordered large printings of books that he could not sell. In the summer of 1931, with the company running up huge losses, Cape fired Smith and replaced him with Ballou, who trimmed the deficit. In May 1932, just after the firm had been renamed Jonathan Cape and Robert Ballou Incorporated, Cape filed for bankruptcy without giving Ballou a chance to buy out his share and continue publishing on his own. Cape had lost more than fifteen thousand pounds, as well as the respect and trust of the New York publishing world. Ballou deeply resented the way he had been treated—with good reason, as Cape later conceded.

The Depression hurt Cape's British operations as well. The year 1929 had been a banner one, with the publication of Hemingway's *A Farewell to Arms*, Graves's *Goodbye to All That*, Margaret Mead's *Coming of Age in Samoa*, Lewis Mumford's biography *Herman Melville*, John Cowper Powys's *Wolf Solent*, and *White-Maa's Saga*, the first novel by Eric Linklater. A year later the book trade was in the doldrums. Arthur Ransome's *Swallows and Amazons* (1930) was a critical but not, at first, a commercial success. Cape started new lines of cheap hardcover books—the four-shilling-sixpence Life and Letters series in 1930 and the two-shilling Florin Books (which cost him barely sixpence to produce) in 1932.

By 1934 Cape was buoyed by the general recovery of the publishing industry. The company briefly took over the monthly magazine *Life and Letters* from Desmond MacCarthy and Lord Esher (Lionel Gordon Baliol Brett). It had a dazzling stable of contributors—W. H. Auden, Elizabeth Bowen, Cecil Day-Lewis, Graham Greene, John Lehmann, Wyndham Lewis, Malcolm Lowry, Louis MacNeice, Malcolm Muggeridge, Herbert Read, Osbert Sitwell, and Stephen Spender—some of whom eventually had books published by Cape. In the early 1930s popular historical books such as Duff Cooper's *Talleyrand* (1932), Jacques Bainville's *Napoleon* (1932), and J. E. Neale's *Queen Elizabeth* (1934) were prominent on the Cape list. Beginning in 1939 Neale would edit the Bedford Historical Series for Cape, and his advice would lead to the acquisition of Garrett Mattingly's classic *The Defeat of the Spanish Armada* (1959).

The death of Lawrence on 19 May 1935 allowed Cape to publish *Seven Pillars of Wisdom* on 29 July. By Christmas more than one hundred thousand copies of the fine thirty-shilling quarto had been sold in Britain; the book was also a bestseller in the United States. That year Cape's sales were up 60 percent over 1934, and profits reached a new high.

Cape's close connections with suppliers and manufacturers made it possible to maintain consistently high production standards. The paper for *Seven Pillars of Wisdom* and for the majority of Cape books came from John Dickinson and Company. Butler and Tanner had done printing for Cape almost from the beginning, but in 1929 the Cape firm (along with Jonathan Cape and Wren Howard as individuals) bought into the Alden

Press. Seven years later Cape drew on the profits from *Seven Pillars of Wisdom* to buy out its binder, A. W. Bain and Company. With full control over printing and binding, Cape was able to minimize production bottlenecks during World War II. The firm sold back its share of the Alden Press in the late 1950s. The Bain plant was closed in 1970.

In 1935 Allen Lane asked Cape for the right to include ten Cape titles in his new paperback venture, Penguin Books. Convinced that the experiment would fail, Cape was happy to sell the rights for forty pounds each. Later he would curse Lane, Penguin Books, and his own lack of foresight: the paperback revolution ultimately killed most cheap hardcover reprints, including Cape's own Travellers' Library, Life and Letters Books, and Florin Books. In 1939, however, Cape joined Harold Macmillan, W. A. R. Collins, Dwye Evans of Heinemann, Harold Raymond of Chatto and Windus, and Alan Bott of the Book Society in founding the Reprint Society, a club that republished popular books in a uniform hardcover format for two shillings, sixpence. Its premiere publication was *Seven Pillars of Wisdom*, in two volumes.

Garnett died on 19 February 1937. Rupert Hart-Davis, who had been a Cape director since 1933, brought in William Plomer to replace him as chief reader. Plomer would have his own fiction and poetry published by Cape, and he edited the three-volume *Kilvert's Diary: Selections from the Diary of the Reverend Francis Kilvert* (1938-1940), a popular and revealing slice of Victorian social history. The Cape list having grown fairly conventional, Plomer tried to make it more avant-garde—with limited success. He could not persuade the firm to publish works by John Betjeman or Nabokov, though he did acquire Arthur Koestler's *The Gladiators* (1939) and *Darkness at Noon* (1940), Derek Walcott's *In a Green Night: Poems 1948-1960* (1962), and Ted Walker's *Fox on a Barn Door* (1965).

Plomer found the Cape poetry list particularly uninspired. It did, however, include Stevie Smith's *Novel on Yellow Paper*, which appeared in September 1936 and sold a respectable thirteen hundred copies by the New Year. Her *A Good Time Was Had by All* (1937) and *Tender Only to One* (1938) were less successful. She worked well with Hart-Davis, though she could be quite assertive about royalties.

The outbreak of World War II initially depressed the market for books. In early 1940

Cape tried to stimulate sales with the St. Giles Library, hardcover books selling for only one shilling, ninepence. Later, as consumer demand returned and paper rationing was imposed, publishers looked for ways to sell their back-list stock before the Luftwaffe disposed of it. Paperbound sheets of Florin Books were sold off as Cape Pocket Books, priced at a shilling. In 1941 several publishers formed a paperback consortium, the British Publishers Guild, headed by Cape; Guild Books were priced from sixpence to a shilling. Cape achieved record sales in 1944, but only by exhausting its old stock. Of ten titles by Hemingway, six went out of print, and few new books could be published.

The firm's relationship with Bates had begun to deteriorate in 1939, when David Garnett—Edward Garnett's son, and a reader for the firm—rejected his World War I novel "San Fairy Ann." Strapped for cash, Bates signed book contracts with Victor Gollancz and B. T. Batsford, provoking an indignant protest from Wren Howard. In the fall of 1941 Bates joined the Royal Air Force, and from February to May 1942 he contributed short stories to the *News Chronicle* under the name "Flying Officer X." When Cape collected the series in *The Greatest People in the World* (1942), the Air Ministry supplied paper over and above the standard ration and ordered 250,000 copies. Since Bates had written the series while working for the government, no royalties were due him. Cape offered him only one hundred pounds each for *The Greatest People in the World* and *How Sleep the Brave* (1943), noting that Bates's earnings from his previous books were still two hundred pounds behind his advances. After some legal squabbling, Bates and Cape parted company in 1944.

During the war Plomer, Hart-Davis, and the rest of the editorial staff went into military service. The historian Cicely V. Wedgwood joined the staff in 1941 and Daniel George Bunting, who had had work published by Cape under the name Daniel George, joined in 1945. Bunting would become an influential man of letters, reviewing books for the *Daily Express* and selecting them for the Book Society. Until 1963, when he was crippled by a stroke, he served Cape as a witty and meticulous reader.

In 1944 both Wedgwood and Bunting recommended the publication of George Orwell's *Animal Farm*. Cape was ready to accept it until a high official at the Ministry of Information urged him not to publish a book that might offend the So-

viet government, Britain's wartime ally. Cape promptly rejected the book; it was published in 1945 by Secker and Warburg. The firm had turned down two other Orwell manuscripts—an early draft of *Down and Out in Paris and London* (published by Gollancz in 1933) and *Burmese Days* (published in America by Harper in 1934 and in England by Gollancz in 1935).

Sinclair Lewis left in a huff in 1949, after Cape ventured some criticisms of his last and worst novel, *The God-Seeker*; the novel was published that year by Heinemann. On the plus side, in 1947 Cape acquired the rights to all the works of Housman in return for a lifetime annuity. Bowen came over from Victor Gollancz, attracted in part by Cape's promise of a uniform edition of her works. Her *The Heat of the Day* (1949) was an immediate best-seller. After quarrelling with his publisher W. A. R. Collins, T. H. White was brought over to Cape by his friend David Garnett. The firm published his *Mistress Masham's Repose* (1947) and would publish Sylvia Townsend Warner's biography of White in 1967. André Maurois produced *The Quest for Proust* (1950), *Lelia: The Life of George Sand* (1953), and *Victor Hugo* (1953).

Cape had brought out Malcolm Lowry's *Ultramarine* in 1933, selling only half of the fifteen hundred copies printed. When Lowry submitted *Under the Volcano* in 1945, Plomer's report on the manuscript complained that it was full of "eccentric word-spinning and stream-of-consciousness stuff" and recommended that it be cut by a third to a half. Cape offered to accept it if it were revised; in response, Lowry sent him a sixteen-thousand word defense of the novel. Plomer was a bit offended when Cape published the text with no changes in 1947. The reviews were not enthusiastic, and the first edition of five thousand copies did not sell out. Lowry would not gain critical recognition until after his death in 1957.

In 1947 Cape paid his first postwar visit to New York. From Scribner's Maxwell Perkins he secured the British rights to Alan Paton's classic novel of South Africa, *Cry, the Beloved Country* (1948). A Book Society selection, it received the *Sunday Times* Book Award in 1949 and had sold almost 1.5 million copies by 1970. Cape would also publish Paton's *Too Late the Phalarope* (1953), *Debbie Go Home* (1961), *Kontakion for You Departed* (1969), *Apartheid and the Archbishop: The Life and Times of Geoffrey Clayton* (1974), and *Ah, But Your Land Is Beautiful* (1981).

Howard (right) meeting in Cape's office with (left to right) the writers E. Arnot Robertson and Arthur Koestler and the historian C. V. Wedgwood in 1944

In spite of these acquisitions, Cape did not immediately share in the postwar growth of the British publishing industry. Sales hit a low point in 1951 but recovered thanks to a series of bestsellers: Herman Wouk's *The "Caine" Mutiny* (1951), Han Suyin's *A Many-Splendoured Thing* (1952), Maurice Herzog's *Annapurna* (1952), and Hemingway's *The Old Man and the Sea*, which won the Pulitzer Prize. In 1953 the house missed a chance to acquire another modern classic, William Golding's *Lord of the Flies*; it was published by Faber and Faber in 1954.

A gold mine for Cape was Ian Fleming. The younger brother of Peter Fleming, a Cape author and editor, he was also a longtime friend of Plomer, having worked with him in naval intelligence during World War II. In 1952 he showed Plomer the manuscript for *Casino Royale*, confessing that he did not have a high opinion of it. Cape was inclined to agree: with the exception of James M. Cain's *The Postman Always Rings Twice* (1934) he generally did not publish thrillers. Wren Howard considered Fleming a "bounder" and was put off by the brutality of the book. Nevertheless, Plomer persuaded Cape to publish it in 1953.

Fleming initially wrote for an elite audience. Although *Casino Royale* sold satisfactorily for a first novel—eight thousand copies in Britain, less than half that in America (where it was published in 1954 by Macmillan)—it took several years for James Bond to attain best-seller status. The 1955 Pan Books edition of *Casino Royale* proved that Fleming had a large potential paperback market. He got invaluable publicity in 1956, when Prime Minister Anthony Eden tried to recuperate from the Suez disaster by vacationing at Goldeneye, Fleming's Jamaican retreat. The *Daily Express* serialized *From Russia, with Love* (1957), and Fleming (against the advice of Plomer) allowed the newspaper to run a James Bond comic strip. The greatest publicity windfall came in March 1961, when *Life* magazine reported that *From Russia, with Love* was one of the ten favorite books of President John F. Kennedy. American sales of *Thunderball*, published in April 1961, were boosted enormously. In 1962 *Dr. No* (1958) became the first Bond novel to reach the movie screen, transforming Agent 007 into the stuff of myth. When Fleming died on 13 August 1964 his books had sold more than forty million copies, and they accounted for nearly all of Cape's profit margin.

Michael Howard, the son of Wren Howard, had joined Cape in 1946 and had been appointed to the board in 1950. He increasingly came to feel that the firm needed new blood and more aggressive marketing. It was he who pressed for the appointment of the company's first sales manager, which was not made until 1955. Robert Knittel, named senior editor in 1956, aggressively made acquisitions in Paris, in New York, and at the Frankfurt Book Fair. As a result, however, the list became lopsidedly foreign, featuring Alice Ekert-Rotholz, Peter Freuchen, Ivar Lissner, Roger Vailland, and Rona Jaffe.

Cape's third wife had died in November 1953. A few months later he had suffered two strokes from which he never fully recovered, though he did return to work. His eightieth birthday was celebrated with a banquet at the Savoy hosted by Lane and tributes from prominent book trade people broadcast over the BBC. He died on 10 February 1960.

Michael Howard had been urging Cape to replace Knittel with Tom Maschler; that summer Knittel resigned and Maschler became senior editor. At twenty-six, Maschler had sympathies and connections with a new generation of young, rebellious, innovative writers, and he brought a new ferment to the Cape list in the 1960s and 1970s. He began by acquiring the plays of Arnold Wesker and Edward Albee. Against the advice of Bunting, he published Joseph Heller's *Catch-22* (1962). Edna O'Brien was brought over from Hutchinson with her second novel, *The Lonely Girl* (1962). Bunting, Maschler, and Plomer all recognized the genius of John Fowles's *The Collector* (1963), which achieved sales and critical praise such as few first novels have ever attained.

In 1961 Len Deighton sent Cape his first thriller, *The Ipcress File*; but he refused to accept Bunting's editorial suggestions and took the manuscript to Hodder and Stoughton, which published it in 1962. When Hodder and Stoughton failed to print enough copies to keep up with demand, Maschler was able to persuade Deighton to give Cape his subsequent books, including his best-selling war novel *Bomber* (1970).

In 1962 Maschler convinced Michael Howard to take on as director the twenty-six-year-old Graham Carlton Greene, nephew of the novelist Graham Greene. Greene inaugurated Cape Paperbacks in 1963. Though the innovations introduced by these three young men were boosting sales and profits, Wren Howard found it difficult

to accept the new regime, and at age seventy he turned over direction of the company to his son.

In 1963 Maschler was handed an odd collection of offbeat jokes and drawings that clearly reflected the influence of Lewis Carroll. The author was the rising pop singer John Lennon of the Beatles, and Maschler induced him to arrange his eccentric scribblings into a book, *In His Own Write* (1964). Booksellers were wary until, just days before publication, Prince Philip and Lennon appeared on television together. As the nation watched, the prince gave the Beatle his book *Birds from "Britannia"* (published by Longmans, Green in 1962), and Lennon reciprocated with an advance copy of *In His Own Write*. An avalanche of orders followed the next morning, and after a year two hundred thousand copies were in print. One Conservative MP rose in Parliament to argue that the book was evidence of the low quality of education in Liverpool. The critics disagreed: "Worth the attention of anyone who fears for the impoverishment of the English language and the British imagination," trumpeted the *Times Literary Supplement* (26 March 1964). Cape published Lennon's *A Spaniard in the Works* the following year.

After Hemingway's suicide in 1961, Maschler worked with his widow, Mary, to edit his unpublished memoir of Paris in the 1920s. They titled it *A Moveable Feast*, and it was published in 1964. Maschler tried to sell the serialization to the *Observer*, but fell afoul of a dispute over rights.

In November 1966 Michael Howard handed over management of the company to Maschler and Greene, who became joint managing directors. Howard succeeded to the chairmanship after the death of his father on 28 July 1968.

Cape's sales continued to soar, boosted by a series of blockbusters. Zoologist Desmond Morris's foray into pop anthropology, *The Naked Ape* (1967), which was translated into twenty-two languages, was followed by Fowles's *The French Lieutenant's Woman* (1969), Philip Roth's *Portnoy's Complaint* (1970), and Kurt Vonnegut's *Slaughterhouse-Five* (1970). Radical politics found a prominent place on the list with Fidel Castro's *History Will Absolve Me* (1968), Eldridge Cleaver's *Soul on Ice* (1969), and the series Writings of the Left.

Elizabeth Jane Howard had been a Cape author since her first novel, *The Beautiful Visit* (1950). In 1965 Kingsley Amis married her and brought to Cape his *The James Bond Dossier*. Cape went on to publish his *I Want It Now* (1968), *Girl, 20* (1971), and *Ending Up* (1974). His son Martin Amis kept Cape in the family with *The Rachel Papers* (1973), *Dead Babies* (1975), *Money* (1984), *The Moronic Inferno and Other Visits to America* (1986), and *Einstein's Monsters* (1987).

To publish experimental poetry Cape formed a partnership with the tiny Goliard Press in 1967. The first venture of the Cape Goliard Press was *TV Baby Poems*, by Allen Ginsberg. The Cape Poetry Paperback series followed in 1969.

Modeled after the quality paperbacks published by the German house of Suhrkamp, Cape Editions were begun in 1967 with *The Scope of Anthropology*, by Claude Lévi-Strauss. The series went on to publish avant-garde work in anthropology and literary criticism by Roland Barthes and Pablo Neruda.

Cape was instrumental in introducing modern Latin American writers to Britain, though at first they attracted little interest. The firm published Cesar Vallejo's *Poemas Humanos* (1969), Gabriel García Marquez's *One Hundred Years of Solitude* (1970) and *Love in the Time of Cholera* (1988), Neruda's *Selected Poems* (1970), Octavio Paz's *Configurations* (1971), Isabel Allende's *Of Love and Shadows* (1987), and the novels of Jorge Luis Borges, Carlos Fuentes, and Mario Vargas Llosa.

By the late 1960s independent publishers were being swallowed up by corporate conglomerates. To protect themselves, Chatto and Windus and Jonathan Cape Limited joined in May 1969 to form Chatto and Jonathan Cape Limited. As Chatto poet Jennifer Couroucli quipped:

Chatto's is merging with Jonathan Cape—
Better to marry than burn,
Better to wed than to give in to rape
By a tempting Big Business concern. . . .

Ian Parsons, of Chatto and Windus, and Howard served as joint chairmen of the new venture. The Bodley Head merged with Chatto and Windus and Cape in 1973, bringing the novelist Greene into his nephew's company. Virago Press, the feminist publisher founded in 1972, joined the consortium in 1982. Each of the four companies preserved its editorial independence.

In addition to thrillers, travel books, and children's books, Cape continued to publish works by the most challenging and important writers of the 1970s and 1980s. The list included Donald Barthelme's *City Life* (1971) and *Sadness* (1973); Anthony Burgess's *MF* (1971) and *The Na-*

poleon Symphony (1974); Gail Godwin's *The Perfectionists* (1971) and *The Odd Woman* (1975); Doris Lessing's *Briefing for a Descent into Hell* (1971), *Shikasta* (1979), and *The Good Terrorist* (1985); Nadine Gordimer's *A Guest of Honor* (1971), *The Conservationist* (1974), *Burger's Daughter* (1979), *A Soldier's Embrace: Stories* (1980), *July's People* (1981), and *The Essential Gesture* (1988); Thomas Pynchon's *Gravity's Rainbow* (1973); Fowles's *The Ebony Tower* (1974), *Shipwreck* (1974), *Mantissa* (1982), and *A Maggot* (1985); Isaac Bashevis Singer's *A Crown of Feathers, and Other Stories* (1974), *Shosha* (1979), and *The King of the Fields* (1989); Judith Rossner's *Looking for Mr. Goodbar* (1975) and *August* (1983); William Styron's *Sophie's Choice* (1979); Tom Wolfe's *The Right Stuff* (1979), *From Bauhaus to Our House* (1982), and *The Purple Decades* (1983); Vonnegut's *Jailbird* (1979), *Galapagos* (1985), and *Bluebeard* (1988); Heller's *Good as Gold* (1979) and *God Knows* (1984); Margaret Atwood's *Life before Man* (1980) and *The Handmaid's Tale* (1986); Salman Rushdie's *Midnight's Children* (1981) and *Shame* (1983); Mary Gordon's *The Company of Women* (1981) and *Men and Angels* (1985); Julian Barnes's *Flaubert's Parrot* (1984) and *A History of the World in 10-1/2 Chapters* (1989); and Jay McInerny's *Ransom* (1986).

Anita Brookner brought out books on an almost annual basis, including her 1984 Booker Prize novel *Hotel du Lac*. John Champlin Gardner wrote *The Sunlight Dialogues* (1973), *Nickel Mountain* (1974), and *The King's Indian: Stories and Tales* (1975); John E. Gardner continued the James Bond novels after Fleming's death with *For Special Services* (1982), *Icebreaker* (1983), and *Role of Honor* (1984). Roth followed up *Portnoy's Complaint* with *The Great American Novel* (1973), *My Life as a Man* (1974), *Reading Myself and Others* (1975), *The Professor of Desire* (1978), *The Ghost Writer* (1979), *Zuckerman Unbound* (1981), *The Anatomy Lesson* (1983), *The Prague Orgy* (1985), *The Counterlife* (1987), and *The Facts: A Novelist's Autobiography* (1988). Cape also published works by Bruce Chatwin, John Cheever, Russell Hoban, John Irving, William Kennedy, Joyce Carol Oates, James Purdy, Frederic Raphael, Alan Sillitoe, David Storey, and Russian dissident Vladimir Voinovich, and science fiction by Brian Aldiss and J. G. Ballard.

From France came Barthes's *Mythologies* (1972), *The Pleasure of the Text* (1976), and *A Lover's Discourse* (1979), as well as Lévi-Strauss's *Tristes Tropiques* (1973). Cape appealed to the countercultural market with *Soledad Brother: The*

Prison Letters of George Jackson (1971), Shulamith Firestone's *The Dialectic of Sex* (1971), Barry Commoner's *The Closing Circle: Confronting the Environmental Crisis* (1972), Antonio Gramsci's *Letters from Prison* (1974), and Jonathan Schell's *The Fate of the Earth* (1982), as well as books by Laurie Anderson, Tariq Ali, Richard Brautigan, Tom Hayden, Terry Southern, and Alan Watts. There were also books of drawings by David Hockney, Ralph Steadman, Quentin Blake, Posy Simmonds, and Ronald Searle.

The Cape tradition of publishing superior historical studies for a lay audience continued with Lacey Baldwin Smith's *Henry VIII: The Mask of Royalty* (1971) and *Treason in Tudor England* (1986), H. R. Trevor-Roper's *Queen Elizabeth's First Historian: William Camden and the Beginnings of English "Civil History"* (1972), Peter Gay's *Style in History* (1975), Jonathan D. Spence's studies of Chinese history, Ronald W. Clark's biographies of Bertrand Russell (1975) and Sigmund Freud (1980), and Ted Morgan's lives of Somerset Maugham (1980) and the young Winston Churchill (1983). In politics Cape published Theodore H. White's *The Making of the President, 1972* (1974), *Breach of Faith: The Fall of Richard Nixon* (1975), *In Search of History: A Personal Adventure* (1979), and *America in Search of Itself* (1983). Books by David Owen and Tony Benn were also on the list of political works, along with the memoirs of Anwar Sadat (1984) and the diaries of Richard Crossman (1974), Hugh Gaitskell (1983), and Hugh Dalton (1986). The psychology list included books by Erich Fromm and B. F. Skinner, and Janet Malcolm's *In the Freud Archives* (1984). Jonathan Miller produced a book version of his popular television series *The Body in Question* (1978).

By 1982 the Cape-Chatto-Bodley Head-Virago combine was quite prosperous, earning £929,000 profit on sales of £9 million. Two years later sales were up to £16 million, but profits were down to £362,000. By 1985 all four divisions were operating at a loss, and in 1986 the consortium was reported to be £3 million in debt. The fundamental problem was that the four companies had failed to take advantage of the merger by streamlining their staffs. As a result, overhead per book was twice that of competing publishers. Greene responded by centralizing operations, reducing office space, and laying off employees. The Bodley Head moved into the Cape offices at 32 Bedford Square. Fearing the disappearance of his old imprint, novelist Graham Greene protested his nephew's business policies in a letter to the *Times* published on 28 March 1987.

In May 1987 Random House took over Jonathan Cape, Chatto and Windus, and the Bodley Head for £17.5 million; Virago arranged a management buyout for a reported £750,000. This fate was precisely the one that the consortium had been designed to avoid. Random House was itself part of the giant S. I. Newhouse, Jr., publishing empire, which included Alfred A. Knopf, Pantheon Books, Villard Books, Times Books, Vintage Books, the Modern Library, Ballantine and Fawcett paperbacks, and many newspapers and magazines.

Graham C. Greene served briefly as chairman of the new parent corporation, Random House UK, before resigning on 15 April 1988. In 1989 Random House and Century Hutchinson merged to form Random Century, with Jonathan Cape and Chatto and Windus remaining as distinct companies. That June the Bodley Head ceased to be a separate division and became an imprint under Jonathan Cape.

References:

Peter F. Alexander, *William Plomer: A Biography* (Oxford: Oxford University Press, 1989);

Brian Appleyard, "The End of the Affair," *Sunday Times Magazine*, 12 July 1987, pp. 14-18;

Dean R. Baldwin, *H. E. Bates: A Literary Life* (Selinsgrove, Pa.: Susquehanna University Press, 1987);

Jack Barbera and William McBrien, *Stevie: A Biography of Stevie Smith* (London: Heinemann, 1985);

H. E. Bates, *Edward Garnett: A Memoir* (London: Parrish, 1950);

Joseph Blotner, *Faulkner: A Biography* (New York: Random House, 1974);

Hugh Brogan, *The Life of Arthur Ransome* (London: Cape, 1984);

Gladys Mary Coles, *The Flower of Light: A Biography of Mary Webb* (London: Duckworth, 1978);

Bernard Crick, *George Orwell* (Boston: Little, Brown, 1980);

Douglas Day, *Malcolm Lowry* (New York: Oxford University Press, 1973);

Lovat Dickson, *Radclyffe Hall at the Well of Loneliness* (London: Collins, 1975);

David Garnett, ed., *The White/Garnett Letters* (London: Cape, 1968);

Robert Graves, *In Broken Images: Selected Letters of Robert Graves 1914-1946*, edited by Paul O'Prey (London: Hutchinson, 1982);

Ernest Hemingway, *Selected Letters 1917-1961*, edited by Carlos Baker (London: Granada, 1981);

Michael S. Howard, *Jonathan Cape, Publisher* (London: Cape, 1971);

George Jefferson, *Edward Garnett: A Life in Literature* (London: Cape, 1982);

A. W. Lawrence, ed., *T. E. Lawrence by His Friends* (London: Cape, 1937);

T. E. Lawrence, *The Letters of T. E. Lawrence*, edited by Malcolm Brown (London: Dent, 1988);

Malcolm Lowry, *Selected Letters of Malcolm Lowry*, edited by Harvey Breit and Margerie Bonner Lowry (London: Cape, 1967);

Jeffrey Meyers, *Hemingway* (London: Macmillan, 1986);

Seán O'Faoláin, *Vive Moi!* (London: Hart-Davis, 1965);

Liam O'Flaherty, *Shame the Devil* (London: Grayson & Grayson, 1934), p. 44;

Michael Parnell, *Eric Linklater* (London: Murray, 1984);

John Pearson, *The Life of Ian Fleming* (London: Cape, 1968);

Mark Schorer, *Sinclair Lewis: An American Life* (New York: McGraw-Hill, 1961);

Martin Seymour-Smith, *Robert Graves: His Life and Work* (London: Hutchinson, 1982);

V. M. Thompson, *"Not a Suitable Hobby for an Airman"—T. E. Lawrence as Publisher* (Oxford: Orchard Books, 1986);

Sylvia Townsend Warner, *T. H. White* (London: Cape/Chatto & Windus, 1967);

Jeremy Wilson, *Lawrence of Arabia: The Authorised Biography of T. E. Lawrence* (London: Heinemann, 1990).

Papers:

The library of the University of Reading has records of Jonathan Cape Limited dating from the founding of the firm to the mid 1970s. Included are correspondence with authors; readers' reports; contracts and royalty statements; records of rejected manuscripts; financial records and accounts; publicity, promotion, and review files; and editorial and production papers.

—Jonathan Rose

Constable and Company Limited
(London: 1910-)
Archibald Constable and Company
(London: 1890-1910)

Archibald Constable and Company was founded in London in 1890 by Archibald Constable, grandson of the Archibald Constable whose Edinburgh publishing house had collapsed in 1826. The new firm pursued, during its more than seventy years of independent existence, a basically conservative and traditional publishing philosophy. As Ralph Arnold, one of the firm's later chairmen, observed, "It was neither large . . . nor small . . . neither strident nor dim. Most Constable books maintained a high standard—but at any moment the firm might produce a best seller."

Constable retired in 1893 and turned the firm over to his nephew, H. Arthur Doubleday, who was joined in 1895 by Otto Kyllmann, formerly of Macmillan, and William Maxsee Meredith, son of George Meredith. Originally trained as an engineer, Meredith had become his father's agent; the father came to Constable as an author at the same time as the son joined the firm as a partner.

As his first task for Constable, George Meredith revised his works for a new collected edition (1896); half of the deluxe thirty-two-volume sets were subscribed even before a prospectus was offered. So that the collected edition could be published concurrently in the United States by Scribners, Kyllmann bought the plates and stock of Meredith's novels from the Boston firm of Roberts Brothers for six thousand dollars. Later, Constable published Meredith's works in an eighteen-volume New Popular Edition (1897-1898), a twenty-seven-volume Memorial Edition (1909-1911), a seventeen-volume Standard Edition (1914-1920), and a nineteen-volume Mickleham Edition (1922). Meredith's first new work for Constable was his last novel, *The Amazing Marriage* (1895). It was followed by three books of poetry— *Odes in Contribution to the Song of French History* (1898), *A Reading of Life with Other Poems* (1901), and *Last Poems* (1909). *Celt and Saxon* (1910) appeared posthumously.

The varied interests of the three directors were evidenced in the diversity of the books published by the firm. One of Kyllmann's early successes was his purchase of the explorer Fridtjof Hansen's *Farthest North* for the unusually large sum of ten thousand pounds. The book was so popular that, on publication day in 1897, 10-12 Orange Street, where Constable was located, was completely blocked by wholesalers' and booksellers' vans. In 1900 publication began of *The Victoria History of the Counties of England*, a series personally planned by Doubleday; each volume was to present the natural history and antiquities of the county as well as ancient and modern sport. Oxford University Press took over the series in 1935. W. M. Meredith was responsible for the various technical books on the firm's early lists. Other offerings were James Boswell's *Life of Johnson* (1896), edited by Augustine Birrell; a translation of René Vallery-Radot's *The Life of Pasteur* (1901); and Constable's Sixpenny Series of novels, featuring such popular authors as R. W. Chambers.

Shortly after the turn of the century Constable began publishing the works and authors whose successes consolidated the firm's reputation. Chief among them was George Bernard Shaw. He had offered his plays to William Heinemann, but Heinemann responded by producing account books recording that many plays sold only enough copies for each of the actors and the prompter. To get his work published— and to make as much money as possible for himself—Shaw adopted the unusual practice of handling all aspects of publishing his plays: he acquired the paper, arranged for printing and binding, and hired Constable as his commission agent. He and Constable worked on this basis from 1903 until Shaw's death in 1950. Although the story was often told that their agreement consisted of only a few lines on a sheet of paper, the firm and Shaw worked out regular agreements regarding payment schedules. The terms were frequently not to Shaw's liking; his correspondence with the firm and with Kyllmann, who personally handled the Shaw business, includes more than one plea for more prompt payment. Shaw's wife,

Charlotte, had the same sort of agreement with Constable when she prepared a selection of passages from her husband's works in 1912.

The arrangement between Shaw and Constable was so generally satisfactory to both parties that it even withstood Shaw's failure to support Constable when he and other bookmen came into conflict with the Times Book Club, which seriously cut into the business of publishers and booksellers. Shaw went so far as to take copies of his *John Bull's Other Island* (1909) and *Major Barbara* (1909), which were already printed, replace the Constable name on the title pages and bindings with that of the Times Book Club, and sell them for less than the listed price.

Among Constable's noteworthy authors were three who are now known primarily as writers of children's literature. In 1912 the firm published *Listeners and Other Poems*, a book for adult readers, which established the reputation of Walter de la Mare. His *A Child's Day: A Book of Rhymes* also appeared that year. From then until 1938, Constable published eleven more books of poetry for children and adults by de la Mare, but only one of his books of children's stories, *Broomsticks and Other Tales* (1925). The American Dorothy Canfield Fisher's first books for Constable were adult fiction and educational works: *The Squirrel Cage* (1912) was followed by two more works of fiction and *A Montessori Mother* (1913), *Mothers and Children* (1915), and *Self-Reliance* (1917). Her children's classic *Understood Betsy* appeared in 1922. Another American writer of children's books was the English-born Ernest Thompson Seton; Constable brought out his *Life Histories of Northern Animals* (1910), *Rolf in the Woods* (1911), and *The Book of Woodcraft and Indian Lore* (1912). Also on Constable's lists were two works by W. E. B. Du Bois—*The Souls of Black Folk* (1905) and *Darkwater: Voices from within the Veil* (1920)—and others by Woodrow Wilson, Hilaire Belloc, and Neville Chamberlain, as well as light fiction.

Michael Sadleir came to Constable in 1912 and became one of the firm's directors in 1920. (The son of the educationist Michael Ernest Sadler, he had added an *i* to his name to distinguish himself from his father.) Although Meredith was still a director through the 1920s, it was Sadleir and Kyllmann who led Constable to its highest levels of achievement during the 1920s and 1930s. Sadleir had a reputation for extravagance; Kyllmann was a penny-pincher who put off paying accounts as long as possible. Sadleir

Michael Sadleir in 1921, the year after he became a director of Constable and Company

was a bibliophile who had the chief voice in manuscript decisions; Kyllmann was interested in international publishing arrangements. Sadleir was daring; Kyllmann was more traditional. Sadleir brought Damon Runyon and John Dos Passos to the firm; Kyllmann brought Theodore Dreiser.

Sadleir recruited Sir Harold Nicolson, suggesting that he write a biography of Paul Verlaine. From the 1920s through the 1950s Nicolson wrote most of his books for Constable and was one of its leading authors. He produced literary biographies of Alfred Tennyson (1923); George Gordon, Lord Byron (1924); Benjamin Constant (1949); and Charles-Augustin Sainte-Beuve (1957), as well as of Verlaine (1921). Political and diplomatic biographies of Erskine Arthur Nicolson, Lord Carnock (1930); George Nathaniel, Lord Curzon (1934); Dwight Morrow (1935); and King George V (1952) joined his works of political and social history—*Peacemaking, 1919* (1933), *The Congress of Vienna* (1946), and *The Evolution of Diplomatic Method* (1954)—along with his literary criticism, essays, and two novels. The quality of these works was such that Sadleir thought Nicolson would come to be considered one of the leading writers of the age. Certainly he was a publisher's ideal author: Arnold reported that Nicolson never complained, his output was steady, his books always sold, and his manuscripts always arrived on the promised day, ready for setting in type.

Almost Nicolson's opposite was Lord David Cecil. He never knew quite when a book he was working on would be finished; if he proposed a date, six months usually had to be added to it; and his proofs, according to Arnold, seemed to be corrected with a blunt pencil in a vibrating railroad car. Nevertheless, he wrote some classics of literary criticism and biography, including *The Stricken Deer; or The Life of Cowper* (1929), *Sir Walter Scott* (1933), *Early Victorian Novelists* (1934), *The Young Melbourne* (1939), *Hardy the Novelist* (1943), *Two Quiet Lives* (1948), *Poets and Story-Tellers* (1949), and *Lord M* (1954).

Helen Waddell had first come to the firm's attention when it published her *Lyrics from the Chinese* (1914). The following year she traveled from her home in Belfast to London to meet the partners, and thus began a lifelong personal and professional relationship. In 1926 she proposed to Kyllmann what was to become *The Wandering Scholars*; released in April 1927, the book paid for itself in two months. It was succeeded by *Medieval Latin Lyrics* (1929). Her selection of Latin short stories and verse, *A Book of Medieval Latin for Schools* (1931), went through ten editions between 1931 and 1962; a novel, *Peter Abelard* (1933), went through three editions in six months, followed by a play, *The Abbé Prévost* (1933). Waddell also worked for Constable as a consultant and adviser.

When Constable's young male staff members were drafted during World War II, Waddell became assistant editor of the *Nineteenth Century and After*, which Constable published from 1921 to 1950. Founded in 1877 as the *Nineteenth Century* by James Knowles, the journal was devoted to signed articles by prominent figures on important public issues. Under Constable, it was edited by Wilson Harris, Arnold Wilson, and F. A. Voigt. They published analyses of national and international affairs, historical articles, biographical pieces, and reports on science; among the contributors were Stephen Spender, Robert Bridges, Hilaire Belloc, Neville Chamberlain, Havelock Ellis,

Ford Madox Ford, Virginia Woolf, and E. M. Forster.

Constable was more briefly associated with *Life and Letters*, which was begun in 1928 and acquired in September 1934. Its first editor had been Desmond MacCarthy, who had featured the Bloomsbury writers; under the editorship of Hamish Miles it had become more daring and had concentrated on emerging literary figures such as Spender, W. H. Auden, C. Day Lewis, Louis MacNeice, Frank O'Connor, and Graham Greene. Although R. Ellis Roberts, the editor at Constable, said he would maintain the journal's innovative character, the two volumes for which he was responsible broke no new ground; he published work by W. B. Yeats, G. K. Chesterton, Clive Bell, and St. John Ervine. Roberts did introduce features that became part of the magazine's permanent format: a monthly commentary on world affairs; reviews of theater, cinema, and gallery exhibitions; essays on science and politics; and a section on noted people of the past and present. The magazine was taken over by Bredin Publishing Company in September 1935.

Sadleir himself was one of Constable's most noted authors of the 1920s and 1930s. As an undergraduate at Oxford he had begun collecting books and writing fiction, and he continued to do both while working for the firm. Constable published his novels; the early ones were of little literary merit, and only *Fanny by Gaslight* (1940) was a best-seller. Of more lasting value were the works that grew out of his interest in book collecting. *Trollope: A Commentary* (1927) almost single-handedly revived interest in the Victorian novelist Anthony Trollope; the following year Constable published Sadleir's Trollope bibliography. In 1930 the first volume of Constable's Bibliographia series presented Sadleir's *The Evolution of Publishers' Binding Styles, 1770-1900*; two more literary biographies followed, *Bulwer and His Wife* (1931) and *Blessington D'Orsay* (1933). His last two books were *Michael Ernest Sadler: A Memoir by His Son* (1949) and *XIX Century Fiction* (1951), a bibliographical record based on his own collection of more than ten thousand first editions.

Constable, like other publishing firms, enjoyed great demand for its books during World War II because of depressed supply. Some firms lost inventory during air raids, and paper rationing cut down on the number of books available for purchase. Even old books that had never sold well were bought by desperate readers. Consequently, when Arnold, who had joined the firm in 1936, returned after the war and became one of its directors, he found that it was financially better off than before the war. Maintaining and improving the firm's profitability, however, required judicious decision making. Like all publishers, Constable found that paper rationing limited its ability to produce new books and, at the same time, reprint its backlist. Production costs rose steeply in the postwar period, but publishers were reluctant to raise the price of books. A new author, Cecil Woodham-Smith, with her biography of Florence Nightingale (1950) and *The Reason Why* (1953), upheld the firm's reputation for quality, as did James Pope Hennessy, Bernard Berenson, Cornelia Otis Skinner, Sir Kenneth Clark, and Patrick Hamilton. And Constable's association with the University of London's newly established Athlone Press promised more opportunities for scientific and technical publishing.

Kyllmann retired in 1954. Sadleir, in ill health, retired in 1957 and died the same year. Left as directors of the firm were Arnold, Sadleir's son Richard Sadler, and D. F. Grover; Arnold became chairman in 1958. Like Sadleir, he was something of a writer, especially of light fiction, short stories, and local history. Two autobiographical works, *A Very Quiet War* (1962) and *Orange Street & Brickhole Lane* (1963), dealt, respectively, with his military and publishing experiences; both were published by Rupert Hart-Davis. Arnold felt that he was not well suited to follow Sadleir as chairman: there had been no period of transition during which Sadleir could have gradually handed over his authors and responsibilities; moreover, Arnold suffered from an incapacitating physical condition and often was not equal to the demands of the work. He did not actively court new authors, and he was disinclined to become involved in the Publishers' Association. There were, as well, certain postwar trends in publishing that Arnold did not lead Constable in following, such as the trend to anthologies and large art books. He did not foresee that after the war the expansion of education both at home and abroad would create a demand for textbooks. But he justified his handling of the firm in two ways: he regarded himself simply as a caretaker maintaining Constable until Richard Sadler was ready to take his father's place, and he believed that a modest general publisher should simply continue to do what it could do best.

Arnold did move into publishing for children, a field that flowered in the 1950s and 1960s. A Constable's list of children's books was started in 1957 under Grace Hogarth, who had begun her publishing career at the Oxford University Press. At Constable she was children's book editor from 1956 to 1963 and managing director of the children's list from 1963 to 1968. Herself a writer of books under the names Amelia Gay, Grace Allen, and Allen Weston, Hogarth brought to Constable many authors and artists who later distinguished themselves. Rosemary Manning, Philippa Pearce, Joan Phipson, Madeleine Pollard, Hilda Van Stocken, Barbara Willard, and Barbara Ker Wilson each wrote several children's books for Constable. One of the most successful authors was Leon Garfield, with adventure stories set in the eighteenth century—*Jack Holborn* (1964), *Devil-in-the-Fog* (1966), and *Smith* (1967). Constable also published the British edition of Madeleine L'Engle's *A Wrinkle in Time* (1963).

With Arnold's retirement in 1962, Constable's independence ended. It was bought by Ben Glazebrook, formerly of Heinemann, and Donald Hyde, an American bibliophile. D. F. Grover was named chairman; he was succeeded by Glazebrook in 1968. By then Sadler had left the firm, and Hyde had died. Paul Marks, from the sales department, and Miles Huddleston, from the publicity department, joined the board along with two nominees from Hutchinson and Company, which had bought a minority holding in Constable. Business, in some respects, continued as usual. The firm became sole distributor in Great Britain for America's Dover Press, the works of Nicolson continued to appear, Cecil's *Max: A Biography* (1964) was published, and a popular travel book, *Journey through Britain* (1968), by John Hillaby, received critical acclaim. But the children's list was sold to Longmans, which incorporated it into its Juvenile Library; Hogarth and most of her staff went along with it. The Orange Street quarters became cramped, and the distribution division moved to Tiptree, where Hutchinson had a distribution company for its own and other publishers' books.

In 1989 Glazebrook, Marks, and Huddleston were still directors, along with Robin Baird Smith, Richard Tomkins, F. C. Bland, J. N. M. Cheetham, R. A. A. Holt, and Jeremy Potter. Constable published seventy new titles in both 1986 and 1987 in the same categories in which the firm had been publishing since 1890—archaeology, architecture and design, biography, fiction, guide books, history, war, natural history, psychology, reference, sociology and anthropology, and travel and topography.

References:

Ralph Arnold, *Orange Street & Brickhole Lane* (London: Hart-Davis, 1963);

Monica Blackett, *The Mark of the Maker: A Portrait of Helen Waddell* (London: Constable, 1973);

Michael Holroyd, *Bernard Shaw*, 2 volumes (New York: Random House, 1989);

Harold Nicolson, *Diaries and Letters*, 3 volumes, edited by Nigel Nicolson (New York: Atheneum, 1966-1968);

Bernard Shaw, *Collected Letters*, 4 volumes, edited by Dan H. Laurence (New York: Viking, 1985-1988);

Lionel Stevenson, *The Ordeal of George Meredith* (New York: Russell & Russell, 1967), pp. 316, 320, 329;

Frederic Whyte, *William Heinemann: A Memoir* (Garden City, N.Y.: Doubleday, Doran, 1929).

—Sondra Miley Cooney

Cresset Press
(London: 1927-   )

The enduring reputation of the Cresset Press derives mainly from its early production of illustrated limited editions and from the quality of editing and production in its later Cresset Reprint Library. The Cresset Press was founded in 1927 by Dennis David Myer Cohen. Born in 1890, Cohen was a man of considerable taste and wealth, educated at Harrow and Trinity College, Oxford. The press began by specializing in limited editions, mainly classical texts illustrated or decorated by contemporary artists.

Several artists who later became well known for their book work received commissions from Cohen early in their careers. Among the most notable were Blair Hughes-Stanton and his wife, Gertrude Hermes, for John Bunyan's *The Pilgrim's Progress* (1928) and again for *The Apocrypha* (1929); Leon Underwood, Eric Kennington, and Eric Ravilious also made wood engravings for the latter. Cohen persuaded Rex Whistler, aged twenty-two, to make exquisite pen drawings for a two-volume edition of Jonathan Swift's *Gulliver's Travels* (1930). Full justice was done to Whistler's delicate originals by printing the full-page plates on a flatbed gravure press from sunken copper plates onto which the drawings had been photographically transferred. In most of the 195 copies the full-page plates were hand-colored by the artist or a copyist.

About twenty limited editions were published between 1927 and 1931. They were print-

Detail from a wood engraving in the Cresset Press edition of John Bunyan's The Pilgrim's Progress, *published in 1928. The illustrations were engraved by Blair Hughes-Stanton and his wife, Gertrude Hermes.*

ed by some of the best presses in England and Scotland, notably R. and R. Clark, Robert Mac-Lehose, Butler and Tanner, the Shakespeare Head Press, the university presses at Oxford and Cambridge, the Curwen Press, and the Shenval Press. Unlike Francis Meynell at the Nonesuch Press, Cohen never took sole responsibility for typographical design when dealing with his printers. Instead he preferred to employ presses run by competent typographers such as Bernard Newdigate, Oliver Simon, and George Jones, who were then left to apply their customary standards of design and production. Consequently, Cresset Press books lacked a distinctive style of their own; but they were nevertheless recognizable as typifying the best qualities of the typographers and presses chosen by Cohen.

In addition to *The Pilgrim's Progress*, *The Apocrypha*, and *Gulliver's Travels*, Cohen published limited editions of several little-known works describing country pleasures and pursuits. He also published works by contemporary writers, such as D. H. Lawrence's *Birds, Beasts and Flowers* (1930) and Sylvia Townsend Warner's *Elinor Barley* (1930). When the Wall Street Crash of 1929 began to affect the market for such editions, the press published more modest works, most of them in the category of belles lettres. During the lean years 1932 to 1945 these works appeared infrequently. Among those whose work Cohen published in unlimited editions were Frances Cornford, Jacquetta Hawkes, Geoffrey Grigson, and H. G. Wells.

From the mid 1930s Cohen lived stylishly in a house in Chelsea designed for him by the firm Chermayeff and Mendelsohn; the house became a salon for writers and artists. The few books he published during World War II included *Low's Political Cartoons* (1941), and it was not uncharacteristic for him to publish political writings. James Shand, who had served from 1925 to 1929 as assistant printer at Oxford and had set up the Shenval Press in 1930, printed several unlimited editions for Cohen during and after World War II. Cohen's obituarist in the *Times* recorded that with Shand in charge of production Cohen's feeling for the look of his books "found a continuing if less luxurious expression."

After serving in the Treasury during World War II Cohen persuaded the bibliophile and anthologist John Hayward to take on general editorship of the new Cresset Reprint Library. Its first volume was *Moby-Dick* (1946). That Cohen and Hayward each had a knowledgeable and appreciative eye for fine typography was reflected in the production standards of the new series. Hayward also scrutinized Cresset Press catalogues and blurbs, many of which were returned marked up like a child's first essay.

Hayward was able to actualize what Cohen modestly called his own "vague ideas." T. S. Eliot, André Gide, and Anthony Powell were among those persuaded to write introductions for the Cresset Press Reprint Library. Figures of equal distinction made new translations from French and Russian. Napoleon's letters (1961) were edited by a director of the firm, John Howard. Howard's wife, Marghanita Laski, was among the authors whose works were published by the Cresset Press, which also published the novels of John O'Hara. Henry Moore illustrated *A Land* (1951), by Hawkes, which went into four impressions during the same year.

Hayward died in 1965. In April 1967 Cohen sold the Cresset Press to the firm of Barrie and Jenkins and retired from publishing. He died in 1970. In 1972 the imprint passed into Walter Hutchinson's ownership. Since 1989 it has been part of the firm of Random Century, which uses the imprint for illustrated reprints of its best-selling titles.

References:

Dennis Cohen, Memoir of John Hayward, *Book Collector*, 14 (Winter 1965): 459-460;

The Double Crown Club Register of Past and Present Members: Privately Printed for Members of the Club in Celebration of the Hundredth Meeting Held in May 1949 (Cambridge: Cambridge University Press, 1949), p. 15;

"Mr. Dennis Cohen, Publisher and Connoisseur [obituary]," *Times* (London), 26 February 1970, p. 12.

—John Dreyfus

Cuala Press
(Churchtown, Ireland: 1908-1923; Dublin: 1923-1968, 1969-1975; Dalkey, Ireland: 1975-1986)
Dun Emer Press
(Dundrum, Ireland: 1903-1908)

Evelyn Gleeson was born in Ireland in 1855, the daughter of a physician. She studied painting at the Atelier Ludovici in London in the 1890s, at a time when Irish culture and Irish literature were experiencing new growth and vitality. In London she became part of the Irish Literary Society, which included the painter John Butler Yeats; his sons, William Butler the poet and Jack Butler the artist; and his daughters, Elizabeth and Lily. Gleeson shared with Elizabeth and Lily Yeats an interest in crafts, a desire to contribute to the Irish cultural revival, and a growing belief in the economic emancipation of women. She was also strongly influenced by the Arts and Crafts Movement. She returned to Ireland in the fall of 1902 and established the Dun Emer Industries in the village of Dundrum, near Dublin, to provide work for Irish girls and women in craft production, including weaving, tapestry, and embroidery. The Dun Emer Press was integral to the movement: it provided employment for local girls and women in the hand printing of books, pamphlets, ephemera, and greeting cards. The name Dun Emer was indicative of the nature of Gleeson's undertaking: in Gaelic legend, Lady Emer, the wife of Cuchulainn, was renowned for her beauty and her skill in needlework and the domestic arts.

The press was supervised by Elizabeth Yeats, who shared Gleeson's enthusiasm for the Arts and Crafts Movement, was a friend of William Morris, and had been strongly influenced by the beautiful productions of Morris's Kelmscott Press. In typographic matters Yeats was advised by Emery Walker, on whose advice she had taken a month-long course in printing at the Women's Printing Society in London early in 1902. The type chosen for the Dun Emer Press was Caslon Old Face in fourteen-point for text, with ten-point for footnotes and larger sizes for titlings; the printing press was a demy Albion handpress bought from a provincial newspaper office. For books the press used handmade rag-based paper from the Swiftbrook Mills in County Dublin measuring 16 1/2 by 11 1/2 inches per sheet, allowing 8 1/4 by 5 3/4 inches for the small quarto page. Separate specifications were drawn up for productions other than books. Advice on bookbinding was given by Sydney Cockerell of the Kelmscott Press.

Dun Emer's first prospectus was unclear about the press's directors, but the daybook entries show that Elizabeth Yeats ran the press with the assistance of Beatrice Cassidy and Esther Ryan. As editorial adviser, William Butler Yeats aimed to establish the press as the first publisher

cations from Dun Emer: they showed that, as the 1903 prospectus had promised, "simplicity is aimed at in . . . composition." Text was elegant and margins were wide, but with few exceptions books from Dun Emer were not illustrated. Elaboration was limited to title-page and colophon devices from woodblocks by Thomas Sturge Moore, AE, Robert Gregory, and Edmund Dulac, or from line drawings by a variety of artists, including Elinor Monsell, Jack B. Yeats, and Elizabeth Yeats. No edition was to be greater than five hundred copies. Productions from Dun Emer cannot be compared with those of the great private presses of late-Victorian and Edwardian England or of the interwar years; but the press's fundamental aim was not fine printing, and the books should be judged on their content rather than their presentation.

The third book from Dun Emer was a collection of Gaelic poetry, *The Love Songs of Connacht* (1904), selected and translated by Douglas Hyde, dedicated to George Sigerson, with a preface by William Butler Yeats. In microcosm, *The Love Songs of Connacht* epitomizes the Irish literary renaissance, for its publication brought together the Gaelic League, of which Hyde was president; the National Literary Society, of which Sigerson was president; and the work of Yeats.

Developments at the Dun Emer Press itself, however, were not harmonious: financial problems proved a constant headache to Elizabeth and Lily Yeats and exacerbated an already difficult relationship with Gleeson. Shortage of capital appears to have been the major problem, and it was aggravated by Elizabeth's eccentric accounting. The summer of 1904 was particularly difficult financially and led to separation of the press from the rest of the Dun Emer workshops. To finance the press, Dun Emer Industries Limited was formed on 29 September 1904. Gleeson, Elizabeth Yeats, Lily Yeats, and the staff of the press became shareholders in the company. This arrangement put the press on a more sound financial footing and, for the time being at least, resolved personality differences between Gleeson and Elizabeth Yeats.

Publication continued early in 1905 with Lionel Johnson's *Twenty One Poems*. This selection, chosen by William Butler Yeats, had been printed by autumn 1904, and the lapse between printing and publication reflects the financial strictures of that period. William Butler Yeats's *Stories of Red Hanrahan* (1905) was similarly delayed. Clear evidence of Yeats's fascination with both

The Dun Emer Press in 1903: Esther Ryan correcting proofs, Beatrice Cassidy rolling out ink, and Elizabeth Corbet Yeats an Albion handpress

of works by contemporary Irish writers and as the reviver of classical Irish poetry and prose. Yeats understood the bringing together of modern and classical Irish literature to be seminal to the Irish literary renaissance: he was inspired by Irish mythology and adhered to a belief in an Irish society which drew strength from a purer sylvan past. During the almost forty years he was responsible for publishing policy he developed an enviable list of authors and achieved some notable coups for the press.

The first book published by the Dun Emer Press was a collection of poems by Yeats, *In the Seven Woods*. Published in August 1903 in an edition of 325, it was bound in full Irish linen and sold at ten shillings, sixpence. The colophon, printed in red ink and celebrating "the year of the big wind 1903," set a pattern for future publications: it became a convention of Dun Emer books to celebrate unusual occasions and saints' days when they coincided with publication. *Seven Woods* was closely followed in 1903 by a selection of George William Russell's poems, *The Nuts of Knowledge*, published under Russell's pseudonym AE. These two books established the style of publi-

the mythical and the magical, *Stories of Red Hanrahan* bore the four provinces of Irish folklore in stylized design on its title page. It cannot have eased the press's financial problems, though, for it was a slow seller. *Some Essays and Passages*, by John Eglington, published in August 1905, was a coup for the press.

Eglington was the pseudonym of William Kirkpatrick Magee, the assistant librarian of the National Library of Ireland, coeditor of a nationalist literary review, and a contributor to the highly influential *Literary Ideals in Ireland* (published by T. Fisher Unwin, 1899). Magee disagreed with Yeats's selection of his writings, but Yeats insisted that his choice go forward for publication. Yeats's opinion prevailed, but *Some Essays and Passages* carried a disclaimer by Magee. Later John Butler Yeats commented to his son, "I think you should treat . . . Magee with great respect—after all a writer knows his own work."

Late in 1905 William Allingham's *Sixteen Poems* was published by Dun Emer. Allingham was an important nineteenth-century poet who drew inspiration from Irish folklore and mythology. His work was much admired by Yeats, who was ever keen to publish writing celebrating ancient Celtic traditions. Lady Gregory's *A Book of Saints and Wonders* (1906), a selection of translations from the Irish, reinforced this tendency in Dun Emer's publications. Lady Gregory, born Isabella Augusta Persse, was a writer and playwright, a friend of William Butler Yeats, a moving figure behind Dublin's Abbey Theatre, and a supporter of the Dun Emer Press who submitted occasional works for publication—predominantly translations which gave new life to otherwise inaccessible literature. In December 1906 a second selection of AE's poetry, *By Still Waters*, was published. Again, literary selection generated disagreement, this time between William Butler and Elizabeth Yeats. During 1904 and 1905 there had been a good deal of friction between them about financial matters, and when the disagreement over selection arose, William Butler could tolerate no more. He refused to continue as literary editor unless he had autonomy in editorial matters.

Tensions had obviously eased before the next publication went to press, for William Butler Yeats acted as literary adviser for Katharine Tynan's *Twenty One Poems* (1907). The title page for Tynan's book carried the Dun Emer pressmark for the first time: Lady Emer standing under a tree engraved from a line drawing by Monsell. The colophon bore the names of the staff of the press—Ryan and Cassidy—a feature that became standard in future publications. Tynan's book was followed in December 1907 by *Discoveries*, an important volume of essays in which William Butler Yeats expressed both his philosophy of poetry and his view of the role of poetry to the Irish people. *Discoveries* was the last book to be printed by the Dun Emer Press.

By 1908 financial tensions between the Yeats sisters and Gleeson made it impossible to continue running the press as part of Dun Emer Industries at Gleeson's home. The Yeats sisters separated the press and embroidery workshops from the rest of Dun Emer Industries and moved to nearby Churchtown, where they established Cuala Industries. The Dun Emer Press became the Cuala Press under Elizabeth Yeats's direction; Lily Yeats supervised the embroidery section. The staff of the press consisted of Ryan, Cassidy, Eileen Colum, and Maire Gill, and like Elizabeth and Lily Yeats they became shareholders in the new venture. The name Cuala was derived from the Irish place-name of the South County Dublin barony in which the new premises were situated. A change of name had been necessary for legal reasons, but the press's publishing policy remained the same. In terms of domestic harmony the change proved highly beneficial: Elizabeth was later to comment to a customer, "we gained so *immensely* . . . in moving from Dun Emer." The move took place in July 1908, the last publication from Dun Emer being the first edition of the monthly *A Broadside* (1908-1915). *A Broadside* was a folio four-page pamphlet carrying ballads and poems by traditional and contemporary artists and writers, and line block illustrations from drawings by Jack Butler Yeats. Its title was set in four-line antique wood letter and its text in fourteen-point Caslon. It was sold by subscription only at twelve shillings a year. The first number, for June, contained "Campeachy Picture," by John Masefield; an anonymous poem, "The Travelling Circus"; and hand-colored and black-and-white illustrations by Jack Butler Yeats. By the time the second number was published in July, the imprint had changed from Dun Emer to Cuala.

Cuala's first book was *Poetry and Ireland* (1908), a collection of essays by William Butler Yeats and Johnson which advocated a poetry shorn of political motivation and a nationalism shorn of jingoism. It bore Monsell's device of Lady Emer standing under a tree, which was to become synonymous with the Cuala Press. At this time John Millington Synge's *Poems and Transla-*

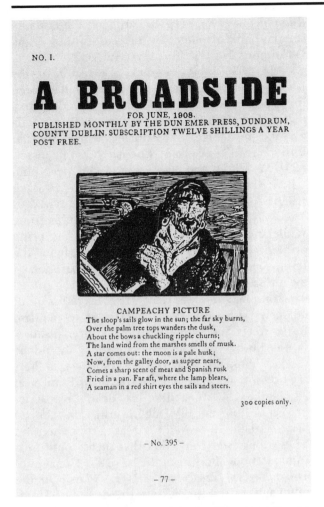

NO. I.

A BROADSIDE

FOR JUNE, 1908.

PUBLISHED MONTHLY BY THE DUN EMER PRESS, DUNDRUM,
COUNTY DUBLIN. SUBSCRIPTION TWELVE SHILLINGS A YEAR
POST FREE.

CAMPEACHY PICTURE

The sloop's sails glow in the sun; the far sky burns,
Over the palm tree tops wanders the dusk,
About the bows a chuckling ripple churns;
The land wind from the marshes smells of musk.
A star comes out: the moon is a pale husk,
Now, from the galley door, as supper nears,
Comes a sharp scent of meat and Spanish rusk
Fried in a pan. Far aft, where the lamp blears,
A seaman in a red shirt eyes the sails and steers.

300 copies only.

– No. 395 –

– 77 –

*First page of the first number of the Dun Emer Press monthly
pamphlet series, published from 1908 to 1915. The poem is
by John Masefield, the woodcut by Jack Butler Yeats.*

tions was in preparation. Synge's work was particularly controversial in 1908: his *Playboy of the Western World* had played in Dublin in 1907, and the ensuing controversy gave him a prominence that was not always benign and a popularity greater than that of any other playwright of his time. William Butler Yeats was a staunch supporter of Synge and appreciated his yearning for the primitive life; it was at Yeats's urging that Synge spent much time in Aran, achieving the quietude needed for writing. Synge was seriously ill during the printing of *Poems and Translations*; it was not until after his death that the book was published on 5 July 1909, with a preface and tribute by Yeats. The Cuala edition was the only edition of *Poems and Translations* available for two years. Over the next few years Cuala published several of Synge's works with commentaries and criticism. *Deirdre of the Sorrows*, possibly Synge's most poignant play, was published in July 1910. The

swift publication of the book, which was ambitiously printed in red and black throughout, had been made possible by a second printing press bought by Cuala in March. The following year Cuala published William Butler Yeats's tribute, *Synge and the Ireland of His Time*.

In December 1910 *The Green Helmet and Other Poems*, a collection of plays inspired by William Butler Yeats's fascination with the Cuchulainn legend, had been published by Cuala; following Yeats's *Synge and the Ireland of His Time* no other substantial publication appeared until autumn 1912, when a busier period of book production began with *Selections from the Writings of Lord Dunsany* (Edward Plunkett). *A Selection of the Love Poetry of W. B. Yeats* and *A Woman's Reliquary* (anonymously edited by Edward Dowden) were published in 1913. The following year William Butler Yeats's new book of poetry, *Responsibilities*, was closely followed by Rabindranath Tagore's treatment of recent political issues in his play *The Post Office*. In 1915 Masefield added his reminiscences to the growing number of published tributes to Synge with *John M. Synge: A Few Personal Recollections*. For the next ten months Cuala was busy with private press commissions and with preparation of William Butler Yeats's autobiographical *Reveries over Childhood and Youth*, which was published in two volumes on 20 March 1916.

In April 1916 the short-lived Irish republic was proclaimed. William Butler Yeats was not directly connected with the republican movement, but his work symbolized the rekindling of the Irish spirit, and he advocated an Irish nation free from English oppression. It was in sympathy with the republican spirit that Cuala undertook to print privately *In Memoriam: Last and Inspiring Address of Thomas McDonagh*; McDonagh was one of the executed republican leaders.

William Butler Yeats added Ezra Pound to Cuala's list of authors in 1916. *Certain Noble Plays of Japan*, chosen by Pound from a translation by Ernest Fenollosa and with a preface by Yeats, was published in September 1916. Pound had recently discovered the Japanese Nō theater, and this book was his first attempt to bring it to a Western audience. Pound's influence on Yeats at this time was significant: Yeats's next published collection of writings, *The Wild Swans at Coole* (1917), and the later *Two Plays for Dancers* (1919) both included plays written in the Nō style. At this time John Butler Yeats was trying to complete his memoirs for publication. Pound edited *Passages from the Letters of John Butler Yeats* (1917), and *Further Let-*

ters of John Butler Yeats was published in 1920, but Yeats's memoirs remained unfinished at his death in New York on 2 February 1922. William Butler Yeats completed his father's manuscript, and it was published as *Early Memories* in 1923.

The early 1920s were not good years for Cuala. Though William Butler Yeats kept the press going with *Michael Robartes and the Dancer* (1921), the autobiographical *Four Years* (1921), and *Seven Poems and a Fragment* (1922), undercapitalization, slow sales, and insufficient profit-making work in the years 1910 to 1920, together with wartime disruption and republican troubles, took their toll. Economic problems dominated throughout 1922, and early in 1923 Lily Yeats was seriously ill. William Butler Yeats and his wife, George, came to the rescue, offering Cuala a home in the basement of their house at 82 Merrion Square, Dublin. The press took up this new residence in August 1923, and George took over Lily's role in charge of the embroidery section. Publication continued in 1924 with Oliver St. John Gogarty's *An Offering of Swans*, the colophon of which commemorated the move to Merrion Square. A small collection of Yeats's poems, *The Cat and the Moon*, followed in July 1924.

In November 1924 William Butler Yeats won the Nobel Prize for literature; the prize's financial benefits meant that a new home could be found for the press at 133 Lower Baggot Street. Publishing began again in 1925 with *The Bounty of Sweden*, Yeats's tribute to Sweden for giving him the Nobel Prize. *Love's Bitter Sweet* (1925), a selection of translations from the Irish by Robin Flower, carried on its title page a drawing of a lone tree on a hillside by Elizabeth Yeats; this drawing became the Cuala pressmark. A conscious effort was made in the late 1920s to publish works by a wider list of authors, and the late 1920s and the 1930s were the most productive years of the Cuala Press. Thomas Parnell's *Poems* was published in August 1926, Lennox Robinson's *A Little Anthology of Modern Irish Verse* in 1928, Seán O'Faoláin's *Lyrics and Satires from Tom Moore* in 1929, and Gogarty's *Wild Apples* in 1930. Publication of William Butler Yeats's books continued: *Estrangement* (1926), *October Blast* (1927), *The Death of Synge and Other Passages from an Old Diary* (1928), *A Packet for Ezra Pound* (1929), *Stories of Michael Robartes and His Friends* (1932), *Words for Music Perhaps and Other Poems* (1932), *The Words upon the Window Pane* (1934), and *The King of the Great Clock Tower* (1934). Lady Gregory's *The*

Kiltartan Poetry Book (1918) had been the last substantial book of poetry in translation until Frank O'Connor's *The Wild Bird's Nest* in 1932.

In 1935 F. R. Higgins, a director of the Abbey Theatre whose *Arable Holdings* had been published by Cuala in 1933, was appointed a director of the press. He worked as coeditor of Cuala for the next six years, during which William Butler Yeats's *Dramatis Personae* (1935), *Essays 1931-36* (1937), and *New Poems* (1938) were published; *Passages from the Letters of AE to W. B. Yeats* (1936) appeared; and *A Broadside* was revived as *Broadsides*, a monthly and an annual publication. While the *Annual Broadside* for 1937 was being printed, O'Connor's prose translation from the Irish, *Lords and Commons*, was in preparation at the press. Its publication late in 1938 reinforced the conjunction of ancient Irish literature with modern Irish authors so significant to William Butler Yeats and to the Irish literary renaissance. It was fitting that *Lords and Commons* should be the last book for which Yeats was to act as literary adviser: he died at Cap Martin in France on 28 January 1939. After his death his long-projected journal of Dublin criticism, *On the Boiler* (1939), appeared. It was a testament to Yeats's long-held conviction that there could be a Dublin school of criticism. In July 1939 Cuala published Yeats's *Last Poems and Two Plays*. On the title page, in red ink, it bore the device of a unicorn engraved by Edmund Dulac, a particular favorite of Yeats.

Yeats's death was a major blow to Cuala; the death of Elizabeth Yeats on 16 January 1940 was devastating. The press never really recovered. Between 1903 and 1940 Elizabeth Yeats had overseen the production of sixty-two books, thirty-six private press commissions, and three series of the *Broadside*, as well as occasional and single-sheet publications, hand-colored greeting cards, calendars, and bookplates. She had kept the press going through difficulties with Gleeson, squabbles with her brother, wartime shortages, republican troubles, and constant financial worries. She managed the staff, wrote to authors, saw to the sales, dealt with the correspondence, and produced stock blocks for publication from her own drawings. On 1 February, after Cuala reopened following Elizabeth's death, a memorial, *Elizabeth Corbet Yeats*, written by her sister Lily for Elizabeth's family, friends, and patrons, was published. In the last paragraph, friends were told that the directorship of Cuala was to be continued by Mrs. William Butler Yeats and F. R.

Higgins, and that Colum, who had worked at the press since 1904, was also to be a director.

The last book published by Elizabeth Yeats had been Gogarty's collection of poems *Elbow Room* in November 1939. Under the new directors Cuala's publishing policy was enlarged to accommodate new authors while its original aims were retained. Louis MacNeice's first work to be published by Cuala, *The Last Ditch*, appeared in April. It was followed in the same year by O'Connor's translation *A Lament for Art O'Leary*, with six hand-colored drawings by Jack B. Yeats; three essays by William Butler Yeats, *If I were Four-and-Twenty*; and Masefield's *Some Memories of W. B. Yeats*, which carried a frontispiece depicting Yeats's London house at 18 Woburn Buildings.

Higgins, the press's coeditor from 1935 and sole literary adviser throughout 1940, died on 8 January 1941. Higgins had been a friend of William Butler Yeats and of Synge and with them had been a director of the Abbey Theatre and a prominent figure in the Irish literary renaissance. His role at Cuala had been short but important: he had helped the press through a difficult and traumatic time. The last book he had advised on, a selection of Donagh McDonagh's poetry titled *Veterans and Others*, was published in April 1941. O'Faoláin and Frank O'Connor were appointed directors in May and also acted as literary advisers to the press. Before the year was out Clifford Bax's edition of the letters of Florence Farr, Bernard Shaw, and William Butler Yeats was published; O'Connor's *Three Tales* followed in 1942. But the financial problems which had troubled Cuala from its inception worsened during the 1940s, when production and distribution were severely curtailed by World War II. Under these circumstances rent for the premises in central Dublin proved to be too onerous. Mrs. Yeats came to the rescue once again, offering the press a home in her house at 46 Palmerston Road. On New Year's Day 1942 the press moved into its new premises; and it was there that Cuala published in June 1942 what was to become one of the most celebrated pieces of twentieth-century Irish poetry: *The Great Hunger*, by Patrick Kavanagh. Later that year Elizabeth Bowen's *Seven Winters* added another important new author to the press's list.

In 1943 Cuala was forty years old. To mark its birthday a list of all the press's publications was bound into the two books published that year, Jack B. Yeats's play *La La Noo* and O'Connor's collection of poems *A Picture Book*, illustrated by Elizabeth Rivers. An ambitious production of *Dafydd ap Gwylym: Selected Poems*, translated by Nigel Heseltine with a preface by O'Connor, was printed in red and black in the winter of 1943 and published in April 1944. William Butler Yeats's *Pages from a Diary Written in Nineteen Hundred and Thirty* followed that year, and *The Love Story of Thomas Davis*, edited by Joseph Hone, in 1945. *Strangers in Aran* (1946), by Rivers, was the press's last book: financial problems finally proved overwhelming. It was fitting that the last book to be produced by Cuala was written, illustrated, printed, bound, and published by women. Hand-colored illustrations and greeting cards continued to be produced until George Yeats's death in August 1968.

On Thursday, 25 September 1969, the Cuala Press was revived at 116 Lower Baggot Street by Anne Yeats and Michael B. Yeats, son and daughter of William Butler and George Yeats. Their fellow directors were the poet Thomas Kinsella and Liam Miller, owner of the Dolmen Press. They declared that the new Cuala's policy was the same as that of the old: to publish "the best work being written in Ireland, printed with the same craftsmanship which made the Cuala Press famous." The revived Cuala was to use the same type and the same press as its forebear, and new paper as near to the old as possible was ordered from Swiftbrook Mills. Its first publication, *Reflections*, from the journals of William Butler Yeats, appeared in February 1971. *A Brief Account of the Cuala Press Formerly the Dun Emer Press Founded by E. C. Yeats in MCMIII*, by Miller, followed later in 1971. Tipped into this celebration of the history of the press was a copy of the first edition of *A Broadside*. To mark the centenary of Synge's birth, *Some Letters of John M. Synge to Lady Gregory and W. B. Yeats*, selected and introduced by Ann Saddlemyer, was also published in 1971. *Notes from the Land of the Dead*, by Kinsella; *A List of Books Published by the Dun Emer Press and the Cuala Press Founded in Nineteen Hundred and Three by Elizabeth Corbet Yeats*, with a preface by Miller; and John Butler Yeats's autobiographical *Letters from Bedford Park* followed in 1972.

To celebrate the Cuala Press's seventieth birthday an exhibition was arranged by the National Book League in London in June 1973, and a catalogue was published by the Dolmen Press. Miller's biographical and bibliographical study *The Dun Emer Press later the Cuala Press*, with a preface by Michael B. Yeats, was published by the Dolmen Press concurrently with a special edition of 250 copies published by Cuala and signed by the author. Also that year John Montague's *A Fair House* enlarged the press's list of poetry in translation, and *The Speckled Bird*, a previously unpublished novel by William Butler Yeats, edited by William H. O'Donnell, was published in two volumes.

In 1975 the Cuala Press moved from the center of Dublin to larger premises at Leslie Avenue, Dalkey, County Dublin. There Patrick O'Carroll joined Anne and Michael Yeats, Miller, and Kinsella as a director. The first publication at Dalkey was *The Revenant*, by MacNeice, a song cycle of previously unpublished poems. The character of Cuala changed with the move to Dalkey: Cuala could only afford a printer for two months of the year, and for the rest of the year the press existed as a sales and mailing operation. Nothing further was published until *Pressmarks and Devices Used at the Dun Emer Press and the Cuala Press* in 1977. The substantial *From a Dark Lantern: A Journal by Arland Ussher*, edited by Roger N. Parisious, was published in 1978, followed the next year by *A Little Book of Bookplates*, by Jack B. Yeats, printed from an original block and edited by Richard Murdoch. *Some Unpublished Letters from AE to James Stephens* (1979), edited by Richard J. Finneran and Mary M. FitzGerald, was the last book published by Cuala; it carried a title-page device first used on AE's *The Nuts of Knowledge* in 1903. The Cuala Press continued at Dalkey as a commercial operation and tourist attraction until various factors made continuation impossible. The press was closed and its equipment and effects auctioned in Dublin in 1986.

From 1903 to 1985 the Dun Emer and then the Cuala Press published ninety-one books; it also produced privately printed works, occasional publications, single sheets, hand-colored prints, calendars, greeting cards, and bookplates. Established to provide employment for Irish girls in the making of beautiful things, it realized its founder's intention; yet in publishing work by William Butler Yeats, AE, Eglington, Tynan, Synge, Allingham, Pound, Masefield, Gogarty, O'Connor, Kavanagh, Bowen, and MacNeice, the Cuala Press made a singular and lasting contribution to the Irish literary renaissance of the twentieth century.

References:

The Cuala Press: A Catalogue of an Exhibition Arranged with the National Book League to Celebrate the Seventieth Anniversary of the Press, 11-30 June 1973 (Dublin: Dolmen Press, 1973);

Michael J. Durkan, "The Dun Emer and the Cuala Press," *Wesleyan Library Notes*, no. 4 (Spring 1970);

Ramsay MacDonald, ed., *Women in the Printing Trades* (London: King, 1904);

Roger B. Mason, "The Cuala Press in 1978," *Antiquarian Book Monthly Review*, 6 (January 1979);

Liam Miller, *The Dun Emer Press, Later the Cuala Press* (Dublin: Dolmen Press, 1973);

Colin Smythe, "The Cuala Press 1903-1973," *Private Library*, 6 (Autumn 1973): 107-113.

Papers:

A complete collection of Dun Emer and Cuala Press publications is in the Belfast Central Library. Substantial collections are in the Dublin City Library; the Manchester Central Library; the Mitchell Library, Glasgow; Queens' University Library, Belfast; Trinity College Library, Dublin; and Wesleyan Library, Middletown, Connecticut. Copies can be found in the Bristol County Reference Library; the British Library; the Church of Ireland Library, Belfast; the Reading University Library; and the St. Bride Printing Library, London.

—Louise Craven

Peter Davies Limited
(London: 1938-1977)
Peter Davies
(London: 1926-1938)

Peter Llewelyn Davies was born on 25 February 1897 to Arthur and Sylvia Llewelyn Davies, and he grew up in a web of literary connections. His mother's father was George du Maurier, the author and *Punch* artist. His family attracted the not always welcome friendship of the playwright J. M. Barrie, and each of the five Llewelyn Davies brothers—Peter, George, John (Jack), Michael, and Nicholas (Nico)—would eventually be identified in the public mind as the model for Peter Pan. Arthur Davies died of a tumor in 1907, followed by his wife in 1910, whereupon Barrie became the guardian of the five boys.

Davies attended Eton, fought at the Battle of the Somme in World War I, and later won the Military Cross. In the 1920s he learned book production at the Edinburgh firm of Walter Blackie. With the help of Barrie and the firm of Hodder and Stoughton, he set up his own publishing business in 1926 at 30 Henrietta Street, London. His brother Nico came to work with him.

The brothers produced many biographies and historical books by popular authors: *François Villon* (1928), by Wyndham Lewis; *Voltaire* (1932), by André Maurois; *Julius Caesar* (1932) and *Gordon at Khartoum* (1934), by John Buchan; *Macaulay* (1932) and *George V* (1936), by Sir Arthur Bryant; *Sarah Bernhardt* (1933), by Maurice Baring; *William the Conqueror* (1933), by Hilaire Belloc; *Mary Queen of Scots* (1933) and *Robert the Bruce* (1934), by Eric Linklater; and *The Hundred Days* (1934), by Philip Guedalla. They also published work by Robert Speaight and by the composer Ethel Smyth.

In 1932 Peter Davies became a limited company, and in 1937 the William Heinemann firm bought a majority interest in it. Heinemann provided financial and distribution services, while

Peter Davies at the funeral of J. M. Barrie, 1937

the Davies brothers retained editorial independence. They put out about twenty books a year—half fiction, half nonfiction.

In 1938 Peter Davies bought out the publishing business of his friend Lovat Dickson for forty-five hundred pounds. It proved to be a highly profitable acquisition. During World War II Peter Davies Limited was allotted the paper ration that would have gone to Lovat Dickson—an extra twenty tons each year, enough to print 350,000 additional books through the course of the war. In the bargain Davies picked up valuable authors: Lloyd C. Douglas, whose biblical novel *The Robe* (1943) became a runaway best-seller; and P. L. Travers, some of whose Mary Poppins books were published by Davies. In 1933 Lovat Dickson had begun publishing Jules Romains's twenty-seven-novel cycle *Les Hommes de bonne volonté* (1932-1946) as *Men of Good Will*; after Davies took over the series, sales increased considerably.

Some of Barrie's writings appeared under the Peter Davies imprint: *The Greenwood Hat* (1937), *M'Connachie and J. M. B.* (1938), and *The Letters of J. M. Barrie*, edited by Viola Meynell (1942). The firm also published Denis Mackail's biography *The Story of J. M. B.* (1941) and Roger Lancelyn Green's *Fifty Years of Peter Pan* (1954). Drawing on other family ties, Peter Davies republished du Maurier's novels in 1947 and published a volume of his letters, edited by his granddaughter Daphne du Maurier, in 1951.

John Dettmer of Heinemann ran the firm during World War II, while Peter and Nico served in the Brigade of Guards. The offices were moved to Heinemann's Windmill Press facility at Kingswood, Surrey. Toward the end of the war Peter Davies Limited relocated, with the rest of the Heinemann editorial staff, to 99 Great Russell Street. In 1959 Davies and Heinemann moved to Heinemann's new custom-built premises at 15 Queen Street, Mayfair.

Peter Davies's working career was brought to an end by a debilitating asthmatic condition. On 5 April 1960 he threw himself under a train at the Sloane Square Underground station. "PETER PAN COMMITS SUICIDE," ran one headline.

By that point the firm he had founded was losing money; it had a record loss of £30,802 in 1961. The Heinemann Group had been bought out by Thomas Tilling, an industrial conglomerate, in 1960; Tilling responded to the crisis by buying Nico's share of Peter Davies Limited, which then became a mere imprint within the Heinemann Group. Nico Davies retired from the chairmanship in 1968. Derek Priestley, who had been moved over from Heinemann in 1964 to be managing director, became chairman and restored profitability for a time.

The underlying problem, however, was not solved. The Peter Davies list had long been dominated by conventional and unexciting authors such as Norah Lofts, Faith Baldwin, and Frances Parkinson Keyes—although there were a few exceptions, including Charles Rickett's *Self-Portrait* (1939), Josephine Tey's *The Daughter of Time* (1951), and Louis Armstrong's *Satchmo: My Life in New Orleans* (1955). Profits fell off again in 1975 and 1976, and in January 1977 Peter Davies Limited was completely absorbed by Heinemann.

References:

Andrew Birkin, *J. M. Barrie and the Lost Boys* (London: Constable, 1979);

Lovat Dickson, *The House of Words* (New York: Atheneum, 1963), pp. 194-197;

"Mr. Peter Davies: The Barrie Circle [obituary]," *Times* (London), 7 April 1960, p. 16;

John St. John, *William Heinemann: A Century of Publishing 1890-1990* (London: Heinemann, 1990).

—*Jonathan Rose*

J. M. Dent and Sons
(London: 1909-   )
J. M. Dent and Company
(London: 1888-1909)

J. M. Dent and Sons has published an impressive list of books by contemporary authors, but it made its mark on publishing history with its inexpensive series of classic literature. Everyman's Library in particular stands as a monument to the firm. It was not the first attempt at a cheap uniform edition of the "great books," but no similar series except Penguin Books has ever exceeded it in scope, and none without exception has ever matched the high production standards of the early Everyman volumes.

Joseph Malaby Dent, born on 30 August 1849, was one of a dozen children of a Darlington housepainter. He acquired his love of literature from the autodidact culture that flourished among Victorian artisans and shopkeepers. Dent attended a "Mutual Improvement Society" at a local chapel, where he undertook to write a paper on Samuel Johnson. Reading James Boswell's biography of Johnson, he was astonished that the great men of the period—such as Edmund Burke, Sir Joshua Reynolds, Oliver Goldsmith—"should bow down before this old Juggernaut and allow him to walk over them, insult them, blaze out at them and treat them as if they were his inferiors. . . . At last it dawned on me that it was not the ponderous, clumsy, dirty old man that they worshipped, but the scholarship for which he stood." Boswell's *The Life of Samuel Johnson, LL.D.* (1791) taught Dent that "there was nothing worth living for so much as literature"—and in 1906 it would become the first book in Everyman's Library. Raised as a

Joseph Malaby Dent (photograph by Frederick H. Evans)

"strict nonconformist," he had become determined to serve the religion of literature—

81

"though only as a door-keeper of the Temple."

Dent became a printer's apprentice but proved so incompetent that he switched to bookbinding—not, however, before he had learned all aspects of the printer's craft. In 1867 he moved to London, where he set up his own bookbinding shop. He often noted that his fine leather bindings put to shame the unattractive Victorian typography of the sheets they bound. It would be some years before Dent came to know and admire the work of William Morris, T. J. Cobden-Sanderson, and the Arts and Crafts Movement; but already he saw a spiritual mission in fine craftsmanship.

In 1888 J. M. Dent and Company began publishing at 69 Great Eastern Street. Its first production was Charles Lamb's *Essays of Elia*, edited by Augustine Birrell and with etchings by Herbert Railton, followed in 1889 by Goldsmith's *Poems and Plays*, edited by Austin Dobson. Dent christened the series the Temple Library, ostensibly because Lamb and Goldsmith had resided at the Temple, but perhaps also to suggest the missionary spirit that motivated the enterprise. In format it resembled Kegan Paul's Parchment Library: the Chiswick Press printed books for both series. The early Temple Library books were produced in limited editions on handmade paper. The eminent antiquarian bookseller Bernard Quaritch endorsed them, and they enjoyed some commercial success.

In 1889 the firm also put out Geoffrey Chaucer's *Canterbury Tales*, with twenty-three hand-colored illustrations reproduced from the Ellesmere manuscript, as well as Johnson's *Selected Essays* and Alfred, Lord Tennyson's *Poetical Works* and *Songs*. Dent next turned to collected editions of the works of eighteenth- and early-nineteenth-century novelists: Thomas Love Peacock in ten volumes, edited by Richard Garnett (1891); Jane Austen in ten volumes (1893); the Brontë sisters in twelve (1893); Maria Edgeworth in twelve (1893); and Goldsmith in six (1893). George Saintsbury edited the works of Henry Fielding (twelve volumes, 1893) and Laurence Sterne (1894). In 1895 Daniel Defoe's *Romances and Narratives* was published in sixteen volumes, with forty-eight photogravure illustrations by J. B. Yeats.

In 1893 Dent's friend the bookseller Frederick H. Evans suggested a series of pocket volumes of the works of William Shakespeare. Dent's familiarity with autodidact culture made him aware of the potential demand for cheap editions of the classics. As secretary of the Shakespeare Society at Toynbee Hall, the Whitechapel settlement house, he noted that the members had to rely on a miscellaneous assortment of "second-hand editions, quartos, Bowdlerized school editions—no two being the same and all without proper machinery for elucidating difficulties. Neither type nor pages gave proper help to reading aloud." Dent's response was the Temple Shakespeare, edited by Israel Gollancz: forty volumes from *The Tempest* (1894) to *The Sonnets* (1896). It offered great value for a shilling a volume, printed on handmade paper, with title pages designed by Walter Crane. Over the next four decades the series sold five million copies—"the largest sale made in Shakespeare since the plays were written," Dent claimed.

Another of Dent's series was inspired by Toynbee Hall—specifically by the Toynbee Travellers' Club, which arranged cheap tours of Europe. Dent visited Florence and Siena and was so entranced by their beauty that he conceived the Mediaeval Towns Series. Margaret Symonds and Lina Duff-Gordon began the series with *The Story of Perugia* (1898). These illustrated volumes were designed to capture the distinctive "personalities" of the old European cities. They also gave Dent an excuse for traveling throughout Europe to scout out new subjects.

The success of the Temple Shakespeare led to two new series in 1896. The Temple Dramatists began with John Ford's *The Broken Heart*, John Webster's *The Duchess of Malfi*, and Christopher Marlowe's *Doctor Faustus*; meanwhile, the Temple Classics commenced with Robert Southey's *Life of Horatio, Lord Nelson*, William Wordsworth's *The Prelude*, and Jonathan Swift's *Gulliver's Travels*. Gollancz edited the Temple Classics until editorial conflicts with Dent led to his replacement by Oliphant Smeaton. By 1918 the series would comprise about three hundred volumes.

When Dent conceived of producing an illustrated edition of Sir Thomas Malory's *Le Morte d'Arthur* (1485), Evans introduced him to the work of a little-known nineteen-year-old artist: Aubrey Beardsley. Dent's tastes were hardly avant-garde, but he at once recognized "a new breath of life in English black-and-white drawing." *The Birth Life and Acts of King Arthur*, with about three hundred Beardsley illustrations, was published in monthly parts at two shillings, sixpence (1893-1894) and in a limited three-volume edition of eighteen hundred copies (1893-1894) that was snapped up by subscribers. The book did much to establish Beardsley as an influential force in English art.

An even more ambitious project was Honoré de Balzac's *Comédie Humaine* (1895-1898) in forty volumes, edited by George Saintsbury and translated by Ellen Marriage, Clara Bell, James Waring, and R. S. Scott. Although it did not sell well in Britain, Macmillan made it profitable by marketing a large number of sets in the United States.

In 1889 Dent had bought the bankrupt Suttaby and Company, a publisher and wholesale bookseller. When he reprinted some of Suttaby's devotional books, he used the firm's printer, Turnbull and Spears of Edinburgh. The two firms would work closely and well together on the Temple Shakespeare, *The Birth Life and Acts of King Arthur*, and many other projects for decades to come.

While the classics remained Dent's forte, the firm began to venture into contemporary literature as well. Maurice Hewlett's *Earthwork Out of Tuscany* and *A Masque of Dead Florentines* appeared in 1895, followed the next year by H. G. Wells's *The Wheels of Chance*. Henryk Sienkiewicz's *Quo Vadis?* was published in 1897 by arrangement with Little, Brown of Boston. In the field of children's books, Kate Greenaway contributed *Almanack and Diary for 1897* (1897) and Edith Nesbit wrote *A Book of Dogs* (1898) and *Pussy and Doggy Tales* (1899).

The firm continued to introduce new series of books. In 1898 Dent undertook to publish Professor Walter Ripman's guides to learning languages via the "Reform Method." Over the course of forty years the series would expand to more than 150 volumes and secure Dent a firm beachhead in the domain of educational publishing. In 1899 Dent scored another success with the Haddon Hall Library. Devoted to the pleasures of the countryman, it included Sir Edward Grey's *Fly Fishing* (1899). The series was decorated by Arthur Rackham and edited by the marquess of Granby (Henry John Brinsley Manners) and G. A. B. Dewar.

Also in 1899 Gollancz suggested producing English translations of the *Sammlung Goschen* (Goschen Collection), a series of German primers in all academic disciplines. Dent secured the rights to many of the Goschen volumes and supplemented them with original works produced by English authors. In 1900 the Temple Primers were launched with Stopford Brooke's *English Lit-*

erature, William Macdougall's *Physiological Psychology*, and Sir William Ramsay's *Modern Chemistry*.

The Temple Biographies commenced in 1902 with *Mazzini*, by Bolton King; they were followed by the Temple Autobiographies, starting with *The Life of Benvenuto Cellini* (1903). H. Warner Allen edited Les Classiques Français, which included François Antoine-René de Chateaubriand's *Atala* (1904). English Men of Science, edited by J. Reynolds Green, began with J. A. Thomson's *Herbert Spencer* (1906). G. Lowes Dickinson and H. O. Meredith edited the Temple Greek and Latin Classics, beginning in 1906 with Euripides' *Medea and Hippolytus*, translated by Sydney Waterlow.

Dent continued to turn out collected editions: the Temple Edition of the works of Henry Fielding (1893) in twelve volumes, edited by George Saintsbury; *The Spectator* (1897-1898) in eight volumes, introduced by Austin Dobson; Sir Walter Scott's Waverley novels in forty-eight pocket-sized volumes (1897-1898) and the Temple Edition of *The Works of Charles Dickens* (1898-1903) in a similar format; Victor Hugo's novels in twenty-eight volumes (1899-1900); the Temple Molière (1900-1902); the works of William Makepeace Thackeray in thirty volumes, illustrated by Charles Brock (1901-1903); and the works of William Hazlitt in twelve volumes, introduced by W. E. Henley (1901-1904). If Dent worshiped literature as a religion, he conversely revered the Bible as great literature, and it was presented as such in the *Temple Bible* (1901-1904). Edited by Smeaton in thirty-one volumes, its sales were disappointing.

Dent suffered a far more costly disaster with the author who began his publishing career. In 1903 he published *The Works of Charles Lamb*, including some ostensibly unpublished letters he had purchased for five hundred pounds. He was not aware that some of those letters had already appeared in a limited edition put out by Macmillan (1899-1900). Macmillan sued and won both the judgment and an appeal; Dent was compelled to pay the costs of the suit. The courts held that a person who first published the work of a dead author thereby acquired the copyright—a precedent that would be altered by the 1911 Copyright Act. The Dent firm would not publish a complete edition of Lamb's letters until 1935-1936, and then it would do so jointly with Methuen.

Anxious to develop his transatlantic market, Dent visited North America in 1893, 1897, 1901,

1913, 1915, 1916, and 1918. Up to 1897 Macmillan handled most of his publications in the United States, but then Dent developed reciprocal arrangements with other American firms. He acquired the complete novels of Alexandre Dumas père (1893-1897) from Little, Brown, and that firm in turn published his set of Frederick Marryat's novels (1896-1898) in America. The works of Ivan Turgenev (1903-1904) came to Dent from Scribners, which distributed the Temple edition of the Waverley novels.

After only seven years in business Dent had published about three hundred volumes and paid off all his debts. Then in January 1897 he was compelled to buy the premises he had leased at 69 Great Eastern Street and had to borrow money again. The previous year he had opened a West End office in St. James's Street, only to be forced out when the building was demolished. At the end of 1897 the firm moved its editorial offices to 29-30 Bedford Street, which had just been vacated by Macmillan—a prestigious but expensive address; the bindery remained at 69 Great Eastern Street. No sooner had his staff moved into Bedford Street than Dent learned that 69 Great Eastern Street did not meet fire regulations. The bindery was therefore moved in October 1899 to Fleur de Lis Street, Bishopsgate.

In 1904, with years of experience in publishing the classics at popular prices, Dent began to plan seriously for a project of which he had long dreamed. Everyman's Library was by no means without precedent: Dent cited as models the French Bibliothèque Nationale and the Reclam series of Leipzig, as well as Henry Bohn's Libraries, the Chandos Classics, Macmillan's Globe Series, Henry Morley's Universal Library, and Charles Knight's British Novelists and Cabinet Shakespeare. But Everyman's Library would far surpass all of them in scope and production quality. Dent's plan was to publish the greatest noncopyright works of English and world literature in one thousand uniform volumes of about five hundred pages, selling for a shilling per volume.

The same general idea had occurred independently to Ernest Percival Rhys, who would edit Everyman's Library from its inception until his death in 1946. Born in 1859, Rhys grew up in Carmarthen, Wales, and worked as a mining engineer in Durham, where he set up a reading room for the colliers. He invited the miner-poet Joseph Skipsey to lecture at the reading room; Skipsey introduced Rhys to publishing when he asked him to edit a volume of the works of George Herbert (1885) for the Newcastle publisher Walter Scott. Rhys went on to edit Scott's Camelot Classics series, advertising it as selling for "the democratic shilling"—a phrase later picked up by Dent. Rhys went to London in 1886 to pursue a full-time literary career. He wrote poems on Welsh themes, and, with T. W. Rolleston and W. B. Yeats, he was a founder of the Rhymers' Club. At their home in Hampstead, he and his wife Grace would later host Sunday literary teas for Yeats, Ezra Pound, Ford Madox Ford, and D. H. Lawrence.

Rhys proposed a series of popular classics in a letter to Dent in 1905. He was clearly the man for the mission. Already he had edited some novels and the Lyric Poets series (begun in 1894) for the Dent firm. He knew the working-class autodidact—an important potential buyer—as well as Dent did. Inspired by the Camelot series, he had spent hours at the British Museum and Dr. Williams's Library sketching out a definitive "world library." And it was Rhys who hit upon the name Everyman's Library, when he recalled the closing lines of a medieval mystery play, which would appear at the front of every volume in the series:

Everyman, I will go with thee, and be thy guide,
  In thy most need to go by thy side.

Rhys would soon discover that J. M. Dent was not an easy man to work for. Frank Swinnerton, who worked as a clerk in the firm from 1900 to 1907, described Dent as dictatorial and temperamental, quick to jump on errors and stingy with praise: "Men and boys scattered before him as street bookies before a policeman." Dent greatly underestimated the capital, labor, and warehouse space he would need for such a mammoth enterprise as Everyman's Library. The plan was to publish a batch of 50 volumes every few months; an incredible total of 152 actually appeared in 1906, the first year. The firm's offices were already cramped, and the staff was wholly inadequate to cope with the huge demand for the first Everyman books. Packers sometimes had to work through the night, Swinnerton recalled: "The staff, united . . . by the common danger, joked like doomed men," chanting:

"Everyman, I will go with thee and be thy curse,
  And at the end will bring thee to thy hearse."

In response to the crisis Dent built a suburban plant at Letchworth Garden City in 1906.

The Temple Press, as it was called, cost a staggering twenty thousand pounds. When workers complained about the quality of available housing in the area, Dent put up two dozen model homes for them. By 1909 the Temple Press had four hundred workers, half of them women, and over the next three decades it would produce sixty million books.

To provide warehouse space for Everyman's Library, in 1911 Dent built an imposing headquarters at 10-13 Bedford Street. Dent himself authorized the Elizabethan/Queen Anne style of the building, which he called Aldine House. (Although Dent's first printer's device had been the Temple sundial, by this point he had borrowed the dolphin and anchor ornament of Aldus Manutius, the Venetian printer who pioneered the production of portable volumes of classic literature at the end of the fifteenth century.)

Having sunk a huge investment in his physical plant, Dent did not pay generous wages or royalties. He quarreled over money with Rhys, who complained that his employer seemed to feel that literary men who had the joy and privilege of contributing to such a noble enterprise as Everyman's Library should not be too insistent on being paid. Rhys's editorial fees were at first only three guineas per volume, which he supplemented by writing 143 introductions to Everyman books.

The entire editorial staff for Everyman's Library consisted of Rhys, Dent and his son Hugh, and two or three researchers. Rhys recalled that J. M. Dent "would often send by post a list of twenty authors, known and unknown, famous and obscure, that had been suggested for Everyman volumes, which he expected me to read before noon, and sum up in a sentence." At the British Museum Rhys would flip through each book at breakneck speed, ashamed of his superficiality, while fending off would-be contributors of prefaces. Each Everyman book was to be introduced by an eminent critic, and the job of getting that copy in under deadlines drove Rhys to distraction. He personally had to go to G. K. Chesterton's house to force him to deliver a promised introduction to Dickens's *Nicholas Nickleby* (1907).

Dent could be quite tough with his printers: he had one of the first Everyman volumes, Lamb's *Essays of Elia* (1906), destroyed because he did not like the look of it. A less demanding man, however, might not have succeeded in producing such attractive books for a shilling. Everyman volumes measured about 7 by 4 1/2 inches, small enough to fit in a pocket but large enough to look respectable on a bookshelf. Margins were narrow, and a new ten-point type was specially cut to provide maximum legibility while fitting as much text on a page as possible. After some experiments a special paper made of esparto grass, wood sulfite, and cotton rag was perfected. Particularly beautiful were the bindings, endpapers, and title pages designed by Reginald Knowles in William Morris style. On the spine a hand-lettered title crowned a distinctive floral ornament, all stamped in gold. For the bindings, thirteen colors were used to identify the various sections of the library: gray for biography, pale green for classics, orange for essays and belles lettres, carmine for fiction, scarlet for history, brown for oratory, olive for poetry and drama, maroon for reference, blue for romance, fawn for science, purple for theology and philosophy, dark green for travel and topography, and light blue for books for young readers.

Dent wanted to impress the book-buying public at once with the broad scope of Everyman's Library. In 1906 he published the plays of Aeschylus, Hans Christian Andersen's *Fairy Tales*, Matthew Arnold's essays, the complete novels of Jane Austen, Robert Burns's *Poems and Songs*, Joseph Butler's *The Analogy of Religion*, Thomas Carlyle's *The French Revolution*, Samuel Taylor Coleridge's poems and essays, Capt. James Cook's *Voyages of Discovery*, Dinah Mulock Craik's *John Halifax, Gentleman*, Charles Darwin's *Naturalist's Voyage in the "Beagle,"* Defoe's *Robinson Crusoe* in an abridged children's edition, Dumas's *The Three Musketeers*, Elizabeth Gaskell's *Cranford, a Tale* (introduced by Dent himself—it was one of his best-loved novels), the three "Breakfast Table" books of Oliver Wendell Holmes, Thomas Hughes's *Tom Brown's School Days*, essays by T. H. Huxley, Lamb's *Essays of Elia* and *Tales from Shakespeare* (the latter illustrated by Arthur Rackham), Thomas Babington Macaulay's *History of England* in three volumes, Malory's *Le Morte D'Arthur, The Golden Book of Marcus Aurelius*, selected works of John Stuart Mill, the letters of Lady Mary Wortley Montagu, *The Diary of Samuel Pepys*, speeches of William Pitt the Younger, Plato's *Republic*, Charles Reade's *The Cloister and the Hearth* (with an appreciation by A. C. Swinburne), the complete works of Shakespeare in three volumes, the plays of Sophocles, Swift's *Gulliver's Travels* in a children's edition illustrated by Rackham, Tennyson's poems, Izaak Walton's *The Compleat Angler* (introduced by Andrew Lang), John Wesley's journal in four volumes, Mrs. Henry Wood's *The Channings*, and the New Testament (the Old Testament and Apocrypha followed in 1907).

To break even, Dent had to sell at least ten thousand copies of each book—twenty thousand to thirty thousand in the case of volumes that were more costly to produce, such as Shakespeare's plays. Though desperately short of capital, Dent was willing to invest in intimidating multivolume classics, especially in the field of history. John Lothrop Motley's *The Rise of the Dutch Republic* (1906) appeared in three volumes; George Grote's *History of Greece* (1907) in twelve; Richard Hakluyt's *Voyages* (1907), introduced by John Masefield, in eight; Henry Hallam's *Constitutional History of England* (1907) in three; J. A. Froude's *History of England* (1909-1912) in ten; Edward Gibbon's *The Decline and Fall of the Roman Empire* (1910) in six; Theodor Mommsen's *History of Rome* (1911) in four; and Livy's *History of Rome* (1912-1924) in six. A revised and updated edition of J. R. Green's *A Short History of the English People* (1915), a mere two volumes, sold twenty-four thousand sets in its first year.

Conscious of the market in the United States, where E. P. Dutton distributed Everyman's Library, Dent and Rhys allotted a large share of their canon to American literature. They included James Fenimore Cooper's five Leather-Stocking tales (1906-1907), six volumes of Nathaniel Hawthorne's works (1906-1911), three volumes of Washington Irving's (1906-1911), five of Ralph Waldo Emerson's (1906-1915), speeches and letters of Abraham Lincoln (1907), Louisa May Alcott's *Little Women and Good Wives* (1907), Benjamin Franklin's *Autobiography* (1908), four volumes of historical works by Francis Parkman (1908), the works of Edgar Allan Poe (1908), Harriet Beecher Stowe's *Uncle Tom's Cabin* (1909), the works of Henry Wadsworth Longfellow (1909), Henry David Thoreau's *Walden* (1910), the works of William Penn (1911), Alexander Hamilton's *The Federalist; or, The New Constitution* (1911), the works of Bret Harte (1911), Richard Henry Dana's *Two Years before the Mast* (1912), James Russell Lowell's *Among My Books* (1912), and Walt Whitman's *Leaves of Grass* (1912). At a time when Herman Melville was little known in England, Everyman's Library ventured to publish *Moby-Dick* (1907), *Typee* (1907), and *Omoo* (1908).

Continental literature was represented by twelve volumes of the works of Dumas père (1906-1912), fifteen volumes of the works of Balzac (1906-1915), Dante's *The Divine Comedy* (1908), Johann Wolfgang von Goethe's *Faust* (1908) and *Wilhelm Meister* (1912), Hugo's *Les Misérables* (1909) and *Notre Dame de Paris* (1910), three volumes of Michel de Montaigne's *Essays* (1910), six volumes of the plays of Henrik Ibsen (1910-1921), Jean-Jacques Rousseau's *Émile* and *The Social Contract and Discourses* (1913), Molière's *Comedies* (1929), and Blaise Pascal's *Pensées* (1931), with an introduction by T. S. Eliot.

Russian literature had a particularly prominent place in Everyman's Library. *Crime and Punishment* (1911) and *The Brothers Karamazov* (1927) appeared in the Constance Garnett translations, along with several other books by Fyodor Dostoyevski. The standard Russian classics were represented—Leo Tolstoy's *War and Peace* (1911) in three volumes and *Anna Karenina* (1912) in two, Turgenev's *Virgin Soil* (1911) and *Fathers and Sons* (1921), Nicolai Gogol's *Dead Souls* (1915), Aleksandr Pushkin's tales (1933), and Anton Chekhov's *Plays and Stories* (1937). The Dent firm also took a chance with Russian authors who were not yet widely read in England—Maksim Gorky's *Through Russia* (1921); Ivan Goncharov's *Oblomov* (1932), just three years after the first English translation had appeared; and Nikolai Shchedrin's *The Golovlyov Family* (1934).

The Greek and Latin classics were, of course, thoroughly represented: the plays of Euripides in two volumes (1906, 1908); the works of Virgil (1907), Tacitus (1908), and Cicero (1909); the comedies of Aristophanes in two volumes (1909, 1911); the works of Epictetus (1910), Herodotus (1910), and Thucydides (1910); Plutarch's Lives from the "Dryden" edition of 1683-1686 (1910); the works of Demosthenes (1911) and Horace (1911); Aristotle's *Nicomachean Ethics* (1911) and *Politics* (1912); and the works of Xenophon (1914), Lucretius (1921), and Ovid (1939). Oddly, the earl of Derby's (Edward George Stanley) 1864 translation of Homer's *Iliad* (1910)—hardly the best one—was used, along with William Cowper's 1802 translation of the *Odyssey* (1910). The war chronicles of Julius Caesar and Josephus were published in 1915, just after the outbreak of World War I.

Philosophy and theology ran the gamut from *The Confessions of St. Augustine* (1907) to

The building at 29-30 Bedford Street, London, where J. M. Dent and Company moved at the end of 1897

Niccolò Machiavelli's *The Prince* (1908), and included Richard Hooker's *Of the Laws of Ecclesiastical Polity* (1907); four volumes by Emanuel Swedenborg (1909, 1912, 1913, 1933); Benedict de Spinoza's *Ethics and "De Intellectus Emendatione"* (1910), introduced by George Santayana; the works of George Berkeley (1910) and David Hume (1911); John Keble's *The Christian Year* (1914); Thomas Hobbes's *Leviathan* (1914); and Friedrich Nietzsche's *Thus Spake Zarathustra* (1933). The library also included seminal works of science that, in the twentieth century, are hardly ever read: Sir Francis Galton's *Inquiries into Human Faculty and Its Development* (1907), Robert Boyle's *The Sceptical Chymist* (1911), Michael Faraday's *Experimental Researches in Electricity* (1912), Sir Charles Lyell's *The Geological Evidence of the Antiquity of Man* (1914), Thomas Malthus's *An Essay on the Principle of Population* (1914), and Darwin's *The Origin of Species* (1928).

A thoroughgoing liberal, Dent included four volumes of Hazlitt's works (1906-1910), John Bright's speeches (1907), the writings of

Giuseppe Mazzini (1907), Adam Smith's *An Inquiry into the Nature and Causes of the Wealth of Nations* (1910), Henry George's *Progress and Poverty* (1911), and William Cobbett's *Rural Rides* (1912). Thomas Paine's *The Rights of Man* (1915) followed Edmund Burke's *Speeches and Letters on American Affairs* (1908) and *Reflections on the French Revolution and Other Essays* (1910). Dent was decidedly opposed to socialism, but after his death his firm would publish Karl Marx's *Capital* (1930), translated by Eden and Cedar Paul, as well as the works of Robert Owen (1927). Feminism was represented by the writings of George Sand (1911), Elizabeth Blackwell's autobiography *Pioneer Work for Women* (1914), and Mary Wollstonecraft's "A Vindication of the Rights of Woman" in a volume with "The Subjection of Women," by John Stuart Mill (1929).

Reflecting Rhys's Welsh literary interests, Everyman's Library published *The Mabinogion* in 1906. In a similar folkish vein, the series would later feature Icelandic literature, including *The Story of Burnt Njal* (1911), *The Saga of Grettir the Strong* (1914), and Snorri Sturluson's *Heimskringla* (1915, 1930). The Finnish epic *Kalevala* appeared in 1907, *The Fall of the Niebelungs* in 1908, and Adam Mickewicz's Polish classic *Pan Tadeusz* in 1930. Everyman's Library made a real effort to be a world library, with some representation of Eastern literature: *Shakuntala* (1907) and other works by the Sanskrit author Kālidāsa; the Koran (1909); *The Ramayana and the Mahábhárata* (1910); *Hindu Scriptures* (1938), introduced by Rabindranath Tagore; and the anthology *Chinese Philosophy in Classical Times* (1942).

Everyman's Library was dominated by the classics of English literature, starting with *The Anglo-Saxon Chronicle* (1912). Needless to say, *Everyman* (1909) was published (in a volume with other miracle plays), as were William Langland's *Piers Plowman* (1907) and Chaucer's *Canterbury Tales* (1908). The works of Shakespeare were joined by those of Marlowe (1909), Ben Jonson (1910), and Francis Beaumont and John Fletcher (1911), as well as the two-volume *Minor Elizabethan Drama* (1910). The poetry of John Keats (1906), Percy Bysshe Shelley (1907), William Wordsworth (1907, 1908), Robert Herrick (1908), John Milton (1909), and Thomas Gray (1912) was represented, as was *The Spectator* (four volumes, 1907), Goldsmith's *The Vicar of Wakefield* (1908), Fanny Burney's *Evelina* (1909), Henry Fielding's *The History of Tom Jones* (1909), Thomas Love Peacock's *Headlong Hall and Nightmare Abbey*

(1910), and Laurence Sterne's *Tristram Shandy* (1912).

Among the Victorians, the complete works of Dickens were published in twenty-two volumes (1906-1921) introduced by Chesterton. John Ruskin was allotted sixteen volumes (1907-1914), including five for *Modern Painters* (1907) and three for *The Stones of Venice* (1907). There were twenty-eight volumes for Sir Walter Scott (1906-1911), ten for Thackeray (1906-1914), nine for Charles Kingsley (1906-1927), and two for his brother Henry (1906, 1909), as well as Anthony Trollope's six Barsetshire novels (1906-1909). By 1914 the works of all the Brontë sisters had been published, along with the romances of William Morris (1907), Benjamin Disraeli's *Coningsby* (1911), and works by John Henry Newman (1912) and Dante Gabriel Rossetti (1912).

Within a few years of its triumphant launch, however, the momentum of Everyman's Library would be broken by two unforeseeable obstacles. When the series began, copyright protection expired forty-two years after publication or seven years after the death of the author, whichever came later. That allowed Dent to publish the great Victorians—Dickens, Tennyson, Ruskin, Huxley, George Eliot—whose copyrights conveniently lapsed around the turn of the century. The Copyright Act of 1911, however, extended protection to fifty years after the author's death. As a result, Robert Browning's work up to 1869 was published in Everyman's Library by 1911, but the final two volumes, covering 1871 to 1890, were delayed until 1940. Wilkie Collins's *The Woman in White* came out in 1910, whereas *The Moonstone* (introduced by Dorothy L. Sayers) did not appear until 1944. Six books by George Eliot were published between 1906 and 1910, but *Middlemarch* (introduced by Leslie Stephen) was held up until 1930.

The impact of World War I was even more devastating. Volume seven hundred had been put out in 1914, but within a few years the publication of additional Everyman books had ground to a halt. In 1921 new titles began to appear again, but only in a slow trickle. Wartime inflation forced the price of each volume up to two shillings, sixpence by 1920, when the gold leaf on the spine was replaced by imitation gold. The price came down to two shillings in 1922, and in 1927 genuine gold leaf was restored, though the spine ornamentation was severely truncated.

The war had literally taken the glitter from Everyman's Library, just as it had tarnished every-

thing else. On the other hand, the postwar atmosphere of sexual freedom did permit the publication of Tobias Smollett's *Roderick Random* (1927); Gustave Flaubert's *Madame Bovary* (1928), translated by Eleanor Marx-Aveling; François Rabelais's *The Heroic Deeds of Gargantua and Pantagruel* (1929); Daniel Defoe's *Moll Flanders* (1930); Giovanni Boccaccio's *The Decameron* (1930); and Rousseau's *Confessions* (1931). All were unexpurgated, although one story in *The Decameron* was printed in Italian.

Copyright law allowed anyone to publish a book twenty-five years after the author's death for a 10 percent royalty payment to the estate; Dent took advantage of this option to publish more recent classics, among them seven volumes of Robert Louis Stevenson's works in 1925. But the real breakthrough into modern literature came in 1935 with the publication of Arnold Bennett's *The Old Wives' Tale*; Joseph Conrad's *Lord Jim*, introduced by R. B. Cunninghame Graham; John Galsworthy's *The Country House*; Henry James's *The Turn of the Screw and The Aspern Papers*; D. H. Lawrence's *The White Peacock*; and Wells's *The Time Machine; and, The Wheels of Chance*. They were followed by anthologies of works by Aldous Huxley (1937), Thomas Mann (1940), and J. M. Synge (1941), as well as a revised edition of *The Georgian Literary Scene* (1938), by Dent's old office boy, Swinnerton. Virginia Woolf entered Everyman's Library with *To the Lighthouse* in 1938, E. M. Forster with *A Passage to India* in 1942; but Bernard Shaw's plays were not published until 1960, and Thomas Hardy's *Stories and Poems* had to wait until 1970.

In March 1935 the format of the Everyman volumes was modernized. The floral designs on the spine, title page, frontispiece, and endpapers were abandoned in favor of simpler abstract ornaments designed by Eric Ravilious, while a biographical note on the author was added facing the title page. The smooth-finish cloth bindings were replaced with rougher natural-grain cloths, in seven colors rather than thirteen. Titlings were set in Eric Gill's Perpetua Roman, which was replaced by Albertus in 1953 and Fournier in 1962. The page size was enlarged slightly in 1953 to 7 1/8 by 4 5/8 inches.

From 1933 to 1936 thirty Everyman books originally published in two volumes were republished in one-volume editions—"Dent's Double-Volumes"—at five shillings each. Everyman's Reference Library was launched in 1951, though reference works had long been a part of the Every-

Ernest Rhys, editor of Dent's Everyman's Library from its inception until his death in 1946 (drawing by W. H. Caffyn; from Ernest Rhys, Everyman Remembers, 1931)

man series. *Everyman's Encyclopædia*—twelve volumes for twelve shillings—had first been published in 1913; the sixth edition appeared in 1978.

World War II—with its attendant paper rationing, inflation, and labor shortages—again stalled the progress of Everyman's Library. From September 1939 to September 1945 nearly four million copies were sold; but only twenty-two new titles were published, more than half of all titles went out of print, and stock on hand was reduced from more than two million copies to fewer than a million. The price gradually increased, reaching five shillings in 1951, and as late as 1955, 30 percent of the nearly one thousand volumes were still unavailable.

Everyman's Library finally reached volume one thousand on its golden jubilee, with the publication of Aristotle's *Metaphysics* on 29 March 1956. In 1960 Everyman Paperbacks were introduced. The postwar expansion of higher education created a demand for textbooks that was addressed by Everyman's University Library. First published in 1972, this series included several anthologies useful in the classroom, such as *Pre-*

Raphaelite Writing (1973), edited by Derek Stanford, and *Pressure Groups in Britain: A Reader* (1974), edited by Richard Kimber and J. J. Richardson.

Critics have questioned whether Everyman's Library fully represents the best that is known and thought in the world; Hugh Kenner, for example, had a hearty laugh over the inclusion of Adelaide A. Procter (1906), the early-Victorian poet who is remembered today only for writing "The Lost Chord" (1858). In 1956 E. F. Bozman, Dent's editorial director, conceded that some of the Victorian novelists, historians, and philosophers were already looking like relics. In selecting books, Rhys and the Dents had been guided by sales potential and by advice from British, American, and Canadian academics, and their choices were not always deathless. Everyman's Library set aside many volumes for the likes of Harrison Ainsworth, Edward Bulwer-Lytton, and R. D. Blackmore—though Blackmore's *Lorna Doone* (1908) proved to be among the top sellers of the entire series. Some readers, moreover, were put off by the sanctimonious air that surrounded Everyman's approach to literature—or, as J. M. Dent pronounced it, "litterchah."

Against such criticisms have to be set the millions of readers who were delighted to spend their shillings on Everyman volumes—among them D. H. Lawrence, who loved the early editions. Everyman's Library was an essential source of cheap texts for the Workers' Educational Association, and generations of university instructors should be grateful to the Dent firm for keeping obscure works inexpensive and in print. The greatest testimonial to the series is its stupendous sales record: by 1975 Everyman's Library had published 1,239 volumes, 64 of them in Everyman's University Library and 348 in paperback. Total sales were more than 60 million.

In 1938 Everyman's best-sellers were Dickens's *The Personal History of David Copperfield* (1907) and the works of Shakespeare, at about three hundred thousand copies each. Just behind them ranked Austen's *Northanger Abbey and Persuasion* (1906), Thackeray's *Vanity Fair* (1908), Peter Mark Roget's *Thesaurus of English Words and Phrases* (1912), and Dickens's *The Pickwick Papers* (1912). First printings usually ranged between eight thousand and twelve thousand copies, reprints from four thousand to twenty thousand copies. Some titles sold as few as four thousand: in 1934 Dent's own list of "worst-sellers" included Scott's *Castle Dangerous* (1906) and *St. Ronan's Well*

(1909), Ruskin's *Pre-Raphaelitism* (1907), George Herbert's *The Temple and A Priest to the Temple* (1908), Thackeray's *Roundabout Papers* (1914), Balzac's *The Country Parson* (1914), and *The Poems of Charles Kingsley* (1927).

Of course, the Dent firm had other publishing activities besides Everyman's Library. In the fall of 1904 Dent inaugurated the *Temple Classics Magazine* to supplement the series, but it only lasted for five issues. He tried again with *Everyman*, a penny literary weekly designed "to foster a taste for books among the proletariat." The editor was Dr. Charles Sarolea, chairman of the French department at the University of Edinburgh. The first issue, for 12 October 1912, sold 150,000 copies on the strength of contributions by Chesterton, Alfred Russel Wallace, Norman Angell, and Saintsbury, as well as articles on J. M. Synge, Oscar Wilde, Tolstoy, George Meredith, and Bennett. The magazine later published contributions by Shaw, Wells, Beatrice Webb, John Masefield, John Middleton Murry, J. C. Squire, Richard Aldington, and Lawrence; nevertheless, circulation fell off. Sarolea also edited Dent's Collection Gallia, a series of French classics begun in 1913; he seriously overextended himself between his editing, teaching, and journalism, and there was growing friction between Dent and Sarolea until the latter purchased *Everyman* in 1914. It ceased publication in 1920.

In 1925 the Dent firm began publishing the *Bookmark* as a threepenny quarterly devoted mainly to publicizing the firm's new books. *Everyman*, edited by C. B. Purdom, was revived as a twopenny weekly on 31 January 1929; but again it was a financial failure, and Sir Robert Donald bought it in January 1932. When *Everyman* closed down again in 1935, the Dent company renamed its house organ the *Bookmark and Everyman* and continued to publish it until 1938.

In 1913 Dent began distributing French-language books in France, first through an agent and then (from December 1915) through its own Paris office. Marketing of the Collection Gallia and the Collection Shakespeare (translations of the bard's works into French) was fraught with difficulties, including employees who embezzled funds. A Toronto branch of the firm was set up in 1913 under the management of Henry Button, but it did not become profitable until the 1920s. A Canadian Aldine House was opened in 1926 at 224 Bloor Street West, opposite McMaster University. An independent Canadian

company was formed in April 1935, with Button and Hugh Dent on the board of directors.

In 1913 Everyman's Library was supplemented by the Wayfarers' Library, devoted to modern literature. The company continued to publish works by important contemporary authors, including *A Sienese Painter of the Franciscan Legend* (1909), by Bernhard Berenson, whom J. M. Dent had met in Florence; *The South Country* (1909), by Edward Thomas; *The Street of Today* (1911), by John Masefield; *Notes on Novelists* (1914), by Henry James; *A Boy in Eirinn* (1915), by Padraic Colum; *Egotism in German Philosophy* (1916), by Santayana; and Mary Webb's *Cordial of Earth* (1916) and *The Spring of Joy* (1917). In 1917 Henri Barbusse's Prix Goncourt novel *Le Feu* (1916) appeared in translation as *Under Fire*; for J. M. Dent, who had lost two sons in combat, it told the horrifying truth about the war. Other ventures into Continental literature included two volumes of plays by Luigi Pirandello (1923, 1925) and *Dostoevsky*, by André Gide (1925).

Dent published the late works of W. H. Hudson, including his autobiographical *Far Away and Long Ago* (1918), *Birds in Town and Village* (1919), *Dead Man's Pluck; and An Old Thorn* (1920), *Birds of La Plata* (1920), and *A Traveller in Little Things* (1921). The company also took over earlier books by Hudson, though they did not sell well. In 1922 author and publisher argued over royalties, with Dent pointing out that Hudson's works had earned only about six hundred pounds for the firm. Nevertheless, Dent offered one thousand pounds for Hudson's last book, *A Hind in Richmond Park* (1922).

Dent published Conrad's *'Twixt Land and Sea Tales* (1912) after it had been rejected by Methuen. Dent would also put out Conrad's *Within the Tides* (1915), *The Shadow-Line* (1917), *The Rescue* (1920), *Notes on Life and Letters* (1921), *Suspense* (1925), *Last Essays* (1926), and a uniform edition of his works (1923-1928).

The company expanded its activities in educational publishing with the Kings' Treasuries of Literature, begun in 1920. Sir Arthur Quiller-Couch edited these school anthologies of the writings of great authors; one of the first volumes was *A Shakespeare Progress* (1920), compiled by J. M. Dent himself. The firm ventured into science texts in 1928, history in 1931, and geography in 1931.

J. M. Dent died on 9 May 1926; he had retired from a managerial role in the business two years earlier. His sons Hugh and Jack, and Jack's

Aldine House, built for J. M. Dent and Sons in 1911 (drawing by the architect, E. Keynes Purchase; from The Memoirs of J. M. Dent, 1849-1926, *1928)*

son F. J. Martin Dent, had, together with the founder, constituted the board of directors; the firm had been known as J. M. Dent and Sons since 1909. Jack had joined the company in 1915 and had supervised the Temple Press; Martin had come in 1924 and directed the production department. After the death of J. M. Dent the board was expanded to include W. G. Taylor, who had been secretary of the firm since 1916; Bozman, editorial director from 1926; and Button. In 1934 A. J. Hoppé, head of sales and publicity since 1925, and H. W. March, chief of the educational department, joined the board. Hugh R. Dent served as chairman from 1926 to 1938, followed by Taylor from 1938 to 1963; Taylor was also managing director from 1934 to 1955. Taylor's two posts were taken over by F. J. Martin Dent. When Rhys died in 1946 the direction of Everyman's Library was assumed by Bozman, who retired in 1965.

J. M. Dent and Sons founded the Phoenix Book Company in 1928 to sell books on the installment plan. Headed by Hugh Dent, the subsidiary began with sets of works of Dumas père, Dickens, and Scott, and later marketed *The Encyclopaedia Britannica* and *The Cambridge Ancient History* as

well as Everyman's Library and Penguin paperbacks.

Phoenix was in turn the parent company of the Readers Union, a book club founded in 1937. It published books by Joyce Cary, Winston Churchill, Forster, Ernest Hemingway, Aldous Huxley, W. Somerset Maugham, Sean O'Casey, Bertrand Russell, John Steinbeck, Dylan Thomas, James Thurber, Evelyn Waugh, Wells, and Woolf at two shillings, sixpence per volume. The early years were a struggle, but the general book hunger during World War II gave the club a boost. By 1947 it had distributed almost two hundred titles and was selling more than four hundred thousand books a year, and by the early 1950s membership was almost forty thousand. In 1970 the Readers Union was sold to the firm of David and Charles. The Phoenix Book Company faded away during World War II, but in 1947 it was revived as Phoenix House, a general publishing imprint.

In 1932 Dent founded the Open-Air Library, which republished the works of Hudson, Edward Thomas, and other observers of country life. During World War I the firm had virtually given up publishing children's books, but in 1935 M. C. Carey of the Junior Book Club was hired

Laugharne 68

Boat House,
Laugharne,
Carmarthenshire
11ᵗʰ September, 1953

Dear E.F. Bozman,

I was sorry I wasn't able to see you when I came to London last; I'd a very short time there — just for a little broadcast, and to see about my daughter's new school — and David Higham told me that, so far as he knew, there was nothing very urgent to discuss. I wanted to meet you anyway; and I do hope now we'll be able to lunch together before I go to the States early in October.

Well before I leave, I'll have finished the final corrections and amplifications of "Under Milk Wood". I think it's much better now — (it sounds as though it had been ill). One of the reasons I'm going to America is to take part in three public readings of it, with a professional cast, at the Poetry Centre, New York. (The other, and main, reason is to go to California to begin work with Stravinsky on a new opera). And, when I return some time in December, I hope that it can be given one or more reading-performances, most likely on a Sunday night, in London; with any luck, I'll be able to get firstrate Welsh actors to read it. Higham, in the meantime, and as soon as he has my complete version, will see to it that someone like Starck has a chance of reading it with this in mind. "Under Milk Wood" will also be broadcast next year, in full, and it should be possible to arrange █████ this broadcast to happen about the same time as publication. I myself have good hopes altogether of the success of Milk Wood; and I'm _very_ _very_ grateful to you for taking it over.

About the Book of Stories — I suggest, tentatively, the title of "Early One Morning," the title of one of the stories: — I have reckoned out that there are now eleven of these, including

First page of a letter from Dylan Thomas to E. F. Bozman, editorial director of J. M. Dent and Sons, written less than a month before Thomas's death (Sotheby's auction catalogue, 23 and 24 July 1987)

to build up a juvenile list. Among the books she published were Noel Streatfield's *Ballet Shoes* (1936) and *Tennis Shoes* (1937). The Aldine Library, a series of inexpensive reprints of modern books, was begun in 1938.

To keep pace with modern scholarship the New Temple Shakespeare was introduced to replace the old series in 1934. It was edited by M. R. Ridley, with wood engravings and layout by Eric Gill. On Gill's suggestion Dent published a fine four-volume edition of the New Testament (1934-1936), edited by M. R. James. Hand typeset by the firm of Hague and Gill, it was illustrated with Gill's woodcuts. Sales were not sufficient to warrant proceeding with the Old Testament. In 1936 Dent bought a share of Hague and Gill, moved its workshop from Piggots to High Wycombe, and supplied it with steady composition work.

Dent published Henry Green's first novel, *Blindness* (1926), as well as the literary history and criticism of Van Wyck Brooks. In addition to producing books for the masses, the company built up a strong list of proletarian writers, including Thomas Okey, a basket weaver who became professor of Italian at Cambridge University; the collier-novelists F. C. Boden and Roger Dataller; the farm laborer Fred Kitchen; the journalist Rowland Kenney; and Labour party politicians James Griffiths and Henry Snell. Dent was also the British publisher of three works by the black American author Zora Neale Hurston: *Their Eyes Were Watching God* (1938), *Voodoo Gods* (1939), and *The Man of the Mountain* (1941).

In 1935 Richard Church, Dent's poetry editor, was introduced to the work of Dylan Thomas. Church was at once fascinated and repelled by Thomas. He was willing to take a chance on the young and difficult Welshman, though he found Thomas's poetry surrealistic (which Thomas indignantly denied), too sexual, and often incomprehensible. (Thomas privately vilified Church as "a cliché-riddled humbug and pie-fingering hack.") Thomas had a contract with Dent by 1936, when *Twenty-five Poems* appeared in a first impression of 730 copies; there were three more printings by 1944. Church suggested that he write about his childhood, and the result was *Portrait of the Artist as a Young Dog* (1940). Dent also put out *The Map of Love* (1939), *Deaths and Entrances* (1946), and *Collected Poems 1934-1952* (1952), though the firm clearly felt more comfortable publishing the verse of Ogden Nash. An early draft of the novel *Adventures in the Skin Trade* was rejected by Dent's readers as "a fragment of frolicsome dirt." The firm scarcely earned any profits from Thomas during his lifetime: advances were paid out for books that lost money or were never written. In one of his last letters (11 September 1953) Thomas effusively thanked Bozman for taking on *Under Milk Wood* (1954) and tried to borrow another advance without the knowledge of his agent, David Higham (Bozman refused).

Dent was able to take advantage of the enormous posthumous interest in Thomas. It published his *Quite Early One Morning* (1954); *A Prospect of the Sea and Other Stories and Prose Writings* (1955); *Letters to Vernon Watkins* (1957); *Miscellany: Poems Stories Broadcasts* (1963); an Everyman edition of his *Collected Poems* (1966); *Selected Letters of Dylan Thomas* (1966), edited by Constantine Fitzgibbon; Andrew Sinclair's dramatization of *Adventures in the Skin Trade* (1967); *A Child's Christmas in Wales* (1968), illustrated by Edward Ardizzone; *The Notebooks of Dylan Thomas* (1968); *Dylan Thomas: Early Prose Writings* (1971); *Dylan Thomas: The Poems* (1971); *The Outing* (1971); *The Collected Stories* (1983); *A Visit to Grandpa's and Other Stories* (1984); *The Collected Letters of Dylan Thomas* (1985), edited by Paul Ferris; *The Notebook Poems 1930-34* (1988), edited by Ralph Maud; and a new edition of *Collected Poems 1934-1953* (1988), edited by Walford Davies and Maud. Dent also put out critical, biographical, and bibliographical studies of the poet, including *The Life of Dylan Thomas* (1965), by Fitzgibbon.

In the 1970s new fiction gradually faded from Dent's list. Everyman Fiction was begun in 1983 as a series of paperback reprints of twentieth-century literature, among them Joyce Carol Oates's *Unholy Lives* (1983), J. G. Ballard's *The Drowned World* (1983), and Aharon Appelfeld's *Badenheim 1939* (1984). Also in 1983 another paperback series, Classic Thrillers, was launched with Sapper's (Herman Cyril McNeile) *Bulldog Drummond* and John Buchan's *Castle Gay*.

J. M. Dent and Sons was purchased by Weidenfeld and Nicolson in January 1988, and the Dent Staff was moved to Weidenfeld's offices at 91 Clapham High Street, London.

References:

J. M. Dent, *The House of Dent 1888-1938* (London: Dent, 1938);

Dent, *The Memoirs of J. M. Dent 1849-1926* (London & Toronto: Dent, 1928);

Paul Ferris, *Dylan Thomas* (London: Hodder & Stoughton, 1977);

A. J. Hoppé, *A Talk on Everyman's Library* (London: Dent, 1938);

Frederick R. Karl, *Joseph Conrad: The Three Lives* (London: Faber & Faber, 1979);

Hugh Kenner, *A Sinking Island: The Modern English Writers* (London: Barrie & Jenkins, 1988);

Ralph Maud, *Dylan Thomas in Print: A Bibliographical History* (London: Dent, 1970);

Ernest Rhys, *Everyman Remembers* (London: Dent, 1931; New York: Cosmopolitan, 1931);

Rhys, *Wales England Wed* (London: Dent, 1940);

J. Kimberley Roberts, *Ernest Rhys* (Cardiff: University of Wales Press, 1983);

Donald Armstrong Ross, ed., *The Reader's Guide to Everyman's Library*, fourth edition (London: Dent, 1976);

Frank Swinnerton, *Swinnerton: An Autobiography* (London: Hutchinson, 1937);

Dylan Thomas, *The Collected Letters of Dylan Thomas*, edited by Paul Ferris (London: Dent, 1985);

James Thornton, *A Tour of the Temple Press* (London: Dent, 1935);

Ruth Tomalin, *W. H. Hudson: A Biography* (London: Faber & Faber, 1982).

Papers:

The Charles Sarolen papers, which deal with *Everyman* magazine, are at Edinburgh University Library. Some J. M. Dent records are held by Weidenfeld and Nicolson, London.

—Jonathan Rose

André Deutsch Limited

(London: 1951-   )

André Deutsch was one of several Central European refugees (others included George Weidenfeld, Walter Neurath, Paul Hamlyn, and Ernest Hecht) who brought a new spirit of enterprise to postwar British publishing. Born in Hungary on 15 November 1917, the son of a Jewish dentist, he was educated in Budapest, Vienna, and Zurich and acquired degrees in economics and political science. His love of English literature, together with the reactionary and anti-Semitic political climate in Hungary, induced him to immigrate to London in 1939, just before the outbreak of World War II. In 1941 he was interned for three months on the Isle of Man; there he met a fellow Hungarian, the publisher Ferenc Aldor, who introduced him to the publishing business. From 1942 to 1945 Deutsch worked for the firm of Nicholson and Watson. When his boss, John Roberts, turned down the manuscript for George Orwell's *Animal Farm*, Deutsch resolved to become a publisher on his own. Orwell then offered *Animal Farm* to Deutsch, but he was not yet ready to take it on; it was published in 1945 by Secker and Warburg.

In late 1945 Deutsch established the firm of Allan Wingate at cramped offices in Great Cumberland Street. He had only one-fifth of the fifteen thousand pounds then considered to be the minimum capital needed to start a new publishing house. He succeeded because of two early best-sellers: *How to Be an Alien* (1946), by his Hungarian friend George Mikes, and Norman Mailer's *The Naked and the Dead* (1949).

Throughout his career as a publisher Deutsch was closely assisted by Diana Athill in what she described as a "fraternal" relationship. There was, however, increasing friction with the other directors of Allan Wingate (Athill called it "guerrilla warfare"), and they compelled him to resign in August 1950.

Assisted by his friends Jack Newth, president of the Publishers' Association, and Edmond Seagrave, editor of the *Bookseller*, he set up the firm of André Deutsch Limited in 1951 with offices at 12 Thayer Street and about sixty-five hundred pounds in capital. Athill and Nicolas Bentley joined Deutsch as directors; Fred Kendall was added to the board later to provide financial expertise. The company published four books that autumn, including two notable successes: a symposium titled *Books Are Essential*, by Sir Norman Birkett and others, and Leah W. Leonard's *Jewish Cookery*. The following year the firm put out twenty-two books, two of them best-sellers: the memoirs of Franz von Papen and the *Reader's Digest Omnibus*, the latter selling eighty thousand copies within a year. Deutsch did, however, miss an opportunity to acquire a modern classic: the firm rejected the manuscript of William Golding's *Lord of the Flies*, which was published by Faber and Faber in 1954.

In 1955 Deutsch took over the Derek Verschoyle list and moved to that firm's offices at 12-14 Carlisle Street. He picked up from Verschoyle the illustrator and children's author Ludwig Bemelmans and went on to publish several of Bemelmans's "Madeline" books. In 1961 André Deutsch Limited relocated to 105 Great Russell Street and bought Grafton Books, which published textbooks on librarianship; it would be sold to Gower Publishing in 1981. Time/Life Incorporated bought a 40 percent share of the Deutsch firm in 1969, but Deutsch found the partnership irksome and soon bought back his equity. He remained an independent—something increasingly rare in the British publishing industry.

Deutsch renewed his connection with Mailer, publishing *Advertisements for Myself* (1961), *Deaths for the Ladies and Other Disasters* (1962), *The Presidential Papers* (1964), *An American Dream*

André Deutsch (center), with his fellow directors Nicolas Bentley and Diana Athill (photograph by Fay Godwin)

(1965), and *Cannibals and Christians* (1967). The early link with Mailer led to the acquisition of many other leading North American authors. The Canadian novelist Mordecai Richler contributed *The Apprenticeship of Duddy Kravitz* (1959). Philip Roth gave *Goodbye, Columbus* (1959) and *Letting Go* (1962) to André Deutsch Limited, but neither Deutsch nor Athill was impressed with his next novel, *When She Was Good*. They offered Roth only a modest advance, so he went to Jonathan Cape, which published the book in 1967. John Updike has remained loyal to the firm for three decades, from *Rabbit, Run* (1961) through *The Centaur* (1963), *Couples* (1968), *Bech: A Book* (1970), *Rabbit Redux* (1972), *A Month of Sundays* (1975), *Rabbit Is Rich* (1982), *Bech Is Back* (1983), *The Witches of Eastwick* (1984), *Roger's Version* (1986), *S* (1988), and *Rabbit at Rest* (1990). Deutsch also brought the work of Jack Kerouac to English readers: *On the Road* (1958), *The Dharma Bums* (1959), *The Subterraneans* (1960), *Lonesome Traveller* (1962), *Big Sur* (1963), *Visions of Gerard, and Tristessa* (1964), *Desolation Angels* (1966), *Satori in Paris* (1967), *Vanity of Duluoz: An*

Adventurous Education, 1935-46 (1969), *Visions of Cody* (1973), *Maggie Cassidy* (1974), and *Doctor Sax* (1977). George Plimpton chronicled his amateurish efforts to play professional sports in *Out of My League* (1962), *Paper Lion* (1968), *The Bogey Man* (1969), *Mad Ducks and Bears* (1974), *Shadow Box* (1978), and *Open Net* (1986). Deutsch also published works by Nelson Algren and Aaron Copland; Brian Moore's first five novels, beginning with *Judith Hearne* (1955); E. L. Doctorow's *Bad Man from Bodie* (1961); John Dos Passos's *Midcentury* (1961); several novels by Howard Fast, writing under the name E. V. Cunningham; and Muriel Rukeyser's *The Orgy* (1966).

Deutsch managed to secure both Andrei Sakharov's *Progress, Coexistence, and Intellectual Freedom* (1968) and Nikita Khrushchev's *Khrushchev Remembers* (1971). He published widely in the field of American politics, including Whittaker Chambers's *Witness* (1953), though most of his selections reflected his own liberal views. Thus Arthur M. Schlesinger, Jr., contributed *A Thousand Days* (1965), *The Bitter Heritage: Vietnam and American Democracy 1941-1966* (1967), *The Crisis of Confidence*

Deutsch (right) with his new partner, Tom Rosenthal, in 1984

(1969), *The Imperial Presidency* (1974), and *Robert Kennedy and His Times* (1978). Schlesinger introduced Deutsch to John Kenneth Galbraith, and Deutsch published Galbraith's *Economics, Peace and Laughter* (1971), a revised edition of *The New Industrial State* (1972), *A China Passage* (1973), *Economics and the Public Purpose* (1974), *A Life in Our Times* (1981), and the fourth edition of *The Affluent Society* (1985). The journalist Hugh Sidey wrote *John F. Kennedy: Portrait of a President* (1964) and *A Very Personal Presidency: Lyndon Johnson and the White House* (1968).

Deutsch continued to publish humor by Mikes, as well as the work of Bentley, David Caute, Mavis Gallant, Natalia Ginzburg, Man Ray, Jean Rhys, and Laurie Lee. He built up a large list of poets, including John Ashbery, Donald Davie, Geoffrey Hill, Elizabeth Jennings, and David Wright. The company also published children's books, books on crafts and hobbies, travel books, and cookbooks. In collaboration with Weidenfeld and Nicolson, Deutsch brought out the writings of Simone de Beauvoir: *The Long March* (1958), *Memoirs of a Dutiful Daughter* (1959), *Brigitte Bardot and the Lolita Syndrome*

(1960), *The Prime of Life* (1962), *Force of Circumstance* (1965), *A Very Easy Death* (1966), *Old Age* (1972), *All Said and Done* (1974), and *Adieux: Farewell to Sartre* (1984).

For a time the Caribbean was a good market for Deutsch, who published works by the historian Eric Williams and other West Indian authors. The most notable was V. S. Naipaul, who contributed a long series of works: *The Mystic Masseur* (1957), *The Suffrage of Elvira* (1958), *Miguel Street* (1959), *A House for Mr. Biswas* (1961), *The Middle Passage* (1962), *Mr. Stone and the Knights Companion* (1963), *An Area of Darkness* (1964), *The Mimic Men* (1967), *A Flag on the Island* (1967), *The Loss of Eldorado* (1969), *In a Free State* (1971), *The Overcrowded Barracoon* (1972), *Guerrillas* (1975), *India: A Wounded Civilisation* (1977), *A Bend in the River* (1979), *The Return of Eva Peron* (1980), *Among the Believers: An Islamic Journey* (1981), and *Finding the Centre* (1984).

Of all his achievements, Deutsch was particularly proud of founding the African Universities Press in Lagos, Nigeria, in 1962 and the East Africa Publishing House in Nairobi, Kenya, in 1964. Kenyan leader Thomas Joseph Mboya had

Deutsch at the time of his investiture as a Commander of the British Empire, 1989

him authors from both houses, including Paul Erdman, Carlos Fuentes, George V. Higgins, Dan Jacobson, Penelope Lively, and Gore Vidal. Thus André Deutsch Limited survived as a mid-sized independent publisher. By the end of the decade it was grossing more than four million pounds on about 150 titles a year.

In the 1980s André Deutsch Limited distributed satirical books for the magazine *Private Eye*, even though *Private Eye* rather nastily portrayed Rosenthal as Snipcock in its cartoon strip "Snipcock and Tweed" and lampooned Deutsch as a penny-pincher. As a young and grossly under-capitalized publisher, Deutsch had had to pester his employees to turn off lights and reuse envelopes. Nevertheless, he had been willing to sink a huge investment in a promising manuscript, as when he snapped up Peter Benchley's *Jaws* (1974).

Deutsch was able to build up two major publishing houses from scratch by dint of almost obsessive hard work. He had total confidence in his own judgment and was not one to delegate authority. One secret of his success was the personal contact he maintained with booksellers throughout the world.

In 1989 Deutsch was made a Commander of the British Empire. Another measure of the professional respect he commands is his seventieth birthday present, a portrait by Leonard Rosoman. More than four hundred friends, authors, publishing colleagues, and Deutsch staff people contributed to its purchase, oversubscribing by nearly ten thousand pounds.

Freedom and After (1963) and *The Challenge of Nationhood* (1970) published by the Deutsch firm.

Deutsch served as chairman and managing director of the company until 1984, when he arranged to share both posts with Tom Rosenthal and sold him a half share of the firm. Rosenthal bought the remaining share in 1987 and became sole chairman and managing director. Deutsch remained a director, though he had no active role in the business. Athill left the board of directors in 1987 but continued to work as literary adviser. Rosenthal had been chairman of Heinemann and of Secker and Warburg, and he brought with

References:

Diana Athill, *Instead of a Letter* (London: Chatto & Windus, 1963);

Ian Norrie, "Seventy not Out!," *Publishing News* (20 November 1987): 10;

Clarence Paget, "André Deutsch Ltd. at 25," *Publishers Weekly*, 210 (8 November 1976): 26-27;

Tom Rosenthal, "A Portrait of André," *Bookseller*, no. 4274 (20 November 1987): 2039-2040;

Liz Thomson, "Rosenthal's Way," *Publishing News* (1 June 1990): 6-7.

—*Jonathan Rose*

Doves Press
(London: 1899-1916)

The Doves Press was the product of the vision of T. J. Cobden-Sanderson, for whom its books were symbols of "a vision of Cosmic Order, Order wrought in rhythm and touched with Beauty and Delight." Thomas James Sanderson was born on 2 December 1840 in Northumberland. He entered Trinity College, Cambridge, in 1860 but left after three years, "refusing both honours and degree (I might, indeed, have failed to get either, but in fact I did not try)." He felt that the competitive system warped all university teaching.

From 1863 until 1871 Sanderson avoided choosing an occupation, spending a great portion of his time reading English literature and German philosophy. During this period he came to know William Morris. In 1871 he chose the law, "by way of stop-gap and to stay inquiries as to what I was doing." He did, however, undertake the arduous task of codifying all the powers, rights, and obligations of the London and North-Western Railway Company. Exhausted from this work, he traveled to Siena, Italy, where he met Annie Cobden, daughter of the politician Richard Cobden. They were married in 1882, and he changed his name to Cobden-Sanderson.

Cobden-Sanderson was greatly influenced by the socialism of his day, with its emphasis on the work of one's own hands. In June 1883 Morris's wife, Jane, suggested that Cobden-Sanderson become a bookbinder. He began to study binding under Roger de Coverly, and in June 1884 he opened his own workshop.

In 1888 Cobden-Sanderson organized a series of lectures held during the Arts and Crafts Exhibition Society's first show. It was in response to one of these lectures, given by Emery Walker, that William Morris decided to turn his hand to

T. J. Cobden-Sanderson in 1890, nine years before he founded the Doves Press

type design. In January 1891 he founded the Kelmscott Press in a cottage near his house in Hammersmith. By 1893 Morris needed more space for the press, and he persuaded Cobden-Sanderson to rent a house opposite as a bindery and to sublet the upper floors to him.

As a result, Cobden-Sanderson established the Doves Bindery, named for Doves Place and

IN THE BEGINNING
GOD CREATED THE HEAVEN AND THE EARTH. ⸿AND
THE EARTH WAS WITHOUT FORM, AND VOID; AND
DARKNESS WAS UPON THE FACE OF THE DEEP, & THE
SPIRIT OF GOD MOVED UPON THE FACE OF THE WATERS.
⸿And God said, Let there be light: & there was light. And God saw the light,
that it was good: & God divided the light from the darkness. And God called
the light Day, and the darkness he called Night. And the evening and the
morning were the first day. ⸿And God said, Let there be a firmament in the
midst of the waters, & let it divide the waters from the waters. And God made
the firmament, and divided the waters which were under the firmament from
the waters which were above the firmament: & it was so. And God called the
firmament Heaven. And the evening & the morning were the second day.
⸿And God said, Let the waters under the heaven be gathered together unto
one place, and let the dry land appear: and it was so. And God called the dry
land Earth; and the gathering together of the waters called he Seas: and God
saw that it was good. And God said, Let the earth bring forth grass, the herb
yielding seed, and the fruit tree yielding fruit after his kind, whose seed is in
itself, upon the earth: & it was so. And the earth brought forth grass, & herb
yielding seed after his kind, & the tree yielding fruit, whose seed was in itself,
after his kind: and God saw that it was good. And the evening & the morning
were the third day. ⸿And God said, Let there be lights in the firmament of
the heaven to divide the day from the night; and let them be for signs, and for
seasons, and for days, & years: and let them be for lights in the firmament of
the heaven to give light upon the earth: & it was so. And God made two great
lights; the greater light to rule the day, and the lesser light to rule the night: he
made the stars also. And God set them in the firmament of the heaven to give
light upon the earth, and to rule over the day and over the night, & to divide
the light from the darkness: and God saw that it was good. And the evening
and the morning were the fourth day. ⸿And God said, Let the waters bring
forth abundantly the moving creature that hath life, and fowl that may fly
above the earth in the open firmament of heaven. And God created great
whales, & every living creature that moveth, which the waters brought forth
abundantly, after their kind, & every winged fowl after his kind: & God saw
that it was good. And God blessed them, saying, Be fruitful, & multiply, and
fill the waters in the seas, and let fowl multiply in the earth. And the evening
& the morning were the fifth day. ⸿And God said, Let the earth bring forth
the living creature after his kind, cattle, and creeping thing, and beast of the
earth after his kind: and it was so. And God made the beast of the earth after
his kind, and cattle after their kind, and every thing that creepeth upon the

27

Page from the Doves Bible, published in five volumes between 1903 and 1905

the Doves public house nearby, as a workshop where others could learn his trade. It opened in March 1893 with a staff of four: Charles McLeish, finisher; Charles Wilkinson, forwarder; Bessie Hooley, sewer; and Douglas Cockerell, apprentice. Cobden-Sanderson created the designs but left the actual binding to his staff.

Morris died in 1896, and the last Kelmscott Press book was published in March 1898. Not only had the Doves Bindery bound Kelmscott Press books, including forty-eight copies of *The Works of Geoffrey Chaucer* (1896), but the shop had rebound many of the books in Morris's personal library. In part to fill the void left by the closing of the Kelmscott Press, Cobden-Sanderson and Walker, with financing from Annie Cobden-Sanderson, founded the Doves Press in 1899. Walker designed a type for the press, working with photographic enlargements of the type used by Nicolas Jenson in his edition of Pliny's *Historia Naturalis* in 1476. The resulting type was a recreation of an ideal font of Jenson's type, not a mere reproduction. It was the only type used by the press.

The first book printed by the Doves Press was Tacitus's *Agricola*, begun in April 1900. Special paper, with a newly designed watermark of two doves and the initials *C-S* and *E-W*, was made by the firm of Joseph Batchelor and Son. The *Agricola* and an edition of T. J. Cobden-Sanderson's tract *The Ideal Book or Book Beautiful* were finished in October. For the third publication of the press, J. W. Mackail's address on the life of William Morris, Cobden-Sanderson directed his compositor J. H. Mason to print the first words of each section in red. The book was finished in April 1901. For an edition of John Milton's *Paradise Lost* (1902), Edward Johnston and Graily Hewitt drew in decorative initial letters in alternating blue and red; they are named in the colophon as "penmen." Shoulder notes were printed in red.

The best-known work of the Doves Press is *The English Bible*, generally known as the Doves Bible. It was published in five large volumes between June 1903 and June 1905. Printed in five hundred paper copies, sold for fifteen guineas, and two vellum copies, not for sale, it was purchased primarily by collectors. The spirit of the work was of unbending righteousness, formal and formidable, as was that of all the Doves Press books. The red headings and the initial letters drawn by Johnston cannot be considered decorations but are an integral part of the design. As

Cobden-Sanderson in 1916, the year he closed the Doves Press (drawing by William Rothenstein; from The Journals of T. J. Cobden-Sanderson, 1879-1922, *1922)*

Holbrook Jackson wrote in *The Eighteen Nineties* (1913), "there is nothing ... quite so effective as the first page of the Doves Bible, with its great red initial I dominating the left-hand margin of the opening chapter of Genesis like a symbol of the eternal wisdom and simplicity of the wonderful Book."

In August 1902 a quarrel began between Cobden-Sanderson and Walker concerning the nature of their partnership in the Doves Press. The primary source of friction was Cobden-Sanderson's developing paranoid concern that he alone have the use of the Doves Press type. In 1903 the partners drew up an agreement that named Cobden-Sanderson the sole proprietor of the press but gave Walker the right to have a font of the Doves type for himself if their partnership was dissolved. In January 1906 Cobden-Sanderson called for an end to the partnership and asked Walker to give up his right to the type. In June 1909, just before the matter was to go to trial, Sydney Cockerell proposed that whichever partner outlived the other would get the type.

Cobden-Sanderson and Walker agreed, but Cobden-Sanderson wrote to Cockerell, "I am, what [Walker] does not appear to realize, a Visionary and a Fanatic, and against a Visionary and a Fanatic he will beat himself in vain." In 1912 Cobden-Sanderson began the destruction of the Doves Press type by throwing the matrices into the Thames from Hammersmith Bridge. On 31 August 1916 he began to throw the type itself into the river, a process that continued throughout the fall and winter as he made many secret midnight pilgrimages to the bridge. When the last page of the last book of the press, the *Catalogue Raisonné* (1916), had been printed, he threw the last of the type into the river. In 1917 Cobden-Sanderson returned his attention to the Doves Bindery. In May 1921 he completed a pattern for binding a copy of John Ruskin's notes on the artists Samuel Prout and William Hunt. In September he closed the bindery. He died on 7 September 1922; his last book, *Cosmic Vision*, was published that year by his son.

The stark simplicity and cleanness of Doves Press books, rather than Morris's extravagant designs, became the model for modern commercial book design. None of the Doves Press books was illustrated, and the uniformity of their type is only relieved by the use of red for headings, initial letters, shoulder notes, and, on occasion, passages of text. The work of the Doves Press shows little development, since, as Francis Meynell pointed out in 1948, Cobden-Sanderson's "ideal" was attained at the very start, as far as it was attainable.

Cobden-Sanderson best defined his ideal in his *Catalogue Raisonné*: "But beyond the immediate purposes of the Press—the solution of typographical problems and the monumental presentment of some of the literary creations of genius—there has always been another and a much greater purpose. . . . In the beginning God created Life, and the Life was with God, and the Life was God. And it is this Life, this Life of each and all of us, which in the language of the press we must Compose, and in the language of the Publisher, Publish."

References:

T. J. Cobden-Sanderson, *The Journals of Thomas James Cobden-Sanderson, 1879-1922* (London: Cobden-Sanderson, 1922);

Colin Franklin, *The Private Presses* (Chester Springs, Pa.: Dufour Editions, 1969);

Holbrook Jackson, *The Eighteen Nineties* (London: Richards, 1913);

Kelmscott, Doves and Ashendene: The Private Press Credos with an Introduction by Will Ransom (New York: The Typophiles, 1952);

Francis Meynell, *English Printed Books* (London: Collins, 1948);

Norman H. Strouse and John Dreyfus, *C-S: The Master Craftsman* (Harper Woods, Mich.: Adagio Press, 1969).

—Jennifer B. Lee

Gerald Duckworth and Company Limited
(London: 1924-   )
Gerald Duckworth and Company
(London: 1898-1924)

Gerald de l'Etang Duckworth was born in 1871 and educated at Eton and at Clare College, Cambridge. After the death of his father, Herbert Duckworth, his mother, Julia, married Sir Leslie Stephen, editor of the *Cornhill* magazine and later of the *Dictionary of National Biography*. Duckworth's half sisters were thus Vanessa Stephen (later Vanessa Bell) and Virginia Stephen (Later Virginia Woolf). In 1898 Duckworth set up his publishing business at Henrietta Street, Covent Garden. A. R. Waller, a literary adviser and bookman, left the firm of J. M. Dent to join Duckworth.

In his first list, issued in May, Duckworth included his stepfather's Ford Lectures, *English Literature and Society in the Eighteenth Century* (1898); a translation of August Strindberg's *The Father* (1899); John Percival's *Agricultural Botany* (1900); Henry James's *In the Cage* (1898); and *Jocelyn* (1898), by the unknown John Sinjohn, an early pseudonym for John Galsworthy.

It was at Waller's instigation that Galsworthy's fiction was published by Duckworth at all. Legend has it that Duckworth, an inveterate first-nighter, turned down *The Man of Property* (1906)—the first of the novels that were to become *The Forsyte Saga* (1922)—with the words: "Stick to plays, my man, stick to plays." (The Forsyte Saga and its component novels—*The Man of Property*, *In Chancery* [1920], and *To Let* [1921]—were published by William Heinemann.) Galsworthy was a lifelong friend of Duckworth,

Gerald Duckworth with his half sister, Virginia Stephen (left), and his sister, Stella, in 1896

whose firm published all of his plays from *The Silver Box* in 1909 to *The Roof* in 1929. An omnibus edition of Galsworthy's plays in an octavo volume of 1,152 pages priced at only eight shillings, sixpence a copy, was published in October 1929 in an edition of forty thousand copies, which Galsworthy thought was far too many; twenty thousand more copies were called for by Christmas, and a total of more than one hundred thousand were sold. A limited edition of the book was also produced, and Galsworthy was extremely irritated at being asked to sign all twelve hundred fifty copies. On being told that he would receive a royalty of fifteen shillings, ninepence on each copy, he placed his watch on the table and said: "It will be interesting to see how long it takes me to earn £984 7s. 6d."

Plays were always an important part of the Duckworth list; volumes in the Modern Plays series, begun in 1898, in distinctive square foolscap format with olive green covers, were usually produced quickly to capitalize on the interest generated by the plays' first London runs. Dramatists represented included Galsworthy, Strindberg, Eden Phillpotts, Alfred Sutro, Patrick Hastings, Aleksandr Ostrovsky, and Gordon Daviot.

Elinor Glyn first appeared on the Duckworth lists in 1900 with her then-daring book *The Visits of Elizabeth*, which was followed by *The Vicissitudes of Evangeline* (1905), *Halcyone* (1912), and *Three Weeks* (1907). The latter novel was considered so shocking that it led to the resignation of one of Duckworth's salesmen, who refused to have anything to do with the book. Legend has it that Glyn would read each new novel aloud to Duckworth in her conservatory after lunch. She died in 1943; despite being one of the best-known romantic authors of the Edwardian era, she is now barely remembered.

In 1901 Waller left Duckworth to become secretary to the Syndics of the Cambridge University Press, where he edited the *Cambridge History of English Literature* (1907-1927). His name was remembered in Duckworth's cable address, "Gerwalduck." He was replaced by George Harry Milsted, who had joined the firm in 1900. In the early years Milsted was a familiar figure driving himself daily to and from Henrietta Street in a phaeton. Until his retirement half a century later he continued to arrive at the office in brown bowler and Harris tweeds.

Also joining the firm in 1901, from William Heinemann, was Edward Garnett; his wife, Constance, was a well-known translator of Russian nov-

els, and he wrote several volumes of plays, novels, and critical works. He served Duckworth as a reader until 1920. Publishers' professional readers are usually anonymous; they have no legal power or responsibility, yet they can greatly affect the authors they recommend and the publishing houses they advise. Garnett was one of the greatest, and he was certainly the best-known reader of his time. Authors he brought to the firm included W. H. Hudson, Charles M. Doughty, Maksim Gorky, R. B. Cunninghame Grahame, Dorothy Richardson, and D. H. Lawrence. Garnett had met Hudson on his last day at Heinemann; he had been trying to persuade Heinemann to publish Hudson's collection of short stories, *El Ombu*, but to no avail. The book made its appearance in the Duckworth list in 1902.

Hudson's South American romances and *The Roadmender* (1902), by Michael Fairless (pseudonym of Margaret Fairless Barber, a social worker who died of tuberculosis at the age of thirty-two) paved the way for other books with a feeling for nature and the simple life by Richard Jefferies, Eric Muspratt, H. M. Tomlinson, and W. H. Davies. The firm failed, however, to publish Davies's best-known book, *The Autobiography of a Super Tramp*, because it could not accept certain modifications to the standard agreement suggested by George Bernard Shaw, who wrote the preface. The book was published in 1908 by Fifield.

Doughty's *The Dawn in Britain* (1906-1907), an epic poem in six volumes, was published two volumes at a time, the last two appearing in January 1907. Doughty called the book his life's work. His *Travels in Arabia Deserta* had been published in an edition of five hundred copies by Cambridge University Press in 1888; with Doughty's help, Garnett edited a two-volume abridgment titled *Wanderings in Arabia*, which Duckworth published in 1908.

Apart from bringing some illustrious authors to Duckworth, Garnett also initiated the inexpensive Popular Library of Art series—pocket-sized books of biography and criticism with forty to fifty illustrations in each two-hundred-page volume. The series, begun in 1902, was edited by Eugénie Sellars Strong, the wife of S. Arthur Strong, librarian to the House of Lords and to the duke of Devonshire at Chatsworth.

An important contributor to the Popular Library of Art was Ford Madox Ford, who wrote volumes on Dante Gabriel Rossetti (1902), Hans Holbein the Younger (1905), and the Pre-Raphaelite Brotherhood (1907). He was the founder of the *English Review*, which was first published by Duckworth in 1908 and was edited by Ford and Joseph Conrad. Ford also started the *Transatlantic Review* in Paris in 1924; it, too, was for a time distributed by Duckworth. Other Ford books published by Duckworth include *The Heart of the Country* (1906), *The Marsden Case* (1923), and *No More Parades* (1925).

Studies in Theology was begun in 1907 as a series of interdenominational religious books for the clergy, divinity students, and laymen. It was edited by Dr. Stuart J. Reid until he retired in 1914. Early contributors to the series included W. R. Inge, A. S. Peake, Sydney Cave, and A. C. McGiffert. Dr. A. W. Harrison, principal of Westminster College, succeeded Reid as editor and remained until his death in 1946, when the position was taken by Dr. Nathaniel Micklem, principal of Mansfield College, Oxford.

In June 1904 Jonathan Cape joined Gerald Duckworth and Company as a salesman. He became manager in 1909, and for the first two years of World War I he ran the company while Duckworth was at the Ministry of Munitions and Milsted was in the army. Cape left Duckworth in 1920 to found his own highly successful publishing firm, taking Garnett with him. Cape's successor as manager was G. Belton Cobb, who remained barely two years before leaving to join Longmans, Green and Company. In his place came A. G. Lewis from the firm of T. Fisher Unwin.

Thomas Balston, O.B.E., M.C., later to become the biographer of the eccentric brothers John and Jonathan Martin (the romantic painter and the incendiary of York, respectively), became a partner in the firm in 1923. Before the war he had trained with T. Fisher Unwin, and he had joined Duckworth in 1921. His interest in the literary avant-garde was reflected in the firm's publications of the 1920s and early 1930s. They included early work by Evelyn Waugh; practically everything produced by Edith, Osbert, and Sacheverell Sitwell; and the complete works of Ronald Firbank, which Duckworth took over after the author's death in 1926.

Waugh, just graduated from Oxford, was commissioned by Duckworth in 1928 to write a book on Rossetti; this invitation was probably extended in response to Waugh's privately printed essay on the Pre-Raphaelites, which had appeared in 1926. Shortly after, the firm received

the typescript for part of Waugh's first novel, *Decline and Fall*. It was accepted, but when the book was completed the publisher suggested some changes. The result was that Waugh took the book to Chapman and Hall, where his father, Arthur Waugh, was managing director; it was published in 1928. Duckworth did publish Waugh's travel books *Labels* (1930), *Remote People* (1931), *Ninety-two Days* (1934), and the collection *When the Going Was Good* (1946).

The Sitwells came to Duckworth in the mid 1920s when their first publisher, Grant Richards, was having financial difficulties. Between 1926 and 1933 Duckworth published almost all their books.

D. H. Lawrence, one of the most controversial authors of the twentieth century, first appeared on the Duckworth list in 1912 with *The Trespassers*. His autobiographical *Sons and Lovers* (1913) was followed by *The Prussian Officer, and Other Stories* (1915), *Twilight in Italy* (1916), and *Amores: Poems* (1916). Lawrence's first novel, *The White Peacock* (1911), first published by Heinemann, was transferred to Duckworth in 1914.

Virginia Woolf, Gerald Duckworth's half sister, rewrote *The Voyage Out* several times before she submitted it to Duckworth; Garnett wrote an enthusiastic report on it, and it was published in 1915. It received good reviews and had moderate sales of about fifteen hundred copies. Her *Night and Day* was published by Duckworth in 1919. In 1917 she and her husband, Leonard Woolf, had set up the Hogarth Press partly as therapy for Virginia, who had suffered bouts of severe mental disturbance since the death of her mother in 1895. Originally the press was to be a printing hobby, but by 1922 it had expanded into a small publishing business. The Woolfs decided to publish Virginia's *Jacob's Room* themselves; Duckworth did not object. Later they bought back the rights in and stock of the two books Duckworth had previously published.

In 1924 Gerald Duckworth became a limited company. Anthony Powell joined the company as literary editor in 1926, and Alan Harris arrived from George Bell and Sons in 1929 to become general editor. So began a vigorous ten-year period of new authors and ideas. Apart from Powell himself, whose first book, *Afternoon Men*, was published by Duckworth in 1931, novelists whose works were published by the company included Godfrey Winn, Barbara Cartland, Harold Acton, and Elizabeth Goudge. In Powell's novel *What's Become of Waring?*, published by

Cassell in 1939, the publishing firm of Judkins and Judkins is based on Duckworth. Powell initiated three series for Duckworth: the New Reader's Library in 1927 and the Great Lives series and the Hundred Years series in 1933. The New Reader's Library was an updated version of the Reader's Library, which had first appeared in 1912. The Reader's Library consisted of crown octavo volumes of up to 350 pages; the New Reader's Library volumes were pocket-sized, reflecting the change in readers' habits.

Humor, children's books, and illustration had not appeared to any large degree on the Duckworth lists, but the 1920s and 1930s saw an explosion of talent in these areas. Duckworth commissioned illustrations from well-known wood engravers, including Paul Nash, Ethelbert White, Robert Gibbings, Vivien Gribble, Clare Leighton, and Eric Ravilious. John Piper's *Brighton Aquatints* (1939), with a preface by Lord Alfred Douglas, was something of a publishing event, since no book of aquatints had appeared for many decades. The plates for the trade edition of *Brighton Aquatints* were printed by the last craftsman in London familiar with the tricky aquatint process, and fifty sets were hand-colored by the artist for a limited edition. A second book of aquatint reproductions, this one of drawings of Stowe House near Buckingham, was published ten years later; it, too, was a limited edition hand-colored by the artist.

Among the authors and illustrators who contributed to the humor and children's books on Duckworth's lists were G. L. Stampa, Lawson Wood, H. M. Bateman, Will Owen, and W. Heath Robinson. A revival of interest in Robinson in the 1970s caused several compilations of his work to be published, including *Railway Ribaldry* (1974), *Heath Robinson at War* (1978), *The Best of Heath Robinson* (1982), and *Great British Industries* (1985). Robinson's brother, Charles, contributed some fine watercolor drawings to an edition of Oscar Wilde's *The Happy Prince and Other Tales* in 1913. Five years later Duckworth published Hilaire Belloc's *Cautionary Tales for Children*, illustrated by "B.T.B." (Lord Basil Blackwood). Other books by Belloc included *The Bad Child's Book of Beasts* (1903; originally privately published in 1896 by Alden in Oxford at the author's expense), *More Peers* (1923; originally published by Swift in 1911), *A Moral Alphabet* (1932; first published by Edward Arnold in 1899), and an omnibus edition of all Belloc's humorous poetry, *Cautionary Verses*—without the illustrations by B.T.B. and Nicolas Bentley—in 1939.

Balston left Duckworth in 1934; he had never forgiven the firm for the loss of Waugh's *Decline and Fall*, which had happened while he was away on vacation in 1928. On 28 September 1937 Gerald Duckworth died while on vacation in Milan. Patrick Crichton-Stuart, after training with an Oxford printer, joined the firm as a learner in 1937. The following year he and Mervyn (later Lord) Horder together bought an interest in Duckworth. Horder had worked for the London branch of the Edinburgh firm Thomas Methuen and Nelson and Sons. Probably as a result of Horder's connections with Nelson, in 1939 an arrangement was made for that firm to handle worldwide distribution of Duckworth books. Editorially, the two firms remained separate, though Nelson did have a seat on the Duckworth board. When Nelson's London offices on Paternoster Row were destroyed in a German air raid in December 1940, the firm moved into Duckworth's premises at 3 Henrietta Street; it remained there until 1959, when it moved to 36 Park Street.

Duckworth did not escape the war unscathed. Just a month before Nelson's offices were bombed, Duckworth's entire stock of unbound books (four hundred thousand copies of six hundred titles) was lost when the firm's warehouse in Enfield was destroyed in an air raid; war damage insurance fell far short of covering the company's losses. In 1946 Crichton-Stuart and Horder returned from military service. That year the Citadel Press was founded at 3 Henrietta Street by E. A. Mundy, a former Duckworth employee. Under license from Duckworth, the Citadel Press republished several titles that would otherwise have remained out of print.

Over the next twenty years Duckworth added to its lists omnibus editions of the works of Anton Chekov (1949), Strindberg (1949), Henrik Ibsen (1950), and Ivan Turgenev (1951). It also set up the Colet Library of Modern Christian Thought and Teaching under the editorship of W. R. Matthews, Dean of St. Paul's Cathedral, in 1947. The volumes were intended to give guidance on the relevance of Christianity to modern problems and included works in philosophy, classics, history, psychology, economics, archaeology, and anthropology.

In 1968 Lord Horder sold the company to a partnership of Colin Haycraft and Timothy Simon. In 1971 Simon died of pneumonia while on a business trip to New York, and Haycraft became controlling shareholder. A year later, with the impending redevelopment of Covent Garden, the office at 3 Henrietta Street was given up. It appeared as the murderer's lair in Alfred Hitchcock's film *Frenzy* (1972).

The firm moved to more spacious premises in Camden Town. The twenty-two-sided Victorian building was once owned by the piano makers Collard and Collard; this history is reflected in the address: The Old Piano Factory, 43 Gloucester Crescent.

In an age of takeovers and specialization, Duckworth remains one of the few independent general publishers in existence. It has a wide range of intellectual interests, a flair for diversification, and a tradition of close editorial contact with books and authors. All operations, from editorial to shipping, are housed under one roof. Books are usually commissioned, and literary agents are not used. No more than fifty books are produced a year. The mix is about 25 percent fiction and 75 percent academic. Many of the academic books are written by Oxford University scholars, including Hugh Lloyd-Jones, Regius

Professor of Greek; Michael Dummett, Wykeham Professor of Logic; W. G. Forrest, Wykeham Professor of Ancient History; and Sir Kenneth Dover, president of Corpus Christi College. In 1989 Richard Sorabji, professor of ancient philosophy at the University of London, started a new series, Articles on Aristotle; forty volumes are envisioned. The series of translations aims to fill an important gap in the history of European thought. Among important writers of fiction is Beryl Bainbridge, who has been on the firm's lists since 1972. In 1989 Duckworth put out an omnibus containing her first three novels to be published by the firm; one of these novels, *The Bottle Factory Outing* (1974), was the winner of the Guardian Fiction Prize. Her *An Awfully Big Adventure* also came out in 1989.

References:
Fifty Years 1898-1948 (London: Duckworth, 1948);
George Jefferson, *Edward Garnett: A Life in Literature* (London: Cape, 1982).

—Geraldine Beare

Edinburgh University Press
(Edinburgh: 1948-   )

In 1943 the Senatus of Edinburgh University, at the urging of Professors William Calder and Sydney Newman, resolved to establish a publishing imprint for the university. According to the resolution, the press's "primary object would be the publication of commercially unremunerative research work, performed by members of the University and others. Part of the cost of such publication would be recovered from the issue of textbooks and other scholarly literature which commands a ready market. Examples elsewhere have shown that the presence in a University of a wisely conducted Press stimulates intellectual activity, canalises its results, and more than pays its cost in the reputation and influence it brings to the University." Implementation of the proposal was delayed until after World War II. In 1948 Edinburgh University Press published its first three titles: R. A. R. Gresson's *Essentials of General Cytology*; *Renart: Le Lai de l'Ombre*, edited by John Orr; and D. E. Rutherford's *Substitutional Analysis*. These works illustrate the scholarly yet unexciting outcome of the worthy but pedestrian objectives which the Senatus had set the press in its 1943 resolution. Georges Poulet's *Études sur le Temps Humain* (1949), however, was awarded the Prix Sainte-Beuve and proved to be a seminal work in critical theory.

Three factors coincided to raise the general standards of the press and to increase its impact on Scotland and the scholarly community. The first was the appointment in 1952 of Archie Turnbull as press secretary (managing director). He brought a professionalism and an enthusiasm that had hitherto been lacking. Titles such as Richard Bell's *Introduction to the Qur'an* (1953), Denys Hay's *Europe: The Emergence of an Idea* (1957), and Thomas Price and George Shepperson's *Independent African* (1958) became mainstays of the back list. Second, Professor William Croft Dickinson exercised his influence and skills in the Press Oversight Committee to establish the Edinburgh University Press as an important outlet for Scottish historical scholarship, laying the foundations for a much fuller understanding of the nation's history and contributing to the debate about its political status in a revival of the Enlightenment com-

David Martin, who became executive director of Edinburgh University Press in 1991

mitment to national rediscovery. Perhaps the title which best embodied that spirit was G. E. Davie's *The Democratic Intellect* (1961). Third, the expansion of higher education in the 1960s produced a parallel increase in the work of Edinburgh University Press: the number of new publications increased from fifteen in 1966 to twenty-four in 1971. Within such an optimistic climate, the Edinburgh University Press undertook the long-term development of key scholarly series such as Comparative Anatomy of the Primates (1954-1974), Flora of Turkey (1956-1985), and Machine Intelligence (1969-1973). It is currently planning the Edinburgh Edition of Sir Walter Scott's Waverley Novels, scheduled to start appearing in 1992. Its traditional values are also seen in the new edition of James, Viscount of Stair's *The Institutions of the Law of Scotland* (1981), edited by D. M. Walker, and in *A Hotbed of Genius: The Scottish Enlightenment 1730-1790* (1986), edited by David Daiches, Peter Jones, and Jean Jones. Under Martin Spencer, who succeeded Turnbull in 1987, the Edinburgh University Press took over the Polygon imprint in 1988 and as a result now publishes the *New Edinburgh Review* as well as a striking list of new Scottish fiction. After Spencer's death in 1990 the university decided to change the status of the press from that of a department to a wholly owned independent company. The executive chairman is David Martin, former managing director of Basil Blackwell, and the publisher is Vivian Bone. Perhaps the key characteristics of the Edinburgh University Press have been the consistent search for quality and an openness to innovation, both tempered with traditional Scots caution.

References:

Catalogue of an Exhibition of Books to Honour Archie Turnbull (Edinburgh: Edinburgh University Press, 1987);

Edinburgh and its College Printers (Edinburgh: Edinburgh University Press, 1973).

—*Alistair McCleery*

Eragny Press
(London: 1894-1914)

The Eragny Press, founded in 1894 by Lucien Pissarro and his wife, Esther Bensusan Pissarro, and named for Lucien Pissarro's home village in Normandy, France, differed from other British small presses of the 1890s and early 1900s in two major respects: more than half of its thirty-two books were in French, and it used unusual colored inks for texts as well as for Lucien's rainbow-hued wood engravings. By selecting the texts; designing illustrations, ornaments, and bindings; commissioning handmade paper; mixing the ink; and setting the type, the Pissarros became cocreators with their authors.

The son of Camille Pissarro, one of the founders of French impressionism, Lucien Pissarro was born in 1863. He lived in London with his parents in 1870 and returned in 1883 to study English; he moved to London in 1890 and married Esther Bensusan in 1892. Charles Ricketts's Vale Press published the Eragny Press's first book, *The Queen of the Fishes*, Margaret Rust's English translation of a French folktale. Between 1896 and 1903 the firm of Hacon and Ricketts published fifteen Eragny Press books, which the Pissarros printed using the Vale type designed by Ricketts.

A typical early Eragny book, such as Pierre de Ronsard's *Choix de Sonnets* (1902), began with an elaborate wood-engraved frontispiece, decorative borders, illuminated wood-cut initial letters, and fleurons used as line endings. The balance of the text was often printed without decorative

Lucien Pissarro (standing, center) in Belgium, 1894, the year he founded the Eragny Press with his wife. Seated is his father, the impressionist painter Camille Pissarro; standing are his brothers Rodo (left) and Félix.

borders and with only a few additional wood-engraved illustrations and illuminated wood-cut initial letters. When the Pissarros were free of financial constraints their books became more elaborate, with more illustrations and a wider use of color.

Believing that a proprietary typeface was essential to a printer-publisher, Pissarro began designing his own type, Brook, in 1901. He first used Brook for Thomas Sturge Moore's *A Brief Account of the Origin of the Eragny Press* (1903), published from the Pissarros' home, The Brook, in Hammersmith. Brook type is lighter in body than Vale; it draws less attention to itself, allowing the reader to concentrate on the ideas presented in the text and reinforced in Lucien Pissarro's illustrations. Pissarro aimed at "a font which would harmonise with my wood-engraving and which would, at the same time, be clear and easy to read." All subsequent Eragny books were published from the Pissarros' home.

Maintaining strong connections with his native France, Pissarro brought impressionist, neo-

impressionist, and symbolist art and literary theory to England in his printing process and in the texts he published. Just as an impressionist painter sat before a landscape and allowed it to stimulate a response that was then recorded in line and color, so Pissarro placed himself before the ideas in a text and allowed images to rise in his mind. A neo-impressionist sense of color, using reds versus greens and yellows versus purples, informs Pissarro's wood engravings. Works of symbolist poetry printed at the Eragny Press included Jules Laforgue's two-volume *Moralités Légendaires* (1897-1898) and Emile Verhaeren's *Les Petits Vieux* (1901). The Pissarros printed Gérard de Nerval's *Histoire de la Reine du Matin et de Soliman Prince des Genies* in 1909 with a subsidy from a French organization of book lovers, the Société des Cent Bibliophiles. The result was a technically innovative work shining with gold and multiple-color block printing.

The Pissarros' experimentation with color began in 1903 with two trial copies of Ronsard's *Abregé de l'Art Poétique François*, one in pale pink and the other in sage green. They also produced five gray and orange versions of Charles Perrault's *Riquet à la Houppe* in 1907. Other French works published by the Eragny Press were Gustave Flaubert's *La Légende de Saint Julien l'Hospitalier* (1900), *Un Coeur Simple* (1901), and *Hérodias* (1901); François Villon's *Les Ballades de Maistre François Villon* (1900) and *Autres Poésies de Maistre Françoise Villon et Son École* (1901); and Judith Gautier's *Poems Tirés du Livre de Jade (Po Yü Shih Shu)* (1911).

A subsidy from another group of French bibliophiles, Le Livre Contemporain, allowed the Pissarros to print their last French work, *La Charrue d'Érable* (1912). They produced a remarkable work of art, combining Emile Chénin's (Emile Moselly) text with Lucien's chiaroscuro woodblock renderings of twelve Camille Pissarro compositions of themes of country work. Lucien and Esther had perfected their chiaroscuro woodblock printing in their frontispiece to Samuel Taylor Coleridge's *Christabel, Kubla Khan, Fancy in Nubis, and Song from Zapolya* (1904).

English titles published by the Eragny Press tended to be collections of poetry and appeared during the press's second decade. Besides the Coleridge book, the Pissarros produced Diana White's *The Descent of Ishtar* (1903), *Some Poems by Robert Browning* (1904), Laurence Binyon's *Dream Come True* (1905), *Songs by Ben Jonson* (1906), John Keats's *La Belle Dame Sans Merci* (1906), and

Page from an Eragny Press book printed in Brook type, designed by Lucien Pissarro

additional copies on vellum.

The Eragny Press ceased publication with the advent of World War I, which left the Pissarros unable to get the paper they needed and cut off from their Continental clients. After Lucien's death in 1944 Esther destroyed the Brook punches; but examples of the type and ornaments were deposited at the Cambridge University Press, and examples of the wood engravings are in the Pissarro Collection at the Ashmolean Museum, Oxford.

References:

Alice H. R. H. Beckwith, *Victorian Bibliomania* (Providence: Museum of Art, Rhode Island School of Design, 1987), pp. 36-37;

David Chambers, *Lucien Pissarro: Notes on a Selection of Wood-blocks Held at the Ashmolean Museum* (Oxford: Ashmolean Museum, 1980);

Alan Maxwell Fern, "The Wood-engravings of Lucien Pissarro," Ph.D. dissertation, University of Chicago, 1961;

W. S. Meadmore, *Lucien Pissarro* (New York: Knopf, 1963);

Thomas S. Moore, *A Brief Account of the Origin of the Eragny Press* (Hammersmith: Eragny Press, 1903);

Camille Pissarro, *Letters*, edited by John Rewald and Lucien Pissarro, third edition (New York: Appel, 1972);

Lucien Pissarro, *Notes on the Eragny Press*, edited by Fern (Cambridge: Privately printed, 1957);

Peter Wick, *The Turn of a Century, 1885-1910* (Cambridge, Mass.: Department of Graphic Arts, Houghton Library, Harvard University, 1970), pp. 39-41.

Verses by Christina Rossetti (1906); prose works included Francis Bacon's *Of Gardens* (1902) and (reflecting Lucien's concern with freedom of the press) John Milton's *Areopagitica* (1904). The last book from the Eragny Press was *Whym Chow, Flame of Love* (1914) by "Michael Field" (Edith Cooper and Katherine Bradley) in an edition of twenty-seven copies. Generally the Pissarros produced about two hundred copies of their titles, and in some instances they printed five to ten

Papers:

The major collection of Lucien Pissarro's papers is at the Ashmolean Museum, Oxford.

—*Alice H. R. H. Beckwith*

Essex House Press

(London: 1898-1902; Chipping Campden, Gloucestershire: 1902-1910)

C. R. Ashbee, cofounder of the Essex House Press, defined a private press as one "whose objective is first of all an aesthetic one, ... that caters for a limited market, and whose aim is not the commercial development of printing by machinery on a large scale, but of printing as an art; whose object is to make of each book—not merely a book, but an artistic unit." Charles Robert Ashbee was born on 17 May 1863 in Middlesex. After obtaining his degree at King's College, Cambridge, in 1886, he was apprenticed to the architect G. F. Bodley. Bodley's office specialized in church work but included much in the way of handicrafts, and it was to the revival of the artistic handicrafts that Ashbee turned his energy.

In 1888 he established the Guild of Handicraft in Commercial Street, London, to bring together and train a body of craftsmen and women in many trades, including furniture making, metalworking, jewelry making, silversmithing, printing, and bookbinding. In 1891 the guild moved to Essex House, Mile End Road. As defined in the guild's book of rules, printed in 1899, "The Guild of Handicraft is a body of men of different trades, crafts and occupations, united together on such a basis as shall better promote both the goodness of the work produced and the standard of life of the producer."

Ashbee and Laurence Hodson founded the Essex House Press in 1898 as part of the guild, "in the hope to keep living the tradition of good printing that William Morris had revived." Morris had died in 1896, and after the last Kelmscott Press book was finished in March 1898, Ashbee purchased Morris's two Albion presses. Thomas Binning and J. Tippett, Morris's compositors, and Stephen Mowlem, his pressman, joined the Essex House Press, as did William H. Hooper and Robert Catterson-Smith, who had turned Edward Burne-Jones's drawings into wood engravings. In 1902 the Guild of Handicraft, including the Essex House Press, moved to Chipping Campden in Gloucestershire. It then numbered 150 men, women, and children. Essex House books were distributed in England by the publisher Edward Arnold from 1898 to 1904, and in

C. R. Ashbee, cofounder of the Essex House Press, in 1900 (photograph by Frank Lloyd Wright)

the United States by Wilfred Buckley of New York from 1901 to 1904.

Ninety-four works were printed by the press between 1898 and 1910 in a variety of sizes but in two general styles: those printed in Caslon type and those printed in type designed by Ashbee. Ashbee's "Endeavour" type was first used in 1901 to print his book of essays, *An Endeavour Towards the Teaching of John Ruskin and William Morris*. Three hundred fifty copies of the book were printed and sold for twenty-one shillings. A larger version of Endeavour, called "Prayer Book," was made for *The Prayer Book of King Edward VII* (1903).

Ashbee's type design was called "obscure and dazzling" by D. B. Updike in his monumen-

Two Albion presses used by the Essex House Press

tal *Printing Types* (1922), and Roderick Cave in *The Private Press* (1971) dismissed it as "without any doubt the worst proprietary type of any cut for private press use in this country." Colin Franklin, however, has argued that these criticisms are unjust, noting that "Ashbee formed his types with very little reference to tradition and history. . . . It was an art nouveau letter, mixing very well with the style of other Campden work and true to his sense of form. Nobody followed his example, but Essex House books printed in his types are more typical of that period than other work from the private presses."

One of the best examples of the Endeavour type is in *The Psalter of Psalms of David From the Bible of Archbishop Cranmer* (1901). It was printed in two columns, with red leaves between verses. Woodcut initial letters designed by Ashbee appear at the beginning of each psalm. Two hundred fifty paper copies, sold for four guineas, and ten vellum copies, sold for sixteen guineas, were printed.

Endeavour and Prayer Book type were used in *The Prayer Book of King Edward VII*, begun in London in 1901 and finished in Campden in Au-

gust 1903. The largest-format book published by the press, it was printed in red and black throughout. An edition of four hundred copies on paper sold for twelve guineas, and ten copies on vellum sold for forty pounds each, of which one vellum copy was presented to the king.

Ashbee's *The Private Press: A Study In Idealism* appeared in November 1909. It included an address on the private press movement that Ashbee had delivered before the Club of Odd Volumes of Boston in February of that year. It also recorded the history of each work printed at the press and included a list of all the members of the Guild of Handicraft. The work also contained full sets of the initial letters made by Ashbee and Edith Harwood for various works, including *The Psalter*; many of the wood-cut illustrations that appear in Essex House books; and the pressmarks used by the Essex House Press. One hundred twenty-five copies were printed on paper and two on vellum.

Ashbee grouped the principal works of the Essex House Press under five headings. Technical books included *The Treatises of Benvenuto Cellini on Metal Work and Sculpture* (1898); religious books included the *Prayer Book* and *Psalter*, as well as John Bunyan's *The Pilgrim's Progress from This World to That Which Is to Come* (1899) and *A Journal of the Life and Travels of John Woolman in the Service of the Gospel* (1901). Humanistic books included Shakespeare's *Poems* (1900) and Erasmus's *The Praise of Folie* (1901), as well as the Great Poems series. The fourteen titles in this series were printed in pamphlet format on vellum and bound in vellum, with a blind-stamped device on the cover bearing the motto "Soul is Form" from Edmund Spenser's hymn *In Honour of Beauty* (1596). Among the works in the Great Poems series are Percy Bysshe Shelley's *Adonais* (1900), Walt Whitman's *Hymn on the Death of President Lincoln* (1901), and Robert Browning's *Flight of the Duchess* (1905). Books on the work of the guild include *The Essex House Song Book* (1904) and Ashbee's *The Guild of Handicraft* (1909). Books on oriental subjects date from 1906, when Dr. Ananda K. Coomaraswamy took over supervision of the press. The chief work of the press in this field was Coomaraswamy's *Mediaeval Sinhalese Art* (1908). The final book published by the Essex House Press was *Two Drawings by Hok'sai*, which appeared in October 1910.

In describing the guild idea, Ashbee wrote, "To me, perhaps, its completed expression in the life of the Guild is to be found in its Song Book"—

his favorite of all the books of the press. Edited by his wife, Janet E. Ashbee, it included songs, written by Ashbee and other guild members, which were sung in the evenings after work was put aside for the day.

In the end, the guild broke up for lack of money, not enthusiasm. Ashbee wrote in 1908, "In plain business terms, the Guild had dropped at the beginning of its twenty-first year and at the end of a period of acute commercial depression a substantial sum of money, upwards of £6,000-£7,000, the money of its shareholders, many of whom are the workmen themselves, in the attempt to carry through certain principles of workmanship and life."

References:

C. R. Ashbee, *The Private Press: A Study In Idealism. To Which is Added a Bibliography of the Essex House Press* (Chipping Campden: Essex House Press, 1909);

Roderick Cave, *The Private Press* (London: Faber & Faber, 1971), pp. 152-153, 321-322;

Alan Crawford, *C. R. Ashbee: Architect, Designer & Romantic Socialist* (New Haven: Yale University Press, 1985);

Colin Franklin, *The Private Presses* (London: Studio Vista, 1969), pp. 64-80, 198-202;

Will Ransom, *Private Presses and Their Books* (New York: Bowker, 1929);

D. B. Updike, *Printing Types: Their History, Forms, and Use. A Study in Survival*, 2 volumes (Cambridge, Mass.: Harvard University Press, 1922), II: 214.

Papers:

The papers of C. R. Ashbee are at the Victoria and Albert Museum, London.

—*Jennifer B. Lee*

Faber and Faber Limited
(London: 1929-   )
Faber and Gwyer Limited
(London: 1924-1929)

ff

Born in Yorkshire in 1889 and educated at Rugby and Christ Church College, Oxford (where he achieved firsts in Classical Moderations in 1910 and *literae humaniores* in 1912), Geoffrey Cust Faber began his career in publishing at the Oxford University Press in 1913. His work there was interrupted by World War I, in which he served on the western front and rose to the rank of captain. In 1919 he was elected a fellow of All Souls College. In 1920 Faber joined the board of directors of his family-connected brewery, Strong and Company, Limited; a year later he was called to the bar by the Inner Temple although he never practiced law. In 1923 Faber was appointed estates bursar at All Souls—a position he held until 1951 and in which he greatly increased the income of the college from its extensive land holdings.

In 1924 Faber left Strong and Company for a partnership with an All Souls colleague, Sir Maurice Gwyer, and his wife, Lady Alsina Gwyer, the owners of the lucrative Scientific Press Limited at 28 Southampton Street, near the Strand. Lady Gwyer had inherited the company from her father, Sir Henry Burdett, who had made it successful by the publication of the weekly *Hospital* and the *Nursing Mirror and Midwives Journal* and a short list of books for nurses. The partnership with Faber was largely motivated by the Gwyers' desire to expand into general publishing, and, as

Sir Geoffrey Faber in 1954

chairman of Faber and Gwyer Limited, which replaced the Scientific Press, Faber immediately reorganized the structure of the firm and began to recruit a vibrant staff.

In 1925 the firm moved to 24 Russell Square in Bloomsbury. That year T. S. Eliot left Lloyds Bank to become literary adviser and to assume responsibility for a poetry list at Faber and Gwyer. He was soon made a member of the board of directors and remained on the board until his death in 1965. Faber recruited Eliot with the understanding that Eliot would continue to

edit the poetry review *Criterion*, which he had been doing since 1922; Eliot edited the review until 1939. From 1925 to 1929 Faber augmented the staff with Richard de la Mare, Frank Morley, and the American Anglophile Morley Kennerley, all of whom were—along with C. W. Stewart, a veteran of the Scientific Press—elevated to the board of directors.

By 1929 the Gwyers had tired of the business and pressed Faber to liquidate the firm. Instead, Faber sold the *Nursing Mirror*, purchased the Gwyers' share of the firm, and changed the name of the company (allegedly at the suggestion of Richard de la Mare's father, the poet Walter) to Faber and Faber Limited. Since there was no other Faber involved in the business, it is assumed that the new name included Faber's supportive wife, Enid.

While he continued the firm's scientific publications, Faber rapidly expanded the company's list to include literature. Within a decade Faber and Faber was producing the works of many promising young writers, especially poets. Himself a poet, Faber gave Eliot a free hand in attracting young poets such as W. H. Auden, Ezra Pound, and Stephen Spender. Other key members of the staff were also accorded extensive autonomy to develop their sectors of the firm—de la Mare, the art and gardening lists; Kennerley, sports; and W. J. Crawley, who became sales director in 1934, children's books. Unlike other publishing houses, Faber and Faber allowed the sales department to participate in deciding what books were to be published. Like Jonathan Cape and Leonard Woolf, Faber insisted that his firm's books appeal to the eye and touch as well as to the mind of the reader: it was important "for the *outside* [of a book] to declare the new firm's personality as distinctively as possible." De la Mare commissioned young artists (many from the Royal College) to develop designs and illustrations. Artists who produced highly successful designs for dust jackets and bindings included Barnett Freedman, Edward Bawden (who worked for most of his career for Faber and Faber), Rex Whistler, John Piper, McKnight Kauffer, Gilbert Spencer, Graham Sutherland, Eric Ravilious, and Paul and John Nash. A distinctive Faber and Faber typeface and a reproduction process were developed by such artists as William and Ben Nicholson, Edward Ardizzone, Reynolds Stone, David Jones, and the eccentric genius Eric Gill. By the end of the 1930s the production department, directed by the gifted designer David Bland, was one of the most important sectors of the firm because of its contribution to the quality and style of Faber and Faber books. Also important was the work of Berthold Wolpe, who joined Faber and Faber at the beginning of World War II and used his typographical and lettering skills to produce thousands of layouts over a period of three decades. That the "Wolpe style" or "tradition" continued to dominate Faber's art department and flourished under Wolpe's successors is apparent in the Royal Society of Art's Presidential Award for 1986 to Faber and Faber.

In its first year Faber and Faber, with a staff of thirteen, produced 60 books; in 1940 the output was 177 titles. The firm's lists included Edith Sitwell's *English Eccentrics* (1933), James Joyce's *Finnegans Wake* (1939), Forrest Reid's fiction, R. H. Wilenski's studies on art, and Alison Utley's children's books.

By the mid 1930s Faber had become one of the most renowned personalities in British publishing. He was elected a member of the Publishers' Association Council in 1934 and five years later was voted president of the association. In 1940 Neville Chamberlain's chancellor of the exchequer, Sir Kingsley Wood, proposed a wartime sales tax which would include books. Faber mobilized the publishers, booksellers, authors, academics, members of Parliament, and Church of England prelates (including the archbishop of Canterbury) in a well-organized campaign to rally public support against this "tax on knowledge"; the government excluded books from the tax before the measure was presented to the House of Commons. In 1944 Faber, Sydney Goldsack of the William Collins firm, and Stanley Unwin founded the National Book League "to involve the book reading public as well as those concerned with writing, printing, publishing and bookselling" in one organization; in 1945 he became the league's first president. Faber's successors in the firm have also been prominently involved in the Publishers' Association and the National Book League.

Since 1940 the reputation of Faber and Faber (already the acknowledged publisher of poetry) has been further enhanced by the publication of the verse of Ted Hughes, Sylvia Plath, Thom Gunn, Philip Larkin, Robert Lowell, E. E. Cummings, Siegfried Sassoon, and Seamus Heaney; the Nobel and Booker Prize novels of William Golding; the Whitbread Book Award author Kazuo Ishiguro; the Booker Prize laureate Peter Carey; Lawrence and Gerald Durrell; and the

works of such playwrights as Samuel Beckett, Jean Genet, John Osborne, Harold Pinter, and Tom Stoppard. To these achievements can be added the publication, in conjunction with the Phoenix, Dent, and Michael Joseph publishers, of the popular *Shell Guides* (begun in 1939), and the success of the Faber Music component.

The staff, which increased from 109 in 1950 to 118 in 1980, produced 216 new titles in 1950, 268 in 1960, 276 in 1970, and 160 in 1980. In 1947 Crawley's son, Peter, was employed in the sales department and succeeded his father as sales director in 1962. Charles Montgomery Monteith (like Faber a fellow of All Souls, and the author of the entry on Faber in the *Dictionary of National Biography, 1961-70*) joined in 1953; he developed the drama list and had much to do with the publication of John Osborne's *Look Back in Anger* in 1957. The first Faber and Faber paperbacks were published in 1957; the popularity of Lawrence Durrell's *Alexandria Quartet* (1957-1960) proved that the firm had a back list which could rival Penguin in paperback sales. This success moved Faber and Faber to reclaim the rights to William Golding's *Lord of the Flies* (1954) and to publish the novel in a paperback edition in 1958. Golding's work and Ted Hughes's poetry provided excellent lead titles in the Faber paperback series.

In 1954 Faber was knighted for his service to British publishing. Six years later he resigned the chairmanship of Faber and Faber Limited and assumed the presidency of the company, which he held until his death on 31 March 1961. He was succeeded as chairman by Peter du Sautoy, who had joined the firm in 1946 and served until 1976. Faber and Faber moved to Queen Square in 1972; since 1960 the company had also possessed a warehouse and distribution point in Harlow, North London. Du Sautoy recruited the young Matthew Evans, who had considerable experience in advertising and bookselling at Dillon's University Bookshop. Evans was promoted to managing director in 1974 and, following the retirement of du Sautoy's successor, Monteith, assumed the chairmanship of the firm in 1980.

Since 1980 the company has regarded itself as a "group"; but aside from the holding company, the only other components of the group are Faber Music Limited and the American company, Faber Incorporated. The Faber family and Eliot's widow, Valerie, owned the majority of shares, with Sir Geoffrey's second son, Thomas

Geoffrey Faber (third from left) and T. S. Eliot (left) at a Faber and Faber editorial meeting in 1948 (Houghton Library, Harvard)

E., a fellow at Corpus Christi College, Cambridge, as chairman of the Faber and Faber holding company. Evans has generally proceeded along the basic lines set by Sir Geoffrey, du Sautoy, and Monteith. He has also established teams of bright and innovative young men and women in all departments of the company.

Evans has carried forward the publication of paperback editions from Faber and Faber's own lists, rather than licensing rights to paperback houses. In 1983 he launched the Faber Paperback series, which by the end of the 1980s comprised 80 percent of the firm's sales. In early 1989 the Faber Children's Paperbacks imprint was inaugurated. Evans and the board of directors have also continued the heavy expenditure—approximately £50,000 per year—on book design, which, according to Evans's reckoning, has "paid off handsomely in staff morale and sales." The investment in design was made possible by the £1 million per year from the worldwide success of the Andrew Lloyd Webber musical *Cats*, based on Eliot's *Old Possum's Book of Practical Cats*, published by the company in 1939. By the first quarter of 1989 the revenues from *Cats* amounted to 12 1/2 percent of Faber and Faber's revenues of £8.5 million; with Faber Music Limited and the American Faber Incorporated, the group's total income approximated £12 million. *Cats*, however, is not the only legacy bequeathed by Eliot to Faber and Faber; there is also the first volume of *The Letters of T. S. Eliot* (1988), edited by Valerie Eliot, which sold well and for which the *Times* paid a handsome sum for the right to publish extracts. The Faber Archive, worth millions of pounds, was carefully nurtured by Sir Geoffrey and his successors; it includes the firm's vast correspondence with Eliot, Pound, Joyce, Golding, Heaney, Auden, Spender, and a host of the most prominent literary and academic lights in twentieth-century Britain and the world. Faber and Faber is planning to exploit this valuable resource by establishing a company to administer the archive and require payment of fees for its use by researchers. A major strength of the firm derived from many of its staff being themselves authors; in 1989 the staff included six successful writers of novels, television and film scripts, poetry, and educational works.

Faber Music Limited was established in 1966 by the musicologist Donald Mitchell, who was then in charge of Faber and Faber's music list, to publish music scores. Since the 1960s Faber Music has become an important and lucrative component of the group with an impressive list of contemporary composers; working closely with the book publishing company, it also produces books that deal with the educational and performing aspects of music. With Robin Boyle as chairman since 1988, Faber Music has attempted to repeat the phenomenal success of *Cats* by developing musicals based on other Faber and Faber literary productions such as Hughes's *The Iron Man* (1968) and Golding's *Lord of the Flies*.

Under Evans, a strong effort has been made by the publicity and promotion department to emphasize "Faber's role as a publisher of creative writing." Faber and Faber has become, as the editorial director, Robert McCrum, averred, "the only publisher in Britain or the United States who publishes fiction and poetry and plays and film scripts, our idea being that whatever form your use of English takes, we are prepared to publish it." From Sir Geoffrey's time onward Faber and Faber has prided itself on nurturing authors—as editor Alan Pringle did with the Durrells and Larkin, and McCrum did with Peter Carey and Ishiguro. Faber and Faber has also sought to maintain "an international perspective" by publishing paperback translations and editions of works by such foreign writers as Milan Kundera, Mario Vargas Llosa, Nikos Kazantzakis, Garrison Keillor, and Breyten Breytenbach—often publicizing the art of the translator as well as that of the author. Approximately one-third of Faber's sales are in the export market; Western Europe ranks first in Faber's total exports, followed by Australia and New Zealand, Canada, and the Far East. The firm participates actively and prominently in bookfairs in Cairo, Calcutta, Jerusalem, and Frankfurt, and at home in the London International Book Fair.

Until 1989, 67 percent of the Faber and Faber holding company shares were owned by Lady Enid Faber and her two sons; 8 percent by the relatives or heirs of Richard de la Mare; and 25 percent by former directors or their heirs. During the previous few years several approaches had been made to Tom Faber, the chairman of the holding company, by other publishing groups, and the staff feared that a takeover would threaten the continuity and stability of the firm for both its authors and its employees. In what the *Daily Telegraph* (18 November 1989) described as "A deal unique in British publishing," the shareholders sacrificed "some immediate advantage" to guarantee the company's continued independence. Under the agreement, the holding company and Mrs. Eliot each retained one third of the shares; the remainder went to a management/staff team. The chairman was accorded the right to purchase 4.9 percent of the shares, the directors 2 percent, and other staff about 1 percent. The arrangement is viewed by many small and medium-sized publishing houses as a means of avoiding absorption by large British or foreign conglomerates.

References:

T. S. Eliot, *Geoffrey Faber: A Memorial* (London: Faber & Faber, 1961);

Geoffrey Faber, *A Publisher Speaking* (London: Faber & Faber, 1934);

Faber and Faber Covers, 1925-1982 (London: Faber & Faber, 1983);

Alan Franks, "Management Buy Faber and Faber," *Times* (London), 18 November 1989, p. 3;

Lynn Gordon, *Eliot's Early Years* (Oxford: Oxford University Press, 1977);

Vivienne Menkes, "Company Profile: Faber and Faber," *British Book News*, 4 (April 1989): 244-248;

F. V. Morley, *T. S. Eliot as a Publisher* (London: Privately printed, 1948);

National Book League, *Faber Books, 1925-1975: Impressions of a Publishing House and Faber Music. Notes of a Decade* (London: Faber & Faber, 1975);

Nigel Reynolds, "Buy Out Keeps Faber and Faber Independent," *Daily Telegraph*, 18 November 1989, p. 2.

—*J. O. Baylen*

Fanfrolico Press

(Sydney, Australia: 1923-1926; London: 1926-1930)

See also the Jack Lindsay entry in *DLB Yearbook: 1984*.

The Fanfrolico Press was inspired by the Australian cartoonist, artist, and writer Norman Lindsay, who founded the "Lindsay Aesthetic": typography in the service of an idea. Lindsay's son Jack elaborated this aesthetic into the Fanfrolico Press.

Its name derived from the French word *fanfreluche* (flummery), from François Rabelais's *La Vie inestimable du grant Gargantua, père de Pantagruel* (1534), the Fanfrolico Press was begun in 1923 in Sydney by Jack Lindsay and John T. Kirtley, a businessman and collector of limited editions who served as financier and typographer; they were assisted by Jack Lindsay's brother Philip. Their early productions included *Fauns and Ladies* (1923), by Jack Lindsay; *Thief of the Moon* (1924), by the Australian poet Kenneth Slessor; and Jack Lindsay's verse translation of Aristophanes' *Lysistrata* (1925). All three books were illustrated by Norman Lindsay.

In 1926 Jack Lindsay and Kirtley went to London—"to invade the area of the fine book at its British fountainhead," according to Lindsay—and established the Fanfrolico Press at 5 Bloomsbury Square. Since they had left their printing equipment in Sydney, Fanfrolico books were printed by other presses. Early productions in London included Slessor's volume of poems *Earth-Visitors* (1926), printed at the Chiswick Press, and Jack Lindsay's *Marino Faliero* (1927), printed at the Curiven Press. Another Jack Lindsay translation, *The Complete Works of Gaius Petronius* (1927), was printed by the Chiswick Press, with illustrations by Norman Lindsay.

Toward the end of 1927 Kirtley returned to Sydney. Lindsay's friend from Australia, P. R. Stephensen, a recent Oxford graduate and advocate of the "Lindsay Aesthetic," replaced Kirtley as business manager. The Fanfrolico Press went on to produce *Robert Eyres Landor* (1927), edited by Eric Partridge; Stephensen's translation of Friedrich Nietzsche's *The Anti-Christ* (1928); and Hugh McCrae's *Satyrs and Sunlight* (1928). Jack Lindsay supplied translations and adaptations of

Jack Lindsay, founder of the Fanfrolico Press, in 1937

works by Greek and Roman authors, including the poems of Theocritus (1929), and wrote *Helen Comes of Age* (1927), *Dionysos: Nietzsche contra Nietzsche* (1928), and *Hereward* (1929), a play with music by John Gough. Lindsay and his father collaborated on *A Homage to Sappho* (1928). Norman Lindsay also provided illustrations for Jack's *Loving Mad Tom* (1927), with a foreword by Robert Graves and musical transcriptions by Peter Warlock, and for John Donne's *A Defence of Women* (1930). Fanfrolico Press works written by Norman Lindsay included *Hyperborea: Two Fantastic Travel Essays* (1928), and a manifesto of the "Lindsay Aesthetic," *Madam Life's Lovers* (1929).

From 1927 to 1929 Fanfrolico Press books were produced by trade printers according to Lindsay and Stephensen's exacting specifications. Among the most celebrated of these efforts was an Elizabethan work, John Eliot's *The Parlement of Pratlers* (1928), illustrated by Hal Collins, a New

THE LONDON

APHRODITE

edited by Jack Lindsey and P. R. Stephensen.

No. 1	CONTENTS	AUGUST 1928
		PAGE
EDITORIAL MANIFESTOS		2
"THE LONDON APHRODITE"	*Lionel Ellis*	2
THE MODERN CONSCIOUSNESS	*Jack Lindsay*	3
MUSIC	*Kenneth Slessor*	25
VARIATION	*Robert Nichols*	28a
PATSA	*Liam O'Flaherty*	29
PASTORALE		35
DUNG OF PEGASUS (Part I)	*Peter Meadows*	39
LEBANON AT APPENRODT'S	*E. Powys Mathers*	47
THE MARRIAGE FLUTE	*Hugh McCrae*	47
BULLETS AND BALLOTS	*P. R. Stephensen*	48
FAREWELL ROCKING HORSE	*Philip Lindsay*	50
THE DAMNED DEITIES	*Jack Lindsay*	54
EX CATHEDRA		64

Only six numbers of *The London Aphrodite* will be issued, bi-monthly. Subscriptions, *nine shillings prepaid*, accepted only for the complete set of six numbers. Orders may be sent to the booksellers or direct to the publishers, THE FANFROLICO PRESS, 5, Bloomsbury Square, London, W.C.1—who are producing this periodical not for profit, but for the fun of the thing, obviously.

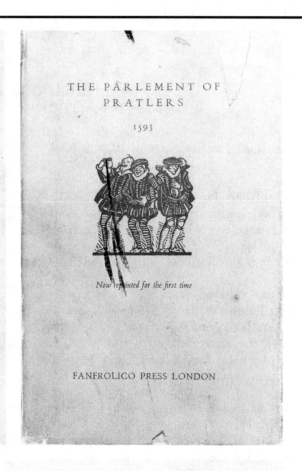

THE PARLEMENT OF
PRATLERS
1593

Now reprinted for the first time

FANFROLICO PRESS LONDON

Three Fanfrolico publications from the late 1920s

DIONYSOS
NIETZSCHE CONTRA NIETZSCHE
an essay in lyrical philosophy

BY JACK LINDSAY

*With reproductions from works by Peter-Paul Rubens
and Norman Lindsay, Titian and Turner, Francesco
Goya and William Blake and the Hellenes*

And a foreword by R. L. Hall, B.A.
Fellow of Trinity College Oxford

THE FANFROLICO PRESS LONDON

Zealander. The book was chosen for special mention and exhibition by the First Edition Clubs of New York and London.

The revenue from each work was used to defray the expenses for the production of the next work. The press's customers ordered through established booksellers. Part of every edition was sent to America.

Lindsay and Stephensen developed their aesthetic in the *London Aphrodite*, an anthology that appeared in six numbers from August 1928 to June 1929. Lindsay called the magazine's title a "polemical joke" directed at the "self-appointed guardians of public morals": John Squire of the *London Mercury* and James Douglas of the *Sunday Express*.

Lindsay credits himself with having conceived the idea in 1928 of publishing a book of D. H. Lawrence's paintings. By 1929, however, according to Lindsay's account, fears of police action against the press because of the *London Aphrodite*, aesthetic differences with Lawrence, and a strain in his relationship with Stephensen led him to suggest that Stephensen start a new press "on the basis of the undoubted profits that would come in from the Lawrence book if it was not suppressed." Lindsay says that with the help of capital from Edward Goldston, a bookseller, Stephensen and Lindsay launched the Mandrake Press.

Stephensen's account differs: he claims that he visited the South of France, met Lawrence, and offered to publish a book of reproductions of his paintings: "but Lawrence did not want to be associated with the Fanfrolico Press, as he disagreed with the Lindsay Aesthetic. I therefore (in partnership with a bookseller named Edward Goldston) founded the Mandrake Press. . . ." A December 1928 letter from Lawrence to Aldous Huxley confirms Lawrence's interest in the reproduction of his paintings by a new press "with no Lindsay stuff in it." Lawrence had serious misgivings about the Fanfrolico Press: "They want to do most of them in black-and-white collotype, but I don't want it. I want colour at any price—I hate collotype reproduction. . . . Stephensen gave me, against my will, about seven massive Fanfrolico books. On the whole, what a waste of good printing!"

In any case, *The Paintings of D. H. Lawrence* (1929) was the first book of the Mandrake Press. The Fanfrolico Press continued without Stephensen, and Lindsay severed his ties with the Mandrake Press (if indeed, he was ever involved with it).

The Fanfrolico Press continued under the management of Jack Lindsay; Brian Penton, a journalist from Sydney; and Philip Lindsay. According to Stephensen, Penton and Philip Lindsay "lacked the peculiar feeling for Limited Editions and Fine Printing that characterizes the true bibliophile. They had ideas to express, but certainly not Dionysian Idealism. . . ." Printing books themselves on a handpress, they produced a few more works—most notably *Morgan in Jamaica* (1930), by Philip Lindsay with illustrations by his brother Raymond Lindsay. Financial difficulties forced the Fanfrolico Press to cease operations in 1930.

References:

Frederick J. Hoffman, Charles Allen, and Carolyn F. Ulrich, *The Little Magazine: A History and a Bibliography* (Princeton: Princeton University Press, 1947);

Aldous Huxley, ed., *The Letters of D. H. Lawrence* (London: Heinemann, 1932);

Jack Lindsay, *Fanfrolico and After* (London: The Bodley Head, 1962);

P. R. Stephensen, *Kookaburras and Satyrs: Some Recollections of the Fanfrolico Press* (Cremorne, Australia: Talkarra Press, 1954).

—Robin Nilon

Folio Society
(London: 1947-   )

The Folio Society was founded in February 1947 by Charles Ede, who declared that its purpose was "to produce editions of the world's great literature in a format worthy of the contents, at a price within the reach of everyman." Ede and his associates Christopher Sandford and Alan Bott believed that beautifully designed books were not antithetical to mass production. As Francis Meynell stated in his preface to the society's 1968 checklist, *Folio 21*, "the outstanding feature of the Folio Society has been the democratization of the fine edition."

The society's first quarters, shared with Sandford's Golden Cockerel Press, were in a building on London's Poland Street that also housed the bindery of Sangorski and Sutcliffe. Bill Green, also of Golden Cockerel served as accountant and production manager. One book per month was planned, and distribution was to be handled by Cassell and Company to trade booksellers. The enterprise had to cope with cramped quarters, Ede's inexperience, and postwar rationing (the paper quota was ten tons a year, enough for only about five titles, and gold leaf was not permitted for bindings). The society's first book, *Tales by Tolstoy*, was published in October 1947, followed by George du Maurier's *Trilby* in November, and the thirteenth-century French tale *Aucassin and Nicolette* in December.

It soon became clear that distribution to booksellers was not sufficient for survival, and in the fall of 1949 an advertising campaign was mounted in an effort to enroll subscribers. The main feature of the campaign—a strategy borrowed from American book clubs—was the presentation copy available to subscribers upon joining.

Undoubtedly aided by Bott's experience and knowledge of book clubs (he had founded the Book Society in 1928), the campaign was so successful that it necessitated a move to a showroom and office at 10 Ryder Street in 1950. Despite its new book-club status, the society continued to sell to booksellers for several years.

The Folio Society moved in 1952 to 3B Dean's Yard, in 1955 to 70 Brook Street, in 1960 to 6 Stratford Place, and during the 1970s to 202 Great Suffolk Street. Ede ran the society until 1973, when it was purchased by John Letts and Halfdan Lynner; in 1983 it was sold to Robert Gavron. The original governing board of the society comprised the founders and Green; other individuals have joined the board, but its membership has remained fairly constant. For example, Brian Rawson became a director in 1956 and served in that capacity until his death in 1975, and Ede has been active in the society since its inception.

Originally the Folio Society's emphasis was on belles lettres, including major works of fiction and some poetry, drama, and memoirs. In the 1960s the society began to publish more nonfiction, including historical accounts, and lesser-known minor classics. Throughout, however, the emphasis has been on developing integrated books; according to Ede, "Our aim in book design has always been to try to create a unity which is in sympathy with, and complements, the text." Often cited as good examples of the society's knack for uniting text and design are Joan Hassall's illustrations for the works of Jane Austen (1957-1962) and Charles Keeping's for Emily Brontë's *Wuthering Heights* (1964). The society retained John Tenniel's illustrations for Lewis Carroll's *Alice's Adventures in Wonderland* (1961) and Jean Cocteau's for *Les Infants Terribles* (1976). Other prominent illustrators for Folio Society editions include Edward Ardizzone, Michael Ayrton, Elizabeth Frik, and Lynton Lamb.

Because it remains a book club, Folio Society editions are sold only to members, although some copies may be found in secondhand bookstores. And although the society does not publish original titles, some Folio imprints have been valued at far above their original purchase price. Society members are asked to select a minimum of four books a year, and books are printed according to demand. All subscribers—not just new members—now receive an annual presentation copy. The Folio Society has been able to keep prices reasonable, averaging fourteen pounds per title in 1988, but the commitment to quality still takes priority in decisions regarding price and design.

Despite its precarious beginnings, the Folio Society has achieved notable success for a limited-edition publisher. In 1989 it claimed nearly forty thousand members worldwide and a backlist of more than 130 titles.

References:

Folio 34: A Checklist of the Publications of the Folio Society, 1947-1980, with Appraisals by John Dreyfuss and John Letts (London: Folio Press, 1981);

Folio 21: A Bibliography of the Folio Society, 1947-1967, with an introduction by Francis Meynell and a historical note by Charles Ede (London: Folio Press, 1968);

Susan Rainey, "The Folio Society: Handsome Books at Minimal Cost," *Syracuse University Library Associates Courier* (1971): 35-45.

—Jean Parker

Golden Cockerel Press

(Watham St. Lawrence: 1920-1933; London: 1933-1959; New York: 1959-1961)

See also the Thomas Yoseloff entry in *DLB 46: American Literary Publishing Houses, 1900-1980: Trade and Paperback.*

Harold Midgeley Taylor and his wife Gay founded the Golden Cockerel Press in 1920 as a cooperative project to publish contemporary writing. It was a modest operation with equipment in a large frame building in their garden at Waltham St. Lawrence, Berkshire. With only one powered press and a bookbinding machine, type cases, and make-up table, they produced seventeen books through 1923. The first was *Adam & Eve & Pinch Me* (1921), the first book by A. E. Coppard; others included Havelock Ellis's first novel, *Kanga Creek: An Australian Idyll* (1922); Peter Quennell's first book, *Masques and Poems* (1922); and Martin Armstrong's *The Puppet Show: Tales and Satires* (1922).

In January 1924 Harold Taylor was compelled by ill health to give up the press; he died the following year. In progress at the time of his death was a translation of Pierre de Bourdeille's *The Lives of Gallant Ladies* with ten wood engravings by Robert Gibbings. Partly to complete this work, Gibbings and his wife Moira bought the press; in July 1924 it became the first book produced by the "New" Golden Cockerel Press.

A founder-member of the Society of Wood Engravers with no previous experience in book printing, Gibbings had a longing to foster fine illustrated books by English wood engravers. The next three Golden Cockerel books were illustrated by Gibbings, including *Miscellaneous Writings of Henry VII*, printed in two colors and published in December 1924. The following year John Nash illustrated Jonathan Swift's *Directions To Servants* with twelve wood engravings, printed in two colors; a special edition was bound in vellum and signed by the artist. This work was soon followed by the press's first association with Eric Gill. Gibbings had asked Gill to illustrate any book of his choosing, but Gill had refused. John Wilson of the bookselling firm of John and Edward Bumpus suggested that if Gibbings would print a selection of poems by Gill's sister,

Robert Gibbings, wood engraver and second owner of the Golden Cockerel Press, in the library at the press, 1931

Enid Clay, Gill could be induced to illustrate it. Thus Clay's *Sonnets and Verses* was printed in 1925 and was chosen by the Double Crown Club of London as the best-printed book of the year. The collaboration of Gill and Golden Cockerel continued with *The Song of Songs* (1925) and *The Passion of the Lord Jesus Christ* (1926) and culminated in 1932 in the magnum opus of the press, *The Four Gospels*. This book was chosen, with the Kelmscott Press edition of *The Works of Geoffrey Chaucer* (1896) and the Doves Bible (1903-1905), to represent the greatest achievements in book production at the Festival of Britain in 1937.

Caslon was the standard type used by the press; for *The Four Gospels* Gill designed a new face, based primarily on Caslon, that became the Golden Cockerel's proprietary type, but it was rarely used afterward. Gill was an "exclusive" illustrator for Gibbings until the establishment of his own Pigotts Press with his son-in-law René

Hague in 1931. Other wood engravers who illustrated Golden Cockerel books included David Jones, a disciple of Gill's; Denis Tegetmeier, Gill's son-in-law; and Eric Ravilious.

The Depression changed the buying habits of collectors, and Gibbings had to sell the press in August 1933 to Christopher Sandford, Francis Newbery, and Owen Rutter, who moved it to 10 Staple Inn, London. From the beginning of the partnership, the active direction of the press was in Sandford's hands; Rutter supplied the financial backing. Arrangements were made with the Chiswick Press to produce Golden Cockerel books, and the Golden Cockerel Press became— like the Nonesuch Press—no more than an imprint. Nevertheless, it was still an important influence on fine presses everywhere. It continued to introduce talented new wood engravers, including John Buckland Wright, Dorothea Brady, John O'Connor, Clifford Webb, John Petts, Gwenda Morgan, and Mark Severin. Newbery was replaced in the partnership in 1936 by Sandford's brother, Anthony.

The press was sold to the New York publisher Thomas Yoseloff in 1959. December 1961 saw the last Golden Cockerel Press book— *Moncrif's Cats* (dated 1962), by François-Augustin Paradis de Moncrif, translated by Reginald Bretnor.

References:

Chanticleer: A Bibliography of the Golden Cockerel Press, April 1921-August 1936 (London: Golden Cockerel Press, 1937);

Cock-a-Hoop; A Sequel to Chanticleer, Pertelote, and Cockalorum; Being a Bibliography of the Golden Cockerel Press, September 1949-December 1961 (London: Golden Cockerel Press, 1962);

Cockalorum: A Sequel to Chanticleer and Pertelote; Being a Bibliography of the Golden Cockerel Press, June 1943-December 1948 (London: Golden Cockerel Press, 1948);

Robert Gibbings, "The Golden Cockerel Press," *Colophon*, 2 (1931): Part 7;

Gibbings, "Memories of Eric Gill," *Book Collector*, 2 (Summer 1953): 95-103;

A. Mary Kirkus, *Robert Gibbings: A Bibliography* (London: Dent, 1962);

Pertelote, a Sequel to Chanticleer: Being a Bibliography of the Golden Cockerel Press, October 1936 - April 1943 (London: Golden Cockerel Press, 1943).

—*Albert Sperisen*

Victor Gollancz Limited

(London: 1927-)

Victor Gollancz was widely recognized as an advertiser nonpareil, whose book jackets and advertising displays employed subtle claims about the books he was selling. Words such as "Best Ever," "Sensational," or "Spellbinding" were intertwined with excerpted comments from reviewers printed in different typefaces to attract the browser. He was also known for demanding huge pressruns, often for unknown authors' first books, and for his lifelong interest in various social issues.

Born in London on 9 April 1893 to Alexander Gollancz, a moderately prosperous jeweler, and Helena Michaelson Gollancz, Victor Gollancz was a member of a prominent Jewish family; his uncles Hermann and Israel Gollancz were noted scholars. After being educated at St. Paul's School in London and at Oxford University, Gollancz served briefly in the army and then as a teacher at Repton School. He began his publishing career in 1921 supervising trade publications for Benn Brothers Limited. Impressed by his talent for advertising and his editorial skills, Sir Ernest Benn soon gave Gollancz additional responsibilities which included the development of a line of technical books. When Benn Brothers—at Gollancz's suggestion—divided into Benn Brothers Limited and Ernest Benn Limited in 1923, Gollancz became the managing director of the latter. Ernest Benn Limited specialized in art books; later, the fiction of such authors as Dorothy L. Sayers and H. G. Wells and the literary nonfiction of Gertrude Bell were added to Gollancz's record of successful acquisitions. Under Gollancz, Ernest Benn Limited's profits increased from £2,000 to nearly £250,000 by 1928. Shortly before Gollancz left Benn, Sir Ernest

Victor Gollancz in the 1920s

wrote in his diary: "*Victor Gollancz* is another story. I spend alternate periods of 3 months each, hating him & loving him. His business ability is tremendous, his energy abnormal & he has made a great thing of E. B. Ltd. We have backed him with about £80,000, more real money, I suppose than any publisher ever had before. The combination of my finance and his flair has produced the biggest thing in publishing history. . . . Most of our books have been successful showing how good is the judgment of Gollancz."

Although Benn was willing to name Gollancz to the directorship of Ernest Benn Limited, the salary and commission Gollancz wanted were too much for Benn to pay; and in September 1927 Gollancz left the firm. Sir Ernest wrote: "The partnership [of Benn and Gollancz] is an unnatural one. First there is the fact that V. G. must be 'boss,' he is a natural leader and in his own interest he should set up for himself."

Using his own savings and capital acquired from his marriage in 1919 to Ruth Lowy, Gollancz established his own company, Victor Gollancz Limited, at 14 Henrietta Street. Gollancz had absolute control over the firm as governing director. One of his immediate tasks was acquiring authors. Susan Glaspell was quickly persuaded to let Gollancz publish her novel *Brook Evans* (1928), but Sir Ernest Benn would not release Dorothy L. Sayers from her obligations to his firm until her contract expired. Gollancz's secretary at Benn, Dorothy Horsman, joined his house as sales manager; Leonard Stein left Benn to be Gollancz's deputy director; and Stanley Morison, a typographer Gollancz met while producing Benn's art books, became a director. Two investors, William Payson of the firm of Payson and Clarke of New York and Frank Strawson, filled out the original group of Victor Gollancz Limited's directors and staff. In 1931 Gollancz published Ford Madox Ford's reflections, *Return to Yesterday*. In 1932 Payson and Clarke withdrew its support for Victor Gollancz Limited, and Morison turned to book design more than management. Strawson was shortly forced to limit his duties because of illness, and the majority of his managerial tasks were assumed by Edgar Dunk, the company secretary. During these early years, Victor Gollancz Limited achieved success with the novels of A. J. Cronin, Phyllis Bentley, and Eleanor Smith. In 1932 Gollancz published Elizabeth Bowen's novel *To the North* with success; in 1934 the firm offered her work *The Cat Jumps and Other Stories*. In 1935 Gollancz published Bowen's *The House in Paris*, followed by *The Death of a Heart* in 1938. Also in 1938 Gollancz published Daphne Du Maurier's best-selling novel *Rebecca*, having published her third novel, *Jamaica Inn*, in 1936. After Gollancz published Hester Chapman's Gothic romances *She Saw Them Go By*

(1933) and *To Be a King: A Tale of Adventure* (1934), she moved to the firm of Jonathan Cape. Backing Chapman's first novels—spending vast sums on advertising and printing thousands of copies when the writer was virtually unknown— was one of the ways Gollancz earned a reputation for recklessness as a publisher. In 1941 Victor Gollancz Limited offered another collection of Bowen's short fiction, *Look at All Those Roses*, and another Du Maurier best-seller, *Frenchman's Creek*. Two other Gothic writers of the 1930s whose books were published by Victor Gollancz Limited were Lady Eleanor Smith, whose central characters in both novels and short fiction were sexually active gypsies in carnivals or circuses, and Marguerite Steen, whose novels *The Wise and the Foolish Virgins* (1932), *Spider* (1933), *Stallion* (1933), *Matador* (1934), and *Return of a Heroine* (1936) were based on her travels in Spain and America.

Although she was not released from her contract with Ernest Benn Limited until 1930, Sayers was able to edit Victor Gollancz Limited's anthology of mystery stories, *Great Short Stories of Detection, Mystery and Horror*, in 1928; a second series appeared in 1931 and a third in 1934. The firm took over from Benn the publication of Sayers's best-selling detective novels depicting the exploits of Lord Peter Wimsey: *Strong Poison* (1930), *The Five Red Herrings* (1931), *Have His Carcase* (1932), *Murder Must Advertise* (1933), *The Nine Tailors* (1934), and *Gaudy Night* (1935). In 1937 another best-selling author, Ivy Compton-Burnett, moved to Gollancz from William Heinemann with her novel *Daughters and Sons* (1937); *A Family and a Fortune* followed in 1939. She continued to have her works published by Gollancz throughout her life. The romance novelist Norah Lofts followed the pattern of Chapman in having her first two novels, *Out of This Nettle* (1938) and *Blossom like the Rose* (1939), published by Gollancz before moving on to another publisher—in her case, the romance publishing specialist Hodder and Stoughton.

Edith Sitwell left the firm of Gerald Duckworth for Gollancz after the latter published her allegorical novel about Jonathan Swift set during World War I, *I Live under a Black Sun* (1937); she had been searching for a publisher for the novel since 1932. Gollancz had originally approached her about writing a biography of the eighteenth-century actor and theater manager David Garrick, but Sitwell had instead persuaded him to publish the Swift novel. Gollancz paid

£350 in advance and printed four thousand copies of the book; twenty-five hundred were sold within the first ten days of its appearance. Another writer whom Gollancz actively sought was the novelist Rose Macaulay; she gave the firm *Personal Pleasures* (1935), a collection of seventy-one brief essays, before returning to William Collins. George Orwell's *Down and out in Paris and London* (1933) was followed by *Burmese Days* (1935); *A Clergyman's Daughter* (1935); *Keep the Aspidistra Flying* (1936); *The Road to Wigan Pier* (1937), for which Gollancz wrote the preface; *Coming up for Air* (1939); and *Inside the Whale, and Other Essays* (1940). But Gollancz rejected Orwell's *Animal Farm* in April 1944 because it was an allegorical attack on the Soviet Union, Britain's wartime ally; the book was published in 1945 by Secker and Warburg, which also received Orwell's best-known work, *Nineteen Eighty-Four* (1949).

The "Gollancz jacket" dates from the early years of the firm. These dust jackets were designed by Morison and Ruth Gollancz using typography instead of photographs or paintings and innovatively featured reviewers' notices on the front cover, the back cover, and the inside flaps. The Gollancz jacket was recognized by book designers as a typographical masterwork, its drama enhanced by the use of gray or yellow as the background color.

Gollancz's short-lived Mundanus series of paperback novels, started in 1930, preceded the Penguin series of Allen Lane by five years. Established as a subsidiary company of Victor Gollancz Limited, Mundanus featured the novels of Charles Williams, whose *The Place of the Lion* appeared as a Mundanus original in 1931. In 1932 Williams's *The Greater Trumps* was published, followed in 1933 by *Shadows of Ecstasy*. The Mundanus line only survived until 1932. Gollancz, Norman Collins, and the former literary agent Michael Joseph went into partnership in 1935 as the codirectors of Michael Joseph Limited. Gollancz treated the Joseph company as if it were his own, rejecting such titles as Richard Llewellyn's *How Green Was My Valley*, which would become a best-seller for Joseph in 1939. The Gollancz-Joseph partnership ended in 1938.

Gollancz created the Left Book Club (LBC) in May 1936 to try to stop the spread of Nazism. He believed that his club was the first to offer mail-order books; in fact, the Book of the Month Club was already active in the United States, although Gollancz was unaware of it. The LBC was, however, the first politically oriented book

by GEORGE ORWELL

KEEP THE ASPIDISTRA FLYING

by the author of

BURMESE DAYS

BURMESE DAYS:

"It can hardly be much more than a year ago that there appeared a remarkable volume of personal experience called *Down and Out in London and Paris*. It is not six months ago that there appeared an even more remarkable novel called *A Clergyman's Daughter*. Last week there was published by the same author a ☞

Dust jacket for one of several books by Orwell that Victor Gollancz Limited published. Gollancz rejected Orwell's Animal Farm, *however, because of its allegorical criticism of the Soviet Union.*

club, and it represented the views of the Labour party in many of its publications. Among the leading LBC titles were *The Intelligent Man's Way to Prevent War* (1933), by Leonard Woolf; *An Outline of Modern Knowledge* (1933), edited by William Rose; and *Nazi Germany Explained* (1933), which was suggested to its author, Vernon Bartlett, by Gollancz himself.

While Gollancz was occupied with LBC rallies, speeches, theatrical performances, and fund-raising activities, Collins was a leading figure in the firm. He had come to Victor Gollancz Limited in 1932 as an editor; by 1934 he was deputy chairman. That year Collins acquired the novel *Anthony Adverse*, Hervey Allen's best-seller.

John Strachey, a political writer, and Harold Laski, a professor of political science at the London School of Economics, assisted Gollancz in the selection of books advertised monthly in the *Left Book News*. Within its first two years the

LBC boasted a membership of ten thousand. In 1937 Continental European branches of the LBC were formed. Before it was interrupted by the outbreak of World War II in September 1939, the LBC achieved a worldwide membership of fifty thousand.

During the war Victor Gollancz Limited published titles by its staple authors—Sayers, Compton-Burnett, Du Maurier, Bowen, and Sitwell; the latter adored Gollancz and thought his efforts to prevent the war were an instance of his nobility. The Left Book Club's membership declined to about ten thousand British members by 1946. Gollancz distributed free to LBC members his own *Our Theatened Values* (1946), one of the seventeen books on issues relating to the war that he wrote between 1939 and 1948. In 1947 Gollancz traveled to Germany to see the ravages of the war firsthand; the trip resulted in one of his more successful war books, *In Darkest Germany* (1947).

While Gollancz traveled, lectured, wrote, and worked for such organizations as Save Europe Now, the management of the publishing company rested with Dunk, the secretary; Sheila Hodges, Gollancz's secretary, deputy, and close friend; Horsman, the production manager; Strawson, the codirector; and John Bush, the assistant company secretary and exports manager. Gollancz did not allow his staff to make management decisions, a policy which often resulted in delayed actions and disappointed authors. Writers such as James Parks, Bob Boothby, and Robert Neumann feared that their timely politically oriented books would be failures without Gollancz's personal attention. By the late 1940s few new authors desired to have their works published by Victor Gollancz Limited because it was widely known that Gollancz's talents for advertising and promoting new authors were being used only sporadically. Gollancz believed that his book-buying trip to America in 1948 would infuse his dying fiction list with new blood, and it did: by 1951 more than half of the fiction list was composed of titles by American authors.

As the house moved into the 1950s, publishing was still secondary to Gollancz's interests in politics, philanthropy, and writing. As his biographer Ruth Dudley Edwards summarizes Gollancz's activities in the early 1950s:

> A considered division of his time between publishing and philanthropy would have been well within his range, but he had three other lives to live. The political Victor would not lie down, and came out to do battle over a succession of domestic and international issues. Victor the author was . . . [compiling] his anthology, *A Year of Grace*. . . . Finally, he was now allowing himself the leisure others took for granted. . . . He complained regularly of overwork, but revelled in it. . . .

Gollancz managed to take regular vacations even while serving as chairman of philanthropical societies such as the Jewish Society for Human Service, on the executive committees of organizations such as the Anglo-Israeli Association, and on the governing boards of institutions such as the Hebrew University.

Communism, racial oppression, and African politics gradually replaced Nazism as topics on Gollancz's lists in the early 1950s; among the titles the firm published were *White Man Boss* (1950), by "Adamastor," and *Scottsboro Boy* (1951), by Haywood Patterson and Earl Conrad. Gollancz's anthology *A Year of Grace*, released at Christmas 1950, sold nearly fifty thousand copies within the first six months and was quickly followed by his pamphlet *Christianity and the War Crisis* (1951), dealing with the Korean War. In February 1951 Gollancz sent Hodges to the United States for the annual book-buying trip; he was too engrossed in Labour party politics and the early stages of his autobiography, *My Dear Timothy* (1952), to leave the country himself. Between 1950 and 1954 Victor Gollancz Limited continued to profit with the novels of Compton-Burnett, *Darkness and Day* (1951) and *The Present and Past* (1953); Sayers's play *The Emperor Constantine* (1951); Du Maurier's *The Apple Tree: A Short Novel and Some Stories* (1952); Edna Ferber's novel *Giant* (1952); Nadine Gordimer's *The Soft Voice of the Serpent and Other Stories* (1953); and Kingsley Amis's first novel, *Lucky Jim* (1954). In 1952 Hilary Rubinstein, Gollancz's nephew, became a director of Victor Gollancz Limited. Both Amis and Gordimer had been recruited by Rubinstein; Gollancz failed to appreciate this achievement fully, viewing Rubinstein as a potential usurper. In 1953 Gollancz's daughter Livia became a member of the board, which was then made up of Bush, Hodges, Horsman, Strawson, and Victor and Ruth Gollancz. In 1954 Hodges retired from the firm but continued to serve as a consulting editor; in 1955 Gollancz hired John Rosenberg as an editor. Rosenberg left after a year and was followed by a succession of one-year replacements.

The firm's publishing activities during the late 1950s included three more Compton-Burnett novels, *Mother and Son* (1955), *A Father and His Fate* (1957), and *A Heritage and Its History* (1959); the first critical work on Compton-Burnett, Robert Lidell's *The Novels of Ivy Compton-Burnett* (1955); Colin Wilson's *The Outsider* (1956); two anthologies by Sayers, *The New Sayers Omnibus* (1956) and *The Sayers Tandem* (1957); James Purdy's *63: Dream Palace* (1957); Ferber's *Ice Palace* (1958); Du Maurier's *The Breaking Point* (1959); and John Updike's *The Poorhouse Fair* (1959). Because of staffing changes, the firm took up more of Gollancz's time until 1954, but by the later part of the decade he was championing the cause of abolition of capital punishment.

Arthur Koestler recruited Gollancz to help in the campaign to abolish the death penalty in England, and in the summer of 1955 Gollancz, Koestler, and Gollancz's longtime friend John Collins organized the National Campaign for the Abolition of Capital Punishment (NCACP). Gollancz's pamphlet *Capital Punishment: The Heart of the Matter* (1955) attracted huge crowds to public lectures, which created excellent fund-raising opportunities. Soon Koestler, who had initiated the campaign and had written the first anti-capital punishment tract, found himself overshadowed by Gollancz, and he broke with the NCACP. By the fall of 1956 the NCACP had done all it could with the Conservative government; Gollancz resigned his chairmanship, turning his attention briefly to the plight of Arab refugees in the Gaza Strip and then to the Campaign for Nuclear Disarmament.

Gollancz received an honorary doctorate of laws from Trinity College, Dublin, in June 1960. That year he was awarded the German Book Trade's Peace Prize; it carried a stipend of one thousand pounds, part of which he donated to the Council for Christians and Jews. In 1961 Gollancz lost the chance to publish Updike's best-selling novel *Rabbit, Run* because Updike refused to remove material the publisher considered pornographic; the novel was published in London by André Deutsch. The firm flourished, however, as Rubinstein managed a respectable deal for the sale of selected Gollancz fiction titles to Penguin; and in 1960 Rubinstein and Livia Gollancz, who were temporary codirectors when Gollancz traveled, were sent to America on the acquisitions trip. By this time American authors such as John Cheever, Art Buchwald, J. F. Powers, Peter de Vries, and Brendan Gill were featured in the Gollancz list alongside the *Treasury of Du Maurier Short Stories* (1960); Compton-Burnett's *The Mighty and Their Fall* (1961); Sayers's *The Sayers Holiday Book* (1963), *The Poetry of Search and the Poetry of Statement* (1963), and *The Lord Peter Omnibus* (1964); and Aleksandr Solzhenitsyn's *One Day in the Life of Ivan Denisovich* (1963). The issue of capital punishment continued to occupy Gollancz, and he filled the lecture halls with his own speeches and those of his authors, including Amis and Ludovic Kennedy. The newly elected Labour government abolished executions in 1965; Gollancz was in large measure responsible for that action.

In the 1960s Gollancz remained unmellowed in his treatment of authors. He fell out with Wilson and also lost John Le Carré, although through Gollancz's puffing Le Carré's *The Spy Who Came in from the Cold* (1968) sold nearly one million copies. Cronin, Edgar Snow, and Elizabeth Spencer also left. Even Du Maurier considered abandoning the firm in 1961, so upset was she at Gollancz's neglect of her interests. Rubinstein and Livia Gollancz initiated new product lines, including a profitable series of children's books, as Victor Gollancz Limited found itself increasingly being offered difficult-to-market books by both British authors and American publishers. To try to save the firm, Gollancz in January 1962 hired as senior director James MacGibbon, a successful agent/editor who had owned the firm of MacGibbon and Kee; it was he who brought Solzhenitsyn to Gollancz. Rubinstein and Livia Gollancz were in America when MacGibbon was hired; taking the move to indicate that Gollancz had little intention of recognizing his potential for running the firm, Rubinstein left in February 1963 to assume an editorial position on the *Observer*. Gollancz went into semiretirement in 1965, leaving Victor Gollancz Limited in the hands of Livia Gollancz as governing director; Bush as chairman; MacGibbon as assistant managing director; and Mary Brash as director. The list for 1965 included a second critical book on Compton-Burnett, by Charles Burkhart, and the novel *The Silence of Herondale*, by Joan Aiken. Gollancz was knighted in June 1965. In 1966 he published his second book on music, *The Ring at Bayreuth and Some Thoughts on Operatic Production*; opera had long been a passion of Gollancz's. His *Journey towards Music: A Memoir* had appeared in 1964.

Gollancz in later years

On 7 October 1966 Gollancz suffered a stroke. He recovered enough to correspond with family members and colleagues; but his health declined, and he died on 8 February 1967. Bush and Livia Gollancz took over the firm; Mac-Gibbon left shortly after Gollancz's death to become managing director of B.P.C. Publishing, Limited. Jiddu Krishnamurti's works brought some financial relief to the company as *Freedom from the Known* appeared in 1969, followed by *The Only Revolution* (1970), *The Urgency of Change* (1971), and *Krishnamurti's Notebook* (1976). Du Maurier returned with *Golden Lads: A Study of Anthony Bacon, Francis and Their Friends* (1975), *Echoes from the Macabre: Selected Stories* (1976), *The Winding Stair: Francis Bacon, His Rise and Fall* (1976), *Growing Pains: The Shaping of a Writer* (1977), *The Rendezvous and Other Stories* (1980), and *The Rebecca Notebook and Other Memories* (1981). In 1972 appeared *The Novels of Ivy Compton-Burnett*; it was followed by three books about the novelist: Burkhart's *The Art of Ivy Compton-Burnett: A Collection of Critical Essays* (1972), Elizabeth Sprigge's *The Life of Ivy Compton-*

Burnett (1973), and Hilary Spurling's *Ivy When Young* (1974). Aiken contributed *A Bundle of Nerves: Stories of Horror, Suspense and Fantasy* (1976) and *A Whisper in the Night* (1982).

Since the 1960s the paperback book list had expanded to include Victor Gollancz Science Fiction, representing authors such as Brian Aldiss, Isaac Asimov, Poul Anderson, Frank Herbert, Robert A. Heinlein, Michael Moorcock, André Norton, Frank Saberhagen, Ursula K. Le Guin, Robert Silverberg, Arthur C. Clarke, Cordwainer Smith, Frederik Pohl, and Kurt Vonnegut. The children's paperback book list was developed by Livia Gollancz. Additional paperbacks were offered in autobiography and biography (including Robert K. Massie's *Nicholas and Alexandra* [1968]), crime, the environment, history, music, religion, and more than fifty books on bridge by Hugh Kelsey, Ron Klinger, Terence Reese, Pat Husband, and Andrew Kambites.

In 1987 Victor Gollancz Limited purchased H. F. and G. Witherby, a natural history and hobbies publisher. Titles on fishing techniques, avian lore, dog breeding, wine, and wildlife painting were added to the Gollancz list, with Witherby retaining its imprint.

In October 1989 Victor Gollancz Limited was sold to Houghton Mifflin of Boston, which retained the Gollancz imprint. In November Livia Gollancz retired as managing director; Stephen Bray now holds the position.

Gollancz's presence was still felt in many of the titles published more than two decades after his death. For example, Vera Brittain's *Wartime Chronicle Diaries 1939-1945* (1990) is a companion to her *Testament of Youth*, published by Gollancz in 1933. John May's *The Greenpeace Book of the Nuclear Age* (1990) is one of the many books on the environment that reflect Gollancz's interest in the subject; his passion for food is recalled in Egon Ronay's *The Unforgettable Dishes of My Life* (1989); and his love of music survives in Helena Matheopoulos's *Bravo* (1989) and Claire Croiza's *The Singer as Interpreter* (1989). Series such as John Creasey's Crime Collection, begun in 1987 and edited by Herbert Harris, continue the

firm's tradition of detective fiction that started with Sayers.

References:

Ernest Benn, *Happier Days: Recollections and Reflections* (London: Benn, 1949);

James Brabazon, *Dorothy L. Sayers: A Biography* (New York: Scribners, 1981);

Ruth Dudley Edwards, *Victor Gollancz: A Biography* (London: Gollancz, 1987);

Victor Gollancz, *More for Timothy* (London: Gollancz, 1953);

Gollancz, *My Dear Timothy: An Autobiographical Letter to His Grandson* (London: Gollancz, 1952; New York: Simon & Schuster, 1953);

Sheila Hodges, *Gollancz: The Story of a Publishing House, 1928-1978* (London: Gollancz, 1978);

John Strachey, *A Strangled Cry, and Other Unparliamentary Papers* (London: Sloane, 1962).

—*Beverly Schneller*

Gregynog Press
(Newtown, Powys, Wales: 1927-1940)
Gwasg Gregynog
(Newtown, Powys, Wales: 1974-   )

The Gregynog Press was founded in 1922 at Gregynog Hall, near Newtown, Powys, Wales, by Gwendoline and Margaret Davies. They had originally intended to set up a crafts center, but, of the various crafts envisaged, bookmaking alone survived. The aim was to stimulate an interest in Wales in fine books and thereby to encourage the art of better book printing; they also hoped to foster the study of Welsh literature. Of the forty-two books published by the press, eight are in the Welsh language, and many others have Welsh associations.

The stables and coach houses at Gregynog Hall were converted into workshops, and every stage of the bookmaking process, with the exception of papermaking, was carried out under one roof. Robert Ashwin Maynard, formerly a scenic artist, was appointed as first controller of the press in July 1922. Assisted by the first binder, John Mason, he produced the press's first book, *Poems by George Herbert*, in December 1923. In February of the following year Horace Walter Bray joined the staff as resident artist. Up to 1930 Maynard and Bray were responsible for the design and illustration of a further seventeen books, which are characterized by sound typography; pleasing woodcut illustrations, some of them hand colored; and well-designed and well-executed woodcut initials. The first four books were printed in Kennerley type; thereafter a Monotype caster was acquired, and subsequent

books appeared in various common book types—the most frequently used being Baskerville, Bembo, Perpetua, and Poliphilus. The first book was printed on an Albion handpress, after which all work was printed from handset type on a Victoria platen press using handmade paper from various mills. Presswork from 1927 to 1936 was by Herbert John Hodgson, whose skill was much admired by other presses.

After the press became a limited company in 1928, its affairs were managed by a board of directors consisting of the Davies sisters; their friend Dr. Thomas Jones, deputy secretary to the cabinet; and W. J. Burdon Evans, a barrister, who was their financial adviser. Jones acted as chairman and was instrumental in securing the services of suitable authors, editors, and translators, who were drawn largely from his wide literary acquaintance.

The most notable works to appear during this first period were *The Life of Saint David* (1927), edited by Ernest Rhys, printed in Poliphilus type in blue, red, and black and bound in limp vellum with a beautifully restrained title page and twenty-five hand-colored, wood-engraved illustrations by Maynard and Bray; *The Autobiography of Edward, Lord Herbert of Cherbury* (1928), a folio printed in Poliphilus and Blado types and illustrated with eight wood engravings by Bray; and *Psalmau Dafydd: The Book of Psalms in Welsh* (1929), a slim quarto that was the most am-

Top: Gwendoline and Margaret Davies, founders of the Gregynog Press; bottom: Gregynog Hall, with the stables (partly visible at the extreme right) where the press was housed

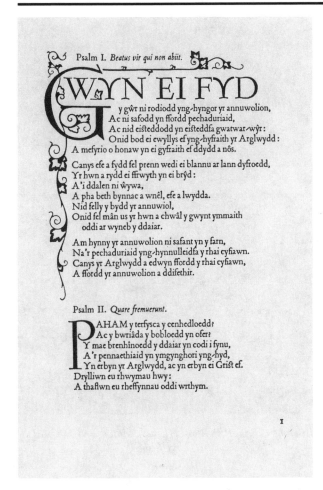

Psalm I. *Beatus vir qui non abiit.*

GWYN EI FYD

y gŵr ni rodiodd yng-hyngor yr annuwolion,
Ac ni safodd yn ffordd pechaduriaid,
Ac nid eisteddodd yn eisteddfa gwatwar-wŷr:
Onid bod ei ewyllys ef yng-hyfraith yr Arglwydd:
A mefyrio o honaw yn ei gyfraith ef ddydd a nôs.

Canys efe a fydd fel prenn wedi ei blannu ar lann dyfroedd,
Yr hwn a rydd ei ffrwyth yn ei brŷd:
A 'i ddalen ni wywa,
A pha beth bynnac a wnêl, efe a lwydda.
Nid felly y bydd yr annuwiol,
Onid fel mân us yr hwn a chwâl y gwynt ymmaith
oddi ar wyneb y ddaiar.

Am hynny yr annuwolion ni safant yn y farn,
Na'r pechaduriaid yng-hynnulleidfa y rhai cyfiawn.
Canys yr Arglwydd a edwyn ffordd y rhai cyfiawn,
A ffordd yr annuwolion a ddifethir.

Psalm II. *Quare fremuerunt.*

PAHAM y terfysca y cenhedloedd?
Ac y bwriâda y bobloedd yn ofer?
Y mae brenhinoedd y ddaiar yn codi i fynu,
A 'r pennaethiaid yn ymgynghori yng-hyd,
Yn erbyn yr Arglwydd, ac yn erbyn ei Grift ef.
Drylliwn eu rhwymau hwy:
A thaflwn eu rheffynnau oddi wrthym.

I

Page from Psalmau Dafydd: The Book of Psalms in Welsh, *published by the Gregynog Press in 1929*

bitious of the books in the Welsh language, with decoration consisting of openings with foliated borders and wood-engraved initials. Perhaps the richest decorative features to be found in any Gregynog book are the initials designed and engraved by Maynard for Abu Obeyd's *The Stealing of the Mare* (1930), translated by Lady Anne Blunt. Here the chaste Garamond type on heavy Japanese vellum is complemented by the gay hand coloring and gold of the floriated initial blocks. In Charles Lamb's *Elia and The Last Essays of Elia* (1931) one sees another side of Bray as an illustrator: each essay is prefaced by a small wood engraving of considerable wit and charm, entirely in keeping with the text. The last work designed by Maynard and Bray was a two-volume folio edition of *The Plays of Euripides* (1931), translated by Gilbert Murray, in which the illustrations are simple wood engravings drawn from Greek vase paintings in the British Museum.

Having firmly established the reputation of the press, Maynard and Bray left early in 1930 to found the Raven Press. The eighteen works they created at Gregynog are a monument of typographic dignity and restraint and set a standard only rarely achieved by those who were to follow.

Maynard was succeeded by William Mac-Cance, an artist, as controller, while Bray's successor was Blair Hughes-Stanton, a noted wood engraver. In the majority of the books produced in their first three years the text may be regarded as subordinate to the illustrations. Though there was a marked drop in typographical standards, artistically these books have great merit. The extraordinary fineness and delicacy of Hughes-Stanton's engravings required presswork of great skill, which was supplied by Hodgson. The most striking books from the MacCance-Hughes-Stanton partnership were John Milton's *Comus* (1931), which displays some fine costume engravings by Hughes-Stanton; the *Fables of Esope* (1932), with thirty-seven lively wood engravings by MacCance's wife, Agnes Miller Parker; and two folios, *The Revelation of Saint John the Divine* (1933) and *The Lamentations of Jeremiah* (1934), the first printed in black and red and the second in black and blue, which allowed full rein to Hughes-Stanton's manual dexterity and power as an imaginative artist. Miller Parker also provided charming wood engravings for *Twenty-one Welsh Gypsy Folk-tales* (1933). *Four Poems by John Milton* (1933) is one of the happier combinations of type and illustration of this era, the long, narrow type areas combining well with Hughes-Stanton's elongated figure engravings. Other contemporary books have initials designed and cut on wood by MacCance, which were frequently printed in a favored combination of sepia and black; these initials are not, however, uniformly successful as decorative devices.

Hughes-Stanton and MacCance resigned their posts in September 1933; in January 1934 Loyd Haberly, an American who had been running his own private press at Long Crendon in Buckinghamshire, was appointed controller on a part-time basis. Of the five books he designed, only one has pretensions to any real typographical merit: Xenophon's *Cyrupaedia* (1936), a handsome folio set in Poliphilus type with chapter heads and marginal notes in red and hand-colored woodcut initials designed by Haberly. Searching for a new type for exclusive use by the press, Haberly chose as a model the type used by Johann Neumeister of Mainz for his edition of

Dante's *Divina Commedia* printed at Foligno, Italy, in 1470. The type was redrawn by Graily Hewitt, the punches were cut by Edward Prince, and the matrices were made by the Monotype Corporation. Its only appearance in a British book was in the Gregynog edition of Robert Bridges's *Eros and Psyche* (1935), which was illustrated with drawings by Sir Edward Burne-Jones that were redrawn by Dorothy Hawkesley; it was further ornamented by initials designed by Hewitt.

James Wardrop was appointed controller in June 1936. His typographical approach was both formal and traditional, and the books produced under his direction are not, with one exception, outstanding. The exception is, however, generally regarded as one of the greatest achievements of the press: *The History of Saint Louis* (1937), by John, Lord of Joinville. It is a superlatively rich folio printed in sixteen-point Poliphilus type with marginal rubrics in Blado and initials in red and blue designed by Alfred Fairbank. Seventeen large hand-colored armorial shields, one at the foot of each page, were drawn by Reynolds Stone. The book's most impressive feature is its several handsome initial openings.

No other British private press paid anything like the attention to the binding of its books that the Gregynog Press did. That it did so was entirely due to George Fisher, the master binder, who presided over the bindery for almost twenty years. Fisher had been apprenticed in his youth to Rivière and Son, the fashionable bindery in London's Regent Street, where he had been responsible for much high-class work. He was appointed to Gregynog in 1925 and was to become the longest-serving member of the press staff. The special bindings, used for between fifteen and twenty-five copies of each edition and mainly executed in Levant morocco, were the work of Fisher himself, with the exception of one or two produced in later years when he was assisted by his apprentice, John Ewart Bowen. These bindings are superbly executed in every detail and distinguished by sound forwarding and faultless tooling.

Artistically, the most satisfying bindings are those designed by the various press artists. Designs from the Maynard regime tend to be basically geometrical, and, though pleasing, they fail to excite the imagination as do some of the bindings designed by Hughes-Stanton and MacCance. MacCance's two designs are of considerable interest. *The Fables of Esope*, bound in buff-colored Levant, has a front cover design consisting of an intri-

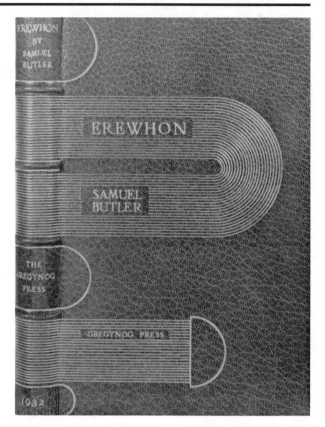

Binding designed by Blair Hughes-Stanton and executed by George Fisher

cate arrangement of the word *ESOPE* inlaid in reddish-brown leather, with the remainder of the title and the author's name tooled in gilt and blind. *The Singing Caravan* (1932), by Robert Vansittart, bound in deep orange Oasis, has a complex arrangement of lines extending over both covers and enhanced by small onlaid shapes in black. The binding incorporates an oriental-type fore-edge flap.

By far the most interesting as a group are those bindings designed by Hughes-Stanton, employing mainly abstract designs and incorporating gold and blind tooling and colored onlays. These bindings are to be found on Milton's *Comus*; *Caniadau gan W. J. Gruffydd* (1932); Samuel Butler's *Erewhon* (1933); *The Revelation of Saint John the Divine*; *Four Poems by John Milton*; *The Lamentations of Jeremiah*; Lope de Vega's *The Star of Seville* (1935), translated by Henry Thomas; Fulke Greville's *Caelica* (1937); and Juan Eugenio Hartzenbusch's *The Lovers of Teruel* (1938), translated by Thomas. Ten special binding were designed by Fisher; of these the most satisfying is that of Sir J. W. Fortescue's *The Story of a Red-Deer* (1936). Technically the most ambitious design is that on Xenophon's *Cyrupaedia*, designed by Lady Cartwright of Aynho, where the covers display an intricate geometrical pattern of intricate strapwork formed from various colored onlays outlined in gilt.

Three books were printed for private circulation: *Elphin Lloyd Jones* (1929), a memoir; *A Theme With Variations: Speeches and Articles* (1933), by Thomas Jones; and *John Davies* (1938), a memoir by Dora Herbert Jones. A considerable amount of more ephemeral printing was also undertaken, including programs for the Gregynog festivals of poetry and music held each year between 1933 and 1938, services, Christmas cards, concert and conference programs, and press prospectuses. The press closed in 1940.

In 1974 the University of Wales reestablished the press under the imprint Gwasg Gregynog, with Michael Hutchins as controller. The first book published by the revived press was R. S. Thomas's *Laboratories of the Spirit* (1976), printed in Janson type on handmade paper. Hutchins was succeeded as controller by Eric Gee, who was succeeded by David Esslemont.

References:

John Ewart Bowen, "Memories of Gregynog," *Manchester Review*, 8 (Spring 1959): 264-268;

Gwenllian Davies, "The Gregynog Press: A Talk to the Manchester Society of Book Collectors, 16 October, 1958," *Manchester Review*, 8 (Spring 1959): 257-263;

Dorothy A. Harrop, "George Fisher and the Gregynog Press," *Book Collector*, 19, no. 4 (1970): 465-477;

Harrop, *A History of the Gregynog Press* (London: Private Libraries Association, 1980);

Thomas Jones, *The Gregynog Press: A Paper Read to the Double Crown Club on 7 April, 1954* (London: Oxford University Press, 1954);

Mary Oldham, "Gwasg Gregynog: The Next Ten Years," *Antiquarian Book Monthly Review*, 16 (March 1989): 88-91.

—Dorothy A. Harrop

Grey Walls Press

(Billericay, England: 1940-1943; London: 1943-1954)

The Grey Walls Press was an outgrowth of the Channing Press, a small imprint in Dawlish operated by E. M. Channing-Renton. In 1933 Channing-Renton founded the quarterly *Poetry Studies*. Later he published the work of a previously unsuccessful writer, Charles Wrey Gardiner, including his autobiography *The Colonies of Heaven* (1938). Early in 1939 Gardiner became assistant editor of *Poetry Studies* and renamed it *Poetry Quarterly*.

After the outbreak of World War II, Channing-Renton, a former army officer, returned to military service, leaving Gardiner to carry on the *Poetry Quarterly*. Gardiner moved to an old house in Billericay known as Grey Walls, where he set up a bookshop to sell the magazine and what remained of the Channing Press backlist. Under his direction, the *Poetry Quarterly* published the work of Alex Comfort, Paul Scott, and the "New Romantic" poets; Denise Levertov's first poems were published in the magazine in 1939. Selling for one shilling, sixpence, the renamed magazine had an initial pressrun of 250 copies; within a few years the circulation would reach 4,000.

Urged on by the poet Samuel Looker, Gardiner began publishing books in December 1940. Of the first ten titles put out by the Grey Walls Press, five were written or edited by Gardiner, including a 1941 republication of his 1938 autobiography. Looker edited *The Nature Diaries and Note-Books of Richard Jefferies* (1941), published in a trade edition and a limited edition.

Gardiner formed a brief partnership with another poet, Nicholas Moore, and the Grey Walls Press was moved to Vernon Place in London. There Gardiner published the first of five volumes of *New Road*, an anthology of literature and art. That first volume (1943), compiled by Alex Comfort, included a section on surrealism edited by Toni Del Renzio.

Grey Walls Press split the cost of a salesman with another small poetry publisher, Peter Baker's Resurgam Books. After the war Baker launched the Falcon Press and persuaded Gardiner to join him. Under this arrangement, Gardiner and Baker became directors of Grey Walls Press, which was made a limited company, and Falcon Press. The two houses shared offices at 6 and 7 Crown Passage near Pall Mall, as well as a common business staff that included the novelist Paul Scott as company secretary, but Gardiner retained editorial control of the Grey Walls Press. The Falcon Press was a much more commercial operation than the Grey Walls Press.

Seán Jennett, who directed production and design for Grey Walls Press, created the firm's most memorable achievement, the Crown Classics series. These thirty-six volumes of classic poetry, published between 1947 and 1954, were beautifully designed and reasonably priced. Each volume was edited and introduced by a contemporary poet—Jack Lindsay for William Morris (1948), Stephen Spender for Walt Whitman (1950), and Geoffrey Grigson for George Crabbe (1951), for example.

Grey Walls Press also published American fiction, including Nathanael West's *Miss Lonelyhearts* (1949) and C. G. Finney's *The Circus of Dr. Lao* (1949). It published the first English edition of F. Scott Fitzgerald's *The Last Tycoon* (1949) and the revised version of his *Tender Is the Night* (1953). The firm also published the first English edition of Zelda Fitzgerald's novel *Save Me the Waltz* (1953), which sold miserably.

In 1953 Gardiner put an end to *Poetry Quarterly*, mainly because he had no sympathy with the newest literary wave, the school of "Movement" poets. Meanwhile, Falcon Press had run up staggering debts, thanks to Baker's freespending habits. In 1954 Baker pleaded guilty to forging signatures on financial documents and was sentenced to seven years in prison. The publisher John Calder wanted to save Grey Walls Press from the wreckage, but it was too closely bound up with Falcon Press. Gardiner was forced to close the enterprise, having published a total of 130 books.

References:

Roderick Cave, "The Grey Walls Press Crown Classics," *Private Library*, fourth series 2 (Autumn 1989): 100-117;

Alan Smith, "Grey Walls Press," *Antiquarian Book Monthly Review*, 13 (September 1986): 328-337;

Hilary Spurling, *Paul Scott* (New York: Norton, 1991).

—*Jonathan Rose*

Hamish Hamilton Limited
(London: 1931-)

Hamish Hamilton, known to his friends as "Jamie," served a two-year apprenticeship with Jonathan Cape and then took over the management of the London office of Harper and Row in 1926 before leaving to establish his own imprint in 1931. Using as his device the green bay tree, he set up his publishing house at 90 Great Russell Street, close to the British Library in the heart of Bloomsbury. Hamilton maintained a close relationship with Harper and Row for years after he embarked on his own, an association which was of benefit to both companies.

The first book put out under the new imprint was W. Graham Robertson's reminiscences, *Time Was* (1931), which sold well. The firm's subsequent literary output was diverse, including *Hotel Splendide* (1942), by Ludwig Bemelmans; *My World and Welcome To It* (1942), *The Thurber Carnival* (1945), *Is Sex Necessary?* (1947), and *The Beast in Me* (1950), by James Thurber; *The English People* (1943), by D. W. Brogan; *The Pursuit of Love* (1945), by Nancy Mitford; *In Camera and The Flies* (1946), by Jean-Paul Sartre; *Me and Mine* (1946), by Jack Jones; *The Outsider* (1946), by Albert Camus; *Inside U.S.A.* (1947), by John Gunther; *Usage and Abusage* (1947), by Eric Partridge; *Brave and Cruel* (1949), by Denton Welch; *The Day's Alarm* (1949), by Paul Dehn; *I Leap over the Wall*

Hamish Hamilton, 1980 (painting by Derek Hill; from Jamie: An 80th Birthday Tribute from His Friends, *1980)*

(1949), by Monica Baldwin; *The Pythoness and*

Other Poems (1949), by Kathleen Raine; *Tokefield Papers, Old and New* (1949), by Frank Swinnerton; *The Simple Art of Murder* (1950), by Raymond Chandler; *From Napoleon to Stalin* (1950), by A. J. P. Taylor; *The God That Failed* (1950), by Arthur Koestler; *The Catcher in the Rye* (1951), by J. D. Salinger; *The Moods of London* (1951), by R. J. Cruikshank; *Seeing More Things* (1951), by John Mason Brown; *The Unquiet Grave* (1951), by Cyril Connolly; *The Villa Diana* (1951), by Alan Moorehead; *World within World* (1951), by Stephen Spender; *Avenues of History* (1952), by L. B. Namier; and *Fancies and Goodnights* (1952), by John Collier.

Hamish Hamilton Limited had great success with the Novel Library, a series of reprints, in the late 1940s. The production editor, Oliver Simon, used patterns by well-known artists on the bindings and dust jackets, and the designs blended together when the books were placed side by side on a bookshelf. Other publishing undertakings were a series of *New Yorker* cartoon books (which are now collectors' items), an educational list, and a uniform edition of Willa Cather in the 1960s. A strong children's list in both fiction and nonfiction was developed by Richard Hough and flourished under Julia Macrae from 1968 until 1980, when she left Hamish Hamilton Limited to set up her own imprint. Elm Tree books, dealing with specialized subjects, were developed under the editorial directorship of Roger Machell, who had joined Hamish Hamilton Limited as a partner after World War II. Hamilton was passionately interested in music, and his firm published many books about musical performers.

Under financial pressure, Hamilton sold the firm to Thomson Publications in 1966 on the condition that he retain personal control of his list during his lifetime. He was managing director from 1931 to 1972, chairman from 1931 to 1981, and president until his death. His personal involvement and the loyal support of his editorial staff, particularly Machell and managing director Christopher Sinclair-Stevenson, ensured that the list remained distinguished and that the imprint continued to attract eminent authors: Georges Simenon, L. P. Hartley, John Hersey, Robert Ruark, Susan Howatch, Raymond Briggs, David Niven, Truman Capote, Hugh Thomas, Ed McBain, Edward Blishen, Philip Howard, Susan Hill, Robert McCrum, Paul Theroux, William Boyd, Jane Gardam, Jennifer Johnston, Clare Boyland, Stephen Vizinczey, Isobel Colegate, Nikolai Tolstoy, Peter Ackroyd—and Prince

Charles, whose children's book *The Old Man of Lochnagar* was published by Hamish Hamilton in October 1981.

On 15 November 1980, on the occasion of Hamilton's eightieth birthday, a limited edition of five hundred copies of *Jamie: An 80th Birthday Tribute From His Friends* was distributed. Twenty-four friends, colleagues, and authors paid tribute to Hamish Hamilton, the man and the firm. All stressed Hamilton's unequivocal commitment to excellence: Harold Acton described the imprint as "a synonym for distinction, discrimination, and catholicity of taste." John Kenneth Galbraith claimed that "Hamish Hamilton volumes are the best printed and the best published books in the English-speaking world." Julia Macrae said that Hamilton's publications were "a touchstone of excellence" and that Hamilton represented "all that was most honourable in publishing." W. Rees-Mogg made it clear that Hamilton was committed to the old tradition of British publishing—a tradition "which argues that publishing is about authors, and that the central theme of publishing is the establishment and maintenance of the relationship between the publisher and the author"; profit is seen to follow "as a natural consequence of publishing good books by good writers." In short, Hamilton had little regard for the new publishing conglomerates and the changes that they wrought on the publishing world, and he made few concessions to the new methods.

After the takeover by the Thomson Organization, Hamish Hamilton Limited distributed the prestigious *Times* publications, such as *The Times Atlas of the World* and *The Times Atlas of World History*. This involvement ceased in early 1982, after the Thomson Organization gave up ownership of Times Newspapers Limited.

Hamish Hamilton authors have consistently been the recipients of literary awards. The Whitbread Literary Award was given to James Buchan for *A Parish of Rich Women* (1984); the book also received the David Higham Prize. Also in 1984 Peter Ackroyd won the Whitbread Best Biography Award for *T. S. Eliot* and the Somerset Maugham Trust Fund Award for *The Last Testament of Oscar Wilde*, and Rose Tremain received the Dylan Thomas Prize for short-story writers for *The Colonel's Daughter and Other Stories*. In 1985 Tremain was given the Angel Literary Award for writers living and working in East Anglia for *The Swimming Pool Season*; Ackroyd picked up a Whitbread Literary Award and a Guardian Fiction Award for *Hawksmoor*, as well as the Royal Society of Literature Heinemann Bequest for *T. S. Eliot*; the John Llewellyn Rhys Memorial Prize for writers under thirty-five went to John Milne for *Out of the Blue*; and a Scottish Arts Council Book Award went to Elspeth Davie for *A Traveller's Room*. In 1988 the Thomas Cook Travel Book Award went to Paul Theroux for *Riding the Iron Rooster*, the Welsh Arts Council Prize for fiction was awarded to Bernice Rubens for *Our Father*, and the Yorkshire Post Book Award for best first book went to Anne Spillard for *The Cartomancer* (1987). In 1989 Tremain again received the Angel Literary Award, and also the Sunday Express Book of the Year Award for fiction, for *Restoration*, while the Time-Life Silver Pen Award for nonfiction went to Brenda Maddox for *Nora: Biography of Nora Joyce*.

In 1985 Penguin bought Thomson Books, thus acquiring the firms of Hamish Hamilton, Michael Joseph Limited, and Rainbird. The price was rumored to be £25 million. At the time of the purchase the managing director of the Thomson Books group, Francis Bennett, who was to join the Penguin board, made it clear that Penguin wanted the companies to retain their individual publishing identities; Penguin issued a press release to the same effect. It was also suggested that the companies would remain in their current premises. In 1986, however, Hamish Hamilton Limited moved from Garden House, 57-59 Long Acre, where it had been since November 1978, into the Penguin building at 27 Wrights Lane.

On 24 May 1988 Hamish Hamilton died at the age of eighty-seven. He had continued to take an active interest in the company, having spoken to the office by telephone that very day. At the end of June 1989 Sinclair-Stevenson, who had been with Hamish Hamilton Limited for almost thirty years, resigned as managing director to set up his own company, Sinclair-Stevenson, in South Kensington. From Hamish Hamilton he took with him Penelope Hoare to be editorial director, and such writers as Ackroyd, Tremain, Galbraith, Theroux, Hunter Davies, Selina Hastings, Susan Hill, Bernice Rubens, Clive Ponting, and A. N. Wilson.

On the resignation of Sinclair-Stevenson, Andrew Franklin took over as managing director of Hamish Hamilton Limited. The firm's publishing areas remain the same, but in an effort to reverse its losses the list has been reduced and Elm Tree publications have been scrapped.

References:

Jamie: An 80th Birthday Tribute from His Friends (Bristol: Privately printed, 1980);

"Penguin Buy Thomson Book Companies," *Bookseller*, no. 4137 (6 April 1985): 1473-1475;

Christopher Sinclair-Stevenson, "At the Sign of the Green Bay Tree," *Bookseller*, no. 3947 (15 August 1981): 530-532.

—Francesca Hardcastle

George G. Harrap and Company Limited
(London: 1917-   )
George G. Harrap and Company
(London: 1901-1917)

Born in 1867, George G. Harrap left school at fourteen. Nevertheless, he had an omnivorous appetite for learning. In 1882 he went to work for the publishing firm Isbister and Company. At Isbister, Harrap had dealings with the American publisher D. C. Heath and Company, which would be the first important business contact for his own publishing house.

In October 1901 Harrap founded George G. Harrap and Company at 15 York Street, Covent Garden. He quickly became the English representative for D. C. Heath and Company and, like Heath, emphasized educational books. His early relationship with D. C. Heath fostered the mistaken belief that Harrap, too, was an American publisher; this myth would persist in the British press even after George G. Harrap and Company had become a major force in English publishing.

In August 1905 George Oliver Anderson became Harrap's partner. Although he kept a low profile, his canny business sense was invaluable, and he helped push the company into publishing literature.

Harrap's Books Beautiful series proved popular despite the relatively high price of the volumes. The firm's entry into the field of illustrated books began when Willy Pogány, a Hungarian who had migrated to Paris and then to London in hopes of earning a living as an artist, visited Harrap in 1906. Harrap commissioned Pogány to illustrate *A Treasury of Verse for Little Children* (1907), which gained an international audience. Pogány illustrated several more books for Harrap, including *The Rubáiyát of Omar Khayyám* (1909) and Samuel Taylor Coleridge's *Rime of the Ancient Mariner* (1910). When World War I broke out in 1914 Pogány, afraid that the British government would deport him, fled to the United States. Harrap always regretted losing Pogány's services.

In 1910 George G. Harrap and Company moved to the second floor and basement of Lincoln Chambers, Portsmouth Street. By that time the firm had become the English representative for the American publisher Thomas Y. Crowell. In 1912 Harrap republished D'Arcy Thompson's *Day-Dreams of a Schoolmaster*, which had first been published in Edinburgh in 1864.

In 1913 George G. Harrap and Company expanded into the ground floor at Lincoln Chambers. Although World War I brought severe pressures on British publishing, with paper in such short supply that companies had to cut back their lists drastically, Harrap continued to grow. Under the guidance of the scholar J. E. Mansion, who took charge of Harrap's modern language department in 1914, work began in 1915 on a French dictionary that would, when it was finally published in two volumes between 1934 and 1939, set the standard for its field. In 1917 Harrap became a limited company. By 1920 it had grown so large that it had had to expand into the basements of 15 and 17 Chichester Rents, Chancery Lane, and in October of that year it leased offices at Great Turnstile, Holborn.

In 1912 Harrap's younger son, Walter, had joined the firm. After serving in the war the

Lincoln Chambers, Portsmouth Street, site of the Harrap offices from 1910 to 1934

elder son, George Steward, also entered the company.

During the 1910s and early 1920s George G. Harrap and Company Limited solidified its prominent standing in the field of educational books for general readers as well as for the classroom. Henry Bernard Cotterill's *Homer's Odyssey: A Line-for-Line Translation in the Metre of the Original* (1911) helped Harrap capture not only an important part of the scholastic market but also a broader popular audience. The book was reprinted many times over the following decades, as were Cotterill's *Medieval Italy during a Thousand Years (305-1313)* (1915), *Italy From Dante to Tasso (1300-1600)* (1919), and *Ancient Greece* (1922). Harrap's Myths and Legends series also moved into a mass market, with Thomas William Rolleston's *Myths and Legends of the Celtic Race* (1911) and Sister Nivedita (Margaret Noble) and Ananda K. Coomaraswamy's *Myths of the Hindus*

and Buddhists (1913). Although not having as much appeal for general audiences, W. H. Hudson's *An Introduction to the Study of Literature* (1910) remained a standard textbook through World War II. In 1925 Francis Henry Pritchard, who edited and wrote several successful books for Harrap, was put in charge of the company's English textbooks. The firm's continuing growth forced it to expand into a warehouse on Pancras Road in May 1926.

The internationally acclaimed artist Arthur Rackham illustrated for Harrap Washington Irving's *The Legend of Sleepy Hollow* (1928), Oliver Goldsmith's *The Vicar of Wakefield* (1929), John Ruskin's *The King of the Golden River* (1932), and Christina Rossetti's *Goblin Market* (1933). Stephen Gooden illustrated George Moore's *Peronnik the Fool* (1933), *Aesop's Fables* (1936), and O. Henry's *The Gift of the Magi* (1939). Such editions helped to keep Harrap among the leading

George G. Harrap (right) with his son George S. Harrap (left) and Winston Churchill, celebrating the publication of the first volume of Churchill's Marlborough: His Life and Times *(1933-1938)*

publishers of illustrated books.

Lily Adams Beck, under the pen name E. Barrington, wrote *The Thunderer: A Romance of Napoleon and Josephine* (1927); the firm also published Laurence Meynell's *Bluefeather* (1928) and Victor MacClure's *The "Crying Pig" Murder* (1929). In addition to these best-selling authors, Harrap's list included Édouard Herriot's *The United States of Europe* (1930) and Jan and Cora Gordon's *Star-Dust in Hollywood* (1930) and *Portuguese Somersault* (1934). The distinguished essayist Thomas Burke contributed *The Flower of Life* (1929). The critic and literary scholar Allardyce Nicoll's books became standard readings in their fields: *William Blake and His Poetry* (1922), *Dryden and His Poetry* (1923), *An Introduction to Dramatic Theory* (1923), *British Drama: An Historical Survey from the Beginnings to the Present Time* (1925), *Readings from British Drama: Extracts from British and Irish Plays* (1928), *Masks, Mimes and Miracles: Studies in the Popular Theatre* (1931), *The Theory of Drama* (1931), *Film and Theatre* (1936), *Stuart Masques and the Renaissance Stage* (1937), *World Drama from Æschylus to Anouilh* (1949), and *The Theatre and Dramatic Theory* (1962). Clennell Wilkinson's biographies *Nelson* (1931), *Bonnie Prince Charlie* (1932), and *Prince Rupert, the Cavalier* (1934) were also successful.

George G. Harrap's love of travel books helped nurture several travel writers, such as Stephen Lucius Gwynn, whose books included *Ireland: Its Places of Beauty, Entertainment, Sport, and Historic Association* (1927), *Burgundy: With Chapters on the Jura and Savoy* (1930), *Ireland in Ten Days* (1935), and *Dublin, Old and New* (1938). Sisley Huddleston contributed *Normandy: Its Charm, Its Curiosities, Its Antiquities, Its History, Its Topography* (1928), *What's Right with America: A Record of a Tour in the United States with Political, Social, Economic and Literary Comments* (1930), and *Between the River and the Hills: A Normandy Pastoral* (1931). William Buehler Seabrook contributed an eccentric series of travel books: *The Magic Island* (1929), *The White Monk of Timbuctoo* (1934), and *Asylum* (1935). Vilhjálmur Stefánsson made traveling an adventure in *The Northward Course of Empire* (1922), *Hunters of the Great North* (1923), *My Life with the Eskimos* (1924), *Ultima Thule: Further Mysteries of the Arctic* (1942), and *Greenland* (1943).

George S. Harrap persuaded one of the prominent travel writers of the day, John Joy Bell, to write for the firm. The first of Bell's books published by Harrap, *The Glory of Scotland* (1932), was a popular success.

During the 1930s Harrap established itself as a prominent publisher of children's books. It had published Hendrik Willem Van Loon's *The*

Story of Mankind in 1922, the year the book won the first Newbery Medal for the most distinguished children's book published in America. The firm went on to publish Van Loon's *The Liberation of Mankind: The Story of Man's Struggle for the Right to Think* (1926), *The Home of Mankind: The Story of the World We Live In* (1933), and *Ships and How They Sailed the Seven Seas (5000 B.C.-A.D. 1935)* (1935). Harrap also published D. M. Stuart's *Women of Plantagenet England* (1932), *The Girl through the Ages* (1933), and *Molly Lepel, Lady Hervey* (1936). Another major children's author, Eleanor Farjeon, contributed *Ameliaranne's Prize Packet* (1933) and *Ameliaranne's Washing Day* (1934), both illustrated by Susan Beatrice Pearse; Harrap sold more than one million copies of these books by 1951. Joyce Lankester Brisley's *Lambs'-Tails and Suchlike: Verses and Sketches* (1930) found a ready children's audience, as did her Milly-Molly-Mandy series, started in 1928.

Of all the distinguished authors whose works the firm published before World War II, the one with whom George G. Harrap seemed proudest to be associated was Winston Churchill. George S. Harrap had first contacted Churchill in 1929; this inquiry resulted in Churchill's four-volume biography *Marlborough: His Life and Times* (1933-1938).

In 1934 Harrap joined with Samuel French Limited to buy and share Cannon House, 182 High Holborn. Anderson became company chairman after George G. Harrap's death on 29 October 1938. In 1941 German bombs hit Harrap's offices, destroying the company's stock of about 250,000 books.

An author who bridged the prewar and postwar eras was Henry Anthony Clement, who produced *The Story of Britain* (1939-1953) in three volumes. Harrap also published his *A History of Europe, from 1789 to 1870* (1961) and *British History, 1865-1965* (1966). Harrap published *James Agate* (1926) as part of its Essays of To-day and To-morrow series, as well as Agate's *The Amazing Theatre* (1939), *Here's Richness!* (1942), and *The Contemporary Theatre, 1944 and 1945* (1946). Agate's autobiography appeared in installments over many years; Harrap took over its publication from Victor Gollancz with *Ego 3: Being Still More of the Autobiography of James Agate* (1938) and continued with *Ego 4: Yet More of the Autobiography of James Agate* (1940), *Ego 5: Again More of the Autobiography of James Agate* (1942), *Ego 6: Once More the Autobiography of James Agate* (1944), *Ego 7: Even More of the Autobiography of James Agate* (1945), *Ego 8:*

George G. Harrap's younger son, Walter, before a picture of his father. Walter Harrap joined George G. Harrap and Company in 1912 and was president at the time of his death in 1967.

Continuing the Autobiography of James Agate (1946), and *Ego 9: Concluding the Autobiography of James Agate* (1948). Janet Payne Whitney's biographies *Elizabeth Fry: Quaker Heroine* (1937), *John Woolman, Quaker* (1943), *Geraldine S. Cadbury, 1865-1941* (1948), and *Abigail Adams* (1949) were well received. Harrap continued to make biography an important part of its list by publishing Hubert James Foss's *Ralph Vaughan Williams: A Study* (1950) and Douglas G. Browne and E. V. Tullett's *Bernard Spilsbury: His Life and Cases* (1951).

The travel writer Mary L. Jobe Akeley contributed *Rumble of a Distant Drum: A True Story of the African Hinterland* in 1948. Harrap published some notable books on crime, including Alan St. Hill Brock's *Inquiries of the Yard* (1950) and Brock and Browne's *Fingerprints: Fifty Years of Scientific Crime Detection* (1953). Janet Dunbar's *The Early Victorian Woman: Some Aspects of Her Life, 1837-57* (1953) was successful, and the firm later published her *Flora Robson* (1960) and *A Prospect of Richmond* (1966).

Harrap broadened its publication of fiction in the 1940s and 1950s. Among its more distinguished books were those of Hans Habe (pen name of Jean Bekessy): *A Thousand Shall Fall* (1942), *Off Limits: A Novel of Occupied Germany* (1956), *Agent of the Devil* (1958), *Ilona* (1962), *Countess Tarnavska* (1964), *Anatomy of Hatred: The Wounded Land* (1964), *The Mission* (1966), *Christopher and His Father* (1967), and *Gentlemen of the Jury* (1967); Harrap also published Habe's *All My Sins: An Autobiography* (1957). The scholar Stanley David Porteus contributed fiction such as *Providence Ponds: A Novel of Early Australia* (1951). An eclectic writer, he produced travel and psychology books as well: *Calabashes and Kings: An Introduction to Hawaii* (1945), *The Restless Voyage: Being an Account by Archibald Campbell, Seaman, of His Wanderings in Five Oceans from 1806 to 1812* (1949), and *Porteus Maze Test Manual* (1952). Harrap also published Elizabeth Ogilvie's *My World Is an Island* (1951) and Ruth Chatterton's *The Southern Wild* (1959).

In 1958 Walter Harrap helped to introduce standardized billing practices to the English publishing industry with the Publishers Accounts Clearing House. At the time of his death in 1967 he was president of the company. He was succeeded by R. Olaf Anderson, the son of G. O. Anderson, who was followed by Walter Harrap's nephew Paull Harrap.

Harrap scored successes with the fiction of Philip McCutchan: *Gibraltar Road* (1960), *Bluebolt One* (1962), *The Man from Moscow* (1963), *Marley's Empire* (1963), *Warmaster* (1963), and *The Screaming Dead Balloons* (1968). Another significant book was George Vaizey's *A Lineage and a City: An Essex Family Cycle* (1970). During the 1960s and 1970s, however, Harrap increased its emphasis on educational books; by the 1980s such works constituted almost the entire list. In 1991 Dobby Eric was the managing director.

References:

Fifty Years of Publishing by Harrap (London: Harrap, 1951);

George G. Harrap, *Some Memories, 1901-1935: A Publisher's Contribution to the History of Publishing* (London: Harrap, 1935);

Partners in Progress: Some Recollections of the Past-Quarter Century at 182 High Holborn (London: Harrap, 1961).

—*Kirk H. Beetz*

Rupert Hart-Davis Limited
(London: 1946-   )

Rupert Hart-Davis began working in the book trade in 1929 as an office boy for William Heinemann; in 1932 he became manager of the Book Society, the first of the modern book clubs. In 1933 he became a director at Jonathan Cape. Even after joining the Coldstream Guards in 1940 Hart-Davis remained on Cape's board of directors, and he was often able to take an active part in the running of the company. In late 1945 he wrote to Cape suggesting negotiable terms for his salary and other financial arrangements. Cape misunderstood Hart-Davis's letter, and his reply referred to Hart-Davis's suggestions as "unreasonable proposals" to which he "could not possibly agree, nor do they offer any basis for discussion: the gap is too impossibly wide. I very much regret it, but can only quote your own phrase to you: 'You've had it.'" Hart-Davis sold his Cape shares and used the money to set up his own publishing firm in 1946 in partnership with David Garnett, who had been a cofounder with Francis Meynell of the Nonesuch Press.

The new company began with an office at 53 Connaught Street. Some Cape authors moved to Hart-Davis; in 1949, for example, Hart-Davis published the second edition of Neville Cardus's *Australian Summer*; the first edition had been published by Cape in 1937. Nor was the traffic all one way; also in 1949 Cape published *The Essential Neville Cardus*, "selected with an introduction by Rupert Hart-Davis." According to Michael Howard, Cape and Hart-Davis never went out of their way to meet after the breach, but at least

Rupert Hart-Davis

there was profitable communication between the two businesses.

Early Hart-Davis successes included Eric Linklater's *Sealskin Trousers and Other Stories*

(1947) and Stephen Potter's *The Theory and Practice of Gamesmanship* (1947); the latter became one of the classics of English humorous writing and was followed by Potter's *Lifemanship* (1950), *One-upmanship* (1952), and *Supermanship* (1958). An interest in Henry James became apparent from the start with the publication in 1946 of *Fourteen Stories*, edited by Garnett. Over the years reprints of James's work and critical works about him appeared regularly. Similar publications by and about Max Beerbohm resulted from Hart-Davis's personal interest in Beerbohm.

Two long-running series were started: The Mariner's Library of books concerned with sailing began in 1949, and The Reynard Library in 1950. The Reynard Library consisted of volumes containing selections from the work of various authors such as *Johnson: Prose and Poetry* (1950), edited by Mona Wilson, and *Memoirs of Laurence Sterne; The Life and Opinions of Tristram Shandy; A Sentimental Journey* (1951), edited by Douglas Grant; the books were well designed and printed, with wood engravings by Reynolds Stone. The title of the series was a reference to the firm's symbol of a fox, designed by Stone again, which was in turn a reference to Garnett's successful first publication under his own name, *Lady into Fox*, published by Chatto and Windus in 1922.

In 1951 the company moved to 36 Soho Square. Hart-Davis had an ability to find well-written books that sold well, sometimes exceptionally well; such works included J. H. Williams's *Elephant Bill* (1950), Alistair Cooke's *A Generation on Trial* (1950) and *Letters from America* (1953); Ray Bradbury's *The Illustrated Man* (1952) and *Fahrenheit 451* (1954); Edward Young's *One of Our Submarines* (1952); Heinrich Harrer's *Seven Years in Tibet* (1953); and Gerald Durrell's *The Bafut Beagles* (1954), *My Family and Other Animals* (1956), *The Drunken Forest* (1956), and *A Zoo in My Luggage* (1960). At the same time as these successful popular titles were appearing, poetry and academic books were also being published. The poets included Charles Causley, Andrew Young, Phoebe Hesketh, Ronald Duncan, R. S. Thomas, W. S. Merwin, and F. T. Prince. Academic publications included Leslie Hotson's *Shakespeare's Motley* (1952), *The First Night of Twelfth Night* (1954), *Shakespeare's Wooden O* (1959), and *Mr. W. H.* (1964); Humphry House's *Coleridge* (1953) and *Aristotle's Poetics* (1956); and Leon Edel's editions of James's works. Bibliographical works included John Carter's *ABC For Book-Collectors* (1952) and

Hart-Davis in later years

Books and Book-Collectors (1956) and the Soho Bibliographies Series, which began in 1951 with Alan Wade's *A Bibliography of the Writings of W. B. Yeats*.

The company had a commitment to good design, not just in the Reynard Library but in all its publications. Garnett's experience with the Nonesuch Press must have been an important influence; in addition, Young, the author of *One of Our Submarines*, was a book designer employed by Hart-Davis who later became a director of the book-design company Rainbird Limited.

Rupert Hart-Davis Limited was a small organization, and despite its string of successful titles (Hart-Davis is reported as claiming that it was *because* of the successful titles) the firm became overextended and suffered from a lack of capital. Young resigned in 1955, and the following year the company was bought by the Heinemann Group. The publishing policy remained unchanged under Heinemann, and the Hart-Davis imprint was allowed its independence. Authors such as Bradbury, Durrell, Hotson, and Williams stayed with the firm; the established series continued, as did the James and Beerbohm books. New authors such as Claude Cockburn and Diana Cooper were added to the list, and an important translation by Michael Meyer of the works of Henrik Ibsen was begun. Hart-Davis himself edited *The Letters of Oscar Wilde* (1962).

But the company was still languishing, and in 1962 it was acquired by the American publisher Harcourt, Brace and World. Harcourt, Brace and World had also acquired another British firm, Adlard Coles, which specialized in books about sailing; perhaps it was thought that Hart-Davis's Mariner's Library would supplement the Adlard Coles list. In any case, American ownership of Hart-Davis was short-lived. The Granada Group, which consisted of MacGibbon and Kee, Staples Press, and Arco, bought both Hart-Davis and Adlard Coles from Harcourt, Brace and World in 1963. Rupert Hart-Davis resigned the next year and left publishing to devote himself to writing and editing. At first the Hart-Davis imprint continued separately under Granada; new authors included Seán O'Faoláin, with *I Remember! I Remember!* (1962) and *Vive Moi* (1965), and Michael Moorcock, with *The Time Dweller* (1969). In 1967 the Hart-Davis office was moved to 1-3 Upper James Street.

The Granada Group acquired Panther Books and Mayflower in 1970 and Crosby-Lockwood in 1972. The general publishing division became known as Hart-Davis, MacGibbon Limited, involving some loss of independence for the two merged imprints. The Hart-Davis element became less and less distinguishable.

In 1983 the Hart-Davis imprint was bought by William Collins and became part of Grafton Books. Rupert Hart-Davis Limited still exists as a registered company, but it has never traded since going to Collins, and it seems unlikely that it ever will. The company is typical of many publishers in the second half of the twentieth century which have been absorbed into the conglomerates. From its foundation to at least 1956 it was the epitome of small British publishers, independently controlled by a few enthusiasts.

Reference:

Michael S. Howard, *Jonathan Cape, Publisher* (London: Cape, 1971).

—*John R. Turner*

Harvill Press Limited
(London: 1946-1955)
Collins Harvill
(London: 1955-)

The Harvill Press was founded early in 1946 by Manya Harari and Marjorie Villiers, taking its name from a conflation of their surnames. Harari had worked on the *Dublin Review* and had founded the *Changing Years*; Villiers had written books. Paper was still being rationed, but the Harvill Press succeeded in having a supply allocated to it. The firm's starting capital was two thousand pounds.

The aims of the founders of the Harvill Press were to build bridges between people of different nationalities and religions, to help in the restoration of the international cultural relations which had been cut off during the war, and to publish translations from French, Italian, Spanish, and Russian. Both were Catholics, and they were to publish many books—both religious and secular—by Catholics. They took over the publication of the *Changing Years* for about two years; the coeditor of the *Changing Years*, a leading Catholic layman, Bernard Wall, was one of Harvill's most influential advisers. Another Catholic adviser was Alec Dru, who brought important German authors to the company. Through the critic and translator Max Hayward the press became particularly well known for contemporary Russian literature in translation. Other sources of advice included René Hague and Fred Davey of the Harvill Press's printers, Hague, Gill and Davey; Davey eventually went to work for Harvill as production manager.

One of Harvill's leading authors was Ylla, whose photographic studies of animals joined books on cookery, gardening, and holiday-making in helping Harvill to stay afloat and to publish the books for which it had been founded. Probably the press's most important publication during its ten years of independence was Roy Campbell's translation of *The Poems of St. John of the Cross* (1951). Those years also saw the publication of English translations of works of many leading European theologians, philosophers, and scholars—including Jacques Maritain, Gabriel Marcel, Jean Guitton, Charles Péguy, Julien Green, Mircea Eliade, Hans Urs von Balthasar, Arnold van Haecker, Michael Hamburger, Le Corbusier, Patrice de la Tour du Pin, G. S. Fra-

ser, George Villiers, Tatiana Tolstoy, and Victor White—and political works on Kurdistan, Jordan, and Turkey.

The Catholic artist David Jones drew a device for use on the press's title pages, jackets, and publicity materials, but it was seldom used. Other artists who illustrated Harvill Press books included Osbert Lancaster, John O'Connor, and the cartoonist Anton.

In 1955 the Harvill Press, which was short on capital, was acquired by the firm of William Collins. Collins allowed the Harvill Press to retain its editorial independence. In 1958 the Harvill Press published Boris Pasternak's *Doctor Zhivago*, translated by Hayward and Harari. Harari died in 1969. Collins Harvill's address is 8 Grafton Street.

Reference:

Manya Harari, *Memoirs, 1906-1969* (London: Harvill Press, 1972).

—John Trevitt

William Heinemann Limited

(London: 1890-)

The history of William Heinemann Limited is virtually a history of modern British book publishing. It is a story of feuds, of company restructuring, of takeovers and mergers, of transatlantic alliances, of near bankruptcy, and of recovery. After a century William Heinemann Limited remains very much a presence in British publishing.

William Heinemann was born at Surbiton on 18 May 1863, the eldest son of Jane Lavino Heinemann of Manchester and Louis Heinemann, a native of Hannover, Germany, who had been naturalized in 1856. William Heinemann received a cosmopolitan education at a gymnasium in Dresden and with an English tutor. He studied music in Germany and became an accomplished musician, but his forte was appreciation.

It was in the publication of books that Heinemann's flair for discovering and guiding the talent of others found expression. He loved books not just for their content but for the craft of bookmaking, of which he became an acknowledged master. He received his training in publishing in the firm of Nicholas Trübner of Ludgate Hill; after Trübner died in 1884 Heinemann was largely responsible for the firm until it was sold to Charles Kegan Paul in 1889.

In 1890 Heinemann started in business for himself with an initial investment of five hundred pounds. The firm occupied two rooms on the third floor at 21 Bedford Street, Covent Garden. The first book published by Heinemann was Hall Caine's *The Bondman* (1890). It had been turned down by Caine's previous publisher, Chatto and Windus, and by Cassell; Heinemann snapped it up for three hundred pounds. The novel not only established the author's popularity but also gave the publisher a triumphant send-off. *The Bondman* received ecstatic reviews and

William Heinemann

sold a total of 450,000 copies. A few months after the appearance of *The Bondman* Heinemann published his friend James McNeill Whistler's *The Gentle Art of Making Enemies* (1890), which became the talk of London and enjoyed remarkable sales.

The International Library was another feature of Heinemann's first list. Edmund Gosse was Heinemann's adviser, reader, and editor for this series of translations of works of fiction. Björnstjerne Björnson's *In God's Way* (1890), translated from the Norwegian by Elizabeth Carmichael, was selected as volume one of the series; it was followed by Guy de Maupassant's *Pierre and*

Jean (1890), translated from the French by Clara Bell; Karl Emil Franzos's *The Chief Justice* (1890), translated from the German by Miles Corbet; and Matilde Serao's *Fantasy* (1890), translated from the Italian by Henry Harland and Paul Sylvester. The press commended warmly Heinemann's efforts to introduce the modern classics of Europe to English readers. In 1890 Heinemann also published Henrik Bernhard Jæger's *The Life of Henrik Ibsen*, translated by Bell, and novels by Lev Tolstoy.

By the end of 1892 Heinemann had more than a hundred books on his list. The International Library was joined by a series of monographs, The Great Educators, which included *Aristotle and the Ancient Educational Ideals* (1892), by Thomas Davidson, and *Loyola and the Educational System of the Jesuits* (1892), by the Reverend Thomas Aloysius Hughes. Volumes on Alcuin, Peter Abelard, Jean-Jacques Rousseau, Johann Heinrich Pestalozzi, Friedrich Wilhelm Froebel, and Horace Mann followed. Under the heading "Dramatic Literature," Ibsen's *Hedda Gabler* (1891) was conspicuous. Heinemann's 1892 list also included Arthur Wing Pinero's plays.

The outstanding commercial success for the firm that year was Maj. Henri Le Caron's *Twenty-Five Years in the Secret Service*. Le Caron's real name was Thomas Beach; he was a government spy who infiltrated the Fenians in America and ascertained their relationship to the Irish Nationalist party in Ireland. These discoveries played a leading part in the Parnell Commission report. The book ran through many editions and led to a formidable list of threatened libel actions against Heinemann, mainly from Irish members of Parliament.

Although no one person or firm can claim the credit for breaking the stranglehold of the fashionable circulating libraries, such as Mudie's, and killing off the "three-decker" novel, Heinemann was one of the first and most successful publishers of six-shilling single-volume novels. He and his firm received a flood of public attention by publishing Caine's *The Manxman* (1894) at six shillings and selling it through the bookshops. At the time Heinemann was benefitting from the advice of Sydney Pawling, a nephew of Charles Edward Mudie and previously one of the managers of and most experienced buyers for the library. Heinemann had persuaded Pawling to join him as a literary adviser and business partner in 1893; they had then taken over the whole build-ing at 21 Bedford Street to meet the growing needs of the publishing firm.

Heinemann's fiction list in the 1890s included books of the caliber of Henry James's *Terminations* (1895), *The Other House* (1896), *Embarrassments* (1896), *The Spoils of Poynton* (1897), and *The Awkward Age* (1899); Rudyard Kipling and Wolcott Balestier's *The Naulahka* (1892); and H. G. Wells's *The Time Machine* (1895), *The Invisible Man* (1896), and *The War of the Worlds* (1898). Heinemann also published most of E. F. Benson's novels, as well as works by John Masefield, D. H. Lawrence, George Moore, Robert Louis Stevenson, Robert Hichens, Sir Gilbert Parker, Israel Zangwill, Elizabeth Robins, Mrs. Dudeney, and William Frend de Morgan. Between 1895 and 1897 Heinemann published the *New Review*, under the editorship of W. E. Henley; Joseph Conrad's *The Nigger of the "Narcissus"* was published in the magazine in 1897.

With Caine, Whistler, and Beach, Heinemann acquired at the outset an essential ingredient for long-term prosperity: best-selling authors who became pillars of the back list. Although Heinemann began to establish a reputation for a cosmopolitan list, the firm did not ignore popular fiction, which was published mainly for the circulating libraries that were so important to the book trade at the time. Sarah Grand's *Heavenly Twins* (1893) and Flora Annie Steel's *From the Five Rivers* (1893), *The Potter's Thumb* (1894), and *On the Face of the Waters* (1897) were enormously profitable. Other financial successes included de Morgan's *Joseph Vance: An Ill-Written Autobiography* (1906) and Clothilde Graves's *The Dop Doctor* (1913), which was published under the pseudonym Richard Dehan and went through some forty editions. Books such as these provided the financial underpinnings for less commercial works of scholarship or translated fiction.

Heinemann became one of London's most respected publishers, exerting a considerable influence on the industry. He played a great part in founding the Publishers' Association of Great Britain and Ireland in 1896 and was president of the association from 1909 to 1911. From 1896 to 1913 he was a British representative on the International Commission and Executive Committee of the International Publishers' Congress; it was largely due to his initiative and energy that the congress came into existence. Through the congress Heinemann played a leading role in the protection of international copyrights. After his resignation from the congress in 1913 and until his

Heinemann advertisement

death in 1920 Heinemann was president of the National Booksellers' Provident Association.

Among the authors who have made a substantial contribution to Heinemann's prosperity is John Galsworthy, whose first book in his own name, *The Island Pharisees*, was published by the firm in 1904. Two years later Heinemann published *The Man of Property*, which was not only a commercial success but eventually became the first part of *The Forsyte Saga* (1922)—a work which, partly because of the BBC television series (1969-1970), has been hugely profitable for Heinemann. Heinemann agreed to publish W. Somerset Maugham's *Mrs. Craddock* (1902) after it had been rejected by other publishers as "improper." With only one exception, Maugham had all of the rest of his books published by Heinemann.

Heinemann published the plays of Pinero but turned down those of George Bernard Shaw because, he said, the public would not buy plays. He would prove his point by producing a ledger showing Pinero's accounts. Over the years, however, he would publish plays by Maugham, Zang-will, Henry Davies, and Charles Haddon Chambers. His own plays—*The First Step* (1895), *Summer Moths* (1898), and *War* (1901)—were published by John Lane.

Heinemann's art books included Arthur Rackham's *Rip Van Winkle* (1905) and W. L. Courtney's adaptation of De la Motte Fouqué's *Undine* (1909). Dr. Salomon Reinach's *Apollo* (1907), a history of art from earliest times, also bore the Heinemann imprint.

In the field of exploration, the house of Heinemann published Ejnar Mikkelsen's *Conquering the Arctic Ice* (1909). Heinemann had advanced Mikkelsen the money to complete the preliminary planning for his expedition, and the book sold sufficiently well to prevent any loss for the publisher. In 1909 Heinemann arranged for the simultaneous publication of Sir Ernest Shackleton's *The Heart of the Antarctic* in nine European languages.

The Loeb Classical Library was financed by Dr. James Loeb, an American banker. The original editors, T. E. Page and William Henry Denham Rouse, were soon joined by E. Capps, L. A. Post, and E. H. Warmington. The first volumes were published in 1912 jointly by Heinemann and the Harvard University Press. The series consists of parallel texts of the major Greek and Latin works from the time of Homer to the fall of Constantinople. Heinemann did not advertise the series because he thought it would find its own market, and it did. Loeb died in 1933; the Heinemann firm continued to publish the series until 1988, when it was sold to Harvard University Press.

Heinemann founded William Heinemann Medical Books in 1917. During his lifetime his firm published new books by more than five hundred writers, half of whom were novelists. He was described as a man of unbounded vitality with an infallible instinct for picking the right book; it was said that he "had a nose for merit like that of a dog for truffles." The device of a windmill, designed by William Nicholson, on the spine of his books seemed to guarantee their sales.

On the morning of 5 October 1920 Heinemann was found dead on the floor of his bedroom in his house on Lower Belgrave Street. His death provoked a crisis for the company. In 1899 Heinemann had married Magda Sindici, a young Italian author (he had published her first novel, *Via Lucis*, written under the pseudonym K. Vivaria, in 1898); they had been divorced

William Heinemann, George Moore, Edmund Gosse, and Haddon Chambers in Heinemann's garden at Ockham, 1919

in 1904. The marriage had produced no children. Heinemann had taken his nephew, Jack Heinemann, into the firm in the hope that Jack would be his successor. Jack Heinemann, however, had been killed in World War I. Pawling, William Heinemann's partner of twenty-seven years, could not afford to buy Heinemann's 55 percent stake in the firm.

Liquidation of the company or its absorption by a rival was averted when the New York publisher F. N. Doubleday, who was in London at the time and who had known Heinemann for thirty years, agreed to Pawling's plea that he buy the controlling interest in the firm and leave the company intact. Theodore Byard was made chairman and Charles S. Evans managing director. It was at Evans's suggestion that nine novels by Galsworthy were turned, with interpolated bridging passages, into *The Forsyte Saga*, *A Modern Comedy* (1929), and *The End of the Chapter* (1934). Evans accepted Graham Greene's first novel, *The Man Within* (1929); he also advised Greene to get a literary agent, a suggestion that Heinemann, who had opposed the rise of agency, would have found disagreeable. J. B. Priestley's *The Good Companions* (1929) and *Angel Pavement* (1930); the collected works of James Elroy Flecker, Max Beerbohm, and Maurice Baring; the essays of J. C. Squire; and novels by Mary Borden, Edna

Ferber, Margaret Kennedy, and Joseph Hergesheimer were added to the Heinemann list.

Doubleday built a printing plant and bindery, the Windmill Press, at Kingswood, Surrey, in 1926-1927. In 1927 the William Heinemann Limited offices were moved to 99 Great Russell Street. The effects of the Wall Street crash of 1929 forced Doubleday in 1932 to sell the firm to its directors, who formed a holding company, Heinemann Holdings Limited. In 1937 Heinemann Holdings acquired a majority interest in the publishing firm Peter Davies Limited; in 1938 Heinemann and Zsolnay was formed to help Paul Zsolnay, a refugee from Hitler's occupation of Austria. Evans died in 1944 and A. S. Frere became chairman of William Heinemann Limited.

After World War II Heinemann enjoyed many successes, such as *Boswell's London Journal 1762-1763* (1950) and Douglas Hyde's *I Believed: The Autobiography of a Former British Communist* (1951). The company reaffirmed its role as a major fiction publisher: Greene became a best-selling author; Nevil Shute, Georgette Heyer, Wilbur Smith, and Catherine Cookson were introduced; Maugham and Priestley went into standard editions; and there was a D. H. Lawrence revival.

In 1946 Alan Hill set about reviving the educational department, which had been discontinued during the war. He was given a tiny office and a small share of the paper allocation, enough to produce only twelve titles in three years. When paper rationing ended in 1949, Hill was able to spread his wings. He concentrated on publishing English literature and science books at the secondary level. In 1961 the department became a separate company, Heinemann Educational Books Limited, with offices first in Charles Street, then in Bedford Square, and subsidiaries in Australia, New Zealand, Southeast Asia, Africa, and Canada. In 1971 a holding company was formed for all Heinemann Educational Book companies. In 1978 a subsidiary called Tinga-Tanga—Swahili for *windmill*—was set up to market foreign educational books in the United Kingdom. The New Windmill series, shortened versions of contemporary works edited for young people, was one of Heinemann Educational Books' great successes. Another was the Drama Library, started by Edward Thompson in 1948. In 1979 Heinemann Educational Books moved into Bedford Square, with Hill as managing director. He retired from this position a few months later but remained to chair the Nigerian subsidiary. A. R. (Tony) Beal and Hamish MacGibbon took control of Heinemann Educational Books into the 1980s. By then, Hill was back as managing director of Heinemann Computers, a group within Heinemann Educational Books.

The firm of Secker and Warburg sought help from Heinemann in 1952. The firm was running out of money because of the rising cost of paper, printing, and binding. Heinemann took over Secker and Warburg's financial responsibilities, not only by purchasing shares of the company but also by the guarantee of an overdraft that grew through the years to more than one hundred thousand pounds. Heinemann took over accounting and the collection of debts and assumed responsibility for sales of Secker and Warburg books throughout the United Kingdom and Ireland—except in London, where Secker and Warburg's representative C. R. Roth continued his work. Heinemann also sold Secker and Warburg books overseas for a time.

When Rupert Hart-Davis's firm faced financial ruin in 1956, he sought refuge in the Heinemann tent. The Hart-Davis firm did not prosper under Heinemann and was sold in 1962 to Harcourt, Brace and World of the United States, which disposed of it to the growing Granada empire in Britain in 1963.

Heinemann in 1920, the year of his death

Although Rupert Hart-Davis and Secker and Warburg were distinguished subsidiaries, they produced some losses for the company. The paperback revolution depressed the sale of hardback books, and Heinemann had not entered the paperback market; stocks of unsold books, which were overvalued in account books, piled up. Though overseas expansion did accelerate schoolbook sales, these were not subject to prudent financial controls. By 1960 Heinemann Publishers Limited—the name had been changed from Heinemann Holdings Limited in 1959—was facing bankruptcy. Thomas Tilling, an important financial group, agreed to provide more capital in return for acquiring control of the Heinemann Group. But W. Lionel Fraser, Tilling's chairman, began to have doubts about a publishing group that had serious liquidity problems and an archaic organizational structure. Frere recommended that Tilling sell Heinemann Publishers Limited, and a deal was nearly signed with McGraw-Hill of the United States. At the last moment it was scotched by Fredric Warburg, and Heinemann became a wholly owned subsidiary of Tilling. That same year a potential merger with the Bodley Head foundered on the rocks of opposition within Heinemann.

At this time Secker and Warburg scored two notable successes: on 12 September 1960 it published in two large volumes David Daiches's *A Critical History of English Literature*. On 7 November William Shirer's *The Rise and Fall of the Third Reich* appeared. These books provided a solid financial foundation for the firm through the 1960s.

In 1961 Frere, who had been "kicked upstairs" to the newly created position of president, and his deputy, H. L. Hall, resigned. Editor James Michie left Heinemann for the Bodley Head, taking the authors Heyer and Greene with him. Dwye Evans, son of C. S. Evans, became managing director of Heinemann; one year later he replaced Peter Ryder, who had succeeded Frere as chairman. Charles Pick moved to Heinemann as managing director from Michael Joseph Limited, bringing with him such strong-selling authors as Monica Dickens and Richard Gordon. At Heinemann, Pick initiated a successful series of omnibus volumes of the works of back-list novelists, published jointly with Paul Hamlyn, that included authors from Franz Kafka to Maugham to Dennis Wheatley. They were greeted by the press as a major breakthrough and sold well. Heinemann Publishers Limited became the Heinemann Group of Publishers Limited in 1963.

John Le Carré was attracted to Heinemann from Victor Gollancz Limited, but he left for Hodder and Stoughton after two books, *The Looking Glass War* (1965) and *A Small Town in Germany* (1968). Maugham, Priestley, and Noël Coward remained large sellers. Kahlil Gibran's *The Prophet*, first published in 1926 and republished in 1966, was the largest selling book on the back list in the 1970s.

In 1977 Ginn and Company, originally an American firm that had opened a London office in 1901, was purchased for £1.7 million. Ginn complemented the Heinemann Educational Book list, but it was run as a separate company. Another acquisition, made in 1980 for six hundred thousand pounds, was Kaye and Ward, originally two small firms which had been combined when purchased by the Straker printing company in 1955. Kaye specialized in sports and topographical titles, Ward in juveniles. The Kaye and Ward purchase complemented the World's Work (1913) Limited list, owned by Heinemann since 1933.

In 1979 William Heinemann Limited moved to 10 Upper Grosvenor Street. At this time the Heinemann group was restructured in three tiers. At the top was the Heinemann Group of Publishers, with Pick as managing director and Michael Kettle, of Tilling, as chairman. Below

this level were William Heinemann International Limited, Heinemann Educational Books International, and Heinemann Distribution, all with Pick as chairman. Then came William Heinemann Limited and Secker and Warburg, with Thomas Rosenthal as chairman; and Heinemann Educational Books, with A. R. (Tony) Beal as chairman.

By 1982 the Heinemann Group was flourishing financially. It turned a pretax profit of £4.3 million on £30.5 million in sales. In April 1983 the industrial conglomerate BTR took over Thomas Tilling. The Heinemann Group remained a subsidiary of BTR until 1985 when BTR agreed to merge it with Paul Hamlyn's Octopus Publishing Group. Octopus paid £100 million for a 65 percent interest in Heinemann; BTR retained a 35 percent interest. The merger with Octopus was welcomed by the book trade, but it disrupted the Heinemann staff. Several authors joined other publishers. The merger put an end to the Heinemann Group as a self-contained entity, and Octopus sold off the Kingswood premises.

The Heinemann Group had scarcely resettled under its new owners when in July 1987 Hamlyn announced its sale to Reed International for £535 million. Again Heinemann found itself caught up in a major organizational and management review, which led to the resignations of Brian Perman, the managing director, and four other directors: Fanny Blake, Susan Boyd, Kate Gardiner, and Peter Grose. In September 1987 Helen Fraser was appointed to the newly created position of publisher. The Heinemann firm came to rest in the Octopus Group's new Michelin House headquarters at 81 Fulham Road.

As of 1989 Heinemann was publishing about eighty new titles a year and producing annual sales of £5 million. About 40 percent of its publications were nonfiction, including about ten titles a year under the Cedar imprint in the fields of self-help and positive thinking.

References:

"Death of Mr. Heinemann," *Times*, 6 October 1920, p. 13;

Guinevere L. Griest, *Mudie's Circulating Library and the Victorian Novel* (Bloomington: Indiana University Press, 1970);

William Heinemann, *The Hardships of Publishing* (London & Edinburgh: Balantyne Press, 1893);

Alan Hill, *In Pursuit of Publishing* (London: Murray, 1988);

Michael S. Howard, *Jonathan Cape, Publisher* (London: Cape, 1974);

"International Publishers' Congress: The Copyright Convention," *Times*, 17 June 1913, p. 7;

"Literature Gifts Endowment," *New York Times*, 14 October 1920, p. 12;

John London, "London Book Talk [obituary of William Heinemann]," *New York Times Book Review*, 20 October 1920, p. 19;

Vivienne Menkes, "William Heinemann," *British Book News* (October 1989): 688-692;

"Scholarship Fund for Literature," *Times*, 12 October 1920, p. 10;

John St John, *William Heinemann: A Century of Publishing* (London: Heinemann, 1990);

Fredric Warburg, *All Authors Are Equal* (London: Hutchinson, 1973);

Frederic Whyte, *William Heinemann: A Memoir* (London: Cape, 1928).

—*Linda Marie Fritschner*

Hogarth Press

(Richmond, Surrey: 1917-1924; London: 1924-   )

See also the Leonard Woolf entry in *DLB 100: Modern British Essayists, Second Series*; the Virginia Woolf entries in *DLB 36: British Novelists, 1890-1929: Modernists* and *DLB 100*; the John Lehmann entries in *DLB 27: Poets of Great Britain and Ireland, 1945-1960* and *DLB 100*; and the Chatto and Windus entry in *DLB 106: British Literary Publishing Houses, 1820-1880*.

In 1917 Leonard and Virginia Woolf set up a handpress in their dining room at Hogarth House, Paradise Road, Richmond, Surrey. What began as a hobby would in seven years develop into a growing commercial concern. Its first handprinted publication was *Two Stories* (1917), containing "The Mark on the Wall" by Virginia and "Three Jews" by Leonard. As Leonard records in his autobiography, *Beginning Again* (1964), he and Virginia decided that if *Two Stories* succeeded, they would "print and publish in the same way poems or other short works which the commercial publisher would not look at." The booklet of thirty-one pages sold well among their

friends; later the Woolfs worked out a more formal arrangement whereby Hogarth Press books were purchased by subscription, either to all publications or by individual title. By 1923 their business had grown to the point that they changed to the more common method of selling to booksellers at a discount.

The success of *Two Stories* led the Woolfs to embark on a more ambitious and, for inexperienced printers, daring project: in 1918 they handset, printed, and published *Prelude*, a sixty-eight-page story by Katherine Mansfield. Also in 1918 they printed for private distribution a book of poems by Leonard's brother, Cecil N. Sydney Woolf.

In 1918 T. S. Eliot introduced the Woolfs to Harriet Weaver of the *Egoist*, who gave them the manuscript for James Joyce's *Ulysses*. Although Virginia expressed personal reservations about it, they recognized its special achievement and decided that they would like to publish it. But the work was too long for them to set it by hand, and all of the printers they contacted turned

Virginia and Leonard Woolf in 1914, three years before they founded the Hogarth Press

down the job for fear of possible prosecution. The Woolfs were forced to return the manuscript. *Ulysses* was published in 1922 in Paris by Shakespeare and Company and in England by the Egoist Press.

In 1919 the Woolfs published Eliot's *Poems*, Virginia's *Kew Gardens*, Hope Mirrlees's *Paris*, and John Middleton Murry's *The Critic in Judgment*. From 1917 to 1932 the Woolfs handprinted thirty-four books, the most well known of which is undoubtedly Eliot's *The Waste Land* (1923).

The handprinted books are now collectors' items. They had colorful covers of heavy paper, sometimes of wallpaper. Some papers were designed by or collected by Roger Fry and his daughter Pamela; some were imported from the Continent. Leonard observed that as the first publisher to use "beautiful, uncommon and sometimes cheerful paper for binding our books, ... we started a fashion which many of the regular, old established publishers followed."

In 1920, having decided to publish two works too long to be printed by hand—Maksim Gorky's *Reminiscences of Leo Nicolayevitch Tolstoi* and Logan Pearsall Smith's *Stories from the Old Testament Retold*—the Woolfs secured the services of the Pelican Press, which had printed the second

edition of Virginia's *The Mark on the Wall* (1919). This was a turning point for the Hogarth Press: almost unintentionally it was transformed from a hobby to a commercial publisher. As Leonard was to put it later, "we found ourselves in the publishing business almost in spite of ourselves."

The early Hogarth Press was literally a cottage industry. The only financial outlay in founding the press was for the press and type; the investment of the owners' time, labor, and talent was gratis; and because the press was in their home there was no overhead. Their only costs were for paper and other materials, postage, hired labor, and royalties. They printed in the larder, bound in the dining room, and wrapped books for mailing and interviewed printers, binders, and authors in the sitting room. From 1918 to 1923 they hired part-time assistants, among them Barbara Bagenal and Ralph Partridge. In 1923 they hired Marjorie Thomson Joad full-time at a salary of one hundred pounds per year and half of the profits; she remained with them for two years. Later assistants were George Rylands, Angus Davison, Richard Kennedy, and John Lehmann.

A daring venture for a small press was Hogarth's early publication of translations from contemporary Russian writing. These translations were in large part the result of the encouragement and guidance of S. S. Koteliansky, a Russian émigré and a friend of the Woolfs. The first was Gorky's *Reminiscences of Leo Nicolayevitch Tolstoi*, translated by Koteliansky and Leonard Woolf. The success of this intimate portrait of the great novelist—a first edition of one thousand copies was quickly followed by a second printing of another thousand—led to a second translation from Gorky the next year. *The Note-Books of Anton Tchekhov with Reminiscences of Tchekhov* (1921) was also translated by Koteliansky and Leonard. In 1922 two more translations from the Russian appeared: the now widely recognized masterpiece by the 1933 Nobelist for literature, I. A. Bunin's *The Gentleman from San Francisco and Other Stories*, translated by Koteliansky and Leonard; and Fyodor Dostoyevski's *Stavrogin's Confessions and The Plan of the Life of a Great Sinner*, translated by Koteliansky and Virginia Woolf. Some copies of the Bunin volume, which contained four stories, carried an errata slip stating that D. H. Lawrence had been one of its translators but that his name had been omitted. "Stavrogin's Confessions" was unpublished chapters of *The Possessed* (1871-1872), and "Plan of the Life of a

The Minerva handpress used by the Woolfs at the Hogarth Press

Great Sinner" was a sketch for a novel that Dostoyevski never wrote. In January 1923 the Woolfs published Leonid Andreyev's *The Dark*, translated by L. A. Magnus and K. Walter; the year 1922 appears on the title page.

In March 1924 the Woolfs moved to 52 Tavistock Square in London; with the press in separate quarters and with a full-time assistant, they settled down to become full-fledged publishers. Although they continued hand-printing books as a hobby, as their publication lists grew they came to depend on commercial printers, working most closely with Clark of Edinburgh and the Garden City Press of Letchworth.

In 1924 the Hogarth Press assumed the publication of the papers of the International Psycho-Analytical Institute in Vienna, including the works of Sigmund Freud. The institute papers were under the general editorship of Dr. Ernest Jones, psychoanalyst and loyal disciple of Freud, assisted by James Strachey, a psychoanalyst and translator. From 1924 to 1946 twenty-seven papers were published, and the series continued into the 1980s.

The Hogarth Essays, First Series (1924-1926), consisted of nineteen titles; it was followed by a second series (1926-1928) of sixteen titles. These booklets sold for an average of two shillings, sixpence. From twenty to sixty pages in length, they dealt chiefly with literature and literary criticism, with an occasional number on aesthetics or politics. Among these essays were such classics as Eliot's *Homage to John Dryden: Three Essays on the Poetry of the Seventeenth Century* (1924), which also included his influential essay on the metaphysical poets; and Roger Fry's *Art and Commerce* (1926). The Hogarth Lectures on Literature, First Series (1927-1931), contained fifteen titles, the second series (1934) only one. All are book-length studies by authors who came to be recognized authorities in their fields, including Allardyce Nicoll's *Studies in Shakespeare* (1927), J. C. Grierson's *Lyrical Poetry from Blake to Hardy* (1928), and G. D. H. Cole's *Politics and Literature* (1929). Two titles sold especially well and became recognized as definitive statements: F. L. Lucas's *Tragedy in Relation to Aristotle's Poetics* (1927) and Edwin Muir's *The Structure of the Novel* (1928).

The Hogarth Living Poets—a first series (1928-1932) of twenty-four volumes and a second series (1933-1937) of five volumes—were collections of original poems published under the sponsorship and general editorship of Dorothy Wellesley, Duchess of Wellington. They featured the work of Robinson Jeffers, C. Day Lewis, Edwin Arlington Robinson, and John Lehmann. Probably the most significant title, however, was *New Signatures: Poems by Several Hands* (1932), edited by Michael Roberts. Including poems by Lehmann, Lewis, W. H. Auden, William Empson, and Stephen Spender, it signaled a modern reaction against "esoteric poetry" in favor of simplicity, using material presented by modern civilization.

The Russians were not the only foreign writers whose works were published by the press. The Italian Italo Svevo's short novel *The Hoax*, translated by Beryle de Zoete, appeared in 1929, and in 1930 his *The Nice Old Man and the Pretty Girl and Other Stories*, translated by L. Collinson-Morley, was published. In February 1931 (the title page says 1930) appeared the first of several translations of works by the German poet Rainer Maria Rilke: *The Notebook of Malte Laurids Brigge*, translated by John Linton. Rilke's *Duineser Elegien*, translated by V. Sackville-West and Edward Sackville-West, was also published in 1931.

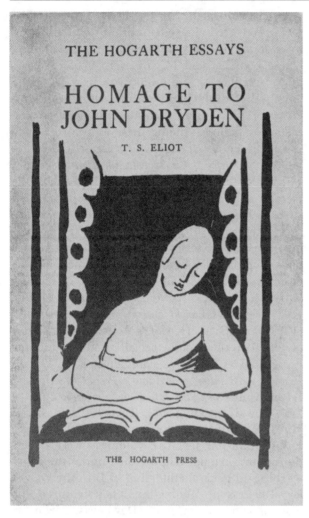

Wrapper for the fourth pamphlet (1924) in the Hogarth Essays series

The forty Day to Day Pamphlets (1930-1939), selling for one shilling, sixpence each, dealt with contemporary social, political, and economic issues. It was for this series that the press device of a highly stylized wolf head was designed by Eric McKnight Kauffer; it replaced a more representational wolf head in a medallion, designed by Vanessa Bell, that first appeared on the title page of Virginia Woolf's *The Common Reader* (1925). The first of the Day to Day Pamphlets, Maurice Dobb's *Russia To-Day and To-Morrow* (1930), an account biased in favor of the Communist state, was highly successful. Other significant works in the series were Aneurin Bevan, E. J. Strachey, and George Strauss's *What We Saw in Russia* (1931), Harold J. Laski's *The Crisis and the Constitution: 1931 and After* (1932), Henry Noel Brailsford's *If We Want Peace* (1932), Arthur Calder-Marshall's *Challenge to Schools* (1935), and Ray-

mond Postgate's *What To Do with the B.B.C.* (1935).

The twelve Hogarth Letters (1931-1933) were short essays on a variety of topics, including new poetry, new novels, the state of the church, what it means to be an Englishman, and childhood and growing up. All but one were republished in an omnibus volume in 1933. An autobiographical novel by Bunin, *The Well of Days*, translated by Gleb Struve and Hamish Miles, was published in 1933; a volume of his stories, *Grammar of Love*, translated by John Cournos, appeared in 1935. Rilke's *Sonnets to Orpheus*, translated by J. B. Leishman, came out in 1936. A series of four short biographies, World-Makers and World-Shakers (1937), included *Socrates*, by Naomi Mitchison and R. H. S. Crossman; *Joan of Arc*, by Vita Sackville-West; *Darwin*, by L. B. Pekin; and *Mazzini, Garibaldi & Cavour*, by Marjorie Strachey.

Lehmann was connected with the press at two different times. His first association, as apprentice manager, lasted from early 1931 to the autumn of 1932. *New Signatures* (1932), the "manifesto" of the new poets of the 1930s, owes much to him. In 1938, when Virginia decided to sell her interest in the press, Lehmann returned as part-owner and general manager. During his tenure as partner Lehmann was responsible for adding to the Hogarth list hardcover editions of *New Writing* (1938, 1939) and *Folios of New Writing* (1940, 1941); for Christopher Isherwood's *Goodbye to Berlin* (1939); and for four novels and an autobiography by Henry Green.

In 1939 the Hogarth Press moved to 37 Mecklenburgh Square. That year it published another translation of Rilke's *Duineser Elegien*, this one by Leishman and Spender and titled *Duino Elegies*. The Hogarth Sixpenny Pamphlets (1939) comprised five titles: E. M. Forster's *What I Believe*, Spender's *The New Realism*, John Betjeman's *Antiquarian Prejudice*, Virginia Woolf's *Reviewing*, and Graham Bell's *The Artist and His Public*.

In September 1940 German bombs destroyed 37 Mecklenburgh Square, and the press moved to the premises of its printers, the Garden City Press, in Letchworth; the title pages of Hogarth Press books, however, continued to show London as the place of publication. Reflecting Lehmann's strong interest in publishing poetry, The New Hogarth Library series (1940-1947) devoted its sixteen volumes to individual poets, including Rilke, Lewis, Arthur Rimbaud, Herman Melville, William Plomer, and Federico García

John Lehmann (left), part owner and general manager of the Hogarth Press, with Leonard Woolf in 1944

Lorca. During World War II the paper ration for the Hogarth Press was quite small. Top priority was given to the Uniform Edition of Virginia's works (she committed suicide in 1941) and to those of Freud; there were ever-increasing requests from America for the latter.

Within seven years after its first publication, the Hogarth Press's annual list had grown to fourteen titles and had branched out from fiction and poetry to include art, travel, biography, literary and art criticism, psychoanalysis, and foreign affairs. The list had reached a peak of thirty-six titles in 1932, falling off to twenty the next year and to seventeen in 1938. In 1939 the list was up to twenty-three, only to diminish gradually to four by 1946. Output was affected by the depression of the 1930s and by World War II but continued to grow in variety: books on economics, trade, government, labor, education, political theory, disarmament, religion, music criticism and music theory, even etiquette and health were published.

By 1946 the two partners were not in agreement on publishing policy, and Lehmann offered to buy Woolf's share of the press. Instead, Woolf bought Lehmann out and then sold Lehmann's share to Chatto and Windus. In 1947 the Hogarth Press became a limited company within Chatto and Windus, with Woolf being a director on the Hogarth board. Woolf died in 1969. Hogarth remains an allied company with Chatto and Windus, which in turn is a member of the Random House UK Limited Group. Chatto and Windus and the Hogarth Press are at 30 Bedford Square; the managing director is Carmen T. Callil.

References:

Richard Kennedy, *A Boy at the Hogarth Press* (London: Whittington, 1972);

John Lehmann, *I Am My Brother* (London: Longmans, Green, 1955);

Lehmann, *Thrown to the Woolfs* (New York: Holt, Rinehart & Winston, 1979);

Lehmann, *The Whispering Gallery* (London: Longmans, 1960);

Donna E. Rhein, *The Handprinted Books of Leonard and Virginia Woolf at the Hogarth Press, 1917-1932*, Studies in Modern Literature, 52 (Ann Arbor, Mich.: UMI Research Press, 1985);

Frederic Spotts, ed., *Letters of Leonard Woolf* (San Diego: Harcourt Brace Jovanovich, 1989);

Leonard Woolf, *Beginning Again* (London: Hogarth Press, 1964);

Woolf, *Downhill All the Way* (London: Hogarth Press, 1967);

Woolf, *The Journey Not the Arrival Matters* (London: Hogarth Press, 1969);

J. Howard Woolmer, *A Checklist of the Hogarth Press, 1917-1946* (Revere, Pa.: Woolmer/ Brotherson, 1986).

Papers:
The chief repositories of Woolf papers with respect to the Hogarth Press are the University of Sussex, the University of Reading, and the Humanities Research Center at the University of Texas at Austin.

—Mary E. Gaither

Hutchinson and Company (Publishers) Limited
(London: 1887-1985)
Hutchinson (Century Hutchinson Limited)
(London: 1985-1989)
Hutchinson (Random Century Limited)
(London: 1989-   )

For almost the whole of its first hundred years, the House of Hutchinson, as it was often called, was the property of one family. Its official title for most of that time was Hutchinson and Company (Publishers) Limited, part of the Hutchinson Publishing Group. Then, within the space of ten years, it changed hands three times.

Born on 18 April 1857 into a Victorian upper-middle-class family that had fallen on hard times, George Thompson Hutchinson started his working life as an apprentice to Alexander Strahan, publisher of various "improving" magazines such as *Good Words for the Young*. After serving his apprenticeship he joined the publishing house of Hodder and Stoughton as a salesman. He made three round-the-world trips while working for the company, and it was on the third of these that he met his future wife, Frances Octa-

via Cornwell, in Melbourne. They were married there in 1886.

Returning to England, Hutchinson started his own business on 10 October 1887 in the basement of 25 Paternoster Row, near St. Paul's Cathedral. The opening capital was three thousand pounds, of which he borrowed one thousand from a friend. Some of the remaining two thousand pounds, it was said, came from the sale of his stamp collection.

A cautious man, Hutchinson did not choose the first two titles to appear under his imprint until the summer of 1888; and when they appeared in the following summer they were, perhaps, a slightly surprising foundation for a list that was to contain so many star attractions in the century to come: a collection of short stories, *In Australian Wilds* (price one shilling), and *The Mod-*

ern Reciter (price sixpence), edited by Alfred H. Miles. Hutchinson commissioned Miles to put together a series of improving anthologies, calculated to appeal to the emerging literate population in the late-Victorian age. They included in 1889 *Our National Songs with Music, Songs of the Queen's Navee,* and *137 English Ballads,* and the first two volumes in the "Fifty-two" series, which was to go on multiplying during the remaining years of the nineteenth century. Each of the "Fifty-two" books contained a story for each week of the year, and fifty-two volumes were planned. The first two were *Fifty-two Stories for Boys* and *Fifty-two Stories for Girls,* and as time went on the titles became increasingly synonymous with Victorian moral values—*Fifty-two Stories of Life and Adventure for Boys* (1895) and *Fifty-two Stories of Life and Adventure for Girls* (1895), *Fifty-two Stories of Pluck and Peril for All Boys* (1896) and *Fifty-two Stories of Pluck, Peril and Romance for Girls* (1896), *Fifty-two Stories of Duty and Daring for Boys* (1897) and *Fifty-two Stories of Duty and Daring for Girls* (1897), and *Fifty-two Stories of Courage and Endeavour for Boys* (1901) and *Fifty-two Stories of Courage and Endeavour for Girls* (1901).

In 1890 Hutchinson launched The Boy's Golden Library and The Girl's Golden Library with children's novels which had gone out of copyright, followed by a series of adult novels in cheap (two shillings and sixpence) editions in Hutchinson's Library of Popular Novels. Seventy titles were published in 1890, including eighteen by Mrs. J. H. Riddell. Many of the names, like hers, are forgotten today, but well-known authors on the reprint lists included Louisa May Alcott, Nathaniel Hawthorne, J. Sheridan Le Fanu, and Jules Verne. Some new popular fiction was also published, much of it in three volumes priced at ten shillings and sixpence each, a standard practice at the time.

The basement office was beginning to become somewhat cramped for this volume of output, and in 1893 the firm moved into larger premises at 34 Paternoster Row. The staff was increased to eighteen, and one of the newcomers was the young Stanley Paul, who soon became one of the company's outstanding salesmen.

In 1894 Hutchinson had its first major success with a new novel when it published *A Yellow Aster,* by Iota, the pseudonym for Mrs. Mannington Caffyn. It was one of the last novels to be published in three volumes for thirty-one shillings and sixpence. By 1895 the leading publishers had decided that in the future novels

should be published in a single volume at seven shillings and sixpence or even six shillings.

At this time Hutchinson was about to take on Marie Corelli, whose *The Sorrows of Satan* (1895), published by Methuen, had made her probably the most popular novelist in Britain. Hutchinson persuaded her to join his list with an advance of four hundred pounds against a royalty of 12 1/2 percent for *The Mighty Atom* (1896). Though she had written to him that she was impressed by "your knowledge of the Colonial trade and your adaptability to the exigencies of the time," Mary Mackay (Corelli's real name) refused to grant him an option on her next novel. The prepublication subscription to *The Mighty Atom* was big enough, however, to convince her that her new publisher knew his job, and she handed over her next novel, *Cameos* (1896), for an advance of five hundred pounds against the same royalty. The two novels were published within three months of each other, and sales topped one hundred thousand within a year.

Even more significant for the future of Hutchinson was the firm's entry into magazine publishing with two lavish productions, the *Lady's Realm,* launched in 1896, and the *Girl's Realm,* for eight- to seventeen-year-olds, started in 1898. Each was priced at sixpence, and they had circulations of one hundred thousand and forty thousand, respectively.

There followed in 1900 an even more spectacular development. Five years earlier the Reverend Henry Neville Hutchinson (no relation) had offered the company an unfinished book titled *The Living Races of Mankind.* He had been working on the text for years but was unable to afford the illustrations or the fees for the quotations that he was amassing. The company advanced him £100 or £150 from time to time but stopped when the total had reached £750 and nothing publishable had been produced. Finally the clergyman sold the firm the whole project. George Hutchinson proceeded to commission articles from various experts; but when these were assembled, together with all the material bought from the clergyman, it became clear that more than one volume would be needed. *The Living Races of Mankind* became the first of the Hutchinson part works, which revolutionized the whole part-work market. Up to this time such works had been down-market and poorly produced; the new book was printed on glossy art paper and illustrated with properly processed halftone blocks. The first printing of one hundred thousand cop-

Walter Hutchinson, son of the founder of Hutchinson and Company and chairman of the firm from 1926 until his death in 1950

ies of part one, priced at sevenpence, went on sale in October 1900; it was to be published fortnightly, but the appearance of part two was held up for two more weeks while part one was being reprinted. The eighteen parts were published in book form in 1901 and received enthusiastic reviews. Lavish part works edited by George Hutchinson followed each other over the next twelve years, culminating in *Marvels of the Universe* (1911-1912) in twenty-four fortnightly parts. They contributed not a little to the financial success of the company. The year 1900 was notable for the sale of ninety thousand copies (in four printings) of a novel, *The Farringdons*, by Ellen Thorneycroft Fowler; there were also novels by Corelli, William Le Queux, and the prolific Annie S. Swan. In 1901 the firm published W. Somerset Maugham's third novel, *The Hero*. Other novelists who joined the imprint in the early years of the

century included Rafael Sabatini; Jerome K. Jerome; Anthony Hope; and Philip Gibbs and Eden Philpotts, who were to stay with the firm for the rest of their lives. (When Philpotts died in 1960 he had had seventy-one novels published by Hutchinson without ever having granted the firm an option on his next work.)

In nonfiction Hutchinson concentrated mostly on big, heavily illustrated works about royalty and natural history, interspersed with biographies and memoirs. There is no doubt, however, that it was popular fiction that made Hutchinson's reputation; it even anticipated Penguin Books by thirty-five years when Hutchinson inaugurated a series of Sixpenny Paper Novels in 1900.

Like many other major figures in the publishing world, Hutchinson was not known for his openhandedness. "Look after the pennies" was his constant admonition to the staff. Nevertheless, he was able to make the big gesture when the opportunity arose, and in 1904 he purchased the distinguished publishing house Hurst and Blackett. This was the first of the major acquisitions which were to transform the House of Hutchinson—though George Hutchinson never showed the same determination to buy every company that came on the market that was to characterize the career of his son.

Walter Hutchinson was born in Camden Town the year his father founded the company. He was educated at Haileybury and at St. John's College, Oxford. In 1909 he entered his father's business and started his publishing career by helping to edit *The Wonders of the World*, published in twenty-four parts in 1910. In 1911 he was called to the bar, but he never practiced law. He appears to have taken over the part works; the last one edited by his father, *Marvels of the Universe*, appeared in 1912.

That year George Hutchinson received a knighthood for "services to literature," the first publisher to be so honored. He continued his highly successful policy of publishing—and advertising extensively—a wide range of titles, mostly novels but some nonfiction, at bargain prices of one shilling, sevenpence, and sixpence.

The early years of the company's second quarter century saw the acquisition of many authors already famous or soon to become so. They included H. de Vere Stacpoole; G. B. Stern with her first novel, *Pantomime* (1914); Mrs. Belloc Lowndes; Berta Ruck; Ethel M. Dell; Upton Sinclair; and Gilbert Frankau. It must all have placed a great strain on Sir George, who, up to 1914, was so insistent on keeping strict financial control in his own hands that he even produced the company's tax returns himself. The Inland Revenue was not happy about this arrangement, and after twenty-seven years Hutchinson and Company acquired its first accountants.

A few months after the outbreak of World War I Walter Hutchinson entered the War Office, where he became superintendent of publications. His duties evidently left him sufficient time to continue his publishing career: his name appears as editor on several of the company's part works, such as *Belgium the Glorious* (1915) and *The Splendour of France* (1918). The war years led to a reduction in output throughout the trade, though not a severe one in the case of Hutchinson. The firm was, however, forced to discontinue the Sixpenny Paper Novel series in 1916.

The company did branch out in other directions. From the time when he had edited his first part work, Walter Hutchinson had resented the firm's dependence on allied trades—having to buy paper from one firm and blocks from another, and then having to send the printed work to a binder. He wanted all these activities to be carried out under Hutchinson and Company's own auspices; but such ambitious proliferation went directly against the cautious philosophy of Sir George, whose guiding principle was "never borrow money." Not only did he insist on having enough cash in the bank to pay for what was ordered; he even deposited cash in advance with his main suppliers, who were required to pay interest until the funds were needed to pay for services rendered. In 1918, however, Sir George authorized Walter to purchase the Anchor Press, a small printing works in Tiptree, Essex, for two thousand pounds. Within two years the Anchor Press's wooden structure had been replaced by a new building, more machinery had been installed, a new manager appointed, and the staff increased from thirty to a hundred.

After the war Walter Hutchinson was made a partner with a seat on the board. In 1919 Sir George purchased the religious publishing house of Skeffington, which had been founded in 1844.

Although the *Lady's Realm* and the *Girl's Realm* had been successful initially, they had ceased publication with heavy losses in 1915. Ignoring his father's warnings, Walter launched three new magazines: *Hutchinson's Story Magazine* in 1919, *Hutchinson's Adventure-Story Magazine* in 1922, and *Hutchinson's Mystery-Story Magazine* in 1923. These magazines, and many more that he started in the years to follow, were to play a substantial role in the firm's later difficulties.

On the book side the situation was a good deal brighter. The biggest success of the immediate postwar years was the novel that made Gilbert Frankau famous, *Peter Jackson, Cigar Merchant* (1920). E. M. Delafield joined the list, and there were new works by old favorites such as Stacpoole, Lowndes, Hope, and E. F. Benson.

Strangely enough, the nonfiction publications included some war memoirs by Germans. The first such work was the two-volume *My War Memories 1914-1918* (1919), by Gen. F. W. E. Ludendorff, which had been strongly recommended for publication by a solicitor, F. A. Holt, who married Walter Hutchinson's sister. Perhaps owing to sensitivity about publishing German war memoirs so soon after hostilities, the book appeared under the Hurst and Blackett imprint rather than that of Hutchinson. (It was also Hurst and Blackett that, in 1933, was to publish Adolf Hitler's *Mein Kampf* [1925, 1927] in an expurgated translation as *My Struggle*; when the full version appeared in 1939, it was under the Hutchinson imprint.)

Immediately after the war an Australian office was opened in Melbourne. South Africa was to follow later. Meanwhile, in London, the cramped offices in Paternoster Row were the headquarters not only of the editorial, production, advertising, and sales departments but also of packaging and shipping. Stocks had to be stored at printers and binders, for which storage charges had to be paid. The strain became intolerable as Walter added a growing chain of magazines to an already overloaded system, and he solved the problem by acquiring Ireland Yard, a three-story warehouse within a few hundred yards of Paternoster Row. It remained the Hutchinson storage, packaging, and shipping headquarters for more than forty years.

An event which was to have an unforeseeable importance for the future of the company was the appointment by Walter Hutchinson in 1922 of a new secretary. Mrs. Katherine Webb was to play a vital role in the firm's survival during the last years of Walter Hutchinson's life and even more so after his death.

Prior to his retirement in 1926, Sir George revived his paper-covered reprints at sixpence to counter the launching of the Readers Library of clothbound reprints at the same price by Woolworth's. His move led to some controversy with the retail booksellers, who were less than enthusiastic. He sold the sixpenny paperbacks extensively through shops other than bookshops, and when the bookshops started a boycott of Hutchinson books he threatened to sell them in Woolworths as well. The boycott was halted.

Walter Hutchinson had recently bought the long-established blockmakers Hill and Company, and the retiring chairman must have been increasingly disillusioned with his son's mania for expansion. He retired with a handsome cash payment and a contract worth £525 a year as publisher's reader. Some preferred shares in the company were made available to the public, but all the common shares were owned by Walter, who became managing director.

Sir George lived for six more years, partly in his town house in Pont Street and partly in a country house in Sussex. Philip Gibbs contributed a warm obituary to the *Sunday Times*: "He had a broad and catholic judgment and as far as fiction went was quick to see quality in the younger writers if they showed any power of storytelling or characterisation. I suppose the House of Hutchinson has produced more first novels than any other publishing firm. That is good for the writers of the first novels, though not perhaps so good for the reading world who are becoming bewildered by so great a tide of fiction."

In the year of Sir George's retirement Hutchinson and Hurst and Blackett between them published 211 new titles. By the end of the year, with Walter in control, they had five hundred more under option or contracted. Among the outstanding novelists who first appeared on the Hutchinson list around this time—some of them making their first appearance in print—were Ethel Mannin, Michael Arlen, Richmal Crompton, Pamela Frankau, and one of the most popular romantic novelists of the day, Ursula Bloom, who stayed on the Hutchinson list for the rest of her life. The novelist, biographer, critic, essayist, and literary adviser Frank Swinnerton made his first appearance on the Hutchinson list in 1923 with *Young Felix*. In nonfiction the tendency was strongly toward biography, autobiography, and travel.

It was said of the new managing director that he seldom met authors or read books but that he was always ready to pay handsomely for a well-known name. He was even more eager to acquire any small, ailing publishing house that came to his notice. His father had added Hurst and Blackett and Skeffington, and in the years to come they were joined by Rider and Company, a publisher of books about oriental religions and the occult; Geographia, a publisher of maps, atlases, and guides; the old established house of Jarrolds; Rich and Cowan, which had been founded by Walter's brother-in-law, Rodney St. John Richard, and had gone into liquidation; Stanley Paul and Company, which had been founded by Hutchinson's former salesman in 1906 and went into liquidation in 1927; John Long; Andrew Melrose; Selwyn and Blount; Denis Archer; Popular Dogs; and probably many others which have vanished into the mists of time.

If Mr. Walter, as he was always known (he never succeeded in his ambition to follow his father's knighthood), was anxious to buy any publishing house that became available, he was even more ruthless in his quest for printers and allied trades. He set up the Hutchinson Printing Trust in 1926, and the following year he bought the Plymouth printing and bookbinding firm William Brendon and Son. In 1928 he set up the Hutchinson Paper Company. A year later he launched Hutchinson Publicity Limited, which allowed the publishing company, as advertising agents, to claim a 10 percent commission on its own advertisements. By 1930 he had added five more printing firms around the country, including the St. Albans firm of Fisher, Knight, and another binder. More were to follow—especially during World War II, when the Greycaine Book Manufacturing Company (later to become Taylor Garnett Evans), the Grout Engraving Company, and the Cheltenham Press were among the more prestigious firms to find shelter under the umbrella of the Hutchinson Printing Trust.

Mr. Walter was to acquire, in addition, racehorses and a racing stable, several farms, an airport with five airplanes, a cosmetics firm, another firm manufacturing sausages, and a splendid collection of paintings including one of John Constable's best-known landscapes.

This eccentric character, who became a legend in the world of publishing, was to remain in dictatorial charge of the House of Hutchinson for a quarter of a century. Robert Lusty worked for him for seven years, starting in 1928 writing blurbs in a doorless cubicle in Paternoster Row, graduating to commissioning jackets, then to overseeing illustrations, and finally to managing Selwyn and Blount. In his 1975 autobiography he wrote of Walter Hutchinson: "His treatment of human beings, dependent upon him for their living, was of a nature so vicious and tyrannical that the only possible defence of those obliged to endure it was to proclaim his insults and humiliations in a sort of riotous spirit of oneupmanship. The more extravagant his excesses, the more unreasonable his attitudes, the more preposterous his requirements, the more outlandish his arrogance and the more bullying his behavior, the greater became accentuated a sort of lunatic happiness experienced by well-nigh every man and woman involved in the madness of those Paternoster Row years. To-day, getting on for half a century later, there still exists among a dwindling few a certain nostalgia for the goings-on which never ceased while Walter Hutchinson was alive. . . . Some of those treated most abominably never ceased in loyalty and even a certain affection."

Hutchinson's eccentricity resulted in many idiosyncracies when it came to producing books. He instituted an outright ban on printing the year of publication—"We can't sell books with dates in them," he insisted—a devastating deprivation for bibliographers. He would sometimes announce two, three, or even more impressions before publication. He also had the season's entire catalogue bound in at the end of every book. Perhaps his most damaging decree was the absolute rule that every advertisement for a Hutchinson title should carry the announcement: "The Largest Publisher in the World." This obsession resulted in a longstanding feud between Hutchinson and Company and the *Bookseller*, the organ of the book trade, whose editor, Edmond Segrave, refused to accept any advertisement bearing such an unauthenticated claim. The outcome was a stalemate in which no advertisement for Hutchinson appeared in the journal until after Mr. Walter's death. He also contrived to upset other publishers and literary agents by inserting an advertisement in a London newspaper in which he invited "authors and agents who think that their books should be selling better, and who wish for greater advances" to "write *in private* to the Chairman, Mr. Walter Hutchinson, Hutchinson & Co."

Nevertheless, as Lusty points out, Mr. Walter was to remain "the pivot around which a very large organisation somehow revolved." Even if he seldom met authors or read books, over the years some remarkable names found their way onto the list, and many of them remained. Naomi Jacob and Barbara Cartland were added in 1930; H. G. Wells stopped for two titles during his peregrination among the London pub-

lishers. Among the 320 authors whose books were published in 1935, two names stand out—R. H. Mottram, with *Early Morning*, and Lion Feuchtwanger, with *The Jew of Rome*. But from the financial point of view perhaps the company's most significant newcomer in the 1930s was Dennis Wheatley, whose first novel, *The Forbidden Territory*, appeared in 1933 and who was to stay faithful to his original publisher for the rest of his life with fifty-five novels of adventure.

Many series, book clubs, and pocket libraries were launched year by year during the 1930s. At the outbreak of World War II Mr. Walter took what many consider to have been the most far-reaching decision of his career: foreseeing the severe rationing of paper that would occur, he bought enormous stocks; the result was that, while many companies had to restrict their output severely, Hutchinson averaged three million copies per year throughout the war, including republications.

Nevertheless, disaster hit the firm, along with other publishers in Paternoster Row, in December 1940. The premises were entirely destroyed in one of the fiercest air raids of the blitz, and with the building all the company's records went up in smoke. The staff moved temporarily to the warehouse in Ireland Yard while Mr. Walter vacated his flat in Princes Gate, Knightsbridge, which was to become the company's wartime headquarters; the overflow was lodged in his father's old house in Pont Street.

Naturally, a good proportion of the list during the early 1940s consisted of books relating to the war; but there were some notable exceptions, such as Sir Thomas Beecham's autobiography, *A Mingled Chime* (1944). The company even launched a magazine, *Printers' Pie*, during the war, and started a specialized imprint, Hutchinson Scientific and Technical. The *Saturday Book* made its first appearance at Christmas 1941; the brainchild of Leonard Russell, literary editor of the *Sunday Times*, who edited it until he was succeeded by John Hadfield in 1951, it was an annual miscellany that was a triumph of wartime production. *Saturday Book* number 3, published in 1943, is described in an editorial note as "a documentary of past and present." Authors of the caliber of Alexander Werth, J. Maclaren-Ross, Dilys Powell, Stephen Potter, Sean O'Casey, Julian Huxley, Peter de Polnay, Francis Iles, and A. A. Milne contributed articles specially written for the volume; these were preceded by an ambitious sixty-four-page section of photographs covering a century of British life, many of them admirably reproduced in photogravure. Needless to say, all the printing and block-making were carried out within the Hutchinson empire.

The end of the war found Walter Hutchinson once again on the move. Not only did the publishing company need a new home, but he must have thought it even more important to find premises which could house his vast collection of paintings and prints, of which the centerpiece was Constable's *Stratford Mill*. Perhaps it was the coincidence of names that persuaded him to settle on Stratford Place in London's West End. The building had originally been called Derby House when it was the London home of the earls of Derby. Then, as Stratford House, it was the prewar headquarters of Christies, the auctioneers. In 1946 it became Hutchinson House. (Today it is Stratford House once more and is the headquarters of the Oriental Club.)

It took some time to organize the paintings in the huge ballroom and magnificent outer rooms, which were opened to the public in 1949 as the National Gallery of British Sports and Pastimes. This arrangement left only a rather cramped space on the other side of the building for the publishing company, and several departments still had to be housed in Princes Gate and Pont Street.

Most of Walter Hutchinson's publishing innovations were fairly short-lived. These included the New Library of Popular Classics, which had been started in 1933; Hutchinson's Universal Book Club, started in 1938; and Hutchinson's Pocket Library of clothbound classics priced at sixpence, also started in 1938. One which lasted longer was the Hutchinson University Library, launched in 1946. Short introductions to academic subjects, for the first few years the books in the series were in the charge of William Kimber; but he, like many other of the company's executives, fell foul of the chairman and was summarily dismissed. In his case, however, Mr. Walter sent an uncomplimentary note to other senior executives, forbidding all contact with him. Kimber won a lawsuit for libel and with the proceeds set up his own publishing house.

In his last years Mr. Walter seldom appeared in the office. He conducted most of the business on the telephone from his Hampshire home, occasionally sending angry memos to his employees. During all this time it was the remarkable Mrs. Webb who kept the train on the rails, acting as a buffer between the chairman and his punch-drunk staff. Since 1934 she had been a director of the firm. Somehow she warded off Mr. Walter's worst excesses, quietly warned his victims when they should lie low, and advised them how to cope with fresh attacks. Never by word or deed did she so much as hint at a criticism of Mr. Walter or permit one to be made in her presence.

Without Mrs. Webb it is doubtful if the House of Hutchinson would have survived his death in 1950. Along with F. C. Thomas, who had joined the firm as company secretary in 1925, Mrs. Webb was appointed joint managing director. She attended to the publishing, Thomas to finance. Walter Hutchinson's widow was named chairman.

Walter Hutchinson had died intestate; his widow, together with the solicitor F. A. Holt, who had married Walter's sister, and their solicitor son, R. A. A. Holt, had to establish the ownership of the Constable and the racehorses, the farms and the sausage factory, the Hampshire School of Flying and its five aircraft. They disposed of Hutchinson House, the National Gallery of British Sports and Pastimes, and other irrelevant pieces of the publishing empire. The publishing companies moved into more suitable premises on the fourth floor of a block of flats in Great Portland Street.

Mrs. Webb's rule lasted for nearly six years. Somehow she juggled the competing imprints, each of which had a manager answerable only to her. Never, apparently, did Jarrolds know anything of Hurst and Blackett's publishing plans, there was nothing to differentiate John Long from Rich and Cowan, and the only imprint which was forced by its name to adhere to a set subject was Popular Dogs.

In 1956 Lusty returned to take control of the company where, nearly thirty years previously, he had served his apprenticeship. In the meantime he had had a distinguished career at Michael Joseph Limited (whose founder had worked for Hutchinson from 1920 to 1924). Some order had been introduced by then. There was a holding company, Hutchinson Limited, of which R. A. A. Holt was chairman. The Hutchinson Printing Trust was separated from the Hutchinson Publishing Group, and it was the latter that Lusty headed as chairman and managing director.

He saw his first job as one of rationalization. It was said that literary agents, having failed

178-202 Great Portland Street W1

LANGHAM 3020

From the Chairman
Hutchinson Publishing Group

12th August 1958.

Dear Swinnerton,

This comes with an early and uncorrected proof copy
of an autobiographical work, Brendan Behan's BORSTAL BOY, of which
we have the highest opinion.   Perhaps you already know the name of
Behan as the author of a successful play of prison life called THE
QUARE FELLOW.   It may be that you know something of his considerable
reputation as a Gaelic poet.   But BORSTAL BOY seems to me a unique
volume in many respects and I hope you will forgive me if I venture
to say a word about it.

Not long before the war, when he was sixteen years
of age, Behan joined the Irish Republican Army in Dublin as a militant
member.   He came to Liverpool, and only a few days after his arrival
he was arrested in his room while he was tinkering with his explosive
stock in trade.   He went first to remand prison and then to Borstal,
on his release from which he was deported to the Republic of Ireland.
BORSTAL BOY tells the story of those years in an Irish-English prose
which, in its nervous accuracy and immediacy, seems to me unsurpassed
even by Sean O'Casey at his best.   Now, Behan is certainly a 'character'
in a very un-English manner; he is extravagent in his conduct and in his
language; but he is no longer a romantic desperado, and this autobiographical
account is not at all an anti-English self-justification.   On the contrary
he came to value England during those years more than many Englishmen do.
It is, rather, in our view, a quite extraordinary delineation of the lower
depths of society, informed in every aspect by deep insight and compassion.
Behan speaks very frankly, to be sure, of prison life and Borstal life,
but while this frankness has its own considerable value (for there is very
little genuine and articulate writing in England about those levels of
society which most of us choose to forget), it seems to me that Behan's
re-creative powers is so intense that his book so far transcends its subject
as to say a good deal of universal and permanent value about humanity
itself.   We are convinced, in short, that this is one of those few pieces
of autobiographical writing which truly illumine the human condition.

/......

THE HUTCHINSON GROUP

First page of a letter from Lusty to the novelist Frank Swinnerton. On the second page of this letter concerning Brendan Behan's Borstal Boy *Lusty asks Swinnerton to contribute a blurb for the book (Hutchinson and Company files, Frank Arthur Swinnerton Papers, Special Collections Division, University of Arkansas Libraries, Fayetteville).*

Robert Lusty, who worked at Hutchinson from 1928 to 1935 and returned in 1956 as chairman of the firm; he retired in 1974 (drawing by Hubert Williams; from Robert Lusty, Bound to Be Read, 1975).

to sell a project at one office on the fourth floor of Great Portland Street, would save time and postage by walking along the corridor to offer it to another imprint. Bearing in mind that at the end of one cricket season three Hutchinson companies had rushed out competing books simultaneously on the current Test matches, Lusty allocated special fields to those imprints which remained extant. Rider reverted entirely to the occult and oriental religions and Stanley Paul to sports and pastimes. Hurst and Blackett became a specialist in romantic fiction under the editorship of Dorothy Tomlinson, who for years had been Mrs. Webb's assistant. John Long, specializing in crime and thrillers, had the distinction of being the first publisher of Ruth Rendell, who was to become one of the country's most respected crime novelists. There were two general lists—

Hutchinson itself and Jarrold's, under Cherry Kearton, which was to be responsible for books of an ephemeral nature.

One of Lusty's most farsighted moves was the establishment of the subsidiary New Authors Limited. This firm was designed as a partnership of writers of first books—almost invariably novels—so that they could learn the realities of publishing. There was a standard advance and royalty, and each author received the imprint's balance sheet. Although the contract contained no option clause, so that the author's second book did not have to be published by the Hutchinson group, Stanley Middleton wrote twenty-eight novels after his first, *A Short Answer*, appeared in 1959, and all were published by Hutchinson. He was the joint winner of the Booker Prize with *Holiday* (1974). Other authors whose first novels were published by New Authors included Julian Mitchell, James G. Farrell, Beryl Bainbridge, Elizabeth Mavor, and Maureen Duffy.

An important part of Lusty's strategy was to give the company some credibility, which it had perhaps lacked at times, as a publisher of long-lasting works of literary distinction. He was delighted when the literary agent A. D. Peters offered him *The Sleepwalkers* (1959), by Arthur Koestler, followed by the other two volumes of the trilogy, *The Act of Creation* (1964) and *The Ghost in the Machine* (1967). Koestler stayed with Hutchinson for the rest of his life. The company published the Danube Edition of his collected works (1965-1969).

Having rationalized the publishing side of the firm's activities Lusty brought in Iain Hamilton, formerly of the *Guardian* and the *Spectator*, as editorial director in 1957. His extensive contacts led to some excellent acquisitions, especially as a result of trips he made to Ireland. Most prominent among the Irish authors was Brendan Behan, whose autobiographical *Borstal Boy* (1958) went through many editions. Many of Behan's later books were dictated into a tape recorder and transcribed by Rae Jeffs, the company's publicity director and a sister of R. A. A. Holt. She gave up her job to be at hand when needed and worked with Behan in London, New York, and Dublin as drink increasingly undermined his health and finally killed him in 1964. Other Irish fiction included Edna O'Brien's first novel, *The Country Girls* (1960); Michael Farrell's classic *Thy Tears Might Cease* (1963), which was published posthumously after it had been edited by his friend Monk Gibbon; and *Strumpet City* (1969), the novel that made James Plunkett famous. Gibbon joined the list with his autobiography *Inglorious Soldier* (1968).

By the time *Thy Tears Might Cease* was published Hamilton had departed to edit the *Spectator*; his place as editorial director was taken in 1962 by another journalist, the literary editor of the London *Evening Standard*, Harold Harris. As Hutchinson reached its seventy-fifth year, it had moved back into the forefront of leading British publishers, with a growing worldwide reputation. Lusty had built up a first-class editorial team that was responsible for a selection of best-sellers and serious literary works during the 1960s and 1970s. Production, jackets, publicity, and sales all had separate departmental managers; printing, warehousing, and distribution were under different management.

Gabriel Fielding wrote most of his best novels for Hutchinson in the 1960s, including *The Birthday King* (1962). W. H. Canaway made his name with *Sammy Going South* (1961), and the novel of the film *2001* (1968) was a notable contribution from Arthur C. Clarke. Francis King wrote twelve books, including novels and volumes of short stories, for Hutchinson. The most phenomenally successful author of the period was undoubtedly Frederick Forsyth, whose first novel, *The Day of the Jackal* (1971), became a best-seller throughout the world and was followed on the Hutchinson list by his next four novels and a volume of short stories. Another successful novelist in the espionage category was Len Deighton. Perhaps the best known of Anthony Burgess's novels to appear under the imprint is *Earthly Powers* (1980). Kingsley Amis's much-praised work *The Old Devils* (1986) won the Booker Prize.

Biography and autobiography have played a major role throughout the company's history. Conor Cruise O'Brien wrote of his experiences with the United Nations in Africa in *To Katanga and Back* (1962). The military historian John Terraine wrote the standard life of Field Marshal Haig, *Douglas Haig: The Educated Soldier* (1963), and was also the author of *The Life and Times of Lord Mountbatten* (1968). The earl of Longford (Frank Pakenham) wrote his autobiography, *Five Lives* (1964), and six years later, with Thomas P. O'Neill, coauthored the official biography *Eamon de Valera* (1970). Edith Sitwell's autobiography, *Taken Care Of*, appeared in 1965. Andrew Boyle joined the list with his biography of Lord Reith (John Charles Walsham Reith) of the BBC, *Only the Wind Will Listen* (1972); he followed it with

Poor, Dear Brendan: The Quest for Brendan Bracken (1974), winning that year's Whitbread Prize for biography. His study of espionage, *The Climate of Treason* (1979), led to the unmasking of Anthony Blunt.

Other biographies included a series by Anita Leslie about the Churchill family, of which she was a member; *Joseph Stalin: Man and Legend* (1974), by Ronald Hingley; *Majesty* (1977), by Robert Lacey, a biography of Queen Elizabeth II; *Robert Graves* (1982), by Martin Seymour-Smith; and *Solzhenitsyn* (1985), by Michael Scammell. Political autobiographies included *Boothby: Recollections of a Rebel* (1978), by Lord Boothby (Robert John Graham), and the diaries of the Rt. Hon. Tony Benn, M.P., of which the first was *Out of the Wilderness* (1987). But certainly the autobiography which caused the greatest worldwide comment was *20 Letters to a Friend* (1967), by Svetlana Allilueva, Stalin's daughter, which she brought with her when she defected from the USSR. Also from the USSR came five volumes of memoirs from Ivan Maisky, culminating in *Memoirs of a Soviet Ambassador* (1967); the novel *Children of the Arbat* (1988), by Anatolii Rybakov; and Andrei Gromyko's *Memories* (1989). American authors include Richard Condon, with several novels; Alex Haley, with *Roots* (1977); William Manchester, with *American Caesar* (1979), his biography of Gen. Douglas MacArthur; and Norman Mailer, with *The Executioner's Song* (1979).

Of the many reference works published since World War II, by far the most successful has been the one-volume *Hutchinson Twentieth Century Encyclopedia*, first published in 1949 and followed by seven completely revised editions. Hutchinson has earned a reputation for poetry under the editorship of Anthony Whittome, with an impressive list of poets including Dannie Abse, Gavin Ewart, and Anthony Thwaite. The Hutchinson reputation for travel books has always been well maintained; the most prominent author in this field today is Tim Severin, starting with *The Brendan Voyage* (1978).

Lusty retired in 1974. By then the rather bleak fourth floor in Great Portland Street had been exchanged for a noble but somewhat impractical townhouse in nearby Fitzroy Square. One legacy Lusty left the company was the device of a bull, which he had commissioned Charles Mozley to design. It was a rather massive, ground-pawing beast, and Lusty's successor, Charles Clark, had it adapted to the present abstract head and horns. By the time of the transfer of power Lusty had become Sir Robert Lusty, knighted no doubt—like the first managing director—for his services to literature, but also in recognition of his services as a governor (and, for some years vice-chairman) of the BBC. He died on 23 July 1991.

Clark came to Hutchinson from Penguin, where he had been in charge of educational publishing. Not surprisingly, therefore, he decided to build up Hutchinson's educational list under the guidance of Mark Cohen; that side of the business has since been sold. He also lent his Penguin expertise to building up the Arrow imprint, which is taking its place among the front-running paperback houses. Cutting back in some areas but expanding in others, he presided over the disappearance of Hurst and Blackett, Jarrold's, and John Long and the acquisition of Barrie and Jenkins, complete with the entire P. G. Wodehouse backlist.

In 1979 R. A. A. Holt, chairman of the publishing group as well as of the holding company, decided that the time had come to sell the firm that had been owned by three generations of his family. The purchaser was London Weekend Television (LWT), under the chairmanship of John Freeman and, when he retired, of Christopher Bland. In 1985 a controlling interest in the Hutchinson publishing group was bought from LWT by Anthony Cheetham and combined with Century Publishing Limited, which he had recently founded. Century Hutchinson, as the combined company was called, moved to Covent Garden. In 1989 Century Hutchinson was sold to the American firm Random House, which had recently bought the British houses Jonathan Cape, Chatto and Windus, and the Bodley Head. The vast new organization was named Random Century, and in January 1990 all the imprints of the new group moved to Random Century House in Vauxhall Bridge Road.

References:

Sir Robert Lusty, *Bound to Be Read* (London: Cape, 1975);

"Mr. W. Hutchinson [obituary]," *Times* (London), 1 May 1950, p. 8;

"Sir G. Hutchinson [obituary]," *Times* (London), 21 December 1931, p. 12.

Papers:

Correspondence relating to Hutchinson and Company is contained in the Frank Arthur Swinnerton Papers, Special Collections Division, University of Arkansas Libraries, Fayetteville.

—*Harold Harris*

Herbert Jenkins Limited
(London: 1912-1965)

Herbert Jenkins Limited was founded in 1912 by the novelist Herbert Jenkins. In its first year the firm published two books of poetry, *Poems to Pavlova*, by A. Tulloch Cull, and *The Days of the Year*, by M. D. Ashley Dodd, with an appreciation by Henry James. In 1913 Jenkins published *The Muse in Exile: Poems, to Which Is Added an Address on The Poet's Place in the Scheme of Life*, by William Watson; it also put out a collected edition of Watson's previously published works. That year the firm published biographical/critical studies of William Morris, by Arthur Compton-Rickett; Leonardo da Vinci, by Jens Thiis; and Francisco Goya, by Hugh Stokes, as well as *The Baconian Heresy: A Confutation*, by J. M. Robertson. Patrick MacGill's *Children of the Dead End: The Autobiography of a Navvy*, appeared in 1914, followed the next year by more autobiographies: *Indian Memories*, by Lieut. Gen. Sir Robert Baden-Powell; *Forty Years in Canada*, by Col. S. B. Steele, a retired Mountie; and *Lodges in the Wilderness*, by W. C. Scully, as well as *Songs of the Fields*, by Francis Ledwidge. Jenkins also published Theodore Watts-Dunton's study of Romantic poetry, *Poetry and the Renascence of Wonder*, and translations of three comedies by the French dramatist Eugène Brieux: *Woman on Her own, False Gods and the Red Robe*.

In 1918 P. G. Wodehouse, who had begun his career in 1902 with A. and C. Black, came over to Jenkins with his novel *Picadilly Jim*. The firm also published Wodehouse's *A Damsel in Distress* (1919), *The Coming of Bill* (1920), *The Girl on the Boat* (1922), *The Adventures of Sally* (1922), and the first Jeeves novel, *Inimitable Jeeves* (1923).

Jenkins died in 1923, leaving his publishing house, all his copyrights, and his estate to the Royal Society for the Prevention of Cruelty to Animals. The RSPCA sold the publishing firm to Derek Grimsdick.

Grimsdick retained Wodehouse as a major author, published several of his books, including his golf stories, *The Heart of a Goof* (1926), during the 1920s. Throughout the 1930s Wodehouse continued to supply Herbert Jenkins Limited with novels and short fiction, including *Blandings Castle and Elsewhere* (1935), *Young Men in Spats* (1936), *Laughing Gas* (1936), and *Lord Emsworth and Others* (1937).

During most of World War II Jenkins must have felt the loss of Wodehouse, who was interned in France first by the Germans and later, because he had recorded some talks that were broadcast on German radio, by the French. Wodehouse was permitted to return to England in 1946. Immediately Jenkins published Wodehouse's *Money in the Bank* and sold twenty-six thousand copies to the eager British public.

Starting in 1948 Jenkins worked out arrangements with American firms for simultaneous publications of Wodehouse's works, starting with *Spring Fever*. The Doubleday edition and the Jenkins edition both appeared on 20 May 1948. In 1949 Jenkins and the New York publisher Didier brought out Wodehouse's *The Mating Season*.

By the 1950s Grimsdick's son J. Derek Grimsdick was in charge of Jenkins and the Wodehouse account, publishing, at the same time as Doubleday, such successful works as *Nothing Serious* (1951), *The Old Reliable* (1952), and *Barmy in Wonderland* (1952, published by Doubleday as *Angel Cake*). Non-Wodehouse books of the 1950s included Homer Ulrich's *The Enjoyment of a Con-*

cert (1951), James Veitch's *I Shall Bury Sorrow* (1953), and Hylton Cleaver's *A History of Rowing* (1957).

Beginning in 1953 Grimsdick and Peter Schwed of Simon and Schuster shared whatever the aging Wodehouse produced. In 1960 they published one of the Jeeves novels as *How Right You Are Jeeves* in the United States and as *Jeeves in the Offing* in Great Britain. On the author's eightieth birthday, 15 October 1961, Jenkins published Wodehouse's novel *Ice in the Bedroom* and Richard Usborne's *Wodehouse at Work*.

Among the last books published by Herbert Jenkins Limited as an independent company was *The Class Music Teacher* (1965), by Charles Proctor. The firm was taken over by Barrie and Rockcliff in April 1965, with Jenkins retaining its imprint in Wodehouse books until 1970. The new company, Barrie and Jenkins, published Wodehouse's novels *The Girl in Blue* (1970); *Much Obliged, Jeeves* (1971); and *Bachelors Anonymous* (1973). In 1971 Simon and Schuster and Barrie and Jenkins began republishing out-of-print books by Wodehouse, and Barrie and Jenkins also released signed editions of Wodehouse's work. Both publishers enjoyed great success with multivolume editions of his novels, especially the Jeeves stories. In 1972 Barrie and Jenkins was acquired by Communica Europe and sold the same year to Hutchinson and Company. In 1985 Hutchinson was purchased by Century Publishing Limited, forming Century Hutchinson. Today, publishing rights to Wodehouse's books are controlled by Random Century, a company formed after Random House purchased Century Hutchinson in 1989.

References:

David A. Jasen, *Wodehouse: A Portrait of a Master* (New York: Mason/Charter, 1974);

Eileen McIlvaine, "A Bibliography of P. G. Wodehouse," in *P.G. Wodehouse: A Centenary Celebration, 1881-1981*, edited by James H. Heineman and Donald R. Bensen (New York & London: Pierpont Morgan Library/Oxford University Press, 1981), pp. 91-197.

—Beverly Schneller

Michael Joseph Limited
(London: 1935-   )

Born in London on 26 September 1897 to Moss and Rebecca Joseph, Michael Joseph received a scholarship to the City of London School, where he studied from 1909 to 1914. During World War I he was commissioned as a subaltern in the Wiltshire Regiment in 1915; the next year he transferred to the Machine Gun Corps and was promoted to lieutenant; and was promoted to acting captain in 1917. He began submitting battle reports to the *Daily Express* in 1916. Joseph was twenty when he embarked on a career as subeditor for a succession of weekly magazines, including the *Nash Weekly*. He joined Hutchinson and Company as advertising manager in 1920.

During the next four years he wrote two books that were to have a major influence on his future career. *Short Story Writing for Profit* (1923) and *Journalism for Profit* (1924) were published by his employer; *Short Story Writing for Profit* was reprinted six times in its first eight months. Thus, when he left Hutchinson in 1924 to work for the Curtis Brown literary agency, he was an accomplished author in his own right. His third book, *The Commercial Side of Literature* (1925), became a best-seller and was ranked by *Publishers' Weekly* in the top eight best-selling books for summer 1925. Joseph followed this success with more books on the subjects of writing and journalism, which enhanced his experience and authority when he decided to start his own publishing house.

Michael Joseph Limited was registered on 5 September 1935. The founding directors with Joseph were Norman Collins and Victor Gollancz. Gollancz not only invested capital but provided rooms at his own publishing company's offices at

Michael Joseph

14 Henrietta Street for three hundred pounds a year in rent.

175

March 14th, 1938.

Messrs. Victor Gollancz Limited and Messrs. Michael Joseph Limited announce that the connection existing between the two firms is by mutual arrangement discontinued from the present date. As part of this arrangement, Mr. Victor Gollancz and Mr. Norman Collins leave the Board of Directors, and their places are taken by Arthur Stanley Craven and Hubert Hessell Tiltman (with Mr. Michael Joseph continuing as Chairman and Managing Director). Messrs. Victor Gollancz Limited have now no financial or other interest in the company of Messrs. Michael Joseph Limited.

Draft announcement of the dissolution of the connection between the firms of Joseph and Gollancz (from Richard Joseph,
Michael Joseph: Master of Words, *1986)*

Two of the initial employees, Robert Lusty and Charles Pick, were destined for greater careers. Lusty would become a chairman of Hutchinson in 1956, and Pick would become managing director of Heinemann in 1962. Pick was Joseph's first salesman. The mermaid logo, designed by Philip Youngman-Carter, was influenced by the popularity of the contemporary penguin logo for Penguin Books.

Gollancz's investment carried stringent conditions: if company losses exceeded twenty-five hundred pounds in any but the first year, then Gollancz could dismiss Joseph; if losses amounted to three thousand pounds in any three consecutive years, Gollancz could terminate the agreement and withdraw his capital. Joseph found galling the large amounts spent by Gollancz on promotion for his own titles while restricting the advertising budget of Michael Joseph Limited, a budget which was already small. In 1938

Joseph sought other investors and bought out Gollancz's shares. He recruited Hessell Tiltman and May Edginton as major shareholders. The company moved from 14 to 17 Henrietta Street for a short time before moving to Bloomsbury Street in 1938.

Joseph had the knack for encouraging new authors, among them Daphne Du Maurier and Monica Dickens, Charles Dickens's great grand-daughter, who was introduced to Joseph in 1938. His advice to Dickens was: "Just imagine you are bursting into a room full of people you know quite well, and you are saying, 'Listen to what happened to me!'" Her first book, *One Pair of Hands* (1939), was written in three weeks and launched her on a highly successful writing career.

Joseph concentrated on fiction, and the company had huge successes with proven authors whose titles had never sold well under other imprints. Notable among these authors was C. S. Forester, who had had thirteen books published by three houses prior to his association with Michael Joseph, which began with the best-selling *The General* (1936). Other authors who enjoyed similar good fortune included Joyce Cary and H. E. Bates; the latter had had twenty-eight titles published before he came to Michael Joseph Limited. Number 26 Bloomsbury Street became a familiar address to Forester, Owen Rutter, Walter Allen, Frank Tilsey, Caryl Brahms, and S. J. Simon. Additional premises were leased at 52 Bloomsbury Street, and these two offices were the company's base until it moved to 44 Bedford Square in 1965.

Joseph met Richard Llewellyn through an introduction by portrait photographer Howard Coster. Llewellyn's first novel, *How Green Was My Valley* (1939), was highly successful, with twenty-eight reprints in the first five years of publication. This one title contributed huge sums to the company and helped sustain it through the difficult years of World War II.

Publishing books while the war raged was extremely difficult and frustrating; paper was scarce and limited by law. In one week the company's trade typesetters, blockmakers, and printers were destroyed by German air raids. Sales increased because reading was popular in the air-raid shelters, and because millions of books were being destroyed by the bombing. Joseph, who had volunteered for military service, was involved in training and participation in home defense. Lusty had been ruled unfit for service and remained at the office. He sent many manuscripts to Joseph, who was invalided out of the army in 1941. While recovering, he wrote *The Sword in the Scabbard* (1942), recalling his recent life in the army. Not only did he avoid the censors but he managed to get enough extra paper to have the book published by his own firm.

After the war Joseph, a cat fancier, published many books about cats, including one he wrote about a Siamese, *Charles—The Story of a Friendship* (1943). His cat catalogue also featured *The Cats in Our Lives* (1949), by film actor James Mason and his wife Pamela. Another of Joseph's interests was music. He had interviewed Noel Cow-

ard in 1931 and had maintained contact with him over the years, and in 1953 the firm published the *Noel Coward Song Book*. Music, cats, racehorses, fishing, and shooting were not only hobbies of Joseph's but were featured in his lists throughout his publishing career.

In 1954 Joseph sold his major shareholding to Sir John Ellerman, who was developing the Illustrated Papers Group. The purchase made Joseph a relatively wealthy man, and he was at last able to indulge as an owner in one of his hobbies, horse racing. One of his jockeys was Dick Francis, who contributed mystery novels to the firm.

Joseph had a wide circle of friends in many walks of life. While managing director and chairman of the company, he gave lectures on the publishing trade, took part in radio broadcasts, wrote articles, and traveled widely. He visited the United States on many occasions, as well as South Africa, Australia, and New Zealand. He died on 15 March 1958.

In 1961 Ellerman sold Michael Joseph Limited to the Thompson Organization. One of the company's subsequent best-sellers was a joint publication with Webb and Bower, *The Country Diary of an Edwardian Lady* (1977), with an initial print run of 147,500 copies. Twenty-one reprints were produced by 1986, taking the sales to more than 2.5 million copies and achieving an entry in the *Guinness Book of World Records*.

In 1985 Penguin UK acquired the business, and in June 1989, in a wave of commercial streamlining, decided to downgrade Michael Joseph Limited from an autonomous company to an imprint. Alan Brooke, the last managing director, resigned, having served the company for fifteen years.

References:

At the Sign of the Mermaid (London: M. Joseph, 1986);

Richard Joseph, *Michael Joseph: Master of Words* (Southampton: Ashford Press, 1986).

—Richard Joseph

Kelmscott Press
(London: 1891-1898)

See also the William Morris entries in *DLB 18: Victorian Novelists After 1885; DLB 35: Victorian Poets After 1850;* and *DLB 57: Victorian Prose Writers After 1867.*

In light of the rather modest, idealistic, and personal origins of the Kelmscott Press, its historical and continuing significance may well seem remarkable. Historically, it turned out to be the last major contribution to the Arts and Crafts Movement by William Morris, the great Victorian designer, thinker, socialist, poet, artist, and master craftsman. Within the world of private-press book collecting, the Kelmscott edition of *The Works of Geoffrey Chaucer* (1896) on vellum joins the Doves Bible (1903-1905) and the Ashendene Dante (1906-1909) as one of the three most highly prized masterpieces; all Kelmscott editions continue to appreciate in value. Most significantly, as the first modern revival of the printed book as a high craft and fine art, the Kelmscott is the wellspring and inspiration of a private-press tradition that immediately began flourishing and has intermittently renewed itself ever since.

Morris was born on 24 March 1834, founded the Kelmscott Press in 1891, and ran it with great energy until he died on 3 October 1896. In effect the press died with him, continuing just long enough to publish books already substantially in progress and a final account of its own history before closing down in 1898.

Morris's immediate inspiration for reforming the printing of books was Emery Walker. A neighbor and a pioneer in process engraving, col-

William Morris (right) and Edward Burne-Jones, the principal illustrator for the Kelmscott Press, in 1890

lotype reproduction, and applied photography, Walker had made himself an expert on the history of printed materials. While the two men discussed the specimens of incunabula in Morris's library over many years, scholars trace the origins of the press to the lecture Walker delivered on 15 November 1888 at the first Arts and Crafts exhibition. What struck Morris most forcibly were the lantern slides of fonts of type and pages from the earliest and from later books. That evening, according to his daughter May, an enthusiastic Morris said to Walker, "Let's make a new fount of type."

Walker's influence fell on well-prepared soil. Morris had always enjoyed purchasing beautiful books, he had helped found the *Oxford and Cambridge Magazine* in 1856, and he had envisioned special ornamented editions of his *The Earthly Paradise* (1868-1870) in 1866 and *Love Is Enough* (1873) around 1871, both to be illustrated by his friend Edward Burne-Jones. Morris's experiments with traditional arts and crafts included manuscript illumination and calligraphy, and illuminated, decorated manuscripts had inspired the earliest printed books. The scribe with his black, red, and blue inks had been replaced by the printer with similar inks; hand lettering had given way to fonts of type based on the same forms. Emery Walker helped Morris to appreciate the continuity of a tradition in which the aim was to integrate worthy words with worthy means of producing books.

More than a year before Morris designed his own font of type he had supervised the typography, layout, and decorative title pages of Chiswick Press editions of his own works. Published in late 1888, *The House of the Wolfings* boasted a Basle Roman typeface, generous margins, and a well-designed typographic title page. For *Roots of the Mountains*, published in late 1889, Morris reproportioned the pages, added shoulder notes, set the chapter headings flush left, and supplied some chintz that he had designed for the bindings of a few copies. He declared the result "the best-looking book issued since the seventeenth century."

His satisfaction proved temporary, however; his letters to his friend Frederick S. Ellis, a bookseller and amateur scholar, reveal him moving toward the decision to handle the printing himself. In December 1889 he began designing his own font of type. Well into 1890 he considered allowing existing printers to use his new typeface, but he was also exploring the option of printing his own books. When Walker furnished him with an estimate of costs, he discovered that he could print a book of his own for the same amount he

was willing to spend on one fine fifteenth-century edition.

Morris had thought about and worked with color and line for decades, and he had mastered many arts and crafts. Even so, mastering this newest and most complex craft proved difficult. He needed to design fonts of type superior to all those currently in use; to learn more about typography and layout; to find sources of high-quality paper, vellum, and ink, or manufacture them himself; and to track down expert binders and pressmen. This extensive research and experimentation continued beyond the preparatory stages into the active years of the press.

Morris invited Walker to join him as a partner; although Walker demurred, he was active as a consultant. Walker played similar roles for the Doves and Ashendene Presses. He maintained a low profile yet helped persuade others to promote readability through well-designed fonts of type based on the earliest models; the elimination of excessive leading and rivers of white space; close word-spacing; generous margins to prevent readers' thumbs from obscuring the print; the integration of type, ornaments, and illustrations into the page; matching the weights of lines in those three constituents; and treating each pair of facing pages as a unit, thereby producing the effect of two columns separated by a narrow gutter. Yet it was not Walker but Morris who took it upon himself to "reattain a long-lost standard of craftsmanship" of the earliest European printers.

To Walker's comparatively utilitarian goal of readability, Morris added the "definite claim to beauty" that he hoped the Kelmscott books would attain. What Morris found beautiful was simple and elegant, with tasteful, restrained ornamentation, coloration, and, when appropriate, illustration. Substance and literary merit were implicit, not stated aims.

As models for Kelmscott volumes Morris depended on incunabula, some owned by friends and acquaintances, others purchased for his own burgeoning collection. But he did not imitate them slavishly. If a modern material or process produced excellent results, he was perfectly willing to adopt it. Major cases in point were cast-iron presses; the distribution of ink via rollers; and electrotypes, a modern photographic method of reproducing decorative elements. When Walker offered a recommendation Morris normally accepted it, but only after testing it and assessing the results with his own eyes. Similarly,

THIS IS THE PICTURE OF THE OLD HOUSE BY THE THAMES TO WHICH THE PEOPLE OF THIS STORY WENT. HEREAFTER FOLLOWS THE BOOK IT. SELF WHICH IS CALLED NEWS FROM NOWHERE OR AN EPOCH OF REST & IS WRITTEN BY WILLIAM MORRIS.

Morris's home, Kelmscott House, from which his press derived its name (frontispiece to the 1892 Kelmscott Press edition of Morris's News from Nowhere)

Morris was happy to modify a traditional typeface to enhance its beauty or legibility; the first typeface he designed was a reshaping of a fifteenth-century Nicolas Jenson font. Neither a purist nor an antiquarian, Morris was a practical idealist, an artist-craftsman, and a creative traditionalist.

Originally Morris intended to design just two fonts of type that would be used for all Kelmscott books. The first, named the Golden after Jacobus de Voragine's *The Golden Legend* (1892), the first book in which it was to appear, was English in size (approximately fourteen points) and Roman in form. Essentially, he subtly Gothicized his Roman models, one designed by Jenson and the other by Jacobus Rubeus, both of which appeared in books published in Venice in 1476. Around the middle of 1891 Morris began to design an eighteen-point (Great Primer) Gothic font. Named the Troy after the first Kelmscott book in which Morris intended to use it, this font represented Morris's attempt to "redeem the Gothic character from the charge of un-

readableness" by resorting to early models, a Peter Schoeffer Bible of 1462 and volumes published by Gunther Zainer in 1473. For both new fonts Walker's firm photographically enlarged the models fivefold; then Morris traced the results, adapted them, and finally drew each letter freehand. In early 1892, when the Troy proved far too large for a one-volume illustrated edition of the works of Chaucer, he designed a third, predictably named the Chaucer, based on photographic reductions of the Troy font to Pica size (twelve points). Toward the end of 1892 he terminated an abortive experiment with a cross between the Roman and the Gothic styles. The only other the Kelmscott actually printed was a Greek type that Selwyn Image designed for Macmillan after consultation with the ubiquitous Walker. Although Morris examined modern papers, those which were available fell short of his hopes and his models. In October 1890 he and Walker took the third volume of Alexander of Hales's *Summa*, printed in Venice in 1475, to show the papermakers Joseph Batchelor and Son in Little Chart, Kent. Confident that the firm would produce superior paper, Morris designed two watermarks, the Flower and the Perch, that same evening. Batchelor would make all the Kelmscott papers of linen rag laid on handmade wire molds, which ensured slight but charming irregularities.

As for vellum, Morris was annoyed to discover that the Vatican was monopolizing the output of an Italian manufacturer that had furnished him more than enough for his earlier calligraphic works. After using up what little was left, he turned to two English suppliers, Henry Band and William J. Turney. Morris himself preferred paper over vellum but felt obliged to humor collectors by printing a few vellum copies of selected works. Similarly, with certain exceptions—such as the pigskin binding which the Doves Bindery devised for forty-eight copies of the Chaucer—J. and J. Leighton bound the vast majority of the Kelmscott books rather simply in quarter linen, stiff vellum, or Morris's eventual favorite, limp vellum.

Manufacturers of ink proved less cooperative than Batchelor; they had trouble seeing why they should rely on traditional materials and avoid modern chemicals, thereby disrupting their normal methods of manufacture. Initially Morris settled on Shackell, Edwards and Company of London for both black and red inks. Walker preferred an alternative black ink manufactured

The Kelmscott Press staff in 1895; seated: Stephen Mowlem, printer; William H. Bowden, foreman; Morris; May Morris, Morris's daughter; W. Collins, pressman; W. L. Tasker, printer; standing: H. Howes, printer; Mr. Carpenter (first name unknown), printer; F. Collins, pressman; Emery Walker, consultant; R. Eatley, printer; Henry Halliday Sparling, secretary; John Tippett, printer; Thomas Binning, printer; G. Heath, printer

more traditionally in Hannover by Gebrüder Janecke, but the Kelmscott printers judged it too stiff. Later, when printing the Chaucer, Morris would see yellow stains emanating from the English ink and would insist that the printers adopt the German alternative.

By 1891, having engaged in over a year of research and preparation, Morris was eager to begin transforming his type, paper, and ink into books. On 12 January he rented a cottage at 16 Upper Mall in Hammersmith, a few doors from his residence, Kelmscott House. He installed a Demy Albion handpress, technologically quite similar to William Caxton's but somewhat more efficient. In May he moved the press to larger quarters in Sussex Cottage at 14 Upper Mall. On 29 November he purchased a second press.

The new premises and the new press reflected marked changes in Morris's plans. In the beginning he had thought of the Kelmscott Press as quite small, experimental, and personal, with himself and his circle of friends as its only beneficiaries. For the first book, his own *The Story of the Glittering Plain* (1891), he had planned just 20 copies, fearing that the printers would find producing more copies so monotonous that the qual-

ity would soon fall off. But he had not anticipated the volume of unsolicited inquiries about the press that soon began flowing into Hammersmith. Somewhat reluctantly, Morris increased the pressrun tenfold and arranged to sell the 180 additional copies of his first book through Reeves and Turner.

Although all but one of the Kelmscott books would be for sale, Morris never concentrated on making a profit or on transforming the fledgling press into a thriving business. Indeed, he was willing to absorb small losses, he refused all but a few outside commissions, and he never allowed advertisers to buy his decorative work. Surviving Morris contracts are rudimentary, to say the least, and bookkeeping could be sloppy. Still, the financial side of the press was not completely irrelevant to Morris. It was partly for financial reasons that he decided in 1893 to take over the publishing and distribution of Kelmscott books. He did sign contracts, he did keep rough track of costs and income, and according to one estimate, the sales of the press eventually mounted to more than fifty thousand pounds. Certainly the commission from Macmillan for Alfred Tennyson's *Maud* (1893) included a generous profit margin; but at the same time, as in the case of profits on smaller books, Morris used the money to subsidize his larger, more ambitious projects. His financial aim seems to have been to cover costs, not including the considerable value of his own services, for the sake of producing beautiful books.

The same kind of reasoning lay behind the expansion of his staff. Originally he persuaded William Bowden, the compositor and pressman who had printed his *News from Nowhere* (1891) for Reeves and Turner, to come out of retirement for the sake of this "little typographical adventure." Soon after the press got underway, however, Morris recognized that the volume of work would require help from other pressmen. Meanwhile, the secretary of the press took on administrative duties for which Morris had little time or inclination. The first secretary was Henry Halliday Sparling, Morris's son-in-law, who had been coeditor of *Commonweal*. In 1894 the meticulous Sydney Cockerell, an admirer whom Morris had hired in August 1892 to catalogue his library, took over. Eventually Cockerell hired his own secretary, Mrs. Sarah A. Peddie. Early on Morris hired a printer's reader, but later Sparling, Cockerell, Ellis, and Morris himself handled most such duties.

Burne-Jones was the Kelmscott illustrator of choice, though Morris called on Walter Crane, Charles M. Gere, and Arthur J. Gaskin for one book each. For the Chaucer a complex process of collaboration helped ensure that illustrations would harmonize with the type, with thins no thinner, thicks no thicker, and a similar black-white ratio. First Walker's firm would produce a "platino," a pale photographic print that scaled Burne-Jones's pencil or silver-point drawing to the proper size for the page. Robert Catterson-Smith would then translate the platino into inked lines that matched the type. Walker's firm would photographically transfer the revised drawing onto a woodblock, which the engraver would then cut. Morris's favorite engraver was William Harcourt Hooper, who had previously transferred art by John Tenniel and John Everett Millais onto woodblocks and had worked for *Punch* and the *Illustrated London News*.

In addition to the typefaces, Morris was responsible for 644 ornamental designs: 384 initial capitals, 33 decorative words, 57 decorative borders for pages, 27 decorative frames for illustrations, 108 marginal ornaments, 28 title pages, 4 line endings, and 3 printer's marks. In designing

them, Morris said, he "always tried to keep in mind the necessity for making any decoration a part of the page of type." Further, he adjusted the amount and style of decoration to the nature of the book. In the majority of Kelmscott books the decoration is quite restrained; indeed, some are quite plain.

The actual order in which the press printed its books differed from the intended one. Morris had planned to inaugurate the press by recreating the first printed book in English, Caxton's 1473 translation of Raoul Lefevre's *The Recuyell of the Historyes of Troye*; but he decided that a second Caxton translation, Voragine's *The Golden Legend*, was more significant. Then the need for a larger version of the Flower paper kept *The Golden Legend* waiting. By the time the book came out in November 1893, the press had completed six small quartos—four featuring Morris's works; a book of poems by his friend Wilfrid Scawen Blunt (1892); and an inspirational favorite of his, *The Nature of Gothic* (1892) from John Ruskin's *The Stones of Venice* (1853). With obvious applicability to Morris's highly skilled and well-paid workers, whom he was willing to overrule but to whom he granted a great deal of autonomy, the Ruskin chapter focuses on the meaningful, individualized work of medieval craftsmen. These six small quartos paved the way for the large Caxton quartos: *The Golden Legend*, edited by Frederick S. Ellis and illustrated by Burne-Jones, in three volumes; and *The Recuyell of the Historyes of Troye* (1892), edited by Sparling, in two volumes. The latter volume marked the first public appearance of the Chaucer and Troy typefaces.

Expansion, elaboration, adjustment, and experimentation characterized the early years of the press. Printers strove to find the best methods for printing on vellum and on Batchelor's papers. The first book, Morris's *The Story of the Glittering Plain* (1891), used black ink only and had twenty initial capital letters. By the second, Morris's *Poems by the Way* (1891), the repertoire had expanded to black and red ink with fifty-nine initial capitals. Morris tried and rejected both hand-colored and printed red initial capitals. He tried hand-lettering on the spine of one volume and wash-leather ties on another, but settled on printed titles and on silk ties manufactured by his design firm, Morris and Company. With Caxton's translation of *The History of Reynard the Foxe* (1893), trimmed edges and limp rather than stiff vellum bindings became stan-

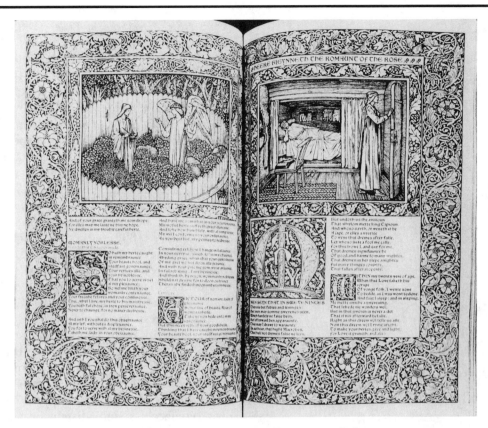

Pages from the Kelmscott Press edition of The Works of Geoffrey Chaucer *(1896), generally considered one of the three greatest private-press books*

dard practice. Meanwhile, the standard press run had risen into the low three hundreds. The press produced books in five different formats—small and large quartos, octavos, sixteenmos, and folios.

At first Reeves and Turner sold the smaller volumes while Bernard Quaritch sold the Caxtons, which appealed to antiquarians and collectors. Disagreements over Quaritch's business practices surfaced early, however, and by the end of 1892 Morris realized that he could save the press and the public money by publishing as well as printing Kelmscott books.

The fifty-three editions in sixty-six volumes that the Kelmscott Press produced fall roughly into five major categories. Seventeen editions in twenty-five volumes feature Morris's own works, some of which had previously been published in serial or volume form: *The Story of the Glittering Plain*, the first Kelmscott book as well as the first to use the Golden typeface, completed on 4 April 1891 and published on 8 May; *Poems by the Way*; *The Defence of Guenevere, and Other Poems* (1892), the first book with a limp vellum binding and the only one with a hand-lettered title on the spine;

A Dream of John Ball and a King's Lesson (1892), with a previously published Burne-Jones frontispiece; *News from Nowhere* (1893); *Gothic Architecture* (1893); a second edition of *The Story of the Glittering Plain* (1894), with illustrations Crane did not complete in time for the 1891 version; *The Wood beyond the World* (1894); *The Life and Death of Jason* (1895); *Child Christopher and Goldilind the Fair* (1895), in two volumes; *The Well at the World's End* (1896), with four Burne-Jones illustrations; *The Earthly Paradise* (1896-1897), in eight volumes; *The Water of the Wondrous Isles* (1897); *The Story of Sigurd the Volsung and the Fall of the Niblungs* (1898); *The Sundering Flood* (1898); *Love Is Enough; or, The Freeing of Pharamond: A Morality* (1898), the second book to be printed in blue as well as red and black inks; and *A Note by William Morris on His Aims in Founding the Kelmscott Press* (1898), which includes Cockerell's annotated booklist and description of the press.

The flavor of Victorian medievalism that permeates Morris's poetry and prose romances rises out of his love of medieval literature, the second major category of books the Kelmscott Press printed. Especially noteworthy are books first

Caricature by Burne-Jones showing himself (right) and Morris being blessed by Chaucer for their publication of his works (from Martin Harrison and Bill Waters, Burne-Jones, 1973)

translated and printed by Caxton, the first English printer. In addition to *The Golden Legend*, printed by Caxton in 1483; *The Recuyell of the Historyes of Troye*, printed by Caxton in 1473; and *The History of Reynard the Foxe*, printed by Caxton in 1481, Morris printed Ramón Lull's *The Order of Chivalry* (1893), printed by Caxton in 1484, and Sparling's edition of Guilelmus, Archbishop of Tyre's *The History of Godefrey of Boloyne* (1893), printed by Caxton in 1481—the first book sold directly by the press and one of its finest. Other medieval works are Francesca Speranza, Lady Wilde's 1849 translation of William Meinhold's *Sidonia the Sorceress* (1893); Morris's translations of three works from Old French, *The Tale of King Florus and the Fair Jehane* (1893), *Of the Friendship of Amis and Amile* (1894), and *The Tale of the Emperor Coustans and of Over Sea* (1894); *Psalmi Penitentiales* (1894), edited by Ellis; a translation by Morris and A. J. Wyatt of *The Tale of Beowulf*

(1895); *Sir Perecyvelle of Gales* (1895), edited by Ellis; *The Works of Geoffrey Chaucer*; *Laudes Beatæ Mariæ Virginis* (1896), a Latin psalter by an English scribe, edited by Cockerell—the first book to add blue ink to red and black; Sir Thomas Clanvowe's *The Floure and the Leafe and The Boke of Cupide, God of Love, or the Cuckow and the Nightingale* (1896), edited by Ellis; two specimen pages of Jean Froissart's *The Chronicles of Fraunce, Ingland, and Other Places* (1897), translated by Lord Berners (John Bourchier); *Sir Degrevaunt* (1897), edited by Ellis; *Syr Isambrace* (1897), edited by Ellis; and *Some German Woodcuts of the Fifteenth Century* (1898), edited by Cockerell. Focusing on medieval subject matter, Ruskin's *On the Nature of Gothic* and Morris's *Gothic Architecture* would raise the total to twenty-one "medieval" editions in twenty-two volumes.

The press produced many masterful editions, some of them comparatively small, brief, and spare; but among them all, the Kelmscott Chaucer has been universally recognized as a masterpiece both because it was so ambitious and because the results were so happy. It demanded its own typeface, as immediately became apparent on 1 January 1892 when the first trial page was printed in the Troy. Despite the much smaller Chaucer typeface, the book is the largest in format, the longest, and the most ornate work produced by the press, with eighty-seven Burne-Jones illustrations, seven borders, eighteen frames around illustrations, twenty-six initial words, three kinds of initial capitals, and the title page by Morris. It even boasts its own printer's mark, which Morris likewise designed. It also took the longest to create, in spite of the extra staff that was employed to produce it. Beginning in February 1893, when Morris designed the first ornament, the volume absorbed three years and four months. Printing took a year and nine months, from 8 August 1894 to 30 June 1896, when Morris's and Burne-Jones's copies were ready. It would have taken longer had Morris not rented an extra building (a small house at 21 Upper Mall), hired eleven printers, and purchased a third press (a larger Albion).

The press also printed postmedieval classics of English literature, the majority by Renaissance and Romantic poets and all edited by Ellis: *The Poems of William Shakespeare* (1893); George Cavendish's *The Life of Cardinal Wolsey* (1893); Ralph Robinson's translation of Sir Thomas More's *Utopia* (1893), based on the second edition (1556); *The Poems of John Keats* (1894); *The Poetical*

Sydney Cockerell, second secretary of the Kelmscott Press

and Lies (1894). Like almost all of the noncommissioned works, the commissioned ones possess considerable literary merit; the publishers must have approached Morris mainly with works they felt he would find worth printing. He turned down other projects because they would take too much time away from the press's proper priorities.

As his third book, Morris produced *The Love-Lyrics and Songs of Proteus* for his friend Blunt and acceded to Blunt's request that he print all the decorative initials in red. Subsequently, he undertook only two other projects for friends: J. W. Mackail's *Biblia Innocentium* (1892) and Charles Fairfax Murray's edition of Girolamo Savonarola's *Epistola de Contemptu Mundi* (1894), the only book the press printed that was not for sale.

Morris alone chose which books to print, though he was subject to lobbying from his secretaries and friends. His criteria included merit as an example of the art of bookmaking when the work was originally printed; literary value; medieval color, romance, learning, and religion; Romantic sensibility; personal friendship; and inspirational value. Books he intended to print (but never got around to) include the Bible, the *Rubáiyát of Omar Khayyám*, Sir Thomas Malory's *Morte d'Arthur*, a complete edition of Berners's translation of Froissart's *Chronicles*, St. Jerome's *Vitas Patrum* (printed by Caxton in 1495), Shakespeare's plays, and works by Walter Scott, Ralph Waldo Emerson, and Charles Dickens.

Critics have attacked the Kelmscott Press for mismatches between illustration and content, choice of inferior works, overly coarse paper, insufficient inner margins, excessive Gothicism in type design, lack of typographical variety and appropriateness, and susceptibility to overdecorated, ugly imitations. Yet later presses and publishers that committed themselves to the highest standards almost invariably acknowledged a substantial debt to the Kelmscott Press. Among Morris's contemporaries, it helped inspire the Doves, Ashendene, and Essex House presses; later it influenced J. M. Dent's Everyman's Library, the Riverside Press, the Nonesuch Press, and the Golden Cockerel Press. Indeed, nearly every small, low-volume, high-quality handpress on both sides of the Atlantic has looked to Morris, as have many high-quality commercial printers and publishers. The press has served not as a pretext for servile imitation but rather as an inspiration for rethinking everything that goes into creating the best possible classic and contemporary

Works of Percy Bysshe Shelley (1894-1895) in three volumes; *Poems Chosen out of the Works of Robert Herrick* (1896); *Poems Chosen out of the Works of Samuel Taylor Coleridge* (1896); and Edmund Spenser's *The Shepheardes Calendar* (1896). Morris's admiration for Victorian literature was selective and often highly qualified, but the press did print Tennyson's *Maud*—the first octavo volume with a woodcut title page; Dante Gabriel Rossetti's *Ballads and Narrative Poems* (1893) and *Sonnets and Lyrical Poems* (1894); Algernon Charles Swinburne's *Atalanta in Calydon* (1894), using Image's type for the Greek passages; and Rossetti's prose work *Hand and Soul* (1895).

Four of the Victorian volumes were printed on commission: the first two Rossettis for Ellis and Elvey, the last Rossetti for Way and Williams of Chicago, and the Tennyson for Macmillan. The only other commission Morris accepted was from Quaritch for Oliver Wardrop's translation of Sulkhan-Saba Orbeliani's *The Book of Wisdom*

books—books that integrate beautiful design, readability, fine typography, sensitive layout, worthy content, and harmonious pages. Morris produced editions that combined painstaking craftsmanship, utility, and beauty. He revived the art of the book, thereby ensuring a continuing influence out of all proportion to the sixty-six books his last brainchild produced during its eight years.

References:

Roderick Cave, *The Private Press*, second edition, revised and enlarged (New York: Bowker, 1983);

Colin Franklin, *The Private Presses* (London: Studio Vista, 1969), pp. 35-49, 200-216;

Martin Harrison and Bill Waters, *Burne-Jones* (London: Barrie & Jenkins, 1973);

Norman Kelvin, ed., *The Collected Letters of William Morris*, volume 1, 1848-1880 (Princeton: Princeton University Press, 1984); volume 2A, 1881-1884 (Princeton: Princeton University Press, 1987); volume 2B, 1885-1888 (Princeton: Princeton University Press, 1987);

John William Mackail, *The Life of William Morris*, 2 volumes (London & New York: Longmans, Green, 1898);

William Morris, *The Collected Works of William Morris*, 24 volumes, edited by May Morris (London & New York: Longmans, Green, 1910-1915; New York: Russell & Russell, 1966);

Morris, *The Ideal Book: Essays and Lectures in the Arts of the Book*, edited by William S. Peterson (Berkeley: University of California Press, 1982);

Paul Needham, comp., *William Morris and the Art of the Book* (New York: Pierpont Morgan Library, 1976);

William S. Peterson, *A Bibliography of the Kelmscott Press* (Oxford: Clarendon Press, 1984);

Peterson, *The Kelmscott Press: A History of William Morris's Typographical Adventure* (Oxford & Berkeley: Clarendon and University of California Presses, 1990);

Will Ransom, *Kelmscott, Doves and Ashendene: The Private Press Credos*, Typophile Chap Book 27 (New York: The Typophiles, 1952);

Henry Halliday Sparling, *The Kelmscott Press and William Morris Master-Craftsman* (London: Macmillan, 1924);

E. P. Thompson, *William Morris: Romantic to Revolutionary* (New York: Pantheon, 1976).

Papers:

The British Library, London, owns Sir Sidney C. Cockerell's diary (Add. MSS. 52623-37), a large body of correspondence addressed to Cockerell (Add. MSS. 52708-71), William Morris's engagement diaries for 1893, 1895, and 1896 (Add. MSS. 45409-11), and some of Morris's correspondence, mostly to his wife and daughters (Add. MSS. 45338-45). A letterbook for the years 1894-1896 is in the William Morris Gallery, Walthamstow. A ledger for 1892 to 1896 and a customer list from 1897 are in the J. Pierpont Morgan Library, New York. Other documents, proof and trial pages, and volumes of ornaments are in the Henry E. Huntington Library, San Marino, California; the Bodleian Library, Oxford; the William Andrews Clark Memorial Library, Los Angeles; the Stanford University Library; the Newberry Library, Chicago; the Victoria and Albert Museum, London; and the Sanford and Helen Berger Collection, Carmel, California.

—*William Lamborn Lee*

John Lehmann Limited

(London: 1946-1952)

See also the Lehmann entries in *DLB 27: Poets of Great Britain and Ireland, 1945-1960* and *DLB 100: Modern British Essayists, Second Series.*

John Lehmann was born on 2 June 1907 to Rudolph Chambers Lehmann, who had been on the staff of *Punch*, and Alice Marie Davis Lehmann. Robert Chambers, Lehmann's great-grandfather, had cofounded the Edinburgh publishing firm W. and R. Chambers Limited.

While a student at Eton, Lehmann edited the literary magazine *College Days*. As an undergraduate at Cambridge, Lehmann worked on both the *Venture* and the *Cambridge Review*. Another Cambridge undergraduate, Julian Bell, the nephew of Virginia Woolf, became a close friend of Lehmann's. Both were novice poets, and they shared long discussions and extended correspondence on poetry.

On graduating, Lehmann was undecided about a career, considering either the foreign service or writing. His future was decided for him when George Rylands, who had worked for Leonard and Virginia Woolf at the Hogarth Press, showed them a collection of Lehmann's poetry. Not only were they interested in publishing the poetry, they proposed that Lehmann become manager of the Hogarth Press. In October 1930 he told Bell that he would begin work for the press and, if not fired after eight months of apprenticeship, had the option of becoming a partner in a year or two. At the Hogarth Press, one of his projects was editing *New Signatures*; through it he became acquainted with young poets such as W. H. Auden, Stephen Spender, Richard Eberhart, William Plomer, Christopher Isherwood, Cecil Day Lewis, and Julian and William Empson.

In 1932 Lehmann took a vacation in Europe, which developed into an extended stay. During that period his relationship with the Woolfs deteriorated, and he broke completely with the press to concentrate on his own writing and to establish *New Writing* to publish poetry and new prose. Lehmann traveled throughout Europe during the 1930s collecting material for his own books and searching for new contributors to *New Writing*.

Lehmann returned to English publishing in 1938. The firm of Lawrence and Wishart, which had published *New Writing*, was not interested in continuing it. Lehmann looked unsuccessfully for another firm to take it on. At the same time the Woolfs, tired of running the Hogarth Press with only the help of a female assistant, suggested that Lehmann take it over. He hoped to do so and—with Isherwood, Auden, and Spender—to make it a publishing center for all the *New Writing* authors; but he was unable to raise the six thousand pounds needed to buy out the business. It was finally agreed that he would buy out Virginia Woolf's half and after two years become Leonard Woolf's full partner as well as the general manager.

Almost at once, tensions developed between Lehmann and Leonard Woolf; but Virginia Woolf helped smooth over their misunderstandings until her death in 1941. By 1944 disagreements between the two men had become more frequent and harder to settle.

Woolf's lack of support for new writers was a major point of disagreement: he rejected Lehmann's suggestion that the press publish work by Jean-Paul Sartre and Saul Bellow. Lehmann had come to Hogarth expecting *New Writing* to have support equal to that given the press's other publications, but wartime exigencies, particularly paper rationing, required that the press's long-standing writers, particularly Virginia Woolf, have first claim to limited resources. Lehmann regarded Woolf's proposal to cut back on the size and publication frequency of *New Writing* as duplicitous. Lehmann also believed that his editorial contributions were overshadowed by Woolf's; he felt he was not given due credit for having brought to the press some of its valued authors, especially Henry Green, William Samson, Jiri Mucha, and Laurie Lee. Aggravating the artistic problems were fiscal ones: Woolf was notorious for his economizing, his idiosyncratic bookkeeping system, and his mania for detail. As for Woolf, in later years he suggested that the fault was Lehmann's for taking himself too seriously.

Finally, on 24 January 1946, Lehmann gave notice that he wished to end their collaboration.

John Lehmann (photograph by Harrods)

Lehmann decided to strike out on his own because he was determined to keep up *New Writing and Daylight*, as it had become known. To do so, he needed supplies of paper, which were strictly controlled. He thought he would have no trouble getting an allotment because of the success of *New Writing* and because of his international literary affiliations. But because he was no longer a partner in Hogarth Press, Paper Control would not give him a quota. He acquired some small amounts, but nothing adequate for his publishing needs. The paper supply problem seemed solved when he learned of a West Country printer, Purnell, which had acquired paper quotas through buying out smaller operations and wanted to get into book publishing. They entered into negotiations, but Purnell's chairman, Wilfred Harvey, insisted on 100 percent financial control; Lehmann could have all the paper and money he wanted if he agreed to be a salaried employee.

His pride stung, Lehmann decided to start his own firm and give it his name, John Lehmann Limited. He invited his mother, his sister Rosamond, and her husband Mountie Bradish-Ellames to become shareholders and directors. They raised ten thousand pounds, an amount that seemed sufficient to start a firm at the time of a book-buying boom. The firm's first offices were at 6 Henrietta Street.

With money in hand and a staff in place, Lehmann moved to acquiring authors. He intended, first, to pick up Hogarth Press authors who were loyal to him and not tied by long contracts. Second, he was interested in writers he had supported in *New Writing*. Third, he especially wanted to identify European and international writers whose works had not been published in England. And, having a long-standing interest in art, he wanted to work with new artists to design and illustrate his firm's books. Many of these artists—including Keith Vaughan, Leonard Rosoman, Leslie Hurry, Michael Ayrton, John Craxton, John Minton, Robert Medley, and Humphrey Spender—had already worked for *Penguin New Writing*, which Lehmann also edited.

Lehmann planned to publish two series of "libraries": the Modern European Library would consist of translations of novels and short stories, and The Chiltern Library would reprint long-unavailable classics. In the autumn of 1946 John Lehmann Limited brought out its first line of nine books. They included an anthology of poems that had appeared in *New Writing*; *That*

Lehmann and Leonard Woolf at Woolf's home in Rodmell, Sussex, in 1939 (photograph by Virginia Woolf)

Summer and Other Stories, by Frank Sargeson; the seventh volume of *New Writing*; *Poems from Giacomo Leopardi*, translated by John Heath-Stubbs; a miniature edition of Herman Melville's *Billy Budd*; *Savage Gold*, an adventure story for boys by Roy Fuller; Bellow's *Dangling Man*; *The Golden Ass of Apuleius*; and Ivan Bunin's autobiographical *The Well of Days*. In hindsight Lehmann admitted that most of his firm's first offerings were highbrow or near-highbrow. But the mood of the times and the success of both *New Writing* and *Penguin New Writing* seemed to indicate that the firm was starting off in the right direction.

By the middle of 1947 John Lehmann Limited was in trouble. The postwar public was less interested in buying books than in acquiring material possessions that had not been available during the war. Because the firm's publications did not move as quickly as expected, Lehmann's capital was locked up. It turned out that ten thousand pounds was too small an amount to keep a publishing firm operating for an extended period. In the winter of 1947 Lehmann reopened negotiations with Purnell, and Purnell agreed to put its full resources—paper and money—behind John Lehmann Limited for 100 percent financial control. The new agreement established Lehmann as managing director on full salary and allowed him to repay his family backers and to hire his sister Rosamond as a salaried reader. In addition, he was free to produce one or two special books outside the Purnell group.

For the next several years Lehmann was able to pursue the course he had originally set for his firm—identifying, hiring, and supporting new writers in Britain, Europe, and America. When he went to the United States in 1948 with a group from Purnell that was studying printing methods and machinery, he used the opportunity to capture a new generation of American writers. Among those he engaged were Gore Vidal, J. F. Powers, Merle Miller, Calder Willingham, Chandler Brossard, Paul Bowles, and Theodore Roethke. On the same trip he saw Marlon Brando in *A Streetcar Named Desire* and set about acquiring the English rights to the works of Tennessee Williams. New European writers the firm introduced were Raymond Queneau, Ennio Flaiano, Mario Soldati, and Nikos Kazantzakis.

Lehmann's long-range plans called for John Lehmann Limited to produce travel books, autobiographies, biographical criticism, and books by experts on the theater, opera, and ballet. In short, he wanted the firm's list to look like *Penguin New Writing*, with attention given to all the arts. He also wanted to start a Library of Art and Travel, which would reprint notable but long-unavailable books in elegant formats, and a Holiday Library, which would reprint between-the-wars fiction and biography.

By the early 1950s, however, John Lehmann Limited, which moved to 25 Gilbert Street in 1951, was in financial difficulty once again. Harvey was not pleased that the firm had made no clear profit, but Lehmann believed that it had; because Purnell charged the firm the normal price for printing, a profit actually was built into every stage of the operations—composition, supply of paper, printing, and binding; Lehmann also thought his firm actually made a concealed profit for Purnell because it provided work for the employees in slack times. While John Lehmann Limited needed time to develop, he contended, it was gaining prestige and would eventually attain financial success as well. In early 1952 Lehmann tried to negotiate a new arrangement with Robert Maxwell, who had bought Simpkin Marshall: with Maxwell's financing, Lehmann hoped to buy back his firm from Harvey. Maxwell and Lehmann were unable to meet Harvey's terms, and on 31 December 1952 Harvey gave Lehmann notice terminating his services.

The causes for the demise of John Lehmann Limited were in some respects like those behind the rupture between Lehmann and Leonard Woolf. Although Lehmann's artistic judgment was never questioned, his business acumen was. He attempted to expand too quickly with too little capital. He also misjudged the temper and needs of the postwar book buyer. Because stock did not move fast enough, his firm did not make enough profit to expand. And, to a degree, Lehmann persisted in overvaluing aesthetics and downplaying economics. The firm's last books were published in 1952: André Malraux's *The Walnut Trees of Altenburg*, translated by A. W. Fielding; Paul Bowles's *Let It Come Down*; Nikos Kazantzakis's *Zorba the Greek*, translated by Carl Wildman; Jean-Louis Curtis's *Lucifer's Dream*, translated by Robin Chancellor; Benjamin Constant's *Cecile*, translated by N. Cameron; Hallam Fordham's *John Gielgud: An Actor's Biography in Pictures*; Annette Hopkins's *Elizabeth Gaskell: Her Life and Work*; and Lehmann's own *Pleasures of "New Writing."* John Lehmann's career as a publisher was ended.

References:

John Lehmann, *The Ample Proposition: Autobiography III* (London: Eyre & Spottiswoode, 1966);

Lehmann, *I Am My Brother* (New York: Reynal, 1960);

Lehmann, *In My Own Time: Memoirs of a Literary Life* (Boston: Little, Brown, 1969);

Lehmann, *Thrown to the Woolfs* (New York: Holt, Rinehart & Winston, 1979);

Lehmann, *The Whispering Gallery: Autobiography I* (New York: Harcourt, Brace, 1954);

George Spater and Ian Parsons, *A Marriage of True Minds: An Intimate Portrait of Leonard and Virginia Woolf* (New York: Harcourt Brace Jovanovich, 1977);

Leonard Woolf, *The Journey Not the Arrival Matters: An Autobiography of the Years 1939-1969* (New York: Harcourt, Brace & World, 1970).

—*Sondra Miley Cooney*

Leicester University Press

(*Leicester: 1957-*)

The Leicester University Press was founded in 1957 to coincide with the granting of the charter of independence to Leicester University. The press developed out of the Small Publications Board, which had begun in 1951 in University College, Leicester. The publications board had the dual function of publishing the official documents of the university, such as calendars, reports and gazettes, and scholarly manuscripts. The university press was established to publish the scholarly manuscripts accepted by the board. In its early years the press was governed by a committee of senior members of the university, with the day-to-day administration under the control of a member of the university registry. Initially the university absorbed overhead costs, and the press operated on a budget of about one thousand pounds per annum. By 1965 the press was producing about a dozen titles annually, and B. J. Roud was appointed full-time press secretary. Peter L. Boulton succeeded him in 1968 together with an assistant, Susan Martin. Both remained in office until September 1988.

In the early years publications of the press strongly reflected the academic interests of the university. Consequently, history, French, and mathematics predominated. The first book published was R. L. Goodstein's *Mathematical Logic* (1957); he had also written the first publication of the original publications board. Professor H. P. R. Finberg of the Department of English Local History produced an extensive series of pamphlets as "Occasional Papers in English Local History," the first of which was his own *The Local Historian and his Theme: An Introductory Lecture* (1952). Some fifty titles have been published in this series.

Historical topics have always been a particular strength of Leicester University Press, and it is renowned for its pioneering interest in urban history, largely the result of the enthusiasm of press board member H. J. Dyos. His *Victorian Suburb: A Study of the Growth of Camberwell* (1961) was reprinted four times. The innovative series Themes in Urban History published the work of recently completed Ph.D. graduates. Other areas of strength have been archaeology, defense studies, international relations, and museum studies.

The establishment of the Victorian Studies Centre in 1967 provided the initiative for The Victorian Library, which provided reasonably priced reprints of out-of-print titles on a wide range of subjects, each with an introduction by a distinguished authority in the field. Charters and records were reprinted, including the *Records of the Borough of Leicester* (starting with volume five in 1965). This commitment to publishing aids to research was continued with the reprinting of C. Gross's *Bibliography of British Municipal History* (1966) and a book by Gareth Shaw, *British Directories* (1988). The *Urban History Yearbook* (1974-) is the only journal still published by the press. Other journals with which the press has been associated include the *Journal of Transport History, Journal of Commonwealth Political Studies*, and a review journal *Philosophical Books*.

Over the years the scope of the publications has widened appreciably, and the press has gained a reputation for scholarly books on subjects as varied as Valerie Marett's *Immigrants Settling in the City* (1988) and *Theodor Storm* (1989), edited by Patricia M. Boswell.

In 1988 it was announced that the London firm Pinter Publishers had acquired Leicester University Press. The imprint Leicester University Press has been retained, and there is an editorial office at Leicester University, but sales and distribution were transferred to Pinter. The University of Leicester continues to influence the publications policy of the press through an editorial advisory committee of academics appointed by the vice-chancellor.

—Diana Dixon

Liverpool University Press
(Liverpool: 1955-   )
University Press of Liverpool
(Liverpool: 1899-1955)

The University Press of Liverpool was established in 1899 by the University College of Liverpool. In 1903 the University College of Liverpool was designated the University of Liverpool, but the imprint remained the University Press of Liverpool until 1955, when it was changed to Liverpool University Press. Dr. John Sampson, whom Thomas Kelly describes in his 1981 history of the university as "a Johnsonian figure . . . , the librarian, portly in build, ponderous in speech, choleric in disposition, immensely learned and yet with an impish sense of humour," is credited "with having initiated the idea of the Press" and was its secretary from its inception until 1910.

Sampson had originally been apprenticed as a printer and engraver. After twelve years he had set himself up in business, but this venture had failed, and he had pursued the life of a self-taught scholar. Inspired by the work of George Borrow, Sampson had embarked on a study of the language and lore of Gypsies. He had become recognized as an authority on the Welsh Gypsies, and it was through these studies that Sampson had become known to the University College staff; he had been appointed college librarian in 1891 and retained the post until 1928.

It was through Sampson that the press was able to call upon the consultancy services of Walter Blackie from the University Press of Edinburgh. A memorandum from Blackie dated 7 September 1900 indicates the working practices established for the University Press of Liverpool. The press was encouraged to act as an agent or broker between University College and the printing office. For its services it would charge a commission of between 10 and 12 percent, plus a 5-percent discount from the printers. The press would not be bound in a formal contract with any one individual printer but would give each piece of work by estimate to any printing office which "seemed able to execute it and willing to accept it." Blackie noted that "The prevalence of competition would keep prices down to the lowest rates." The memorandum ends with the comment: "On mature consideration it would be very risky to establish a printing office to do such work as Liverpool University requires without experience—and I do not think that £2,000 would be sufficient capital. The outlets for expenditure are so endless and without experience would be ruinous." Blackie's system was tried for a few years while the Printing and Stationery Committee learned the trade and prepared to take control of the whole enterprise.

In 1901 the press was registered as a limited company separate from the college. This company—first under the secretaryship of Sampson and then under Professor B. Moore from 1910 to 1914, Professor Garstang (first name not known) from 1914 to 1915, Professor E. T. Champagnac from 1916 to 1918, and Professor Patrick Abercrombie from 1918 to 1922—survived until 1922. Its records show the employment of a succession of printers and the practice of arranging sales and distributions through established trade publishers—Longmans, Green from 1901 to 1904; Williams and Norgate from 1904 to 1908; and Constable from 1909 to 1921.

192

In the years before the outbreak of World War I the press published twenty books and twice that number of pamphlets. These early publications included learned works such as R. Caton's *The Temples and Ritual of Asklepios* (1900); medical expositions, such as J. W. W. Stephens and S. R. Christopher's *The Practical Study of Malaria and Other Blood Parasites* (1903) and A. M. Paterson's *The Human Sternum* (1904); and literary studies, such as J. Weightman's *The Language and Dialect of the Later Old English Poetry* (1907). Other early publications were based on the activities of scholars both at the university and in the locality of Liverpool, including R. Muir's *A History of Liverpool* (1907) and a 1911 publication by the students of the University of Liverpool, *Primitiae: Essays in English Literature*. At the same period the press was also involved in the launching of some important—and for the most part profitable—periodicals: the *Biochemical Journal* (1906-1912), later the official *Journal of the Biochemical Society*; *Annals of Tropical Medicine and Parasitology* (1907-1946); *Annals of Archaeology and Anthropology* (1908-1914; 1921-1940); and *Town Planning Review* (1910-1915; 1918-1946), one of the mainstays of the press. In 1909 the University of Liverpool was the first university in the world to have a department of town planning. During the interwar period this department was headed by Press Secretary Abercombie, who was also editor of the *Town Planning Review*.

In 1922 the press received a donation from Edward Whitley of twenty-five hundred pounds in response to a university appeal. This money made it possible for the press to dissolve the original company of 1901 and establish a new one. This new company was still called the University Press of Liverpool Limited. Each partner contributed capital of five thousand pounds. All profits went to the press, but Hodder and Stoughton received 10 percent of net receipts as a commission on works it published and distributed. In 1924 Hodder and Stoughton withdrew.

Between 1922 and 1928 the press published forty-seven books. Kelly notes that "the University Press had little or nothing in the way of financial resources, and yet continued to struggle to publish worthwhile books of scholarship." In 1928 the press ceased to be an independent organization and passed under the control of a press committee responsible to the university council.

Even though the press had become technically part of the University of Liverpool, it received little financial help apart from the provision of a modest office. The press's only income was the commission earned on publishing books financed from outside sources, plus approximately fifty pounds per annum in interest on invested capital.

The backbone of the press during the interwar years was the continued publication of journals: the *Town Planning Review*, published quarterly, was joined by the *Journal on Tropical Medicine* and the *Journal Bulletin of Hispanic Studies*, all of which reflect pioneering work carried out by the University of Liverpool. In 1949 the press published what is regarded as a seminal Hispanic text, *A Short History of the Romantic Movement in Spain*, by Edgar Allison Peers. In 1950 one of its most prestigious works was published, Clarence S. Stein's *Toward New Towns in America*, with an introduction by Lewis Mumford. Because of the difficulties in marketing a thin but wide-ranging catalogue, however, the press deliberately moved into such new fields as history and English literature and language, while retaining its small but profitable periodical markets. The initiator of these developments was John O'Kane, secretary of the press from 1954 to 1981. He was a colorful and eccentric personality who left his mark on the character of the press. He had an aversion to paperbacks and continued the press's policy of producing works that met high production standards, a practice that has led at times to costly publications.

In the 1960s and 1970s the press published works in the social sciences. The best known of these is John Barron Mays's *Growing up in the City: A Study of Juvenile Delinquency in an Urban Neighborhood* (1964), which was based on research in the Toxteth area of Liverpool. In 1979, following its decision to expand the literature section, the press produced two seminal critical Shakespearean studies by Kenneth Muir: *Shakespeare's Tragic Sequence* and *Shakespeare's Comic Sequence*. English literature and language is now the biggest subject area of the press.

In other areas the press's "best-sellers" include specialist publications such as the veterinary handbook *Notes for the Sheep Clinician* (1983), by M. J. Clarkson and W. B. Faull. Other successes include a series of translated texts for historians, notably *Glory of the Martyrs*, by Gregory of Tours (1988), translated by Raymond Van Dam.

The second half of the 1970s was dominated by endless debates with the university in relation to subsidies, and the press experienced little in the way of expansion—in contrast, for example, to Manchester University Press, which expanded rapidly during this period. In 1980 a report recommended the closure of the press; but following heated discussions the press was permitted to survive, though with a much lower profile. This decision, however, meant a relocation into the university administration building, which brought to an end the press's warehousing and distribution services. The press is now responsible to the registrar and the university in a more direct way, and while it is supposed to seek outside sponsorship, it is largely reliant on funds from the university.

Liverpool University Press now operates cautiously, publishing one book at a time. Books are still published on commission, usually from departments in the university. Hence, the academic departments and the publishing house are locked in to a certain extent and are mutually supportive. Some external, self-financing publications are also produced for other institutions, such as museums and art galleries.

In 1988 the press published sixteen books— the largest number in one year since World War II—though its journals continue to provide its backbone. Sales for the financial year 1987-1988 were forty-five thousand pounds for books and sixty-five thousand pounds for journals.

Liverpool University Press continues to hold its own, with publisher Robin Bloxsidge leading a team of five full-time employees and one part-time worker. In 1990 the press had some one hundred books in print and sixty-seven authors receiving royalties. The press continues to publish works of academic and scholarly worthiness, and its authors, according to Bloxsidge, "are paid in glory rather than in money."

References:

J. P. Droop, *The University Press of Liverpool—A Record of Progress 1899-1946* (Liverpool: University Press of Liverpool, 1947);

Thomas Kelly, *For Advancement of Learning: The University of Liverpool, 1881-1981* (Liverpool: Liverpool University Press, 1981).

—Joss West-Burnham

Macdonald and Company (Publishers)
(London: 1942-)
T. T. MacDonald
(London: 1938-1942)

Theodore Thomas MacDonald began publishing cheap hardback fiction under the imprint T. T. MacDonald in August 1938 from offices at Ludgate House, 110 Fleet Street. MacDonald published three-penny books for sale in Woolworth's stores and novels for three shillings and sixpence.

A significant factor in the firm's development was a link with Purnell and Sons, the printing group based at Paulton, near Bristol. MacDonald's first company secretary, S. E. Jackson, was an associate of Wilfred Harvey, Purnell's chairman.

Ambitious to become a mainstream publisher as well as a large-scale printer, Harvey seized the opportunity presented when, at the outbreak of World War II, T. T. MacDonald resigned and had no further connection with the company he founded. Jackson was appointed as a director in his place, and in December 1940 Harvey became joint managing director.

Harvey was able to obtain a surprisingly generous paper allocation under strict wartime rationing, and he had first-class printing facilities available to him from the outset. In July 1942 E. R. H. (Eric) Harvey, stepson of the chairman, became literary director of T. T. MacDonald (although he was away in the army), and J. Murray Thompson, a director of Purnell's London office, became joint managing director with Wilfred Harvey.

In October 1942 the company's name was changed to Macdonald and Company (Publishers), and it moved to 19 Ludgate Hill. The new company secretary, H. E. (Ewart) Taylor, was based at Paulton, and Thompson, with his range

of valuable contacts and publishing experience, was the principal driving force in London.

The first title from the reorganized company appeared on 13 March 1943: *The Britain I Want*, by Emanuel Shinwell, MP. Another early publication was *Selected Verses* (1943), by Gilbert Frankau—the first in a many-volume series of reprints of that popular author's works, followed after the war by three original novels by Frankau.

Macdonald's most notable success was the British edition of American author Kathleen Winsor's historical romance *Forever Amber* (1945). No other publisher had been willing to expend its paper quota for this sensational eight-hundred-page blockbuster. But whatever the literary merits of *Forever Amber*, the novel significantly lifted Macdonald's fortunes and encouraged the company to promote Margaret Campbell Barnes, another historical novelist, into a second, this time homegrown, success. Dorothy Eden, yet another of the company's women novelists, was a writer of best-selling crime fiction. Macdonald has always been remarkable for the variety of its lists. By the end of the war one found the epic novelist John Cowper Powys on the same lists as popular cartoonist Ronald Searle, the novels of Henry Williamson were offered alongside the Macdonald Illustrated Classics. In 1946 Macdonald began publishing *Film Review*, an annual edited by F. Maurice Speed. The firm also produced authoritative aviation books.

Catherine Cookson was forty-four in 1950 when Macdonald accepted her first novel, *Kate Hannigan*; she became one of Britain's best-selling authors. All of her novels and children's stories are set in and around her native Tyneside. Macdonald also published her autobiography, *Our Kate* (1969). Today, devotees flock to Tyneside from all over the world, and commemorative plaques abound. By 1991, 85 million copies of Cookson's books in seventeen languages had been sold. Her overwhelming success in Britain was reflected by her top ranking year after year in the Public Lending Rights "league table" (the yardstick of popularity with library readers).

Steady development led to progressive moves of the company's London headquarters to 43 Ludgate Hill; 16 Maddox Street; Gulf House, Portman Street; and St. Giles House, Poland Street. During the 1950s and 1960s, Purnell, under the direction of Wilfred Harvey, acquired a succession of other publishing lists—among them Max Parrish, Oldbourne Press, Queen Anne Press (with Ian Fleming among its authors), T. V. Boardman, John Lehmann, Latimer House, and Sampson Low, Marston and Company. Many of the titles on these lists were republished under the Macdonald imprint. The Sampson Low imprint was retained, and the Jane's imprint it brought to Macdonald played a central role in the company's growth and character in the 1970s.

Harvey's expansion of printing and allied interests led to a merger of Purnell with Hazell Sun in 1964 under the name British Printing Corporation (BPC). Macdonald at that juncture was publishing fiction (including science fiction) and general nonfiction, as well as technical, scientific, and educational books. After a dispute regarding expenses, Harvey resigned from BPC in the following year. Even the arrival of the charismatic James MacGibbon failed to arrest losses caused elsewhere in BPC largely by overinvestment in part works. It took the appointment of Ronald Whiting as managing director to steady the firm.

Whiting was brought in specifically to reorganize the Jane's imprint. *All the World's Fighting Ships* had been founded by Fred T. Jane in 1898; his other historic reference annual, *Jane's All the World's Aircraft*, was first published as *All the World's Airships, Aeroplanes and Dirigibles* in 1909—the year Louis Blériot flew across the English Channel. Sampson Low had produced these and all the other Jane's publications from the outset.

Thus Macdonald entered the arena as a general hardback publisher, taking full advantage of the accumulated backlist, notably Enid Blyton's "Noddy" books. Launched by Sampson Low in 1949, these books have remained—despite fierce denunciation by educationalists and children's librarians—firm favorites with generations of young readers worldwide. Under Whiting the company had its share of other best-sellers. Macdonald and Jane's published Yehudi Menuhin's memoirs, *Unfinished Journey* (1977), and Colleen McCullough's *Thorn Birds* (1980), thus satisfying two very distinct mass markets.

Futura, mainly a paperback imprint, was founded in 1973. Under Anthony Cheetham, this venture proved an immediate success. After a cash crisis and troubles in both staff and labor relations led to the sale of Jane's to the Thomson Group in 1980, Futura moved into Shepherdess Walk in its place, and a merged company, Macdonald/Futura, was founded with Whiting as chairman and Cheetham as managing director.

Even more radical changes have taken place since 1982, when Robert Maxwell took over BPC, which he renamed British Printing and Communication Corporation (BPCC). Most of the Macdonald staff was concentrated into Holywell House, Worship Street; the building was soon renamed Maxwell House. Later the firm moved to Greater London House, Hampstead Road, and still later to 66-73 Shoe Lane—a short distance from T. T. MacDonald's premises in 1938.

In 1987 the parent company became Maxwell Communication Corporation (MCC), with Maxwell Pergamon Publishing Corporation (MPPC) as an intermediate holding company for the publishing division. Macdonald Educational and all the children's books (except the Noddy books) were sold to Simon and Schuster in January 1989. The present-day Macdonald and Company (Publishers) comprises Macdonald hardback books; paperback imprints Futura, Optima, Orbit, Sphere, Cardinal, and Abacus (the last three acquired from Penguin in April 1989); Scribners; and Queen Anne Press (sports titles). The company moved in late 1989 to Orbit House, New Fetter Lane, and in 1991 to 165 Great Dover Street in Southeast London. That year MPPC became Maxwell Macmillan Publishing Corporation.

—David Linton

Manchester University Press
(Manchester: 1904-   )

The institutional origins of Manchester University Press lie in the charter conferring independence on the Victoria University of Manchester on 15 July 1903. The university had promoted the publication of significant lectures and volumes before 1903, but it is appropriate to regard 1904 as the press's foundation year. The University Publications Committee, chaired by Professor T. F. Tout, was constituted in the summer term of 1904. In the same year the Manchester firm of Sherratt and Hughes was appointed as printers and publishers for the university and rented a cramped room in university property on Burlington Street.

In the 1904-1905 academic year the committee financed the publication of three books, including James Tait's *Mediæval Manchester and the Beginnings of Lancashire* (1904) and Sydney J. Chapman's *The Lancashire Cotton Industry: A Study in Economic Development* (1904). In addition, it published three medical textbooks and thirteen lectures, and sanctioned the use of the university press imprint for eleven further publications. It arranged for book exchanges with some hundred universities and learned societies throughout the world, ranging from the Berlin and Leipzig Academies to Harvard University and the New York Public Library.

In 1906 the press published posthumously W. T. Arnold's *Studies of Roman Imperialism*, with a long memoir by his sister, the novelist Mrs. Humphry Ward, and his colleague C. E. Montague of the *Manchester Guardian*. In its report for 1906-1907 the Publications Committee announced *An Introduction to Early Welsh*, by John Strachan, for publication in 1908; but it was delayed in consequence of legal proceedings taken by Dr. J. Gwenogvryn Evans on grounds of copyright infringement. The case came before the

T. F. Tout, chairman of the Manchester University Publications Committee from 1904 to 1925 and founder of the Manchester University Press

High Court (Chancery Division) in February 1909 and was settled on the third day. Evans's copyright claim was admitted, and the book was well received on its publication in March 1909; a second impression was printed in 1937.

In 1909 the press list included A. C. Bradley's Adamson lecture *English Poetry and Ger-*

man *Philosophy in the Age of Wordsworth*; the lecture had been delivered at the university. The publishing links that were to develop between the university press and the Rylands Library in Manchester are foreshadowed in the report for 1908-1909, which notes that the first volumes of the library's catalogues, produced by the Oxford University Press, bore the Manchester University Press imprint.

The period 1909-1910 was one of great depression in the book trade, and the university assisted the press with a special grant of two hundred pounds. This session saw the publication of the first of a series of English studies, Phoebe Sheavyn's *The Literary Profession in the Elizabethan Age* (1909); in 1967 a second edition of this standard book, revised by J. W. Saunders, was published. The 1909-1910 report also listed the first of a series of facsimiles of the rarest documents in the Rylands Library—*Propositio Johannis Russell* (1909), a short tract printed by William Caxton in 1476.

During the academic year 1909-1910 the Publications Committee concluded arrangements whereby the New York branch of Longmans, Green and Company would act as American agent for future publications; the success of Longmans, Green in promoting sales was apparent as early as 1912. Meanwhile, both in 1908 and 1910 the committee had pointed out the need for a "real University Press," acting as both printer and publisher under the immediate direction of the university. Printing was not, and has not been, undertaken; crucially important developments were to take place, however, between 1911 and 1915.

In October 1911 the University Council appointed a full-time secretary to the Publications Committee, H. M. McKechnie; he had previously managed the Edinburgh publisher E. and S. Livingstone. He took office early in 1912. That year the office and storeroom of the committee were established at 12 Lime Grove, a university property. During the 1912-1913 session eleven new works in the Manchester University Series were published, bringing the total to eighty-two volumes. A record sale was reported for a volume of five lectures, *Germany in the Nineteenth Century* (1912); more than fourteen hundred copies were sold within fifteen months. The 1913 report expressed the view that the committee's position as one of the country's leading publishing agencies was completely established.

Sherratt and Hughes undertook all the press's printing for the 1913-1914 session; in the next session, however, the firm resigned as the university's publisher. In 1915 the committee itself became a publisher and was admitted as a member of the Publishers' Association under the designation of the Manchester University Press. On 27 October 1915 the Publications Committee was authorized by the University Council to rename itself the University Press Committee. Its policy remained that of publishing works of scholarship that would be unlikely to command the interest of a commercial publisher. Distribution was transferred to Longmans, Green and Company, with a view to covering a wider European and American area. All Manchester University Press publications were listed in Longmans, Green's catalogues. The success of this development can be gauged from the committee's 1915-1916 report, which included a special "expression of gratitude" to Charles J. Longman.

This same report noted that the press had become publisher for the Chetham Society, founded in 1843 for the publication of historical and literary research concerning Lancashire and Cheshire. The first Chetham text to be published by Manchester University Press was Tait's *The Domesday Survey of Cheshire* (1916). Thirteen of the society's publications were listed in the press's 1989 catalogue, including Thomas Short Willan's *Elizabethan Manchester* (1980).

In 1915 it was estimated that more than 150 books had been given the university imprint since 1904. The year 1918 saw the posthumous publication of Mark Hovell's *The Chartist Movement*, edited and completed with a memoir by Tout; it remained on the list for almost seventy years. Tout was the most productive author in the next decade. To existing knowledge of the role of the Chancery and the Exchequer in medieval England he added his fully detailed research on three less well known departments of the royal household: the Wardrobe, the Chamber, and the Small Seals. The first two volumes of *Chapters in the Administrative History of Mediaeval England* appeared in 1920, volumes three and four in 1928, and volume five, posthumously, in 1930. A 317-page index by Mabel Mills was the chief feature of volume six (1933); at the time it was regarded as the fullest and most scientifically arranged guide to the contents of any historical work in English. With Tout's death on 24 October 1928 the press lost its founder and the chairman of its Publications Committee from 1904 to

H. M. McKechnie, secretary of the Manchester University Press from 1912 to 1949, and Terence L. Jones, secretary from 1949 to 1973

1925. During his time in office 250 volumes were published. The 1929 committee report paid tribute to his "grit and determination" and said that the university owed a great debt to his "unselfish devotion."

In June 1925 Tout had been succeeded as chairman by Tait, who continued until the end of 1934 and monitored the publication of more than 370 books, pamphlets, and volumes of serial publications. In 1927 the agreement with Longmans, Green and Company Limited was terminated; the New York branch of Longmans terminated its agreement as of 31 March 1929. Manchester University Press had decided in December 1927 that it could conduct its business without the aid of any other firm of publishers, thereby effecting a considerable saving in discounts and commissions. Meanwhile, in the 1921-1922 session the press had moved from 12 Lime Grove to more commodious premises at 23 Lime Grove; when this site was required for a new library the press transferred in February 1935 to 8-10 Wright Street.

Tout's scholarship continues to be valued;

volumes two and three of his principal work are listed in the catalogues of the late 1980s. Other highly important books—not least of all in the field of economic history—appeared concurrently with his, and continued through the 1930s. It was at Tout's instigation that the first chair of economic history in England was established. Its holder was George Unwin, who opened up new lines of inquiry into the social aspect of history. In 1924 the press published his *Samuel Oldknow and the Arkwrights*; a second edition, with a preface by W. H. Chaloner, appeared in 1968. The 1924 list also included T. S. Ashton's *Iron and Steel in the Industrial Revolution*; a fourth edition was printed in 1968. In 1926 came Arthur Redford's *Labour Migration in England, 1800-50*; the second edition, revised and edited by Chaloner, was published in 1964. *The Cotton Trade and Industrial Lancashire, 1600-1780* (1931; second impression, 1964), by A. P. Wadsworth and J. de Lacy Mann, was regarded as marking a significant advance in the study of the cotton industry and was widely praised. In European history, the first of A. J. P. Taylor's books, *The Italian Problem in European Diplomacy, 1847-1849*, was listed in 1934. Its publication by Manchester University Press was subsidized from the Tout Memorial Publication Fund established in 1929.

In the field of English language and literature many noteworthy volumes were published from 1910 to 1930. Among these was W. J. Sedgefield's edition of *Beowulf* (1910), its third printing (1935) remaining listed until 1959. The year 1913 saw the two-volume *The Poetical Works of William Drummond of Hawthornden*, edited by L. E. Kastner. The press's report for 1921-1922 singled out Eilert Ekwall's *The Place Names of Lancashire* (1922) as an important work "marking a new era in the study of place-names in this country." In 1925 came Edward H. Sugden's authoritative compilation, *A Topographical Dictionary to the Works of Shakespeare and His Fellow Dramatists*. It was listed for thirty-five years and subsequently made available in a microfiche edition.

In 1949 McKechnie retired after thirty-seven years' service. He was succeeded as secretary by T. L. Jones, who came to Manchester from the London publisher Routledge and Kegan Paul. By 1950 the press's offices in Wright Street became due for demolition before redevelopment, and in 1951 the press moved to larger premises at 316-324 Oxford Road. During World War II and its aftermath there had been little scope for expansion, but during Jones's long term as secretary, which lasted until 1973, there was a marked growth of publication in social anthropology, social history, and the social and political sciences. Whereas in 1953 the press published seventeen new books and eight new editions, in 1968 the figures were thirty-one new books and twenty-eight reprints from the backlist. The volume of reprints was the result of the expansion of British universities and polytechnics during the 1960s and, particularly in the case of economic history titles, of American copublication.

In the 1950s two significant texts in political science were Harold J. Laski's *Reflections on the Constitution* (1951; fourth impression, 1963) and E. J. E. Hobsbawm's *Primitive Rebels* (1959; third impression, 1972). The university's postwar initiatives in social anthropology and comparative religion were reflected in the publication of Max Gluckman's *Rituals of Rebellion in South-East Africa* (1954) and Samuel G. F. Brandon's *Man and His Destiny in the Great Religions* (1962), respectively. The university's links with Zambia were evident

in its publication of the *Rhodes-Livingstone Institute Journal* and institute papers from 1954 to 1966, and of their successors, the Institute for African Studies' journal *African Social Research* and sixteen Zambian Papers from 1966 to 1980.

History has remained the press's largest publishing category. Marc Bloch's *The Historian's Craft* (1954) was an important account of the practical methods of a first-class historian and sold well. In 1958 came *The Strutts and the Arkwrights, 1758-1830*, by Robert S. Fitton and Alfred P. Wadsworth, a study of the early factory system. A local social historian, Robert Roberts, was responsible for two examples of "the good-selling serious book" that the press has promoted since the early 1950s. His *The Classic Slum* (1971; reprinted in 1972 and 1978) was a firsthand account of Salford life in the early decades of the twentieth century. Roberts followed it with a depiction of his childhood and youth in *A Ragged Schooling: Growing Up in the Classic Slum* (1978). In 1975 a major publication was Gordon Leff's *William of Ockham*, the first comprehensive study in English of Ockham's system of thought. A popular work published in 1983 was Colin D. Rogers's *The Family Tree Detective*, a definitive manual for analyzing and solving genealogical problems; it is marketed in North America under the title *Tracing Your English Ancestors*. In 1985 the American Gary S. Messinger's *Manchester in the Victorian Age* won the first Portico prize (fifteen hundred pounds) for a book of fiction or nonfiction based on the northwest region. Manchester's Hallé Orchestra has been the subject of Michael Kennedy's *The Hallé Tradition* (1960) and *The Hallé: 1858-1983* (1983).

The 1980s have seen the development of series such as Lives of the Left, original biographies of leading figures in the European and North American socialist and labor movements exemplified by Joel Wiener's *William Lovett* (1989) and Stephen Coleman's *Daniel De Leon* (1990). Cross-disciplinary approaches to imperialism have resulted in a variety of titles, such as John M. MacKenzie's *Propaganda and Empire* (1984) and *Imperialism and Juvenile Literature* (1989), edited by Jeffrey Richards—both in the series Studies of Imperialism. Since 1980 the press has published the first specialist historical journal devoted to transport, the *Journal of Transport History*.

In the postwar period up to the 1970s Manchester has typically listed some thirty works in English studies in its catalogues. A landmark in

The building at 316-324 Oxford Road that served as the Manchester University Press headquarters from 1951 to 1973

1952 was Florence E. Harmer's *Anglo-Saxon Writs*; this standard work is never likely to be superseded. In 1959 R. W. V. Elliott's introductory study, *Runes*, was chosen by the National Book League for exhibition among the best-produced books of the year. A new edition was published in 1989. The Press Committee report for 1961-1962 noted that "for the first time for many years" there had been a return to publishing books on modern English literature. Bernard Bergonzi's *The Early H. G. Wells* (1961), a study of Wells's early scientific romances, was taken by Toronto University Press for publication in Canada and the United States. The centenary of Mrs. Elizabeth Gaskell's death in 1865 was particularly significant to a press based in the region where much of her work is set. Arthur Pollard's *Mrs. Gaskell: Novelist and Biographer* (1965) preceded a volume scheduled to appear concurrently, *The Letters of Mrs. Gaskell*, edited by J. A. V. Chapple and Arthur Pollard. Publication of the latter was postponed until 1966, following the release of an additional 120 letters when the book was already in page proof; the letters were edited and set in appendix form, the complete text running to 1,010

pages. Both volumes were copublished by Harvard University Press. Among the literary studies were John Beer's *Blake's Visionary Universe* (1969); Marcia Pointon's *Milton and English Art, 1638-1860* (1970); D. G. Scragg's *A History of English Spelling* (1974); *The Achievement of Ted Hughes* (1986), edited by Keith Sagar; and *The Black Presence in English Literature* (1986), edited by David Dabydeen.

In 1973 the press moved from its Oxford Road headquarters to mid-campus premises on Coupland Street. In July 1973, on Jones's retirement, J. M. N. Spencer joined the press as publisher. Spencer had gained previous experience with the Longman firm. During his term in office there was a substantial increase in the annual production of new books, from thirty in 1977 to seventy in 1987. The expansion of titles in English studies was particularly marked. In 1974 the press began a new series, Manchester Medieval Classics, with each book presenting the original text and a modern version on facing pages. Under the general editorship of G. L. Brook, the first to appear was *Sir Gawain and the Green Knight* (1974), edited by W. R. J. Barron. The

Old and Middle English Texts series was enlarged in 1972, when the press published second impressions of six texts from Nelson's Medieval and Renaissance Library. Among them were *The Owl and the Nightingale*, edited by Eric G. Stanley, and Geoffrey Chaucer's *The Parlement of Foulys*, edited by D. S. Brewer; both works had originally been published in 1960.

In 1973 Manchester University Press took over the journal *Critical Quarterly*, edited by C. B. Cox and A. E. Dyson, from Oxford University Press. It combines accessible literary criticism with the publication of new poetry; contributors have included Thom Gunn, Seamus Heaney, Ted Hughes, and R. S. Thomas. Since the 1980s it has also published articles on cinema, television, radio, and recorded music; new fiction has been presented since 1986. Colin MacCabe joined the journal as criticism editor in 1988, with Cox continuing as general editor. The press had published MacCabe's *Theoretical Essays: Film, Linguistics, Literature* in 1985.

In 1976 the press acquired the complete stock of and future publishing rights to the Revels Plays from Methuen and Company Limited. This series, devised by the late Clifford Leech, presents texts by sixteenth- and seventeenth-century dramatists other than William Shakespeare; one of its hallmarks is the thoroughness of the scholarly annotations. In 1976 the series comprised some twenty-one volumes; by 1989 it totaled forty-three, with such dramatists as George Chapman, Ben Jonson, Christopher Marlowe, Thomas Middleton, and John Webster well represented. A background series, The Revels Plays Companion Library, was launched in 1984.

Shakespeare's plays are the subject of the Shakespeare in Performance series, initiated in 1984 with *All's Well That Ends Well*, edited by J. L. Styan. In 1985 two important studies of Shakespeare were published. E. A. J. Honigmann's *Shakespeare: The "Lost Years"* includes evidence that Shakespeare worked as both schoolmaster and player for a wealthy Catholic landowner in Lancashire. *Political Shakespeare: New Essays in Cultural Materialism* (1985), edited by Jonathan Dollimore and Alan Sinfield, contests the idea of Shakespeare as a universal genius whose work transcends politics and history. A similar interdisciplinary approach can be found in a new series of the late 1980s, Cultural Politics. Its texts cross traditional subject boundaries, drawing on literary theory, feminism and sexual politics, and Marxist and cultural studies. Among the works already published are *The Shakespeare Myth* (1988), edited by Graham Holderness; *Poetry, Politics and Language* (1988), by John Barrell; and *Comics: Ideology, Power and the Critics* (1989), by Martin Barker. This innovative series has proved commercially successful and can be seen as challenging the traditional literary monograph. Manchester also copublishes the series Theory and History of Literature, including such works as Jean-François Lyotard's *The Postmodern Condition* (1984).

In European languages, a program for publishing French and German texts was established as early as 1917; today the press lists more than thirty texts in French, German, Italian, and Spanish. Under the editorial guidance of Kathleen Speight, Manchester's Italian texts are unrivaled; the Spanish texts and the Manchester New German Texts, launched in 1988, are also noteworthy. Among the press's publications in European languages and literature have been Mildred K. Pope's *From Latin to Modern French* (1934; third edition, 1961); Joseph Chiari's *Contemporary French Poetry* (1952), to which T. S. Eliot contributed a foreword; and Roy Pascal's *The German Sturm und Drang* (1953).

In other subject areas, Sir Alexander and Lady E. C. Ewing's *Teaching Deaf Children to Talk* (1964) and John Reed's *The Schubert Song Companion* (1985) carried authoritative status. Similarly, through the publication of specialized studies and journals, the press has made substantial contributions in the areas of education, voluntary organizations, international law, Anglo-American affairs, and engineering. It has also promoted American, Latin American, East Asian, and African studies. The North American market is an important feature in budgeting for each book. Before the early 1980s the press would often assign the North American rights to a suitable American university press, under whose imprint it would appear. Specialist import agencies, such as Barnes and Noble Books, Rowman and Littlefield, and Humanities Press, were also used. The role of both types of distributor has diminished. Apart from scientific and technical books, joint publication had declined by 1983. The press was then in the process of setting up its own warehouse and distribution center in New England. After some unanticipated problems the distribution agency was assigned in 1988 to St. Martin's Press, a subsidiary of Macmillan of London. Manchester began acting as a distributor for Michigan University Press in the United Kingdom and Europe in 1990; this development was initiated

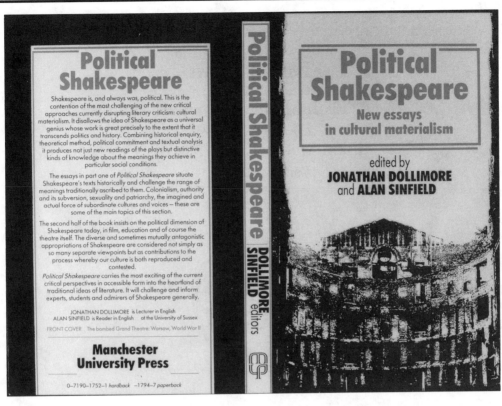

Dust jacket for a 1985 publication of the Manchester University Press

by Francis Brooke, who succeeded Spencer as publisher in 1987. The press regularly participates in the Frankfurt international book fair, which provides opportunities for contact with the European book trade as well as for negotiating rights.

In 1983 the Press Management Board was established, responsible to the University Council for the management and development of the press's activities. In October 1983 the Press Committee was replaced by the Editorial Committee, chaired by Cox. This committee makes recommendations to the board and monitors the publishing program. In its last year (1982-1983) the Press Committee had reviewed 156 projects and accepted 72 for publication. In 1984 a business computer was installed in the trade department, and accounting procedures were transferred from the university bursar's office. By 1986 computer-based production information systems and a progress control section, concerned with the scheduling and budgeting of the publishing program, were fully operative.

Manchester University Press ranks third in the United Kingdom after the university presses of Oxford and Cambridge. It is substantially larger than the remaining university presses, comparing in output with such medium-sized commercial publishers as Heinemann.

By the late 1980s the press was publishing up to 120 titles each year; if republications and paperback editions are included, the total rises to some 150. Virtually all printing and binding is carried out by British firms, but approximately one-quarter of typesetting work is placed overseas, principally in Hong Kong. In the financial year ending in 1989 sales were £1.2 million, the highest in the press's history and almost eight hundred times higher than the receipts of £1,563 recorded in McKechnie's first set of accounts for 1912-1913.

References:

H. B. Charlton, *Portrait of a University 1851-1951* (Manchester: Manchester University Press, 1951);

T. L. Jones, "University Presses," in *Libraries and the Book Trade*, edited by Raymond Astbury (London: Bingley, 1968), pp. 81-90.

—Ian Jackson

Elkin Mathews
(London: 1887-1921)
Elkin Mathews Limited
(London: 1921-1926)
Elkin Mathews and Marrot
(London: 1926-1945)

After dissolving his partnership with John Lane in the Bodley Head on 30 September 1894, Charles Elkin Mathews continued publishing under his own name at 6B Vigo Street in London. Observing that the Bodley Head was "fast becoming identified with fiction of a very modern character—made-up emotion and no morals," Mathews determined to conduct his business along the lines of the early Bodley Head by selling rare books and publishing poetry and some rather fanciful fiction.

Mathews brought out books and periodicals central to the Decadent and Symbolist movements of the 1890s, as well as the work of leading authors in the Celtic movement. He also published many books by Ezra Pound expressing the seminal ideas behind the poetry of the 1910s and 1920s, ideas often opposed by the so-called Georgian poets whose works Mathews also published. A list of his most significant publications reads like a roll call of books crucial to the rise of modern literature: William Butler Yeats's *The Wind among the Reeds: Poems* (1899); John Masefield's *Ballads* (1903); Pound's *Personae* (1909), *Cathay: Translations* (1915), and *Lustra of Ezra Pound* (1916); and Richard Aldington's *Images of Desire* (1919). Mathews also published such significant first books as Lionel Johnson's *Poems* (1895), Vincent O'Sullivan's *Poems* (1896), Wilfred Gibson's *Urlyn*

Elkin Mathews in 1894, the year he dissolved his partnership with John Lane; chalk drawing by Jack B. Yeats (Elkin Mathews Archives, University of Reading Library)

the Harper (1902), John Millington Synge's *The Shadow of the Glen and Riders to the Sea* (1905), Lord Dunsany's (Edward John Moreton Drax Plunkett) *The Gods of Pegana* (1905), Ronald Firbank's *Odette d'Antrevernes: A Study in Temperament* (1905), James Joyce's *Chamber Music* (1907), Eleanor Farjeon's *Pan-Worship, and Other Poems* (1908), and F. S. Flint's *In the Net of the Stars* (1909), as well as A. E. W. Mason's first novel, *A Romance of Wastdale* (1895), and Nancy Cunard's first book of poems, *Outlaws* (1921). The tasteful design and format of Mathews's books, by innovative designers and illustrators such as Selwyn Image, H. P. Horne, Aubrey Beardsley, S. H. Sime, Jack B. Yeats, and Pamela Colman Smith, were important to the evolution of the modern book.

One of Mathews's most important vehicles for young, avant-garde writers was several series of booklets in paper wrappers selling for a shilling. The first of these series, Elkin Mathews' Shilling Garland, published between 1896 and 1898, boasted twelve booklets by such authors as Laurence Binyon and Robert Bridges. Stephen Phillips's *Christ in Hades, and Other Poems* (1896) sold more than five thousand copies, and Henry Newbolt's *Admirals All, and Other Verses* (1897) sold some twenty-five thousand.

The Vigo Cabinet series of paperback booklets comprised 145 titles between 1900 and 1918, leading Mathews to claim that it was "the longest series of original contemporary verse in existence." Among its most noted titles were Masefield's *Ballads*, W. B. Yeats's *The Tables of the Law and The Adoration of the Magi* (1904), Synge's *The Shadow of the Glen and Riders to the Sea*, James Elroy Flecker's *The Bridge of Fire: Poems* (1907), and Max Weber's *Cubist Poems* (1914). Mathews also published the Satchel series, which included Masefield's *A Mainsail Haul* (1905), with a frontispiece by Yeats, and E. H. Visiak's *Buccaneer Ballads* (1910); and the Burlington series, which featured William Carlos Williams's first commercially published book of poems, *The Tempers* (1913).

Mathews championed the Irish literary movement, which he believed was "destined to exercise a lasting influence on the national character." Among the Irish Renaissance books he published were Lionel Johnson's *Ireland, with Other Poems* (1897), W. B. Yeats's *The Wind among the Reeds*, and Synge's *The Shadow of the Glen and Riders to the Sea*. He also aided the movement by publishing the two books of poetry produced by

the Rhymers' Club, which included a large Celtic element.

Then a young, unknown American poet, Pound arrived on Mathews's Vigo Street doorstep in the autumn of 1908 "*sans sous*" (penniless), as Pound later reported it. At this crucial stage of Pound's career, Mathews played an indispensable role as his publisher and as his entrée to London literary society. Though of quite different temperaments, the brash young poet and the middle-aged publisher seem to have taken a liking to each other from the start, Pound seeing Mathews through youthful eyes with a slight case of hero-worship and Mathews viewing the youth from a fatherly perspective. Pound's *Personae* was followed by *Exultations of Ezra Pound* (1909) and *Canzoni* (1911).

In January 1913 Mathews moved to 4A Cork Street. By this time his relationship with Pound had begun to change. Mathews had at first seen Pound as an attractive, spirited, and talented young poet destined to carry on the tradition of the Pre-Raphaelites, A. C. Swinburne, and the poets of the 1890s in the twentieth century. But he was increasingly unable to ignore the note of modernity—clear imagery, flexible language, free verse—sounded strongly and persistently for the first time in *Ripostes of Ezra Pound* (1915). Pound's clear emergence as a modern poet in *Ripostes* weakened the bond between the two men. Although the second phase of the relationship was marked by controversy, a highlight of Mathews's Cork Street years was his publication of several of Pound's most influential books, including the highly praised *Cathay* and the collection of contemporary poetry that Pound edited titled *Catholic Anthology 1914-1915* (1915). The anthology included not only poems by Pound but the first publication of T. S. Eliot's "The Love Song of J. Alfred Prufrock," as well as poems by Williams, Carl Sandburg, Edgar Lee Masters, and Harriet Monroe. Although Mathews's advertisements attempted to alert the public to the precise nature of the anthology, describing it as "representing the more active tendencies in contemporary verse," the book designer Francis Meynell objected vehemently to the book's title.

If Mathews's discomfiture over the anthology had been considerable, it was nothing compared to the anguish in store for him as a result of his decision to publish *Lustra of Ezra Pound*. The "long and comic" history (as Pound later referred to it) of the controversy began in the spring of 1916 when Mathews sent the typescript

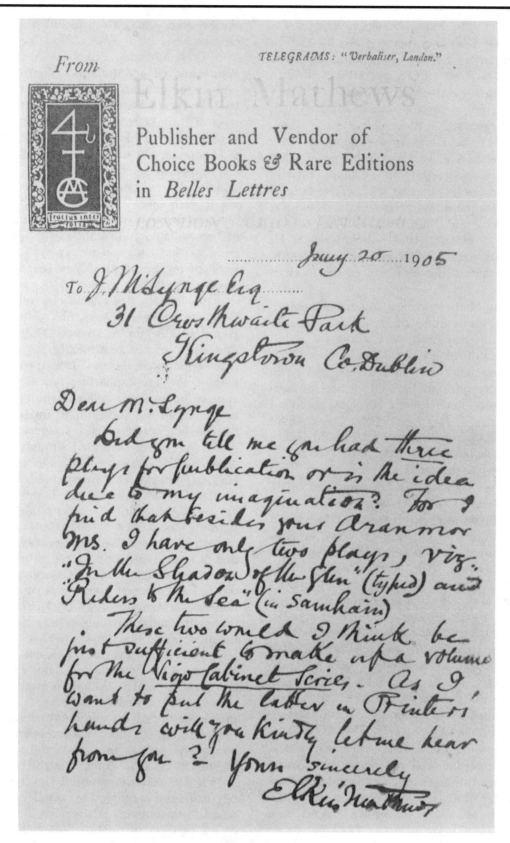

Letter from Mathews to J. M. Synge concerning the publication of Synge's The Shadow of the Glen *and* Riders to the Sea
(Trinity College Library, Dublin)

Mathews circa 1912

After digesting the opinions of W. B. Yeats and Augustine Birrell, Mathews wrote Pound a letter listing nine poems that were to be deleted from the text, as well as other emendations and corrections. Ultimately poet, publisher, and printer reached a compromise. Clowes would print the commercial edition of *Lustra* with all the emendations and corrections Mathews had listed earlier; as a concession to Pound and his friends, Clowes consented to produce a privately printed edition of two hundred unexpurgated copies, with the exception of four poems that Clowes declined to print in any form whatsoever. Pound reluctantly agreed, and *Lustra* appeared in its two versions in the autumn of 1916.

Despite the strains in their relationship that resulted from the struggle over *Lustra*, Pound and Mathews remained on friendly terms, Mathews continuing to be Pound's best hope of getting published in England. Mathews was on the verge of publishing Pound's *Quia Pauper Amavi*, but his insistence on the deletion of several poems led Pound to withdraw the manuscript; the book was published in 1919 by the Egoist Press. Unable to agree on the new, poet and publisher got together on the old: Mathews brought out a selection of Pound's early poems titled *Umbra* in 1920. This last venture in publishing together was an appropriate one, bringing the relationship full circle.

Looking back over Mathews's publishing career of some thirty years, one must concede that his support for young, often unknown poets earned him many successes and, indisputably, the place of honor Robert Scholes assigns him among that handful of "small publishers who were so influential in British literary developments around the turn of the century," those courageous "men who had a direct hand in the shaping of new literature."

After Mathews's death on 10 November 1921, the firm was sold to a group headed by A. W. Evans and became known as Elkin Mathews, Limited. In 1926 the publishing business (as distinct from the antiquarian book business) restyled itself Elkin Mathews and Marrot. Percy Muir became a director in the firm in 1929 and kept it alive through the Great Depression and World War II largely on his own. The publishing business was sold to George Allen and Unwin toward the end of the war, and Elkin Mathews and Marrot ceased to exist. In 1986, however, *The Company We Kept*, by Muir's widow Barbara Kaye, bore the Elkin Mathews imprint for senti-

to the printing firm of William Clowes and Sons. At the last minute the page proofs were brought to the attention of the senior director of the firm, the elderly W. C. K. Clowes, who had held many distinguished positions in his profession. In light of the recent suppression of D. H. Lawrence's novel *The Rainbow* (1915), published by Methuen, he concluded that he did not want his firm's name associated with a book of poetry whose contents included such irreverent parodies as "Winter is icummen in, / Lhude sing Goddamm," bore such titles as "Coitus," commanded the reader to "Dance the dance of the phallus," and referred to the "scrawny but amorous" whore Phyllidula. Clowes communicated his views to Mathews, who, alarmed, extensively blue-penciled the proofs. (A note in Pound's hand on the half-title page of the first proofs of *Lustra* in the Harry Ransom Humanities Research Center at the University of Texas reads: "First proofs. Deletions by E. Mathews instigated by Clowes, pres. master printers assn., pres. printers pension ass.")

mental reasons; the book was published by Werner Shaw.

References:
Percy Muir, *Minding My Own Business* (London: Chatto & Windus, 1956);
James G. Nelson, *Elkin Mathews: Publisher to Yeats, Joyce, Pound* (Madison: University of Wisconsin Press, 1989).

Papers:
The Elkin Mathews archives are in the library of the University of Reading and are reproduced on microfilm by Chadwyck-Healey of Alexandria, Virginia, and Cambridge, England.

—*James G. Nelson*

Merlin Press
(London: 1956-   )

Merlin Press was founded by Martin Eve in the summer of 1956, between the revelations of the Soviet Twentieth Congress, when Nikita Khrushchev denounced Stalinist policies, and the ensuing Hungarian revolution, but it was conceived somewhat earlier in a different political climate. At that time it was planned as a cultural supplement to the Communist party publishing house, Lawrence and Wishart. More particularly it was started to publish one title, *Folksong—Plainsong* (1956), by George Chambers, which had been accepted and then rejected by publisher Dennis Dobson during one of his recurrent financial crises. The book was a difficult one, including Latin, Greek, and some musical settings, and it challenged the then-prevailing orthodoxy. Ralph Vaughan Williams wrote a preface in which he referred to musicologists as "bat-eyed," prompting a critical reception that was decidedly hostile.

During the lengthy preparation of Chambers's book various other projects were initiated. Two translations of works by Stendhal (Marie Henri Beyle) were commissioned—*Love*, published by Merlin in 1957 and *The Life of Henry Brulard* (1958). Stendhal, a Bonapartist living in an era of reaction, spoke with special resonance to radicals in the 1950s. The historic events of 1956, however, soon created new perspectives and new possibilities.

Two of the first Merlin files were labeled "Brecht" and "Lukács." Both authors were almost totally ignored in Britain at that time; each had

only one work in translation. Bertolt Brecht went to Methuen, but, with the help of István Mészáros, negotiations were begun with Georg (György) Lukács. Lukács had at that time recently been released from prison in Hungary, the only member of Imre Nagy's cabinet to escape execution. A nonperson, he had been deprived of his post at Budapest University, and his books were banned throughout the Eastern bloc. The translation by Hannah and Stanley Mitchell of his *The Historical Novel* was published in 1962, followed by *The Meaning of Contemporary Realism* (1963), *Essays on Thomas Mann* (1964), and *Writer and Critic* (1965). Critical response to *The Historical Novel* was wide and appreciative; the British and American literary establishments admitted Lukács to honorary membership. Other projects in a new-left direction included a Polish anthology, *The Broken Mirror* (1960), which sold three hundred copies. Lengthy negotiations were undertaken with the editorial board of the *New Left Review*, but their only book was published elsewhere.

The decisive breakthrough for the Merlin Press was the launching of the *Socialist Register* in 1964, under the editorship of Ralph Miliband and John Saville and with the active encouragement of Isaac Deutscher. That publication's Marxist commitment and freedom from any party line set the tone for the whole Merlin list. With the revival of the left in the universities, the new journal was well received and became a forum for such writers as Ernest Mandel, E. P. Thompson, Ken

Martin Eve, founder of the Merlin Press, and Norman Franklin, who bought a half interest in the firm in 1988

Coates, and Dorothy Wedderburn, as well as Deutscher and the editors. An ambitious undertaking at this time was the translation of Mandel's great work of popularization, *Marxist Economic Theory* (1968), which took four years to translate and print.

Merlin was not so much underfinanced as unfinanced in its early years. Eve's intention had been to find a partner rather than to launch out on his own. He had only enough capital to finance one book at a time—a stringent form of quality control. It was obvious that some money-making sidelines were needed, and the first of these made its appearance in 1960—Hugh Burnett's *Top Sacred* (1960), a collection of cartoons about monks published under the pseudonym Phelix. It was followed by *Sacred and Confidential* (1961) and *Nothing Sacred* (1962). The original ran through a dozen printings, and American and other foreign rights were sold. Another sideline which was to make a steady contribution over the years was the Seafarer Books imprint. As with the Merlin list, titles were few and carefully chosen; there was never the imperative to expand felt by larger publishers. More significant

throughout the 1960s was a series of historical reprints which began with *The English Yeoman under Elizabeth and the Early Stuarts* (1961), by Mildred Campbell (first published by Yale University Press in 1942), and culminated in the four volumes of *Poor Man's Guardian* (1969), a London leftist weekly.

In the early 1970s the main list began to attract attention with the publication of *The Unknown Mayhew* (1971), by E. P. Thompson and Eileen Yeo; István Mészáros's *Marx's Theory of Alienation* (1970), which went through half a dozen editions and foreign sales in most major languages; and Lukács's *History and Class Consciousness* (1971). The latter had been written in 1922 and had been attacked by Lenin. Disowned by its author and suppressed, it had become a legend over the years. By the late 1960s it was the object of considerable publishing interest. There were also threats—by no means empty—of piracy. Sinister interpretations were placed on the delay in publication, but the reasons were uncomplicated: Lukács wanted to be known for other works that he rated more important, and he also wanted to write a long introduction explaining the circumstances of the original publication, his recantation, and the ways in which his ideas had changed since then. Other significant Merlin books were a paperback edition of Ralph Miliband's *Parliamentary Socialism* (1972) and *Beyond the Fragments: Feminism and the Making of Socialism* (1980), by Sheila Rowbotham, Hilary Wainwright, and Lynne Segal—a key text for the left.

In 1972 Merlin moved from its small office in Fitzroy Square to a warehouse on the Isle of Dogs. From there paperback editions of works by Mandel, Lukács, and Mészáros, as well as Thompson's *William Morris* (1977), were sent. At the same time paperback rights were sold to Penguin for *The Historical Novel* and the two Stendhal translations. These developments enabled the purchase in 1976 of larger premises on the Isle of Dogs with space for a warehouse.

The 1980s began with the publication of the complete translation of Stefanos Sarafis's *Elas:*

Greek Resistance Army (1980). This work led to a series of Greek and Balkan studies, including *British Intervention in Greece* (1985), by Heinz Richter, and Svetozar Vukmanovic-Tempo's *Struggle for the Balkans* (1990). The press was committed to European nuclear disarmament, which led to books and pamphlets including Thompson's *Beyond the Cold War* (1982), which ran through three printings of ten thousand copies each, and his *The Defence of Britain*, which was written, printed, and sold during the 1983 election campaign.

In 1988 the Isle of Dogs premises were sold, and Merlin moved to Camden. A half interest in the company was sold to Norman Franklin, formerly of Routledge and Kegan Paul, and the newly formed Greenprint imprint was acquired, along with its editor, Jon Carpenter.

—Martin Eve

Methuen and Company
(London: 1889-1972)
Eyre Methuen
(London: 1972-1981)
Methuen London
(London: 1981-   )

See also the Chapman and Hall and Eyre and Spottiswoode entries in *DLB 106: British Literary Publishing Houses, 1820-1880*.

Algernon Methuen Marshall Stedman was born on 23 February 1856 in Southwark, the son of John Buck Stedman, a doctor and former mayor of Godalming, Surrey. He was educated at Berkhamsted School and Wadham College, Oxford. After obtaining his degree in classics in 1878 he was employed as a tutor at Friar Park, Henley-on-Thames; that same year he had a book on Oxford published by Trübner and Company.

Two years later he started a prep school, Highcroft, at Milford, near Godalming, where he gave the students tasks to keep them occupied while he wrote textbooks that were published by George Bell and Sons. Eventually Stedman decided to start his own publishing firm, and he began to solicit books from well-known authors; he was fortunate to secure the services of the Reverend Sabine Baring-Gould, composer of "Onward Christian Soldiers" (1890), and Edna Lyall. Choosing the family name Methuen—an ancestor, John Methuen, had negotiated a trade treaty between Britain and Portugal in 1709—he set up his business in June 1889 in a small back room at 19 Bury Street, Bloomsbury. The building was owned by W. W. Gibbons, a remainder merchant, who became the new company's trade manager.

Sir Algernon Methuen (originally Algernon Methuen Marshall Stedman), founder of Methuen and Company

One of Stedman's initial moves was to take back from George Bell and Sons the publication of his textbooks and of his volume on Oxford, which had been republished by Bell in 1887. His first published work of fiction, *Derrick Vaughan, Novelist* (1889), by Lyall, had great success, with sales of more than twenty-five thousand in its first year. Stedman's other new author, Baring-Gould, contributed two nonfiction works, *Historic Oddities and Strange Events* (1889-1891) and *Old Country Life* (1890). Within twelve months the company produced twenty books. In 1892 Methuen published Rudyard Kipling's *Barrack-Room Ballads and Other Verses*, which was greeted with acclaim by the press; the *Times* (1 May 1892) said that "unmistakeable genius . . . rings in every line." Methuen published Kipling's next volume of verse, *The Seven Seas*, in 1896.

In April 1894 the firm moved to 36 Essex Street, off the Strand. With the move a new manager was appointed: G. E. Webster, from Kegan Paul, Trench, Trübner and Company. Despite a trade depression in the mid 1890s, Stedman's business was booming, and he began to broaden his list. Of Marie Corelli, who had achieved a huge sale with *Barabbas* in 1893, he wrote in the first issue of *Methuen's Gazette and Literary Notes*, published to coincide with the move to Essex Street: "Few books in late years have received such savage and merciless treatment from the critics. . . . Meanwhile. . . . The first large issue of the cheap edition and a second reprint were sold before publication, and an eighth edition is now nearly exhausted, so that there is still balm in Gilead." Corelli followed this success with another best-seller, *The Sorrows of Satan* (1895), and was to remain the company's leading woman novelist until her death in 1924. Apart from popular fiction, the company in 1891 had published the first English edition of Henrik Ibsen's *Brand* (1866), thus starting a long and distinguished modern drama list.

In 1894 a move by the circulating libraries W. H. Smith and Mudie's to pay only four shillings a volume for the then-popular two- and three-part novels led Stedman to decide to publish only one-volume novels. The following year he gave up teaching to devote himself full-time to Methuen. The fiction list included such well-known names as E. F. Benson, Anthony Hope, and H. G. Wells, who in 1897 had his volume *The Plattner Story and Others* published by Methuen. Arthur Morrison's *A Child of the Jago* (1896), describing life in the poverty of the East

End, made a great impact and won the approval of the Prince of Wales. Among the editors Stedman employed at this time was W. E. Henley, who was also editor of the *National Observer*; he was responsible for introducing Kipling, Wells, W. B. Yeats, and Henry James to the list. The increased profitability of the firm meant that in 1897 Stedman could rebuild his home at Haslemere, Surrey, and employ Gertrude Jekyll and Charles Voysey to redesign his twenty-acre garden. Much of his time, therefore, was spent in the country, but he insisted on receiving daily reports from the firm by overnight mail.

For the children's market Methuen published a wide range of works, from illustrated nursery stories to mystery tales for older children. Baring-Gould's adventure story for boys, *The Icelander's Sword; or, The Story of Oraefa-dal* (1893), was to be a regular in the publication lists for many years. The first children's best-sellers were the series of books about King Wallypug and his entourage, by G. E. Farrow, beginning with *The Wallypug of Why* (1895). As the century drew to a close the firm was one of the leading publishers of theological works, with four series: The Churchman's Library, Handbooks of Theology, Leaders of Religion, and the Library of Devotion. In 1899, under the editorship of Professor Edward Dowden, The Arden Shakespeare was launched with *Hamlet*. *The Works of Charles Dickens*, with introductions by George Gissing and notes by F. G. Kitton, was published in 1900.

In its quest to publish books by popular authors, Methuen would normally offer a royalty of 10 percent on the first five hundred copies and a minimum of 12 1/2 percent thereafter. Production costs for one thousand copies of an average-sized book were approximately fifty pounds for printing and paper and twenty-five pounds for binding. In 1899 Stedman took the innovative step of offering shares in the company to his employees. That same year he changed his surname: henceforth he was to be known as Algernon Methuen. Finally in 1899 he launched Methuen's Library of Fiction, which would publish new novels by the leading authors of the day in sixpenny paperback volumes. By 1902 more than thirty titles had been published; that year the company launched its Sixpenny Library of "great and popular books of past years."

Joining the firm in the new century was E. V. Lucas, who, after editing Charles Lamb's *The Essays of Elia* (1901), was commissioned by Algernon Methuen to edit *The Works of Charles*

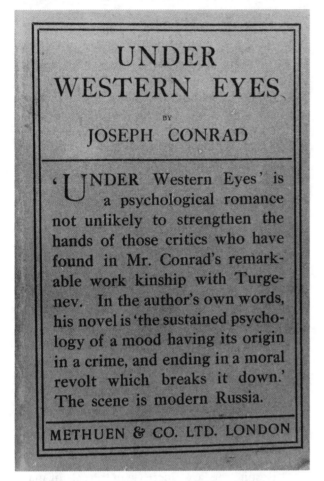

UNDER
WESTERN EYES
BY
JOSEPH CONRAD

'UNDER Western Eyes' is
a psychological romance
not unlikely to strengthen the
hands of those critics who have
found in Mr. Conrad's remarkable work kinship with Turgenev. In the author's own words,
his novel is 'the sustained psychology of a mood having its origin
in a crime, and ending in a moral
revolt which breaks it down.'
The scene is modern Russia.

METHUEN & CO. LTD. LONDON

*Dust jacket for one of several novels by Conrad published by
Methuen and Company; this one appeared in 1911.*

and *Mary Lamb* (1903-1905) and to write a biography of Lamb (1905). Lucas became a reader for
the firm. Joseph Conrad was also a newcomer,
with *Mirror of the Sea* (1906). It was not a success,
but he made amends with *Chance* (1914). Nevertheless, throughout Conrad's period with the
firm, sales of his novels tended to be modest.

In 1904-1905 Methuen published a deluxe
set of four Shakespeare volumes, priced at twelve
guineas for the set, and a sixpenny paperback
edition of the works of Alexandre Dumas. The
firm's most daring venture, also started in 1904,
was Methuen's Standard Library; edited by Sidney Lee, who was also editor of the *Dictionary of National Biography*, the series was planned to embrace more than fifty classic titles, selling at
sixpence each in paperback and one shilling in
cloth. In its advertising the firm proudly proclaimed: "Thus when fifty volumes have been published, you will have a shelf-full of the finest literature of the world for under thirty shillings. Here

is indeed the Poor Man's University." The announcement met with wide approval, and among
the many letters of congratulation received were
those from the prime minister and the archbishop of Canterbury. It was not the hoped-for
success, however: it met stiff competition from
J. M. Dent's Everyman series, clothbound and selling for one shilling each.

In popular fiction, the firm had two best-
sellers in 1904 with Corelli's *God's Good Man* and
Robert Hichens's *The Garden of Allah*; the latter
book was to reach thirteen editions by 1913 and
to start a vogue with Garden of Allah parties.
Other fiction writers of note were the husband-
and-wife team C. N. and A. M. Williams, with
The Lightning Conductor (1902) and *The Princess
Passes* (1904), both of which made early references to the automobile. Hilaire Belloc first appeared on the Methuen list in 1904 with his
novel *Emmanuel Burden, Merchant*, with thirty-four
illustrations by G. K. Chesterton; within the next
few years the firm published Belloc's *Hills and the
Sea* (1906), *Paris* (1907), *On Nothing and Kindred
Subjects* (1908), and *The Pyrenees* (1909). In 1905
Henry James's *The Golden Bowl* proved a popular
success, running into three editions. Chesterton
made his initial appearance as an author for Methuen with his biography of Charles Dickens in
1906.

One of the most controversial events of this
period—indeed, of the decade— was the decision
to publish Oscar Wilde's *De Profundis* (1905), obtained from Wilde's literary executor, Robert
Ross. In his memoirs Lucas recalled that "it was I
who was asked by Ross to prepare the printed version from Wilde's very disorderly draft. The title
was mine and, rightly or wrongly, I left out a
great deal." In promoting the book Methuen
noted that it "should take an enduring place in
the literature of misfortune" while expressing
"with unfailing lucidity the philosophy which he
gathered in two years' imprisonment." Within
two months *De Profundis* had run to three editions and won rave notices from the London newspapers. In 1908 Methuen published Wilde's complete works under the editorship of Ross.

The growing success of the firm meant that
more and more well-known writers were attracted, including Laurence Binyon, W. H. Davies, John Masefield, and Francis Thomson; but
it was Kenneth Grahame, with *The Wind in the Willows*, who provided the next best-seller. Published
in 1908, within five years it had run to eight editions; it was not until 1913 that the first set of illus-

trations, by Paul Branson, appeared. A. A. Milne made his debut on the Methuen list in 1910 with *The Day's Play*. Milne was an assistant editor of *Punch*, and the book was the first of four collections of his contributions to the magazine; the others were *The Holiday Round* (1912), *Once a Week* (1914), and *The Sunny Side* (1921).

In 1910 Algernon Methuen decided to turn the business into a private company and invited Lucas to become a director. The board then consisted of Methuen, as chairman; Lucas, and Webster, as managing director. The new company secretary was Frederick Muller, who had been responsible for the education list and for illustrations. Within two years C. W. Chamberlain was appointed head of the trade department, and Spencer Killby was made production chief. Nineteen members of the staff had taken up Methuen's offers of shares. By 1913 the company was able to announce sales of £107,000 and declare a 2 1/2 percent dividend three times a year.

At that time the firm had almost 170 authors on its fiction list, including—in addition to Belloc, Wells, James, Gissing, Milne, Conrad, and Corelli—Arthur Conan Doyle, Jack London, and A. E. W. Mason. A newcomer to the list was Arnold Bennett, already well known for his "Five Towns" series of novels published by Chatto and Windus. His initial novel for Methuen was *Clayhanger* (1910), followed by *Hilda Lessways* (1911).

In 1914 the onset of World War I brought a flurry of titles with a military background, including much poetry: Alfred Noyes was prominent with *The Searchlight* (1914) and *A Salute from the Fleet and Other Poems* (1915); there was a reprint of Bret Harte's *The Reveille* (1914); and Kipling's *Recessional* was republished. Other works related to the war were Hope's *The New-German-Testament* (1914) and Chesterton's *Letters to an Old Garibaldian* (1915). Anticipating a shortage of materials during wartime, Methuen ordered enough paper for fifty thousand books; and, with staff volunteering for the army, the company took on its first females as replacements.

D. H. Lawrence's *The Rainbow* was published on 30 September 1915 and greeted with hostile reviews. In the *Star* James Douglas wrote: "The young men who are dying for liberty are moral beings. They are the living repudiation of such impious denials of life as *The Rainbow*. The life they lay down is a lofty thing. It is not the thing that creeps and crawls in these pages." Within days Scotland Yard had impounded all cop-

ies of *The Rainbow*, and on 11 November a summons was issued. The case came up two days later at the Bow Street magistrate's court. Methuen expressed deep regret, no defense was offered, and the books were ordered destroyed.

On a more positive note for the firm, Bennett's new novel, *These Twain*, sold more than thirteen thousand copies in its first week of publication in January 1916. Lucas himself appeared in print that year with *The Vermilion Box*; it was dedicated to his brother, Percy, who had been killed in the war.

With the ever-growing demand for reading matter—especially on subjects related to the war—Methuen's list expanded, with a wide range of novels, poetry, humor, and personal reminiscences. The company's sales rose to more than £145,000 in 1917. Making a name for himself at this time was A. P. Herbert, with his collection of war poems *The Bomber Gipsy and Other Poems* (1918); he followed it with *The Secret Battle* (1919), considered by many to be one of the finest works of fiction from World War I. Bernard Adams's *Nothing of Importance* (1917) was a firsthand account of trench warfare on the Western Front; the author was later killed in the trenches. Capt. C. A. L. Brownlow's *The Breaking of the Storm* (1917) told of the early months of the war.

Despite the large increase in the cost of materials, the company's profits continued to rise. At the first postwar annual meeting, Sir Algernon—he had been knighted in 1917—announced that sales were at record levels, and that to commemorate the thirtieth anniversary of the firm he would be making a further distribution of shares to the staff. One result of the war was that Methuen had a mixed staff of men and women, and it was a policy that was to remain.

One of the great successes for the firm at this period was Edgar Rice Burroughs, whose *Tarzan of the Apes* (1917) was followed by the first volume in his Martian series, *A Princess of Mars* (1920). In the early 1920s his works provided the escapism that a war-weary public sought. Their huge popularity further increased Methuen's profits. The company's fortunes were marred only by a six-week packers' strike in 1920, during which the clerical staff helped with the distribution of books.

T. S. Eliot made his debut on the list with his anthology of modern poetry, *The Sacred Word* (1920). That same year, through the efforts of A. Watson Bain, the new educational manager, the

Memorial plaque to Sir Algernon Methuen in the Methuen offices

firm published Albert Einstein's *Relativity: The Special and the General Theory.*

Sir Algernon's final book, *An Alpine ABC and List of Easy Rock Plants,* was published in 1922. He died on 20 September 1924. He was succeeded as chairman by Lucas, with Chamberlain as managing director. Frederick Muller was assistant managing director, and Killby was head of production. There was one resignation from the board: Webster, who had been Methuen's right-hand man for many years, decided to leave. Under the terms of Sir Algernon's will, employees received £5 for each year's service—although Lady Methuen had to contribute half of the £970 needed to make up the sum.

E. V. Rieu had been appointed educational manager in 1923. In 1924 he outlined his plan for Methuen's Modern Classics, abridged versions of popular classics ranging from 160 to 192 pages and selling at the low price of one shilling, sixpence. The books were to be marketed as read-ers for elementary schools. Rieu sought the opinions of educational experts, including J. C. Stobart, director of education for the BBC. Stobart turned down the offer to edit the series, and Rieu undertook the task himself. Among the works published in the series in 1925 were *The Wind in the Willows* and London's *White Fang,* which had originally been published by Macmillan in New York in 1905 and by Methuen in 1907. The series was greeted with acclaim by the teaching profession.

In 1926 the trustees of Sir Algernon's estate decided to exercise their option to sell his shares, worth £250,000. With the aid of Lady Methuen the management tried to buy in the shares themselves so as to prevent the company from being taken over; but they were unable to raise the money to do so. The uncertainty lasted until November 1927, when it was announced that the business was no longer for sale. It was, however, to be a short respite; in 1928 George Roberts, a biscuit manufacturer, purchased Sir Algernon's interest in the firm for slightly more than £3 a share and indicated that he would not change the current management.

For his investment, Roberts had secured a successful publishing business with profits of more than thirty thousand pounds per annum over the past decade; and he allowed Lucas to carry on the principles laid down by Methuen. The lists were still headed by Kipling, Hope, and Herbert. Travel was recognized as a potential revenue earner, and Lucas engaged H. V. Morton, already well known to readers of the *Daily Express,* to start a new series for Methuen under the title "In Search Of." Beginning with *In Search of England* (1927), it was to be a huge success. Morton insisted that his books be priced at no more than three shillings, sixpence, thereby reaching a wider audience. On 13 February 1928 another children's classic was added: Milne's *The House at Pooh Corner.* It followed his two earlier great successes: a book of verses for children, *When We Were Very Young* (1924), and the immortal *Winnie-the-Pooh* (1926), both illustrated by E. H. Shepard. Apart from his own prolific output, Milne acted as chief reader for the firm and also found time to dramatize Grahame's *The Wind in the Willows* as *Toad of Toad Hall* (1929).

As Methuen moved into the 1930s it had more than fifteen hundred titles in print. Humor was becoming increasingly popular and was well represented by the cartoonists David Low, W. Heath Robinson, and H. M. Bateman. In humorous fiction, the firm published some of P. G. Wodehouse's non-"Jeeves" books.

In 1931 the firm sponsored a "Novels of English Life Today" competition with a first prize of £1,000 and a second of £350. The contest was not the hoped-for success; the judges—Herbert, Rose Macaulay, and Gerald Gould—were unable to award the prizes, although they considered six of the entries worthy of publication. The following year was notable for publication of the chairman's memoirs, *Reading, Writing and Remembering*, but it was marred by the death of Grahame, so long a pillar of Methuen's success. The previous year *The Wind in the Willows*, with illustrations by Shepard, had reached its thirty-eighth edition.

It was also in 1932 that Roberts decided that the appearance of Methuen books needed modernizing and gave orders that all designs should be submitted for approval to Colin Summerford, a young man in the production department. The directors threatened to resign en bloc, and Roberts called their bluff by accepting the resignations. Lucas reconsidered and signed a new contract, but Chamberlain, Muller, and Killby left the firm.

The new managing director was E. V. Rieu, the creator of the Methuen Modern Classics series. Peter Wait was made educational manager, J. Alan White was appointed director, and J. W. Roberts was named company secretary. In 1934 Lucas was able to declare a dividend of 10 percent. Newcomers to the list at this time were Pearl S. Buck, with *The Good Earth* (1934), and the Chinese writer Chiang Yee, with his illustrated "Silent Traveller" series. The Methuen Library of Humour was started in 1933 under the editorship of E. V. Knox of *Punch*; it included works by Bateman and Nicolas Bentley. Among political books were *A History of National Socialism* (1934), by Konrad Heiden; *The Science of Peace* (1933), by Lord Raglan (FitzRoy James Henry Somerset Raglan); *In Pursuit of Peace* (1933), by G. P. Gooch; and Milne's *Peace with Honour* (1934). The Gateway Poets series, launched in 1933, included John Pudney's *Spring Encounter* (1933) and Randall Swingler's *Difficult Morning* (1933). A series of distinguished academic works in philosophy, psychology, physics, biology, and chemistry began in the early 1930s and ran for more than a decade. On the children's list the 1930s were notable for the huge success of Enid Blyton, a schoolmistress whose tales had appeared in the magazine *Teacher's World*. Rieu recognized their merits and persuaded her to allow the company to publish collections of them. Her works were best-sellers for the next twenty years. Another best-selling author introduced to the children's list at this time was Jean de Brunhoff, who was discovered by Tegan Harris, Rieu's sister-in-law and an editorial assistant at the firm. Beginning with *The Story of Babar* (1934), the Babar series was a great success. A competition for stories for children between eight and twelve, with a first prize of two hundred pounds and a second prize of one hundred pounds, attracted more than four hundred entries.

In 1936 Roberts's accountant proposed that Andrew Dakers, a literary agent, be appointed to the board. The directors opposed the appointment; but their counterproposal was not accepted, and Dakers joined the board in May. Five months later Rieu resigned and was replaced as managing director by Dakers; Rieu remained with the company as an external adviser on educational and academic matters. The following year was not a good one for the company, with the dividend down to 4 percent and arrangements being made for an overdraft for up to twenty-five hundred pounds. Meanwhile, Roberts had engaged in an unsuccessful speculation in real estate; Lloyds Bank, which held his Methuen shares as collateral, foreclosed in 1938. Lloyds immediately appointed a new chairman, Philip Inman; a principal shareholder in Chapman and Hall, Inman soon sold that firm to Methuen. Dakers was replaced as managing director by the returned Chamberlain. Lucas, who had served the company as author, editor, director, and chairman, died in June 1938. He had produced nearly one hundred titles, highlighted by his best-selling *The Open Road*; originally published in 1899 by Grant Richards and republished in 1905 by Methuen, the anthology had run to forty-two editions.

The company continued to publish some three hundred new books each year, including Wells's *Brynhild* (1937) and—taken over from the liquidated firm of Arthur Barker, which had published them in 1934—Robert Graves's *Claudius, the God and His Wife Messalina* (1936) and *I, Claudius* (1937). Nevertheless, profits of the company were only £14,500 on sales of £180,000 in 1938. The imminence of war was reflected in the spring of 1939 with the publication of R. W. Seton-Watson's *Munich and the Dictators*. On the lighter side, the firm published for amateurs a series of one-act plays priced at one shilling, and the six-penny fiction market was catered to for the first time in twenty years. During the opening weeks of World War II the firm closed briefly. Many of the male staff joined the armed forces or the Thames Auxiliary Patrol, including Herbert and Wait. Rieu returned to act as editorial adviser in education four days a week. The success of the first wartime winter for Methuen was Milne's autobiography, *It's Too Late Now*, published on 29 September 1939. The first edition of three thousand copies and a second of fifteen hundred quickly sold out. Overall, however, sales were down, and directors and employees earning more than £250 a year agreed to a reduction in salaries. In March 1940 the Methuen board was strengthened by the inclusion of J. L. Bale and A. W. Gatfield, both from Chapman and Hall.

Like all other publishing houses, Methuen was subject to paper rationing. In the spring of 1940 its quota was fixed at 60 percent of its previous year's usage; later the allowance was further reduced to five hundred tons, one-third of its prewar requirements. Sales of most books, with the exception of humor, continued to be depressed; and the government's War Risk Insurance Scheme, costing twelve thousand pounds a year, made further inroads into profits. Fortunately for London publishers, the public once more wanted to find escapism in books, and Methuen was able to sell off many of the older titles from its list. In the winter of 1940-1941 all four of the firm's London binders were destroyed in German air raids, and the entire stock of Babar books was lost.

Methuen was fortunate in early 1941 with Alice Duer Miller's *The White Cliffs*, a novelette in verse about a love spanning two wars. Already a best-seller in the United States, where it had been published by Coward-McCann in 1940, it rapidly reached sales of more than forty thousand in Great Britain. W. Hooper's *Behind the Spitfires* (1941), published under the pseudonym Raff, also did well, with seven thousand copies ordered before publication. *The Men of the Burma Road* (1942), written and illustrated by Chiang Yee, was another "hit" at this time, with three editions in quick succession.

In December 1943 the firm acquired a new chief shareholder when Lloyds Bank sold Roberts's shares to H. Nutcombe Hume, a financier. Hume brought with him to the Methuen board the publishers James Pitman and Stanley Unwin. The new board was delighted to hear on 30 March 1944 that the company had shown a profit for 1943 of £127,251 before taxes, compared with £73,796 for the previous year. That

same month, however, the Essex Street premises had been hit by incendiary bombs. More than thirty thousand educational books and five thousand novels, with a market value of £1,400, had been destroyed. Concentrating on selling books from its backlist rather than publishing new works, in 1945 Methuen listed only fifteen hundred titles in print compared with nearly five thousand five years earlier.

On 8 May 1945 the war in Europe formally ended. About the same time Chamberlain suffered a massive stroke. White assumed the role of acting managing director. In January 1946 the sixty-nine-year-old Chamberlain retired as managing director and was replaced by White. Chamberlain remained as chairman, but in July his continuing ill health compelled him to resign from the board. He died two months later. Hume assumed the chairmanship. The paper shortage persisted; stocks would not return to normal until early 1948. Nevertheless, in the spring of 1946 Methuen was able to announce seventy new titles, including novels by Buck and Milne and the initial appearance on the list of Christopher Isherwood, with *Prater Violet*. Isherwood was to be one of the firm's postwar successes, contributing *The Condor and the Cows* (1949), *The World in the Evening* (1954), *Down There on a Visit* (1962), and *A Single Man* (1964). In nonfiction Methuen launched the Home Study Series, edited by B. Ifor Evans and embracing titles in chemistry, politics, history, literary criticism, and farming. An unexpected success for Methuen was Einstein's *The Meaning of Relativity* (1946); all twenty thousand copies were quickly sold. In 1946 the firm relaunched its Arden Shakespeare series under the general editorship of Una Ellis-Fermor.

In the summer of 1947 Unwin resigned from the boards of Methuen and Chapman and Hall. Hume continued as chairman and White as managing director; John Cullen and Wait were made directors; and L. A. G. Strong was named chief literary adviser. Thanks to the first rebates of the wartime Excess Profits Tax, the company was able to buy a large share in the Foster Bookbinding Company in July 1947. But in the autumn the firm arranged with its bank for an overdraft of seventy thousand pounds. Also in 1947 Methuen joined other publishers at the Book Centre distribution operation in Neasden; the space released at 36 Essex Street meant that Chapman and Hall could share the offices of its sister company.

Memorial plaque in the Methuen offices to C. W. Chamberlain, who served as managing director of the firm from 1938 to 1946

It was through Cullen's efforts that the French influence on Methuen became more pronounced. Cullen's first signing was Jean-Paul Sartre, who caused a sensation in 1948 with his *Existentialism and Humanism*, followed in 1950 by *What Is Literature?* Cullen was also responsible for W. J. Strachan's *Apollinaire to Aragon* (1948), a translation of thirty modern French poets. Other notable translations from the French were André Malraux's *Man's Estate* (1948), Jean Anouilh's *Ring round the Moon* (1950) and *Antigone and Eurydice* (1957), Marguerite Duras's *A Sea of Troubles* (1953), and Jean Giraudoux's *Tiger at the Gates* (1955).

In 1949 Hesketh Pearson's biography of Dickens appeared, three years after his biography of Oscar Wilde. Also in 1949 Pearson edited a complete version of Wilde's *De Profundis*, with

an introduction by Wilde's son Vyvyan Holland. In 1949 Methuen took over the Pilot Press's educational list for thirty-five hundred pounds, retaining its editor, Patrick Thornhill. In fiction the firm's leading author at this time was Wyndham Lewis. Methuen published a biography of Lewis, by Hugh Kenner, in 1954 and published Lewis's *The Human Age* trilogy in 1955-1956. The company was fortunate to secure R. K. Narayan's *Waiting for the Mahatma* (1955), which soon assumed cult status. Enid Blyton's books, despite opposition from some parents and teachers, continued to sell in the thousands.

In May 1957 Methuen and Chapman and Hall merged with Eyre and Spottiswoode. Col. Oliver Crosthwaite-Eyre was made deputy chairman of Methuen. In June 1958 a parent company, Associated Book Publishers, was established, with White as managing director. Although the editorial independence of the three publishing houses was maintained, their production and distribution departments were merged.

Methuen's drama list, under the direction of Cullen, introduced such plays as Brendan Behan's *The Quare Fellow* (1956) and *The Hostage* (1958). Another new playwright was Shelagh Delaney, with *A Taste of Honey* (1959). From these works emerged the successful Methuen's Modern Plays series. Interest was not, however, confined to modern playwrights; at about this time Wait launched The Revels Series of plays by Shakespeare's contemporaries. In the humor area, Norman Thelwell of *Punch* made his debut for Methuen with *Angels on Horseback and Elsewhere* (1957). In the children's list a new name was added in 1958 with the *Tintin* series, by Hergé (pseudonym of Georges Remy). Strong died in August 1958. The firm published his autobiography, *Green Memory*, in 1961. Through his European connections, Cullen was responsible for securing the plays of Bertolt Brecht for the company. Wait, meanwhile, through his university contacts, was able to sign some of the best academic writers, including Peter Medawar and Konrad Lorenz. Herbert was still a valued author on the lists with *Made for Man* (1958). The art critic John Berger was coming to the fore as a novelist, and he followed *A Painter of Our Time* (1958), published by Secker and Warburg, with *The Foot of Clive*, published by Methuen four years later.

The 1960s were notable for the launch, under the aegis of Wait and Tony Forster, of the University Paperback series on 6 October 1960; the first dozen titles released included two best-

The Methuen offices at 36 Essex Street in the 1950s

selling republications, Einstein's *Relativity: The Special and the General Theory* (1960) and Eliot's *The Sacred Wood* (1960). Appearing in batches twice a year and moderately priced at around ten shillings, the University Paperbacks won instant approval; sales of ten thousand copies a title were not uncommon.

Another new scheme was Talking Books, a series of recordings started in the autumn of 1960; among the first titles was John Betjeman reading *The Story of Jesus*. In 1961 the series was expanded with language courses in French, German, Italian, and Spanish. Called The Traveller Pocket Language Courses—each title came with a thirty-two-page book of the most common phrases—they were designed for the ever-increasing number of holiday travelers to the Continent.

During the early 1960s several important new playwrights found their way onto the list, including John Arden, with *Serjeant Musgrave's Dance* (1960); Harold Pinter, with *The Caretaker* (1960) and *The Birthday Party* (1960); Max Frisch, with *Three Plays* (1962); and Rolf Hochhuth, with *The Representative* (1963). Methuen's influence in

theater publishing was extended even further in 1965 with the launch of its Playscripts series of plays by new writers in paperback. Among the plays featured was Edward Bond's *Saved* (1966), which had been refused a public license and had to be performed by the English Stage Society at the Royal Court Theatre. Joe Orton was another controversial playwright, with *Loot* (1967) and *Crimes of Passion* (1967).

One experiment of the 1960s failed. The decision was taken to publish simultaneous editions of novels in hardback and paperback; the first title selected was Jakov Lind's *Landscape in Concrete* (1966). More copies of the hardback edition were sold than of the paperback, and the experiment was swiftly concluded.

In 1961 40 percent of Methuen shares were bought by Penguin, and Penguin chairman Allen Lane joined the board. A fourth publishing company, Sweet and Maxwell, specializing in legal works, joined Associated Book Publishers in 1961. In 1962 the Eyre Family Trust, which held more than 50 percent of the shares, bought back the Penguin holding, and Lane resigned from the board. In 1964 the group of companies moved from 36 Essex Street to 11 New Fetter Lane, a modern high rise and the home of Sweet and Maxwell. White remained as chairman, with Cullen and Wait as vice-chairmen; John Burke, from Sweet and Maxwell, took over as managing director. In 1968 Methuen became purely a publisher of university books, Chapman and Hall specialized in scientific and technical books, and the general publishing division was renamed Methuen, Eyre and Spottiswoode. The end of the decade saw the retirement of White; he was replaced by Cullen as chairman of Methuen, Eyre and Spottiswoode. In 1972 the general lists were amalgamated as Eyre Methuen.

The great success for Methuen during the 1970s was the Monty Python books. *Monty Python's Big Red Book* (1971) sold 70,000 copies before going into paperback the following year and recording a further 140,000 in sales; ultimately, sales reached more than 400,000 copies. *The Brand New Monty Python Bok* [*sic*] (1973) sold more than 750,000 copies. A further Python book, *The Life of Brian* (1979), was also a success; and two years later Robert Hewison discussed the genre in *Monty Python: The Case Against*, also published by Eyre Methuen. Despite the success of the Python books, in 1974 there was a need for a tightening of finances at Methuen; many workers were laid off. There were also changes at the top: Cullen retired from full-time work, and Geoffrey Strachan was appointed managing director.

As the firm moved into the 1980s, two new senior managers joined: Christopher Falkus, as chairman of Eyre Methuen, and Alan Miles, as managing director of the parent company. The dwindling of the Eyre and Spottiswoode general list meant that it was unreasonable to continue with the Eyre Methuen imprint; in 1981 it was changed to Methuen London. By 1986 Associated Book Publishers was structured so that the Methuen General Books Division was responsible for Methuen London—general books, especially fiction, history, biography, humor, and plays; Methuen Children's Books—including Magnet paperbacks and Methuen Educational schoolbooks; Eyre and Spottiswoode—Bibles, prayer books, and religious titles; and Pitkin Pictorials—illustrated guides to historical buildings and institutions. In the United States, Methuen Incorporated, which included Routledge and Kegan Paul Incorporated, published and distributed scientific books. In Canada, Methuen of Canada Limited had a majority share in the Carswell Company Limited, publisher of law reports and law books, while Methuen Publications Division served as a general college and school publisher. In Australia Methuen LBC Limited included The Law Book Company Limited and Methuen Australia Pty Limited, general, children's, and schoolbook publishers. In New Zealand, Reed Methuen Publishers Limited published works on New Zealand life, countryside, flora, and fauna.

In 1986 Strachan was still managing director of Methuen London. The chairman was Peter Allsop, who had come over with Sweet and Maxwell in the early 1960s, and the vice-chairman was Antony F. J. Crosthwaite-Eyre. Michael Turner was deputy chairman and group managing director and chief executive.

With the gradual reduction in the Crosthwaite-Eyre family shareholding to 35 percent, Associated Book Publishers was vulnerable to a takeover. Plans for board members to stage a management buy-out with the aid of a merchant bank fell through, and in 1987 Thomson International bought the firm. Within months it sold the Methuen general and children's lists to Paul Hamlyn's Octopus Publishing Group, a subsidiary of Reed International. In April 1988 Methuen London moved to its new home at Octopus's headquarters in Michelin House, Fulham Road, west London.

References:

Maureen Duffy, *A Thousand Capricious Chances: A History of the Methuen List 1889-1989* (London: Methuen, 1989);

E. V. Lucas, *Reading, Writing and Remembering* (London: Methuen, 1932);

Sweet and Maxwell Limited, *Then and Now, 1799-1974: Commemorating 175 Years of Law Bookselling and Publishing* (London: Sweet & Maxwell, 1974).

—Dennis Griffiths

Mills and Boon

(London: 1908-1986; Richmond, Surrey: 1986-   )

Mills and Boon was founded by Gerald Mills and Charles Boon in 1908 with a capital of £1,000. Both men had previously been with Methuen, Mills as education director and Boon as sales manager. They set up offices in Whitcombe Street, London, moving in 1909 to 49 Rupert Street and beginning their connection with the printers Hazell, Watson and Viney. In its first year the firm achieved respectable sales of £16,650, publishing in the general, educational, and romance literature fields. Its early general publications included theatrical and other reminiscences, plays, travel stories, travel guides, game-playing manuals, self-help books, and children's books. Among its better-known authors in the general fields were Padraic Colum, Robert Lynd, and H. B. Marriott Watson; its fiction-list writers included E. F. Benson, Beatrice Grimshaw, Georgette Heyer, William Le Queux, Jack London, Dorothea Mackellar, Hugh Walpole, P. G. Wodehouse, and May Wynne.

The firm published Colum's *My Irish Year* (1912) and Lynd's *The Book of This and That* (1915), *Home Life in Ireland* (1909), and *Rambles in Ireland* (1912). In fiction Mills and Boon published Benson's *The Room in the Tower* (1912) and Grimshaw's *When the Red Gods Call* (1911), *Guinea Gold* (1912), *Kris-Girl* (1917), and *The Coral Palace* (1920). Mills and Boon republished Le Queux's novel *Who Giveth This Woman* (first published in 1905) in 1915. None of these writers stayed with the firm for long, most of them spreading their wares far and wide among other publishers.

One writer who did remain for some time was Jack London. London's *White Fang* (1905) was a great success, and Mills and Boon published many of his books between 1912 and 1923, including *South Sea Tales* and *When God Laughs, and Other Stories* in 1912; *Smoke Bellew, A*

John Boon, son of the cofounder of Mills and Boon, who served as managing director of the firm from 1964 until the early 1970s

Son of the Sun, and *The Cruise of the Snark* in 1913; and *The House of Pride and Other Tales of Hawaii* and *John Barleycorn, or, Alcoholic Memoirs* in 1914. The firm took over his *Children of the Frost* (1913) from Newnes in 1915, and *Adventure* (1911) from Nelson in 1916. Not all were successful. *The Iron Heel* (1915) was too earnestly socialist to attract many readers at the time in Britain or the United States, though it became popular in Eastern Europe. The firm also published *Voyaging in Wild Seas* (1915), by London's wife, Charmian K. London.

In 1911 Mills and Boon published Hugh Walpole's *Mr. Perrin and Mr. Traill* and in 1912 his *The Prelude to Adventure*. *The Prince and Betty* (1912) was the only one of P. G. Wodehouse's many novels to appear in two completely different versions that shared the same title. One version, about gangsters in New York City, was published in March 1912 in the United States by W. J. Watt, while in May, Mills and Boon's version appeared as a love story. May Wynne, a prolific writer since 1900, provided the firm with *For Church and Chieftain* (1909) and *A Blot on the Scutcheon* (1910). Apart from publishing these already-established authors, Mills and Boon achieved a reputation as a publisher of first and early novels, including Dorothea Mackellar's *Outlaw's Luck* (1913) and Georgette Heyer's *The Transformation of Philip Jettan* (1923) written under the pseudonym Stella Martin.

From the beginning, Mills and Boon put out books at prices within the reach of a wide readership. Its Shilling Cloth Library books sold well after World War I, as did its romance library series, both in hardback and paperback. The firm used a variety of printers apart from Hazell, Watson and Viney, sending work to Morrison and Gibb, Baylis and Son, and Butler and Tanner in the 1950s; Richard Clay and C. Nicholls in the 1960s; and Cox and Wyman in the 1970s.

Mills died in 1928, and Boon continued the firm alone. In 1930, responsive as always to market changes, he noticed the rapid rise of the commercial libraries and their users' growing appetite for escapism in the Depression years. Among the favored escapist forms was romance, and the company saw its sales of nurse-doctor and general romances rise rapidly. General books were dropped, and the firm concentrated on this form, at first producing only hardback romances. Romance authors who came to the firm included Mary Burchell, who wrote more than one hundred books for Mills and Boon between 1930 and 1970; Sara Seale, who produced more than forty titles; Betty Neels, who has produced more than one hundred titles; and Jean Macleod, whose first novel for the firm, *Life for Two*, appeared in 1936.

In the 1950s the firm moved to 50 Grafton Way, Fitzroy Square. In 1955 it returned to publishing general books with *Discovering Embroidery*, by Winsome Douglass. In the late 1950s the commercial libraries began to decline, and Mills and Boon responded by increasing its general-book output and by taking over Allman's and its educational textbook list in 1961. Mills and Boon realized that a demand for romances would remain after the library closures, but that sales would depend as much on readers having easy access to the books as on the books being reasonably priced. The firm decided that because the lack of bookshops in the smaller towns would cause sales problems, Mills and Boon should find alternative sales points and selected newsagents to offer the books.

In 1964 John Boon, son of Charles Boon, took over as managing director. Boon maintained the steady pace of publication, taking the firm to a significant lead in Britain's romance publishing field. He also served as president of the Publishers' Association from 1961 to 1963 and of the International Publishers' Association from 1972 to 1976. In 1970 Mills and Boon moved to 50 Grafton Way, Fitzroy Square.

In 1958 Harlequin Books of Winnipeg, Manitoba had begun distributing some of the Mills and Boon hardback romance novels. In return, Harlequin allowed the English firm to import its books for distribution. Harlequin merged with Mills and Boon in 1972 under the name Harlequin Enterprises Limited. In 1975 a controlling interest in Harlequin was sold to Torstar Corporation, a Canadian communications company. At this time separate publishing organizations (not just sales outlets) were set up in France, Germany, Italy, Holland, Greece, Japan, South America, Australia, and New Zealand. By 1981 Harlequin was the world's largest publisher of romances, with 80 percent of the world market, translations into 18 languages, and sales of 107 million copies in 98 countries.

After the merger Mills and Boon also went from strength to strength. It had British sales of 27 million copies in 1972, producing 14 hardback and 9 paperback novels per month; by 1973 sales had increased to 30 million. By 1978 the firm was the fifteenth largest British publisher of new books.

Mills and Boon quickly moved in a more focused way into paperback publishing. It also moved, with Harlequin, into marketing techniques that previously had been used more for consumables and household goods. Publicity was directed as much to the name of the firm as to individual volumes, encouraging a brand loyalty that was supported by the firm's policy toward its writers, requiring them to adhere to certain narrative lines, to write to a certain length (55,000 to 60,000 words), and to have their characters conform to a certain pattern of romantic behavior. Consequently, a Mills and Boon romance became a consistent product, resulting in reader familiarity. Sales displays encouraged multiple buying, as did the creation of a subscription service (called "Jane Lovell") through which readers could purchase each month's output by mail. In 1980 Mills and Boon sold its textbook list to Bell and Hyman. The following year it moved to 15-16 Brook's Mews.

Mills and Boon has had several managing directors since the early 1970s: John Rendall, Paul Scherer, Mark Abbott, and Robert Williams. In 1983 it became the third most profitable publishing company in the United Kingdom; at a time when many publishing houses were threatened by the high costs of printing and production as well as competition from other media, particularly television, Mills and Boon not only survived but thrived.

Competition began to arise, however, in the early 1980s, and continues with such names as Silhouette, Dell, and Avon all increasing their output. Harlequin rapidly lost sales in the United States, with its share of the market dropping to 58 percent. Mills and Boon, not as badly hit, responded to the competition by spending £5.1 million in 1982 on magazine, radio, and television advertisements. Although it continued to market the firm and the romance series more than individual authors, some attempts were made to render its authors more visible.

Mills and Boon is said to be the only British publishing firm whose readers ask for it by name when making their romance purchases. Its redrose logo and its well-designed covers make it a highly visible and distinctive product. As competition increased during the 1980s, the firm used another marketing strategy to great effect: selling its books through supermarkets, thereby targeting its female readers in the shop they most fre-

quently use. The firm has been able to reach its audience more effectively since the sociological surveying done on its books by Dr. Peter H. Mann, of Loughborough University. In 1969 he produced a major study (extended in 1974) which found that the typical Mills and Boon reader is female, between nineteen and forty-four years old, married, and works in a clerical job. She does not exclusively read romance, yet it is her favorite fiction form.

Mills and Boon has recognized this readership, as well as the changing social conditions for women, by updating the content of its romances. Where in the 1960s a heroine was young, virginal, and rarely in the work force, now she is older, more sexually experienced, may even have been married and have produced a child, and may have an important job. Also, the interaction between hero and heroine is now more likely to have a strongly sexual basis. Certain rules persist, however: the story's action should be in good taste, fit the general perception of community standards, and culminate in marriage, seen always as a happy ending.

Since 1986 the firm's address has been Eton House, Paradise Road, Richmond, Surrey. In 1989 its sales were 250 million copies worldwide, with 30 million in the United Kingdom.

References:
Phyllis Berman, "They Call Us Illegitimate," *Forbes*, 6 (March 1978): 37-38;

Peter H. Mann, *A New Survey: The Facts about Romantic Fiction* (London: Mills & Boon, 1974);

Mann, *The Romantic Novel: A Survey of Reading Habits* (London: Mills & Boon, 1969);

Janice A. Radway, *Reading the Romance* (Chapel Hill: University of North Carolina Press, 1984);

Ken Worpole, *Reading by Numbers: Contemporary Publishing and Popular Fiction* (London: Comedia, 1984).

—Joan Mulholland

Eveleigh Nash
(London: 1902-1921)
Nash and Grayson
(London: 1921-1929)
Grayson and Grayson
(London: 1929-circa 1939)

James Malcolm Eveleigh Nash was born on 5 November 1873. He was educated in Edinburgh, and at the age of sixteen, inspired by Thomas Constable's three-volume work *Archibald Constable and His Literary Correspondents* (1873), decided to go into publishing. In 1889 he joined John Menzies and Company, wholesalers and bookstall owners, of Edinburgh and Glasgow.

Four years later William Sands of the publishing firm Bliss, Sands and Foster offered Nash the post of country representative. In 1896, the same year he edited *The Poetical Works of Robert Burns* for the firm under the pseudonym John Fawside, Nash left Bliss, Sands and Foster and joined Frederick Warne and Company. Two years later he left Warne to set up on his own as a literary agent.

In 1900 Nash accepted the post of literary adviser to Constable and Company. While there he arranged for George Gissing's *An Author at Grass*, a series of papers that had first appeared in the *Fortnightly Review*, to be published by Constable under the title *The Private Papers of Henry Ryecroft* (1902).

In 1902 Nash became a publisher. With financial help from the author Edward Morton he set up business at 32 Bedford Street, Strand, in London. The first book to be published under the Eveleigh Nash imprint was *The Promotion of the Admiral* (1903), by Morley Roberts. Six months later he published *Rachel Marr* (1903), also by Roberts. Nash's first year as a publisher was so successful that he was able to repay

Eveleigh Nash (photograph by Elliott & Fry)

Morton's loan, plus one thousand pounds as Morton's share of the profits.

Algernon Blackwood was another of Nash's successes. His first book, *The Empty House*, was published in 1906, and over the next few years sev-

SOME
REMINISCENCES

By
JOSEPH CONRAD
AUTHOR OF
"TALES OF UNREST," "TYPHOON AND OTHER STORIES,"
"UNDER WESTERN EYES," ETC.

Dust jacket for the Eveleigh Nash edition of Conrad's autobiography, published in 1912

magazines to attract the best authors and illustrators of the day. If successful, the stories that first appeared in the magazines were then published in book form. Nash did particularly well, publishing works by authors as diverse as Thomas Hardy, Robert Louis Stevenson, Arthur Morrison, Bret Harte, H. G. Wells, E. W. Hornung, and Ambrose Bierce.

Nash was not averse to suggesting changes in titles if he did not like them. In 1910 he published Haggard's *Queen Sheba's Ring*, which was initially called "Maqueda."

Nash was not noted for adventurous publishing, but he did occasionally have flashes of inspiration—as when, in 1912, he decided to publish twelve volumes of O. Henry stories that had been published by Doubleday, Page and Company of New York and had been turned down by other English publishers. Also in 1912 Nash published Joseph Conrad's autobiography, *Some Reminiscences* (republished by Thomas Nelson and Sons in 1916 as *A Personal Record*). Two editions of the work were brought out, and both sold well.

When World War I broke out, Nash put the company into voluntary liquidation; all authors and trade creditors were paid in full. After the war the business moved to 148 Strand. Capt. Thomas Crease, former secretary to the Allied Naval Council, became a shareholder and director of Eveleigh Nash. One of the first books Nash published after the war was *The Sheik* (1919), by Edith Maude Hull. More than one million copies were sold, and the book was made into a highly successful film starring Rudolph Valentino in 1921. Nash published four more books by Hull: *The Shadow of the East* (1921); *The Desert Healer* (1923); *The Sons of the Sheik* (1926), which also became a film that year; and *The Lion Tamer* (1928).

In 1921 Sir Henry Grayson became a shareholder and director of Eveleigh Nash, and the firm was renamed Nash and Grayson. As a result of Grayson's joining the company, Nash was able to bring out at a reduced price some of the best copyright fiction published since 1890. Nash's Great Novel Library and Nash's Famous Fiction Library were the two most popular series and included authors such as Thomas Hardy; Conrad; Sir Arthur Conan Doyle; Arnold Bennett; Emmuska, Baroness Orczy; Compton Mackenzie; Sinclair Lewis; and Samuel Butler. Nash's Masterpieces of French Fiction included works by Honoré de Balzac, Guy de Maupassant, Gustave

eral others appeared, including *The Listener and Other Stories* (1907), *John Silence, Physician Extraordinary* (1908), and *The Lost Valley and Other Stories* (1910).

In 1908 Nash successfully published three books by Hilaire Belloc: *Cautionary Tales for Children*—a runaway best-seller, *Mr. Clutterbuck's Election*, and *The Eye-Witness*. At about this time Edward Hewish Ryle became codirector of the company, and the offices were moved to Fawside House, King Street, Covent Garden.

In 1909 Nash began *Nash's Magazine*. It was a popular-fiction magazine, though atypically for the period it was not illustrated. The first issue contained pieces by Rudyard Kipling, Anthony Hope, and H. Rider Haggard. Up to World War II, magazines were the ideal place for new and popular authors to reach a huge audience. Nash vied with Sir George Newnes, Sir Cyril Arthur Pearson, Alfred and Harold Harmsworth, William Randolph Hearst, and others who owned

Flaubert, Prosper Mérimée, and Théophile Gautier. Other popular series were the Lothian (1925-1927) and Colinton (1928) editions of Robert Louis Stevenson's works and the Georgian edition, in large type, of Jane Austen's novels (1927).

In 1929 Grayson offered to buy Nash out, and Nash decided it was time to retire. Nash and Grayson became Grayson and Grayson and continued as such until it was merged with Purnell around the time of World War II. Nash died after a short illness on 9 July 1956 at the age of eighty-two.

References:

Eveleigh Nash, *I Liked the Life I Lived* (London: John Murray, 1941);

"Mr. Eveleigh Nash: Founder of 'Nash's Magazine [obituary],'" *Times* (London), 11 July 1956, p. 13.

—Geraldine Beare

George Newnes Limited
(Manchester: 1881-1884; London: 1884-1968)

George Newnes Limited principally comprised a magazine empire, but it also published cheap classics, popular fiction, annuals, educational books with a special emphasis on practical manuals, and cricket and football albums. Sir George Newnes described his publishing enterprise as one that was "content to plod on year after year, giving wholesome and harmless entertainment to crowds of hard-working people, craving for a little fun and amusement. It is quite humble and unpretentious." While this description perhaps captures the tenor of much of the work his firm published, it disguises the commercial acumen with which the company was directed and which made George Newnes Limited a significant influence on popular publishing and allowed the imprint to survive until 1968.

Newnes was born in Matlock on 13 March 1851 to Thomas Mold Newnes, a congregational minister, and Sarah Urquhart Newnes. After schooling in Yorkshire, Birmingham, and London he was apprenticed at age sixteen to a London wholesale firm. In 1881 he was managing the Manchester branch of another London merchant firm when he got the idea for a magazine consisting of interesting or entertaining items, or "tit-bits." After failing to secure financial backing, he used his own savings to found the penny weekly *Tit-Bits*, which first appeared on 22 October 1881. This first printing of 5,000 copies sold out two hours after it went onto the streets; by 1883 the magazine had a steady circulation of 200,000, and by Easter 1897 it sold 671,000 copies in a week and had become known as "the working man's *Times*." Newnes was the first to focus entrepreneurial attention on the increase in literacy at the end of the nineteenth century as the board schools began to turn out graduates and as working hours dropped and living standards improved. He understood that massive circulations

Sir George Newnes; cartoon by "Spy" (from Reginald Pound, Mirror of the Century: The Strand Magazine 1891-1950, 1966)

depended on reaching lower down on the social scale. The future owner of another magazine empire, Arthur Pearson, and the future press baron Alfred Harmsworth both worked for Newnes, the former as a clerk and later as business manager, the latter as a contributor. It was in his offices that they became familiar with the kinds of gimmicks which, combined with an aggressive sales and distribution policy, became synonymous with popular newspaper and magazine journalism.

Newnes was the first to raise circulation figures to enormous proportions by buying readers. *Tit-Bits*, which included jokes, short articles, snippets from elsewhere in the press, statistics, fiction, and answers to correspondents, came with an insurance policy against railway accidents as well as competitions with prizes ranging from moderate sums of money to a seven-room house or a pot of buried treasure. In 1897, in an article titled "Ourselves in Figure and Diagram" in his most popular magazine, the *Strand*, Newnes calculated that by that time more than twenty-six thousand pounds had been given away in prizes and insurance benefits to the readers of *Tit-Bits*. He did not add that by then the annual profit of *Tit-Bits* fluctuated between twenty-two thousand and twenty-eight thousand pounds.

In addition to seeking outlets through newsagents Newnes sold his magazine direct to newsboys on the street, often involving them in eye-catching sales stunts. The launch of the weekly had seen the Boys' Brigade marching up and down Market Street wearing wide sashes bearing the name *Tit-Bits*. He stormed the rest of the country in the same way. At an Easter parade in Brighton, asses bore the slogan "We don't read *Tit-Bits*."

In 1884 Newnes moved his operations to Farringdon Street in the City of London; in 1886 he moved to Burleigh Street, off the Strand. Always on the leading edge of technical innovation, Newnes ensured that production of *Tit-Bits* would match demand by installing new machines that printed seven copies a second, or twenty-five thousand per hour.

In 1891 the business was incorporated as a company with a nominal capital of £400,000 under the sole directorship of Newnes, who guaranteed a dividend of 10 percent for the next five years. The company was restructured in 1897; its nominal capital then was £1 million. Two new directors joined the board, one of whom was Newnes's son Frank, and the firm moved into a new building on Southampton Street.

Newnes entered Parliament as a Liberal member for Newmarket in 1885 and remained there until 1895, when he was made a baronet. When the *Pall Mall Gazette* changed hands and political orientation in November 1890, the Liberals were left without a newspaper. Newnes stepped into the breach by founding the *Westminster Gazette*, an evening paper which—because of its color, meant to be restful to the eyes of tired commuters—rapidly became known as "the pea-green incorruptible." It made its first appearance on 31 January 1893, the first day of the Home Rule Session of that year. The circulation seldom exceeded twenty-five thousand; nevertheless, as J. A. Spender, perhaps its most eminent editor, noted, the paper was "appealing to a select audi-

Cover, drawn by G. H. Haite, for the first issue of the Strand Magazine

book contained 80-120 closely printed pages; longer novels were spread over two or three volumes. These books were neither durable nor attractive; their low price, however, represented a triumph of technology from which Newnes was, once again, among the first to profit. The first forty-four penny novels sold an average of 96,587 copies.

In the late 1890s George Newnes Limited acquired the Weldon Brothers printing works and interests in a wine merchant and in the Darracq Car Company. The prosperity of the firm, however, was built on the enormous number of magazines it published. Out of the offices in Southampton Street came the *Million*, one of the first magazines to use color illustrations; *Woman's Life*; the *Hub*; *British Boys*; *Wide-World Magazine*; the *Captain*; *Ladies Field*; *Grand*; *Navy & Army Illustrated*; *C. B. Fry's Magazine*; the *Home Magazine*; and the *Strand Musical Magazine*. Newnes also had an interest in *Country Life Illustrated* that lasted from 1897 until 1908. Not all of these magazines were long-lasting; for example, the *Million* and the *Home Magazine* had short lives. On the other hand, the *Review of Reviews*, *Country Life Illustrated*, and the *Strand Magazine* became national institutions.

It was Newnes's short involvement with the *Review of Reviews* that was instrumental in bringing the *Strand* into existence. In January 1890 Newnes and W. T. Stead launched a sixpenny monthly that made pungent comments on news items and summarized major articles that had appeared in the periodical press in the past weeks. The venture was a great success, but Newnes soon recognized that Stead's combative journalism was neither to his liking nor appropriate to the kind of business that he had developed. In early April Stead bought Newnes out for a rumored ten thousand pounds.

Newnes's withdrawal from the enterprise left him with surplus production facilities. He had for a long time noticed the appeal in Britain of the American magazines *Harper's* and *Scribner's*; they were smarter and livelier than anything that the home market was producing. Newnes decided to challenge them with the *Strand Magazine*. As he would note when he celebrated its hundredth number, the *Strand* revolutionized magazines in Britain and provided a model for many that came after it.

It was innovatory in a technical sense, because it carried a picture on every page. In January 1891, when it began, there was no process engraving and the illustrations had to be cut on

ence of politically instructed readers, who, in those days, were the makers of opinion, and from whom an immense influence radiates outwards to the multitude." Financially, however, the paper was not a success. During the fifteen years he owned it Newnes was out of pocket by sums varying from five thousand to ten thousand pounds. The *Westminster Gazette* was sold in 1908 to Sir Alfred Mond; it ceased publication in 1928.

George Newnes Limited was able to sustain these losses because of its multifarious operations. By the mid 1890s it had a book list and was publishing a Penny Library of Famous Books that included unabridged editions of works by Oliver Goldsmith, Edgar Allan Poe, Sir Walter Scott, Mayne Reid, Frederick Marryat, and Charles Dickens, with translations of works by Alexandre Dumas, Eugène Sue, and Prosper Mérimée. Each

wood; not until 1898 were photographic blocks employed. Three different kinds of press were used, including a Rotary Art Press, the only one of its kind in Europe at that time, which could print sixty-four illustrated pages at one revolution of the cylinders. The art editor of the *Strand* was William Henry James Boot; in twenty years in this post he encouraged and furthered the careers of such well-known illustrators as Will Owen, W. Heath Robinson, and G. H. Haite, who designed the distinctive cover of the magazine.

Cardinal Henry Edward Manning and Queen Victoria were readers of the magazine, and the latter corrected proofs of articles about the royal family. Yet the circulation figures showed that the *Strand* was equally popular with the masses. By July 1896 it was selling 392,000 copies per month, with 60,000 copies going to America. Much of the credit for this success was due to the literary editor, Henry Greenhough Smith. During his forty years in the position the authors whose work appeared in the *Strand* included Arthur Conan Doyle, Rudyard Kipling, H. G. Wells, Edith Nesbit, Winston Churchill, W. W. Jacobs, P. G. Wodehouse, Sapper, W. Somerset Maugham, Agatha Christie, Arnold Bennett, and Dorothy L. Sayers.

The author who was most closely associated with the *Strand*, and whose contributions always ensured a boost in the circulation figures, was Doyle. After reading two stories submitted to him by the author, Greenhough Smith realized, as he recalled later, that "here was the greatest short-story writer since Edgar Allan Poe." Newnes agreed and bought the copyright on all of Doyle's previously published work. Sherlock Holmes had first appeared in 1887 in *A Study in Scarlet* in *Beeton's Christmas Annual*; the novel was published in book form by Ward, Lock in 1888. He was also featured in *The Sign of Four* (1890). His enormous popularity, however, stemmed from July 1891, when he appeared in a short story titled "A Scandal in Bohemia" in the *Strand*.

Doyle had written that story with magazines such as the *Strand* in mind. He recalled in his autobiography: "Considering these various journals with their disconnected stories, it had struck me that a single character running through a series, if it only engaged the attention of the reader, would bind that reader to that particular magazine. On the other hand, it had long seemed to me that the ordinary serial might be an impediment rather than a help to a magazine, since,

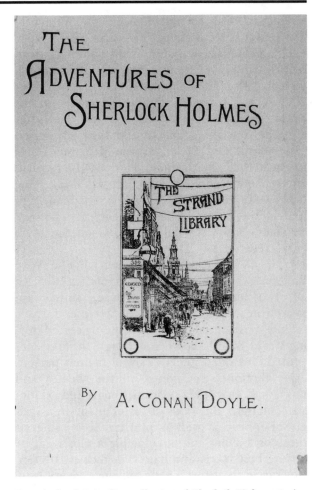

Dust jacket for the first collection of Sherlock Holmes stories, all of which originally appeared in the Strand. *The detective had previously been featured in two novels.*

sooner or later, one missed one number and afterwards it had lost all interest. Clearly the ideal compromise was a character which carried through, and yet instalments which were complete in themselves so that the purchaser was always sure that he could relish the whole contents of the magazine. I believe I was the first to realise this and *The Strand Magazine* the first to put it into practice." Again, therefore, George Newnes Limited was on the leading edge of innovations in the magazine world of the 1890s.

Sherlock Holmes's public proved to be more enthusiastic about him than was his creator, who, having had more than enough of him by July 1893, ended his existence in "The Final Problem." Doyle went on to write other short-story sequences, including those featuring Brigadier Gerard, and to contribute articles on subjects as far afield as spiritualism, the cricketer W. G. Grace, and the escape artist and magician Harry Houdini. The public, however, still demanded

Holmes. Doyle revived him in the *Strand* in *The Hound of the Baskervilles* (August 1901 - April 1902), a case that was supposed to have occurred before Holmes's plunge into the Reichenbach Falls in "The Final Problem." Then, in October 1903, it was revealed in "The Adventure of the Empty House" that Holmes had not died after all. The detective's sixtieth and final adventure, "Shoscombe Old Place," appeared in the *Strand* in April 1927. By this time Sherlock Holmes had entered popular mythology and was influencing many young crime writers, just as the pictures of him in the *Strand* by Sidney Paget had become the models for his impersonators on the stage and screen.

P. G. Wodehouse's first story, "The Wire Pullers," was published in the *Strand* in 1905. In all, two hundred of Wodehouse's stories appeared in it, and after 1910 he wrote exclusively for the magazine. His link with it only ceased during World War II. Apart from fiction, the *Strand* included illustrated interviews with famous personages, reminiscences, items on the theater and music hall, puzzles, a curiosities page, and symposia containing the views of the eminent on a variety of topics, as well as practical series such as those on buying and maintaining a motor car or on the best foods and patent medicines. Its fare was varied to attract a wide audience. Every issue carried a hundred pages of advertisements, and many would-be advertisers were turned away.

In 1930 Doyle died and Greenhough Smith retired. The magazine gradually became less popular as it faced competition from cinema, radio, and paperback books. During World War II the magazine was forced to reduce its size and increase its price from one shilling to one shilling and threepence. It struggled on until March 1950.

The demise of the *Strand* was no indicator of the general health of the company in the twentieth century; it had gone from strength to strength. Although Frank Newnes had become a director in 1898, it was Sir George (later Lord) Riddell, the proprietor of the *News of the World*, who took over the running of the firm when Sir George Newnes died on 10 June 1910. Riddell had acquired an interest in the company in 1905.

In July 1914 C. A. Pearson Limited, the other magazine "empire," entered into a working alliance with George Newnes Limited to expand business and effect economies. In 1921 the firms merged to form Newnes and Pearson Limited, although both companies maintained their indepen-

dence. A subsidiary, the Newnes and Pearson Printing Company, was also formed. By 1934 George Newnes Limited had acquired all the ordinary shares in C. A. Pearson Limited and had become the managing partner. In 1959 there were rumors of a takeover of George Newnes Limited. Eventually, News of the World Limited emerged with a bid of nine million pounds; but this offer was bettered by Odhams Press Limited, and its bid of more than twelve million pounds was accepted on 20 May. George Newnes Limited maintained a semi-independent position in the Odhams Fleetway organization, which in 1961 was bought by Daily Mirror Newspapers Limited, which in turn soon became part of International Publishing Corporation Limited.

George Newnes Limited had shown a remarkable resilience in adapting itself to the varying conditions of twentieth-century magazine publishing. The BBC had given it the franchise to publish the *Radio Times*; it had originated *Woman's Own*, *Homes and Gardens*, and *Amateur Gardening*; and it had continued to publish *Country Life*. It owned the National Trade Press and magazines such as *Flair* (started in 1960), *Nova* (started in 1965), and *19* (started in 1968), designed to appeal to younger women. It also published the *New Musical Express*, which was hugely popular in the 1960s, and it capitalized on the do-it-yourself craze in England by producing *Practical Electronics*, the *Practical Householder*, *Practical Motorist and Motor Cyclist*, *Practical Television*, *Practical Wireless*, and *Practical Woodworking*. All of these magazines indicate the capacity of George Newnes Limited to continue to discover new readerships. It was, of course, a characteristic which had been responsible for the success of the firm from the outset. Although magazine publishing had always remained the main focus of the firm's activity, it owned Temple Press and had formed the Newnes Educational Publishing Company Limited. The latter published cheap editions of the classics, popular history, children's storybooks, and illustrated new fiction, as well as manuals on such subjects as plumbing, metric and decimal tables, chemistry in commerce, carpentry, and photography. Clearly, the distinguishing feature of George Newnes Limited was its ability to gauge the changing nature of popular interests and produce magazines and books that reflected them.

In 1968 the IPC Magazine Division was created, and George Newnes Limited was absorbed into it to eliminate competition between it, Od-

Letter from Arthur Conan Doyle to H. Greenhough Smith, editor of the Strand, *dated 28 August 1893 and discussing the proposed second collection of Sherlock Holmes stories (Harry Ransom Humanities Research Center, University of Texas at Austin)*

hams, and Fleetway. In May 1970 IPC became a subsidiary of Reed International Limited.

References:

Geraldine Beare, *Index to the Strand Magazine 1891-1950* (Westport, Conn.: Greenwood Press, 1982);

"A Description of the Offices of *The Strand Magazine*," *Strand Magazine*, 4 (December 1892): 594-606;

Sir Arthur Conan Doyle, *Memories and Adventures* (London: Hodder & Stoughton, 1930);

Hulda Friederichs, *The Life of Sir George Newnes Bart* (London: Hodder & Stoughton, 1911);

Stephen Koss, *The Rise & Fall of the Political Press in Britain*, volume 1: *The Nineteenth Century* (London: Hamilton, 1981);

"Ourselves in Figure and Diagram," *Strand Magazine*, 14 (July 1897): 37-42;

Reginald Pound, *Mirror of the Century: The Strand Magazine 1891-1950* (New York: Barnes, 1966);

H. Simonis, *The Street of Ink: An Intimate History of Journalism* (London & New York: Cassell, 1917), pp. 285-290;

J. A. Spender, *Life, Journalism and Politics*, 2 volumes (London: Cassell, 1927).

—Ann Parry

Nonesuch Press
(London: 1923-1953)
Nonesuch Press Limited
(London: 1953-1968)

Named after the Tudor Nonesuch Palace, the Nonesuch Press began modestly in the basement of 30 Gerrard Street, London, in 1923; it was founded by Francis Meynell, with Vera Mendel and David Garnett as partners. Meynell, a typographer, designed the books; Mendel handled accounts and organization; and Garnett acted as literary adviser. The press quickly won acclaim for its affordable and beautifully produced books, sold almost entirely by subscription. In his autobiography Meynell writes that he set out "to be a new kind of publisher-designer, an architect

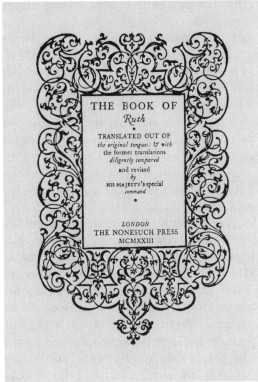

Francis Meynell in 1923, the year he founded the Nonesuch Press; title page for one of the first twelve books published by the press

of books rather than a builder, seeking the realisation of my designs by marshalling the services ... of the best printing houses, papermakers, builders."

Its first publication, *Love Poems of John Donne* (1923), was followed in that same year by eleven others, all but one in limited editions. These represent the range of subjects the press would cover in the next forty-five years: poetry (Johannes Secundus's *Kisses*); drama (*The Complete Works of William Congreve*); classics (the *Anacreon*); the Bible (*The Book of Ruth*); letters and biography (*The Letters of George Meredith to Alice Meynell*; *153 Letters from W. H. Hudson*); and nonfiction (John Donne's *Paradoxes and Problemes* and *X Sermons*, and Ernst Toller's *Masses and Man*). The only significant genre missing from the first year's list was fiction, which, after poetry, was to be the press's chief output. Most Nonesuch books were in the public domain; they were books for which Meynell wanted to establish texts, "sometimes rescuing from the past great writing that had gone out of favour or out of print."

The press did so well its first year, fulfilling in every way its founder's intentions, that it outgrew its quarters. At the end of 1924 it moved to a more commodious office at 16 Great James

Street. Its reputation for well-made and attractive books soon reached America, and Bennett Cerf initiated an arrangement in 1927 whereby Random House acted as sole agent for the press in the United States.

In its first years Nonesuch distinguished itself for ambitious undertakings, publishing books still highly regarded for their literary significance or for their quality of production. *The Complete Works of William Congreve* in four volumes, edited by Montague Summers, was the first collected edition of Congreve's work and the first in the press's series of Restoration dramatists. The dramatic discovery of the true circumstances of Christopher Marlowe's death was presented in J. Leslie Hotson's *The Death of Christopher Marlowe* (1925). The Holy Bible (Authorized Version) appeared in four volumes in 1925, with decorations by Stephen Gooden. Robert Burton's *The Anatomy of Melancholy* (1925) had illustrations by Eric McKnight Kauffer, and Geoffrey Keynes edited the *Poetry and Prose of William Blake* (1927), which is still admired. Dante's *Divine Comedy* (1928) included the Botticelli illustrations, and an edition of Donne's *Complete Poetry and Selected Prose* (1929) was edited by John Heyward. D. H. Lawrence's *Love among the Haystacks and Other*

Pieces (1930) consists entirely of previously unpublished rejections.

As much attention was given to the physical making of the books as to their contents and editing. On one occasion Meynell invited subscribers to cancel their order for Secundus's *Kisses* because he felt that the page size was too large for the delicate contents and that the title page was too gaudy. The Lanston Monotype Company was the printer most consistently employed by the press; others included William Brendon and Son, R. and R. Clark, and the Oxford and Cambridge university presses.

By 1936, when Nonesuch published *The Nonesuch Century*, celebrating its first one hundred books, it had fallen on hard times. It had grossed sixteen hundred pounds in its first year and eleven thousand pounds in 1929, its best year, but by 1933, generally as a result of the Depression, gross profits were down to eight hundred pounds. By 1936 Nonesuch needed help to avoid the real possibility of closure, and George Macy of the American Limited Editions Club came to Meynell's aid. In an amicable arrangement, Macy took over financial control of Nonesuch, assumed its debts, kept Meynell as a director and designer, and moved the press to Russell Square, London. In the sixteen years of Macy's administration Nonesuch published the twenty-four-volume *Nonesuch Dickens* (1937-1938) as well as some American literature classics, such as Samuel Clemens's *The Adventures of Tom Sawyer* (1936) and Nathaniel Hawthorne's *The Scarlet Letter* (1936). The series Ten Great French Romances included Emile Zola's *Germinal* (1942), Honoré de Balzac's *Old Goriot* (1949), and Gustave Flaubert's *Madame Bovary* (1950).

Macy decided to give up his interest in Nonesuch, and in an agreement signed in September 1951 he returned to Meynell the right to use the name and style of "The Nonesuch Press." Meynell also recovered the copyrights to Herbert Farjeon's text of Shakespeare's *Works* (1929) and the popular *Week-end Book* (1924), a game, song, and verse book compiled by Meynell and Mendel. In 1953 Meynell formed a new company,

the Nonesuch Press Limited, with himself as managing director and Max Reinhardt of the Bodley Head Press, Pamela Zanker, and Meynell's son Benedict as directors.

In the remaining years of the Nonesuch Press twenty-three books were published, from offices at 66 Chandos Place until 1956 and then from 10 Earlham Street. Three titles and one series stand out: the Coronation Shakespeare—*The Complete Works* (1953), in honor of the coronation of Elizabeth II and dedicated to her; the bicentenary edition of *The Complete Writings of William Blake* (1957); and another Holy Bible (1963). These three publications were printed on a paper made especially for Nonesuch by the Imperial Tobacco Company. It was as thin and opaque as India paper but with enough roughness to keep the pages from sticking together. Its use resulted in volumes of lighter weight with stronger pages that had all the fineness of India paper.

Between 1963 and 1968 Nonesuch published a series of children's literature classics that Meynell named Cygnets. He believed that special, well-made editions for children would encourage them to build libraries and perhaps become collectors. With the last of the Cygnets, the Nonesuch Press came to an end. Six years after Meynell's death in 1975, *A History of the Nonesuch Press*, by John Dreyfus, was published nominally by the Nonesuch Press but was distributed by the Bodley Head.

References:

John Dreyfus, *A History of the Nonesuch Press* (London: Nonesuch Press, 1981);

David Garnett, *The Familiar Faces* (London: Chatto & Windus, 1962);

M. H., "Sir Francis Meynell and the Nonesuch Press," *Bookseller*, no. 3413 (22 May 1971): 2274-2275;

Francis Meynell, "Cygnets," *Bookseller*, no. 2958 (1 September 1962): 1144-1146;

Meynell, *My Lives* (London: Bodley Head, 1971; New York: Random House, 1971).

—*Mary E. Gaither*

Octopus Publishing Group
(London: 1979-   )
Hamlyn Publishing
(London: 1950-   )
Octopus Books Limited
(London: 1971-   )

Paul Hamlyn was an assistant at a bookshop and then purchased remainders and sold them in department stores before he started Hamlyn Publishing in 1950 with an investment of £350. Then twenty-four years old, he began by publishing an extensive range of illustrated leisure books that he had printed at low cost in Czechoslovakia. He concentrated on books with a mass-market appeal, such as children's books and works on arts and crafts, cookery, and gardening. Hamlyn soon became the leading British publisher of "coffee-table books."

In 1964 Hamlyn sold his company to the International Publishing Company, which owned the *Daily Mirror*, for £2.3 million. Between 1964 and 1970 he headed the division of the International Publishing Company that owned both the Hamlyn and Butterworth publishing firms.

In 1970 Hamlyn joined Rupert Murdoch's News International. He left the following year to form his own publishing company, Octopus Books Limited. Hamlyn repeated his earlier success by using the same mass-marketing strategies and publishing the same types of books. In 1976 Octopus Books joined with William Heinemann and Secker and Warburg in a successful reprinting of novels by authors ranging from Franz Kafka to Dennis Wheatley. Three years later Hamlyn set up the Octopus Publishing Group.

In 1983 Hamlyn formed a subsidiary, Conran Octopus, with Sir Terence Conran. In 1985 the Octopus Group merged with the Heinemann Group, which included William Heinemann and Secker and Warburg; thus Octopus acquired a backlist of authors including D. H. Lawrence, W. Somerset Maugham, and George Orwell, as well as contemporary novelists such as J. M. Coetzee, Catherine Cookson, Patricia Highsmith, and Graham Swift. The merger included Heinemann Educational Books and Ginn and Company, which together formed the largest British educational publishing operation. Hamlyn's Octopus Publishing Group had become the second largest publishing conglomerate in the United Kingdom; its pretax profits in 1985 were £20.4 million, and it published a total of 340 titles that year. In 1986 Hamlyn repurchased his original company, Hamlyn Publishing, from International Publishing Corporation, which was then owned by Reed International. In 1987 the Octopus Publishing Group acquired Mitchell Beazley, which was best known for its illustrated books on wine, travel, gardening, and interiors. During the 1980s Octopus published a wide variety of books, ranging from sports, cookery, and travel to a classic-authors series that included works by Herman Melville, Beatrix Potter, John Steinbeck, and Isaac Asimov. Heinemann continued to specialize in fiction by best-selling authors such as Jackie Collins, while Secker and Warburg published serious literary works, including translated fiction.

Hamlyn sold Octopus Publishing Group to Reed International in 1987 for £535 million and

Ian Irvine, chief executive of the Octopus Publishing Group, and Paul Hamlyn, founder of Hamlyn Publishing, Octopus Books Limited, and the Octopus Publishing Group

became executive director of Reed. Reed was also the owner of Butterworth, which was known for its large list of legal titles. Hamlyn was the largest individual shareholder in Reed; the combined financial interests of Octopus and Reed totaled more than £1 billion, making Reed the largest British-owned publisher. After the Octopus Publishing Group lost Pan Books, the paperback house, to Macmillan in 1987, Hamlyn launched Mandarin Paperbacks. In 1988 Octopus Publishing Group bought Methuen, Eyre and Spottiswoode, and George Philip, the leading atlas publisher and cartographer. Hamlyn finished off the year by purchasing 50 percent of Book Club Associates, Britain's largest book club.

In 1990 the sixty-four-year-old Hamlyn remained chairman of Octopus Publishing Group, including Hamlyn Publishing. Octopus Publishing Group was located at Michelin House, 81 Fulham Road, London.

References:

Anna Foster, "The Battle of Britain's Books," *Management Today* (March 1987): 38-45;

Vivienne Menkes, "How Octopus Grew," *Publishers Weekly*, 234 (18 November 1988): 22-24;

Menkes, "Reed Acquires Octopus, Leads British Publishing," *Publishers Weekly*, 232 (17 July 1987): 11;

"Octopus Group to Go Public in London," *Publishers Weekly*, 223 (8 April 1983): 17;

"Paul Hamlyn Buys Back Hamlyn Group," *Publishers Weekly*, 229 (11 April 1986): 23;

Ion Trewin, "Paul Hamlyn's Octopus Group Acquires Heinemann in Merger," *Publishers Weekly*, 228 (16 August 1985): 16.

—Neil L. Kunze

Odhams Press Limited
(London: 1920-1983)
Messrs. Biggar and Odhams
(London: 1847-1892)
William Odhams
(London: 1892-1898)
Odhams Limited
(London: 1898-1920)

William Biggar and William Odhams, compositors with the *Morning Post,* founded the printing firm of Messrs. Biggar and Odhams on 4 September 1847. Their first premises were at 15 Beaufort Buildings, Strand, London. The printing equipment of this first plant, which printed newspapers and magazines, was valued at £423 2s. 4d. In the early 1860s Bigger and Odhams moved to 5 Burleigh Street, Strand.

Biggar died in the 1870s, and his son, who succeeded him as a partner in the business, neglected his duties. In 1892 Odhams became sole proprietor of the company and changed the name to William Odhams. Its capital was five thousand pounds.

In 1893 Odhams sold the printing side of his business to his two sons, John Lynch and William James Baird Odhams. Under the name Odhams Brothers Limited, the firm was converted into a private company, with seven or eight friends of the brothers as shareholders and a capital of seven thousand pounds. William James Baird Odhams was appointed chairman and managing director. In 1893 Odhams Brothers established itself at 19 Hart Street, later Floral Street, Covent Garden; the premises were expanded the next year to include 19A and 24 Floral Street.

In 1898 William Odhams and Odhams Brothers Limited amalgamated under the name Odhams Limited. The Odhams brothers; Julius Salter Elias (later Lord Southwood), who had been hired as a clerk in 1894; and C. J. Potter were appointed directors of the company. The firm's capital in 1898 was fifty thousand pounds. From 1898 to 1912 Odhams Limited was a private company; thereafter it was a public company.

Odhams Limited turned from printing to publishing in 1906. In that same year the firm moved to 93 and 94 Long Acre and soon expanded to include 92 and 67 Long Acre. This location, designated an official shelter during World War I, was bombed by the Germans at 12:30 A.M. on 29 January 1918. An estimated thirty-five persons were killed in the explosion, and the damage caused by the bomb was massive, costing Odhams more than £250,000.

For more than half a century, beginning on 9 June 1906, Odhams was associated with the controversial weekly *John Bull,* first as its printer and from 1909 as its publisher. The newspaper was edited by Horatio Bottomley, whose editorial policy was reflected in his paper's slogan: "Politics without Party—Criticism without Cant; Without Fear or Favour—Rancour or Rant." Odhams profited from the wide readership of *John Bull* that was ensured by the paper's policy of explicitness and its editor's notoriety as a public figure; but as a defensive measure, in 1908 Odhams purchased from

Top: William James Baird Odhams, chairman of Odhams Press Limited from 1920 until 1933 (photograph by Lafayette); Julius Salter Elias, chairman and managing director from 1933 until 1946; bottom: the Odhams Press headquarters, Long Acre, in 1927 (drawing by Hanslip Fletcher; from R. J. Minney, Viscount Southwood, *1954)*

Lloyd's of London the first insurance policy issued in Britain against the possibility of libel. Odhams also published *Bottomley's Book* (1909), a memoir, and *Bottomley's Battle Cry: A Speech on the War Crisis* (1914). The connection with the outspoken Bottomley, who also neglected to pay his bills, eventually threatened the success of the firm's other ventures. Hence, at the end of 1921 Odhams paid Bottomley twenty-five thousand pounds, and their relationship was effectively severed—though Odhams continued to publish *John Bull* until its demise on 20 February 1960.

In 1920 Odhams Limited and John Bull Limited amalgamated to form Odhams Press Limited. That year the capital of Odhams Limited was £295,000; the capital of the newly founded Odhams Press Limited was £1.5 million. Elias became managing director, William James Baird Odhams became joint managing director and chairman, and Grant Morden was appointed chairman of the firm. On Odhams's retirement at the close of 1933, Elias became chairman and managing director. Under Elias, Odhams expanded and prospered. It published books; magazines such as *Pictures and the Picturegoer* (21 February 1914-August 1922); and newspapers—in particular the Sunday newspaper the *People* (7 March 1925 - 19 December 1971) and the Labour party newspaper the *Daily Herald* (17 March 1930 - 14 September 1964). Odhams's public image was increasingly that of a trade-union house.

Around 1934 Odhams acquired sole British rights to the color photogravure process used in the production of magazines. Odhams's large Watford printing plant began operations in the autumn of 1936. Elias died on 10 April 1946; Arthur George Cousins succeeded Elias as chairman and held that position until his death on 25 September 1949. A. C. Duncan succeeded him.

Odhams published a general list that included encyclopedias, reference and educational works, children's books, how-to books, histories, biographies, and some literary works. *Debrett's Peerage* (1934) was an Odhams title. *The Works of Charles Dickens* (1930), a sixteen-volume set bound in cloth or imitation leather, served as a gift incentive to increase subscriptions to Od-

hams's newspapers. Other literary works published by Odhams were the Lewisham Edition of the works of H. G. Wells (1930); *The Complete Plays of Bernard Shaw* (1934); *Prefaces by Bernard Shaw* (1938); and *William Shakespeare: The Complete Works* (1954). Among the many biographies on the firm's list were Malcolm Thomson's *The Life and Times of Winston Churchill* (1945), Willi Frischauer's *Goering* (1951) and *Himmler* (1953), Alan Bullock's *Hitler* (1952), Rosalie Glynn Grylls's *William Godwin and His World* (1953), Cyril Falls's *Mountjoy* (1955), Rubeigh James Minney's *Viscount Addison* (1958), Joachim Joesten's *Nasser* (1960), Charles Wighton's *Eichmann* (1961) and *Heydrich* (1962), Edward Ashcroft's *De Gaulle* (1962), and Ivone Kirkpatrick's *Mussolini* (1964). Odhams's histories included the *War Memoirs of David Lloyd George* (1938), Winston Churchill's *The World Crisis, 1911-1918* (1939), Vladimir Halpérin's *Lord Milner and the Empire* (1952), and Asa Briggs's *Victorian People* (1954) and *Victorian Cities* (1963).

In 1964 Odhams Books Limited was established as a subsidiary company of Odhams Press Limited. Two years later, in 1966, Odhams Books was absorbed by the International Publishing Company, which continued to publish books under the Odhams imprint.

After difficult years of labor strife and economic hardship, the Watford plant ceased operation in 1983. Its closure marked the end of 136 years of printing and publishing by Odhams.

References:

Viscount [William] Camrose, *British Newspapers and Their Controllers* (London: Cassell, 1947);

Bernard Falk, *Five Years Dead: A Postscript to "He Laughed in Fleet Street"* (Plymouth, U.K.: Mayflower, 1938);

R. J. Minney, *Viscount Southwood* (London: Odhams, 1954);

Julian Symons, *Horatio Bottomley: A Biography* (London: Cresset Press, 1955);

W[illiam] J[ames] B[aird] Odhams, *The Business and I* (London: Secker, 1935).

—*Ruth Panofsky*

Osgood, McIlvaine and Company

(London: 1891-1897)

See also the Harper and Brothers and James R. Osgood and Company entries in *DLB 49: American Literary Publishing Houses, 1638-1899*.

The firm of Osgood, McIlvaine and Company published for only six years, but it marked the opening of a new era in the transatlantic book trade. The company was the creation of an important figure in American publishing, James Ripley Osgood. Born on 22 February 1836 in Fryeburg, Maine, he entered the trade in 1855 as a clerk for the Boston publisher Ticknor and Fields. He became a partner in 1864 and in 1871 reorganized the firm as James R. Osgood and Company. Most major American authors of the period could be found on his list: Ralph Waldo Emerson, Henry Wadsworth Longfellow, William Dean Howells, Nathaniel Hawthorne, Harriet Beecher Stowe, Mark Twain, William Cullen Bryant, William Ellery Channing, Charles Francis Adams, Edward Everett Hale, Joel Chandler Harris, and Edward Bellamy. Osgood produced the early works of Henry James; the first American edition of the *Rubáiyát of Omar Khayyám* (1878), in the Edward FitzGerald translation; and the seventh edition (1881-1882) of Walt Whitman's *Leaves of Grass*, which public protests forced him to withdraw. He also published many important English authors, including Matthew Arnold; Robert Browning; George Eliot; William Makepeace Thackeray; Charles Dickens; Jane Austen; Walter Scott; Alfred, Lord Tennyson; Thomas De Quincey; Charles Reade; and Harriet Martineau.

Osgood's firm went bankrupt in May 1885. He then worked for Harper and Brothers in

James Ripley Osgood

New York for several months, and in 1886 he set up as Harper's London agent at 30 Fleet Street.

On 4 December 1890 Osgood learned that the United States House of Representatives had just passed copyright legislation (the Chace Act) that would protect the work of British authors in America. Immediately he wrote to Thomas Hardy proposing a uniform edition of Hardy's collected works. Previously there had been no reciprocal Anglo-American copyright agreement, with the result that (according to Carl J. Weber's count) no fewer than thirty-four American publishers had pirated Hardy's work. The prospect of adequate legal protection enabled Osgood to set in motion his plans for transatlantic publishing. He persuaded the Harper firm to set him up in a publishing subsidiary in London to secure English authors for the American market. In partnership with Clarence W. McIlvaine, a young Harper employee, he established Osgood, McIlvaine and Company at 45 Albemarle Street in 1891.

Hardy had had difficulty placing *Tess of the D'Urbervilles* (1891) with English editors, but Osgood immediately snapped it up along with another Hardy volume, *A Group of Noble Dames* (1891). Osgood arranged for *Tess of the D'Urbervilles* to be published first as a serial in *Harper's Bazar*, then as a book, and finally in a uniform edition of the Wessex Tales. He hired twenty-four-year-old Charles Ricketts to design the bindings for *Tess of the D'Urbervilles* and other Osgood, McIlvaine books—experience that Ricketts would draw upon when he founded the Vale Press in 1896. After *Tess of the D'Urbervilles* was published on 29 November 1891, scandalized clergymen and critics raised a great outcry, which sent sales soaring.

Osgood died on 18 May 1892. He had already made plans to publish James's *Essays in London and Elsewhere* and *The Private Life*, both of which appeared in 1893. McIlvaine carried on the business, publishing Hardy's *Life's Little Ironies* (1894) and *Jude the Obscure* (1895); the latter aroused an even greater furor than had *Tess of the D'Urbervilles*. Although Osgood had set in motion plans to publish Hardy's collected works, they had to be assembled from several publishers; consequently, the edition did not appear

until 1895-1897, with the texts revised and prefaces contributed by Hardy. The Osgood, McIlvaine list also included works by E. F. Benson, Rebecca Harding Davis, and her son Richard Harding Davis; several works by Harris; George Kennan's *Siberia and the Exile System* (1891); Vernon Lee's *Althea* (1893); Violet Hunt's novel *The Maiden's Progress* (1894); the writings of Count Helmuth von Moltke (the architect of German victory in the Franco-Prussian War); and fiction by Henryk Sienkiewicz.

Osgood had arranged for *Harper's Monthly* to feature George Du Maurier's cartoons and his novel *Peter Ibbetson*. The latter sold modestly when Osgood, McIlvaine published it in book form in 1891, but sales were belatedly boosted by the phenomenal success of Du Maurier's next book, *Trilby* (1894). Osgood, McIlvaine's three-volume edition of *Trilby* sold seventy-five thousand copies; two one-volume versions, one illustrated and one "deluxe," were even more popular. As Du Maurier had sold the manuscript for a flat fee of two thousand pounds, Harper reaped enormous profits—six hundred thousand dollars. When it became clear that *Trilby* was a best-seller, Harper generously restored dramatic rights to the author and paid him a royalty on every copy sold after January 1895.

Osgood, McIlvaine and Company published no more British authors after 1897. McIlvaine stayed on at 45 Albemarle Street as Harper's representative in England, with the young Jonathan Cape working for him as a traveling salesman.

References:

Eugene Exman, *The House of Harper: One Hundred and Fifty Years of Publishing* (New York: Harper & Row, 1967);

Leonée Ormond, *George Du Maurier* (London: Routledge & Kegan Paul, 1969);

L. Edward Purcell, "Trilby and Trilby-Mania: The Beginning of the Bestseller System," *Journal of Popular Culture*, 11 (Summer 1977): 62-76;

Carl J. Weber, *The Rise and Fall of James Ripley Osgood* (Waterville, Maine: Colby College Press, 1959).

—*Jonathan Rose*

Peter Owen Limited

(London: 1951-   )

Peter Owen was twenty-four years old when he founded his publishing company in 1951. He had served his apprenticeship at the Bodley Head in London, and his subsequent experience had been with small publishers. His initial capital was one thousand pounds.

Owen had broad experience in publishing—typography and design, editing, sales, and publicity. For the first two years he worked alone, except for occasional part-time assistance. His first list included two books of the French surrealist writer Julien Gracq, *A Dark Stranger* (1951) and *The Castle of Argol* (1951); Ezra Pound's *The Spirit of Romance* (1952), Henry Miller's *The Books In My Life* (1952), and an anthology of Russian stories, all of which were produced in England by Owen and copublished with New Directions in the United States. The practice of producing books by important authors for copublication with other houses helped establish and finance the fledgling Peter Owen imprint.

The second list, for 1952-1953, included Hermann Hesse's *Siddhartha*, then an unknown book by an obscure author. A small advance secured the book, which went into nine hardback British editions and also sold well in paperback. Subsequently the company published Hesse's *Gertrude* (1955), *Journey to the East* (1956), *The Prodigy* (1957), *Death and the Lover* (1959), *Peter Camenzind* (1961), and *The Hesse/Mann Letters* (1976). The Hesse boom of the 1960s helped to bring Peter Owen Limited to prominence, and in the 1990s the Hesse titles continue to generate substantial paperback sales for the firm.

Peter Owen's lists are literary in character, including works by Pound, Jean Cocteau, James Agee, Paul Bowles, Jane Bowles, Cesare Pavese, Anna Kavan, Blaise Cendrars, Anaïs Nin, Octavio Paz, Violette Leduc, Peter Vansittart, and James Purdy. The firm published Marc Chagall's

Peter Owen in 1967

My Life (1965) and Salvador Dali's novel *Hidden Faces* (1973).

242

The company specializes in translations, notably of Japanese, South American, Scandinavian, and Eastern European writers. Japanese authors include Shusaku Endo, whom Owen represents throughout the world; Osamu Dazai; Yukio Mishima; Yasushi Inoue; and Yasunari Kawabata. Guatemalan Miguel Angel Asturias won the Nobel Prize in 1967, the year Owen published his *The Cyclone* and *The Multatta and Mr. Fly*. Brazilian authors published by Owen are Machado de Assis and Autran Dourado. Eastern European writers on the list include Joszef Lengyel, author of the controversial dissident novel *Confrontation* (1973). *The Ice Palace* (1966), the first book of the Norwegian author Tarjei Vesaas won the Nordic Council Prize. Owen has published almost all of Vesaas's books, as well as those of Cora Sandel, and Knut Faldbakken's *The Sleeping Prince* (1988), *Adam's Diary* (1989), and *Insect Summer* (1991). For a short period in the early 1960s Peter Owen Limited was publisher to the Council of Europe, and since that time it has published books with UNESCO. Owen is editor in chief, but he has employed notable editors. The first of these, in 1955, was the novelist Muriel Spark, who went to work for Owen after he published her biography *Emily Brontë* (1953). Her successor in 1956 was another writer, Elizabeth Berridge. Other editors have been Dan Franklin, Beatrice Musgrave, and Michael Levien.

During the 1960s and the 1970s Peter Owen Limited published some thirty books annually. In the early 1980s the list decreased to fifteen or twenty new publications a year but increased in 1986 to thirty-five to forty books annually; the paperback list was also expanded in 1986. The staff continues to be small but highly skilled. The firm emphasizes sound editing, good design, energetic promotion, and a determined approach to the sale of subsidiary rights. As it entered the 1990s Peter Owen Limited's stated goal was to remain independent and to continue the publication of quality literature.

—Peter Owen

Pan Books Limited
(London: 1944-)

The publishers William Collins, Macmillan, Heinemann, and Hodder and Stoughton founded the Reprint Society in 1939. Discussions between Leonard Cutts of Hodder and Stoughton and Alan Bott of the Book Society resulted in the establishment of Pan Books Limited as an independent subsidiary of the Book Society in 1944, with Aubrey Forshaw as managing director. Until the 1950s Pan's books were printed in Paris. They were carried down the Seine and across the channel in the *Laloun*, which flew the Pan house flag.

Pan was the second largest paperback imprint after Penguin by 1950. Its policy, unlike Penguin's, was to keep the number of its titles to a minimum and to promote each title. Thus in 1955 Pan sold 8 million copies of 150 titles. By the late 1950s Pan, together with Corgi and Panther, were serious rivals to Penguin in the paperback market.

Hodder and Stoughton had invested in Pan in 1947. John Attenborough, whose family owned Hodder and Stoughton with the Hodder-Williamses, was a director from 1951 to 1962. Macmillan purchased a half share in 1962, while Collins held the other half. In was in the early 1960s that Pan made its name with the James Bond books. Ian Fleming, who was an officer in British Naval Intelligence during World War II and foreign manager of the London *Sunday Times* after the war, wrote his first James Bond adventure, *Casino Royale*, in 1953. His James Bond novels, which appeared annually from 1953 until 1964, were first published by Jonathan Cape in hardback, then by Pan in paperback. In 1965, of Pan's 21 million sales 6 million were Bond titles, and Pan claimed that out of its first 18 million sales in Britain, 10 million were Bond novels.

Heinemann bought a one-third share of Pan in 1969, with Macmillan and Collins holding the other two thirds. Annual sales in the early 1970s were around 17 million books. *The Diary of Anne Frank*, first published by Pan in 1954, sold its millionth copy in 1971.

Ralph Vernon-Hunt replaced Aubrey Forshaw as managing director in 1970. As the firm's sales director in the 1950s, Vernon-Hunt had encouraged booksellers to make their shops less intimidating and offered bonuses and, later, large credit notes as incentives to increase sales. In 1975 he initiated the bookselling side of the business by opening Pan's first retail bookshop below the offices on Fulham Road.

In the 1970s Pan was the paperback publisher of several international best-sellers, including such fiction as Richard Bach's *Jonathan Livingston Seagull* (1973) and Peter Benchley's *Jaws* (1975), and such nonfiction as *Linda Goodman's Sun Signs* (1972), Thomas Harris's *I'm O.K.—You're O.K.* (1973), and James Herriot's accounts of veterinary life. In 1974 Pan published a one-thousand-page edition of Margaret Mitchell's 1936 novel *Gone with the Wind*.

Pan had sales of almost £16 million in 1980, of which nearly a third was from exports; profits were more than half a million pounds. At this time Pan was still owned by Collins, Heinemann, and Macmillan, each holding 660,000 shares, but in 1986 Octopus Publishing (of which William Heinemann Limited is a subsidiary) held a one-third share. In 1987 Collins sold its share to the other two shareholders, Macmillan and Octopus, at a profit of £6.05 million.

The number of employees at Pan fluctuated between 210 and 293 in the 1980s and stood at 255 in 1988. Nicholas Byam Shaw, previously with Macmillan, was chairman in that year, and Alan Gordon Walker, who succeeded Simon Master, was managing director. Sales were £33 mil-

Executives of Pan Books, and of the consortium of companies that owned the firm in 1960, selecting books to be republished by Pan: (left to right) G. Wren Howard of Jonathan Cape, J. H. Barrett of the Reprint Society, W. A. R. Collins of William Collins, Ian Parsons of Chatto and Windus, A. D. Forshaw of the Reprint Society and Pan Books, H. Lovat Dickson of Macmillan, Ralph Vernon-Hunt of Pan Books, and A. Dwye Evans of William Heinemann

lion in 1988, of which export sales were £15 million; profits were more than £2 million.

Of the 2,019 Pan titles listed in print in 1988, 340 had been published that year. Pan's areas of publishing include paperback originals and reprints of distinguished fiction and nonfiction. Subjects covered range from travel, adventure, and war books to biography, memoirs, current affairs, and humor. Reference books, study aids, and practical handbooks are also on its lists, including *Brodie's Notes on English Literature*, which originated from the firm of James Brodie, estab-

lished in 1907. In addition, children's nonfiction titles are published under the Pan Piccolo imprint and children's fiction/picture books under Pan Piper. Pan is presently part of Pan Macmillan Limited, the trade publishing arm of the Macmillan Group.

Reference:

J. A. Sutherland, *Fiction and the Fiction Industry* (London: Athlone Press, 1978).

—Betty Princep

Stanley Paul and Company Limited
(London: 1906-   )

In 1893 Hutchinson and Company (Publishers) Limited moved from 25 Paternoster Row to larger offices at number 34. Five new employees were hired, bringing the staff to eighteen; one of the five was Stanley Paul, who quickly became one of the trade's outstanding salesmen. So successful was he that in 1906 he left to form his own firm.

From premises at 31 Essex Street Paul began to build a general-interest list which would soon range from popular nonfiction to frothy escapist novels. Among publications of the former kind were a set of handbooks on recreational activities such as golf, cricket, and chess, while for the less-leisured housewife there was *Paul's Penny Pudding Book*, a cookery series in monthly parts—each of which served up thirty or so daily recipes and some doggerel: "If these recipes you try / You'll be happy all July." The fiction list included a few titles by such popular authors as Eden Phillpotts; but on the whole its Sixpenny Novels were the thrillers and romances of now mostly forgotten writers. The same held true for another series, the New Shilling Novels, launched early in 1911 and distinguished by eye-catching pictorial covers. In an item which could well have been written by Paul himself, the *Bedford Guardian* declared that this new series was "an attractive feature on the book stalls, and the numbers seen in the hands of travellers by train is sure testimony to the great popularity of these books."

But for all the purported appeal of at least some of its fiction in the early years, the firm was ultimately unable to compete with the larger general houses. In 1927 Stanley Paul and Company went into voluntary liquidation. The following year the imprint was acquired by Walter Hutchinson, son of the founder of Hutchinson and Company, and registered as a subsidiary of that firm with a nominal capital of one hundred pounds. Paul was soon at loggerheads with the testy Walter, who clashed with many of the staff. In 1930 Paul was replaced, thus severing his connection with the imprint that bears his name.

His successor, Frank Cowling, saw no sense in trying to compete on all fronts and concentrated instead on his own passions: sports and hobbies. He signed many of the leading sports stars of the day to write their autobiographies, and Stanley Paul became one of the leading publishers of sports autobiographies, instruction books, annuals, analysis, and humor. By the post-World War II years Stanley Paul's lists included—alongside books by H. Rider Haggard, Emile Zola, Alexandre Dumas, and an assortment of popular fiction—Learie Constantine's *Cricket in the Sun* (1946) and Walter Hammond's *Cricket My Destiny* (1946). Other sports best-sellers included Bobby Riggs's *Tennis Is My Racket* (1950), Sir Alfred Ramsey's *Talking Football* (1952), and several books by the former England football captain Billy Wright. On the hobbies and handicrafts side were titles on everything from gardening to building a house and from postmark collecting to a boatman's encyclopedia.

In the 1960s Stanley Paul's sports list grew to include Percy Cerutty's classic *Athletics* (1960) and Test cricketer Fred Trueman's *Fast Fury* (1961), as well as Frank Taylor's moving tribute to Manchester United after the 1958 Munich air crash, *The Day a Team Died* (1960). In 1966, when the company published England's Cup-winning captain Bobby Moore's autobiography, *My Soccer Story*, a Spanish firm did a translated edition. An advance copy arrived with the author's name spelled *Booby* in bold letters on the jacket. Libel suits were averted by a corrected version.

Stanley Paul is fortunate in having a stable team, with only three publishing directors in thirty years: Bob Luscombe from 1958 to 1966, Robert Anderson from 1966 to 1969, and Roddy Bloomfield beginning in 1969. During Bloomfield's first decade there was a proliferation of craft-series titles and several major new sports books, including Michael Parkinson's official biography of George Best (1975); Arthur Ashe's *Portrait in Motion* (1975), written the year he won Wimbledon; and the charismatic Formula One champion Graham Hill's autobiography (1978), based on interviews taped before he died. In 1972 *Practical Golf*, by John Jacobs with Ken Bowden, established itself as the instructional bible, selling more than one hundred thousand copies in hardback. Titles by Arnold Palmer, Gary Player, and Jack Nicklaus strengthened Stanley Paul's position as one of the leading golf publishers in the world. The instructional Tackle series became renowned throughout the trade and featured *Tackle Squash* (1976), by Jonah Barrington, the greatest British squash player of all time; the books used "flicker" pictures to bring the action to life. Cricket was still a strong suit, with the autobiography of Sir Leonard Hutton (1984) and E. W. Swanton's biography of "Gubby" Allen (1985). Michael Parkinson's humor books were also a great success. In the field of sports autobiographies the company had a runaway best-seller in *Gareth*, the life of the legendary Welsh rugby scrum-half Gareth Edwards, which appeared in 1978 and sold more than eighty-four thousand copies in hardback. The Hutchinson group's printers at Tiptree, Colchester, enabled the company to have six reprints out in six weeks.

But one of Stanley Paul's biggest successes of the 1970s was not on a major sport. In the late 1970s a young woman came to Bloomfield with a book proposal and announced over lunch that she intended to sail single-handedly around the world. Bloomfield backed his hunch that she would do it, and the result was *At One with the Sea* (1979). The author, having circumnavigated the globe in record time, was made Dame Naomi James.

The group to which Stanley Paul belongs was owned by the Hutchinson family for three generations, but in 1979 it was sold by R. A. A. "Bimby" Holt, a nephew of Walter Hutchinson, to London Weekend Television. On 20 March 1985 Hutchinson merged with Century to form the Century Hutchinson Group, headed by Anthony Cheetham, who had founded Century in 1982. The Stanley Paul imprint was broadened to include books on animals as well as popular military history, although sport has remained its central subject of interest.

Stanley Paul continued through the 1980s to produce books by legendary sporting heroes— from Bill Beaumont, captain of England's 1980 Grand Slam-winning rugby team, to the golfing superstars Nick Faldo and Seve Ballesteros. There were instructional television tie-ins, both on sports and crafts. Stanley Paul has collaborated with sponsors where there has been a mutual interest and a target audience and in this way has produced *The Willis Faber Book of Tennis and Rackets* (1980), *With Flying Colours—The Pirelli Album of Motor Sport* (1987), and *The Pimms Book of Polo* (1989).

Other highlights have included *Princess Anne and Mark Phillips Talking about Horses with Genevieve Murphy* (1976) and Wing Commander P. B. "Laddie" Lucas's biography of Douglas Bader, *Flying Colours* (1981), the first of several major titles by legendary war heroes. But for the supreme back-list book it would be hard to beat Capt. Matthew Horace Hayes's *Veterinary Notes for Horse Owners* (1987), originally published in 1887, the year Hutchinson was founded; a standard work for a century, it was completely revised and updated by the Newmarket veterinary surgeon P. D. Rossdale for its thirty-fourth edition.

On 6 June 1989 the Century Hutchinson Group was sold to the American giant Random House for sixty-four million pounds. Random Century is one of the largest publishing groups in the country. Stanley Paul continues to flourish and now has the backing of the group's strong service departments. In 1990 it moved to Random Century Houses, Vauxhall Bridge Road.

—R. B. Bloomfield

Pear Tree Press

(Ingrave, Essex: 1899-1900; Shorne, Kent: 1900-1901; Harting, Sussex: 1901-1908; Flansham, Sussex: 1908-1952)

James Guthrie was born in Glasgow in 1874 and moved to London with his family in 1878. As a young man he rebelled against the world of commerce, particularly the grind of working in his father's office, and sought to develop his talents as an artist. While serving as apprentice, and later assistant on a miniscule salary, to the painter Reginald Hallward, he accepted commissions for illustrations from periodicals such as the *Pall Mall Gazette* and the *Windmill*. This experience of creativity impotent in the clutches of mammon stimulated his second rebellion: in 1899 he bought a small Albion press and struck out on an independent path as the Pear Tree Press, named after the cottage at Ingrave, Essex, where he moved that year. In 1900 he moved to Shorne, Kent. By 1905 he had acquired a second press, a Stanhope. Not all of the Pear Tree Press books were hand-printed by Guthrie; some were produced by commercial printers.

In his manifesto, *An Account of the Aims and Intentions of His Press, With a List of Books*, published by Pear Tree in 1905, Guthrie wrote: "My work in black and white had so developed out of all reasonable chance of being adapted to the requirements of the magazines for which I previously had drawn, that it seemed necessary to preserve my identity and carry into practice a theory which had long been germinating in my mind, and which, in spite of many vexatious defeats, still seems as true as it did then. It was, in fact, apparent to me that the artist suffered chiefly from dependence upon others whose aims were as far as possible from those which ought to be his. I

ANNOUNCEMENT OF THE HAND PRESS NEWLY SET UP AT THE PEAR TREE PRESS, & OF PLATE AND TYPE BOOKS PRINTED THERE.

AFTER working for a number of years exclusively with plates in order to explore the art of printing in a different direction, we have now acquired the hand press upon which William Morris printed the Kelmscott Chaucer.

Our aim is not to imitate that or any other master, but with due regard for the past to carry out our own ideas by both methods. The type in use is shown in this circular.

The Pear Tree Press, the oldest private press in this country, was founded in the year 1899 and is now in its majority.

Prospectus, circa 1920, for the Pear Tree Press

saw that he was ready to submit to any conditions which an absurd commercial system cared to impose upon him. There, I was determined to part company with him and stand by what seemed,

James Guthrie at the Pear Tree Press in the late 1930s

and does seem, an undertaking which was bound to be interesting, and perhaps important, even if it should also prove sometimes trying beyond my strength." This enterprise was to be no slavish emulation of William Morris, whose influence continued to dominate the private press movement after his death in 1896. Indeed, even though in 1920 he acquired the press on which Morris's Kelmscott Press had printed *The Works of Geoffrey Chaucer* (1896), Guthrie bridled against the example of Morris, who left the execution of his conceptions to the craftsmanship of others. Guthrie's actual guiding light was William Blake, who also attempted to retain his artistic integrity by taking over all publishing functions himself: editing, production, and marketing.

The first decade of the Pear Tree Press was its most prolific period. Two volumes (four numbers) of a periodical, the *Elf*, appeared in 1899 and 1900, illustrated by Guthrie and containing poems such as "The Glow-Worm's Light" and "The Moon Fairies." The first work to carry the Pear Tree Press imprint was *Some Poems of Edgar Allan Poe*, published in six parts in 1901. A limited edition of *Pillow Fancies in Silver Grey* (1901), by Helen Beardsell, featured decorations de-

signed by Guthrie and engraved on wood by Clemence Housman, sister of the poet A. E. Housman. Her other brother, Laurence, had sought fame initially as an illustrator but found it as an author. With W. Somerset Maugham he edited *The Venture: An Annual of Art and Literature*, the first volume of which Pear Tree published in 1903. In 1938 Guthrie decorated and printed a limited edition of Laurence Housman's *Hop-O'-Me-Heart: A Grown-Up Fairy Tale*.

The essayist and poet Edward Thomas lived in Petersfield, near the cottage in Harting, Sussex, to which Guthrie moved with his family in 1901. Poet and publisher initiated a close friendship. Thomas would walk over to Harting and share with the reclusive Guthrie news and opinions about people he visited and met on his trips to London. The Pear Tree Press published Thomas's *Six Poems*, under the pseudonym Edward Eastaway, in 1916. *To the Memory of Edward Thomas* appeared in 1937 in a limited edition of 250 copies. In 1938 Thomas's *The Friend of the Blackbird* was produced in an edition of 100 copies.

John Johnson of Oxford University Press, who invited Guthrie to read his paper, "The

Hand Printer and His Work," at a Double Crown Club lunch at the Café Royal in 1934, began in 1937 to gather support from such figures as James M. Barrie, George Bernard Shaw, and William Butler Yeats for a Civil List pension for Guthrie; it was granted in 1939. The number of new works from the Pear Tree Press had already declined considerably, but Guthrie's love of Sussex led to the appearance in 1951 of his *From a Sussex Village*, as a late companion to Eleanor Farjeon's *A Sussex Alphabet* (1939). The village of the title was Flansham, where he had lived since 1908.

Guthrie's work on a hand-colored edition of Blake's *Songs of Innocence* (1789), the long-term magnum opus of the press initiated for the centenary of Blake's death in 1927, continued until his death. Copies bear the date 1939, but Guthrie was still engaged on it in 1952. Because of a sprained wrist and generally poor health, he managed to complete only seventeen out of the planned edition of two hundred. All the production work except the binding was Guthrie's. The Pear Tree Press ceased with Guthrie's death in 1952.

References:
Colin Franklin, "James Guthrie," *Private Library*, second series 9 (Spring 1976): 2-17;
James Guthrie, *An Account of the Aims and Intentions of His Press, With a List of Books* (Sussex: Pear Tree Press, 1905);
Guthrie, "The Hand Printer and His Work," *Private Library*, second series 9 (Spring 1976): 25-43;
Robin Guthrie, *James Guthrie: Biographical Notes*, Margaret I. King Library Occasional Papers No. 54 (Lexington: University of Kentucky Libraries, 1953).

—*Alistair McCleery*

Penguin Books
(London: 1935-1937; Harmondsworth: 1937-)

See also the Penguin Books and New American Library entries in *DLB 46: American Literary Publishing Houses, 1900-1980: Trade and Paperback.*

Penguin Books, launched in 1935 by Allen Lane, transformed many aspects of the publishing industry not only in Britain but worldwide. Lane's company virtually invented the modern paperback, significantly altering publishers' approaches to book production and marketing. Along the way Lane became something of a legend, and the company he formed has become a cherished institution.

Lane was born Allen Williams in Bristol in 1902. His uncle, John Lane, was chairman of the Bodley Head publishers in Vigo Street, London. John agreed to take the seventeen-year-old Allen into the business. At that time Allen, his parents, two brothers, and sister changed their surname to Lane at John Lane's request. Allen immediately took to the trade, performing every function from packing and delivering to sales. He soon showed himself particularly adept at what would now be called public relations: his easy affability and business sense helped him befriend and retain authors and gained him entrée into the circles of the influential, from important London publishers to the Prince of Wales.

John Lane died in 1925; Allen became a member of the board, rising to chairman in 1930. The Bodley Head had become conservative, even staid, and Allen Lane's ideas often clashed with those of the other board members. The first indication that their relationship was not going to be harmonious involved Lane's wish to publish a volume of cartoons by Peter Arno; when the board balked, he announced that he would personally take on the financial risk. *Peter Arno's Parade* appeared in 1931. Not long after, he further alarmed the old guard with an even bolder project: publishing James Joyce's *Ulysses*, first published in Paris by Shakespeare and Company in 1922. This plan was not quite as reckless as it might have seemed, for in December 1933 Bennett Cerf and Random House had won their victory in the American courts for the book, and *Ulysses* was not hard for the British reader to come by in Continental and pirated editions. Printing Joyce's work at this time was, therefore, a risk quite worth taking. The Bodley Head edition finally came out in 1936, the board's fears of prosecution proved groundless, and the book was a great financial success. The *Ulysses* affair set a pattern for Penguin: Lane was an innovator and a risk-taker, but his risks were based on sound business thinking, and the risks in retrospect seem minimal.

The idea for Penguin Books came to Lane in 1934 when he was returning to London from a weekend with Agatha Christie and her husband

*Allen Lane about three years before he founded
Penguin Books*

and could find nothing to read on the train; the railway stands offered only slick magazines and tenth-rate fiction reprints. The next morning he presented to his brothers, Richard and John, who by then were also involved in running the Bodley Head, a radical scheme: the Bodley Head would gain the rights to reprint good fiction and nonfiction, produce the titles in attractive and tasteful paperback covers, and sell each copy for sixpence. An integral part of the scheme was mass marketing. His brothers were skeptical, and so, needless to say, were the directors of the Bodley Head.

All the publishing wisdom of the day foretold failure for Lane's scheme. The two key concepts in the plan—the price and the paperback format—were the sticking points. A sixpenny book, Lane calculated, would have to sell at least seventeen thousand copies to break even, and no one could be assured of that kind of sale with every title. Paperbacks, moreover, were virtually synonymous with low-quality books. Lane's ideas had been tried in one form or another before, but it was his combination of them that would eventually guarantee the success of the scheme. Cheap reprints had been around since the Victorian era, in series such as Routledge's Railway Library. These series contained some valuable titles, but the great majority of books were ephemeral fiction and romances. And there had been inexpensive editions of classic books since the turn of the century in Grant Richards's World's Classics and J. M. Dent's Everyman's Library, but these were not sixpenny paperbacks. Lane's idea was to combine quality—both in production and in literary content—with low prices and mass marketing. He was convinced that the time was right for such a combination; the Bodley Head directors disagreed. Lane at length managed to get the directors' approval, however, to solicit Bodley Head writers and their agents, and to approach authors and agents signed with other publishers, for their reprint rights. Lane's new series would be allowed to come out under the Bodley Head imprint, but with the stipulation that it should not interrupt normal Bodley Head business.

When Lane announced his scheme at the annual booksellers' convention, the other publishers were unanimous in their conviction that the enterprise must fail. The chief reason given was production cost: in their view, a series could not survive at sixpence a title. Some, however, took another tack: if Lane did succeed, it would mean disaster for conventional publishing, for nobody would be willing to pay conventional prices when good books could be had for sixpence. The contradictions in these objections only spurred Lane and his brothers on; they became ever more sure that the idea would succeed.

Lane had decided that they must produce a set of ten titles immediately, to convince retailers and customers that this was a real series and not just an isolated and eccentric venture. As things turned out, only two of the initial ten were Bodley Head titles. Several others came from Jonathan Cape Limited—Cape, convinced that the enterprise would fail, saw no reason not to sell rights to Lane.

By no definition a literary man, Lane believed that a mix of middlebrow fiction and biography would appeal to a wide range of educated readers. He was intent on avoiding the scholarly

The crypt at Holy Trinity Church that served as Penguin's headquarters during 1936 and 1937

and the avant-garde, on the one hand, and vulgar pulp works, on the other. Either extreme might have guaranteed him a market, but he wanted a series that would cross almost all existing markets. The list that was finally put together illustrates Lane's own tastes and the sort of reader he was looking for: *Ariel*, by André Maurois, published by the Bodley Head in 1924; *The Unpleasantness at the Bellona Club*, by Dorothy L. Sayers, published by Ernest Benn in 1924; *A Farewell to Arms*, by Ernest Hemingway, published by Cape in 1929; *Poet's Pub*, by Eric Linklater, published by Cape in 1929; *Madame Claire*, by Susan Ertz, published by the First Novel Library in 1923; *Twenty-five*, by Beverly Nichols, published by Cape in 1926; *William*, by E. H. Young, published by Cape in 1925; *Gone to Earth*, by Mary Webb, published by Archibald Constable in 1917 and by Cape in 1930; *Carnival*, by Compton Mackenzie, published by Newnes in 1907; and *The Mys-*

terious Affair at Styles, by Christie, published by the Bodley Head in 1920. The emphasis was on readable but respectable works of contemporary fiction and biography, with a special nod in the direction of detective fiction; Christie's appearance on the list is especially appropriate, given her indirect role in inspiring Penguin Books. Richard Lane was put in charge of negotiating with authors and agents. His standard offer was twenty-five pounds in advance with one pound in royalties for every thousand copies sold. This was hardly a princely sum; but the market for reprints was not strong, and some of the authors must have felt (like Cape) that since the enterprise was doomed anyway, there was nothing wrong with taking the advance.

It was critical to Lane that the books not be confused in the public's mind with ordinary paperbacks; they must have an image befitting their contents. The typical paperback of the day had an illustrated cover calculated to catch the eye of the browser; lurid covers often adorned quite tame novels. Lane's contemptuous term for such illustrations was "bosoms and bottoms," neither of which, he insisted, would ever appear on the covers of Penguin Books. Much later, when the series was well established, he maintained this anti-illustration bias over the arguments of his board and advisers. Lane settled on a design that was at once dignified and highly visible on the shelf. The front of each cover had the title and the author's name centered, set in simple, nonserif type, with a bright band of color above and below. Green was used for detective fiction, orange for novels, and blue for nonfiction. The result was bright without being gaudy and respectable without being stodgy—exactly the balance Lane was aiming for with the content of the books.

The next item was the choice of a name for the series that would complement the carefully designed image. Lane shied away from serious-sounding names like Everyman and World's Classics, which would have seemed too ponderous and scholarly. Dolphin Books was proposed, but this name had already been used. Eventually the Lanes decided on Penguin, which seemed to them to fit the spirit of the enterprise perfectly. Edward Young, a junior employee of the Bodley Head, drew the first version of the now-famous device.

Lane contracted with the printing firm of Hazell Watson and Viney (which still prints many Penguin titles) to produce a dummy version of

Poet's Pub, and he and his brothers began to make the rounds with it—Richard taking London, John the foreign markets, and Allen the rest of England and Scotland. When they came together to compute the orders they had received, things looked dark: they had only seven thousand orders for each title, with seventeen thousand the bare minimum for breaking even. A bold move was called for, and Allen Lane decided to approach Woolworth. The variety chain had the enormous customer base Lane needed, but it was hardly a natural choice for a publisher. Woolworth had in the past sold some books under its own Reader's Library imprint; but books were never a high-profit item for the firm and were certainly not what one thought of when one thought of Woolworth.

Lane met with a Woolworth buyer named Prescott, who was unimpressed with the dummy book; he thought the cover too severe (dismaying Lane considerably), particularly when compared with the Reader's Library covers (which were closer to the "bosoms and bottoms" school of design). As fate would have it, Prescott's wife turned up at just that moment, and Lane showed her the dummy and the list of titles. She was charmed, saying that at sixpence apiece, she would probably pick up all ten titles at once. Prescott gave in and told Lane that he would order a dozen copies of each title. The order was not enough to go ahead with the series. A few days later, however, Prescott phoned Lane to clarify that he meant a dozen copies of each title for every Woolworth's store—63,500 copies. The break-even point was clearly in sight, and Mrs. Prescott would forever be revered as the company's patron saint.

Plans were set for twenty thousand copies of each of the ten titles to be ready on 30 July 1935. Last-minute fears caused Lane to cut back the order from twenty thousand to ten thousand, but the immediate and enormous success of the series made him rush to the printer and go back to the original number. Many buyers reacted as Mrs. Prescott had and bought a complete set of the ten titles—which quickly became a collector's item. There was a cool reception from the press; the *Times Literary Supplement* (25 July 1935) mentioned the new series only in a footnote and confidently predicted failure for sixpenny books.

Lane's second ten titles, hurriedly prepared and distributed, were in keeping with the tone of the first list: *The Thin Man*, by Dashiell Hammett; *Erewhon*, by Samuel Butler; *The Purple Land*, by

W. H. Hudson; *South Wind*, by Norman Douglas; *Patrol*, by Philip MacDonald; *Four Frightened People*, by E. Arnot Robertson; *The Edwardians*, by Vita Sackville-West; *The Informer*, by Liam O'Flaherty; *Debonair*, by G. B. Stern; and *The Strange Case of Miss Annie Spragg*, by Louis Bromfield. All were published in 1935. Again the list was dominated by respectable but not intimidating authors and titles, and again the variety was calculated to appeal to the widest range of readers possible. The success of this list matched the success of the first, and only the most confirmed skeptics (who still, however, included most of the publishing establishment) could doubt that Lane had a highly promising concept.

On 1 January 1936 the Lane brothers officially founded a separate company, Penguin Books Limited. This move was inevitable, since a true alliance of Penguin with the Bodley Head was ideologically impossible—and physically impossible, for the great success of the Penguins had pushed the production capacity of the old company to the limit.

The Penguin staff worked out of a makeshift warehouse and packing area in a crypt below Holy Trinity Church in Euston Road. In this bizarre setting Allen Lane would dole out pennies as needed for the women employees to go out down the road to the public lavatories; the men used a bucket and pulley. In late 1937 the firm moved out of London to Bath Road in Harmondsworth, Middlesex. Successful publishers had always located themselves in Bloomsbury or the West End; by moving to Harmondsworth, Lane was again setting himself off from the conventional.

In April 1937 the first six volumes of the Penguin Shakespeare, edited by G. B. Harrison, appeared. Inexpensive editions of Shakespeare's works were not new, but Lane showed his instincts for public relations by throwing a large launching party with a guest list of leading actors and directors.

During 1937 Lane met William Emrys Williams, secretary of the British Institute of Adult Education. Williams and H. L. Beales, a reader in history at the London School of Economics, developed the idea of a more serious, more overtly educational sort of book. Lane was immediately enthusiastic. The new series was named Pelican, and the first title, selected to capture the public's attention, was George Bernard Shaw's *The Intelligent Woman's Guide to Socialism, Capitalism, Sovietism and Fascism* (1937), an enlarged edition of a

Covers for the first Penguin and Pelican titles

work first published by Constable in 1928; the chapters on Fascism and Sovietism were the first original material Penguin ever produced. Shaw showed his enthusiasm for Penguins and Pelicans in a typically clever preface.

Pelicans, like Penguins, were priced at sixpence. Many of the first set were reprints of standard and authoritative works by such authors as Sigmund Freud, Roger Fry, Clive Bell, and Julian Huxley; but Lane, working with Williams, commissioned new books on subjects ranging from English literature to ballet and ornithology. Over the next decade the Pelican list became dominated by original titles. Owing to Penguin's rapidly solidifying reputation and Lane's market sense, Pelicans quickly became an equally successful line. The emphasis in the early Pelican lists was on works by authors who tended toward socialism, but Lane made sure that Pelicans represented a broad range of subjects and opinions.

In addition to Williams, other key additions to the Lane brothers' nucleus during the early years were Young, who had drawn the first Penguin device, and Eunice Frost. Young worked in the editorial department and was a frequent source of ideas for unconventional promotional schemes. During World War II Young would be one of the first submarine commanders, and Pen-

guin would publish his *One of Our Submarines* in 1954. Frost began as secretary to Lane but moved gradually into editorial work and eventually became one of the company's primary decision makers; she referred to herself as the firm's "principal literary midwife." She was one of the first women to rise so high in British publishing.

Williams's dedication to adult education colored Lane's view of the mission of Penguin. For Lane, good adult reading matter, such as one might relish on a train journey, was the original objective. But Williams believed that Penguins could have solid educational value. His approach appealed to Lane as simple good business sense and a way to broaden the market.

Political developments in Europe inspired a new series, Penguin Specials, designed to explain and clarify the issues for the British reader. The first title was Edgar Mowrer's *Germany Puts the Clock Back* (1937). Mowrer's book was a revision, but the Specials in 1938 included original titles such as *Mussolini's Roman Empire*, by G. T. Garratt, and *Blackmail or War*, by Geneviève Tabouis. Many of the Specials were enormously popular—the Tabouis title sold 250,000 copies in a few weeks—and they helped enhance Penguin's image for the British public; nearly fifty titles were published from 1937 to 1939.

Lane (center) with his brothers Richard (left) and John, his partners in Penguin, outside the firm's headquarters in Harmondsworth in 1940

Not everything Penguin did during these years was a complete success. Lane authorized a foray in 1938 into the field of illustrated books; but the books were badly produced, the illustrations being difficult to fit in with the Penguin size and format, and Lane discontinued the series after its tenth title. The experience kept him thinking of a way to produce a more lavish Penguin, and he hit on the idea that came to be called King Penguins. King Penguins were a direct imitation of the popular German Insel series, books that combined a brief monograph treatment of a subject with lavish color illustrations. The first title was a reprint of *Les Roses* (1817-1824), by Pierre-Joseph Redouté; it was published in 1939 as *A Book of Roses* and was soon followed by John Gould's *British Birds on Lake, River and Stream* (1939). The King Penguins remained a success into the 1950s, but rising production costs finally caused the firm to drop them in 1959.

Penguin was set up to produce books; its attempts at magazine publishing were less than perfectly planned and were poorly integrated into the company. Begun in 1937, in the first flush of Penguin success, *Penguin Parade* tried to cast its net wide, encouraging over-the-transom submissions rather than seeking out the literary elite. In one sense, the strategy worked quite well: in 1938 the editor, Denys Kilham Roberts, reported receiving an average of thirty submissions a day. The plan was to publish mostly short stories, and though *Parade* encouraged amateur fiction, it also printed works by Stephen Vincent Benét, Sherwood Anderson, and Katherine Anne Porter. Publication of *Parade* was spotty and irregular. Roberts continued as editor until 1945, when the magazine was discontinued. In 1947 it was reestablished under the editorship of J. E. Morpurgo, but the firm again discontinued it the following year.

Penguin New Writing was begun in November 1940 under the editorship of John Lehmann, who had been a partner in Virginia and Leonard Woolf's Hogarth Press and had been printing a magazinelike anthology of contemporary authors called *New Writing*. Lane allowed Lehmann to run the publication as he saw fit; it had tremendous success for a venture of its kind, selling as many as a hundred thousand copies and enjoying great prestige in the literary world. George Orwell, an early critic of the Penguin enterprise, had his now-classic essay "Shooting an Elephant" published in the first issue. Other frequent contributors included Stephen Spender, Louis MacNeice, C. Day Lewis, and W. H. Auden, and Lehmann vigorously sought out pieces from Russian, Chinese, Indian, American, and European authors. *Penguin New Writing* appeared monthly throughout most of the 1940s. At one point Lane told Lehmann he would have to cut the magazine back to a quarterly, and Lehmann did so under protest. Finally, in 1949, Lane said that *Penguin New Writing* would have to become a biannual. At that point Lehmann let the magazine die; the last issue appeared in 1950.

But for every Penguin failure, there was at least one stunning success. Another visionary taken on by Lane was Noel Carrington, who saw a market for well-written and well-produced though inexpensive children's books. Under Carrington's aegis, Puffin Books were begun with four titles in December 1940. Puffins were at first meant to be primarily educational rather than entertaining. Early titles such as *War on Land* (1940) and *War at Sea* (1940), both by James Holland, fit both the mission and the times, though today Puffins are primarily known for their fiction titles.

The war was good to Penguin Books Limited. The books' format, size, and content made them ideal for British soldiers to carry in Europe and for mailing abroad as gifts. And British government agencies saw a role the books could play in the war effort; as a result, paper allocations—a nightmare for other British wartime publishers—were never a problem for Penguin. Lane returned the favor by printing titles suggested by the government, one of the most popular being a book on recognizing types of aircraft. Moreover, Lane won a huge order from the Canadian government to produce books for its troops. Following this deal, Lane and Williams approached the British government with an idea for an Armed Forces Book Club, which was met with enthusiasm; the club was launched in July 1942. The numbers involved were staggering: Lane would produce ten titles a month, seventy-five thousand copies of each. Later the club was expanded to mail out parcels to British prisoners of war. The club put Penguin Books in the forefront of British publishing and the home-front war effort. It was one of the biggest public rela-

E. V. Rieu, who created, edited, and translated the Penguin Classics series

tions triumphs in publishing history. But Lane was not merely a profiteer. His motivations were strongly patriotic; the loss of his brother John, whose ship was sunk off Africa in 1942, certainly strengthened his personal investment in the war effort above and beyond the business gains he was making from it.

Lane had long desired to break into the American market. Setting up a fully American firm was essential to circumvent the import laws, and after some false starts he established Penguin Books, Incorporated in New York in 1941. The first American Penguins were published in December 1941, just before the attack on Pearl Harbor. The American branch was not as immediately successful as its parent had been, in part because there were already American firms competing for the paperback market; Penguins were not the novelty in 1941 America that they had been in 1935 England. Moreover, there were stormy episodes when Lane disagreed with some of the ideas and policies of the American managers. One such case came when the American firm published Erskine Caldwell's *God's Little Acre* in 1946. The book was a big success for the company, but Lane never approved of it; he suggested that the American branch open a separate subsidiary and name it Porno Books. Lane also disapproved of other authors whose works were published by the Americans, including James M. Cain and James T. Farrell. Lane forced out, or encouraged the departure of, several American directors. Some of them took the Penguin philosophy with them to start new and highly successful firms. In 1948 the partnership with the American branch was dissolved; the American directors, Kurt Enoch and Victor Weybright, bought out Lane's interest in the firm and reorganized the company as the New American Library (NAL). A new Penguin Books, Incorporated was started in 1951 under the direction of Harry Paroissien.

In 1947 Lane expanded the firm to Australia. Until 1955, when his brother Richard became involved in running the branch, Penguin Books Proprietary Limited, based in Melbourne, suffered from being not quite independent of Allen Lane. According to an often-repeated story, on one of his infrequent visits to the branch Lane virtually ignored the directors there in favor of parties and sporting events. Finally, three of the heads of the company drove him to the airport for his flight back to England. He left them at the gate and walked toward the plane, stopped, came back, and said, pointing to each of them in turn: "*You're* out—*you're* out—and *you're* in." He then turned around and boarded the plane. Even with such leadership turmoil, the Australian firm did quite well, selling around 750,000 books a year by the mid 1950s. In addition to the full-scale operations in America, Australia, and Canada, agencies were set up in South Africa, Europe, and South America by the mid 1950s.

In 1945 the British parent firm inaugurated what was to become one of the most popular series of all: Penguin Classics, edited by E. V. Rieu. Rieu was a scholar who had worked in the publishing industry since before World War I, having played significant roles at Oxford University Press and Methuen. He began a prose translation of *The Odyssey* in late 1940, planning to put Homer into an idiom approachable by the contemporary lay reader. He brought the idea to Lane, who was enthusiastic. Rieu's *Odyssey* was the first title in the Penguin Classics series; over the next

Lane celebrating Penguin's victory in the Lady Chatterley's Lover *obscenity case in 1960*

fifteen years it was in constant demand, selling well over a million copies. A rival translation by W. H. D. Rouse was produced in America by the New American Library's Mentor imprint in 1955 to try to take away Penguin's monopoly on Homer, but with little success: the American Penguin sold more than a half million copies of Rieu's translation in the 1950s. Another highly successful title that Rieu oversaw was Nevill Coghill's modernized version of Geoffrey Chaucer's *The Canterbury Tales* (1951). One factor in the Classics series' success was the high-school and college textbook market, which the American branch of Penguin in particular was quick to exploit. Rieu stayed with Penguin until his death in 1964. The Classics series remains a mainstay of Penguin today.

Another innovation that had great public relations value was the publication of the Shaw "million." Lane's idea was to publish, on the occasion of George Bernard Shaw's ninetieth birthday on 26 July 1946, ten of his works in editions of one hundred thousand each. Shaw liked the idea, but he insisted on his own peculiar system of spelling in the books, which so bedeviled the Penguin printers that the job was given to a Scottish printer who had had extensive dealings with Shaw. The series sold out in less than six weeks, so there were several other "million" series in the years to come. Probably the most noteworthy was the D. H. Lawrence million planned for 1960, the seventy-fifth anniversary of Lawrence's birth and the thirtieth of his death. There had been many earlier Penguin editions of Lawrence's works, but this one was different because it was to include *Lady Chatterley's Lover* (1928). In 1959 a new and more liberal Obscene Publications Act went into effect. The new act said that a book had to be judged as a whole—an obscene passage was not enough to condemn it; also, a book could not be condemned if it could be shown to tend to the public good in some way, and the act allowed witnesses to be called to testify in the book's behalf. Lane and the directors knew that the government would try to prosecute, so they prepared themselves well. So that no bookstore would be involved in the case, they handed the first copy of the book to the police themselves. And the government did prosecute.

The government's case was not well handled. At the trial, which began on 20 October 1960, the prosecutor's contention was not that the book should be absolutely banned but that it should not be published in a cheap paperback version in which, he said repeatedly, "even maidservants" would be able to read it. The absurdly anachronistic paternalism of the prosecution certainly lost points with the jury. Penguin countered with an impressive array of expert witnesses in the book's behalf, including E. M. Forster, Rebecca West, and C. Day Lewis; Lane himself also testified. The prosecution brought forth no witnesses other than the policeman who had purchased the book and served the summons. The trial took six days, and the jury brought in a verdict of not guilty; the court refused to award Penguin costs, however. Penguin was vindicated, and the case made headlines everywhere—yet another public relations triumph.

Throughout the 1960s Penguin's British and foreign sales grew. Illustrated covers—though not, of course, the "bosoms and bottoms" variety—began to appear on Penguins during this period; today Penguins, and especially Penguin Classics, are renowned for their beautifully reproduced cover art. These years were publicly good ones for the firm, but there was turmoil in the inner circle as Lane cast about him for the ap-propriate successor, creating bitterness and division within the ranks. Among the plans that came and went were partnerships with other firms, including Atheneum and Houghton Mifflin. One particularly difficult episode involved Tony Godwin, who in 1965 was chief editor. Godwin was trying to get the company to go into hardback books, and his plan eventually ran afoul of Lane, who abruptly announced his own, quite different, hardback plan. Relations between the two worsened as it became evident that Godwin was aiming for control of the firm. The episode reached its low point when Godwin contracted to publish a volume of satirical drawings that were on the mildly obscene side (though probably not much worse than the Arno volume Lane himself had pushed through years earlier against the wishes of the Bodley Head directors). Lane vigorously objected, but Godwin lobbied the board and had Lane overruled. Lane reacted in dramatic form: under cover of night he and a worker gathered up all the copies of the book before they could be distributed, took them to his farm, and burned them. Godwin was soon forced out, and Lane reasserted control of the firm. He was still in charge when he died on 7 July 1970 after a two-year struggle with bowel cancer.

Following his death, there was a short period of confusion among the directors. They finally settled on selling the firm to Pearson Longman, but at the last minute the American company McGraw-Hill sought to halt the sale and merge with Penguin. Finally, on 21 August 1970 Penguin became part of Pearson Longman, with Christopher Dolley, selected by Lane as his heir apparent, as managing director. As is not unusual with a buyout, the firm was not as well run in succeeding years. The early 1970s were Penguin's darkest period by far, with decisions, it was said, being made by financial people rather than publishers.

During this gloomy period, there was one dramatic announcement: the American branch of Penguin, which had remained healthy, merged with Viking Press in November 1975. Penguin brought its great strength in paperbacks to the merger, and Viking brought its fifty years of experience in hardbacks. The newly formed company was named Viking Penguin, Incorporated. Viking's moderately successful paperback lines, Compass and Seafarer, were blended into the Penguin lists; henceforth, all of the firm's paperbacks would appear under the Penguin imprint.

Portrait of Lane in 1960 by Bryan Kneale (from W. E. Williams, Allen Lane: A Personal Portrait, *1973)*

In 1978 Peter Mayer became chief executive of the parent British firm. Mayer came from a similar post at Avon Books, and he came to a company with increasingly heavy debt and mounting financial troubles. For 1978 Penguin had a loss of $800,000, but under Mayer's guidance the company posted a pretax profit of $8 million three years later. Mayer revamped almost everything about the company, swiftly putting together a move to a new location in King's Road. He was anxious to keep Penguin close to its roots in Allen Lane's vision, including keeping up a backlist of close to five thousand titles. He also took on highly profitable books that never would have fit with the old Penguin—books on solving Rubik's Cube, diet books, and hugely profitable popular fiction such as M. M. Kaye's *The Far Pavilions* (1978). Mayer's stated aim was to have from 5 to 10 percent of the company's list allotted to such broadly popular books.

As the company returned to strength, acquisitions followed. In 1983 Pearson bought out Frederick Warne on behalf of Penguin, and in 1985 Penguin purchased five subsidiary publishers from the International Thomson Organization. Among the authors brought into the Penguin fold by these acquisitions were Beatrix Potter, James Herriot, Dick Francis, Paul Theroux, and Danielle Steel. All of the new subsidiaries are hardback publishers. One of the most poignant signs of Penguin's robust new health was the 1986 buyout of New American Library, which had split off from Penguin in 1948. With NAL, Penguin had roughly equal interests in the United States and Britain.

In 1989 the company found itself embroiled in a highly dramatic situation. Viking Penguin had published Salman Rushdie's novel *The Satanic Verses* toward the end of 1988; the book received some favorable early reviews, but its experimental structure and dense, allusive text promised no tremendous sales or interest outside its limited market. Then, in February 1989, Iran's Ayatollah Khomeini pronounced a death sentence on the book's author on grounds of blasphemy against Islam and called on all devout Moslems to carry out the sentence; he extended the sentence to all those involved in the publication of the book. Rushdie went into hiding, and some Viking Penguin executives and employees had to arrange for twenty-four-hour police protection for themselves and their families; in 1990 the company was paying an estimated $3 million a year for this security, with no quick resolution in sight. Mayer faced a further dilemma in determining when to reprint *The Satanic Verses* in paperback. He hoped to delay the printing until the sentiment surrounding the book had abated, but there was no sign of that happening. Meanwhile, liberals were insisting that Viking Penguin go ahead with the printing, seeing the paperback edition as a dramatic symbol of the freedom to publish without fear of religious repression. The cases of *Ulysses* and *Lady Chatterley's Lover* seemed quite sedate by comparison; Khomeini had made the stakes higher than they had been in any previous publishing controversy in modern times. Rushdie pressed Mayer on the issue, feeling that his life would never have a chance of returning to normal until the entire publishing cycle was complete. Viking Penguin published the paperback edition in 1989; as of late 1991, Rushdie was still in hiding.

Apart from the Rushdie controversy, Penguin continues to enjoy great goodwill from the public—especially the British public, which has seen it as a national institution since World War II—and it has won the respect of writers as well.

One piece of evidence for this respect is the publication in 1989 of Saul Bellow's *A Theft* and *The Bellarosa Connection* in Penguin paperbacks before the books appeared in hardback. Bellow settled on this scheme, he said, because the high cost of hardback books prevents serious novelists from getting the wide readership they need. Allen Lane would have been delighted by the Bellow episode, for it confirms the principle on which he had founded the company: that the public would welcome quality books at an affordable price even in paperback. If this principle seems obvious today, with dozens of highly successful publishers following the same path, it is because Allen Lane and Penguin did it first and did it right.

References:

Rosemary Brady, "Between Scylla and Charybdis," *Forbes*, 130 (November 1982): 230-232;

J. E. Morpurgo, *Allen Lane, King Penguin: A Biography* (London: Hutchinson, 1979);

Penguins: A Retrospect, 1935-1951 (Harmondsworth: Penguin, 1951);

Penguins Progress, 1935-1960 (Harmondsworth: Penguin, 1960);

W. E. Williams, *Allen Lane: A Personal Portrait* (London: Bodley Head, 1973);

Williams, *The Penguin Story, MCMXXXV-MCMLVI* (Harmondsworth: Penguin, 1956).

—*Raymond N. MacKenzie*

Phaidon Press Limited

(Vienna: 1923-1936; London: 1936-1947; Oxford: 1947-1948; London: 1948-1977; Oxford: 1977-)

Phaidon Verlag

(Vienna: 1923-1936)

Phaidon Press, which was to become a prestigious name in art-book publishing and a pioneer in producing fine art books for a mass market, was founded in Vienna in 1923 by Bela Horovitz; Ludwig Goldscheider; and Frederick Unger, who remained with the enterprise for only two years. The firm's original name was Phaidon Verlag. Born in 1898, Horovitz spent his early adulthood in Vienna at a time when, after the devastation of World War I, the city was beginning to revive its artistic and intellectual traditions. He attended Vienna University and took a degree in law, but he was also a classical scholar who could speak ancient Greek and loved reciting Greek poetry. He was a great admirer of both Plato and the eighteenth-century philosopher Moses Mendelssohn, and he named the company after Mendelssohn's *Phädon* (1767)—a dialogue on immortality in imitation of Plato's dialogue *Phaedo*, in which Socrates expounds on the immortal qualities of the soul.

The press was originally to be a literary publisher; its first publication was a German translation by Goldscheider of the works of Shakespeare, followed by translations of works by William Wordsworth, Algernon Charles Swinburne, and Plato. These 1923 limited editions featured luxurious leather bindings, elegant handset type, handmade paper, marbled inside covers, and woodcut silhouette illustrations. Horovitz and Goldscheider's vision, however, was founded on the belief that a wide readership existed for reasonably priced quality books on cultural subjects,

Bela Horovitz, one of the founders of the Phaidon Press

and Horovitz was convinced that such an idea could work in both commercial and publishing terms. Phaidon's innovation was the now-accepted concept of coeditions: multitranslations that gave access to a worldwide mass market, with large enough print runs to enable high quality illustrated books to be sold at relatively low prices.

Phaidon's first art books were published in the mid 1930s in Vienna. The attention to the aesthetics of book design displayed in these volumes, though applied to the requirements of the mass market, was to remain a principle of Phaidon publishing. The design and typography were done by Goldscheider, who was Phaidon's art consultant. He also chose, edited, wrote, and collaborated on many of the texts; supervised the color reproduction process; and became a successful Phaidon author in his own right, with a marked interest in Renaissance studies. Born in Vienna in 1896, he had attended school with Horovitz and remained a lifelong friend. During his long association with Phaidon, Goldscheider became a valuable and much-respected editor, particularly among the many Phaidon authors of German and Austrian origin, with whom he shared a common intellectual background. Goldscheider's close involvement with artistic production ensured a finished product that combined quality reproductions, good design, and scholarly text.

George Allen and Unwin Limited bought control of the Phaidon Press in 1936, enabling Horovitz and Goldscheider to transfer their firm to London before Adolf Hitler annexed Austria to Germany in 1938. In 1937 Phaidon published the highly successful *Vincent van Gogh*, by Wilhelm Uhde. Edited by Goldscheider, who also selected extracts from van Gogh's letters, it contained folio-size pages with 120 hand-tipped reproductions that captured the brilliance of van Gogh's original colors. The first art book to achieve popular appeal, it is still in print. The Phaidon Press continued to publish during the war years, bringing out books on such English artists as Stanley Spencer. After World War II Horovitz renewed business links with Germany. He started a publishing company, Phaidon Verlag Cologne, in association with Kiepenheuer and Witsch, rescuing many of the prewar German cultural histories and providing German translations of new English titles. The firm did not close until 1970, long after Horovitz's death.

In 1947 Phaidon moved from London to Oxford. In 1948 offices at Cromwell Place were acquired, and Phaidon moved back to London. It took over the marketing of its books from Allen and Unwin, while Hamish Hamilton took over distribution and warehousing (a relationship that lasted until 1969). By the late 1940s the list created by Horovitz and Goldscheider had established Phaidon's international reputation as a publisher of prestige books on art and art history; and the art scholarship of many of its authors was well regarded in academic circles.

With the company's move back to London came the adoption of the Phaidon logo, designed by Goldscheider, based on the appearance of the Greek letter *phi*. The design of this symbol evolved from the elaborately decorative art-nouveau monogram of the letters *PhV* (Phaidon Verlag) of the Vienna original, to the plainer elegance of the single stylized *phi* contained within a triple-framed rectangle, and from this to the even plainer, present-day stylization against a solid color background, designed by Ted Gould.

A special interest of Phaidon authors was the Renaissance and its artists. Goldscheider designed and edited many of the distinctive, lavishly illustrated volumes on the period, including *Donatello* (1941), *Ghiberti* (1949), *Michelangelo* (1953), and *Leonardo da Vinci* (1954). Bernhard Berenson's wide-ranging *The Italian Painters of the Renaissance* (1952) considered the art not only of Florence but also of the central and northern Italian schools. Another area of interest of Phaidon's German-speaking art historians concerned the analysis of the psychology of perception and the consequent breakdown of the barriers between science and art.

One of Phaidon's most popular and long-lasting successes has been Ernst Gombrich's *The Story of Art*, designed by Goldscheider and first published in 1949; by 1984 fourteen editions had appeared. Translated into twenty languages, it sold tens of thousands of copies each year and is still regarded as an unequaled introduction to the world of art. Its basic principles, as stated by Gombrich, are to recount the historical development of art through closely related words and images; to ensure that each illustration appears on the same page as its analytical text; and to express the text in clear, comprehensible terms without loss of scholarship. Gombrich's *Art and Illusion* (1960) has also gone into many editions and has been translated into eleven languages. His *Meditations on a Hobby Horse* (1963) was followed in 1966 by *Norm and Form*. His *The Sense of Order*, the application of the psychology of perception to design, was published in 1979, reprinted in 1980, and has been translated into Spanish and German. His *The Image and the Eye* was published in 1982.

Following Horovitz's death in New York on 8 March 1955, his daughter and son-in-law, Elly and Harvey Miller, took over the firm's management. After 1955 scholarship rather than mass marketing became the focus. Under Harvey Miller's directorship, with Goldscheider as codirector and Elly Miller as editor and designer, Phaidon published *The Drawings of Rembrandt* (1955) in six volumes. Oxford University Press of New York published Phaidon editions from 1936 until 1954; Doubleday distributed Phaidon books from then until 1958; and the New York Graphic Society served as American distributor from 1958 until 1968. In 1967 Phaidon was sold to the American publisher Frederick A. Praeger of New York, itself a newly acquired subsidiary of Encyclopaedia Britannica, with scope for expansion provided by the Britannica reputation and financial backing.

With Praeger's acquisition of the British publishing house, the Phaidon list, which under Horovitz's direction had produced carefully selected titles each year, broadened its appeal to a wider and more popular readership. Marketing of Phaidon titles in the United States included paperback editions of the more popular titles, such as *The Story of Art*, but Phaidon's essential character—and its emphasis on dignified, well-produced art books—was retained. Harvey Miller left after eighteen months, and Elly Miller remained in a free-lance capacity until 1972. Today they are publishing under the imprint Harvey Miller Publishers, carrying on the Phaidon tradition of producing prestige art books.

In 1974 the Dutch publishing firm Elsevier purchased Phaidon. Elsevier moved the company back to Oxford in 1977 and expanded its publishing program to cover a more general interest in the arts, including illustrated reference works and encyclopedias. In September 1981 Phaidon was reestablished as an independent company in a management buyout. In 1982 Phaidon and the auction house Christie's International formed a separate publishing company, Phaidon-Christies, which produces books on collecting. Emphasis in these books is placed on high-quality reproduction and the latest scholarship, a combination in line with the original founders' philosophy toward book production.

Since 1983 Phaidon has been part of the Musterlin Group, which subsequently purchased two complementary publishing companies, Lennard Books and Canongate. In 1983 Phaidon celebrated sixty years of continuous publishing, and an anniversary catalogue was brought out to commemorate what the firm called its "Diamond Jubilee." Phaidon's publishing program continues to maintain its traditional involvement in editing and manufacturing books on the fine arts and art history, together with associated subjects in the fields of applied, decorative, and performing arts. Phaidon is also distributor for National Gallery Publications in London.

References:

Diamond Jubilee Anniversary Catalogue (Oxford: Phaidon Press, 1983);

Phaidon Jubilee Catalogue 1923-1973 (London: Phaidon Press, 1973).

—Pamela Shorrocks

Porpoise Press
(Edinburgh: 1922-1939)

The Porpoise Press was founded in 1922 by Roderick Watson Kerr and George Malcolm Thomson, undergraduates at Edinburgh University. Their primary interests lay in the discovery and dissemination of literary talent within Scotland; the press was to provide an outlet for new work by native writers. It was part of a rebellion against the kailyard, considered not simply as a fairly homogeneous group of authors but also as a collection of agents, salesmen, editors, and publishers. As the larger houses sought to consolidate and expand their publishing by exploiting the kailyard, the only recourse open to the young was to set up their own publishing ventures.

From 1922 to 1926 the Porpoise Press was based on the enthusiasm and energy of Kerr and Thomson rather than on sound finance or expertise. Eighteen poetry pamphlets—including *Thus Her Tale: A Poem* (1923), by Walter de la Mare, and *Poobie* (1925), a piece of juvenilia by Eric Linklater—and editions of Robert Fergusson's *Scots Poems* (1925) and Robert Henryson's *The Testament of Cresseid* (1925), the initial two volumes of what was envisaged as a series of long-overdue reprints of Scottish classics, were published.

The Porpoise Press did not share any of the features associated with, for example, the Kelmscott Press or the Pear Tree Press. All production work was contracted out. Any concern that its owners might have had for their publications as aesthetic objects was limited not only by their lack of knowledge of, and perhaps of interest in, design and production but also by the time they could devote to publishing.

Thomson and Kerr left Edinburgh in 1925 and 1926, respectively, to further their careers in journalism. The Porpoise Press was taken over in 1926 by Lewis Spence and then in 1927 by Charles Graves. The latter's drive and verve did much to rescue it from the doldrums. The production of pamphlets was expanded to include such works as *The Lucky Bag* (1927), by Hugh MacDiarmid (C. M. Grieve); new authors were encouraged; and the foundations of a notable prose list were laid with Neil M. Gunn's *Hidden Doors* (1929) and MacDiarmid's *Annals of the Five Senses* (1930).

The pressures of running the part-time operation began to tell on Graves, who was also working for the *Scotsman* newspaper. In 1930 he agreed to a takeover by Faber and Faber in cooperation with George Blake and, in his second involvement with the Porpoise Press, Thomson. Blake and Thomson retained a degree of editorial independence, while Faber and Faber relieved them of such chores as sales and design. The new arrangement was flawed from its inception. Faber and Faber was based in London, and its sales team had little knowledge or understanding of the Scottish market. Blake, moreover, took up a new post on the *Glasgow Evening News*; the demands of this job and the furtherance of his own career as a novelist left little time for the Porpoise Press. Thomson remained in London. The Porpoise Press title pages, including that of Gunn's *Morning Tide* (1931), a Book Society choice, continued to carry an Edinburgh address even though none of its principals worked there.

The difficulties of this situation were resolved, but only to the detriment of the Porpoise Press. Thomson was eased out in 1933. Sporadic conflict, polite rather than acrimonious, characterized the relationship between Blake and Faber and Faber. The difficulties of a one-man, part-time operation once more became apparent, despite the delegation of further duties, such as reading of manuscripts, to Faber and Faber. The Porpoise list of new publications grew smaller each year after a spate in 1934 that included Lewis Grassic Gibbon's *Niger* and Gunn's *Butcher's Broom*. Faber and Faber abandoned the imprint in January 1939, retaining the backlist and at least one significant author nurtured by the Porpoise Press, Gunn, whose *Highland River* (1937) had achieved both popular and critical success.

Reference:

Alistair McCleery, *The Porpoise Press 1922-1939* (Edinburgh: Merchiston, 1988).

—*Alistair McCleery*

Review of Reviews Office
(London: 1890-1908)
Stead's Publishing House
(London: 1908-1920)

After almost twenty years of daily paper journalism as the innovative and sensationalist editor of the *Northern Echo* (1871-1880) in Darlington and the *Pall Mall Gazette* (1880-1890) in London, William Thomas Stead in 1890 launched the *Review of Reviews*, which he intended to be an influential voice in national and international affairs. In announcing the inauguration of his project, Stead said that the sixpenny monthly would not only provide a readable summary of all that was best in the magazines and reviews and of "the best writers of our time" but would communicate to the reading public his own "gospel and ideals," which included the union of all English-speaking peoples; the expansion of the British Empire; Irish home rule; the "quickening of spiritual life" in the nation; morality in political life; political and social reform, especially complete equality for women; and a commitment to the world peace movement and its emphasis on international arbitration and the limitation of armaments. In brief, it was the creed of an advanced radical, a liberal imperialist, and the projection of the Nonconformist conscience in British life.

To finance the establishment of the new journal Stead formed a partnership with George Newnes, the publisher of the successful weekly, *Tit-Bits*; Stead was to be the editor and Newnes the publisher of the new venture. The first issue of the *Review of Reviews* was published on 6 January 1890, and the magazine quickly became a success. Each issue contained a news commentary for the past month; a "Character Sketch" of a prominent personality; summaries of the leading articles in the major British and foreign periodicals; brief notes on the contents of British, American, and Continental magazines; a condensation of a new book; a list of new books published; some book reviews; and a section reproducing many of the best cartoons of the past month. Although Newnes was pleased with the general makeup and sales of the *Review of Reviews*, he was unhappy with Stead's use of the journal to air his views on current issues and his plans to use the office as a publishing center for other publications.

W. T. Stead in 1890, the year he founded the Review of Reviews

Stead, in turn, charged that Newnes was unduly interfering with the editorial direction of the *Review of Reviews*. In early April 1890 the partnership was dissolved.

Stead established the Review of Reviews Office in Mowbray House, near the Temple, and recruited a staff which included young women employed at the same salary as their male counterparts. In early 1891 he hired Edwin H. Stout as business manager; until his departure after Stead's death in 1912, Stout restrained Stead's prodigality and kept the journal and Stead's other publishing ventures solvent. A major problem was to keep the circulation—about 220,000 copies a month by 1897—and advertising revenues stable in the face of Stead's "social purity" campaigns and other crusades. The first pamphlet published by the Review of Reviews Office in 1891 was *The Pope and Labour: The Encyclical of Pope Leo XIII*, which included a republication of Stead's "Letters from the Vatican," previously published in the *Pall Mall Gazette* in 1889, and the complete text of the pope's encyclical on the condition of labor. This pamphlet was followed during 1891 by two editions of Stead's *The Discrowned King of Ireland* demanding that the Irish Nationalists and the British Liberal party repudiate Charles Stewart Parnell because of his "immoral" relationship with Mrs. Katherine O'Shea and the "principle" that immorality in private life disqualifies a person for public life. In these tracts Stead also mentioned the sexual transgressions of Sir Charles Dilke, whom he had helped oust from Parliament in a campaign in the *Pall Mall Gazette* in 1886. When Dilke sought to resume his political career in Parliament in the general election of 1892, Stead published three pamphlets—*Sir Charles Dilke: An Examination of the Evidence given at the Two Trials of the Crawford Divorce Case*, *Has Sir Charles Dilke Cleared His Character?*, and *Deliverance or Doom? or the Choice of Sir Charles Dilke*—declaring that the Forest of Dean constituency must reject Dilke because he was a liar morally unfit to sit in Parliament. Neither these polemics nor the sixpenny *Handbook for the General Election and Electors' Guide* which Stead edited and published for the enlightenment of voters, persuaded the Forest of Dean electors, and Dilke was easily returned to Westminster. But Stead's sixpenny *Electors' Guide: A Popular Hand-Book for the Election of the London County Council in 1892*, along with his penny *Unionist Electors' Guide, 1892* and *The Liberal Electors' Guide . . . 1892* were genuinely nonpartisan and welcomed by both parties; they sold quite well. The Parnell and Dilke tracts yielded no profit, but Stead was always ready to stand the expense of publishing materials that communicated his views on issues and causes close to his heart. One of these causes, the case of Dr. Charles Augustus Bynoe, imprisoned for forgery, moved Stead to write and publish the sixpenny booklet *Wanted: A Sherlock Holmes!* (1895), a plea for the exoneration of Bynoe as "a victim of mistaken identity and circumstantial evidence." At about the same time he reprinted a sharp critique of the upper house of Parliament, *Fifty Years of the House of Lords* (1894), in support of pop-

ular discontent with the Tory-dominated Lords' obstruction of progressive legislation.

In 1896 Stead launched the short-lived (five issues) sixpenny *Papers for the People* pamphlet series, which included *The Haunting Horrors in Armenia* and *"The Assassin," or St. George to the Rescue! What We Ought to Do*, both of which attempted to rally the British public against the Turkish massacres of Armenians; *Always Arbitrate Before You Fight*, urging international arbitration to resolve disputes between nations; *Russia and England: "Proposals for a New Departure,"* by Stead's longtime friend, the Slavophile propagandist Mme Olga Novikoff, calling for joint Anglo-American action to punish the Turks for the Armenian massacres; and *Wake Up John Bull!*, by Ernest Williams, warning that German competition threatened Britain's world trade. More profitable was the publication in 1897 of the five-shilling books *Her Majesty the Queen: Studies of the Sovereign and The Reign* and *Notables of Britain. An Album of Portraits and Autographs of the Most Eminent Subjects of Her Majesty in the 60th Year of Her Reign*, which celebrated the Diamond Jubilee of Queen Victoria. In 1898 the death of William Ewart Gladstone was memorialized in a lavishly illustrated monograph, *Gladstone 1809-1898: A Character Sketch*, and the best-selling *Gladstone in Contemporary Caricature: Being a Collection of Cartoons*.

Two of Stead's last great campaigns were the Peace Crusade of 1898-1899 on behalf of the First Hague Peace Conference in 1899 and his opposition to the Boer War in South Africa from 1899 to 1902. At great personal expense Stead published the weekly *War Against War: A Chronicle of the International Crusade of Peace* from 13 January through 21 March 1899; the paper was distributed to almost all involved in the crusade and to members of Parliament. As the many national delegations convened at The Hague in May 1899 Stead wrote and published the profusely illustrated *The United States of Europe on the Eve of the Parliament of Peace*, which disseminated his view of the conference as a possible prelude to the "Federation of the World." At the close of the Hague Conference, which he attended, Stead produced a twenty-eight-page pamphlet, *The Parliament of Peace and Its Members* (1899), and in 1901 two onepenny tracts, *The Hague Conference of Peace: What it Was, What it Did, and What we have Done Since* and *The International Union*, in an attempt to unify the various pacifist organizations.

Because of his strong commitment to the peace movement and his conviction that Britain

To My Readers. Programme and Principles

I Programme.

Of the making of magazines there is no end. There are already more periodicals than any one can find time to read. That is why I have today added another to the list. For the new comer is not a rival but rather an index and a guide to all those already in existence, & so far from seeking to gain circulation at the cost of others one object of this new venture will be to advertize all the other monthlies and to promote their welfare by calling attention to the articles with which they are filled. In the mighty maze of modern periodical literature, the busy man wanders confused, not knowing exactly where to find the precise article that he requires and fearing often losing altogether all his scanty time in the search he departs unsatisfied. It is the object of the Sixpenny Monthly to supply a clue to that maze. in the shape of a readable compendium of all the best articles in the magazines and reviews. However short of the ideal the performance may come, my aim is simple. I shall try to help the busy man to find quickly what he wants in the periodicals of the month. and I still try to give my readers some general idea of the drift and character of the more important articles in the monthlies of England, Europe and America.

Page from the manuscript for Stead's introductory address in the first issue of the Review of Reviews *(from Frederic Whyte,* The Life of W. T. Stead, *1925)*

provoked the war with the Boer republics in South Africa, Stead was prominently involved in the antiwar or pro-Boer movement and in the organization of the Stop-the-War Committee. In spite of the loss of revenue from advertisements and the decline in the sales of the *Review of Reviews* and the Review of Reviews Office enterprises, Stead persisted in his campaign against the war. At considerable expense and with limited funds from other pro-Boers, beginning in 1899 he wrote, published, and widely distributed a series of antiwar tracts on behalf of the Stop-the-War Committee: *The Scandal of the South African Committee* (1899); two editions of *Joseph Chamberlain: Conspirator or Statesman? An Examination of the Evidence as to His Complicity in the Jameson Conspiracy* (1899 and 1900); *Shall I Slay My Brother Boer? An Appeal to the Conscience of Britain* (1899); two editions of *Are We in the Right? An Appeal to Honest Men* (1899 and 1900); *The Truth about the War* (1900); *The Truth about the War: Told in Plain Answers to Straight Questions* (1900); *How We are Waging War* (1900); *Hell Let Loose! What is now Being Done in South Africa* (1900); *How Not to Make Peace: Evidence as to Homestead Burning* (1900); *"Methods of Barbarism": The Case for Intervention* (1901); and *Candidates of Cain: A Catechism for the Constituencies* (1900). But neither these publications nor the weekly *War Against War in South Africa,* published from 20 October 1899 through 26 January 1900, greatly turned public opinion against the war until the last year and a half of the conflict.

Immediately after the Boer War Stead's major venture was the publication of *The Last Will and Testament of Cecil John Rhodes* (1902). A close friend of Rhodes, Stead was largely responsible for publicizing Rhodes's exploits and imperial ambitions and for making Rhodes something of a national hero in Britain. But following Rhodes's involvement in precipitating the Boer War, Stead broke with Rhodes and was removed as an executor of his will before his death in 1902. In spite of their estrangement, Stead sought to honor Rhodes's memory by publishing his last will with a discussion of Rhodes's ideas and concepts, which led to the bequest for the Rhodes Trust and Scholarships. Rhodes's will was a profitable publication for the Review of Reviews Office and has since become a major source for biographical studies.

This success was followed by a disastrous enterprise in which Stead sought to realize his great dream of a new type of newspaper with features that would appeal to all classes. With all the personal and publishing resources he could muster, Stead launched the *Daily Paper* on 3 January 1904. Mismanagement and a breakdown of his health led to the demise of the *Daily Paper* after only five weeks and left Stead facing bankruptcy. Loyal friends and the Rhodes Trust saved him from financial ruin.

From 1891 until 1903 Stead wrote and published the *Review of Reviews Annual,* either as a novelette based on some important events of the past year or as a description and commentary on some occurrence of national and international significance; the annual was sold at the end of each year for a shilling. The paperback annual usually comprised about one hundred pages of text, with artists' illustrations and/or photographs. The annuals included the popular *Real Ghost Stories* (1891) and *More Ghost Stories* (1892), reflecting Stead's increasing interest in the occult; *From the Old World to the New* (1892), the story of a party of English tourists traveling to the Chicago World's Fair in 1893; *Two and Two Make Four* (1893), a mystery story based on the celebrated "Liberator Swindle"; *The Splendid Paupers: A Tale of the Coming Plutocracy* (1894), dealing with the intermarriage of wealthy Americans with impoverished British peers; *Blastus, the King's Chamberlain* (1895-1896), a semifictionalized account of the career of Stead's bête noire, Joseph Chamberlain; *The History of the Mystery: A Sequel to Blastus* (1897), an attempt by Stead to shift the blame for the disastrous Jameson Raid from his friend Cecil Rhodes to the colonial secretary, Chamberlain; and *The United States of Europe* (1898-1899), an explanation of the purpose and hopes of the First Hague Peace Conference. One of Stead's best annuals, *The Americanization of the World or the Trend of the Twentieth Century* (1902), prophesied and explained the impact of American life and industry on the world. Stead's last annual, *In Our Midst: The Letters of Callicrates to Dione, Queen of the Xanthians concerning England and the English* (1903), was a fictionalized commentary on the social and economic condition of Edwardian Britain. All of Stead's annuals were profusely illustrated and largely financed by advertisements in the publication.

An unsuccessful venture of Stead's publishing firm was *Borderland: A Quarterly Review and Index of Psychical Phenomena.* Modern bibliographical guides rate *Borderland* as the most important of the many spiritualist periodicals in the Victorian era because of its broad coverage of psychic

Stead in his office at Mowbray House (photograph by Ernest H. Mills)

phenomena. When Stead established *Borderland* in July 1893, he declared that his major objective was to bring to the study of psychic phenomena "the scientific spirit which accepts nothing on trust." The periodical was indeed a bold experiment, which evoked considerable comment and controversy. The journal finally proved too costly to publish, and he terminated it in October 1897.

The most successful, lasting, and best-remembered publishing enterprise of the Review of Reviews Office and, later, of Stead's Publishing House, was the paperback Books for the Bairns series. In 1895 Stead sought to make books available to adults and children of all classes by establishing the Review of Reviews Circulatory Library. For six pounds per year a subscribing center could obtain the loan of a box of fifty books of children's literature every quarter. At the same time Stead launched the Masterpiece Library with the publication of the Penny Poets series. By early 1896 approximately two million copies of the Penny Poets had been printed. As the weekly issue of the Penny Poets was drawing to a close, Stead launched the Penny Popular Novels

in January 1896; the first of the series, an abridgment of H. Rider Haggard's *She*, sold almost 500,000 copies. By the end of 1896 more than 7.2 million copies of the Penny Novels had been published. Encouraged by these successes, in March 1896 Stead launched the Books for the Bairns series; it quickly became the most popular of the threepenny paperback series. A new title in the Books for the Bairns series was published monthly and, unlike the other series, was profusely illustrated with line drawings by such artists as Brinsley Le Fanu. Within a year sales of the Books for the Bairns—covering a wide range of well-known classics—rose to 150,000 copies. Stead wrote the forewords for many of the books, often explaining any changes he had made in the text—such as his substitution in *More Nursery Rhymes* of the word "Screw" for the words "rascally Jew."

The Penny Novels series ended in 1900, but Books for the Bairns continued with excellent sales. In 1907 Stead negotiated the publication of a French edition, Collection Stead, of thirteen of the best-selling Books for the Bairns titles, following the successful use of the series for teaching English in French schools. By 1916 Collection Stead included 191 Books for the Bairns titles.

From 1896 through 1901 the Books for the Bairns series was published in the Review of Reviews Office; from August 1901 until October 1908 at the Books for the Bairns Office—a branch of the Review of Reviews Office; and from November 1908 until June 1920 at Stead's Publishing House. The series was terminated in 1920 with number 228, *The Story of the Bent Pin*, but all titles remained available for sale. Stead had died on the *Titanic* in 1912; Stead's Publishing House continued to operate under his eldest daughter, Estelle, until the company ceased to exist in 1920. In late January 1923 Estelle Stead introduced a new series of Books for the Bairns at twopence each, but it was discontinued in early August after the publication of twenty-eight new titles because of lack of sales. During 1926-1927 Ernest Benn Limited republished twenty-five titles at sixpence each and offered the remaining stock of the series at inflated prices with little success. But the original Books for the Bairns still evoke warm memories among the older generations. The *Review of Reviews* continued under several owners and various titles until it was liquidated in 1953.

References:

J. O. Baylen, "The Review of Reviews," in *British Literary Magazines: The Victorian and Edwardian Age, 1837-1913*, edited by Alvin Sullivan (Westport, Conn.: Greenwood Press, 1984), pp. 351-360;

Baylen, "Stead's Penny 'Masterpiece Library,'" *Journal of Popular Culture*, 9 (Winter 1975-1976): 710-725;

Baylen, "W. T. Stead as Publisher and Editor of the 'Review of Reviews,'" *Victorian Periodicals Review*, 12 (September 1979): 70-84;

Baylen, "W. T. Stead's *Borderland: A Quarterly Review and Index of Psychic Phenomena*, 1893-1897," *Victorian Periodicals Newsletter*, no. 4 (April 1969): 30-35;

Baylen, "William Thomas Stead (1849-1912)," in *Biographical Dictionary of Modern British Radicals*, volume 3: *1870-1914*, part 2, edited by J. O. Baylen and N. J. Gossman (Hemel Hempstead: Harvester, Wheatsheaf, 1988), pp. 783-792;

J. W. Robertson Scott, *The Life and Death of a Newspaper* (London: Methuen, 1952);

Estelle W. Stead, *My Father: Personal and Spiritual Reminiscences* (London: Nelson, 1913);

W. T. Stead, "After Seven Years: To My Readers," *Review of Reviews*, 15 (January 1897): [95]-[99];

Frederic Whyte, *The Life of W. T. Stead*, 2 volumes (London: Cape, 1925);

Sally Wood, *W. T. Stead and His "Books for the Bairns"* (Edinburgh: Salvia Books, 1987).

—J. O. Baylen

Grant Richards
(London: 1897-1905)
E. Grant Richards
(London: 1905-1908)
Grant Richards Limited
(London: 1908-1927)
Richards Press
(London: 1927-1963)

The reputation of Grant Richards rests not only on the quantity of his publishing but also on his choice of authors and his forthright advertising. He published some of the most enduring literature of his day. Yet the same confidence that led him to take chances on unknown authors—some of whom became major literary figures—also encouraged a cavalier attitude toward finances, contributing to his drastic swings of fortune.

Franklin Thomas Grant Richards was born in Glasgow on 21 October 1872. His father, a member of the classics faculty at the University of Glasgow, accepted a post at Oxford two years after Richards's birth. Richards spent his childhood in Oxford and attended the City of London School in his teens.

Richards had little interest in school; he found city life and the theater more compelling. An emotionally distant father left a void in Richards's life that was filled by Grant Allen, who had married the sister of Richard's mother. As a philosopher, scientist, and fiction writer (most remembered for his novel *The Woman Who Did*, published by John Lane in 1895), Allen was able to offer Richards a social entrée into London's literary world. Allen arranged an interview for Richards with Arthur E. Miles, the head of the wholesale booksellers Hamilton, Adams and Company. Richards seized the opportunity to leave school and begin working as a clerk with the firm on 1 September 1888. In early 1890 Allen again assisted his nephew with an introduction to W. T. Stead, publisher of the *Review of Reviews*, and on 1 May 1890 Richards went to work for Stead. He performed a variety of clerical and editorial tasks and wrote brief notices in the "New Books of the Month" section of the *Review of Reviews*. It was during his years with Stead that he became acquainted with prominent London publishers such as Andrew Chatto, William

Grant Richards, 1909 (drawing by Henry Lamb; from Grant Richards, Author Hunting, *1934)*

Heinemann, and John Lane. Richards's work in Stead's office brought him into contact with Walter Haddon, advertising representative and publisher of *Phil May's Illustrated Winter Annual*. Haddon asked Richards to edit the 1895 issue; Richards was able to secure a poem from John Davidson, an article from Allen, and a story from H. G. Wells. He also included a story of his own, "The Mislaid Child."

Richards opened his first publishing venture on 1 January 1897 at 9 Henrietta Street, Covent Garden. Financial backing consisted of £750 from Allen; £200 from another uncle, T. W. Jerrard; and a £500 bank loan guaranteed by his father. Youthful confidence and earlier contacts with authors served Richards well. The previous autumn he had begun approaching established writers who could lend their reputations to his list. The titles Richards published in his first year show a flair for diversity and a careful choice of authors—qualities that would distinguish his lists for the rest of his career. His first book, Edward Clodd's *Pioneers of Evolution: From Thales to Huxley*, was published on 15 January 1897. Between sales of the book and the sale of American publishing rights to Appleton, it made a gross profit for Richards of £100. In the same year he published E. V. Lucas's *A Book of Verse for Children*, his former employer Stead's *Real Ghost Stories*, and Edward Spencer's *Cakes and Ale*. Lucas became a reader for Richards during the next few years. The 1897 list featured the first titles in the Grant Allen's Historical Guides series, *Paris* and *Florence*, along with Allen's *The Evolution of the Idea of God*. Richards also published his first novel, Leonard Merrick's *One Man's View*, in 1897; it was a commercial failure. Richards published several other books by Allen, including the novels *An African Millionaire* (1897) and *Linnet* (1898). After Allen's death in 1899 Richards continued his Historical Guides in print.

Richards was aggressive in his pursuit of authors. He had followed George Bernard Shaw home after the theater one night in November 1896 in an attempt to win an agreement to publish Shaw's first collection of plays. Richards's persistence prevailed, and he published *Plays Pleasant and Unpleasant* in 1898. A flurry of letters between Shaw and Richards records Shaw's meticulous concern for typographic design, binding, and price—he preferred to charge seven shillings for the two volumes, in the hope of stimulating sales; Richards again prevailed, and the set was priced at ten shillings. In the next few years Richards published Shaw's *The Perfect Wagnerite* (1898), *Fabianism and the Empire* (1900), *Three Plays for Puritans* (1901), a revised edition of *Cashel Byron's Profession* (1901), and *Mrs. Warren's Profession* (1902).

Confidence in his acumen in identifying successful writers led Richards to A. E. Housman, at the time a professor of Latin at University College in London. Housman's collection of poems *A Shropshire Lad* had been published in 1896 by Kegan Paul. Housman responded coolly to Richards's overtures but finally agreed to let Richards publish a new edition, which appeared in September 1898. Housman, considering himself more of a classical scholar than a poet, declined royalties. Although sales were slow at first, the book's popularity steadily increased, and it thrived for years as a staple of Richards's backlist. Richards later sold American rights to *A Shropshire Lad* to Henry Holt, who published it in 1924; in return Richards received Robert Frost's *New Hampshire*, which he published in the same year.

While his books do not differ greatly in physical appearance from those of other British trade publishers of the early twentieth century, Richards was attentive to their design and ornamentation. The title pages of the Shaw books are particularly striking, featuring unadorned but bold capitals for the titles and for the author's name. The 1908 edition of *A Shropshire Lad* has an embossed white binding, illustrated endpapers, untrimmed pages, a gilt top edge, and eight color illustrations by William Hyde. Many of Richards's books have a fleuron on the title page.

Richards helped further the careers of many fledgling writers, but they often went on to larger or more financially stable publishing houses after one or two books with Richards. He was the first publisher of G. K. Chesterton, with *The Wild Knight and Other Poems* (1900); of Alfred Noyes, with *The Loom of Years* (1902); and of John Masefield, with *Salt-Water Ballads* (1902). Other prominent authors Richards was able to attract near the beginnings of their careers included the poets Laurence Binyon, with *Porphyrion and Other Poems* (1898), and Laurence Housman, with *Spikenard* (1898); Hector H. Munro, who was later to become well known for short stories he wrote under the pseudonym "Saki," with *The Rise of the Russian Empire* (1900); Arnold Bennett, with *Fame and Fiction: An Enquiry into Certain Popularities* (1901); and Maurice Baring, with *Gaston de Foix and Other Plays* (1903).

Near the end of his life Samuel Butler had some of his most important works published by Richards, who was the first of Butler's publishers to bear the expense of publishing. Richards published *Erewhon Revisited* and a companion revised edition of *Erewhon* in October 1901. Butler had completed *The Way of All Flesh* in 1884, but did not give permission for it to be published until shortly before his death in 1902. Richards published it in 1903 and followed it with Butler's *Essays on Life, Art, and Science* in 1904.

J. W. N. Sullivan, Richards, and A. E. Housman at Bigfrith, Cookham Dean (photograph by Mrs. Grant Richards)

Richards's first years of publishing were fruitful—his announcement for Spring 1898 lists sixty-two titles in print. His first major commercial success, the now-forgotten novel *No. 5 John Street*, by Richard Whiteing, came in 1899. John Davidson had established himself as a poet with *Fleet Street Eclogues*, published by Elkin Mathews and John Lane in 1893; Richards published his play *Self's the Man* in 1901. Until Davidson's death in 1909, Richards was his primary publisher of works of drama and poetry, including the first two plays in a projected trilogy titled *God and Mammon* (1907-1908) and *Fleet Street and other Poems* (1909). Richards arranged with the poet Alice Meynell to edit an anthology of English poetry, *The Flower of the Mind* (1897); although the book was a financial loss, he felt that it added to his reputation. Richards published English editions of the American novelist Frank Norris's *McTeague* (1899) and *The Octopus* (1901). He published multivolume editions of *The Novels of Jane Austen* (1898) and *The Works of Shakespeare* (1901-1904), edited by W. E. Henley. During the same years appeared the first titles in the Dumpy Books for Children series, including the now infamous *Story of Little Black Sambo* (1899), by Helen Bannerman. Seventy republished works, including Charlotte Brontë's *Jane Eyre* (1901), were featured in the World's Classics series. The Paris Exposition of 1900 included four of Richards's titles: *The Novels of Jane Austen*, Lucas's *Book of Verse for Children* and *The Open Road* (1899), and Wilfred Whitten's *London in Song* (1898).

Yet Richards's judgment was not infallible, and his agreements were sometimes unsound. He declined to publish books for which he saw little demand, including Theodore Dreiser's *Sister Carrie* (1900) and John Millington Synge's *The Aran Islands* (1906). In 1899 he agreed to an unusual, and probably not well-considered, arrangement with Frederick Rolfe (who also used the pseudonym Baron Corvo) to compile a history of the Borgia family. Richards agreed to pay Rolfe £1 per week for not more than seven months during the course of his research, a flat £10 upon publication, and £25 upon the appearance of a second edition, with no other royalties or rights. In August 1900 Rolfe produced a manuscript that Richards's reader criticized substantially. Rolfe responded in a haughty letter that he would make changes in the manuscript but would only allow it to be published under a pseudonym unidentified with him. When the contemporary Count Borgia offered to allow Rolfe to examine the family archives, Rolfe requested 260 guineas for the journey to Italy. Richards was not about to forward such an extravagant sum; fruitless negotiations continued until Richards unexpectedly published the unrevised *Chronicles of the House of Borgia* in October 1901.

It took two years for Richards's business to become profitable. But profits increased between 1899 and 1903, and in 1902 Richards moved his offices to larger quarters at 48 Leicester Square. Notices in the *Publishers' Circular* during these years show Richards toasting his successes at dinners for his staff at the Restaurant Frascati. By 1904, however, increasing debts from heavy borrowing and his own substantial drawings of cash from the business put the firm in serious financial trouble. Bankruptcy proceedings took place in April 1905; Alexander Moring of the De La More Press purchased the firm's remaining assets, and Oxford University Press took over the World's Classics series.

Still in his early thirties, and with plentiful business and literary connections throughout London, Richards lost little time in starting a new publishing venture. He moved to a small office at 7 Carlton Street, and, with his wife, Elisina, as nominal head of the firm (her name appears on contracts from these years), he began publishing as E. Grant Richards. The firm's first book was one of Housman's classical editions, Juvenal's *Satires*, in mid 1905. By 1908 Richards was again publishing under his own name, and in April 1915 he moved his offices to 8 St. Martin's Street.

The ensuing two decades were successful for Richards. His catalogues, with their decorative typography, plentiful illustrations, and literate blurbs, were much more than just lists; they addressed a sophisticated audience. His catalogue for Christmas 1908 advertises the first volumes of Charles Stonham's five-volume *The Birds of the British Islands* (1906-1911) in two expensive gilt editions, and a selection of other "books in beautiful bindings." A 1913 catalogue lists more than three hundred titles in print. The publication for the 1916 Christmas market during World War I of Bruce Bairnsfather's tales of battle experiences, *Bullets and Billets* (dated 1917), was a marketing coup—the book sold tens of thousands of copies. Richards's publications included children's books, works on gardening, cookbooks, art books, biographies, travel books, and literary criticism—but his pride rested on the works of fiction and poetry that launched or furthered the careers of their authors.

Richards was a continual traveler, both to the Continent for pleasure and to the United States on business. On a trip to New York in 1911 he encountered Dreiser, dismal over his then-limited success and over his inability to afford to travel to Europe, where he claimed he

Seven Carlton Street, London, where Richards conducted business from 1905 until April 1915 (painting by Hester Frood; from Grant Richards, Author Hunting, *1934)*

needed to go to absorb a particular milieu for a projected novel. Richards arranged for the Harper and Century companies in New York to fund a several-month-long trip to Europe for Dreiser. He accompanied Dreiser for much of the trip, which Dreiser recounted in *A Traveller at Forty* (published by Century in 1913 and by Richards in 1914).

The name of one of Richards's most important authors appears nowhere in either of the two volumes of his autobiography. James Joyce's offer in 1905 of the manuscript for *Dubliners* elicited from Richards both praise and a sense of caution. Filson Young, his reader at the time, liked it; but Richards, still recovering from financial failure, doubted the commercial viability of books about Ireland and of collections of short stories—and *Dubliners* was both. Yet Richards was intrigued enough by the stories to offer to publish them with no royalty on the first five hundred copies but rights of first refusal for future manuscripts for five years after publication. Joyce agreed to the arrangement.

The beginning of many years of censorship for Joyce began in 1906 when Richards's printers, fearing prosecution for obscenity, refused to print the story "Two Gallants." Richards asked Joyce to lighten sexual innuendoes in "Counterparts" and to remove the word *bloody* from "Grace." Joyce at first objected and then acquiesced, leading only to further objections by Richards, who continued to reiterate his admiration for the stories but also his fear of the public response. Joyce resubmitted *Dubliners* in November 1913, and Richards finally published it in the somewhat relaxed moral climate of 1914. In 1918 Richards published Joyce's play *Exiles*.

Richards's increasing willingness to take risks led him to publish *The Ragged Trousered Philanthropists* (1914). He acquired the manuscript of this novel of the lives of workingmen circuitously through the daughter of the author, a deceased housepainter named Robert Noonan who had used the pseudonym Robert Tressall. The book enjoyed only a minor success in its first few months. But in 1918, when a bookseller in Glasgow advised Richards that a lower price would attract working-class purchasers, he brought out an inexpensive abridged edition that sold many thousands of copies.

As with *Dubliners*, Richards was forced to skirt the obscenity laws in his publication of Thomas Burke's collection of stories of a seedy London Chinatown, *Limehouse Nights* (1916). Though wary of its sexual innuendoes and violence in the wake of the recent prosecution for obscenity of D. H. Lawrence's *The Rainbow* (published by Methuen in 1915), he was convinced of its worth. *Limehouse Nights* was a critical success and became a financial one as well when D. W. Griffith bought the film rights for one thousand pounds and used a story from it, "The Chink and the Child," as the basis for his film *Broken Blossoms* (1919). Burke followed the collection with a novel in a similar vein, *Twinkletoes* (1917).

Richards was able to publish representative works of some of London's most noted authors. His list included two Sitwells—Osbert, with *Out of the Flame* (1923), *Triple Fugue* (1924), and *Discursions on Travel, Art and Life* (1925); and Sacheverell, with *The Hundred and One Harlequins* (1922) and *Southern Baroque Art* (1924). He pub-

lished some eleven books by the prolific Eden Phillpotts, including the poetry collections *Cherry-Stones* (1923), *A Harvesting* (1924), and *Brother Man* (1926). He also published *The Sea Is Kind* (1914) and *Judas* (1923), by T. Sturge Moore, a poet who is now little remembered but was praised at the time by Ezra Pound and Yvor Winters. Alec Waugh's *The Loom of Youth* (1917) was an exposé of public-school life that he wrote while still at school. His long-standing friendship with A. E. Housman no doubt won Richards the publication of Housman's *Last Poems* in 1922. Richards published the first of his own novels, *Caviare*, in 1912; during ensuing years he wrote and published *Valentine* (1913), *Bittersweet* (1915), *Double Life* (1920), and *Every Wife* (1924).

In 1914 Ronald Firbank, having had his manuscript for *Vainglory* rejected by Martin Secker, offered it to Richards. Richards published it in an edition of five hundred copies in April 1915. Except for an early title and a hiatus during which Firbank had two novels published by Brentano's in New York, Richards published all of Firbank's books during the author's lifetime, including *Inclinations* (1916), *Odette: A Fairy Tale for Weary People* (1916), *Caprice* (1917), *Valmouth* (1919), *The Princess Zoubaroff* (1920), *Santal* (1921), *The Flower beneath the Foot* (1923), and *Concerning the Eccentricities of Cardinal Pirelli* (1926). Richards published Firbank's books in small editions and stipulated that Firbank bear production costs. Firbank was intensely interested in the physical appearance of his books and had several illustrated with frontispieces by Augustus John. Despite a flurry of sales in the United States, there was little interest in his work until after his death in 1926. A five-volume collected edition of his works (published in London by Duckworth and in New York by Brentano's in 1929) signaled a continuing demand and vindicated Richards's judgment.

The 13 September 1917 issue of the *Times Literary Supplement* carried the first of Richards's distinctive advertisements. Each week Richards would address his potential readers in a signed half-column of tightly-spaced bold print on the upper right corner of the page. In an easy, familiar manner he would introduce his authors and forthcoming titles, quote reviews, and discuss critical and popular reactions—both pro and con—to his firm's publications.

During these years Richards lived outside of London, commuting by train from Cookham Dean. He and his first wife had divorced, and he

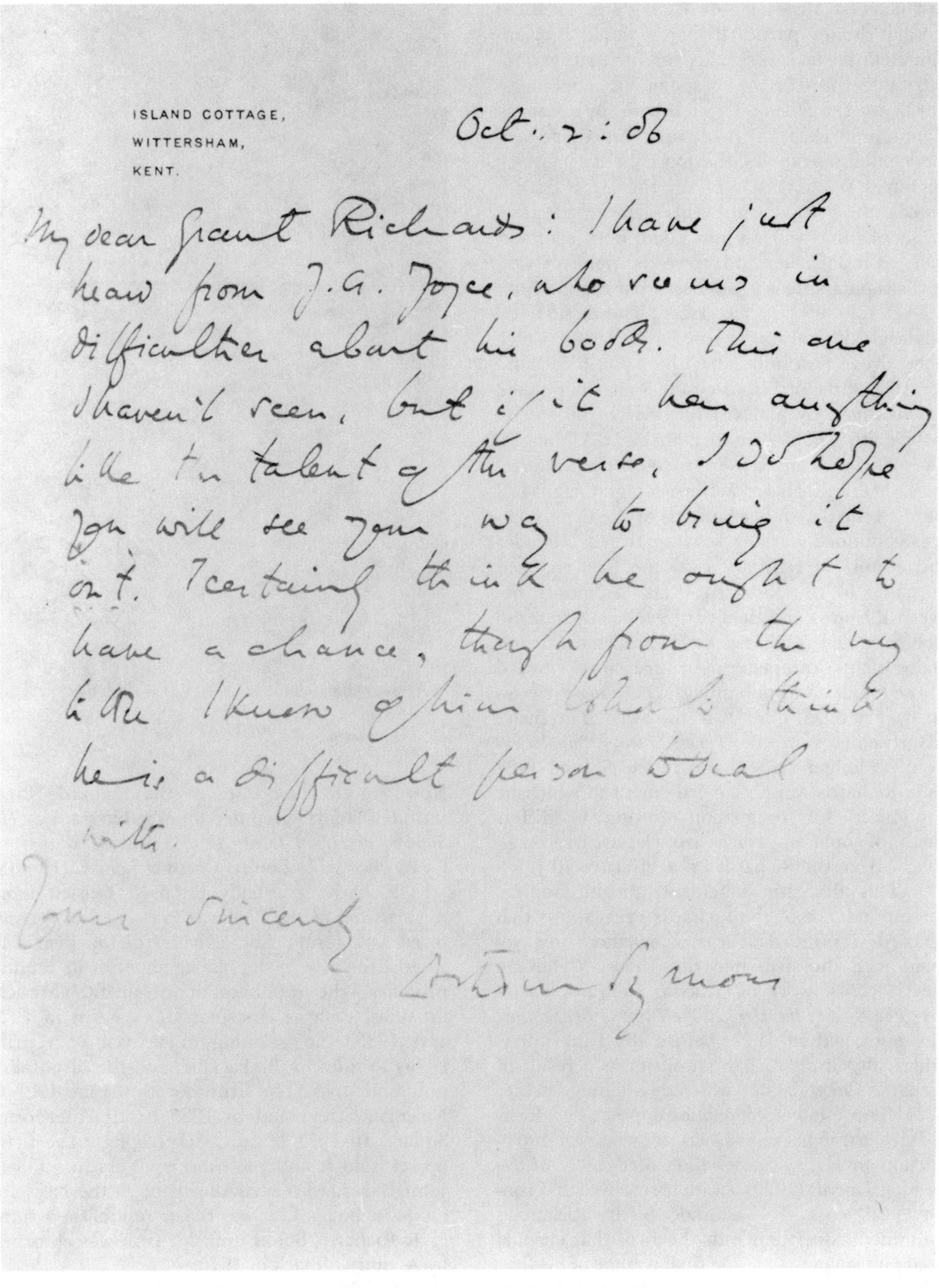

ISLAND COTTAGE,
WITTERSHAM,
KENT.

Oct. 2: 06

My dear Grant Richards: I have just heard from J. G. Joyce, who seems in difficulties about his book. This one I haven't seen, but if it has anything like the talent of the verse, I do hope you will see your way to bring it out. I certainly think he ought to have a chance, though from the very little I know of him what I think he is a difficult person to deal with.

Yours sincerely

Arthur Symons

Letter to Richards from Arthur Symons, who had been urging Richards to publish James Joyce's Chamber Music *and* Dubliners
(Christie's auction catalogue, 7 February 1986)

had married Madeleine de Csanady in 1915. At Sunday dinner parties Richards would mix authors and friends. Sociability for Richards was inextricable from his business—in his autobiography, *Author Hunting* (published by Hamish Hamilton in 1934), he notes that "The more people a publisher knows, the more circles in which he mixes freely, and specially the more friends he has, the greater will be his chance of finding the books that will do him good, both commercially as a publisher and, from the point of view of his reputation, as a judge of what is good."

Despite literary successes, Richards suffered financial difficulties in the mid 1920s which again drove him into bankruptcy. On 6 September 1926 directorship of Grant Richards Limited was assumed by a board headed by Sir Joseph Dobbie (to whom Richards, in his 1941 biography of Housman, spitefully refers as a "dictator"). Maxwell Hicks, as receiver and manager, handled the day-to-day business of the firm; Richards continued working with the firm as a reader and editor. In February 1927 the firm changed its name to the Richards Press. Animosity between Richards and the board grew: in a letter to Dobbie dated 7 February 1927 Richards complains of his "complete subordination to a Board whose literary and publishing experience is necessarily very much inferior to my own." The firm's advertisements in the *Times Literary Supplement* were no longer signed, and in the 9 June 1927 issue Richards ran an advertisement in which he announced his resignation—"owing to differences of opinion which are clearly irreconcilable"—from the Richards Press effective 10 July.

This dramatic statement notwithstanding, correspondence of the Richards Press shows that Richards continued at least a desultory involvement with the firm into the 1930s. Wyndham Lewis's classic work of criticism *The Lion and the Fox: The Role of the Hero in the Plays of Shakespeare* was published in 1927, before the bankruptcy, under the Grant Richards imprint as a result of Richards's negotiations with Lewis dating back to 1925. This established relationship enabled Richards to arrange with Lewis to write an introduction to Henry Somerville's *Madness in Shakespearian Tragedy* (1929), a widely reviewed and controversial work. It was undoubtedly Richards's continued association with the firm that encouraged Housman to have the final volume of his five-volume translation of Manilius's *Astronomicon* published in 1931 by the Richards Press; Richards had begun publishing the translation in 1903.

Richards in 1930

Now-forgotten successes of the Richards Press include Henry Arthur Jones's biography *The Shadow of Henry Irving* (1931) and E. Beresford Chancellor's *The Literary Ghosts of London* (1934).

Richards gradually removed himself from the activities of the Richards Press, and its list suffered as a result. The activities of the firm consisted primarily in the management of its literary property—the republication of profitable backlist titles, such as Housman's *Last Poems* in 1928 and 1933; the granting or refusal of reprint rights to titles in the backlist; and the disposal of unbound stock. The firm moved in June 1927 to Newman Street and in 1935 to 10 Paternoster Square. In 1937 Martin Secker bought the firm; Secker sold it and his Unicorn Press in 1963 to John Baker, who used the firms as the basis for his John Baker Limited. Baker republished some early Richards books until his firm was absorbed by A. and C. Black in 1970.

In 1928, with the financial support of Humphrey Toulmin, Richards bought the Cayme Press. In cooperation with Crosby Gaige at the

Fountain Press in New York the firm published limited editions of several literary titles, as well as Richards's own guide to the French Riviera, *The Coast of Pleasure* (1928). His involvement with the Cayme Press lasted little more than a year. Richards chose to have his novel *The Hasty Marriage* (1928) published by Jonathan Cape rather than the Richards Press.

Through the 1930s and 1940s Richards lived in retirement. He wrote his autobiographical volumes *Memories of a Misspent Youth, 1872-1896* (1932) and *Author Hunting* (1934), and the biography *Housman, 1897-1936*. Apparently with a new publishing venture in mind, Richards wrote in 1947 to the Ministry of Supply and to the Rye House Press in an attempt to buy paper, which was still under postwar restrictions. He traveled to Monte Carlo in August 1947 to recover from a heart attack and died there on 24 February 1948.

References:

Mervyn Horder, "Grant Richards: Portent & Legend," *London Magazine*, 31 (April/May 1991): 36-46;

"Mr. Grant Richards: An Adventurous Publisher [obituary]," *Times* (London), 25 February 1948, p. 7;

"Mr. Grant Richards's Affairs," *Publishers' Circular*, new series 31 (22 April 1905): 434;

Grant Richards, *Author Hunting by an Old Literary Sportsman: Memories of Years Spent Mainly in Publishing, 1897-1925* (London: Hamilton, 1934; New York: Coward-McCann, 1934);

Richards, *Housman, 1897-1936* (London: Oxford University Press, 1941; New York: Oxford University Press, 1942);

Richards, *Memories of a Misspent Youth, 1872-1896* (London: Heinemann, 1932);

Robert Scholes, "Grant Richards to James Joyce," *Studies in Bibliography*, 16 (1963): 139-160;

George Sims, "Grant Richards: Publisher," *Antiquarian Book Monthly Review*, 16 (January 1989): 14-27;

A. J. A. Symons, *The Quest for Corvo: An Experiment in Biography* (New York: Macmillan, 1934).

Papers:

The major collection of letters, account books, announcements, and clippings of reviews and advertisements from Grant Richards's enterprises is in the Rare Book Room at the University of Illinois at Urbana-Champaign. The Special Collections Division of the Georgetown University Library in Washington, D.C., holds manuscripts, letters, photographs, and clippings pertaining to his publishing career. The Grant Richards archives at the University of Illinois are reproduced on seventy-two reels of microfilm by Chadwyck-Healey of Cambridge, England, and Alexandria, Virginia. The Library of Congress holds manuscripts, letters, and other materials relating to Richards's publication of A. E. Housman's works.

—*William S. Brockman*

St. Dominic's Press

(Ditchling, Sussex: 1916-1936)

For twenty years St. Dominic's Press published and printed books, posters, and ephemera concerning philosophy, political economy, art, poetry, Roman Catholic liturgical practices, and local activities in the village of Ditchling, Sussex. Roderick Cave described St. Dominic's as the most private and at the same time the most commercial of the presses founded after the example of William Morris's Kelmscott Press. The diversity of the clientele served by St. Dominic's resulted from the intentions of its founder, Hilary Dominic Clare Pepler, born Harry Douglas Clark Pepler in 1878. Pepler was well aware of Kelmscott, but he hoped to serve a wider public by printing everything from poetry to beer-bottle labels. During the first decade of the twentieth century Pepler was a neighbor of Kelmscott House in Hammersmith. He bought the last batch of handmade Kelmscott paper from Joseph Batchelor, using it for one of his earliest and most praised books, Francis Thompson's *The Mistress of Vision* (1918). Also, Brocard Sewell suggests in *Three Private Presses* (1979) that Pepler's Stanhope handpress may originally have been Morris's.

Pepler developed his knowledge of printing during 1915 and 1916, as seen in four early books. (He was the prime mover behind all four, although they were printed by his friend Gerard T. Meynell at the Westminster Press, and the Hampshire House Workshops was listed as publisher.) Pepler's *The Devil's Devices; or, Control versus Service* (1915) is dedicated to G. K. Chesterton and contains wood engravings by Eric Gill; *Emblems Engraved on Wood* is a separate volume of Gill's wood engravings from *Devil's Devices; A Carol and Other Rhymes* (1915) was produced by the noted calligrapher Edward Johnston; and *Cottage Economy* (1916), by William Cobbett, contains an introduction by Chesterton and diagrams by Gill. This association with Gill, Johnston, and Chesterton led Pepler to move to Ditchling, where Gill and Johnston were already living.

By 1913 a group of artists had gathered in Ditchling under the influence of the socioeconomic theory of distributionism, propounded by Chesterton and Hilaire Belloc. The central tenent of distributionism was that freedom could be safeguarded by having workers own their own tools, workshops, and products. *The Distributionist Program* was printed at St. Dominic's Press for the Distributionist League in 1934.

When Pepler arrived at Ditchling, he was a Quaker. By the end of 1916 he had become a Roman Catholic layman associated with the Dominican Order of priests as a tertiary member, and had changed his name. In 1916 the artisans at Ditchling formed the Guild of St. Dominic and St. Joseph. Pepler's affiliation with the Dominicans was reflected in more than just the name of his press. Dominican influence found expression in the way the workday was organized at Ditchling, in the authors of some of the books he printed, and in the patrons for his liturgical texts. Members of the Ditchling community gathered to sing and pray the Dominican Little Office four times daily.

In 1934 Pepler gave two lectures for the Society of Typographic Arts in Chicago, which were published as *The Hand Press* (1934). In this last book from St. Dominic's Press, Pepler retrospectively outlined his aims as a publisher and his attitude toward printing. He told the Chicago printers that he went to Ditchling to "print books about crafts which machinery threatened with extinction." Some examples are *A Book of Vegetable Dyes* (1916), by Ethel M. Mairet, the weaver in the Ditchling community; *Wood-work* (1918), by A. Romney Green; *Wood Engraving* (1920), by R. John Beedham; and Bernard Leach's *A Potter's Outlook* (1928).

Pepler believed that satisfied workers, simple methods, and good materials produced the best printing. He purposefully chose a kind of printing and a resultant life-style dependent on restricted output as opposed to mass production. The number of copies published by his press was determined by the process of production and its effect on the workers rather than by the pressures of the marketplace. After experiencing the printing process firsthand, he decided to print no more than five hundred copies of anything, because above that number the work became tedious. Pepler felt free to print small numbers of posters for village events; these attracted interna-

Hilary Pepler (center), founder of St. Dominic's Press, with his family in 1921

tional attention, and an exhibition was held in Stockholm in 1922.

Sewell, an early staff member at St. Dominic's Press, recalled that Pepler's printers changed positions at the press so that each would know all of the tasks and avoid the boredom associated with repetition. Besides Pepler and Sewell, the press workers were Pepler's son Mark; Cyril Costick; Truscott Hargrave, who also kept the accounts, handled correspondence, and packed books; and a man always referred to only as "Old Dawes." Dawes learned printing in the 1860s, becoming foreman of the Cape Argus Printing Company pressroom in Cape Town, and by all accounts he was a crucial employee in the early years of St. Dominic's Press. Wood engraving for books and pamphlets was done by Gill, David Jones, Desmond Chute, Philip Hagreen, and Mary Dudley Short. Handmade paper from Joseph Batchelor, Caslon Old Face type from Stephenson Blake and Company, and ink from Mander Brothers or Lorilleux and Bolton gave even the simplest production of the press a well-made appearance.

A major contribution to twentieth-century printing can be observed in one of the significant first editions by St. Dominic's Press, *The Philosophy of Art* (1923), by the French philosopher Jacques Maritain, translated by the Reverend J. O'Connor. This book was the first English translation of Maritain's work. Typographically the book is important because the right-hand margin is not justified. Pepler preferred evenness of word spacing to an even block of type on the page, and he also understood that a ragged right edge aids the reader's eye in distinguishing between the lines. Similar ragged right margins characterize other books from St. Dominic's, including Gill's *Songs without Clothes* (1921). Two important first editions from 1930 printed at the press were James Joyce's short pieces *James Clarence Managan* and *Ibsen's New Drama*, published by the Ulysses Bookshop in London. From 1916 to 1922 St. Dominic's Press produced a magazine, the *Game*, with contributions from Pepler, Gill, and others.

It was in the area of liturgical printing that St. Dominic's Press excelled visually. The *Horae Beatae Virginis Mariae Juxta ritum Sacri Ordinis Praedicatorum* (1923) is displayed in the permanent fine-printing exhibit in the British Museum and described as the "best example of English

Page from Horae Beatae Virginis Mariae Juxta ritum Sacri Ordinis Praedicatorum, *a book of liturgical music published by St. Dominic's Press in 1923*

liturgical music printing extant." This large quarto, printed in red and black, is enhanced with twelve wood engravings by Gill and two by Chute. The most elaborate book from St. Dominic's Press, *Cantica Natalia* (1926), was printed after Gill's departure. The ninety-five copies of this folio volume of twenty Latin carols were printed in red and black with wood engravings (some hand colored) by Chute, David Jones, and Philip Hagreen.

In spite of the appreciation his works received, Pepler was finally unable to compete with automated print shops. He turned over St. Dominic's Press to Mark Pepler, Cyril Costick, and Gerard Falkner in 1936. The new owners moved operations to the center of Ditchling Village, purchased machine-operated presses, and changed the firm's name to the Ditchling Press.

References:

Aylesford Review, "Hilary Pepler Memorial Number," 7, no. 1 (Spring 1965);

Roderick Cave, *The Private Press* (London: Faber & Faber, 1971), pp. 206-208, 266, 358;

Conrad Pepler, O.P., "H.D.C.P.," *Catholic World,* 178 (March 1954): 445-450;

Hilary Dominic Clare Pepler, *The Hand Press* (Ditchling: St. Dominic's Press and Society of Typographic Arts, 1934; new edition, Ditchling: Ditchling Press, 1952);

Will Ransom, *Selective Check Lists of Private Press Books: Part II* (New York: Duschnes, 1946-1950);

Brocard Sewell, O. Carm., *A Descriptive Check List of Books, Pamphlets, Broadsheets, Posters etc. Printed by H. D. C. Pepler at St. Dominic's Press, Ditchling, 1916-1936.* (Ditchling: Ditchling Press, 1979);

Sewell, *Three Private Presses* (London: Skelton, 1979).

—Alice H. R. H. Beckwith

Scholartis Press
(London: 1927-1929)
Eric Partridge at the Scholartis Press
(London: 1929-1931)
Eric Partridge Limited
(London: 1929-1935)

Eric Honeywood Partridge was born on 6 February 1894 at Waimata Valley, New Zealand. He went to Britain to study at Oxford University and later lectured on English at the University of London. In 1927 he abandoned lecturing to set up his own publishing firm, Scholartis Press, without experience and with only one hundred pounds capital. Partridge, later to become a noted lexicographer, explained the firm's name in his *The First Three Years: An Account and a Bibliography of the Scholartis Press* (1930): "The name Scholartis refers to two qualities on which we insist in every reprint: the scholarly and the artistic."

In 1927 Partridge wrote an introduction to *Robert Eyres Landor: Selections from his Poetry and Prose* and edited a volume of Landor's poetry, *Selections from Robert Landor*, both published by Jack Lindsay's Fanfrolico Press. Partridge was later able to publish these titles under the Scholartis Press imprint and was to use the firm to publish his own work, consisting of scholarly research, novels (under the pseudonym of Corrie Denison), and editing or introductions for various reprints. Partridge consciously followed the example of the sixteenth-century scholar-printers, who had been simultaneously editors and publishers.

In September 1927 Scholartis produced its first book, *Ixion in Heaven and Endymion* by Benjamin Disraeli and W. E. Aytoun, edited by Partridge. It was followed by *Poetical Sketches, by William Blake* (1927), with an essay by Lindsay. The press was first located at 18 New Oxford Street, London, moving in October to 5 New Oxford Street. The firm moved again in 1928 to 30 Museum Street, previously the address of Fanfrolico.

Scholartis published both contemporary fiction and scholarly reprints, usually in one or two limited editions; between twenty and thirty titles were brought out each year. The reprints were designed to form a specific literary program, comprising four series: Elizabethan Gallery, Eigh-

Eric Partridge, founder of Scholartis Press

teenth Century Novels, Nineteenth-Century Highways and Byways, and Oriental Bazaar. Uniformly high standards of production were achieved, a few copies being sumptuously produced with handmade paper and autographed. A characteristic device was used for the catalogues: three maidens bearing the caption aspired to by the press, "Liberality, Originality, Distinction."

Scholartis discovered several new writers. Norah Hoult's first work, *Poor Women!* (1928), a collection of short stories that had been rejected by nineteen publishers, received critical acclaim. An early work by H. E. Bates, renowned for his representations of pastoral life, was *Alexander and Seven Tales* (1929). Notable contributions to scholarship were *The Poetry of Sir Thomas Wyatt: A Selection and a Study* (1929), edited by E. M. W. Tillyard, and *The Works of François Villon* (1930), edited by Geoffroy Atkinson.

In 1929 the press became a private company, using the names Eric Partridge Limited for the fiction and Eric Partridge at the Scholartis Press for the reprints. Bertram Ratcliffe joined Partridge as director; Wilson Benington became a director in 1930.

Partridge had served in World War I with the Australian infantry and contributed to a notable autobiographical collection, *Three Personal Records of the War* (1929), along with Ralph Hale Mottram and John Easton. In 1930 Partridge published *The Soul of a Skunk*, by George Baker, the autobiography of a conscientious objector.

In 1929 *Sleeveless Errand*, the first work of Norah C. James, was suppressed shortly before publication on the grounds of immorality. Partridge lost the subsequent court case and was forced to pay legal expenses. This experience occasioned him to write an article defending publishers' rights, "Literary Censorship," for the May 1929 *Controversialist*. An unexpurgated edition of the novel in English was published in Paris later that year and achieved some success, followed by translations into several foreign languages.

By 1930 the press's fortunes were looking precarious because of the Depression. It was at this time that Partridge published *The First Three Years: An Account and a Bibliography of the Scholartis Press*. This self-advertisement is a curious mixture of immodesty and self-deprecation; for example, Partridge thus describes his annotated edition of *Lettres à Malesherbes* (1928), by Jean-Jacques Rousseau: "Now a text-book for the Oxford 'schools' it is fervently hoped that it will become a text-book at other universities and colleges, for there are plenty of copies left." He occasionally claims an unusually symbiotic relationship between an author and the published text; the typography for *The Man of Feeling* (1928), by Henry Mackenzie, is described as "Garamond: a delicate type for a sensitive author."

The *Window*, a quarterly magazine edited by Partridge and Ratcliffe, was published from January to October 1930 and included work by H. E. Bates, Dorothy Richardson, and Edmund Blun-

den. *Songs and Slang of the British Soldier: 1914-1918*, edited by Partridge and John Brophy, appeared in 1930. Brophy was best known for his portrayals of sensitive young soldiers amid the brutality of war. The book was published in a limited edition of fifty copies, but following critical success it was revised and enlarged the following year.

One of the last books Partridge published, *A Classical Dictionary of the Vulgar Tongue* (1931), from the 1796 edition by Francis Grose, ideally suited the publisher's tastes and abilities. Not content with publishing, introducing, and editing it, Partridge wished to rewrite it, his stated aim being "to complete Grose . . . by enriching his entries with contemporary colloquial senses that he omitted or overlooked . . . by rectifying Grose's etymologies and by supplying etymologies to the more interesting words that elicit none from him." This work proved to be one of Partridge's most acclaimed publications, going into three editions. It and *American Tramp and Underworld Slang* (1931), by Godfrey Irwin, with an introduction by Partridge, marked his growing absorption with lexicography.

In December 1931 the press went bankrupt, but *Literary Sessions*, an anthology of Partridge's writings, was published the following year. Partridge went on to a renowned career in lexicography, his works including *Usage and Abusage: A Guide to Good English* published by Hamish Hamilton in 1942. He died on 1 June 1979. In *A Covey of Partridge: An Anthology from the Writings of Eric Partridge* (1937) Partridge wrote that "the slump . . . killed the Scholartis Press (which went out of business in November 1935)." No record, however, has been discovered of the firm's activities after 1932.

References:

Eric Partridge, *A Covey of Partridge: An Anthology from the Writings of Eric Partridge* (London: Routledge, 1937);

Partridge, *Eric Partridge in His Own Words*, edited by David Crystal (London: Deutsch, 1980);

Partridge, *The First Three Years: An Account and a Bibliography of the Scholartis Press* (London: Scholartis Press, 1930).

—Tim Randall

Walter Scott Publishing Company Limited

(London: 1882-1931)

Walter Scott was born in 1826. Despite his name and the fact that he was made a baronet in 1907, he had no connection with the author of the Waverley novels. He received a minimum of formal education, and by 1849 he was in business on his own as a builder and contractor in Newcastle-on-Tyne, soon becoming one of the most successful men of his day in the north of England. By the early 1880s Scott had founded or acquired businesses in the fields of construction, railways, steel manufacture, and coal mining.

The beginning of the Walter Scott Publishing Company Limited is obscure; even the year of commencement is not certain, although it was probably 1882. Scott took over, prior to its impending bankruptcy, the Tyne Publishing Company, which had itself begun from the acquisition of an even more obscure publisher, Adam and Company. Printing and publishing were unexpected and completely new lines of business for Scott.

The Tyne Publishing Company had a printing works in Felling, a district of Newcastle, and a publishing office at 14 Paternoster Square, London. The Tyne Company had only a short list of publications, and at first Scott simply continued to advertise Tyne's titles under his own name. The publishing office moved to 24 Warwick Lane, Paternoster Row, in July 1885. A further move took place in October 1894 to 1 Paternoster Buildings.

To succeed in his new business Scott had to overcome two obstacles: a failing printing and publishing concern had to be revived, and some attention had to be diverted from building, railways, coal mines, and his other business concerns so he could learn the methods of printing and publishing. Scott appears to have solved both problems by delegating the responsibilities to managers.

In September 1883 a reprint line of popular classics was advertised alongside the old Tyne titles. Twenty-seven reprints were listed including *The Pickwick Papers* and *Oliver Twist*, by Charles Dickens; the other Sir Walter Scott's *Ivanhoe*; and Tobias Smollett's *Roderick Random*. Reprints were to become the backbone of Scott's publishing department. This first advertisement does not list the books in a series, but as time went by there were at least fifty named series in Scott's catalogues. Reprints included the Hero, Emerald, and Million series; practical manuals included the Useful Red series; music was offered in the Music Story series. It is now usually impossible to decide in which series a particular book belongs because there is rarely any indication in the book itself, titles were seldom dated, and the same title could appear in more than one series; *Ivanhoe*, for example, was listed in nine separate series.

In 1884 the Canterbury Poets series was announced, with Joseph Skipsey as general editor. Each volume was to be an edition of the work of a particular poet together with a critical introduction, and one volume would be published every month at one shilling. The remarkable Skipsey was apparently a part-time editor; within a few years he had to give up the work due to "lack of leisure." Like Scott, Skipsey had no formal education. At seven he had left school and gone to work in a coal mine. He had taught himself to read and write, practicing with bits of chalk on a trapdoor by the light of a candle in the mine. He had gradually made progress with his education and by 1863 had found work in a library, but an insufficient salary had forced him back down into the mines. He had begun to write poetry, and his early collection *Poems, Songs and Ballads*, had been published by Hamish Hamilton in 1862 (and in a new edition as *Carols, Songs, and Ballads* by Scott in 1888). His writing brought him to the attention of William Morris, Dante Gabriel Rossetti, Sir Edward Burne-Jones, and their circle, and these people tried with only meager success to help him. For the rest of his life Skipsey would move from what appeared to be congenial work—for example, in 1889 he was curator of the Shakespeare Birthplace Trust in Stratford—to working in a coal mine, usually because he could not live on the wages from other jobs. William Sharp took over as editor of the Canterbury Poets series in 1886. In total 113 volumes were published, covering the work of most of the major English and American writers. The series also contained a few translations.

Another major series, the Camelot Classics, made its appearance in February 1886 with Ernest Rhys as the general editor. Rhys was certainly the right man for the job, but he was chosen by mistake, as he explains in his autobiography, *Wales England Wed* (1940). He had already done some work for Scott when Skipsey asked him to edit the works of George Herbert for the Canterbury Poets (the volume was published in 1885). Some months later Rhys received an unexpected call at his London home from "two prosperous-looking men in top hats." They were Scott's representatives, and they offered the editorship of the new series to Rhys; but it became clear in the course of conversation that they thought they were talking to Professor John Rhys, a well-known Celtic scholar. Nevertheless, it was Ernest who got the job.

Camelot Classics was a series of editions of the major works of English prose and translations of important foreign language works. Altogether there were 131 volumes, and the series received praise for its overall balance and careful editing. Without explanation the series changed titles, in May 1887 to the Camelot series and in February 1892 to the Scott Library.

Rhys often chose one of his friends to edit or introduce a particular volume, as William Sharp did for Thomas De Quincey's *Confessions of an English Opium-eater* (1886), Havelock Ellis for Walter Savage Landor's *Imaginary Conversations* (1886), and W. B. Yeats for *Fairy and Folk Tales of the Irish Peasantry* (1888). For certain titles Rhys did not hesitate to approach the author in person, as occurred with the edition of Walt Whitman's *Leaves of Grass*; in this case the direct approach led on to other publications in which original material appeared.

A feature of the Canterbury Poets and Camelot series was that they were well produced and also cheap. Both series began as "shilling monthly volumes." The prospectus for Camelot Classics shows that this was deliberate policy, offering "a comprehensive Prose Library ... cheap, without the reproach which cheapness usually implies.... A complete Prose Library for the People." By 1906 Rhys had left Scott to engage in almost identical work for J. M. Dent as the editor of the Everyman series. Thus it is clear that the Camelot/Scott Library series was the forerunner of Everyman.

Another important series, which ran from 1889 to 1915, was the Contemporary Science series, with Ellis as general editor. Soon after Rhys introduced Ellis to Scott, Ellis put his own ideas for this series to the publisher. He met with no opposition and was given complete freedom. The intention was to deal with the latest advances in all branches of science in terms "an intelligent layman" could understand. The definition of science was broadly based, with a bias toward sociology, anthropology, and psychology. There were forty-eight titles in all, of which the best-seller was Albert Moll's *Hypnotism* (1889), with four separate editions; but the series as a whole was always successful, and it provided Ellis with his main source of income until about 1914.

In addition to Skipsey, Rhys, and Ellis, employed as editors of series, there was also a full-time managing editor, David Gordon. The source of what little information there is on him is Ellis's *My Life* (1940). Ellis mentions that Rhys and Will H. Dircks worked for Scott, with Dircks "in the publishing office." Walter Scott had "chosen a manager and given him fairly full powers. This manager, Gordon, of little education but whom Dircks once described to me as 'a Napoleon of business', quickly made the publishing house ... a great success; he flooded the whole country with good cheap editions of the English classics in prose and verse and was at the same time ready to encourage new ability wherever he could find it...."

Yet another series was the Great Writers, begun in 1887, consisting of forty-four biographies of authors and edited by Eric S. Robertson and Frank T. Marzials. Each volume also contained a bibliography compiled by J. P. Anderson. Most of the subjects were literary figures—Charles Dickens, Charlotte Brontë, Nathaniel Hawthorne, Ralph Waldo Emerson, Victor Hugo, and Johann Wolfgang von Goethe, for example—but biographies of nonliterary authors such as Charles Darwin and Adam Smith were also included.

Scott's publications were not confined to works by British authors. In 1887 the company began to publish translations of Leo Tolstoy's works, and besides the two great novels, *Anna Karenina* (1889) and *War and Peace* (1889), several of his short stories and works of nonfiction appeared. The first to be published was *A Russian Proprietor, and Other Stories* (1887). Other volumes include *Ivan Ilyitch and Other Stories* (1887), *What To Do?* (1888), and *My Religion* (1889). *The Kingdom of God Is Within You*, an "authorised translation" with a new preface by Tolstoy, caused a few problems. The book was due to be published in

1894 when it was discovered that the same work in a different translation was about to be published by William Heinemann. In the ensuing confusion Tolstoy explained that he did not consider it right to accept money for his writing, and therefore he was in the habit of granting permission to print, translate, or use his work in any way to anyone who asked. He had given permission to both Scott and Heinemann, and he had no further interest in the matter. Both companies published their translations of the work in 1894.

Scott's second important translation project concerned the works of Henrik Ibsen—the one achievement for which this publisher has received some slight recognition. The translations began in December 1888 with a volume in the Camelot series containing *The Pillars of Society, Ghosts*, and *An Enemy of Society* (usually translated as *An Enemy of the People*) by three different translators—William Archer, H. F. Lord, and Eleanor Marx—and edited by Ellis. The book sold well, and consequently Archer had no difficulty in persuading Scott to bring out a collected edition of Ibsen's plays in Archer's translation. At this point there was another clash with William Heinemann. Ibsen had agreed to the Scott collected edition, and because of a misunderstanding he had also agreed that Heinemann should have exclusive rights to the English translation of *Hedda Gabler*, thus preventing a true "collected" edition from Scott. In the end Heinemann published *Hedda Gabler* in 1890 but allowed Archer's translation to appear in Scott's edition (1891). As the translations began to be published, interest in Ibsen grew beyond expectations; it is not too much to claim that Scott's edition changed the course of modern English drama.

George Bernard Shaw was a close friend of Archer and a great supporter of Ibsen, and he too was published by Scott. His first novel, *Cashel Byron's Profession*, was originally published in the periodical *To-day* between 1885 and 1886 and then as a book in 1886 by the Modern Press. In 1889 Scott brought out a revised second edition in the Novocastrian Novels series. The following

year Scott republished Shaw's edition of *Fabian Essays in Socialism*. Scott's most important Shaw publication was the first edition in 1891 of *The Quintessence of Ibsenism*.

Works by the Irish novelist George Moore were also published by Scott. Eight of his works appeared between 1893 and 1895, including first editions of *Modern Painting* (1893), *The Strike at Arlington* (1893), *Esther Waters* (1894), and *Celibates* (1895).

A new managing editor, Frederick J. Crowest, was appointed in the early years of the twentieth century. Before joining Scott, Crowest had written several books on music, and he introduced the Music Story series in 1902 with Annie W. Patterson's *The Story of Oratorio*. Over the next years a total of fifteen titles appeared.

One new series on music, however, was not sufficient to revive the firm's flagging fortunes. Scott died in 1910, and almost immediately afterward a decision was made to sell the publishing company. Finding a buyer proved difficult, and publishing activities were left in limbo for many years. Some of the stock was sold to Simpkin Marshall and some to William Reeves, but the majority seems to have been sold as waste paper. Liquidation proceedings dragged on and on, and the company was not finally dissovled until 1931.

It is difficult to explain why such a dynamic publishing house lost its way. Crowest was not as strong a leader as Gordon, but in any case, the impetus seems to have gone before Crowest was appointed. Similarly, it is not easy to understand why in later years the publisher of Ibsen, Tolstoy, Bernard Shaw, and George Moore should have been so neglected.

References:

Havelock Ellis, *My Life* (London: Heinemann, 1940);

Ernest Rhys, *Wales England Wed* (London: Dent, 1940).

　　　　　　　　　　　　　　　　—John R. Turner

Martin Secker
(London: 1910-1917)
Martin Secker Limited
(London: 1917-1935)

Martin Secker was born in 1882. A legacy of £1000 enabled him to enter publishing in 1908. He made unsuccessful approaches to three publishers before coming to an agreement to learn the trade under James Eveleigh Nash. After eighteen months he removed his premium to found his own business at "Number Five John Street Adelphi," as it was printed on his title pages. He rented the ground floor and basement for £110 a year, later taking the second floor, too. In 1916 the novelist Rafael Sabatini became a partner in the firm, which became Martin Secker Limited the following year. Sabatini was replaced after World War I by Percival Presland Howe, who had been a reader for Eveleigh Nash when Secker was there. Howe remained with the firm until the end, having the formal standing of director. He shared with Secker a strong interest in contemporary theater, and his five books were all published by Secker.

Secker's publishing house, though small, is in the front rank of twentieth-century literary publishers. The literature of the 1890s, which attracted him in his youth, informed his judgments as a publisher. His first general list of nine titles earned the congratulations of the *Publishers' Circular* (17 September 1910) and exemplified Secker's breadth of reading and his commitment to the production of aesthetically pleasing books. Secker regarded *Old English Houses: The Record of a Random Itinerary* (1910), by Allan Fea, as his first book. A work by Arthur Ransome, *Edgar Allan Poe: A Critical Study* (1910), was the first in a Critical Studies series.

Martin Secker, 1912 (photograph by E. O. Hoppé)

Secker's first fiction list, announced for publication in early 1911, included a new writer, Compton Mackenzie. Secker had read the manuscript of Mackenzie's romance of eighteenth-century life, *The Passionate Elopement* (1911), while he was with Nash and had recommended publication but had been overruled. After setting up on his own, he tracked down the still-unpublished manuscript, which justified his judgment by the reviews and by the sales; he was able to claim it as the best reviewed of any modern novel. Mackenzie volunteered to put his royalties into advertising the book, and Secker contributed his profits. Advertisements were placed in the elevators of selected London Underground stations, an innovation in advertising books. Within six months of publication, sales in Britain, America, and the colonies reached more than twenty-two hundred copies. This six-shilling edition continued to sell into the 1920s, by which time total net sales had more than doubled. A two-shilling edition had sold more than forty-eight hundred copies by 1919.

Secker's contract with Mackenzie was made through the Authors' and Playwrights' agency on the basis of English royalties of 10 percent for one thousand copies, 12 1/2 percent for the next five hundred, and 15 percent thereafter; colonial royalties were at 10 percent and American royalties at 15 percent. Secker paid royalties of this order to most of his authors, with whom he sustained good working relationships either directly or through literary agencies. More than a half century later, *The Passionate Elopement* was shown in a national Book League exhibition as an example of how Secker improved the appearance of the six-shilling novel. Sales of Mackenzie's two-volume *Sinister Street* (1913-1914) were clearly not diminished by the ban imposed by the libraries. Secker was anxious, nonetheless, about the risk in publishing Mackenzie's *Extraordinary Women* (1928) in the wake of the prosecution of *The Well of Loneliness* (published in 1928 by Jonathan Cape), by Radclyffe Hall, but agreed to an expensive limited edition; the title page stated that the type had been broken up. The Home Office decided against prosecution.

Secker's early titles included works by published authors whom he had met while with Nash; one was Oliver Onions's collection of ghost stories, *Widdershins* (1911); Secker thought Onions to be an unjustly neglected novelist. By the end of Secker's first decade he had published the fiction of Sabatini, Laurence North, Frederick Niven, Christopher Stone, Viola Meynell, Hugh Walpole, Eric and Francis Brett Young, Phyllis Bottome, Gilbert Cannan, Norman Douglas, and Frank Swinnerton. Cannan's *Round the Corner* (1913) was banned by the libraries, and Secker took out advertisements to defend it; sales had reached nearly five thousand copies when it was sold to T. Fisher Unwin in 1917. Almost all the copies of Walpole's *The Dark Forest* (1916) were destroyed by fire at the binders a few days before

publication and had to be reprinted. Swinnerton considered his *Nocturne* (1917) the first of the novels of concentrated time and chance meetings; it was stimulated by Secker's request that he write a novel of only fifty thousand words. On the verso of the title page is an explanation of the eleventh-hour title change from "In the Night," which remains the running title. Between 1915 and 1919 Secker published a uniform edition of tales by Henry James.

The poetry published in Secker's first decade included works by Ford Madox Hueffer, James Elroy Flecker, and T. W. H. Crosland, and *Poems 1914-1917* (1918), by Maurice Baring. Twice as many copies of the last were sold as of D. H. Lawrence's *New Poems* (1918), which Secker published in a first edition of five hundred copies.

The Critical Studies series dealt mainly with the works of late-nineteenth-century writers. The second in the series, *Oscar Wilde: A Critical Study*, was written by Ransome. Within a month of its publication on 14 February 1912 Ransome was lured by Charles Granville, who traded as Stephen Swift, to transfer the rights of his published work from Secker for immediate pecuniary gain. On the day after Secker agreed to sell his rights to Ransome's books on Poe and Wilde, Lord Alfred Douglas caused writs to be served with respect to the Wilde work on Secker, Ransome, and others. Secker, although the original publisher, no longer had any rights to the book and successfully negotiated with Douglas to have the writ against him be withdrawn. The Secker production ledger records that sometime in 1911 or 1912 two advances of one hundred pounds each were paid to Douglas for a book to be called "The Wilde Myth"; the work was set in type but never published. In 1919 Secker purchased from Grant Richards the stock and rights of Douglas's *The City of Soul* (1899), enabling him to republish it as *The Collected Poems of Lord Alfred Douglas* (1919); but few copies were sold. Further volumes in the Critical Studies series included *William Morris: A Critical Study* (1912), by John Drinkwater; *Thomas Hardy: A Critical Study* (1912), by Lascelles Abercrombie; and *Fyodor Dostoevsky: A Critical Study* (1916), by John Middleton Murry.

A series of a different character was launched in 1913 under the title John Street Booklets. The first of these sixpenny booklets was *Malthus and the Publishing Trade*, a reprinted article by P. P. Howe. Within was announced the second in the series, *Poetry and the Modern Novel*, by Mac-

THE
WILDE MYTH

BY LORD ALFRED DOUGLAS

This is to certify that this is the only remaining set of proofs of this book: it contains the Author's final corrections. No copies were ever printed, and the type was distributed.

Martin Secker

LONDON
M A R T I N   S E C K E R
NUMBER FIVE JOHN STREET
ADELPHI

Title page for the only set of proofs for a book that Secker refused to publish in 1916, after he and Douglas argued over revisions

kenzie, presumably to be a reprint of the article of the same title. No copy of the second booklet has been found, and the series was probably aborted.

In 1914 Secker launched a series devoted to literary criticism, The Art and Craft of Letters. Whereas the Critical Studies editions were sold at seven shillings and sixpence, the little Art and Craft of Letters books were sold for one shilling and aimed at a much wider market; the first title had a print run of five thousand copies. Secker paid Abercrombie twenty-five pounds for the copyright to *The Epic*, the work that led the series. Basil de Selincourt's *Rhyme* (1914) appears to have been the first in the series for which the copyright was not bought outright for about twenty pounds; it was negotiated on a royalty basis. For most of the titles Secker secured distinguished scholars such as Frank Sidgwick, who wrote *The Ballad* (1915).

Independently of any series, Secker published works of literary criticism, many by Abercrombie; the critic R. A. Scott-James came onto his list first in 1913 with *Personality in Literature*. Secker's travel books were aesthetically pleasing,

examples of belles lettres rather than guides. Norman Douglas first came onto Secker's general list with his book about Tunisia, *Fountains in the Sand* (1912), but it was his unique near-novel *South Wind* (1917) that attracted more critical attention.

Secker developed a list of drama and dramatic criticism, although it did not reach the distinction of his fiction list. In 1913 he published in association with Ben Huebsch the first four volumes of the authorized edition of *The Dramatic Works of Gerhart Hauptmann*, edited by Ludwig Lewisohn. Hauptmann had won the Nobel Prize for literature in 1912. In 1913 Secker published cheap editions of G. K. Chesterton's *Magic: A Fantastic Comedy*.

Secker's early excursion into magazine publishing was short-lived. In November 1912 he took over *Rhythm: Art, Music, Literature*, the ailing periodical edited by Murry. It survived as a monthly until March 1913. In May it was transformed into a quarterly, the *Blue Review: Literature, Art, Drama, Music*; only three numbers were published.

By 1920 Secker had sixty-five authors on his list and 143 titles, of which 47 were fiction. In that year there was apparently some suggestion that D. H. Lawrence and Mackenzie might become partners in Secker's house. Mackenzie could see, however, that Secker was apprehensive about an arrangement that would give Mackenzie a one-third share in the house in exchange for all his books, and nothing came of the idea.

Secker's notable achievement in the 1920s was to acquire Lawrence's fiction, which he had sought in 1911, and to publish English translations of works by European authors who were little known in England. The first of Lawrence's novels to be published by Secker, *The Lost Girl* (1920), won the James Tait Black Memorial Prize. Secker undertook *Women in Love* (1921), which had been refused by other publishers, and, with some reluctance, *The Rainbow*, which its previous publisher, Methuen, had had to suppress in 1915. Secker made publication of *The Rainbow* in 1926 conditional upon there being no legal action against *Women in Love*. Philip Heseltine complained that he was libeled in *Women in Love*; some changes were made to the offending passages, and—to Lawrence's annoyance—Secker paid Heseltine fifty pounds in compensation. These titles were, as a matter of policy, highly priced at nine shillings each. Secker continued to publish Lawrence's work until the author's death in 1930.

Writers who joined Secker's list in the 1920s included Robert Graves, Conrad Aiken, Edna St. Vincent Millay, Arthur Symons, John Dos Passos, and Noel Coward. Secker's contract with John Gunther for *The Red Pavilion* (1926) included an option on Gunther's next two novels. In 1923 Secker published Jane Austen's novels in seven volumes, beginning with *Lady Susan and The Watsons*. His drama list, too, was extended by cheap reprints of works within the literary canon: John Gay's *The Beggar's Opera*, (1920), William Congreve's *The Way of the World*, (1924), and Richard Brinsley Sheridan's *The Duenna* (1924). Secker published the *Complete Poems* (1925) of Emily Dickinson; only ninety-three copies at twenty-one shillings each had been sold by 1928.

J. C. Squire edited three highly salable volumes: *Selections from Modern Poets* (1921), *Second Selections from Modern Poets* (1924), and *Younger Poets of To-day* (1932). The 1924 volume announced that its predecessor had reached the "12th thousand." Sales of *Modern American Poets* (1922), edited by Aiken, reached only 831 by 1935. The production ledger notes that the volumes were published on the basis of half profits to authors.

Secker introduced Thomas Mann's *Buddenbrooks* to English readers in a translation by H. T. Lowe-Porter in 1924, nearly a quarter of a century after its first publication in German. He published *Jew Suss* by Lion Feuchtwanger in a translation by Edwin and Willa Muir in 1926, one year after the first German edition, acquiring the English rights through Ben Huebsch. *Jew Suss* was a best-seller from the first; by March 1928 sales were 54,685, turning a profit of £8000. In 1928 Secker brought out another winner in Arnold Zweig's *The Case of Sergeant Grischa*, the second novel in a trilogy written in 1926-1927; a translation fee of £150 was paid to Eric Sutton. By 1932 sales reached 37,259, with a profit of about £3000. For translations of *Thérèse Desqueyroux* (1928), by François Mauriac; *Steppenwolf* (1929), by Hermann Hesse; Franz Kafka's *The Castle* (1930); and Hermann Broch's trilogy *The Sleepwalkers* (1933), he paid fees totaling about £470. By 1935 the trading balance on the four titles showed a loss of about £300.

The New Adelphi Library, Secker's reprint series, was launched in 1925. Most titles reached sales of 1000 or 2000 by 1935 and returned a small profit. The reprint of *South Wind* (1927) by Norman Douglas sold 15,988 copies. Fifty-five titles were in print when Secker sold out. In 1935 there were five titles in print in another series, Fa-

Secker and D. H. Lawrence in Spotorno, Italy,
January 1926

mous Fiction, with copies selling at three shillings and sixpence each.

In the 1930s the literary strength of Secker's house continued to lie in the translations from European authors and the works of Lawrence. In 1932, four years after Lawrence had written to Secker that he was "expurgating" *Lady Chatterley's Lover*, Secker published the authorized British edition. The works of Lawrence did not attract as many readers as hoped, and Secker sold the rights to Heinemann in 1934. This did not avert the financial collapse that had been threatening for several years.

The decline of Secker's publishing house is indicated by comparison of a stock valuation dated 31 December 1925 with the final sale price of the business in 1935. The 1925 summary valued trading stock at £7,846. In 1935 the business was sold for £3,100. The solvency of the house was in doubt when the printing bill for *The Tales of D. H. Lawrence* (1934) could not be met. A first printing of 10,000 copies in 1934 was in fact sold within a year, but it was only by Walter Hutchinson's goodwill that the printer's bill was deferred. In the 1930s Secker had to pay substantial advances to retain Feuchtwanger, and the three-shilling-and-sixpenny edition of *The Oppermanns*, of which 6,610 were printed in June 1934, barely broke even. In April 1935 the Feuchtwanger titles were sold to Hutchinson.

In its final year Martin Secker Limited published 5,500 copies of *The Tales of Elinor Mordaunt*, along with a similarly high print run of a three-shilling-and-sixpence edition of Compton Mackenzie's novels. For May 1935 the ledger shows first printings of 5,000 copies of each of the first six titles in a new two-shilling-and-sixpenny fiction series; by October 1935 about 500 copies of each had been sold. A valuation of quire and bound stock made on 31 March 1935 and updated to 1 October 1935 amounted to £5,471. Martin Secker Limited was placed in the hands of a liquidator, owing creditors about £5000. Hutchinson and a partnership of Fredric Warburg and Roger Senhouse made identical sealed bids of £3000 by the due date of 15 March 1936. Warburg was present when the bids were opened and raised his to £3,100, which was accepted.

Together with published stock, Warburg had bought the manuscript of *Clochemerle* (1936), by the unknown Gabriel Chevallier, which proved to be a best-seller and could have made Secker solvent again if he had been able to trade on for another few months. Howe did not join the new firm, Secker and Warburg. Secker himself, who stayed on in charge of production, remained only two years.

References:

Mervyn Horder, "Conversations with Martin Secker," *Times Literary Supplement*, 10 December 1976, pp. 1565-1566;

Horder, "Last Conversations with Martin Secker," *London Magazine*, new series 18 (December 1978 / January 1979): 93-104;

Horder, "Martin Secker," *Blackwood's Magazine*, 325 (February 1979): 126-131;

D. H. Lawrence, *Letters from D. H. Lawrence to Martin Secker 1911-1930* (Bridgefoot, U.K.: Privately printed, 1970);

"No. 5, John Street," *Publisher's Circular*, 42 (17 September 1910): 339;

Martin Secker, "Publisher's Progress," *Cornhill Magazine*, 1076 (Summer 1973): 20-32;

Secker, "Publisher's Progress: 2," *Cornhill Magazine*, 1079 (Spring 1974): 256-263;

George Malcolm Thomson, *Martin Secker & Warburg: The First Fifty Years* (London: Secker & Warburg, 1986).

Papers:

The Archives of Martin Secker Limited are in the library of the University of Reading.

—Dorothy W. Collin

Martin Secker and Warburg Limited
(London: 1936-   )

In 1935 Fredric Warburg, who had recently been fired by Georg Routledge and Sons, noticed that the small, distinguished firm of Martin Secker had gone bankrupt. With one thousand pounds borrowed from an aunt and three thousand pounds supplied by Roger Senhouse, he made an offer; Secker eventually sold the firm to Warburg and Senhouse on 15 March 1936 for thirty-one hundred pounds. The working capital of eighty-three hundred pounds came from friends of Senhouse; Secker stayed on in charge of production for two years. He died in 1978.

Warburg had a radical streak: he set out to publish both unusual novels and antifascist, anticommunist, anticonservative nonfiction. Thirteen of the seventeen books published in the first year were novels, including *Clochemerle* (1936), by Gabriel Chevallier. After more than twenty thousand copies had been sold in hardback, *Clochemerle* was brought out in a cheaper Penguin edition, and its continued success helped to make up for Secker and Warburg's early overspending on advertisements. Nevertheless, on a gross of £7,618, the firm sustained a net loss of £3,283 in 1936-1937, made good by a loan from Warburg's banking family.

Up to 1939 Secker and Warburg published more than thirty left-wing books, including *World Revolution, 1917-1936: The Rise and Fall of the Communist International* (1937), by the Trinidadian Trotskyist writer C. L. R. James; *Back from the U.S.S.R.* (1937), by André Gide, of which forty-five hundred copies were sold in six months; and *Homage to Catalonia* (1938), by George Orwell, of which the first impression was still in print when Orwell died in 1950. Orwell's *Road to Wigan Pier*, originally published in 1937 by Victor Gollancz, was reprinted in 1959 by Secker and Warburg with his earlier, relatively unsuccessful novels.

Fredric Warburg, who joined with Roger Senhouse to buy the bankrupt firm of Martin Secker in 1936

During the 1930s Warburg also managed to lure H. G. Wells, who boasted that no publisher made money on his books. After Wells's *The Fate of Homo Sapiens* (1939) sold thirteen thousand copies and reduced the firm's losses by half, the firm published eight of Wells's last ten books, among them *All Aboard for Ararat, Babes in the Darkling Wood,* and *The New World Order* (all 1940); *You Can't Be Too Careful* (1941); and *The Outlook for Homo Sapiens* and *Phœnix* (both 1942).

Two books published in 1938 were to prove their value during the postwar revival of interest in Africa and in town planning: *Facing Mount Kenya: The Tribal Life of the Gikuyu*, by Jomo Kenyatta, who finally became president of an independent Kenya, and *The Culture of Cities*, by Lewis Mumford, the American urban historian. In three years, the first had sold only 517 copies; the other 983 were destroyed by bombs in 1941. The book was profitably reprinted during the Mau Mau emergency in the early 1950s. One thousand copies of Mumford's book were bought from Harcourt Brace; a cheaper edition of 2,650 copies appeared in December 1940, when the blitz concentrated British minds on problems of rebuilding. By 1959 seventeen thousand copies of the book had been sold.

Like all other publishers, Secker and Warburg suffered from a paper shortage during World War II. In 1939 the Board of Trade worked out the average tonnage of paper used by each firm in the "reference period" 1936, 1937, and 1938. Beginning on 31 March 1940, the board allocated 60 percent of the average as the paper ration for each firm. When Norway and Denmark were invaded, two prime sources of wood pulp for British paper disappeared, and the ration dropped to 30 percent. It rose to 60 percent in June 1940 but fell to 50 percent later. Secker and Warburg could draw on extra paper it had sent to Plymouth for safekeeping in 1939. At first, therefore, the shortage was not deeply felt. But in March 1941 the Plymouth premises of William Brendon, where the additional paper was stored, were badly damaged in two air raids; all unused paper and 150,000 books in sheets went up in flames. Yet even this ironic catastrophe failed to subdue the firm: Secker and Warburg received help from an Edinburgh printing firm that had laid in almost three thousand tons of paper against just such a crisis. As the war progressed, the shortage became even more acute until, in 1945, the Board of Trade made no provision at all for publishers. Because the rationing system lasted until 1949, many firms experienced real difficulties well into the peacetime years.

In the hope of reducing overhead costs, Secker and Warburg began in 1940 to employ the Book Centre created by Sir Isaac Pitman and Sons for invoicing and distribution. After Sunday, 29 December 1940—when the heart of the London book trade in Paternoster Row near St. Paul's Cathedral was smashed by bombs—the wholesalers Simpkin Marshall, on which many firms depended for a distribution service, no longer existed. The air raid destroyed six million books in a single night. Until 1941 Secker and Warburg found profits elusive. There was a loss of £3,197 in 1938, of £3,766 in 1939, and £2,159 in 1940. The firm could not even afford to evacuate the four flimsy rooms it occupied on the top floor of 22 Essex Street, however desirable such a move might have seemed during the blitz.

The radical tone of Secker and Warburg publishing was, if anything, intensified by war. The firm continued to support writers with revolutionary, even eccentric, views. One of these writers, T. R. Fyvel, suggested a series of Searchlight Books on the future of Britain. From February 1941 to March 1942 ten titles were published in the series, among them Orwell's *The Lion and the Unicorn: Socialism and the English Genius* (1941), offering a six-point program of social reform that probably influenced the Labour government of 1945. Another Searchlight title, *The English at War* (1941), by Cassandra (the *Daily Mirror* columnist W. N. Connor), sold thirty thousand copies in six months. The Scottish science writer Ritchie Calder, the drama critic T. C. Worsley, the poet Stephen Spender, and the novelist Joyce Cary, all in their different spheres, tapped a radical vein in British opinion. Books and authors such as these, as well as the wartime hunger for reading of any sort, lifted the firm out of the doldrums. In 1941 it actually showed a small profit of £440; in 1942 and 1943 the profits were substantial.

Secker and Warburg feared that its popular authors would move to other firms with more paper. Warburg led a group of small publishers in a campaign to improve the allocation, but the so-called Moberley Pool gave 250 tons of extra paper to the Publishers' Association only to reprint scarce scientific, technical, and cultural books seldom to be found on the Secker and Warburg list. Therefore, the firm did lose authors in the six years of war. Nevertheless, some significant writers stayed. The American literary critic Edmund Wilson contributed *To the Finland Station* (1941), on the history of Marxist-inspired revolutionary theory, and *The Wound and the Bow* (1942), on the Freudian element in modern literature. The writer on social administration Richard Titmuss; the French-born American scholar Jacques Barzun; the biologist, philosopher, and expert on William Blake, Jacob Bronowski; and the novelist and historian John Prebble all helped to establish the firm's adventurous reputation in this period.

Its later prosperity owed most perhaps to Orwell, a personal friend of Warburg. They served

together (Warburg as a corporal, Orwell as a sergeant) in the same unit of the Home Guard. Between November 1943 and February 1944, Orwell wrote *Animal Farm*. It was rejected by Victor
Gollancz, Jonathan Cape, and Faber and Faber,
partly on account of its brevity (it was only thirty
thousand words long) and partly because it attacked Britain's ally, the Soviet Union, which Orwell had come to mistrust during the Spanish
Civil War. He offered the book to Secker and Warburg at the end of July 1944, and it was accepted
within a month. The paper shortage held up publication for a year, and it appeared in August
1945 in an edition of 4,500 copies. Within days it
was out of print. As a Book of the Month Club
choice it sold 460,000 copies from 1946 to 1949.
More than five million copies were sold in the
New American Library series, and it continues to
sell in that series at the rate of 350,000 copies a
year. Three million copies have been sold in the
United Kingdom; 140,000 copies a year are sold
in paperback. Foreign-language rights have been
extensively sold.

The war did not dampen Secker and Warburg's interest in publishing original work by foreign writers. Thomas Mann's *Lotte in Weimar*
(1940) and *Joseph the Provider* (1945) helped to
maintain Mann's reputation in Britain. A more
surprising success was the establishment of Franz
Kafka as an author of world importance. Martin
Secker had acquired the British rights to Kafka's
The Castle (1926) and a collection of short stories
called *The Great Wall of China* (1933), but two-
thirds of the editions of fifteen hundred copies
each that Secker had printed were still unsold
when the new firm took them over in 1936.
Senhouse hoped to publish a collected edition of
Kafka's works in the translation by Edwin Muir,
but this scheme seemed too ambitious in the later
1930s. The firm did, however, reprint *The Castle*
just before the war. Rights to *The Trial* (1925),
strangely prescient of Bolshevik interrogations,
were bought from Gollancz; rights to *America*
(1927) from Routledge; and rights to *Metamorpho-
sis* (1937) from the Parton Press. It proved, however, hard to discover—even from Kafka's literary executor Max Brod—who owned the copyrights. Eventually, an agreement was reached to
publish Kafka's complete works in English in conjunction with the Schocken Publishing House Limited of Tel Aviv.

In August 1944, having escaped damage
thus far, the Secker and Warburg premises in
Essex Street were destroyed by a bomb; the care-

*Roger Senhouse (portrait by Clemence Dane; The Stone
Gallery, Burford)*

taker was killed. After camping out in the offices
of W. H. Allen in the same road, and in rooms
loaned by Pitman near Kingsway, the firm moved
in 1945 to 7 John Street, Bloomsbury.

Despite upheavals, and the constant shortage of paper, Secker and Warburg seemed likely
to continue the prosperity of 1942 to 1944 into
the postwar years. In 1946 David Farrer, who
had studied at Oxford and had worked for
Odhams Press before the war, came into the firm
from Beaverbrook Newspapers. He was made a director within a year. His first great discovery was
Defeat in the West, by Milton Shulman, which
Secker and Warburg published to substantial success on 17 April 1947. Based on Shulman's interrogations of German generals, the book gave English readers a picture of the war from the
enemy's point of view.

Secker and Warburg both maintained and extended its publishing of Continental authors
after the war. Hoping to repeat the success of
Chevallier's *Clochemerle*, the firm brought out his
Sainte-Colline in 1946, but with less gratifying results. When Jean-Paul Sartre's existentialism became fashionable in the late 1940s, a British
market opened for the work of his friend and con-
sort Simone de Beauvoir, which the firm began

to publish in 1948. The year before, the Italian writer Alberto Moravia figured on its list for the first time, with *The Fancy Dress Party*. His unique brand of Latin eroticism was popular with English readers. There followed *The Woman of Rome* (1949), *The Conformist* (1952), *The Time of Indifference* (1953), *Roman Tales* (1956), and *Two Women* (1958), which helped to compensate for the isolation of Italy during and immediately after the war.

Sales of Gide's works predictably improved after his receipt of the Nobel Prize in 1947. Four volumes of his *Journals* were published by the firm between 1947 and 1951, and his *Strait Is the Gate* (first published in 1924) came out in 1948. Another French writer of Gide's generation, Sidonie-Gabrielle Colette, enjoyed a delayed popularity in Britain during this period. The firm brought out *Chéri* (first published in 1920) in 1951, and there followed more than a dozen novels, including the autobiographical Claudine series.

Of writers in German, Mann continued to be the most distinguished on the Secker and Warburg list up to his death in 1955. *Essays of Three Decades* (1947) was followed by *Dr. Faustus* (1949) and *The Confessions of Felix Krull, Confidence Man* (1955); the latter sold twelve thousand copies in its first few months. As Mann's writing career was coming to an end the Austrian author Robert Musil began to attract English readers. The suggestion that Secker and Warburg should publish his work came from Ernst Kaiser, a Jewish refugee from Vienna who, with his wife Eithne Wilkins, undertook the translation. A 1949 article in the *Times Literary Supplement* created great interest in Musil. Secker and Warburg published *Young Törless* in 1955 and *Tonka and Other Stories* in 1965, but Musil's huge novel *The Man without Qualities*, begun in the early 1930s, made his reputation. The firm published volume one in 1953, volume two in 1954, and volume three in 1960. The fourth and final volume was incomplete when the translators died.

The year of the discovery of Musil, 1949, was perhaps the high point of Secker and Warburg publishing. The firm published volume two of *The Diaries of Franz Kafka*, having published volume one in 1948. Kafka's *America* was reprinted, and his *In the Penal Settlement* came out for the first time in English. Orwell's *Nineteen Eighty-Four*, a more savage and terrifying satire than *Animal Farm*, appeared in June. A reprint of his novel *Coming up for Air* (first published in 1939) came

out in 1948. The immediate success of *Nineteen Eighty-Four* led to the reprinting of *Burmese Days* (1934) and *Down and Out in Paris and London* (1933), and the publication of *Shooting an Elephant and Other Essays* (1950). Antiauthoritarianism and the plain, direct style of these books suited the atmosphere of Britain in the late 1940s. *Nineteen Eighty-Four* received a first printing of 26,000 copies; frequent reprints followed. It still sells at the rate of 150,000 copies a year. Orwell died in London in 1950; the authorized *George Orwell: A Life* (1981), by Bernard Crick, was published by Secker and Warburg.

Angus Wilson was one of Secker and Warburg's most significant postwar discoveries. His *The Wrong Set, and Other Stories* (1949); *Such Darling Dodos, and Other Stories* (1950); and his first novel, *Hemlock and After* (1952), revealed a delicate gift for satire and good writing. *The Wrong Set*, almost unprecedentedly for a short-story collection, sold five thousand copies in its first year; the novel sold nearly twelve thousand copies. Secker and Warburg also published his *Anglo-Saxon Attitudes* (1956) and *The Middle Age of Mrs. Eliot* (1958), and an acclaimed critical study, *The World of Charles Dickens* (1970).

In 1953 the firm faced a charge of obscene libel for publishing *The Philanderer*, by Stanley Kauffmann. The verdict of not guilty, based on the principle that a book has to be read and judged as a whole and not on the alleged obscenity of its parts, influenced the Obscene Publications Act of 1959 and the test case on the Penguin Books publication of D. H. Lawrence's *Lady Chatterley's Lover* (1928) in 1960.

Since the mid 1950s the firm has published Japanese books, including *The Sound of Waves* (1957), by Yukio Mishima, and *Snow Country* (1957), by Yasunari Kawabata, who was awarded the Nobel Prize in 1968. Japanese writing continued to appear on the Secker and Warburg list into the 1980s. In 1976 the firm undertook a reprint of Murasaki Shikibu's *The Tale of Genji*, originally published in six volumes by Allen and Unwin from 1925 to 1933. The profits on these books were modest.

The firm sustained its reputation by publishing the work of prizewinning authors apart from Kawabata. One of the most notable was Heinrich Böll, Nobel Prize winner for 1972. His books, from *Group Portrait with Lady* (1973) to *What's to Become of the Boy?* (1985), all came out under the Secker and Warburg imprint. *Humboldt's Gift* by Saul Bellow appeared in 1975, the year before he won the Nobel Prize. The award encouraged the firm to bring out *The Dean's December* (1982) and *Him with His Foot in His Mouth and Other Stories* (1984). In 1977 *In the Heart of the Country* introduced a South African writer, J. M. Coetzee, who, after two other novels, won the Booker Prize with *Life and Times of Michael K.* (1983). An author of "campus novels," David Lodge won the Hawthornden Prize with *Changing Places* (1975). Malcolm Bradbury, another satirist of college life, began a series of novels for Secker and Warburg with *Eating People Is Wrong* (1959); the best known of his works are *The History Man* (1975) and *Rates of Exchange* (1983). Yet another gifted writer of academic comedy is Tom Sharpe, whose *Porterhouse Blue* (1974) opened a highly successful series of books that included *Blott on the Landscape* (1975), and *Wilt* (1976).

Despite an impressive publishing record after the war, Secker and Warburg underwent several financial crises; one of the worst occurred in 1951. The main problem was a shortage of working capital, due to inflation in the costs of paper, printing, and binding. The firm also found its overhead costs excessive. It simply could not pay big advances, even on the most promising novels. Under an agreement reached in 1952, William Heinemann Limited made an investment in Secker and Warburg in return for a preference dividend. Thereafter, the profits, if any, were divided. Heinemann guaranteed an overdraft that grew to one hundred thousand pounds, despite the condition that Secker and Warburg should keep its advances below three hundred pounds. The chairman and finance director of Heinemann sat on the Secker and Warburg board, and Heinemann's staff took over the firm's accounting, distribution, and domestic and overseas sales. Secker and Warburg, however, retained complete editorial freedom. This experiment in group publishing worked well for a time, but at the end of the 1950s, it was Heinemann's turn to experience financial difficulties. In 1960 both the Heinemann Group and Secker and Warburg were taken over by the Thomas Tilling Group.

Secker and Warburg moved to 14 Carlisle Street, Soho. Senhouse resigned in 1962. In 1967 Barley Alison, an Australian who had worked for Weidenfeld and Nicolson, was engaged as an unsalaried editor with her own imprint, the Alison Press. She was to share profits if her publishing proved successful. Her first effort, *The Attempt* (1968), by John Hopkins, made only forty-three pounds in two years. A new author, Piers

Paul Read, had more success with *The Junkers* (1968) and five subsequent novels under the Alison Press imprint. In 1973 the press found prosperity with *Governor Ramage R. N.*, by Dudley Pope, a naval historian who produced about a dozen "Ramage" novels in the manner of C. S. Forester's "Hornblower" series. Having established herself, Alison joined the Secker and Warburg board.

In 1968 Warburg, then seventy, began to contemplate retirement. Maurice Temple Smith entered the firm as a replacement managing director but resigned after a few months to found his own business. The prospect arose that Heinemann would completely absorb the firm, which was losing money every year during the late 1960s. Graham C. Greene, nephew of the novelist and head of Jonathan Cape, offered to buy shares to protect the firm's editorial independence, but Heinemann rejected the bid and took control. Profits increased in 1969 and 1970, and in 1971 were the highest ever. Warburg retired on 30 April of that year; he died in 1981. Tom Rosenthal, from Thames and Hudson, became managing director in 1971, working closely with Farrer. Charles Pick became chairman in 1973. In 1978 the firm moved to 54 Poland Street, Soho. In the early 1980s Rosenthal, who became chairman in 1981, reconstructed the firm, bringing Leo Cooper (formerly of Longmans and Hamish Hamilton) onto the board, and becoming chairman both of Secker and Warburg and Heinemann. During Rosenthal's time Secker and Warburg's sales gross rose from £250,000 to £2,750,000 a year, and profits, previously modest, rose to £300,000 a year. Rosenthal began the Secker and Warburg Poets series, edited by the poet and critic Anthony Thwaite. The series opened with *Cannibals and Missionaries* (1972), by John Fuller and came to include the *New and Collected Poems, 1934-1984* (1985) of his father, Roy Fuller. Cooper was encouraged to bring out military books, among them *No Picnic* (1985) by Julian Thompson on the Falkland Islands war.

Cooper later merged his publishing with that of Seeley, Service (founded in 1744), an established publisher of sports and military books. Rosenthal, too, resigned his chairmanships in 1984. Peter Grose, who had been appointed publishing director in 1980 after twelve years with the literary agents Curtis Brown, took over as managing director of Secker and Warburg when Rosenthal left. But he stepped down when, in August 1985, the Octopus Group took over the

Heinemann Group, including Secker and Warburg. Nicolas Thompson moved from Sir Isaac Pitman and Sons to become managing director of the Heinemann Group and chairman of Secker and Warburg. By 1986, however, he had been succeeded as chairman by Paul Hamlyn, proprietor of the Octopus Group, with David Godwin as managing director. Godwin departed to join Jonathan Cape in 1988, after the purchase of the entire Octopus Group by Reed International in July 1987 for £535 million. Despite these rapid changes of ownership and personnel, characteristic of the disturbed state of publishing in the 1980s and a world away from the modest beginnings of Secker and Warburg in 1936, the firm has managed to remain an autonomous editorial unit. The firm is currently located at 81 Fulham Road.

References:

George Malcolm Thomson, *Martin Secker and Warburg: The First Fifty Years* (London: Secker & Warburg, 1986);

Fredric Warburg, *All Authors Are Equal: The Publishing Life of Fredric Warburg, 1936-1971* (London: Hutchinson, 1973);

Warburg, *An Occupation for Gentlemen* (London: Hutchinson, 1959).

—*J. A. Edwards*

Seizin Press

(London: 1928-1929; Deya, Majorca: 1929-1936; London: 1936-1939; occasional titles thereafter)

See also the Robert Graves entries in *DLB 20: British Poets, 1914-1945*, *DLB 100: Modern British Essayists, Second Series*, and *DLB Yearbook: 1985*; and the Laura Riding Jackson entry in *DLB 48: American Poets, 1880-1945, Second Series*.

The Seizin Press was established in 1927 as a private press by the American poet Laura Riding and the British poet Robert Graves in a two-story apartment at 35a St. Peter's Square, Hammersmith, London. The proprietors had each had works published by the Hogarth Press of Leonard and Virginia Woolf, and it is possible that the Woolfs' example had some influence on their decision to set up as printers and publishers. The more immediate impetus, however, came from the enthusiasm of Vyvyan Richards, who had recently acquired a handpress. It was through Richards's agency that the poets acquired an 1872 Crown Albion press. "The idea of a press, and publishing one's own poems," Riding said, "seemed to spell freedom; it intrigued us, then excited us." Riding was the chief manager of the press.

Like Hogarth's, Seizin's concern was with publishing original literary material and not with creating beautiful books. The poets' plan was "to print necessary books by various particular people. Our editions are decidedly not addressed to collectors but to those interested in work rather than printing—of a certain quality." In looking back on the press many years later Riding wrote that its orientation was "not to a kind or kinds of writers, but to questions of word-use—the kind of use writers made of words."

The press's name, a legal term denoting possession, was deliberately chosen. Not only was possession involved, but one may, Riding wrote, "read back into the launching of the Press with 'Seizin' for its name a spirit of moral resolve to use it well."

Seizin's first book, published toward the end of 1928, was Riding's *Love as Love, Death as Death*, a collection of poems in an edition of 175 copies. Seizin's hand-printed books were numbered sequentially; Seizin One was to be, at sixty-four pages, the longest of the hand-produced volumes. Two more books were published during

Poets Laura Riding and Robert Graves, founders of the Seizin Press

Seizin's London years, Gertrude Stein's *An Acquaintance with Description* (Seizin Two, 1929) and Graves's *Poems, 1929* (Seizin Three, 1929), each in editions of 225 copies.

Late in 1929 Riding and Graves left London; after brief sojourns in France and Germany they settled in Deya on the Spanish island of Majorca, where their printing press subsequently joined them. There they printed and published Seizins Four through Seven, limited to two hundred copies each: Len Lye's *No Trouble* (1930), Riding's *Though Gently* (1930), Graves's *To Whom Else?* (1931), and Riding's *Laura and Francisca* (1931). A pamphlet and some ephemera were also printed. The last hand-printed books of the press were Riding's *The First Leaf* (1933) and *The Second Leaf* (1935).

Seizins One through Seven were printed on the Crown Albion press. In London the type for the books was set by Monotype in Caslon Old Face and reworked by Riding and Graves. After relocating on Majorca they continued to print on English paper, but they bought Dutch type in Spain and employed a printer from Palma to set type for them. In *Laura and Francisca* there is a glimpse of Riding and Graves at the press: "I

ink, he pulls, we patch a grayness / Or clean the thickened letters out"; the colophons of some of the books state: "hand-set and hand-printed by ourselves on hand-made paper." The first Seizin had a title-page decoration by Len Lye, a filmmaker credited with making the first abstract film, and a surrealist artist. Lye designed many of the distinctive Seizin bindings.

In 1935 Seizin established a copublishing arrangement with Constable and Company Limited in London, bringing to an end its activity as a producer of hand-printed books. Thenceforth Seizin's books were commercially printed and published trade books, and ten titles were so issued. Among the authors whose works were published under Seizin sponsorship, in addition to Graves and Riding under their own names and a pseudonym, were Thomas Matthews, Norman Cameron, Alan Hodge, and James Reeves. All of these authors were associated with *Epilogue: A Critical Summary*, the "Twice a Year" hardbound periodical with Riding as editor and Graves as assistant (and later associate) editor. *Epilogue*, with its literary and cultural program, is perhaps the most important and influential of the Seizin/Constable publications. Only three issues of *Epi-*

logue appeared, dated autumn 1935, summer 1936, and spring 1937. In 1937 Seizin broke with Constable and moved to the firm of Cassell.

With the outbreak of the Spanish civil war in 1939 Riding and Graves left Majorca; later that year they terminated their partnership. Riding, as first partner in the press, formally turned over to Graves, its second partner, all rights to the imprint. After his return to Majorca in 1946 Graves sold the printing press but continued to use the imprint. Graves's biographer, Martin Seymour-Smith, identifies two such widely separated Graves-sponsored Seizin publications: *Nineteen Poems*, by the Canadian poet Jay Macpherson in 1952, and *As It Was . . .* , by Terence Hards in 1964. The former was printed in Palma; the latter was printed in London and was distributed by Heinemann.

Bibliographies exist for both Riding and Graves, but not for the Seizin Press. Information on the press is widely scattered and often inaccurate in detail.

References:

Roderick Cave, *Private Press*, second edition (New York: Bowker, 1983);

Hugh Ford, "The Seizin Press," *Private Library*, second series 5 (Autumn 1972): 121-138; reprinted in *Published in Paris* (New York: Macmillan, 1975), pp. 385-403;

Rigby Graham, "T. E. Lawrence & the Seizin Press," *Private Library*, second series, 6 (Spring 1973): 16-21;

Fred H. Higginson, *A Bibliography of the Writings of Robert Graves*, second edition (Winchester: St. Paul's Bibliographies, 1987);

Laura (Riding) Jackson, "A Postscript," *Private Library*, second series 5 (Autumn 1972): 139-147;

Jackson, "Correspondence: The Cult of Connections," *Private Library*, second series 6 (Autumn 1973): 133-141;

James Moran, "The Seizin Press of Laura Riding and Robert Graves," *Black Art*, 2 (Summer 1963): 34-39;

Will Ransom, *Private Presses and Their Books* (New York: Bowker, 1929);

Martin Seymour-Smith, *Robert Graves: His Life and Work* (London: Hutchinson, 1982);

Joyce Piell Wexler, *Laura Riding: A Bibliography* (New York: Garland, 1981).

—Francis O. Mattson

Shakespeare Head Press

(Stratford-upon-Avon: 1904-   )

Arthur Henry Bullen, founder of the Shakespeare Head Press
(plaque by an unknown artist)

See also the Basil Blackwell Publisher entry in *DLB 106: British Literary Publishing Houses, 1820-1880.*

Arthur Henry Bullen, son of George Bullen, keeper of printed books at the British Museum, founded the Shakespeare Head Press with the express purpose of printing and publishing the works of William Shakespeare in Stratford-upon-Avon. Bullen became involved in publishing after he left Worcester College, Oxford, where he had acquired an extensive knowledge of English classics of the Tudor and Stuart periods. In the 1880s he published his own editions of works by the poets Michael Drayton and Thomas Campion and two volumes of seventeenth-century love poems. In the 1890s he went into partnership with Harold Lawrence and, under the imprint Lawrence and Bullen, published many pretty editions of the poets in the Muses Library series. Three volumes in the series were printed at the Chiswick Press, one of which, *Lyrics from the Song-Books of the Elizabethan Age* (1891), is believed to have had considerable influence on the anthologists F. T. Palgrave and Arthur Quiller-Couch. Bullen claimed that in a dream in which he visited Shakespeare's birthplace, his attention was drawn to "the noble edition of Shakespeare that is being printed here." On awakening, he determined to set up a printing press in Stratford and realized that ambition within twelve months. With his partner, Frank

Sidgwick, and four compositors, work on *The Tempest* began on 6 June 1904. Bullen had acquired premises at 21 Chapel Street, two doors from the site of New Place, the house Shakespeare bought in 1597.

It took two and a half years to produce the Shakespeare, well printed in Caslon Old Face, and Bullen was "not sorry to write Finis." During this time several booklets together with *A Cypress Grove* (1907), by William Drummond of Hawthornden, and two volumes of *Collectanea* (1906, 1907), by Charles Crawford, were published, doubtless to help finance *The Works of William Shakespeare*. Bullen was a weak businessman, and Sidgwick, who left in 1907 to start a publishing house, lost heavily in his involvement with the Shakespeare Head Press. Although the Stratford Town Shakespeare, as it became known, was a scholarly edition of ten volumes, handsomely bound and moderately priced at ten guineas, only half the edition of one thousand sets had been sold by 1915.

Following completion of the Shakespeare, Bullen embarked on *The Collected Works in Verse and Prose of W. B. Yeats* (1908). Other major works were *The Elizabethan Playhouse and Other Studies* (1912-1913), by W. J. Lawrence, and *The Works of Aphra Behn* (1915), edited by Montague Summers. Bullen's final work, an edition of *Shakespeare's Sonnets*, appeared posthumously in 1921. In matters of book design, nothing produced after the splendid *Works of William Shakespeare* was above the ordinary.

Basil Blackwell acquired the press in February 1920, the month of Bullen's death, for £1,500 plus £492 for stock. Wilfrid Blair-Fish was appointed manager, H. F. B. Brett-Smith became literary editor, and Bernard H. Newdigate took charge of design and printing of the books, which were to be published in Oxford under the Basil Blackwell imprint. The policy of the new company was spelled out by Brett-Smith in his foreword to *Shakespeare's Sonnets*, where he stressed that the present directors were anxious that the press should produce no work unworthy of its traditions, whether in scholarship or printing.

From the publication of Drayton's *Nimphidia* in 1921, the Shakespeare Head Press produced many books, most of them of high quality. Apart from slight volumes of verse, many of which are examples of vanity publishing, Blackwell embarked on a program of publishing important books in scholarly editions to the standards achieved by the best private presses. These expensive productions were supported by the publication of collected editions of the works of standard authors such as Jonathan Swift, Henry Fielding, and Anthony Trollope, handsome sets priced attractively.

Typical of the truly fine books published by the Shakespeare Head Press are *Froissart's Cronycles* (1927-1928), with color added by hand, and *The Works of Geoffrey Chaucer* (1928-1929), with illustrations based on those in the Ellesmere Manuscript. Lynton Lamb, Paul Woodroffe, Thomas Lowinsky, and John Farleigh were among the notable illustrators used by the press. In addition to printing for the Blackwell imprint, editions of *The Essayes, or Counsels Civill and Morall, of Francis, Lord Verulam, Viscount St. Alban* (1928), John Bunyan's *The Pilgrim's Progress* (1928), and John Milton's *Paradise Lost and Paradise Regained* (1931) were printed for the Cresset Press, all in Cloister typeface, an unusual departure from Newdigate's preferred Caslon Old Face. In 1930 the Shakespeare Head Press was commissioned by the Limited Editions Club of New York to print Thomas De Quincey's *Confessions of an English Opium Eater*.

Blackwell still continued to push Newdigate for fine editions well into the depressed 1930s. Sir Thomas Malory's *Morte DArthur* (1933) and Giovanni Boccaccio's *The Decameron* (1934) were set in double column, leading to one of Blackwell's most daring projects. *The Works of William Shakespeare* in one volume was designed by Newdigate and printed in double columns in an edition of fifty thousand copies by Billing and Sons in 1934, to be sold at six shillings. Two years later a reprint was necessary.

Effectively, World War II ended the firm as a source of distinguished printing. Since then Blackwell has used the Shakespeare Head Press as an imprint for limited editions printed elsewhere—notably Richard De Bury's *Philobiblon*, published in 1960 in honor of Basil Blackwell's seventieth birthday.

References:

B. H. Blackwell, *Bernard Newdigate, Typographer: An Address to the Double Crown Club, 8 March 1945* (London: Curwen Press, 1945);

A. H. Bullen, *The Shakespeare Head Press, Stratford-upon-Avon* (Stratford-upon-Avon: Shakespeare Head Press, 1908);

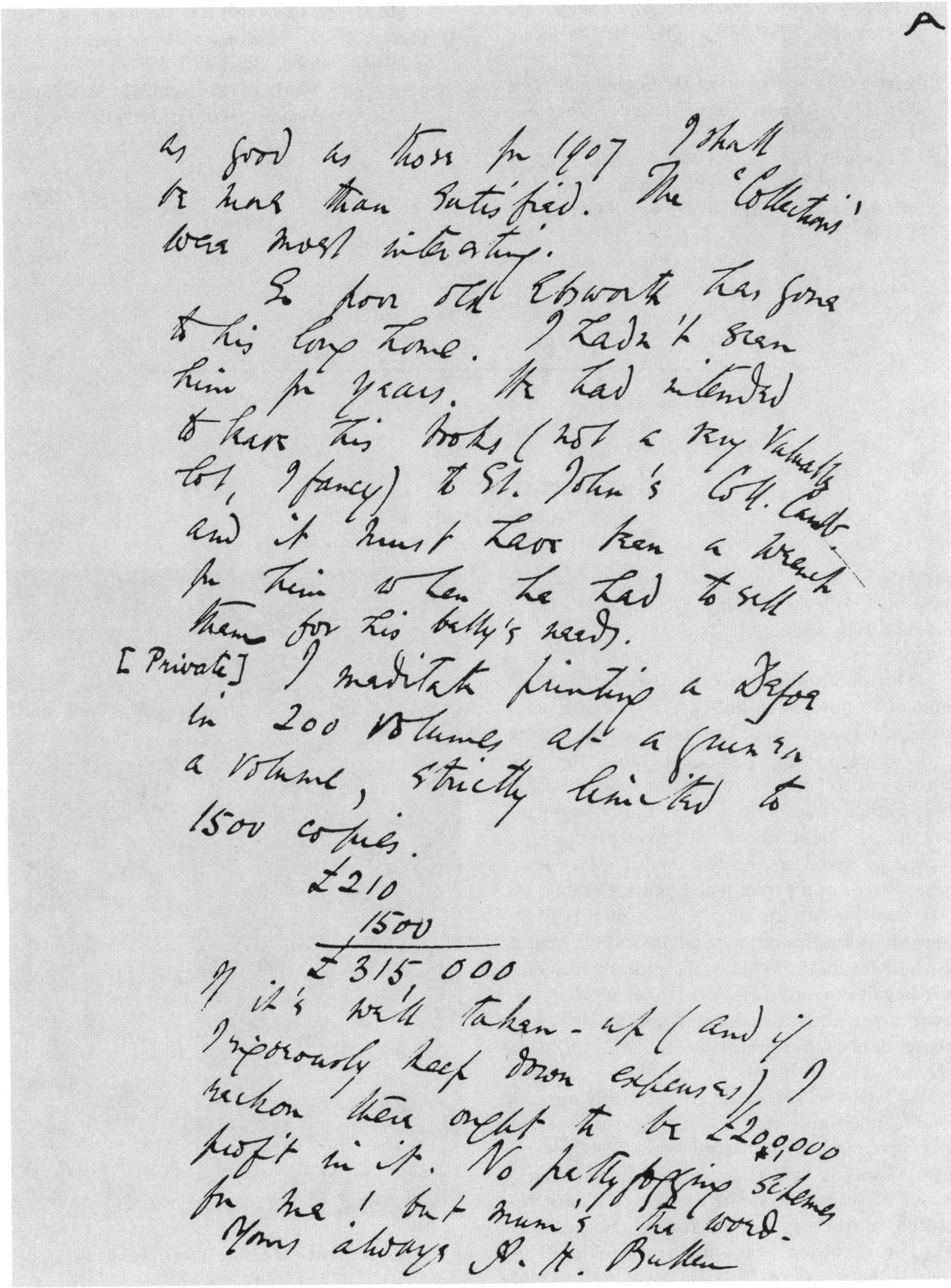

as good as those for 1907 I shall
be more than satisfied. The "Collections"
were most interesting.

So poor old Elworth has gone
to his long home. I hadn't seen
him for years. He had intended
to leave his books (not a very valuable
lot, I fancy) to St. John's Coll. Camb.
and it must have been a wrench
for him when he had to sell
them for his belly's needs.

[Private] I meditate printing a Defoe
in 200 volumes at a guinea
a volume, strictly limited to
1500 copies.

£210
1500
£315,000

If it's well taken-up (and if
I rigorously keep down expenses) I
reckon there ought to be £200,000
profit in it. No pettifogging schemes
for me! but mum's the word.
Yours always A. H. Bullen

Page from a letter to an unknown correspondent, in which Bullen reports expenses and expected profits for the 1927 Shakespeare Head edition of The Novels and Selected Writings of Daniel Defoe (from Frank Sidgwick's Diary and Other Material Relating to A. H. Bullen, & The Shakespeare Head Press at Stratford-upon-Avon, 1975)

A. L. P. Norrington, *Blackwell's 1879-1979: The History of a Family Firm* (Oxford: Blackwell, 1983);

I. Rogerson, *Books Printed at the Shakespeare Head Press* (Manchester: Manchester Polytechnic Library, 1988);

Frank Sidgwick's Diary and Other Material Relating to A. H. Bullen, & The Shakespeare Head Press at Stratford-upon-Avon (Oxford: Shakespeare Head Press by Basil Blackwell, 1975);

J. Thorp, *B. H. Newdigate, Scholar Printer, 1869-1944* (Oxford: Blackwell, 1950);

Thorp, "The Work of Bernard H. Newdigate," *Printing Review* (Winter 1938-1939): 803-809.

—Ian Rogerson

Sheed and Ward Limited

(London: 1926-   )

See also the Sheed and Ward entry in *DLB 46: American Literary Publishing Houses, 1900-1980: Trade and Paperback.*

The publishing house of Sheed and Ward commenced business in 1926 with a view to disseminating the full range of Catholic thought. In the words of its opening policy statement, the new firm set out to "make a real effort to express the whole Catholic mind." Sheed and Ward was the inspiration of the Catholic lay theologian Frank (Francis J.) Sheed and his wife Maisie (Mary Josephine) Ward, of a prominent English Catholic literary family. With an initial capital of twenty-six hundred pounds and a small stock of manuscripts by distinguished Catholic authors, the company began operation from premises at 31 Paternoster Row. Among its earliest publications were Hilaire Belloc's *Companion to Mr. Wells's "Outline of History"* (1926); his *Mr. Belloc Still Objects to Mr. Wells's "Outline of History"* (1926), probably the earliest of Sheed and Ward's twelvepenny series of pamphlets; and, in the same year, *The Queen of Seven Swords,* a collection of poems on Mary, mother of Jesus, by one of the period's most renowned converts to Catholicism, G. K. Chesterton. The following year the firm published his play *The Judgement of Dr. Johnson,* as well as two works by Christopher Hollis, *The American Heresy* and *Glastonbury and England.* Hollis would become one of the firm's most prolific authors, as

Frank Sheed and Maisie Ward (right) on their wedding day, 1925

would C. C. Martindale, S.J., whose translation of *The Marriage of St. Francis* by Henri Ghéon and book of sermons, *The Kingdom and the Word*, appeared in 1927 and 1928, respectively.

In her autobiography, *Unfinished Business* (1964), Ward recalled that the firm's first few publications attracted a good deal of positive critical attention; this response was not immediately reflected in the sales figures, however, and both the company and its founders were, as Ward put it, "desperately poor for many years." To make matters worse, the couple remained firm in their resolve not to follow the example of other Catholic publishers who augmented their revenues by trading in such staples of the faith as rosaries. As the house newsletter, *This Publishing Business*, announced in its first number, "We do not sell crucifixes, statues, rosary beads or medals: we sell books."

Despite its initial financial difficulties, the firm managed to expand its list steadily. At the end of two years it could boast some one hundred titles, and by 1933 revenues were sufficient to permit the establishment of an American branch in New York. At this time, as it had already done for some years, and would continue to do, Sheed and Ward was riding the crest of a Catholic literary revival. The last years of the 1920s and the whole of the 1930s were thus a time of prolific and quality output for the firm.

Among its notable publications during this period were Alfred Noyes's *The Opalescent Parrot* (1929); Belloc's *Survivals and New Arrivals* (1929; reprinted, 1939), *Essays of a Catholic Layman in England* (1931), and *Characters of the Reformation* (1936); Chesterton's *The Thing* (1929; reprinted, 1939 and 1957), *Greybeards at Play* (1930), and *Sidelights on New London and Newer York* (1932); and C. S. Lewis's *The Pilgrim's Regress* (1935; published in 1933 by Dent). Other Sheed and Ward publications included Fr. Hugh Pope's *Layman's New Testament* (1928), Hollis's *The Monstrous Regiment* (1929), a study of the religious policies of Queen Elizabeth I; and Martindale's *Our Blessed Lady* (1938). Works in translation also bore the Sheed and Ward imprint, including Ghéon's *The Comedian* (1927), as well as several of his other works; Karl Adam's *The Spirit of Catholicism* (1929; reprinted 1969); and Sheed's own translation of Jacques Maritain's *Theonas: Conversations of a Sage* (1933).

The late 1920s also saw the first appearance of two important Sheed and Ward authors. The theologian, journalist, broadcaster, and convert from Anglicanism Ronald Knox began publishing with the firm in its early years and would continue to do so for about thirty years. Among his early contributions to its list were *Essays in Satire* (1928; reprinted, 1930 and 1954); *Anglican Cobwebs* (1928), part of the twelvepenny series; and, in the same year, *The Mystery of the Kingdom, and Other Sermons*. The wide-ranging scholar Christopher Dawson was yet another convert who would become one of Sheed and Ward's most prolific authors, producing works throughout the 1930s, 1940s, and 1950s. Ward remembered his 1929 book, *Progress and Religion*, as "the immense sensation early in our career." Later works by Dawson that carried the Sheed and Ward imprint were *Christianity and the New Age* (1931), a collection of essays; *The Making of Europe* (1932); and *Religion and the Modern State* (1935).

During this period the firm's founders began to contribute their own writings to the house list with Ward's *The Oxford Groups* (1937) and Sheed's *Communism and Man* (1938). Both would continue to write prolifically until their deaths. Ward produced *Gilbert Keith Chesterton* (1944), *Young Mr. Newman* (1948), and *To and Fro on the Earth* (1973). Sheed's works included *Theology and Sanity* (1947; reprinted, 1978), *Theology for Beginners* (1958), and *To Know Christ Jesus* (1962).

The 1930s and the first part of the 1940s were a time of remarkable activity for Sheed. In addition to writing and lecturing he coordinated the operations of the London and New York offices, crossing the Atlantic fifteen times during World War II. It was at this time that the London firm suffered a major setback. The bombing of 30 December 1940 destroyed all office records and the entire stock of three hundred books. Not long deterred, however, Sheed took another office nearby and was operating more or less normally within a few months.

By the postwar period Sheed and Ward was "publishing full-blast"—or so Wilfrid Sheed recollected in his *Frank and Maisie: A Memoir with Parents* (1985). Output was in any event steady and included such works as Dawson's *Religion and Culture* (1948), *Understanding Europe* (1952), and *The Makers of Christendom* (1954); Martindale's *The Queen's Daughters* (1951), a study of female saints; John Courtney Murray's *We Hold These Truths* (1961); and Knox's *The Layman and his Conscience* (1962). In the wake of the Vatican Council II (1962-1965) Sheed and Ward added to its list such theologians as Hans Kung, Karl Rahner, and Edward Schillebeeckx. Kung would have his works published by the firm until the late 1970s, Rahner and Schillebeeckx into the 1980s.

Sheed retired from active publishing in the 1960s, leaving the London firm under the managing editorship of his son-in-law, Neil Middleton. Some years later, in an attempt to resolve its financial difficulties, he went back to work at the New York branch. He sold it in 1973, and since that date the English and American firms have operated independently. The London firm now serves a primarily English and Commonwealth market and has expanded its activities to include distribution for some half-dozen other publishers. Presently located at 2 Creechurch Lane, Sheed and Ward remains a small, private company, still in part family-owned. It continues to publish books, mostly by Catholics, on history, philosophy, and theology.

References:

"Frank Sheed [obituary]," *National Catholic Reporter*, 4 December 1981, p. 13;

A Second Sheed and Ward Anthology (London: Sheed & Ward, 1933);

Francis J. Sheed, *The Church and I* (London: Sheed & Ward, 1975);

Sheed, Foreword to *Sidelights on the Catholic Revival* (London: Sheed & Ward, 1941);

Wilfrid Sheed, *Frank and Maisie: A Memoir with Parents* (New York: Simon & Schuster, 1985; London: Chatto & Windus, 1986);

A Sheed and Ward Anthology (London: Sheed & Ward, 1931);

A Third Sheed and Ward Anthology (London: Sheed & Ward, 1937);

Maisie Ward, *Unfinished Business* (London & New York: Sheed & Ward, 1964).

—*Patricia J. Anderson*

Sidgwick and Jackson Limited

(London: 1908-   )

A Certificate of Incorporation was granted to Sidgwick and Jackson Limited on 2 November 1908. At the first meeting of directors, held on 11 November 1908 in the offices of the company at 3 Adam Street, Adelphi, Frank Sidgwick was appointed chairman of directors and Robert Cameron Jackson company secretary. The third director was Ronald Brunlees McKerrow. Since 1902 Sidgwick had been a partner with A. H. Bullen in the Shakespeare Head Press, Stratford-upon-Avon, and he sold the new company premises at Stratford with goodwill, stock, and other assets for two thousand fully paid one-pound shares and a further fifteen hundred shares to James Tennant, who had held a mortgage over the Stratford premises, which were leased by Sidgwick and Jackson back to Bullen. Other shares were allotted to Jackson; to R. B. McKerrow, the bibliographer; to Arthur Sidgwick, the father of Frank; and to A. C. Benson, nephew of Arthur Sidgwick and later president of Magdalene College, Cambridge.

On 19 February 1909 Byam Shaw was commissioned to draw sixteen pictures in color for Edgar Allan Poe's *Tales of Mystery* (1909). *The Publishers' Circular* announced on 10 October 1908 that the company's autumn and Christmas lists were in preparation; but there was nothing from Sidgwick and Jackson in that journal's Christmas supplement, and it was not until March 1909 that the company's first catalogue was prepared.

In March 1909 the directors offered to sell the Shakespeare Head Press to Bullen for £750, of which £500 was to be paid on 1 June 1909

Frank Sidgwick in 1910, two years after he founded Sidgwick and Jackson with Robert Cameron Jackson and Ronald Brunlees McKerrow

and the balance in installments; but Bullen was not in a position to purchase the press. The Shakespeare Head Press was not sold until 1920, following Bullen's death.

When Sidgwick and Jackson began, the publishing trade was in the midst of a general depression and the six-shilling novel was at death's door. Against this background the company developed a list strong in modern poetry. It began with a backlist of a hundred Shakespeare Head books. These ranged from the volumes of Shakespeare at ten pounds each to the Watergate series of literary selections. In 1909 a few titles in a Pocket Book series of easily digestible literature were published, and the company advertised three "dainty volumes" of lyrics in the Savoy series, sold at one shilling or, in crushed morocco, at five shillings. None of these series extended beyond a few titles. The first volume of literary substance with the Sidgwick and Jackson imprint was *Letters of James Boswell to the Rev. W. J. Temple* (1908), with an introduction by Thomas Seccombe. The next entry in the production ledger was *Selected Poems* (1908), by Laurence Housman. The curiosity of the 1909 list must be *Rose's Universal Code Economiser*. The company advanced thirty pounds to Sydney Rose for the English and colonial copyright and agreed to pay 40 percent royalties on the first one thousand and 50 percent thereafter. The hardcover book of sixteen pages was sold at ten shillings and sixpence, and the publishers took every precaution to secure international rights. Rose's code was a key for checking and deciphering messages sent through any of the principal existing systems.

The directors' report delivered in September 1909 recorded a trading loss of £187 to 30 June, resulting from poor sales of the older publications and delay in issuing the first catalogue. Country sales had improved since Jackson and Sidgwick, in turn, had themselves undertaken country traveling. In the three months from June to the date of the report sales exceeded the whole of the previous total, and American sales were satisfactory.

Twelve months later the trading account showed a profit of £350, with sales increased fourfold. The company was expanding and rented the ground floor under its existing offices for stock and trading departments. Publication of the *Englishwoman*, a monthly which supported the enfranchisement of women, was undertaken on commission in February 1910 and continued until January 1914. From an analysis of company accounts the directors concluded that large expensive books were more profitable than small books and cheap series. Harley Granville Barker's *Three Plays* (1909) and E. Keble Chatterton's *Sailing Ships* (1909) showed high profits, and John Masefield's *The Tragedy of Pompey the Great* (1910) established the house as a publisher of the new drama. The success of Ethel Sidgwick's *Promise*

(1910) encouraged the publishers to take on more novels. In the autumn of 1910 the *Westminster Gazette* opened within its columns a debate on the proper length of a novel and invited Sidgwick to contribute his opinion. He referred to the 40,000-word novel by Rosalind Murray, *The Leading Note* (1910), which his firm had just published at three shillings and sixpence and announced that in a short while he proposed as an experiment to publish a novel of only 30,000 words. The *Westminster* dryly noted that *Promise* ran to 130,000 words. The directors agreed to publish an adaptation of Arthur Schnitzler's *Anatol* (1911), by Granville Barker.

The company's acquisition of works by E. M. Forster, Rupert Brooke, and Masefield made 1911 a year of distinction. Forster's *The Celestial Omnibus and Other Stories* (1911), illustrated by Roger Fry, sold fairly well, although not as well as the firm's novels. The response to Brooke's manuscript was cautious; the directors offered only to publish on commission and to do their best for the book. They made suggestions about omissions and substitutions, and there was difficulty over printing the long lines, which the printers had turned over to save expense. The first edition of *Poems* was published in August 1911, and by the end of December the return amounted to £12. The volume was reprinted with corrections in April 1913, the only reprint in Brooke's lifetime, and a third impression, for which Brooke had given permission before he left for the Dardanelles, was printed in 1915; by August 1930 *Poèms* had reached its thirty-sixth impression. After Brooke's death Sidgwick and Jackson published *1914 and Other Poems* (1915), which reached its twenty-fourth impression by June 1918. Sales of these two titles amounted to 17,500 by November 1916. *Selected Poems* was published in 1917, and in July 1918 the firm published *The Collected Poems of Rupert Brooke* with a memoir by Brook's literary executor, Edward Marsh, to which Mrs. Brooke had raised objection. The latter volume remained in copyright because of Marsh's contribution after the other Brooke copyrights had expired. The company came to an agreement over American rights with John Lane in New York and for many years received requests and fees for broadcasts of the poems in several Commonwealth countries.

Masefield's narrative poem *The Everlasting Mercy* (1911) was considered a risk because of its experimental lack of punctuation; in such a matter the firm preferred to conciliate the reader.

Sidgwick advised Masefield to stick to drama and lyrics; too much narrative verse would not be good for his reputation. Publication of Masefield's *The Widow in the Bye Street* (1912) was postponed for a year.

In 1911 the company also published Bram Stoker's *Famous Imposters*, which had been postponed from the previous year; Katherine Tynan's *New Poems*; the poems of Gerald Gould on commission; *The Footpath Way*, with an introduction by Hilaire Belloc; and a volume by Laurence Housman that was to be called "The Child's Guide to Knowledge." Shortly before publication a salesman noticed a book of that title already on sale, and so it became *The New Child's Guide to Knowledge*. In April 1911 Alfred Ollivant, author of *The Gentleman* (1908), complained in the *Publishers' Circular* about the use of the title *Le Gentleman* for Ethel Sidgwick's second novel, published the previous month. The editor pointed out in a footnote that Ollivant was not the first to use the title nor its moral owner. In 1911 the company began to publish its first uniform edition of the works of a novelist, George Gissing.

The 1911 board meeting heard that satisfactory growth continued, although not sufficiently strongly to achieve a net profit. The trading profit was nearly double that of the previous year, and sales had increased by one thousand pounds. Twenty-eight of the forty-seven books published since the company was founded showed a gross profit; all publications in drama and fiction were profitable, with the exception of juvenile fiction from America.

Authors' agents took a hard line on contracts in late 1911; the firm of Curtis Brown and Massie secured a contract for J. D. Beresford's *The Early History of Jacob Stahl* (1911) that included a guarantee that £50 would be spent on advertising. The publishers had to increase Masefield's royalties for a second time, giving him 20 percent on copies from one thousand to fifteen hundred and 25 percent thereafter, and a few months later had to agree to a royalty of 25 percent on all three-shillings-and-sixpeny copies of *The Widow in the Bye Street* with an advance of one hundred. During January and February 1913 they failed to agree with C. E. Cazenove of The Literary Agency on terms for the publication of Masefield's *The Dauber* and *The Daffodil Fields*. In the course of negotiations the publishers proposed a method of valuing the rights in Masefield's works based on sales for a certain number of years previous to transfer of the rights. Their

final offer was an advance of forty pounds on each of the new works and the addition of a termination clause to existing contracts. Cazenove broke off negotiations and sold the poems to William Heinemann Limited, which published them in 1913. In contrast, for Ethel Sidgwick's third novel, *Herself* (1912), which was one of the company's most lucrative publications, the publishers paid royalties of 10 percent on the first five thousand and 15 percent thereafter and secured an option on her next three novels. In May 1912 the Associated Booksellers' Society complained that the company was selling J. C. Stobart's *The Glory That Was Greece*, published in October 1911 at thirty shillings, to libraries for twenty-five shillings; this claim was acknowledged to be correct.

In 1912 the firm had to balance an increase in sales and commissions against a decline in trading profits. In December the registered capital was increased by the creation of three thousand one-pound shares, and two thousand of these were issued to Alfred F. Schuster.

The annual report delivered in November 1913 announced a trading profit of £1,671, which exceeded the sum of all previous years. Three new books were particularly profitable: Stobart's *The Grandeur That Was Rome* (1912); Ethel Sidgwick's fourth novel, *Succession* (1913); and Stanley Houghton's *Hindle Wakes* (1912), which was to prove a lasting success—unlike the two plays by Edward Garnett that Sidgwick and Jackson published: *The Trial of Jeanne d'Arc* (1912) under his own name and *Lords and Masters* (1911) pseudonymously as James Byrne. A branch office in Toronto was opened and a new representative was appointed for Australia and New Zealand.

In September 1914 the country was at war. The general meeting was postponed because so many clerks enlisted that the auditor's report was not ready. Trading profits had fallen by half, and sales had decreased slightly because of a bookbinders strike at Christmas 1913. Loss of commissions following withdrawal of the *Englishwoman* magazine was not made up by publication of the quarterly *Folk-lore*, which the company had begun to publish in 1914. Most of the year's profit came from fiction, including new novelists.

The year 1915 brought a much graver outlook. Schuster was killed at the front; he had contributed his scholarship to only a few of Sidgwick and Jackson's books. The company had to borrow one thousand pounds from Dr. E. J. Schuster, to whom his son's shares had passed,

65

MEMORANDUM OF AGREEMENT made this Twelfth day of August 1911
BETWEEN Rupert Brooke Esq, of The Old Vicarage, Grantchester,
Cambridge., hereinafter called the Author, his heirs, executors,
and assigns, of the one part, and Sidgwick & Jackson Limited, of
3 Adam Street, Adelphi, London, W.C., hereinafter called the Publishers, of the other part; WHEREBY it is agreed as follows:-

(1) The Author having supplied the Publishers with the M.S. of
his poems, the Publishers undertake at the Author's charge to print
an edition of ~~Egg~~ *five* hundred copies and bind and advertise the
same as required and publish the said work in the Author's behalf
and offer it for sale through the ordinary trade channels at the
published price of two shillings and sixpence net.

(2) The Publishers shall produce the said work in accordance
with the specimens and estimates submitted to and approved by the Au
Author, who undertakes to bear all costs of production in accordance with the Publishers' letters to him, together with the charges
for Author's corrections on the proofs.

(3) The Publishers shall render to the Author an account of the
sales of the said work, reckoning thirteen copies as twelve, and
shall pay over to him the net amounts derived therefrom as received
less their commission of fifteen per cent. on such amounts. Accounts
shall be rendered half-yearly as at June 30th and December 31st in
each year and shall be settled in cash within three months of the
said dates respectively.

(4) The Publishers shall include the said work in their lists
and catalogues free of further charge, but all costs of newspaper
advertising shall be borne by the Author and debited to his account;
but the sum so spent shall not exceed the sum of £ 3 (three) pounds
without written instructions from the Author.

(Agreement continued to Folio 2.)

Publication agreement for Rupert Brooke's Poems *(1911), the only volume of his verse published during his lifetime (from* Letters from Rupert Brooke to His Publisher, 1911-1914, *1975). Brooke's signature was witnessed by Virginia Stephen
(later Woolf).*

65

Folio 2 of Agreement
Between Rupert Brooke Esq and Sidgwick and Jackson Ltd.

(5) If after two years from the date of publication the demand for the said work shall in the Publishers' opinion have ceased, they shall be at liberty to return to the Author the unsold stock of the work, and this agreement shall thereupon determine.

(6) The Author undertakes to keep the Publishers indemnified against all actions claims and demands which may be brought against or made upon them by reason of the said work containing or being alleged to contain any libellous or other actionable matter or to be an infringement of any right or rights belonging to any other party.

(7) The Publishers shall be allowed six free copies of the said work for their file and travellers' use, and five copies for the Statutory Libraries gratis.

SIGNED.

SIX PENCE

Rupert Brooke

In the presence of

Virginia Stephen
29 Fitzroy Square
London W.

and trade was reduced by a third. All stock was insured under the Government Aircraft Insurance Scheme, on which claims had to be made in June 1916 after losses in fires. There were unprecedented sales of poetry books of which the great majority were Brooke's first two volumes.

One of the house's most successful productions, launched on the flood of this revival of interest in poetry, was *Poems of To-day* (1915), an anthology published for the English Association. Sales of the volume justified the publication of *Poems of To-day Second Series* (1922), and then a combined volume in 1924 simultaneously with *French Poems of To-day*. When Macmillan published *Poems of To-day Third Series* (1938) Sidgwick and Jackson protested against the use of the title and later expressed the view that the English Association had not acted honorably in the matter. This series was intended for the upper forms of secondary schools; for the lower and middle forms the company published *The Daffodil Poetry Book* (1920), by Ethel L. Fowler, which reached the twenty-fourth thousand in 1922, and in 1931 *The Second Daffodil Poetry Book*.

In 1916 Jackson was called to military service and resigned as secretary to the company, while remaining a director. The year was extraordinarily profitable; gross sales exceeded the sum of the two preceding years. More than half the total was from Brooke's two volumes; of every £7, £5 came from modern poetry published during the war. The trading profit rose from £660 in the previous year to £4,926.

Sidgwick secured exemption from war service for a period but was called up on 1 July 1917. Before his departure the company negotiated reductions in royalties to authors to compensate for increases in production costs. Half of the loan from Dr. Schuster was repaid, and a £50 advance was paid to John Drinkwater for transfer of his agreements with David Nutt. The first Drinkwater book published by Sidgwick and Jackson was *Swords and Ploughshares* (1915). Six thousand copies of Brooke's *1914 and Other Poems* were printed.

On 23 September 1917 Jackson was killed in action in France. The company was left with one director on hand—McKerrow, who had been appointed managing director when Sidgwick was called up. Miss E. A. Vigor (later Mrs. Sisley) had been appointed acting assistant secretary, and she continued to perform the duties of secretary until 1922.

Reconstruction of the board of directors waited until Sidgwick's return from war service in December 1919, when he and McKerrow were appointed joint managing directors. In February 1920 H. R. Hall was engaged as educational manager. In the same month Bullen died, and the Shakespeare Head Press was sold; after Bullen's debt was set against the sale, two thirds of the proceeds went to Frank Sidgwick and one third to Sidgwick and Jackson Limited. In 1922 McKerrow was appointed to succeed Jackson as company secretary. In 1925 the firm bought 44 Museum Street, and these premises became the registered address of the company. Benson, one of the original shareholders, died in 1925. In the early 1920s the company appointed copyright agents in many commonwealth countries.

The appointment of an educational manager was consistent with the directors' intention to move into educational publishing after the war. An educational list was developed which encompassed English and European literature and language and biological and physical sciences. The individual volumes of Text Books of Animal Biology, a series under the editorial direction of Julian Huxley, were written by scientists of the caliber of Lancelot Hogben. A series of Biological Handbooks was edited by J. Arthur Thomson. In humanities the company published New Term French Texts and New Term German Texts.

The 1920s were a time of consolidation and expansion of the partnerships between Sidgwick and Jackson and some of the authors whose work the firm had published since its establishment, rather than of the attraction of works by authors new to the list—although Edmund Blunden's *The Waggoner* (1920) and an edition of Erskine Childers's *The Riddle of the Sands* (1926) were exceptions. Sidgwick and Jackson had published the plays of Harley Granville Barker from its first years, including *Waste* (1909), which had been refused a license for public performance, and *The Madras House* (1911), which was slow to meet its production costs. Nevertheless, the firm assured him, "our faith in you shall move mountains." In the 1920s their mutual devotion to the drama bore fruit. A series, The Players' Shakespeare, was proposed, which would include Barker's performance notes; eight titles were published, beginning in 1923. From the ashes of this enterprise arose the five volumes of *Prefaces to Shakespeare*, published between 1927 and 1948. In coming to terms with Barker the fiction of his wife, Helen, had to be part of the package. That package came to include adaptations into English by Barker and his wife of works by Gregorio Martinez-Sierra and Jules Romains, as well as Barker's *Clark* (1931) and *Romanes Lectures* (1937).

Laurence Housman was another author who had been on the firm's list since its early years and whose connection with Sidgwick and Jackson developed profitably in the 1920s. His first commission was to illustrate the text of *Prunella* (1911), on which he had collaborated with Barker. In 1922 the company published Housman's *Little Plays of St. Francis*, followed by a Second Series in 1931. His narrative poem, *Cynthia* (1947), after postponement in wartime, was published in a limited edition of five hundred copies signed by the author with deletions to meet censorship requirements; attempts were made to provide purchasers with typescripts of the deletions.

McKerrow edited the *Review of English Studies* from 1925, and in 1931 it was agreed that he should be free from work for Sidgwick and Jackson for two days a week to perform editorial work for the Clarendon Press. At this time James Knapp-Fisher organized a foreign department of Sidgwick and Jackson. In 1932 staff salaries were reduced by 10 percent and directors' salaries by 11 1/9 percent. In March 1933, on the death of Mrs. Jackson, her shares were divided between T. Gordon Jackson and the Reverend H. Murray Jackson. In 1937 the 10 percent cut in salaries was restored.

In August 1939 Frank Sidgwick died. He had led his house for a generation and had published the work of many contemporary poets. He was a scholar-publisher; editor with E. K. Chambers of a standard work, *Early English Lyrics* (published by Bullen in 1907); and sole author of several others. If Sidgwick and Jackson's lists seemed a little less brilliant in his last decade, it was perhaps because the public had turned from poetry to fiction and Sidgwick had not.

On 21 August 1939 Knapp-Fisher and Mrs. E. A. Sisley were appointed directors. On 12 September 1939, nine days after the outbreak of World War II, the directors passed a resolution to limit expenditure on the publication or translation of any title to fifty pounds, except by a vote of the board of directors.

In January 1940 David Balfour invested fifteen hundred pounds in the company, and the registered capital was increased to twelve thousand pounds. On 20 January 1940 McKerrow died, thus breaking the living link with the foundation of the firm. The *Review of English Studies* was transferred to the Clarendon Press. By the end of January there were several changes: two new staff members were engaged, a production consultant and another on a retainer to produce not less than two ideas each month for new books (this experiment failed); four hundred unissued one-pound shares were sold to Knapp-Fisher, and he became a permanent director (a security held by Sidgwick and McKerrow in the past). Resolutions to rejoin the Publishers' Association and the National Book Council were passed, and on future occasions the firm turned to the association for advice on such matters as an application to the Board of Trade for Knapp-Fisher to visit the United States during the war.

On the outbreak of war the first concern of the directors was to obtain stocks of paper, but shortages continually caused books to be rejected or postponed. In November 1940 the directors reviewed the finances of the company, and although they discerned some improvement they affirmed that the policy of not publishing new books should stand. Balfour was called to military service in December.

Under Knapp-Fisher the Sidgwick and Jackson list took on a different coloration. An approach by Edward Lyndoe led to the publication in 1941 of *Your Next Ten Years*, with the imprint of Lyndoe and Fisher, a new subsidiary company. Knapp-Fisher secured *Lyndoe's Year Book for 1941* and, with it, much-improved finances for the company. Prices of major titles on the backlist were increased, and five hundred pounds cash was voted for transfer of the business of J. Marby and Company to Sidgwick and Jackson. In August 1941 an associated company, Feature Books Limited, was set up with 44 Museum Street as its registered address and a nominal capital of one thousand pounds. The directors were Shirley Long of the *Sunday Pictorial*; Rupert Crew, literary agent; and Knapp-Fisher as managing director.

At the end of 1941 Knapp-Fisher left the country on government business for the duration of the war. Margaret Dowling was appointed a director until his return. The staff was awarded a 10 percent bonus. During the war profits were maintained in spite of the shortage of paper. The company refused to sign the undertaking regarding reversion of rights to authors as requested by the Publishers' Association, owing to the difficulty of reprinting. The company paid compensation ex gratia to Lyndoe because it was impossible to reprint *Your Next Ten Years*. A dispute between Sidgwick and Jackson and the printer Morrison and Gibb was referred to the Publishers' Association. It concerned the large number of corrections required for a reprinting of Brooke's *Collected Poems*; Morrison and Gibb wrote in terms which implied that it was too busy with more important work to do a better job. Behind the issue of financial damage lay the perceived assumption of control of the press by printers.

Relations with Feature Books deteriorated. Lyndoe proposed a merger which was rejected, demanded a five-year contract for his yearbooks, and complained that decisions by committee were destroying Sidgwick and Jackson. When Knapp-Fisher returned in September 1945 Lyndoe was told that no further contract could be made until sales of the 1946 *Year Book* were known. There was renewed activity in book production, although it was still restricted by paper rations; by 1947 arrangements had been made to print books in Europe. A publicity department was established to promote Sidgwick and Jackson books, and a reference library of the firm's own publications was begun.

The incorporation of Watergate Classics in November 1946 led to a fruitful association with John Betjeman resembling the literary partnerships of earlier days. Knapp-Fisher and Betjeman selected old favorites, such as Charles Kingsley's *The Water Babies* (1948), and chose contemporary illustrators. In 1952 the Watergate Classics series was sold to Bear Hudson Limited.

In 1946 registered capital was increased by sixty-five hundred pounds to a total of seventeen thousand pounds, and preference shares were redeemed. In January 1947 the directors decided to reject all poetry manuscripts except under special circumstances. Sales in 1947 increased by a third, and the trading results of Sidgwick and Jackson were satisfactory; but Feature Books Limited lost badly.

In the 1950s Sidgwick and Jackson began to publish science fiction and had an active relationship with the literary agency Pearn, Pollinger, and Higham, which frequently sent proposals for English rights of American science fiction, most of which were rejected as too expensive. The company was the first publisher of the works of Arthur C. Clarke, who was occasionally asked for an opinion on a work of science fiction. In the mid 1950s the company started its own science fiction and jazz book clubs, but they did not last long. Publication of *The Black Diaries: An Account*

of *Roger Casement's Life and Times* (1959), by Peter Singleton-Gates and Maurice Girodias, was accomplished after searching and anxious inquiries into copyright ownership and the likelihood of prosecution. The volume was published with the Sidgwick and Jackson imprint pasted over the imprint of Grove Press, New York, and on the verso a second label stating that it was a special edition limited to two thousand numbered copies.

Since 1955 the address of the company has been 1 Tavistock Chambers, Bloomsbury Way. As the company entered the 1960s it was short of capital, and for a period there were only two directors, Knapp-Fisher and Mrs. Sidgwick. Charles, Lord Forte, became a majority shareholder. Knapp-Fisher retired in 1970; Sidgwick and Jackson then became a subsidiary of Fortes Holdings Limited (later Trust Houses Forte). Knapp-Fisher was succeeded as managing director by John P. Chancellor, who had joined the firm in 1968 as vice-chairman, and Francis Pakenham, the seventh Earl of Longford, became chairman of the board.

In 1986 Sidgwick and Jackson came under the aegis of Macmillan Limited, whose president is Daniel Alan Macmillan, the second Earl of Stockton. The managing director is William Armstrong, who joined the company as editor at the invitation of Chancellor. The company's interest lies in general publishing, especially the works of celebrities such as Edward Heath and Richard Nixon. It has achieved several best-sellers, including *Their Trade is Treachery* (1981), by Chapman Pincher, and Lee Iacocca's autobiography (1985).

References:

Editorial, *Publishers' Circular*, 2216 (19 December 1908): 881;

"How long is a novel?," *Westminster Gazette*, 36 (5 September 1910): 5; (12 September 1910): 9;

"Obituary: Mr. F. Sidgwick," *Times* (London), 15 August 1939, p. 14b;

"Sidgwick & Jackson present a new list—and a new look," *Bookseller*, 3378 (19 September 1970): 1792-1793;

Trade Notes, *Publishers' Circular*, 2206 (10 October 1908): 531;

Elizabeth Turner, *Report on the Records of Sidgwick & Jackson Ltd Publishers 1903-1966* (London: Royal Commission on Historical Manuscripts, 1985).

Papers:
The archive of Sidgwick and Jackson is at the Bodleian Library, Oxford University. An eight-page typescript by William Armstrong, summarizing events immediately preceding the association with Macmillan Limited, is at the company office in London.

—*Dorothy W. Collin*

Leonard Smithers
(London: 1894-1900)

Born in 1861, Leonard Charles Smithers was a London publisher whose work was crucial to the careers of some fin de siècle writers and artists—Oscar Wilde, Aubrey Beardsley, Arthur Symons, and Max Beerbohm among them. Smithers collaborated with Sir Richard E. Burton in translating and producing erudite editions of the *Priapeia* (1890) and *The Carmina of Caius Valerius Catallus* (1894). Smithers came to London from his native Sheffield, where he had practiced as a solicitor, in 1891, entering into the already-established publishing business owned by his old Sheffield friend, the rather shadowy and sinister H. S. Nichols. Unhappy with his partner's penchant for bringing out what he considered hardcore pornography, Smithers set up in business for himself toward the close of 1894 in Effingham House, 1 Arundel Street, the Strand. Growing more prosperous, toward the close of 1896 Smithers moved his business to 4 and 5 Royal Arcade, Old Bond Street. By 1897 the renowned bookman Bernard Quaritch was calling him the "cleverest" publisher in London. His love for beautifully bound and illustrated books as well as his excellent taste in book design and typography made him, in the words of one critic, "the most extraordinary publisher, in some respects, of the nineties, a kind of modern Cellini, who produced some wonderfully finely printed books and was himself just as much a part of the movement as any of its numerous writers."

After Wilde went to prison, Smithers almost singlehandedly saved the avant-garde writers and artists from extinction, providing them with both employment and encouragement. When in April 1895 John Lane of the Bodley Head succumbed to the ultimatum of his "respectable" authors and

Leonard Smithers

dismissed Beardsley as art editor of the *Yellow Book*, Smithers came to the rescue. He launched a rival journal, the *Savoy*, appointing Beardsley art editor and Symons literary editor. The finest aesthetic journal of the 1890s, the *Savoy* (eight numbers, all during 1896), included stories and essays by Symons, Ernest Dowson, Bernard Shaw, Max Beerbohm, William Butler Yeats, Edmund Gosse, Ford Madox Hueffer (Ford), Joseph Conrad, and Havelock Ellis, as well as artwork by Beardsley, Beerbohm, Joseph Pennell, Charles Conder, Charles H. Shannon, and James McNeill

Whistler. At a time when Beardsley was ill, depressed, and all but destitute, Smithers offered him a regular income for life in exchange for anything he might draw or write.

Smithers declared that he would "publish anything that the others [that is, London publishers] are afraid to." That audacity enabled him to bring out some of the most important books of the nineties: Symons's *London Nights* (1895) and *Amoris Victima* (1897), Dowson's *Verses* (1896) and *The Pierrot of the Minute* (1897), Vincent O'Sullivan's *A Book of Bargains* (1896) and *The Green Window* (1899), and the writings of others whom, like Beardsley, the public had erroneously associated with Wilde and treated as pariahs. As O'Sullivan later wrote, for the "young poets" Smithers took under his wing, he was "a benediction. They would have been hard put to it to find another publisher in London." After Wilde was released from prison in 1897, Smithers dared to publish *The Ballad of Reading Gaol*, a work no other publisher would touch. Printed at the Chiswick Press, *The Ballad of Reading Gaol* was published on 14 February 1898 in an initial printing of eight hundred copies on handmade paper and thirty on Japanese vellum. Five further printings soon appeared under Smithers's imprint. There is little doubt that without Smithers the avant-garde movement of the 1890s might have been snuffed out.

During the late 1890s Smithers was a familiar personage among the avant-garde writers and artists of London, Dieppe, and Paris. He was a distinctive figure, described by Wilde as wearing ties "delicately fastened with a diamond brooch of the impurest water—or perhaps wine, as he never touches water: it goes to his head at once. His face, clean-shaven as befits a priest who serves at the altar whose God is literature, is wasted and pale—not with poetry, but with poets, who, he says, have wrecked his life by insisting on publishing with him. He loves first editions, especially women: little girls are his passion. He is the most learned erotomaniac in Europe. He is also a delightful companion, and a dear fellow, very kind to me."

But as Smithers poured large sums of money into finely produced books such as Honoré de Balzac's *La Fille aux Yeaux d'Or* (1896) and Alexander Pope's *The Rape of the Lock* (1896) with Beardsley's stunning illustrations, he fell into financial difficulties. Partly as a result of his generosity to impecunious authors such as Wilde,

Smithers moved steadily downward toward bankruptcy, which occurred on 18 September 1900.

After the bankruptcy Smithers, in order to survive as a publisher, began pirating books to which he no longer had legal rights. He published Wilde's plays *Lady Windermere's Fan* and *A Woman of No Importance* in 1903 in pirated editions with the place of publication listed as Paris. He set up an office at 14 Cliffords Inn, where he continued to do business under various surreptitious names, such as Hampden and Company and Burton and Company, Publishers. Moreover, he became associated with Alfred Cooper, who operated under the name of Wright and Jones. After Wilde's death in November 1900 Smithers and Cooper published many pirated editions of Wilde's work. In 1904, under the imprint Mathurin Press, Smithers published a pirated edition of Wilde's *The Harlot's House* with illustrations by Althea Gyles, who had done the beautiful cover design for Yeats's *The Wind Among the Reeds* (1899). Also in 1904 Smithers published under the imprint Melmoth and Company an edition of Wilde's *Salomé*. Because Lane had bought up most of the copyrights to Beardsley's artwork after the artist's death in 1898, Lane had the Smithers edition seized and suppressed. One of Smithers's last publications was the pirated pamphlet *Wilde v Whistler: Being an Acrimonious Correspondence on Art between Oscar Wilde and J. A. McNeill Whistler* (1906).

During his later years, Smithers's problems were augmented by what George Sims called "Muscular rheumatism," the ravages of which drove him to alcohol and narcotics abuse. Smithers died in poverty at 4 Kent House, Peterborough Road, Fulham, on 19 December 1907. In his *Aspects of Wilde* (1936), O'Sullivan gives a fair estimate of Smithers's career: "I said to him [Smithers] one day that as there were among those he had published two or three who were bound to survive, he would go down to posterity with them. He shook his head. 'If the publisher is remembered at all, he is never remembered well.' And, as a fact, Smithers seems to be remembered, but remembered in a bad sense. That is not just: he was worth more than that."

References:

Rupert Hart-Davis, ed., *The Letters of Oscar Wilde* (New York: Harcourt, Brace & World, 1962), pp. 630-631;

Vincent O'Sullivan, *Aspects of Wilde* (London: Constable, 1936);

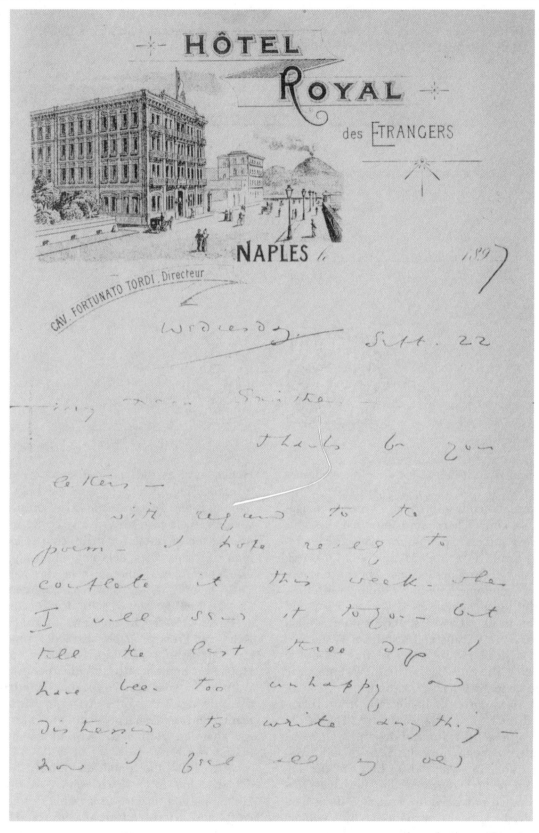

First page from a letter in which Oscar Wilde informed Smithers of his plans for completing The Ballad of Reading Gaol, *which Smithers published in 1898 (Christie, Manson & Woods International, Inc., auction catalogue, 17 and 18 October 1988)*

George Sims, "Leonard Smithers: A Publisher of the 1890s," *Antiquarian Book Monthly Review*, 10 (July 1983): 248-251; (August 1983): 294-299;

Jack Smithers, *The Early Life and Vicissitudes of Jack Smithers* (London: Secker, 1939).

—*James G. Nelson*

Studio
(London: 1893-1963)
Studio Vista
(London: 1963-   )

Founded in 1893, the *Studio: An Illustrated Magazine of the Fine and Applied Arts* became the first internationally influential European magazine of its kind. There were four main reasons for its early success: a philosophy that accorded respect to applied as well as fine arts; profuse, high-quality illustrations facilitated by the development of photomechanical halftone reproductions; the leading position of British artists and craftsmen in its early years; and its international dissemination of crafts and arts from Eastern as well as Western cultures. Out of this periodical sprouted a thriving book-publishing enterprise with the same governing philosophy.

As an importer of handicrafts from Turkestan, India, China, and Japan, Charles Holme developed an eye for crafts and design. By 1886 he had joined a men's club, the Sette of Odd Volumes, whose "Brothers" knew him as "the Pilgrim." There he fraternized with Bernard Quaritch, who had published the earliest William Caxton-inspired volumes produced by William Morris's Kelmscott Press, and C. W. H. Wyman, who printed limited editions of the members' lectures and related miscellanies. The first lecture

Holme gave at the club centered on Arab culture, focusing on carpets, wool weavings, and the happiness and "earnest simplicity" of artisans developing their own art. In his second lecture he praised the Japanese for their "courtesies of common life" and the "delicate rendering of cultivated and artistic thought" in the New Year's cards they printed in color from woodblocks.

In 1889 he moved into Morris's Red House at Bexley Heath, Kent. News of the fledgling Kelmscott Press probably sparked Holme's interest in publishing, and Morris certainly deepened Holme's commitment to the diffusion of arts and crafts in everyday life. On the other hand, the relative provincialism of the Arts and Crafts Movement contrasted sharply with the internationalism that led Holme to help found the Japan Society in 1891.

In 1892 the publisher John Lane introduced Holme to C. Lewis Hind, a young editor. Holme wanted to start a magazine devoted to the crafts and arts of different cultures; Hind sent Holme a proposal and a dummy magazine but then accepted the editorship of the *Pall Mall Budget*. In need of a founding editor, Holme turned

Charles Holme, who became a book publisher after the success of special issues of his magazine, the Studio *(portrait by P. A. de László; from* The Studio: A Bibliography, The First Fifty Years, 1893-1943, *1978)*

to Gleeson White, who had written *Practical Designing* (published in 1893 by George Bell and Sons) and had designed book covers for Elkin Mathews and the Bodley Head. White edited the first four volumes of the *Studio* and continued to write extensively for it on applied art and handicrafts until he died in 1898.

Among the founders of the magazine, Holme exerted the strongest and most lasting influence. Having collaborated with White from the beginning, he was ready to take over as editor on White's resignation in 1895. With the issue for 15 October 1898 he began to take credit for his contributions: "Edited by Charles Holme" appeared above the table of contents. Though he relinquished the editorship in 1919, his vision continued to shape both the *Studio* and the firm's books as long as the enterprise remained in his family. For more than sixty years the Holme family remained true to his belief that useful crafts and beautiful art could communicate across cultural boundaries and enrich the daily lives of people of all classes and countries.

Under Holme the *Studio* championed the Arts and Crafts movement, French and British

Art Nouveau, the Vienna Secession and the Wiener Werkstatte, Japanese arts and crafts, European peasant arts and crafts, the design of everyday objects, and photography as an art. The magazine so successfully injected British Domestic Revival architecture into the Continent that the Dutch began to refer to "the Studio style."

In its first issue the *Studio* "discovered" Frank Brangwyn and Aubrey Beardsley; one of the latter's designs graced the cover, a subtly phallic faun having been expurgated. While it praised traditional techniques such as the woodcut and raised the status of traditional media such as lithography, formerly besmirched by association with caricature and commercial art, it was the first publication that wholeheartedly exploited both line and halftone photomechanical processes to create superior reproductions of arts and crafts on superior paper. In the fourth volume it began to expand its repertoire of color as well as black-and-white originals and reproductions. By contrast with its rather motley predecessors, it achieved visual coherence, a look and feel of its own. Via "supplements" it could include more expensive, more sophisticated illustrations, among which five original lithographs by James McNeill Whistler are the best known.

Through accessible articles and reviews of books and exhibitions, the *Studio* rather painlessly educated its readers. Through international competitions and reviews of exhibitions it encouraged the development and recognition of younger artists. Inclusively embracing the artistic and the decorative, the beautiful and the useful, the pure and the commercial, the traditional and the new, the upscale and the homey, it reached an increasingly large and varied international audience. Students, teachers, and schools; amateur and professional craftsmen and artists; and consumers of arts and crafts were eager to augment and apply their knowledge of the newest developments around the world. Meanwhile, ordinary middle-class readers wanted to participate, if only vicariously, in aesthetic currents and in the art of living.

There were limits to the *Studio*'s inclusiveness. It admired the original impressionists for their vibrant, psychologically realistic treatment of color and light, but more radical impressionist and postimpressionist experiments such as those of Paul Gauguin and Vincent van Gogh struck early reviewers as ugly, self-indulgent, badly crafted, and disconnected from real life. It loved the beauty and craftsmanship of Beardsley's art

Cover, designed by Aubrey Beardsley, for the first issue of the magazine Holme founded to promote the arts and crafts of various cultures

but resisted his "unhealthy" subject matter. The decadents and aesthetes were often dismissed as foppish, narcissistic, and useless. At the same time, the *Studio* opposed the Royal Academy and the so-called Old Criticism, which exclusively valued the Old Masters and the old realism while rejecting all "modern" movements. Thus the *Studio* successfully occupied a broad middle ground between hidebound traditionalists and radical experimenters. While drawing on the oppositional heritage of Matthew Arnold, John Ruskin, and Morris, it seldom alienated its readers. That positioning helps explain how the magazine managed to turn a profit in its first year and how it built its pre–World War I circulation to around sixty thousand. It spawned foreign imitators such as *Art et Décoration*, *Deutsche Kunst und Dekoration*, *Kunst und Handwerk am Oberrhein*, *Dekorative Kunst*, and *Arte Italiana Decorativa ed Industriale*; it also influenced such British successors as *Pan* and *Ver Sacrum*.

The Studio's book publishing emerged from special issues of the periodical. In 1895 a special Christmas number by Gleeson White, "Christmas Cards and Their Chief Designers," surveyed artists including Walter Crane, Kate Greenaway, and Randolph Caldecott. In 1896 a special winter number focused on Robert Louis Stevenson's work as an artist, and the next winter White edited "Children's Books and Their Illustrators," including Crane, Greenaway, and Howard Pyle. These special issues were the same length as the regular numbers of the magazine but set the precedent for extended treatment and heavy illustration that evolved into the publication of books.

The first true books were surveys. *The Art of 1897* (1897) focused on London and Paris exhibitions, with 224 full-page illustrations; *A Record of Art in 1898* (1898) followed suit. The special winter number for 1898-1899 was "Modern Book-Plates and Their Designers," while the next year's was "Modern Bookbindings and Their Designers." In 1899 the Studio put out *Beauty's Awakening*, a masque created by members of the Art Workers' Guild, including Crane, C. R. Ashbee, and Selwyn Image. Ashbee designed the in-text illustrations and initial capitals, and he printed the book at the Guild of Handicraft, Essex House. Published in 1900, *Pictures from the Studio* was limited to three hundred copies. By that time almost all the elements of the Studio's book publishing operation were in place: profuse, high-quality illustration; extensive, usually international treatment of a single art or craft in a single volume; attention to the art of the book; and occasional limited editions that focused on art, literature, or both.

World War I badly wounded the Studio's prosperity and its influence. The firm immediately lost its European audience, approximately half its total circulation, and half its revenue. Paper and other materials, in short supply, skyrocketed in price and plummeted in quality. Subject matter reverted almost exclusively to England, so that the magazine grew physically thinner and culturally more provincial. The resulting strains weighed heavily on Holme. In 1919 failing health forced him to transfer the editorship to his son; in 1922 he retired completely, and he died on 14 March 1923.

Under Charles Geoffrey Holme, known as Geoffrey, the *Studio* slowly recovered its high quality. It appealed more strongly to its domestic audience while expanding its international readership in the face of economic hardship and national prejudice. By 1927, with the help of business manager F. A. Mercer, the firm had established a distribution network in Paris, Berlin, Leipzig, Milan, and New York. In 1932, assisted by William S. Hall, a former salesman; Kathleen Frost, a longtime staff member; and Bryan Holme, Geoffrey's younger son, Mercer launched a separate New York office, Studio Publications, Incorporated. Mercer left Hall in charge of the American office; but the two soon fell out, and Bryan Holme took over in 1933 at the age of twenty. Originally the New York office acted solely as a book importer, mostly from the mother company; but later, as the threat of World War II mounted, Bryan Holme started publishing books intended to appeal specifically to a growing American audience. Particularly successful were two series called How to Do It and How to Draw, which featured better-illustrated handbooks than competitors were publishing.

Charles Geoffrey Holme circa 1918, about four years before he took over the editorship of the Studio

Mercer was innovative not only as a business manager but also as an editor. Beginning in 1926, he edited a magazine called *Commercial Art*; its title was changed to *Commercial Art and Industry* in 1932 and to *Art and Industry* in 1936. In 1928-1929, when two volumes titled *Posters and Publicity* proved popular, Mercer and William Gaunt, perhaps the firm's most talented critic of art between the wars, began to edit a new series of annuals, *Modern Publicity* (1930-1961). Mercer also edited *Gardens and Gardening* from 1932 to 1940 and coedited a new series under the same title from 1950 to 1955. As usual, Charles Holme had set the precedent, having launched one of the most successful series of annuals, *Decorative Art* (1906-1960). In 1931 Geoffrey Holme began editing an innovative annual, *Modern Photography*, which ran until 1943. Here too his father had pointed the way, in this case by writing two groundbreaking books, *Art in Photography* (1905) and *Colour Photography and Other Recent Developments of the Art of the Camera* (1908).

The firm was attuned to new art forms that could enhance the lives of ordinary people, especially photography, poster art, and industrial design. One of the most culturally significant books the press ever published was *Aircraft* (1935), by Le Corbusier, which combined poetic prose, photography, and prophecy. The other two books in the same series, called The New Vision, were *World Beneath the Microscope* (1935), by W. Watson-Baker, in which reproductions of photomicrographs revealed the "astonishing design" of microscopic nature, and *The Locomotive* (1937), in which Raymond Loewy brought out the design possibilities of streamlining. Geoffrey Holme wrote *Industrial Design and the Future* (1934) to accompany the 1935 Exhibition of British Art in Industry, which featured the work of such pathfinders as Norman Bel Geddes.

Similarly, the Studio came to admire "The New Movement" in architecture, whereby Walter Gropius, Le Corbusier, and Frank Lloyd Wright strove to combine the useful and the beautiful in a minimalist, functional aesthetic. Here the most significant volumes are Bruno Taut's *Modern Architecture* (1929), Herbert Hoffmann's *Modern Interiors in Europe and America* (circa 1932), Alfred C. Bossom's *Building to the Skies: The Romance of the Skyscraper* (1934), and *Industrial Architecture* (1935), introduced by L. H. Bucknell and edited by Geoffrey Holme.

The Studio between the wars was neither as timely nor as influential as it had been before World War I. England was no longer a leader in arts and crafts, so the rest of the world was no longer as interested in English news. Meanwhile, the international competition was stiffer and more varied. In the fine arts, such movements as postimpressionism, formalism, and abstraction largely ignored the careful technique and the connection with ordinary life that writers for the Studio preferred. For some time, the publication fought a rearguard action against almost all aspects of modernism. Even in the teeth of World War II Geoffrey Holme was still confident that "pictures speak all languages" and that arts and crafts could act as "a bridge between countries and continents." Earlier, however, in *What Is Wrong with Modern Painting?* (1932), he had inveighed against internationalist homogenization and leveling in modern art, insisting that each country should continue to make its own distinctive contributions and that England should stop looking toward the Continent and America as sources of inspiration. The year before Gaunt,

usually more open-minded, had criticized Pablo Picasso in "Picasso and the Cul-de-Sac of Modern Painting" (June 1931) for poor technique and lack of human interest. Only gradually, and with considerable ambivalence, did the firm make its peace with the realization that modernism was not only unlikely to go away but was actually winning the cultural battle.

His stress on ordinary life notwithstanding, Charles Holme, like Morris before him, had been willing on occasion to produce books aimed at collectors and at prosperous bookbuyers. In 1900 and in 1901 he had overseen the production of the Studio's first two limited editions of art books. In 1921, with the firm still feeling the economic pinch of the war and facing a shortage of capital, Geoffrey Holme revived the practice with *The Etchings of Charles Meryon*, by Campbell Dodgson, an edition printed on handmade paper, bound in full vellum gilt, boxed, and limited to two hundred copies.

Many of the ensuing limited editions were of literary interest, including *The Drawings and Engravings of William Blake* (1922), by Laurence Binyon; *Thomas Rowlandson: His Drawings and Water-Colours* (1923), by A. P. Oppé; and *The Highway and Its Vehicles* (1926), by Hilaire Belloc. Two dazzling facsimiles combined art, literature, and the exotic in both regular and special deluxe editions—*The Poems of Nizami* (1928), by Binyon, and *The Lights of Canopus* (circa 1929), by J. V. S. Wilkinson. Among its customers the deluxe edition of *The Poems of Nizami* claimed Queen Mary, who purchased a dozen copies as Christmas presents. In 1930 the firm published *The Chronicler of European Chivalry: A Study of Jean Froissart*, by G. G. Coulton, which reproduced all eighty miniatures from the Harley manuscripts. In 1937 came *Treasures of Illumination: English Manuscripts of the Fourteenth Century (c. 1250-1400)*, described by Frederick Harrison.

Once more Charles Holme had set the precedents for these volumes. In 1910 he had sponsored a version of Edward FitzGerald's *Rubáiyát*, illustrated by Abanindro Nath Tagore; in 1914 he had published the first facsimile edition of *The Book of Kells*, described by Sir Edward Sullivan, which went through five editions; in 1916 he had published *Shakespeare in Pictorial Art*, by Malcolm C. Salaman; and in 1919 he had brought out *A Carol: Good King Wenceslas*, with illustrations and a cover design by Jessie M. King.

The Studio published some books for juvenile readers, notably *Art for Children* (circa 1929),

Bryan Holme, who took over the New York division, Studio Publications, Incorporated, in 1933 (photograph by Fritz Henle)

by Ana M. Berry; *Children's Books of Yesterday* (1933); and *The Children's Art Book* (circa 1937). Books on the performing arts included *Design in the Theatre* (1927), by George Sheringham; *Settings and Costumes of the Modern Stage* (1933), by Theodore Komisarjevsky and Lee Simonson; *Design for the Ballet* (1937), by Cyril Beaumont; and *Theatre in Action* (1938), by Geoffrey Whitworth, which updated *Settings and Costumes of the Modern Stage*. Four books featured caricature: *Daumier and Gavarni* (1904); *Thomas Rowlandson: His Drawings and Water-Colours* (1923), by Oppé; *Caricature of Today* (1928), edited by Geoffrey Holme; and *Ye Madde Designer* (1935), by David Low. *Movie Parade 1888-1949: A Pictorial Survey of World Cinema* (1950), by Paul Rotha and Roger Manvell, updated and enlarged *Movie Parade* (1936), by Rotha. Another series of books, Peasant Art, illustrated peasant art in various cultures: Sweden, Lapland, and Iceland (1910); Austria and Hungary (1911); Russia (1912); Italy (1913); Switzerland (1924); and Romania (1929). Raymond Firth's *Art and Life in New Guinea* (1936) pointed out ties between primitive art and modern primitivist art, while *Man and Art* (1959), by Cottie Arthur Burland, surveyed folk art from around the world.

True to its Morrisian roots, the firm published volumes on calligraphy and the book arts. Among these books were *The Art of the Book* (1914), edited by Charles Holme; *Modern Book Illustrators and Their Work* (1914), by Malcolm C. Salaman, edited by Geoffrey Holme and Ernest G. Halton; *British Book Illustration Yesterday and Today* (1923), with commentary by Salaman and edited by Holme; *The New Book-Illustration in France* (1924), by Leon Pichon; *Modern Book Production* (1928), edited by Bernard H. Newdigate and printed at the Curwen Press; *Modern Book Illustration in Great Britain and America* (1931), by F. J. Harvey Darton; *Mise en Page: The Theory and Practice of Lay-Out* (1931), by A. Tolmer, a spectacular book which immediately sold out; *William Morris, Designer* (1934), by Gerald H. Crow; *Lettering of Today* (1937), edited by Holme; *The Art of the Book* (1938), by Bernard H. Newdigate; and *The Art of the Book: Some Record of Work Carried out in Europe and the U.S.A. 1939-1950* (1951), edited by Charles Ede and designed and produced by the Folio Society.

Like World War I, World War II seriously wounded the *Studio*. Although the firm had almost fully recovered by the time Geoffrey Holme died in 1954, ruinous death duties forced the family to sell the business to Sir Edward Hulton, the publisher of the *Picture Post*, who soon resold it to Reed International, which owned the *Daily Mirror*. In November 1963 Reed International sold it in turn to the Reverend Timothy Beaumont, who retained the book publishing side but sold the periodical to Hearst's National Magazines.

Charles Holme had originally agreed, evidently without a formal contract, to allow William Randolph Hearst to add a brief American section to the English version of the magazine, to call the combination the *International Studio*, and to distribute it in America beginning in March 1897. In 1927 Hearst unilaterally decided to publish the entire American edition himself, and in 1931 he incorporated it into the *Connoisseur*. Meanwhile, the London office distinguished its periodical from Hearst's by publishing it under a succession of alternative names—*Creative Art* (October 1927 - March 1931), *Atelier* (April 1931 - February 1932), and the *London Studio* (March 1932 - January 1939)—before reverting to the *Studio* (February 1939 - May 1964). In June 1964 the name of the periodical on both sides of the Atlantic became *Studio International*.

Since then the periodical has changed

hands several times and undergone major changes in editorial policy. Although the current publisher, Arthur Sackler, seems to have returned to its original theme, "The Creative Arts and Design," the magazine since 1954 has focused nearly exclusively on contemporary international fine arts, with occasional gestures toward its origins when anniversaries roll around.

Under Hulton, Edmund Penning-Rowsell of Longacre Press managed not only the Studio book imprint but also the Vista imprint that Hulton originated as an umbrella for general nonfiction titles. In 1963 Beaumont purchased both imprints and amalgamated them under the name Studio Vista. David Herbert, formerly chief editor at Reed, became the new firm's editorial director. Crowell, Collier, and Macmillan bought Studio Vista in 1969; Herbert stayed on as chief executive until 1972, affording some continuity under increasingly difficult circumstances.

Like the editors of *Studio International*, Herbert actively fostered avant-garde art. Studio Vista published what may well have been the first books in the world on their subjects: *Pop Art and After* (1965), by Mario Amaya; *Kinetic Art* (1968), by Guy Brett; *Minimal Art* (1969), by Gregory Battcock; *Art Povera: Conceptual, Actual or Impossible Art?* (1969), by Germano Celant; and *Op Art* (1970), by Cyril Barrett. Groundbreaking volumes on the cinema included *The Silent Cinema* (1965), by Liam O'Leary; *The Films of Alfred Hitchcock* (1965), by George Perry; *New Cinema in Europe* (1966), by Roger Manvell; *Fritz Lang in America* (1967) and *John Ford* (1967), by Peter Bogdanovich; and *Ingmar Bergman* (1969), by Robin Wood. The firm opened its doors to new techniques and trends in design with *Design Coordination and Corporate Image* (1967), by F. H. K. Henrion and Alan Parkin, and *Sign Systems Manual* (1970), by Alan Fletcher, Colin Forbes, and Bob Gill. Among its successes were practical books such as *The Nature of Design* (1964), by David Pye; *New Movement in Cities* (1966), by Brian Richards; a revised version of *Thoughts on Design* (1970), by Paul Rand; sophisticated manuals edited by John Lewis for design students; how-to books for experienced practitioners of arts and crafts; and a Pocket How-to-Do-It series for beginners. Studio Vista continued to publish two of the veteran annuals, *Decorative Art in Modern Interiors* and *Modern Publicity*. Books that looked back to the past included *Seurat's Drawings* (1965), by Robert L. Herbert; *William Morris as Designer* (1967), by Raymond Watkinson; *The Bauhaus*

Dust jacket for the first volume in the New Vision Series (1935-1937), "devoted to the forms of today, and the fresh outlook with which, aided by the camera, we survey machines, the work of man, and nature"

(1968) and *The Arts and Crafts Movement* (1971), by Gillian Naylor; and *Colour in Turner* (1969), by John Gage. Beaumont himself created some ideas for books, including Charles Spencer's *Erté* (1970), which helped revive interest in that artist. Brian Reade's *Beardsley* (1967) was one of many volumes Herbert copublished with Bryan Holme, who was by that time at the head of the Studio Books division of Viking in New York. Studio Vista books ranged through various cultures, arts and crafts, graphic design, architecture, the decorative arts, and vibrant new movements, just as Charles Holme's had.

On the other side of the Atlantic, separate incorporation and ownership protected Studio Publications, the American book publishing venture, from death duties and therefore from a forced sale in 1954. Although Bryan Holme still imported Studio books, he had long since developed considerable independence from the parent house in England. In 1951 he had entered into a trial marriage with the Thomas Y. Crowell firm, which agreed to relieve him of the responsibilities of distribution so that he could concentrate on creating books. That union issued some worthy offspring, including Alice Ford's *Audubon's Animals* (1951), Erwin O. Christensen's *Primitive Art* (1955), and Francis Robinson's *Caruso: His Life in Pictures* (1957). Holme, however, felt more and more pressure from Crowell to produce practical books, so he exercised his option to repurchase at cost all the books bearing the Studio imprint. By contrast, his 1959 merger with Viking under Harold Guinzberg, and after 1961 under Guinzberg's son Thomas, proved challenging and remarkably fruitful. As director of the Studio Books department of Viking, Holme was able to revitalize the Studio tradition. In publishing around forty books a year, including imports, he exercised all but complete freedom; and his small, independent staff ensured that his books would boast superior reproductions and production values. With pressruns of major books seldom dropping below fifteen thousand, Studio Books were reaching a wider audience than ever before.

Holme published dozens of fascinating volumes, ranging from *Edith Wharton: A Woman in Her Time* (1971), by Louis Auchincloss, to *Georgia O'Keeffe* (1976), by the artist herself. Arthur Miller collaborated with his wife Inge Morath, the photographer, for *In Russia* (1969). Robert Graves and Joseph Campbell contributed introductions to Alexander Liberman's *Greece, Gods, and Art* (1968) and *Bulfinch's Mythology* (1979), respectively. In *America and the Americans* (1966), photographs by American masters enhanced John Steinbeck's text; while in *Lincoln and His America 1809-1865* (1970), Lincoln's own words accompanied the historical and contemporary photographs selected by David Plowden. Holme published books in collaboration with several major museums, including two catalogues for the Whitney: *The Flowering of American Folk Art, 1776-1876* (1974), by Jean Lipman and Alice Winchester, and *Calder's Universe* (1976), by Lipman. In *The Artist in His Studio* (1960) Alexander Liberman revealed Henri Matisse, Picasso, and other great artists at work. Holme wrote several volumes, including *The Kate Greenaway Book* (1976), and edited and designed most others, including *The Kennedy Years* (1964) and Jacqueline Onassis's *In the Russian Style* (1976), which coincided with a major exhibition at the Metropolitan Museum of Art. With books featuring the work of Alfred Eisenstaedt—*Witness to Our Time* (1966) was the first of eight—Henri Cartier-Bresson, Horst P. Horst, and Ernst Haas, photography was a strong point.

In November 1975 Penguin USA acquired Viking. Holme retired in 1979, and the Viking division of Penguin allowed the Studio imprint to lapse in the early 1980s; in the fall of 1988 Michael Fragnito revived it. Certain themes carry over from the Holme years—notably, generous illustrations and attention to the "art of living," including fine homes, interior decoration, gardening, and the fine arts. The appeal is to an upscale audience, hence the illustrated books on fine dining, cooking, and fashion design. The old emphases on the art of the book, volumes of literary interest, and the arts and crafts of different cultures seem to have faded.

After Herbert left in 1972, the Studio Vista imprint gradually trailed off because of international competition, failure to adapt to changing times, and the ill effects of conglomeratization, including the loss of key people. In 1986 Philip Sturrock resurrected the imprint under Cassell. Studio Vista publishes works on design, architecture, commercial art, and the arts and crafts of various countries.

Overall, the Studio reflected, disseminated, and at times helped to originate and foster major movements in crafts and arts. As cultural indicators, its publications are indispensable.

References:

Martha Sue Bean, "History and Profile of the Viking Press," M.S. thesis, University of North Carolina, 1969;

David Herbert, "Publishing Style," *Bookseller* (28 October 1988): 1718-1722;

Charles Lewis Hind, *Naphtali: Being Influences and Adventures While Earning a Living by Writing (Essays in the Sphere)* (London: Lane, 1926);

Haldane Macfall, *Aubrey Beardsley: The Man and His Work* (London: Lane, 1928);

The Studio: A Bibliography; The First Years, 1893-1943 (London: Sims & Reed, 1978).

Papers:

The Studio offices at 44 Leicester Square were bombed in World War II, destroying the fullest extant collection of books and periodicals as well as all records of the business. What papers survive are in the hands of members of the staff, their families, and Holme family members.

—William Lamborn Lee

Thames and Hudson Limited

(London: 1949-   )

Walter Neurath was born in Vienna in 1903. He studied philosophy and the history of art at Vienna University and then worked for Harry Fischer (later to found Marlborough Fine Art Gallery in London), assisting him with his gallery and in publishing books until 1938, when they fled from the Nazis. Neurath settled in London and took a job as production director of Adprint, a small company started the previous year by Wolfgang Foges, another Austrian émigré publisher, mainly to produce greeting cards. Together they developed the concept of packaging— that is, conceiving book ideas and then overseeing the editorial development and the production of finished books, which would be sold to a publisher for distribution under the publisher's imprint. At Adprint, Neurath produced the series *Britain in Pictures*, which eventually ran to 130 volumes, and *The New Naturalist Library*, both published by Collins.

In 1949 Neurath left to set up his own publishing company. With capital of seven thousand pounds and credit assistance and contributions from founding directors John Jarrold, a Norwich printer, and Wilfred Gilchrist, managing director of block-makers Gilchrist Brothers of Leeds, Thames and Hudson was incorporated on 21 September 1949. The company was set up simultaneously in New York with the assistance of Sanford Greenberger, an influential New York literary agent. This transatlantic collaboration was reflected in the decision to name the company after London and New York rivers. Limited capitalization dictated a warehousing and distribution agreement with Constable for books sold in United Kingdom and Commonwealth markets.

An important early book, *Art Treasures of the Louvre* (1952), marked the beginning of a relationship between the New York publishing house Harry N. Abrams, responsible for the books' design and manufacture, and Thames and Hudson. Both companies have reciprocated on the production of books originated by the other and cooperated on copublishing ventures involving Continental publishers. In 1953 the New York office of Thames and Hudson was closed down, and an agreement was signed with Vanguard Press for American publication of certain Thames and Hudson books. Neurath also copublished books under other American imprints. By the end of 1957 twenty-seven titles had been published by Atlantic Press, an imprint created to handle British editions of books originated by Frederick A. Praeger of New York. A new American company, Thames and Hudson, Incorporated, was set up in 1977 primarily to copublish with the parent firm and to arrange copublications with other American publishers and American book clubs, although occasionally it has commissioned and published some titles of its own.

From the outset Neurath's strong personality stamped itself on the identity of Thames and Hudson. Trevor Craker, who joined the company in 1952 and became a director in 1966, knew him well. In his book *Opening Accounts and Closing Memories* (1985) Craker remembers him as energetic, risk-taking, optimistic, and innovative, "always seeing the new approach, the original idea"; as possessing great confidence in his own judgment; and with an "uncanny flair" for knowing which subjects to publish. Producing well-designed books was integral to his concept of publishing, and he was dismayed to hear his products so often referred to as "coffee-table books." He concerned himself with all aspects of book production, including printing, binding, sales, and

Henry J. Heinz II; Walter Neurath, managing director of Thames and Hudson; Bryan Robertson; and Stefan Munsing, cultural-affairs officer at the American Embassy in London, at a November 1960 party given by the embassy to honor Robertson on the publication of his book Jackson Pollock *by Thames and Hudson*

art production, as well as financial matters, and he understood the advantages of economies of scale. His wife, Eva, a talented book designer and organizer whom he had met when both worked at Adprint, headed the art production department. Together they exerted a strong influence on the nature and direction of the company's development.

Starting with a few titles bought from foreign publishers, Thames and Hudson published its first original book, *English Cathedrals*, in 1950. Illustrated with 166 photographs by Dr. Martin Hurlimann (a Swiss photographer, publisher, and music critic who by 1966 would have twenty-one books in print with Thames and Hudson), it was reprinted by the end of the year and remained in print for more than twenty years.

Other books that established the company's reputation for quality followed in 1951, including Hurlimann and Jean Bony's *French Cathedrals* and Carl Kerényi's *The Gods of the Greeks*, and in 1952 Graham Hutton and Edwin Smith's *English Parish Churches*, whose publishing success was given impetus by the Council for the Preservation of Historic Churches' press campaign.

In 1956 came the first of the World of Art series (nicknamed the "little black books" series because of the all-black jackets), *Picasso*, by Frank Elgar and Robert Maillard. With nearly 400 illustrations, 75 in color, it sold 6,500 copies in less than three months, reaching 12,500 copies in fourteen months. Books on Picasso continued to appear on the Thames and Hudson list, and by 1982, 27 Picasso books had been published. *The Louvre* (1957) and *Impressionist Paintings in the Louvre* (1958), both by Germain Bazin, were published before the success of *Picasso* was repeated in 1958 by *Van Gogh*, by Elgar. The World of Art series sold more than 22 million copies in 16 languages. More than 100 titles are currently in print, including some early classics such as Herbert Read's *A Concise History of Modern Painting* (1959), the first book commissioned by Thames and Hudson, and consistently the most successful, with 500,000 copies sold to date. *Impressionism* (1967), by Phoebe Pool, was second in popularity only to the Read title, and world sales of Michael Levey's *A Concise History of Painting from Giotto to Cezanne* (1962) exceed 150,000.

In 1962 the first two World of Art paperbacks were published. Read's *Concise History of Modern Painting* and Bazin's *Impressionist Paintings in the Louvre* sold out in two months and had to be reprinted, without the dramatic decrease in hardback sales that had been feared. Paperback sales continued to increase, rising 7 percent by 1965, 23 percent by 1970, and 37 percent by 1980. Today the World of Art series is generally available only in paperback, with occasional higher-priced special volumes such as *Women, Art and Society* (1990), by Whitney Chadwick. Under the editorial control of Nikos Stangos, the series continues to commission authors expert in their field, such as Anna Moszynska for *Abstract Art* (1990).

The idea of series publishing, which Neurath had enthusiastically supported from the beginning, proved to be a most successful aspect of Thames and Hudson's publishing program. Over the years many more series were created, such as Pictorial Biographies (1959), the Library of the Early Civilisations (1965), the Library of Medieval Civilisations (1966), the highly successful Library of European Civilisations (1966), the paperback Dolphin Art Books (1967), and the Art and Imagination series (1973). The Ancient People and Places series, whose first four titles had appeared in 1957, required extensive contacts with archaeologists and led Thames and Hudson to undertake the sale and distribution of publications of the Society of Antiquaries of London to booksellers throughout the world. In 1981 the company celebrated the one hundredth volume in this series with the publication of *A Short History of Archaeology*, by Glyn Daniel.

Thames and Hudson's international outlook has been the key to its success from the outset. By 1985 overseas publishers and booksellers accounted for three quarters of total books sold, and the company's present international sales represent a third of its sales. As sales director, Craker made an important contribution. In his

first ten years he discharged twelve sales agents and replaced seven of them, including those in Israel, India, Canada, Mexico, and West Germany. He awarded the important Australian agency to Cassell and appointed agents in sixteen areas not previously represented, among them Greece, Iceland, and the Middle East. For twenty years, beginning in 1962, Craker traveled regularly to such countries as India, Japan, and Australia, forging social and business links with Thames and Hudson's most important export markets.

By 1960 the Constable organization was finding it difficult to satisfy Thames and Hudson's expanding warehousing and distribution requirements, so those functions were transferred to the Reprint Society, which built a new warehouse in a converted aircraft hangar at its premises in Farnborough in 1963 solely to handle the still-increasing Thames and Hudson operation. Four years later, when W. H. Smith and the Doubleday group of American book clubs bought the Reprint Society, Thames and Hudson agreed to purchase the Farnborough facilities. A new warehouse and distribution center, six times the size of the original derelict hangar, was designed, and by 1968 Thames and Hudson was the owner of a modern facility capable of storing more than one million books. Thames and Hudson earned an excellent reputation for its distribution organization and in 1979 was voted "Publisher of the Year" by the Booksellers' Association—the first time such an honor had been awarded.

A fine example of international copublishing, *The Dawn of Civilisation*, edited by Stuart Piggott, dominated the 1961 catalogue. Described by Craker as a "marvel of book production," it was the first volume of the Great Civilisations series. With 172 color plates, 440 monochrome illustrations, 205 original line drawings, and 48 maps, it required three years of intensive study and research by fourteen leading archaeologists. Simultaneous editions were produced in France, Germany, Holland, Italy, Sweden, Denmark, Norway, the United States, and other countries, necessitating a first print run in excess of two hundred thousand copies.

Neurath died of cancer in 1967. In 1969 an annual Walter Neurath Memorial Lecture was established at the University of London; the first, "Ruskin and Viollet-le-Duc," was given by Nikolaus Pevsner.

With the death of the firm's founder, Eva Neurath was appointed chairman and their son Thomas was named managing director. They maintained the firm's prominence. By 1968 Thames and Hudson dominated art book publishing. In the National Book League's autumn catalogue of the Tate Gallery's first exhibition of international art books, of the sixty-two publishers from the United Kingdom, Europe, and America showing a total of 897 books, 219 carried the Thames and Hudson imprint.

Thames and Hudson has a history of prestigious Australian book publishing, with links with National Trust projects, the National Gallery of Victoria, and several of the teaching staff at Melbourne University's Department of Fine Arts. In 1961 Thames and Hudson published a comprehensive volume on the Australian artist Sidney Nolan, by Colin MacInnes, with photographs by Graeme Robertson, and in 1981 the lavishly illustrated *The Wharncliffe Hours*, a facsimile edition of three illuminated thirteenth- , fourteenth- , and fifteenth-century manuscripts belonging to the National Gallery of Victoria, was published. To achieve the quality of transparencies required for the reproductive process, these priceless manuscripts had to be flown to London to be photographed by the book's Swiss printer/producer.

When the American publishing house Crowell, Collier and Macmillan took over Cassell, which had represented Thames and Hudson's Australian interests for many years, the company decided to establish its own Australian organization. Thames and Hudson (Australia) Proprietary Limited (which had already been set up as a nontrading company) commenced business in November 1970. Herb Longmuir was appointed general manager, a position he held until he retired in 1981. Today Australia is the firm's largest export market.

In 1974 Thames and Hudson published *The Book of Kells* with text by Françoise Henry, described by the *Times* of London (22 March) as "one of the year's biggest publishing coups." Ambitiously illustrated with 126 pages of high-quality, technically complex color reproductions, the project represented close collaboration between Thames and Hudson and Trinity College, Dublin. Despite a high price, by 1982 world sales had exceeded one hundred thousand.

Also in 1974 Thames and Hudson signed a contract with British Museum Publications Limited to provide sales and warehousing for its titles. To coincide with the major 1980 British Museum exhibition "The Vikings," Thames and Hudson published *The Northern World: The History and Heritage of Northern Europe AD 400-1100*, ed-

ited by David Wilson, director of the British Museum, and a revised large-format paperback edition of Wilson's *The Vikings and Their Origins*.

Another notable coup was *David Hockney* (1977), a collection of 414 illustrations that reproduced almost all of Hockney's existing paintings and graphics. A printing of 23,000 was needed to satisfy demand in the United Kingdom alone, and large preprint orders came from America and other European countries. Hockney books published by Thames and Hudson have continued to be popular, including his *Pictures* (1979), a large-format paperback edited by Stangos; the international best-seller *Paper Pools* (1980); and *China Diary* (1982), coauthored with Stephen Spender.

In 1989, with an eye to benefiting from the single-market potential created by the European Economic Community, Thames and Hudson launched a French publishing program operated by a new Paris-based subsidiary, Editions Thames et Hudson. A few months later Thames and Hudson's involvement in the French book trade was extended to include a distribution role with the opening up of Interart, a subsidiary of the London-based Arts Distributors (itself a joint venture between Thames and Hudson and Onslow Books), to distribute art and illustrated books to Paris bookshops and museum outlets.

Apart from family members, the firm has always been able to rely on loyal staff. Craker came from bookselling to be the company's first sales manager and remained for more than thirty years; Tom Rosenthal joined in 1959 and left in 1971; Werner Guttman retired in 1989 as production director after thirty years. Among those still with the firm in 1991, Stanley Baron, the editor in chief, has been employed there since 1969; Stangos since 1974; and Simon Huntley, head of sales and marketing, remains after thirty years.

Today Thames and Hudson is Britain's leading art book publisher, with about 160 titles a year and annual sales of £12 million. It remains an independent, medium-sized company and is still a family concern. The company's headquarters since 1956 have been in Bloomsbury, where it occupies five Georgian houses. The company's publishing principles remain true to those of the founder—to produce intelligently written, well-illustrated books appealing to the student, the professional, and the public alike, whenever possible in international copublications. While constantly broadening its range, Thames and Hudson has remained a specialist publisher in arts and humanities. Its strong backlist of sixteen hundred titles, including several first published decades ago and still selling well in new or revised editions, provides Thames and Hudson with a traditional and commercially sound base.

References:
Trevor Craker, *Opening Accounts and Closing Memo-*

ries (London: Thames & Hudson, 1985);

Vivienne Menkes, "Thames and Hudson: 40 Years of International Publishing," *British Book News* (March 1990).

—*Pamela Shorrocks*

University of Wales Press
(Cardiff: 1922-   )

The University of Wales Press (Gwasg Prifysgol Cymru) is administered by the University of Wales Press Board, first established in 1922 as part of a vigorous movement toward the promotion of education and research in Wales, emanating primarily from the university colleges. The need for a university press had already been recognized among Welsh academics, and the idea received a timely endorsement from the Report of the Royal Commission on University Education in Wales (1918). Not only were the fruits of academic research in Wales often failing to achieve a wider currency because of the lack of publishing opportunities, but there was also a dire shortage of texts, particularly in Welsh, suitable for university teaching in all faculties.

The first meeting of the new board was held on 6 January 1922 in London, with seven members present. These were the deputy chancellor, Lord Kenyon; the vice-chancellor, Professor A. H. Trow; John Ballinger, the first librarian of the National Library of Wales and a member of the university court; Professor J. H. Davies, principal of University College, Aberystwyth; W. J.

Gruffydd, professor of Celtic, University College, Cardiff; Sir John Morris-Jones, professor of Welsh, University College, Bangor; and Professor I. Franklin Sibly, principal of University College, Swansea.

Ballinger (made Sir John Ballinger in 1930) was elected as the first chairman of the press board because of his experience as the national librarian. Of these original members, Davies, Gruffydd, and Morris-Jones remained on the board until their deaths, providing some continuity in the early years of the board. The university press device, a crest of four lions set in a circle surrounded by the words *Gwasg Prifysgol Cymru* (the press's Welsh name), was designed by Morris-Jones, a scholar still well known for his contributions to the study of the Welsh language.

In its first few meetings, the board arranged for the University Registry in Cardiff to act as the publishing office, and appointed Humphrey Milford of the Oxford University Press Warehouse to act as the London agent for the board's publications. Some of the books published between 1923 and the early 1930s bear the

John Humphreys Davies, a founding member of the University of Wales Press Board

double imprint of the University Press Board and Oxford University Press, London.

Booksellers in the four university towns and other large centers in Wales were approached to stock books from the University of Wales Press. In addition, the board invited suggestions from the colleges, the County Schools Association, the National Eisteddfod Association, the Welsh Folksong Society, and similar organizations regarding the kind of material the board should be publishing.

The first venture of the new board was to take over responsibility for the publications put out by the Guild of Graduates. The stock was transferred to the board, forming the basis of its first list of publications circulated in July 1922. The list comprised books and journals which had been published in London or Wales before 1922, such as the transactions of the Guild of Graduates; a series of texts transcribed from medieval Welsh manuscripts; and the first part of volume one of the *Bulletin of the Board of Celtic Studies*. The first two bound volumes of this journal were published by Humphrey Milford for Oxford University Press, London, in 1923 and 1925, but by the time the third volume appeared in 1927 the University Press Board imprint appeared together with that of Humphrey Milford. The

press continues to publish the *Bulletin*, one of Wales's most authoritative academic journals.

From its beginnings and up to the present day, some of the most illustrious names in Welsh scholarship have been appointed to the University of Wales Press Board. Other members during the first decade of the board included Ifor Williams, professor of Welsh at University College, Bangor; J. E. Lloyd, professor of history at Bangor; E. A. Lewis, inaugural professor of Welsh history at University College, Aberystwyth; and T. H. Parry-Williams, professor of Welsh at Aberystwyth, who remained on the board until 1970.

During the 1920s and 1930s many of the standard texts of Welsh scholarship were published by the press. Many early editions of important Welsh poetry surviving in manuscripts were also produced during this period, such as *The Poetical Works of Dafydd Nanmor* (1923), edited by Ifor Williams, a revision of an earlier edition by Thomas Roberts, and one of the first publications to appear from the press; and *Gwaith Tudur Aled* (1926), by T. Gwynn Jones.

Ballinger retired from the board shortly before his death in 1933 and was replaced as chairman by the Right Reverend Gilbert Joyce, Bishop of Monmouth, who became pro-chancellor of the university in the following year. Members of the board at this time included Glyn Davies, Parry-Williams from the University College at Aberystwyth, and E. A. Lewis, representing the court of the university.

Publications of the 1930s continued to support academic research in Wales and the editing of standard texts of early Welsh literature. Ifor Williams was particularly prolific, with *Pedeir Keinc y Mabinogi* appearing in 1930, making this important group of medieval Welsh prose tales available in print for the first time. His editions of some of the earliest Welsh poetry, *Canu Llywarch Hen* and *Canu Aneirin*, having appeared in 1935 and 1938, respectively, are standard editions.

In 1929 the Board of Celtic Studies began its History and Law series with *A Catalogue of Star Chamber Proceedings Relating to Wales*, by Ifan ab Owen Edwards, which was published by the press. With the aim of making available primary sources for the study of Welsh history, this series has continued to form a valuable resource for historians. Number two in the series, *A Calendar of Ancient Correspondence concerning Wales*, edited by Goronwy Edwards, appeared in 1935. In 1940, when Bishop Joyce resigned from the chairmanship of the board, Professor Ifor L. Evans was elected chairman, holding the position until his death in 1952.

Evans was principal of the University College at Aberystwyth, and also served as vice-chancellor of the university from 1937 to 1939, 1946 to 1948, and 1950 to 1952. He was highly regarded as a financier and administrator, and as a man of great social skills and vigorous initiative in promoting university activities. More than his predecessors on the press board, Evans held definite ideas about the kinds of books the board should recommend for publication, and during his term of office the press began to produce a wider range of books on religion, music, and general-interest areas which sold to a reading public beyond the colleges themselves.

During World War II publishing activity was slow in Wales as elsewhere in Britain, but the postwar period saw a resurgence in Welsh scholarship. In 1945 Thomas Parry, who succeeded Ifor Williams as professor of Welsh at Bangor in 1947, published the first major history of Welsh literature, *Hanes Llenyddiaeth Gymraeg Hyd 1900*, later translated into English. Parry's most significant work, the first authoritative and thorough edition of the works of the great medieval Welsh poet Dafydd ap Gwilym, appeared in 1952.

In 1950 the press embarked on one of its major projects, the publication in fascicles of the *University of Wales Dictionary* (*Geiriadur Prifysgol Cymru*), the standard multivolume dictionary of the Welsh language. The dictionary is still being produced and is expected to reach completion before the end of the 1990s.

From 1952 to 1958 Sir Emrys Evans was chairman of the press board. He was succeeded by Parry, who occupied the position until 1969. Parry made a major contribution to Welsh scholarship over a period of fifty years and wrote some of the most influential books published by the press up until the 1960s.

Parry was succeeded by Sir Goronwy Daniel, who held the position until 1979. The 1970s saw new initiatives such as the beginning of the Writers of Wales series, English-language accounts of significant writers or periods of literature, with *An Introduction to Anglo-Welsh Literature* (1970), by Raymond Garlick; *Caradoc Evans* (1970), by Trevor Lloyd Williams; and *Alun Lewis* (1971), by Alun John, and more than seventy titles published since then on behalf of the Welsh Arts Council. The series of Social Science Mono-

Ifor Leslie Evans, chairman of the University of Wales Press Board from 1940 until his death in 1952

graphs began in 1975 with *Colliery Closure and Social Change* by John Sewel. Since 1979 the chairman of the board has been J. Gwynn Williams, Emeritus Professor of Welsh History at the University College of North Wales, Bangor.

From the beginning of the board in 1922, the post of secretary, or administrative officer, of the press board was held by the secretary of the university council, whose duties included the management of several different university boards. This post was held by Jenkin James when the press board was first set up, and he remained as secretary until 1944, when he was succeeded by Elwyn Davies.

In 1963, after the post of secretary of the university council was abolished, the management of all the university boards, including the press board, reverted to the registrar of the university. However, there was clearly a need for someone to take full-time responsibility for the management of the press, and R. Brinley Jones was appointed for this purpose in 1966. Three years later he was given the title of director of the University of Wales Press and continued to hold the position until 1976. He was succeeded by John Rhys, who, on his retirement in 1990, was succeeded by E. M. (Ned) Thomas. The director is responsible for the administrative management of the press, while the press board continues to decide the kind of books which the press should be publishing.

The press has always been aware of its responsibility to serve not only an academic community but also a bilingual community. As well as academic books in areas of Welsh interest, the press publishes studies of other European literatures and general books on economics, politics, history, geography, and other areas. There is no formal quota of Welsh-language books published by the press, but the proportions are roughly two-thirds English to one-third Welsh. The press continues to be the publisher for the Board of Celtic Studies, and has published its journals *Llên Cymru* (1950-), *Welsh History Review* (1960-), *Studia Celtica* (1966-), and *Contemporary Wales* (1987-) since their inception.

Over the years, the press has received many awards and prizes for its publications. Among these awards are the Welsh Arts Council Annual Award for J. Beverly Smith's *Llywelyn ap Gruffydd, Tywysog Cymru* (1985); the Wolfson Literary Award for History for R. R. Davies's *Conquest, Coexistence and Change: Wales 1063-1415* (1987), a copublication with Oxford University Press; and the John Bartholomew Design Award for the *National Atlas of Wales* (1989), edited by Harold Carter.

The press has never had its own printing house but confines itself to publishing, making use of various printers in Wales and elsewhere. Most of its titles still carry the press device designed by Morris-Jones in 1922.

Having been located for many years at the University Registry in Cathays Park, Cardiff, the press moved to Merthyr House, James Street, Cardiff Docks, where it remained from 1971 to 1975. Since 1975 its address has been 6 Gwennyth Street, Cathays, Cardiff.

—*Helen Fulton*

Vale Press
(London: 1893-1904)

While studying engraving at the London City and Guilds Technical Art School, Charles de Sousy Ricketts met the painter Charles Haslewood Shannon, with whom he formed a lifelong friendship. The Vale Press was named for Ricketts and Shannon's home, "The Vale," where they first began printing and publishing their magazine the *Dial*. In it they presented the beauties of wood engraving, color lithography, good paper, and contemporary French and Belgian symbolist literature. Five issues of the *Dial* appeared sporadically between 1889 and 1897, with Ricketts and Shannon executing most of the artwork.

Ricketts gained experience with commercial publishing during the early 1890s. Several of his most memorable commercial bindings for the publishers Elkin Mathews and John Lane reveal Ricketts's ability to combine geometric abstraction with striking color while retaining a sense of organic rhythm, as in his design for the cover of Oscar Wilde's *Poems*, published by Mathews in 1892.

Distinguishing between his commercial work and the Vale private press in his *A Defence of the Revival of Printing* (1899), Ricketts defined Vale works as texts selected by him, produced in volumes over which he had complete design control, and which were ornamented with his wood engravings. Two books published by John Lane for the Vale Press fulfilled these requirements. The first was George Thornley's version of Longus Sophista's *Daphnis and Chloe* (1893), with wood engravings by Ricketts and Shannon. Ricketts cited a work by the Venetian Renaissance scholar-printer Aldus Manutius, *Hypnerotomachia Poliphili* (1499), as inspiration for the illustrations in *Daphnis and Chloe*. The second Vale Press book published by Lane, Christopher Marlowe's *Hero and Leander* (1894), was the first to be printed on hand-made paper carrying the *VP* watermark.

The year after *Hero and Leander* appeared, Ricketts met Llewellyn Hacon and through him gained the financial backing needed to transform the Vale Press from a printing establishment into a publishing house. Hacon, a wealthy lawyer, advanced one thousand pounds. At this point

Charles Ricketts (holding woodblock), with his partner in the Vale Press, the painter Charles Shannon

Ricketts took on total responsibility for the Vale Press while Shannon concentrated on his career as a painter, becoming a member of the Royal Academy in 1921.

Ricketts opened his publishing business at 52 Warwick Street at Regent Street in 1896, later moving to 17 Craven Street in the Strand, London. Woodblock engraving and business affairs were conducted at these locations. The books were printed at the Ballantyne Press's London shop under Ricketts's supervision. His anxiety over the quality of contemporary type had increased as he designed Wilde's *The Sphinx* for John Lane during 1894; therefore, for his new venture he designed the Vale type. All books printed with the Vale type appeared under the

334

The Vale, Chelsea, the house of Ricketts and Shannon, from which the press derived its name

names of Hacon and Ricketts as publishers. The Vale type, more Roman in form than William Morris's Golden type, anticipated the well-known Times Roman in its simple clarity. In addition to editions of the Bible and thirty-nine volumes of the works of Shakespeare, between 1896 and 1904 the Vale Press published works by John Milton; Sir John Suckling; Thomas Chatterton; Thomas Gray; Michael Drayton; William Blake; Elizabeth Barrett Browning; Sir Philip Sidney; Percy Bysshe Shelley; John Keats; Dante Gabriel Rossetti; Samuel Taylor Coleridge; Alfred, Lord Tennyson; Sir Thomas Browne; William Wordsworth; William Meinhold; and T. Sturge Moore.

There is a Venetian Renaissance inspiration in the designs for some of Ricketts's books, such as John Gray's *Spiritual Poems* (1896), *A Defence of the Revival of Printing*, and the book often proclaimed as the masterpiece of the Vale Press, *De Cupidinis et Psyches Amoribus* (1901). Ricketts also drew inspiration from hand-illuminated medieval manuscripts, as had Morris, but he was always able to design outside the bounds of his sources. For instance, his medieval wild bryony border for the *Rowley Poems of Thomas Chatterton* (1898) is more precise in its depiction of the vines and flowers, and at the same time more open, than borders by Morris. As had Morris in his Kelmscott Press books, Ricketts saw the page as a block of type with the narrowest margin on the inside, and the other margins increasing in size from the top to the outside (fore edge) to the bottom. Whether he was following Italian Renaissance or medieval formats, Ricketts always treated decoration as an enhancement of the text that should not distract the reader.

The binding of *Rowley Poems* is decorated in two contrasting printed papers: bird and rose and vine-and-diamond domino. Such printed covers were an innovation of Ricketts and Lucien Pissarro, as seen in their jointly produced *De la Typographie et de l'Harmonie de la Page Imprimée* (1898), the only French text published by the Vale Press. This book covered Morris's contributions to the advancement of fine printing in England and his relationship with the Arts and Crafts Movement in general.

A fire at the Ballantyne Press in 1899 resulted in the loss of many of Ricketts's engraved woodblocks. In spite of this disaster, he brought out thirty-nine volumes of the Vale Shakespeare between 1900 and 1903. These editions differ from the earlier Vale Press books in that they are printed with Ricketts's small-pica Avon font, and

Two pages from the Vale Press's second book, Hero and Leander *(1894)*

brass-cut borders as well as wood engravings decorate the texts. All ornamental work in the Vale Shakespeare is minimized in a manner seen in *De la Typographie,* pointing the way to the forceful simplicity of later twentieth-century printing. Ricketts's impact on the return to simplicity in printing can be seen in books from Daniel B. Updike's Merrymount Press; Updike singled out the Avon font for praise in his *Printing Types: Their History, Forms and Use* (1937).

Citing his losses in the Ballantyne Press fire, Ricketts announced the closing of the Vale Press in 1904, and in the same year published *A Bibliography of the Books Issued by Hacon & Ricketts,* in which he reiterated his desire to "give a permanent and beautiful form to that portion of our literature which is secure of permanence." The punches, type, and ornaments were destroyed at the closing of the press because Ricketts did not want them to fall into general circulation, but some of Ricketts's woodblocks are preserved in the British Museum Print Room. Ricketts occasion-

ally designed books for others after 1904, and he had a career as a painter, sculptor, author, art connoisseur, and successful stage designer until his death in 1931.

References:

Joseph Darracott, *The World of Charles Ricketts* (London: Eyre Methuen, 1980);

J. G. P. Delaney, *Charles Ricketts: A Biography* (Oxford: Clarendon Press, 1990);

Charles S. Ricketts, *A Bibliography of the Books Issued by Hacon & Ricketts* (London: Hacon & Ricketts, 1904);

Ricketts, *A Defence of the Revival of Printing* (London: Hacon & Ricketts, 1899);

Ricketts, *Self-Portrait,* edited by Cecil Lewis, compiled and collected by T. Sturge Moore (London: Davies, 1939);

John Russell Taylor, *The Art Nouveau Book in Britain* (London: Methuen, 1966).

—Alice H. R. H. Beckwith

Vine Press
(Steyning, Sussex: 1919-1930; 1947)

The Vine Press was one of many small, privately owned presses active in England during the first three decades of the twentieth century. Founded in 1919 in Steyning, Sussex, by the poet Victor Neuburg, who had been born in 1883, in its brief existence it produced at least eighteen volumes of poetry and prose. Four of these books were wholly, or in part, by Neuburg. The remainder were by writers who, with the exception of Rupert Croft Cooke and G. D. Martineau, remain little known. The press produced books in both deluxe and ordinary editions, with attractive woodcuts that were often hand-colored by Neuburg's wife Kathleen. The books were all produced in limited editions, and at least one was published for private circulation. The press also printed stationery for local businesses.

Marketing was never undertaken on an organized basis. Local sellers would take a few books on a sale-or-return basis; other booksellers were approached personally by Neuburg, rarely to any great effect. Advertisements in journals and in local papers, or simple word of mouth, were the major means of promoting sales. The bookseller W. H. Smith and Sons had some dealings with the press; but since Smith objected to paying the postage for books it ordered, it advised customers wanting Vine Press books to order them directly.

The press was a financial disaster. The handpress with which Neuburg had begun was damaged by a storm, and printing had to be done elsewhere. Also, at seven shillings and sixpence or more, his books were expensive by contemporary standards. Neuburg's habit of giving away books to anyone expressing an interest in him and the press did not help the business, and sometimes individuals would renege on payments for orders. The failure of the press must be attributed to Neuburg's own poor business sense. It closed in 1930, although there was an attempt to revive it in 1947 when Runia MacLeod, Neuburg's mistress for the last ten years of his life, pub-

Victor Neuburg, founder of the Vine Press, in 1923

lished her play *Wax* under its imprint. Neuburg died in May 1940.

References:
Jean Overton Fuller, *The Magical Dilemma of Victor Neuburg* (London: Allen, 1965);

Victor E. Neuburg, *Vickybird: A Memoir by His Son* (London: Polytechnic of North London, 1983);

Caroline Robertson, Introduction to *The Triumph of Pan*, by Victor B. Neuburg (London: Skoob, 1990).

—Caroline Robertson

Weidenfeld and Nicolson
(London: 1949-   )

George Weidenfeld immigrated to England from Austria in August 1938 at the age of nineteen, following the imprisonment of his father and the confiscation of most of his family's property by the Nazis. With the assistance of a London family, he was subsequently able to secure passage for his parents to England as well. Having studied law and attended the Diplomatic Academy in Vienna, he spent a year at London University and in 1939 landed a job with the BBC, where he eventually became diplomatic-news commentator on European affairs.

At that time, with the advice and assistance of Gerald Barry of the *News Chronicle*, Tangye Lean of the BBC, and H. de C. Hastings of the *Architectural Review*, Weidenfeld conceived *Contact Magazine*, which he intended to pattern after the *New Statesman*, the *New Yorker*, and *Fortune*. He planned to publish the magazine simultaneously in several countries, in several different languages. When the war ended, however, paper rationing forbade the publication of new magazines; so, on the advice of his attorney, John Foster, Weidenfeld published the magazine in hardcover format under the imprint Contact Books. While he was well versed in politics and international affairs, Weidenfeld recognized the need to find a literary editor for his venture. Stephen Spender, Weidenfeld's first choice, was unavailable; Spender recommended Philip Toynbee, who served in that capacity during the first years of the firm. Among the first Contact publications was Harold Wilson's *New Deal for Coal* (1945).

Weidenfeld met Nigel Nicolson, who was also looking for a job in publishing. Their partnership, Weidenfeld and Nicolson, was begun in 1949. Early success was achieved with Rose Macaulay's *Pleasure of Ruins* (1953) and Cyril Connolly's *Ideas and Places* (1953) and *The Golden Horizon* (1953). Although the firm retained his

Lord Weidenfeld with Dame Edna Everage, 1990

name, and he remained on the board of directors, Nicolson sold his interest in the firm in 1956.

Although it has published some notable fiction, Weidenfeld's long suits have been history, biography, and memoirs. Some of the firm's authors have been Winston Churchill, Kurt Waldheim, Lyndon Johnson, Henry Kissinger, Albert Speer, Saul Bellow, Mary McCarthy, Edna O'Brien, and Margaret Drabble. It initiated the History of Civilisation series, the Asia-Africa se-

Sir George Weidenfeld, Secretary-General of the United Nations Kurt Waldheim, and Austrian publisher Fritz Molden in February 1973, the month in which Weidenfeld and Nicolson published Waldheim's book The Austrian Example

ries, and the eighty-volume World University Library. Weidenfeld also published such lavish art books as Douglas Cooper's *Great Private Collections* (1963), Peter Thornton's *Authentic Decor* (1984), and Arabella Lennox-Boyd's *Traditional English Gardens* (1987). According to a 1986 article by Stephen Schiff, the firm has been among the most successful of British publishers, with an annual list of over 160 titles.

One of the hallmarks of Weidenfeld's approach to publishing was an idea he preserved from the Contact Books days: that of having books published simultaneously in as many different countries as possible. In 1964 the *New Statesman* reported that "No other publisher in the world, probably, has brought international collaboration to such a system." Weidenfeld believed strongly in what he called "internationalism in publishing" and practiced it by seeking out and publishing a wide range of foreign authors. His success in the effort owed a great deal to his global life-style and facility with languages (in addition to English and German, he speaks or reads French, Italian, Dutch, and Spanish). Schiff described the typical Weidenfeld and Nicolson publishing project: it begins with an idea by

Weidenfeld himself and proceeds to sales of the rights to an American publisher, to book clubs, to other foreign firms, and to Sunday supplements. Ideally Weidenfeld and Nicolson will recoup any investment before the book is even published.

In 1986 Gigi Mahon called Weidenfeld the "ultimate networker," describing his flair for and pleasure in entertaining: "He realized that if he were going to compete with more established firms, he couldn't wait around for agents and authors to come calling. He had to approach *them*— or, better still, invite them to a party." Weidenfeld has often called on his wide circle of acquaintances to produce books for his firm. According to Fred Newman in a 1989 article, Weidenfeld kept a notebook filled with at least one hundred ideas for future books. Then, when "the right author [came] along," he could approach him or her and commission the work. Such commissioned books included Lady Antonia Fraser's *Mary, Queen of Scots* (1969) and *Cromwell, Our Chief of Men* (1973). He persuaded Arianna Stassinapoulos to try a different kind of writing with her *Maria: Beyond the Callas Legend* (1980). His friendship with Vladimir Nabokov

Prince and Princess Michael of Kent with Lord Weidenfeld at Kensington Palace, 8 July 1986. Weidenfeld and Nicolson published the princess's Crowned in a Far Country: Portraits of Eight Royal Brides *later that year.*

led to the republication of Nabokov's 1955 novel *Lolita* in 1957. Personal connections led to Kissinger's *The White House Years* (1979) and Nancy Reagan's *My Turn* (1989). A long-awaited autobiography by Mick Jagger, however, was eventually dropped, and the substantial advance was repaid.

Weidenfeld, who took what he called a sabbatical year in 1949 to serve Israel's first president, Chaim Weizmann, as political adviser and chief of cabinet, has remained committed to Israel and the Zionist cause, and his firm has benefited from his connections with influential Israelis. He published *Golda Meir Speaks Out* (1973), Moshe Dayan's *Story of My Life* (1976), Teddy Kollek's *For Jerusalem: A Life* (1978), and Shimon Peres's *From These Men: Seven Portraits* (1979).

Having secured the firm's reputation in England and abroad, Weidenfeld had long been interested in expanding into the lucrative American market. In the mid 1980s Weidenfeld and J. Paul Getty's widow, Ann Getty, established the Wheatland Corporation and purchased Grove Press from Barney Rossett for nearly $2 million, assuming the latter firm's $690,000 debt. At

about the same time Weidenfeld and Nicolson New York was established, with Getty as president and Weidenfeld as chief executive. Getty also invested in the London firm. In 1989 Weidenfeld and Nicolson was merged with Grove Press, forming Grove Weidenfeld. Although there were reports in the British and American press that both firms sustained heavy losses, Weidenfeld said that "start-up losses were well within the budget," partly because Getty was so secure financially.

Charges of mismanagement and rumors of financial difficulties have appeared in various publications. The *New Statesman* in 1979 accused Weidenfeld of injudiciously expanding into the area of illustrated books and offering overgenerous advances to authors. In 1986 Schiff repeated similar charges but noted that Getty believed that Weidenfeld was a good businessman and that the charges of financial mismanagement were overstated. A *Manhattan, Inc.* article in 1986 detailed the long and expensive lawsuit brought by Rosset against Weidenfeld and Getty. As of 1990, however, the firm had suffered financial losses in only three of its forty-one years—quite a remarkable achievement for a serious literary publishing house.

Ultimately the success of Weidenfeld and Nicolson rests on the energy and creativity of its founder, who was knighted in 1969 and made a life peer in 1976. On his seventieth birthday in 1989 Lord Weidenfeld showed no sign of retiring and no interest in giving up the controlling interest in the firm that bears his name. On that occasion Paul Johnson wrote in the *Spectator*, "No publisher in our time has had so many ideas . . . his enthusiasm makes the world of books glitter for his authors."

References:

Adam Begley, "Ann Getty: Publish and Perish?," *New York Times Magazine*, 22 October 1989, p. 36;

Miriam Gross and George Weidenfeld, "Portrait of a Publisher," *Observer Magazine*, 19 October 1980, pp. 60-66;

Christopher Hird and Patrick Wintour, "Publishing is Damned: Why Lord Weidenfeld is in Trouble," *New Statesman*, 98 (2 November 1979): 665-666;

Paul Johnson, "A Talent to Enthuse," *Spectator* (26 August 1989): 15;

Gigi Mahon, "Lord on the Fly: Peripatetic Publisher George Weidenfeld," *New York*, 19 (24 February 1986): 40-45;

Fred Newman, "The Great Commissioner," *Publishing News* (13 October 1989): 7;

"Rise of Stout Party," *New Statesman*, 67 (19 June 1964): 944;

Stephen Schiff, "Lord BIG," *Vanity Fair*, 49 (March 1986): 62-68;

John Seabrook, "Endgame," *Manhattan, Inc.* (September 1986): 95-106.

—Jean Parker

Allan Wingate
(London: 1944-1970)
Allan Wingate (Publishers) Limited
(London: 1970-1984)

André Deutsch, born in Budapest in 1917, arrived in London in 1942. That year he began his publishing career with Nicholson and Watson. While there, he saw an opportunity to acquire George Orwell's *Animal Farm* and became discontented when the principals of the firm were unwilling to make the deal. As a result Deutsch left to start his own imprint, which he named Allan Wingate. (*Animal Farm* was published by Secker and Warburg in 1945.)

Deutsch met Diana Athill, employed by the BBC, while he was working for Nicholson and Watson, and he invited her to join him in the new firm. By all accounts, Allan Wingate was started on three thousand pounds at a time when the accepted estimate of the minimum required to start a publishing house was fifteen thousand pounds.

Deutsch directed the Allan Wingate firm from 1944 to 1950. In 1946 he published François Villon's *Ballades, French and English*, and, in 1949, Norman Mailer's *The Naked and the Dead* for the Collector's Book Club with the Wingate imprint. He also published the works of satirist George Mikes, his boyhood friend from Hungary, who had also emigrated. Mikes wrote *How to be an Alien* (1946), now considered a classic view of the English, with pictures contributed by Nicolas Bentley.

Diana Athill, in her autobiography, *Instead of a Letter* (1963), described the working environment at Allan Wingate as stimulating and creative, even though the physical facilities left much to be desired. She wrote, "Our first office was two rooms with a w.c. and a box room with a skylight next to the w.c. in which sat a sequence of morose little men who did our accounts. The chief thing I remember about those first few years was the agony of the bills coming in: the agony of paying when we had to and the agony of not paying when we could get away with it."

André Deutsch had little patience with accounting practices, and he had an overly high regard for Englishmen. He believed that a gentlemen's agreement was completely trustworthy, and too many times Deutsch took on new di-

André Deutsch, director of the Allan Wingate firm from 1944 to 1950, and Norman Mailer, whose novel The Naked and the Dead *was published by Allan Wingate in 1949*

rectors of Wingate for their money rather than for their creative abilities. Business ends were rarely tied neatly, and Deutsch and Athill would fairly quickly become enraged by the other directors' ineptitude in creative matters. Neither of them was reluctant to speak his or her mind, and when money became the primary issue, the financial directors removed André Deutsch and Diana Athill from Allan Wingate. They promptly set about organizing and setting into operation the new firm of André Deutsch Limited, where they were later joined by Nicolas Bentley. Allan Wingate's new executive officers were Anthony Gibbs, son of the novelist Sir Philip Gibbs, and A. L. C. Savoy.

Wingate published several books on publishing and bookselling, the most notable of which were Michael Joseph's *The Adventures of Publishing* (1949); *Battle of the Books*, edited by Gerald Hopkins (1947); and *The Bookman's London*, by Frank Swinnerton (1952). *Fred Bason's Diary*, the memoirs of a secondhand bookseller, was edited and introduced by Nicolas Bentley in 1950; a second volume was published in 1952.

In 1959 Allan Wingate fell into receivership and was purchased by William Kimber, a small independent publisher who subsequently gained rights to the works of Leon Uris. The Wingate imprint appeared on *Battle Cry* (1953), *The Angry Hills* (1956), and *Exodus* (1959). After Wingate was acquired by Kimber, *Topaz* (1968) and *QBVII* (1971) carried the Kimber imprint.

In 1960 Allan Wingate became one of the subsidiaries of Paul Hamlyn's publishing venture known as the Books for Pleasure Group. By 1966 the Books for Pleasure Group had disappeared, but Allan Wingate continued to be a subsidiary of Paul Hamlyn Limited. Michael Gibson, the chief editor of Books for Pleasure, had become the editor of Hamlyn.

By 1970 Allan Wingate (Publishers) Limited was a separate company directed by two Americans, Peter Abramson and David Rowan, along with chief editor Anthony Gibbs. Wingate imprints were distributed in the United States by Universal Publishing and Distributing Corporation. The output of the publishing house continued to be fiction, history, and biography. Peter Abramson formed a new partnership in 1972 with Ralph Stokes and Richard Sharland, both British; Carola Edmond was named editor, and Howard Moorepark was the American representative of the Wingate imprint.

By 1976, Allan Wingate (Publishers) Limited had become a division of W. H. Allen and Company Limited. Jeffrey Simmons and Donald Morrison were directors of the subsidiary company and continued with Wingate until 1984, the apparent end date for the imprint.

References:

Diana Athill, *Instead of a Letter* (London: Chatto & Windus, 1963);

C. Paget, "Andre Deutsch Ltd. at 25," *Publishers Weekly*, 210 (8 November 1976): 26-27.

—Deanna B. Marcum

Wishart and Company
(London: 1925-1935)
Lawrence and Wishart
(London: 1935-   )

Although Ernest Edward Wishart had an impeccably respectable upbringing, he became one of the most radical publishers of the interwar period. He was born on 11 August 1902, the only son of Sir Sidney Wishart, lieutenant and sheriff of the City of London. While studying at Cambridge University he met the poet Douglas Garman, and, in 1925, shortly after graduation, they founded the house of Wishart and Company at 19 Buckingham Street, London.

From March 1925 to July 1927 Wishart published the *Calendar of Modern Letters*, first as a shil-ling monthly and then as a half-crown quarterly. It was edited by Edgell Rickword, assisted by Garman and later by Bertram Higgins. The *Calendar of Modern Letters* was a leftist response to T. S. Eliot's *Criterion* (1922-1939), and it in turn inspired F. R. Leavis to found *Scrutiny* in 1932. Circulation started at about seven thousand and swiftly sank to one thousand, but in its brief life the *Calendar* published works by D. H. Lawrence, Aldous Huxley, E. M. Forster, Robert Graves, Wyndham Lewis, Edmund Blunden, Desmond MacCarthy, Edwin Muir, Luigi Pirandello, John

Crowe Ransom, Bertrand Russell, Siegfried Sassoon, Roy Campbell, Hart Crane, and Allen Tate.

Wishart books included Geoffrey Gorer's *The Revolutionary Ideas of the Marquis de Sade* (1934) and, most notably, *Negro* (1934), Nancy Cunard's anthology of black culture. Mutual involvement in protests against the Scottsboro trial brought Cunard and Rickword together. He arranged for Wishart to publish *Negro* under Cunard's imprint and at her expense after the book had been turned down by Jonathan Cape and Victor Gollancz. It was a mammoth tome of 854 pages, weighing almost eight pounds, with about 250 contributions by 150 writers, both black and white. A thousand copies were printed, priced at two guineas each, and many went unsold. Some British colonies banned the book, and even the black press and leftist periodicals paid scant attention to it. Recently, however, it has gained some recognition as a pioneering work in its field.

In 1935 Wishart merged with the firm of Martin Lawrence, which had been publishing at 26 Bedford Row. Relocated to 2 Parton Street, Red Lion Square, the new imprint of Lawrence and Wishart was, like Martin Lawrence before it, the publishing arm of the Communist party of Great Britain. Rickword was by then a member of the party; Wishart never joined, though he had embraced Marxism-Leninism.

The Lawrence and Wishart list featured mainly Marxist intellectuals such as J. D. Bernal, Christopher Caudwell, Maurice Dobb, Ilya Ehrenburg, Maksim Gorky, Antonio Gramsci, J. B. S. Haldane, Christopher Hill, Eric Hobsbawm, T. A. Jackson, and Georgy Plekhanov, and Communist party leaders such as William Gallacher, Ho Chi Minh, Dolores Ibárruri, Nikita Khrushchev, Vladimir Ilyich Lenin, Vyacheslav Molotov, Harry Pollitt, and Mao Tse-tung. In cooperation with the Institute of Marxism-Leninism and Progress Publishers in Moscow, Lawrence and Wishart undertook the publication of the complete works of Karl Marx and Friedrich Engels in English. The first of fifty volumes was brought out in 1975. One author whose works Wishart came to regret publishing was Joseph Stalin. Lawrence and Wishart produced six volumes of the *Little Stalin Library* in 1941-1942. Lawrence and Wishart moved to 2 Southampton Place in 1945, to 81 Chancery Lane around 1954, to 46 Bedford Row around 1967, to 39 Museum Street in 1972, and to 144A Old South Lambeth Row in 1989.

Wishart was not much involved in Lawrence and Wishart after 1939. Until his death on 16 September 1987 he devoted himself to the study of ornithology, architecture, and local history at his Tudor manor house near Arundel.

References:

Malcolm Bradbury, "A Review in Retrospect," in *The Calendar of Modern Letters*, volume 1, edited by Edgell Rickword and Douglas Garman (London: Cass, 1966; New York: Barnes & Noble, 1966), pp. vii-xix;

Anne Chisholm, *Nancy Cunard* (London: Sidgwick & Jackson, 1979);

"Mr. E. E. Wishart [obituary]," *Times* (London), 23 September 1987, p. 18.

—Jonathan Rose

Contributors

Patricia J. Anderson..*Simon Fraser University*
J. O. Baylen ....*East Sussex, England*
Geraldine Beare...*Surrey, England*
Alice H. R. H. Beckwith ....*Providence College*
Kirk H. Beetz...*National University, Sacramento*
Bryan Bennett ....*London*
R. B. Bloomfield ....*London*
William S. Brockman...*University of Illinois*
Peter W. H. Brown ....*London*
John Calder..*London*
Dorothy W. Collin..*University of Western Australia*
Sondra Miley Cooney..*Kent State University*
Louise Craven ....*St. Bride Printing Library*
Diana Dixon...*Loughborough University of Technology*
John Dreyfus...*London*
J. A. Edwards ....*Hampshire, England*
Martin Eve..*London*
Linda Marie Fritschner ....*Indiana University at South Bend*
Helen Fulton...*University of Sydney*
Mary E. Gaither ....*Indiana University at Bloomington*
Dennis Griffiths ....*Buckinghamshire, England*
Anthony Hamilton...*London*
Francesca Hardcastle...*University of Reading*
Harold Harris ....*London*
Dorothy A. Harrop ....*Powys, Wales*
John Hewish..*London*
Ian Jackson...*Lancashire, England*
Richard Joseph...*Hampshire, England*
Neil L. Kunze ....*Northern Arizona University*
Jennifer B. Lee...*Brown University*
William Lamborn Lee..*Yeshiva University*
David Linton ....*Kent, England*
Raymond N. MacKenzie ....*Minneapolis, Minnesota*
Deanna B. Marcum ....*Catholic University of America*
Francis O. Mattson ....*New York Public Library*
Alistair McCleery ....*Napier Polytechnic*
John M. McEwen ....*Brock University*
Joan Mulholland..*University of Queensland*
James G. Nelson ....*University of Wisconsin—Madison*
Robin Nilon...*University of Delaware*
Peter Owen..*London*
Ruth Panofsky..*York University, Canada*
Jean Parker ....*St. Olaf College*
Ann Parry...*Staffordshire Polytechnic*
Betty Princep...*Nantwich, Cheshire*
Tim Randall..*University of Sussex*

Caroline Robertson ....*Hampshire, England*
Ian Rogerson..*Manchester Polytechnic*
Jonathan Rose ....*Drew University*
Beverly Schneller ....*Millersville University of Pennsylvania*
Pamela Shorrocks ....*Vancouver, British Columbia*
Albert Sperisen ....*University of San Francisco*
John Trevitt ....*Cambridge University Press*
John R. Turner ....*University College of Wales*
Joss West-Burnham..*Cheshire, England*

Cumulative Index

Dictionary of Literary Biography, Volumes 1-112
Dictionary of Literary Biography Yearbook, 1980-1990
Dictionary of Literary Biography Documentary Series, Volumes 1-9

Cumulative Index

DLB before number: *Dictionary of Literary Biography,* Volumes 1-112
Y before number: *Dictionary of Literary Biography Yearbook,* 1980-1990
DS before number: *Dictionary of Literary Biography Documentary Series,* Volumes 1-9

A

F

G

K

M

P

Cumulative Index

T

U

(Continued from front endsheets)

80: *Restoration and Eighteenth-Century Dramatists*, First Series, edited by Paula R. Backscheider (1989)

81: *Austrian Fiction Writers, 1875-1913*, edited by James Hardin and Donald G. Daviau (1989)

82: *Chicano Writers*, First Series, edited by Francisco A. Lomelí and Carl R. Shirley (1989)

83: *French Novelists Since 1960*, edited by Catharine Savage Brosman (1989)

84: *Restoration and Eighteenth-Century Dramatists*, Second Series, edited by Paula R. Backscheider (1989)

85: *Austrian Fiction Writers After 1914*, edited by James Hardin and Donald G. Daviau (1989)

86: *American Short-Story Writers, 1910-1945*, First Series, edited by Bobby Ellen Kimbel (1989)

87: *British Mystery and Thriller Writers Since 1940*, First Series, edited by Bernard Benstock and Thomas F. Staley (1989)

88: *Canadian Writers, 1920-1959*, Second Series, edited by W. H. New (1989)

89: *Restoration and Eighteenth-Century Dramatists*, Third Series, edited by Paula R. Backscheider (1989)

90: *German Writers in the Age of Goethe, 1789-1832*, edited by James Hardin and Christoph E. Schweitzer (1989)

91: *American Magazine Journalists, 1900-1960*, First Series, edited by Sam G. Riley (1990)

92: *Canadian Writers, 1890-1920*, edited by W. H. New (1990)

93: *British Romantic Poets, 1789-1832*, First Series, edited by John R. Greenfield (1990)

94: *German Writers in the Age of Goethe: Sturm und Drang to Classicism*, edited by James Hardin and Christoph E. Schweitzer (1990)

95: *Eighteenth-Century British Poets*, First Series, edited by John Sitter (1990)

96: *British Romantic Poets, 1789-1832*, Second Series, edited by John R. Greenfield (1990)

97: *German Writers from the Enlightenment to Sturm und Drang, 1720-1764*, edited by James Hardin and Christoph E. Schweitzer (1990)

98: *Modern British Essayists*, First Series, edited by Robert Beum (1990)

99: *Canadian Writers Before 1890*, edited by W. H. New (1990)

100: *Modern British Essayists*, Second Series, edited by Robert Beum (1990)

101: *British Prose Writers, 1660-1800*, First Series, edited by Donald T. Siebert (1991)

102: *American Short-Story Writers, 1910-1945*, Second Series, edited by Bobby Ellen Kimbel (1991)

103: *American Literary Biographers*, First Series, edited by Steven Serafin (1991)

104: *British Prose Writers, 1660-1800*, Second Series, edited by Donald T. Siebert (1991)

105: *American Poets Since World War II*, Second Series, edited by R. S. Gwynn (1991)

106: *British Literary Publishing Houses, 1820-1880*, edited by Patricia J. Anderson and Jonathan Rose (1991)

107: *British Romantic Prose Writers, 1789-1832*, First Series, edited by John R. Greenfield (1991)

108: *Twentieth-Century Spanish Poets*, First Series, edited by Michael L. Perna (1991)

109: *Eighteenth-Century British Poets*, Second Series, edited by John Sitter (1991)

110: *British Romantic Prose Writers, 1789-1832*, Second Series, edited by John R. Greenfield (1991)

111: *American Literary Biographers*, Second Series, edited by Steven Serafin (1991)

112: *British Literary Publishing Houses, 1881-1965*, edited by Jonathan Rose and Patricia J. Anderson (1991)

Documentary Series

1: *Sherwood Anderson, Willa Cather, John Dos Passos, Theodore Dreiser, F. Scott Fitzgerald, Ernest Hemingway, Sinclair Lewis*, edited by Margaret A. Van Antwerp (1982)

2: *James Gould Cozzens, James T. Farrell, William Faulkner, John O'Hara, John Steinbeck, Thomas Wolfe, Richard Wright*, edited by Margaret A. Van Antwerp (1982)

3: *Saul Bellow, Jack Kerouac, Norman Mailer, Vladimir Nabokov, John Updike, Kurt Vonnegut*, edited by Mary Bruccoli (1983)